26th Italian Symposium on Advanced Database Systems (SEBD 2018)

AA004988

Castellaneta Marina, Italy
24-27 June 2018

Editors:

Sonia Bergamaschi
Andrea Maurino
Tommaso Di Noia
Letizia Tanca

ISBN: 978-1-5108-6963-9

Printed from e-media with permission by:

Curran Associates, Inc.
57 Morehouse Lane
Red Hook, NY 12571

Some format issues inherent in the e-media version may also appear in this print version.

Printed by Curran Associates, Inc. (2018)

Edited by:
Sonia Bergamaschi
Tommaso Di Noia
Andrea Maurino
Letizia Tanca

Additional copies of this publication are available from:

Curran Associates, Inc.
57 Morehouse Lane
Red Hook, NY 12571 USA
Phone: 845-758-0400
Fax: 845-758-2633
Email: curran@proceedings.com
Web: www.proceedings.com

TABLE OF CONTENTS

Preface

This volume collects the papers selected for presentation at the twenty-sixth Italian Symposium on Advanced Database Systems (SEBD 2018), held at Castellaneta Marina (Taranto), Italy, at Ethra Reserve from the 24th to the 27th of June 2018.

Databases and, more generally, data management is a well-established key player in the digital transformation we are witnessing nowadays. This reflects in the papers presented in this volume whose topics span from Data mining and knowledge Discovery to Information Extraction to Semistructured Data Management and Intelligent Web Information Systems, just to cite a few. Each submission was evaluated by three independent referees. Besides regular paper, the program also featured three invited talks by Amr El Abbadi, Wenfei Fan, and Michel Dumontier, and an invited tutorial given by Massimo Bartoletti. Finally, SEBD 2018 hosted a session devoted to the discussion of ongoing research activities form Ph.D. students.

The wide spectrum of database-related topics addressed in the volume is a clear clue of the vibrant activity in the Italian scientific community, and we hope that SEBD will continue to be a gathering forum where people from academic and industrial environments meet, discuss and exchange experiences on the theory and practice of information storage and management.

We wish to thank all the authors who submitted papers and all the conference participants. We are also grateful to the members of the Program Committee and the external referees for their thorough work in reviewing submitted contributions with expertise and patience, and the members of the SEBD Steering Committee.

We gratefully acknowledge CC ICT-SUD for its sponsorship and the patronage of Politecnico di Bari, Università degli studi di Modena e Reggio Emilia, and Università degli studi di Milano Bicocca.

June 24, 2018
Castellaneta Marina (TA), Italy

Sonia Bergamaschi
Tommaso Di Noia
Andrea Maurino
Letizia Tanca

An approach to extracting thematic views from highly heterogeneous sources of a data lake

Claudia Diamantini[1], Paolo Lo Giudice[2], Lorenzo Musarella[2], Domenico Potena[1], Emanuele Storti[1], and Domenico Ursino[1]

[1] DII, Polytechnic University of Marche
[2] DIIES, University "Mediterranea" of Reggio Calabria

Abstract. In the last years, data lakes are emerging as an effective and efficient support for information and knowledge extraction from a huge amount of highly heterogeneous and quickly changing data sources. Data lake management requires the definition of new techniques, very different from the ones adopted for data warehouses in the past. One of the main issues to address in this scenario consists in the extraction of thematic views from the (very heterogeneous and generally unstructured) data sources of a data lake. In this paper, we propose a new network-based model to uniformly represent structured, semi-structured and unstructured sources of a data lake. Then, we present a new approach to, at least partially, "structure" unstructured data. Finally, we define a technique to extract thematic views from the sources of a data lake, based on similarity and other semantic relations among the metadata of data sources.

1 Introduction

In the last years, data lakes are emerging as an effective and efficient answer to the problem of extracting information and knowledge from a huge amount of highly heterogeneous and quickly changing data sources [13]. Data lake management requires the definition of new techniques, very different from the ones adopted for data warehouses in the past. These techniques may exploit the large set of metadata always supplied with data lakes, which represent their core and the main tool allowing them to be a very competitive framework in the big data era. One of the main issues to address in a scenario comprising many data sources extremely heterogeneous in their format, structure and semantics, consists in the extraction of thematic views from data sources [3], i.e., the construction of views concerning one or more topics of interest for the user, obtained by extracting and merging data coming from different sources. This problem has been largely investigated in the past for structured and semi-structured data sources stored in a data warehouse [26, 8, 22], and this witnesses its extreme relevance. However, it is esteemed that, currently, more than 80% of data sources are unstructured

SEBD 2018, June 24-27, 2018, Castellaneta Marina, Italy.

[9]. As a consequence, it is just this type of source that represents the main actor of the big data scenario and, consequently, of data lakes.

In this paper, we aim at providing a contribution in this setting. Indeed, we propose a supervised approach to extracting thematic views from highly heterogeneous sources of a data lake. Our approach represents all the data lake sources by means of a suitable network. Indeed, networks are very flexible structures that allow the modeling of almost all phenomena that researchers aim at investigating [7]. Thanks to this uniform representation of the data lake sources, the extraction of thematic views from them can be performed by exploiting graph-based tools. We define "supervised" our approach because it requires the user to specify the set of topics $T = \{T_1, T_2, \ldots, T_n\}$ that should be present in the thematic view(s) to extract. Our approach consists of two steps. The former is mainly based on the structure of involved sources. It exploits several notions typical of (social) network analysis, such as the notion of ego network, which actually represents the core of the proposed approach. The latter exploits a knowledge repository, which is used to discover new relationships, other than synonymies, among metadata, with the purpose to refine the integration of different thematic views obtained after the first step. In this step, our approach relies on DBpedia.

This paper is organized as follows: Section 2 illustrates related literature. In Section 3, we present the proposed approach. In particular, first we describe a unifying model for data lake representation; then, we present our approach to partially structuring unstructured sources; finally, we discuss the two steps of our approach for thematic view extraction. In Section 4, we present our example case, whereas, in Section 5, we draw our conclusions and discuss future work.

2 Related Literature

The new data lake scenario is characterized by several peculiarities that make it very different from the data warehouse paradigm. Hence, it is necessary to adapt (if possible) old algorithms conceived for data warehouses or to define new approaches capable of handling and taking advantage of the specificities of this new paradigm. However, most approaches proposed in the literature for data integration, query answering and view extraction do not completely fit the data lake paradigm. For instance, [8] proposes some techniques for building views on semi-structured data sources based on some expected queries. Other researchers focus on materialized views and, specifically, on throughput and execution time; therefore, they a-priori define a set of well-known views and, then, materialize them. Two surveys on this issue can be found in [16, 1]. The authors of [26] investigate the same problem but they focus on XML sources. The approach of [25] addresses the same issue by means of query rewriting; specifically, it transforms a query Q into a set of new queries, evaluates them, and, then, merges the corresponding answers to construct the materialized answer to Q. [4] proposes an approach to constructing materialized views for heterogeneous

DBpedia: http://dbpedia.org

databases; it requires the presence of a static context and the pre-computation of some queries.

Another family of approaches exploits materialized views to perform tree pattern querying [24] and graph pattern queries [12]. Unfortunately, all these approaches are well-suited for structured and semi-structured data, whereas they are not scalable and lightweight enough to be used in a dynamic context or with unstructured data. An interesting advance in this area can be found in [23]. Here, the authors propose an incremental approach to address the graph pattern query problem on both static and dynamic real-life data graphs. Other kinds of views are investigated in [6] and [3]. In particular, this last paper uses virtual views to access heterogeneous data sources without knowing many details of them. For this purpose, it creates virtual views of the data sources.

Finally, semantic-based approaches have long been used to drive data integration in databases and data warehouses. More recently, in the context of big data, formal semantics has been specifically exploited to address issues concerning data variety/heterogeneity, data inconsistency and data quality in such a way as to increase understandability [17]. In the data lake scenario, semantic techniques have been successfully applied to more efficiently integrate and handle both structured and unstructured data sources by aligning data silos and better managing evolving data models. For instance, in [15], the authors discuss a data lake system with a semantic metadata matching component for ontology modeling, attribute annotation, record linkage, and semantic enrichment. Furthermore, [14] presents a system to discover and enforce expressive integrity constraints from data lakes. Similarly to what happens in our approach, knowledge graphs in RDF are used to drive integration. To reach their objectives, these techniques usually rely on information extraction tools (e.g., Open Calais) that may assist in linking metadata to uniform vocabularies (e.g., ontologies or knowledge repositories, such as DBpedia).

3 Description of the proposed approach

3.1 A unifying model for data lake representation

In this section, we illustrate our network-based model to represent and handle a data lake, which we will use in the rest of this paper. In our model, a data lake DL is represented as a set of m data sources: $DL = \{D_1, D_2, \cdots, D_m\}$. A data source $D_k \in DL$ is provided with a rich set $\mathcal{M}_k$ of metadata. We denote with $\mathcal{M}_{DL}$ the repository of the metadata of all the data sources of DL: $\mathcal{M}_{DL} = \{\mathcal{M}_1, \mathcal{M}_2, \ldots, \mathcal{M}_m\}$.

According to [21], our model represents $\mathcal{M}_k$ by means of a triplet: $\mathcal{M}_k = \langle \mathcal{M}_k^T, \mathcal{M}_k^O, \mathcal{M}_k^B \rangle$. Here: *(i)* $\mathcal{M}_k^T$ denotes *technical metadata*. It represents the type, the format, the structure and the schema of the corresponding data. It

RDF Concepts and abstract Syntax: `http://www.w3.org/TR/2004/REC-rdf-concepts-20040210/`

`http://www.opencalais.com`

is commonly provided by the source catalogue. *(ii)* $\mathcal{M}_k^O$ represents *operational metadata*. It includes the source and target locations of the corresponding data, the associated file size, the number of their records, and so on. Usually, it is automatically generated by the technical framework handling the data lake. *(iii)* $\mathcal{M}_k^B$ indicates *business metadata*. It comprises the business names and descriptions assigned to data fields. It also covers business rules, which can become integrity constraints for the corresponding data source.

In this paper, we consider only business metadata. Indeed, they denote, at the intensional level, the information content stored in the data lake sources and are those of interest for supporting the extraction of thematic views from a data lake, which is our ultimate goal. In order to represent $\mathcal{M}_k^B$, our model adopts a notation typical of XML, JSON and many other semi-structured models. According to this notation, Obj_k indicates the set of all the objects stored in $\mathcal{M}_k^B$. It consists of the union of three subsets: $Obj_k = Att_k \cup Smp_k \cup Cmp_k$. Here: *(i)* Att_k indicates the set of the attributes of $\mathcal{M}_k^B$; *(ii)* Smp_k represents the set of the simple elements of $\mathcal{M}_k^B$; *(iii)* Cmp_k denotes the set of the complex elements of $\mathcal{M}_k^B$. In this context, the meaning of the terms "attribute", "simple element" and "complex element" is the one typical of semi-structured data models.

$\mathcal{M}_k^B$ can be also represented as a graph: $\mathcal{M}_k^B = \langle N_k, A_k \rangle$. N_k is the set of the nodes of $\mathcal{M}_k^B$. There exists a node $n_{k_j} \in N_k$ for each object $o_{k_j} \in Obj_k$. According to the structure of Obj_k, N_k consists of the union of three subsets: $N_k = N_k^{Att} \cup N_k^{Smp} \cup N_k^{Cmp}$. Here, N_k^{Att} (resp., N_k^{Smp}, N_k^{Cmp}) indicates the set of the nodes corresponding to Att_k (resp., Smp_k, Cmp_k). There is a one-to-one correspondence between a node of N_k and an object of Obj_k. Therefore, in the following, we will use the two terms interchangeably. Let x be a complex element of $\mathcal{M}_k^B$. Obj_{k_x} indicates the set of the objects directly contained in x, whereas $N_{k_x}^{Obj}$ denotes the set of the corresponding nodes. Finally, let y be a simple element of $\mathcal{M}_k^B$. Att_{k_y} represents the set of the attributes of y, whereas $N_{k_y}^{Att}$ denotes the set of the corresponding nodes.

A_k indicates the set of the arcs of $\mathcal{M}_k^B$. It consists of two subsets: $A_k = A'_k \cup A''_k$. Here: *(i)* $A'_k = \{(n_x, n_y) | n_x \in N_k^{Cmp}, n_y \in N_{n_x}^{Obj}\}$, i.e., there is an arc from a complex element of $\mathcal{M}_k^B$ to each object directly contained in it. *(ii)* $A''_k = \{(n_x, n_y) | n_x \in N_k^{Smp}, n_y \in N_{n_x}^{Att}\}$, i.e., there is an arc from a simple element of $\mathcal{M}_k^B$ to each of its attributes.

3.2 An approach to partially structuring unstructured sources

Our network-based model for representing and handling a data lake is perfectly fitted for representing and managing semi-structured data because it has been designed having XML and JSON in mind. Clearly, it is sufficiently powerful to represent structured data. The highest difficulty regards unstructured data because it is worth avoiding a flat representation consisting of a simple element for each keyword provided to denote the source content. As a matter of fact, this kind of representation would make the reconciliation, and the next integration, of an unstructured source with the other (semi-structured and structured) ones of the data lake very difficult. Therefore, it is necessary to (at least partially) "structure" unstructured data.

Our approach to addressing this issue consists of four phases, namely: *(i)* creation of nodes; *(ii)* derivation and management of part-of relationships; *(iii)* derivation of lexical and string similarities; *(iv)* management of lexical and string similarities.

Phase 1. During this phase, our approach creates a complex element representing the source as a whole, and a simple element for each keyword. Furthermore, it adds an arc from the source to each of the simple elements. Initially, there is no arc between two simple elements. To determine the arcs to add, the next phases are necessary.

Phase 2. During this phase, our approach adds an arc from the node n_{k_1}, corresponding to the keyword k_1, to the node n_{k_2}, corresponding to the keyword k_2, if k_2 is registered as a lemma of k_1 in a suitable thesaurus. Taking the current trends into account, this thesaurus should be a multimedia one; for this purpose, in our experiments, we have adopted BabelNet [20]. When this arc has been added, n_{k_1} must be considered a complex element, instead of a simple one.

Phase 3. During this phase, our approach starts by deriving lexical similarities. In particular, it states that there exists a similarity between the nodes n_{k_1}, corresponding to the keyword k_1, and n_{k_2}, corresponding to the keyword k_2, if k_1 and k_2 have at least one common lemma in a suitable thesaurus. Also in this case, we have adopted BabelNet. After having found lexical similarities, our approach derives string similarities and states that there exists a similarity between n_{k_1} and n_{k_2} if the string similarity degree $kd(k_1, k_2)$, computed by applying a suitable string similarity metric on k_1 and k_2, is "sufficiently high" (see below). We have chosen N-Grams [18] as string similarity metric because we have experimentally seen that it provides the best results in our context. Now, we illustrate in detail what "sufficiently high" means and how our approach operates. Let $KeySim$ be the set of the string similarities for each pair of keywords of the source into consideration. Each record in $KeySim$ has the form $\langle k_i, k_j, kd(k_i, k_j)\rangle$. Our approach first computes the maximum keyword similarity degree kd_{max} present in $KeySim$. Then, it examines each keyword similarity registered therein. Let $\langle k_1, k_2, kd(k_1, k_2)\rangle$ be one of these similarities. If $((kd(k_1, k_2) \geq th_k \cdot kd_{max})$ and $(kd(k_1, k_2) \geq th_{kmin}))$, which implies that the keyword similarity degree between k_1 and k_2 is among the highest ones in $KeySim$ and that, in any case, it is higher than or equal to a minimum threshold, then it concludes that there exists a similarity between n_{k_1} and n_{k_2}. We have experimentally set $th_k = 0.70$ and $th_{kmin} = 0.50$. At the end of this phase, our approach has found some (lexical and/or string) similarities, each stating that a node n_{k_i} is similar to a node n_{k_j}.

Phase 4. During this phase, our approach aims at managing the similarities found during Phase 3. In particular, if there exists a (lexical and/or string) sim-

In this paper, we use the term "lemma" according to the meaning it has in BabelNet [20]. Here, given a term, its lemmas are other objects (terms, emoticons, etc.) contributing to specify its meaning.

ilarity between two nodes n_{k_i} and n_{k_j}, it merges them into one node $n_{k_{ij}}$, which inherits all the incoming and outgoing arcs of n_{k_i} and n_{k_j}. After all similarities have been considered, it could happen that there exist two or more arcs from a node n_{k_i} to a node n_{k_j}. In this case, our approach merges them into one arc.

3.3 An approach to extracting thematic views

Our approach to extracting thematic views operates on a data lake DL whose data sources are represented by means of the model described in Section 3.1. It is called "supervised" because it requires the user to specify the set of topics $T = \{T_1, T_2, \cdots, T_l\}$, which should be present in the thematic view(s) to extract. It consists of two steps, the former mainly based on the structure of the sources at hand, the latter mainly focusing on the corresponding semantics. We describe these two steps in the next subsections.

Step 1. The first step of our approach receives a data lake DL, a set of topics $T = \{T_1, T_2, \cdots, T_l\}$, representing the themes of interest for the user, and a dictionary Syn of synonymies involving the objects stored in the sources of DL. This dictionary could be a generic thesaurus, such as BabelNet [20], a domain-specific thesaurus, or a dictionary obtained by taking into account the structure and the semantics of the sources, which the corresponding objects refer to (such as the dictionaries produced by XIKE [10], MOMIS [5] or Cupid [19]).

In this step, the concept of ego network [2, 11] plays a key role. We recall that an ego network consists of a focal node (the ego) and the nodes it is directly connected to (the "alters"), plus the ties, if any, between the alters.

Let T_i be a topic of T. Let $Obj_i = \{o_{i_1}, o_{i_2}, \cdots, o_{i_q}\}$ be the set of the objects synonymous of T_i in DL. Let $N_i = \{n_{i_1}, n_{i_2}, \cdots, n_{i_q}\}$ be the corresponding nodes. First, Step 1 constructs the ego networks $E_{i_1}, E_{i_2}, \cdots, E_{i_q}$ having $n_{i_1}, n_{i_2}, \cdots, n_{i_q}$ as the corresponding egos. Then, it merges all the egos into a unique node n_i. In this way, it obtains a unique ego network E_i from $E_{i_1}, E_{i_2}, \cdots, E_{i_q}$. If a synonymy exists between two alters belonging to different ego networks, then these are merged into a unique node and the corresponding arcs linking them to the ego n_i are merged into a unique arc. At the end of this task, we have a unique ego network E_i corresponding to T_i.

After having performed the previous task for each topic of T, we have a set $E = \{E_1, E_2, \cdots, E_l\}$ of l ego networks. At this point, Step 1 finds all the synonymies of Syn involving objects of the ego networks of E and merges the corresponding nodes. After all the possible synonymies involving objects of the ego network of E have been considered and the corresponding nodes have been merged, a set $V = \{V_1, \cdots, V_g\}$, $1 \leq g \leq l$, of networks representing potential views is obtained.

If $g = 1$, then it is possible to conclude that Step 1 has been capable of extracting a unique thematic view comprising all the topics required by the user. Otherwise, there exist more views each comprising some (but not all) of the topics of interest for the user. If $g = 1$, Step 2 is performed to make more precise and complete the unique view representing all the topics of T. If $g > 1$, Step 2 aims at finding other relationships, different from synonymies, among the objects of the views of V in such a way as to try to obtain a unique view embracing all the topics of interest for the user.

Step 2. This step starts by enriching each view $V_i \in V$. For this purpose, it connects each of its elements to all the semantically related concepts taken from a reference knowledge repository.

In this work, we rely on DBpedia, one of the largest knowledge graphs in the Linked Data context, including more than 4.58 million entities in RDF. To this aim, first each element of V_i (including its synonyms) is mapped to the corresponding entry in DBpedia. In many cases, such a mapping is already provided by BabelNet. Then, for each DBpedia entry, all the related concepts are retrieved. In DBpedia, knowledge is structured according to the Linked Data principles, i.e. as an RDF graph built by triples. Each triple $\langle s(ubject), p(roperty), o(bject)\rangle$ states that a subject s has a property p, whose value is an object o. Both subjects and properties are resources (i.e., nodes in DBpedia's knowledge graph), whereas objects may be either resources or literals (i.e., values of some primitive data types, such as strings or numbers). Each triple represents the minimal component of the knowledge graph. This last is built by merging triples together. Therefore, retrieving the related concepts for a given element x implies finding all the triples where x is either the subject or the object.

For each view $V_i \in V$, the procedure to extend it consists of the following three substeps:

1. *Mapping*: for each node $n \in V_i$, its corresponding DBpedia entry d is found.
2. *Triple extraction*: all the related triples $\langle d, p, o\rangle$ and $\langle s, p, d\rangle$, i.e., all the triples in which d is either the subject or the object, are retrieved.
3. *View extension*: for each retrieved triple $\langle d, p, o\rangle$ (resp., $\langle s, p, d\rangle$), V_i is extended by defining a node for the object o (resp., s), if not already existing, linked to n through an arc labeled as p.

These three tasks are repeated for all the views of V. As previously pointed out, this enrichment procedure is particularly important if $|V| > 1$ because the new derived relationships could help to merge the thematic views that was not possible to merge during Step 1. In particular, let $V_i \in V$ and $V_j \in V$ be two views of V, and let V_i' and V_j' be the extended views corresponding to them. If there exist two nodes $n_{i_h} \in V_i'$ ad $n_{j_k} \in V_j'$ such that $n_{i_h} = n_{j_k}$, then they can be merged in one node; if this happens, V_i' and V_j' become connected. After all equal nodes of the views of V have been merged, all the views of V could be either merged in one view or not. In the former case, the process terminates with success. Otherwise, it is possible to conclude that no thematic views comprising

Whenever this does not happen, the mapping can be automatically provided by the DBpedia Lookup Service (`http://wiki.dbpedia.org/projects/dbpedia-lookup`).
Here, two nodes are equal if the corresponding name coincide.

all the topics specified by the user can be found. In this last case, our approach still returns the enriched views of V and leaves the user the choice to accept of reject them.

4 An example case

In this section, we present an example case aiming at illustrating the various tasks of our approach. Here, we consider: *(i)* a structured source, called *Weather Conditions* (W, in short), whose corresponding E/R schema is not reported for space limitations; *(ii)* two semi-structured sources, called *Climate* (C, in short) and *Environment* (E, in short), whose corresponding XML Schemas are not reported for space limitations; *(iii)* an unstructured source, called *Environment Video* (V, in short), consisting of a YouTube video and whose corresponding keywords are: *garden*, *flower*, *rain*, *save*, *earth*, *tips*, *recycle*, *aurora*, *planet*, *garbage*, *pollution*, *region*, *life*, *plastic*, *metropolis*, *environment*, *nature*, *wave*, *eco*, *weather*, *simple*, *fineparticle*, *climate*, *ocean*, *environmentawareness*, *educational*, *reduce*, *power*, *bike*.

By applying the approaches mentioned in Section 3.2, we obtain the corresponding representations in our network-based model, shown in Figure 1.

Assume, now, that a user specifies the following set T of topics of her interest: $T = \{Ocean, Area\}$. First, our approach determines the terms (and, then, the objects) in the five sources that are synonyms of *Ocean* and *Area*. As for *Ocean*, the only synonym present in the sources is *Sea*; as a consequence, Obj_1 comprises the node *Ocean* of the source V (*V.Ocean*) and the node *Sea* of the source C (*C.Sea*). An analogous activity is performed for *Area*. At the end of this task we have that $Obj_1 = \{V.Ocean, C.Sea\}$ and $Obj_2 = \{W.Place, C.Place, V.Region, E.Location\}$.

Step 1 of our approach proceeds by constructing the ego networks corresponding to the objects of Obj_1 and Obj_2. They are reported in Figure 2.

Now, consider the ego networks corresponding to *V.Ocean* and *C.Sea*. Our approach merges the two egos into a unique node. Then, it verifies whether further synonyms exist between the alters. Since none of these synonyms exists, it returns the ego network shown in Figure 3(a). The same task is performed to the ego networks corresponding to *W.Place*, *C.Place*, *V.Region* and *E.Location*. In particular, first the four egos are merged. Then, synonyms between the alters *W.City* and *C.City* and the alters *W.Altitude* and *C.Altitude* are retrieved. Based on this, *W.City* and *C.City* are merged in one node, *W.Altitude* and *C.Altitude* in another node, the arcs linking the ego to *W.City* and *C.City* are merged in one arc and the ones linking the ego to *W.Altitude* and *C.Altitude* in another arc. In this way, the ego network shown in Figure 3(b) is returned. At this point, there are two ego networks, E_{Ocean} and E_{Area}, each corresponding to one of the terms specified by the user.

Here and in the following, we use the notation *S.o* to indicate the object *o* of the source *S*.

Fig. 1. Network-based representations of the four sources into consideration.

Now, Step 1 verifies if there are any synonyms between a node of E_{Ocean} and a node of E_{Area}. Since this does not happen, it terminates and returns the set $V = \{V_{Ocean}, V_{Area}\}$, where V_{Ocean} (resp., V_{Area}) coincides with E_{Ocean} (resp., E_{Area}).

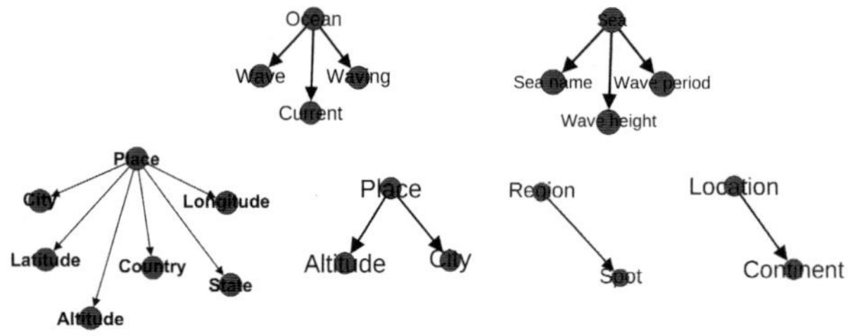

Fig. 2. Ego networks corresponding to *V.Ocean*, *C.Sea*, *W.Place*, *C.Place*, *V.Region* and *E.Location*.

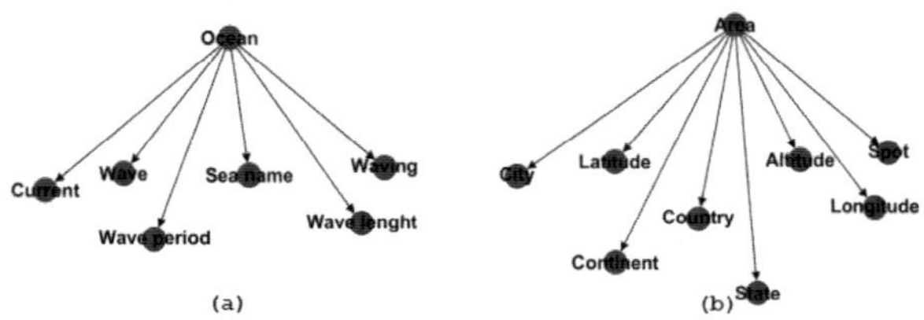

Fig. 3. Ego networks corresponding to *Ocean* and *Area*.

At this point, Step 2 is executed. As shown in Figure 4, first each term (synonyms included) is semantically aligned to the corresponding DBpedia entry (e.g., *Ocean* is linked to *dbo:Sea*, *Area* is linked to *dbo:Location* and *dbo:Place*, while *Country* to *dbo:Country*, respectively). After a single iteration, the triples ⟨*dbo:sea rdfs:range dbo:Sea*⟩ and ⟨*dbo:sea rdfs:domain dbo:Place*⟩ are retrieved. They correspond to the DBpedia property *sea*, which relates a country to the sea from which it is lapped. Other connections can be found by moving to specific instances of the mentioned resources. In this way, the following triples are retrieved: ⟨*instance rdf:type dbo:Sea*⟩, ⟨*instance rdf:type dbo:Location*⟩, ⟨*instance rdf:type dbo:Place*⟩, meaning that there are resource instances having types *Sea*, *Location* and *Place* simultaneously (e.g., *dbr:Mediterranean_Sea*). Furthermore, a triple ⟨*instance dbo:country dbo:Country*⟩ can be retrieved, meaning that those instances being a *Sea*, a *Location* or a *Place* specify in which *dbo:Country* they are located through the *dbo:country* property. In this example case, Step 2 succeeded in merging the two views that Step 1 had maintained separated.

5 Conclusion

In this paper, we have presented a new network-based model to uniformly represent the structured, semi-structured and unstructured sources of a data lake. Then, we have proposed a new approach to, at least partially, "structuring"

Prefixes *dbo* and *dbr* stand for `http://dbpedia.org/ontology/` and `http://dbpedia.org/resource/`

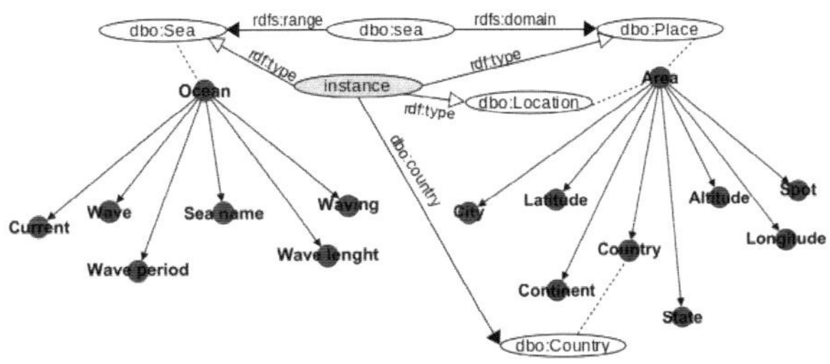

Fig. 4. The integrated thematic view.

unstructured data. Finally, based on these two tools, we have defined a new approach to extracting thematic views from the sources of a data lake consisting of two steps, based on ego networks (Step 1) and semantic relationships (Step 2). This paper is not to be intended as an ending point. Actually, it could be the starting point of a new family of approaches aiming at handling information systems in the new big data-oriented scenario. By proceeding in this direction, first we plan to define an unsupervised approach to extracting thematic views from a data lake. Then, we plan to define new approaches to supporting a flexible and lightweight querying of the sources of a data lake, as well as approaches to schema matching, schema mapping, data reconciliation and integration strongly oriented to data lakes based mainly on unstructured data sources.

References

1. S. Abiteboul and O.M. Duschka. Complexity of answering queries using materialized views. In *Proc. of the International Symposium on Principles of database systems (SIGMOD/PODS'98)*, pages 254–263, Seattle, WA, USA, 1998. ACM.
2. V. Arnaboldi, M. Conti, A. Passarella, and F. Pezzoni. Analysis of ego network structure in online social networks. In *Proc. of the International Conference on Privacy (PASSAT'12)*, pages 31–40, Amsterdam, Netherlands, 2012. IEEE.
3. L. Aversano, R. Intonti, C. Quattrocchi, and M. Tortorella. Building a virtual view of heterogeneous data source views. In *Proc. of the International Conference on Software and Data Technologies (ICSOFT'10)*, pages 266–275, Athens, Greece, 2010. INSTICC Press.
4. C. Bachtarzi and F. Bachtarzi. A model-driven approach for materialized views definition over heterogeneous databases. In *Proc. of the International Conference on New Technologies of Information and Communication (NTIC'15)*, pages 1–5, Mila, Algeria, 2015. IEEE.
5. S. Bergamaschi, S. Castano, M. Vincini, and D. Beneventano. Semantic integration and query of heterogeneous information sources. *Data & Knowledge Engineering*, 36(3):215–249, 2001.
6. J. Biskup and D. Embley. Extracting information from heterogeneous information sources using ontologically specified target views. *Information Systems*, 28(3):169–212, 2003. Elsevier.
7. M. R. Bouadjenek, H. Hacid, and M. Bouzeghoub. Social networks and information retrieval, how are they converging? A survey, a taxonomy and an analysis of social

information retrieval approaches and platforms. *Information Systems*, 56:1–18, 2016.
8. S. Castano and V. De Antonellis. Building views over semistructured data sources. In *Proc. of the International Conference on Conceptual Modeling (ER'99)*, pages 146–160, Paris, France, 1999. Springer.
9. A. Corbellini, C. Mateos, A. Zunino, D. Godoy, and S.N. Schiaffino. Persisting big-data: The NoSQL landscape. *Information Systems*, 63:1–23, 2017. Elsevier.
10. P. De Meo, G. Quattrone, G. Terracina, and D. Ursino. Integration of XML Schemas at various "severity" levels. *Information Systems*, 31(6):397–434, 2006.
11. R. DeJordy and D. Halgin. Introduction to ego network analysis. *Boston MA: Boston College and the Winston Center for Leadership & Ethics*, 2008.
12. W. Fan, X. Wang, and Y. Wu. Answering pattern queries using views. *IEEE Transactions on Knowledge and Data Engineering*, 28(2):326–341, 2016. IEEE.
13. H. Fang. Managing data lakes in big data era: What's a data lake and why has it became popular in data management ecosystem. In *Proc. of the International Conference on Cyber Technology in Automation (CYBER'15)*, pages 820–824, Shenyang, China, 2015. IEEE.
14. M. Farid, A. Roatis, I.F. Ilyas, H. Hoffmann, and X. Chu. CLAMS: bringing quality to Data Lakes. In *Proc. of the International Conference on Management of Data (SIGMOD/PODS'16)*, pages 2089–2092, San Francisco, CA, USA, 2016. ACM.
15. R. Hai, S. Geisler, and C. Quix. Constance: An intelligent data lake system. In *Proc. of the International Conference on Management of Data (SIGMOD/PODS'16)*, pages 2097–2100, San Francisco, CA, USA, 2016. ACM.
16. A. Halevy. Answering queries using views: A survey. *The VLDB Journal*, 10(4):270–294, 2001. Springer.
17. P. Hitzler and K. Janowicz. Linked Data, Big Data, and the 4th Paradigm. *Semantic Web*, 4(3):233–235, 2013.
18. G. Kondrak. N-gram similarity and distance. In *String processing and information retrieval*, pages 115–126, 2005. Springer.
19. J. Madhavan, P.A. Bernstein, and E. Rahm. Generic schema matching with Cupid. In *Proc. of the International Conference on Very Large Data Bases (VLDB 2001)*, pages 49–58, Rome, Italy, 2001. Morgan Kaufmann.
20. R. Navigli and S.P. Ponzetto. BabelNet: The automatic construction, evaluation and application of a wide-coverage multilingual semantic network. *Artificial Intelligence*, 193:217–250, 2012. Elsevier.
21. A. Oram. *Managing the Data Lake.* Sebastopol, CA, USA, 2015. O'Reilly.
22. L. Palopoli, L. Pontieri, G. Terracina, and D. Ursino. Intensional and extensional integration and abstraction of heterogeneous databases. *Data & Knowledge Engineering*, 35(3):201–237, 2000.
23. K. Singh and V. Singh. Answering graph pattern query using incremental views. In *Proc. of the International Conference on Computing (ICCCA'16)*, pages 54–59, Greater Noida, India, 2016. IEEE.
24. J. Wang, J. Li, and J.X. Yu. Answering tree pattern queries using views: a revisit. In *Proc. of the International Conference on Extending Database Technology (EDBT/ICDT'11)*, pages 153–164, Uppsala, Sweden, 2011. ACM.
25. J. Wang and J.X. Yu. Revisiting answering tree pattern queries using views. *ACM Transactions on Database Systems*, 37(3):18, 2012. ACM.
26. X. Wu, D. Theodoratos, and W.H. Wang. Answering XML queries using materialized views revisited. In *Proc. of the International Conference on Information and Knowledge Management (CIKM '09)*, pages 475–484, Hong Kong, China, 2009. ACM.

Discussion paper: Filling the gap between business rules and technical requirements in Business Analytics: The Fact - Centered ETL approach

Antonella Longo[1], Mario Bochicchio[1], Marco Zappatore[1], Lucia Vaira[1]

[1] Set-Lab, Dept. of Engineering for Innovation, Univ. of Salento,
via per Monteroni, 73100 Lecce, Italy
{antonella.longo, mario.bochicchio, marcosalvatore.zappatore,
lucia.vaira}@unisalento.it

Abstract. In real-time Business Analytics scenarios, like Business Activity Monitoring (BAM) or Operational Intelligence, using modeling language to describe ETL processes is fundamental to provide business users with up-to-date data in order to support decision-making process and to optimize business operations. To bridge the gap between business and technical requirements and encapsulate business requirements into technical specifications, it can be very convenient to design ETL processes starting from business facts; this would effectively support business users in decision-making processes and would represent business rules and entities as soon as possible in the BI process design. Moreover a fact centered approach to ETL process design can split the traditional black-box approach into several fact-centered flows, which can be processed in parallel exploiting the advantages of distributed multi-threaded process models, typical of big data scenario. In this context we propose a control-flow- based approach to ETL process modeling, which starts from business facts identification, and represents ETL processes using BPMN notation, which is the foundation for machine-readable code. Our main contribution consists in a proposal for structuring ETL processes and related objects and in its application to a business case. The paper has been already published at Procedia Technology, Volume 16, 2014, Pages 471-480, and this version shows only minor updates

Keywords: Business Intelligence; ETL; Process & Conceptual Models; Operational Intelligence.

1 Introduction

Business Intelligence (BI) can be defined as the process of getting information about the business from available data sources [6]. It assists managers to take correct decisions based on facts given at the right time/place throughout the life of the business.

The exponential growth of data streams is a big challenge for BI and Business Analytics (BA) as decisions based on fresh information represent a competitive advantage. This challenge is addressed by Real-time BI and Operational Intelligence (OI) that provide visibility into Business Processes (BPs), streaming events, and operations as they are happening. These topics go under Big Data challenges, where the new frontier of data management must combine big data volumes with event-centric, speed up processing that allow delivering and accessing information with low latency. Conceptually similar to OI, Business Activity Monitoring (BAM [7] is an enterprise

SEBD 2018, June 24-27, 2018, Castellaneta Marina, Italy.

solution that allows monitoring business activity across operational systems and BPs. It refers to the aggregation, analysis, and presentation of real-time data about customers' and partners' activities inside and across organizations. BAM is the real-time and event-driven extension of BI: while BI products usually handle historical data stored into a Data Warehouse (DWH), BAM technologies provide managers with real-time business analyses obtained by operational data sources, more and more integrated with cloud-based resources for achieving faster Return of Investments and lowering costs [3]. The success of OI, BAM and BI systems depends mostly on the adequacy of the populating system: ETL (Extract-Load-Transformation) processes are, therefore, the critical feeding component of DWH/BI systems as they retrieve data from operational systems and pre-process them for further analysis [12]. An ETL system translates specific decision-making processes into system rules but there are several challenges: volatile business rules, heterogeneous operational data schemas, proprietary ETL tools, different notations, complex ETL porting processes. As of today, there is no widely adopted methodology covering the ETL development cycle, with an easy notation for user profiles, allowing to map the model on the execution environment and offering pre-implementation validation features. We believe that in order to bridge the gap between business and technical requirements and encapsulate business requirements into technical specifications, ETL processes should be designed by starting from business facts (BFs), thus supporting business users in decision-making processes and representing business rules and entities as soon as possible in the BI process design. Such a fact-centered approach to ETL process design can split the traditional black-box approach into several fact-centered flows, which can be processed in parallel exploiting the advantages of distributed multi-threaded process models, typical of big data scenario. In this paper, the advantages of control flow models and BPMN notation are applied to ETL process design, as defined in [4, 1, 5]. First, design patterns allow structuring the process and selecting required data. Second, a uniform notation for BPs and DWH modelling eases the communication between IT and business roles. Third, non-functional requirements (e.g., performance indicators, data freshness) can be specified more easily. We propose to structure the ETL design process starting from the identification of BFs and to define a reference model for representing the ETL process. The integration between the fact-centered approach and control flow models allows identifying relevant business objects and isolating related facts in order to handle them independently.

The paper is organized as follows. Section 2 analyzes existing works on ETL process conceptual models; Section 3 discusses our case study; the proposed approach and application are described in Section 4; conclusions are presented in Section 5.

2 Related Works

Several efforts have been proposed for the conceptual modeling of ETL processes, including ad hoc formalism approaches based on standard languages like UML [10] or MDA [11]. Conceptual models that use BPMN notation for ETL design have been also already proposed. The work we present in this paper is built along the lines of [1] and [4, 5]. In the former Akkaoui, Mazón and others present a conceptual model based on the BPMN standard and provide a BPMN representation for frequently used ETL design constructs. They propose a meta-model for conceptual modeling of ETL processes based on the separation between control and data processes, and on the classification of ETL objects resulting from a study of the most used commercial and open source ETL tools. The issue of ETL conceptual view is also addressed in [4, 5]; authors propose the use of BP models for a conceptual view of ETL, and show how to translate this conceptual view to a logical and a physical ETL view that can be optimized. Our work differs from those described because we propose a fact centered approach to ETL design which allows obtaining analytical up-to-date data in a timely and efficient manner, and a control flows based modeling of ETL processes, represented with BPMN notation.

3 Preliminaries and running example

A BI system is based on data sources analysis, design and implementation of the DWH that store analytical data and on related ETL procedures, according to its typical 4-level architecture (Fig. 1) [8]. The integration of heterogeneous sources is composed of ETL procedures for extracting, integrating, cleaning, validating, filtering data and then loading them into a staging area, posed in a reconciled model which creates a central data reference model for the whole enterprise and introduces a clear separation between extraction and integration problems and issues related to DWH loading process. The DWH can be directly consulted or used as a source to build data marts (i.e., data subsets/aggregations in the DWH). The concepts of interest in the decision-making process are named facts, which typically match with events that occur within the enterprise. Every fact represents a set of events, quantitatively described by measures and analysis dimensions, detailed with hierarchies of attributes. They are modeled as Dimensional Fact Models (DFMs) [8] so that the efficient consultation of integrated data is available for reports, analyses and simulations.

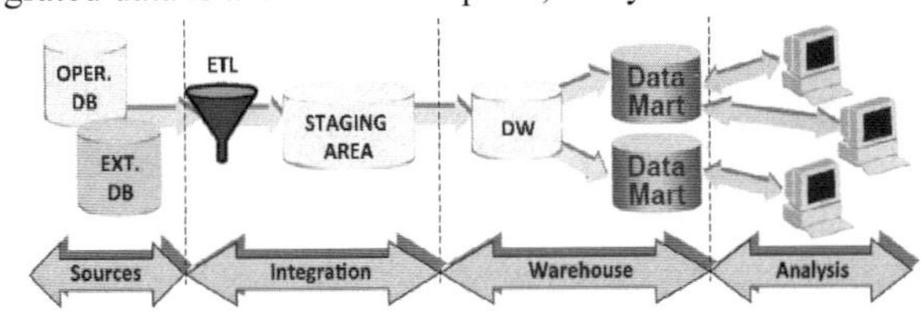

Fig. 1. Data warehousing system architecture [8]

ETL procedures require constraints checks for filtering data according to quality rules in terms of business rules and format inconsistencies. Some these rules (e.g., exception handling, data workflow patterns) can be derived from control-flow patterns. Wrong data feed a specific database that logs error types, source tables and execution dates. In our approach we propose a method to structure ETL processes based on relevant BFs, and to model them according to control-flow models.

Let us now discuss our running example: an Italian company needs a Service Level Agreement (SLA) management platform to calculate and present service levels associated with fidelity cards printing and delivery services. Operational data from several relational data sources must be mapped into hyper-cubes via an ETL process in order to produce reports and booklets for controlling the quality of services according to SLAs. Starting from the operational data sources, the system runs ETL procedures to populate the reconciled model and then the hyper-cubes. Data stored into the operational database is about fidelity cards details, and related events, which correspond to facts defined into the DWH. In this running case we describe the application of the proposed approach to fidelity cards printing, delivery and complaint events.

4 The fact-based ETL process

BFs are business artifacts meaningful to business. They can be modeled as business domain objects for transactional aims or as DFM for analytical processing. Once a BF has been defined in the domain, it must be populated starting from heterogeneous data sources. As in [1], we consider the ETL process as a combination of two perspectives. First, a *control flow process*, which manages the branching and synchronization of the flows, handles execution errors and exceptions and coordinates information exchange with external processes. Second, a *data process* that sends operational to the DWH, thus providing insights about inputs and outputs of each process element. Therefore, in Fig.2 we propose our fact population data process, which exploits the conceptual separation between quality management, data and fact population processes.

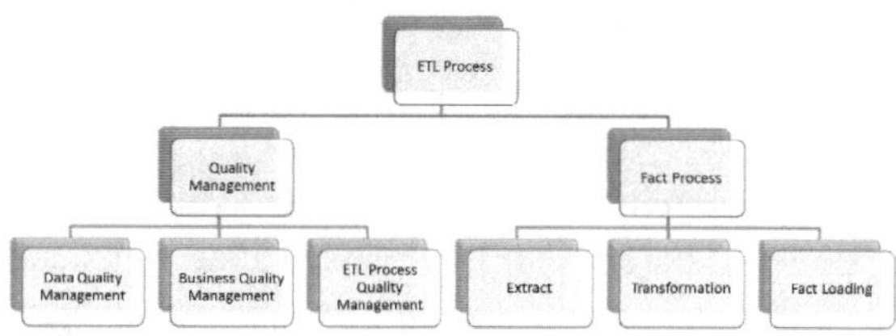

Fig. 2. ETL Process Model

The Quality Management can be further specialized as it includes data quality, ETL process and BP management; it can be considered as an event generator that checks the compliance with given constraints on business rules, data formats, integrity and ETL rules. The Quality Management handles quality checks within the whole ETL process, at different levels, via transformations exploiting syntactic and semantic rules, or business and ETL constraints. In particular, the Data Quality Management phase considers the syntactic accuracy of collected data and applies syntactic constraints to extract and load data into the reconciled model. These rules allow discarding incorrect data coming from errors that may affect the population process.

In addition to the rules on syntactic data accuracy, ETL processes need the definition and application of business rules that assess data coherence/consistency within the specific reference domain and which are defined into the Business Quality Management phase, which includes the procedures for applying business rules to data, in order to filter records out of constraints. The ETL Process Quality Management aims to filter data on constraints related to the ETL procedures (e.g., they verify correctness of data produced by ETL modules to prevent duplicated or contradicting data).

The output of the Quality Management process is the storage of filtered data into the reconciled model according to the Fact management process or into the log database that include a record for each violated constraint, with the following information: source table name, record identification, error code, error description, date check. This approach allows tracking data source errors, easily identifying reasons for records' discards and obtaining statistics such as the most violated constraint, and so on. The Fact Management Process handles data entry into data structures that can be staging area tables of reconciled models or facts inside a DWH. In both cases, the population process is constituted by a first phase of data extraction, followed by a transformation step and finally by the loading of transformed data into the specific reconciled or fact tables. In particular, the Extract activity performs the initial collection of data that will be transformed and loaded into the destination and for the integration of multiple data sources, managing topics such as format/conceptual heterogeneity, due to differences in communication protocols, data formats, schemas, vocabularies, etc. The Transformation process handles activities related to the second step of the ETL Process, which aims to obtain analytical data from operational ones, and to match input data with output data structures. Typical ETL transformation procedures include data summarization, derivation, aggregation, conversion, constants substitution, setting of values to null or default based on particular conditions, and so on. Finally, the Load module administers the population of the target table, which can be part of a reconciled database, a fact or a dimension, including the management of primary keys, integrity constraints and indexes.

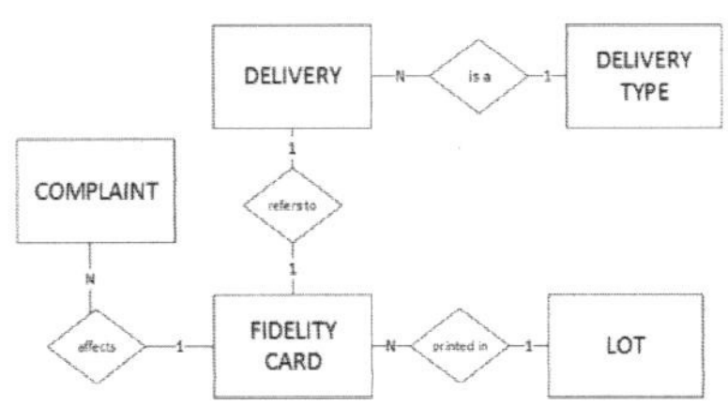

Fig. 3. Conceptual representation of reconciled model

In our model, we design an ETL process for each BF; therefore the whole ETL process can be considered as a set of fact processes and quality rules checks, which can be integrated and managed through control flow processes. We propose to design ETL starting from the definition of BFs and to split ETL process in order to isolate them within the flow. This approach: 1) allows managing facts independently, in a framework providing the integration aspects; 2) helps to structure ETL design; 3) allows business users working on their BFs even if the whole process is not completed yet. The result is the reduction of BF processing cycle, and the timely provision of analytical data. Splitting and fastening the ETL process is one of the steps for speeding BA process up enabling higher response times, which are fundamental in real-time BA systems. Furthermore, ETL process representation based on control flow models, and in particular on BPMN notation, adds information about accountability, as it allows linking process activities with the involved user profiles. Profiles typically involved in an ETL process include: 1) *Data Provider* (who assesses data readiness); 2) *Data Quality Supervisor* (who checks for data accuracy and correctness from a business point of view); 3) *Technician* (who handles the technical cycle). Roles definition, together with a BPMN-based conceptual modeling of the ETL process, improves accountability: at any time a problem occurs, managers are able to immediately know the activity that generates the problem and who is accountable for it.

Now we apply the proposed approach to our running example described in the previous section. Starting from a portion of the conceptual schema of the reconciled model, and from the DFM model corresponding to fidelity cards delivery, we illustrate the ETL process and the transformation that load the Delivery table of the reconciled model, both modeled with BPMN notation.

Fig. 3 shows the Entity-Relationship (ER) model that represents fidelity cards printing, delivery and complaints events. The printing event is modeled by the relationship between Fidelity Card and Lot entities: a printing lot includes several cards, and each card can be associated only with a lot. A delivery event is linked to each fidelity card: delivery detailed data, such as delivery date or payment, are included into Delivery entity, whereas Delivery Type entity is used to classify feasible delivery typologies, according to adopted procedures. The relationship between Fidelity Card and Complaint models complaint events: one or more complaint events can be registered on the same card, and each of them is linked to a single card.

Once the reconciled model is populated, a second step of ETL procedures elaborates data and store them into hyper-cubes. Fig. 4 (left side) shows the DFM for analytical data on fidelity cards delivery events (i.e, one of the outputs in the ETL process). Delivery events can be analyzed along many dimensions (e.g., state, card, delivery and registration date, etc.). By applying the proposed approach to ETL process that loads reconciled model tables, we represent the process in BPMN notation; Fig. 4 (right side) refers to fidelity cards printing, delivery and complaint events loading.

The process is represented as a set of complex activities, aggregated in sub-processes (each of them corresponds to a table of the reconciled model). Activity execution is modeled through the Parallel Split workflow control pattern, used when a single thread of control splits into multiple threads that can be executed in parallel [9]. In BPMN notation, the pattern is represented with a parallel gateway, to highlight the fact-centered approach that allows independently running and handling single tables' loading. The whole process ends when all the activities are concluded, according with Synchronization workflow control pattern, used when multiple parallel activities converge into one single thread of control, thus synchronizing multiple threads [9].

Each activity of the previous ETL process representation is a sub-process that can be further detailed and modeled with BPMN notation. As an example, Fig. 5 shows the BPMN representation of the fact process related to the Delivery table loading process. The fact process starts collecting operational data related to cards delivery

(Extraction phase), and this activity is in charge of the Data Provider. The process goes on with two quality controls, through which card identifier validity and delivery date existence are checked; the Data Quality Supervisor is accountable for these checks, whereas the Technician is responsible for error handling and event insertion into the appropriate table. Quality checks are modeled with the Exclusive Choice workflow control pattern, used when one of several branches is chosen, based on a decision or workflow control data [9]. Technician is also accountable for the following steps, related to lookups made in order to obtain cards and delivery codes, and to record sorting; this activity closes the Transformation phase. The last step of the fact process is the Loading phase, which inserts data into the Delivery table of the reconciled model. Activities inserted into this process are executed for each record of the data source Delivery table. The proposed approach applied to the running example allows organizing ETL process, by a conceptual separation between data quality management and facts loading procedures, and graphically representing the process, thanks to control flow models, design patterns and BPMN notation, in a fact-centered perspective, oriented to real-time BA.

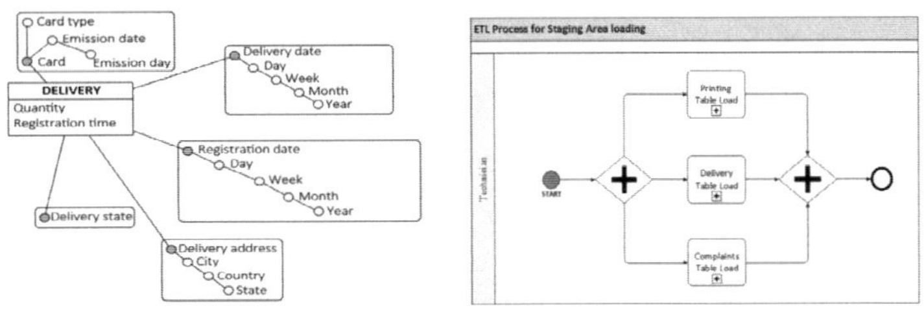

Fig. 4. DFM of cards delivery (on the left) and ETL process representation (on the right)

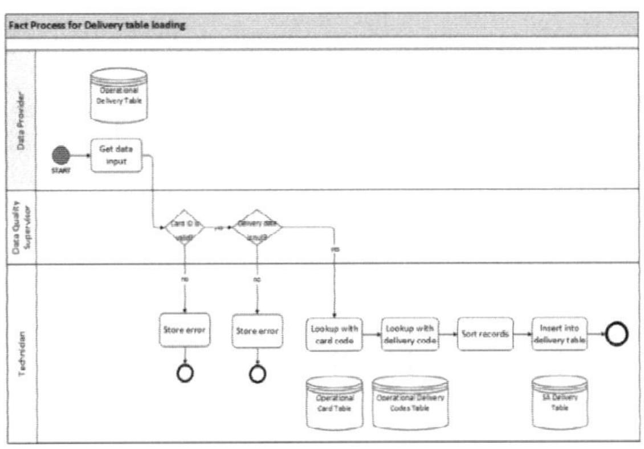

Fig. 5. Delivery Table Loading

5 Conclusions

The paper links conceptual ETL modeling with real-time BA and Big Data concepts. The changes in business requirements and needs as well as the growth of data volumes to be analyzed, lead to the introduction of new solutions to provide users with analytical data that support efficiently the decision-making process. In this context, we presented a fact centered approach to ETL design that aims at reducing ETL process granularity according to the identification of BFs so that they can be processed independently. Our proposal also structures ETL processes by distinguishing data quality management activities from fact processes, and by using control flow models, workflow patterns and the BPMN notation to support the conceptual representation of the ETL process. The proposed approach has been applied to a SLA Management platform managing service levels related to cards printing and delivery services.

Next steps will include the specification of a tool for graphically design and transform ETL process into ETL platform specific language. Moreover we are designing a wizard to support the definition of BFs, according to the business artifact theory [13].

Acknowledgement

This work is partially funded by Engineering S.p.A. and Essentia s.r.l.

References

1. El Akkaoui Z, Mazón JN, Vaisman A, Zimányi E. BPMN-Based Conceptual Modeling of ETL Processes. LNCS vol. 7448, 2012, pp 1-14.
2. Mell P, Grance T. The NIST Definition of Cloud Computing. Special Publication 800-145, National Institute of Standards and Technology, 2011.
3. Birst. Why Cloud BI? The 9 Substantial Benefits of SaaS BI. Birst, 2010.
4. Wilkinson K, Simitsis A, Dayal U, Castellanos M. Leveraging Business Process Models for ETL Design. Conceptual Modeling – ER 2010, pp 15-30.
5. Dayal U, Wilkinson K, Simitsis A, Castellanos M. Business Processes Meet Operational Business Intelligence. Bulletin of the IEEE Comp. Soc. TC on Data Engineering, 2009.
6. Azimuddin K, Karunesh S. Business Intelligence: a new dimension to business. Institute of Business Management, Pakistan Business Review, 2011.
7. Schmidt W. Business Activity Monitoring (BAM). Business Intelligence and Performance Management, Advanced Information and Knowledge Processing, 2013, pp 229-242.
8. Golfarelli M, Rizzi S. Data Warehouse. McGraw-Hill, 2006.
9. Van Der Aalst W. et al., Workflow Patterns. Distributed and Parallel Databases, 2003.
10. Luján-Mora S, Vassiliadis P, and Trujillo J. Data Mapping Diagrams for Data Warehouse Design with UML. In ER, pages 191–204, 2004.
11. Mazón JN, Trujillo J, Serrano MA, Piattini M. Applying MDA to the development of data warehouses. In DOLAP, pages 57–66, 2005.
12. Kimball R, Caserta J: The Data Warehouse ETL Toolkit: Practical Techniques for Extracting, Cleaning, Conforming, and Delivering Data. 2004.
13. Cohn, D., & Hull, R. Business Artifacts. Bulletin of the IEEE Comp. Soc. TC on Data Engineering, vol. 32, pp. 1-7, 2009.

First Steps towards Reasoning on Big Data with DLV

Nicola Leone[1], Simona Perri[1], Francesco Ricca[1],
Pierfrancesco Veltri[1,2], and Jessica Zangari[1]

[1] Department of Mathematics and Computer Science,
University of Calabria, Italy
{lastname}@mat.unical.it

[2] DLVSystem s.r.l.
P.zza Vermicelli, Polo Tecnologico, Rende, Italy
veltri@dlvsystem.com

Abstract. Answer Set Programming (ASP), that extends Datalog with powerful knowledge modeling constructs, is suitable for modeling both database-oriented applications and more complex combinatorial optimization tasks arising in decision-making. However, ASP systems were not conceived having the challenges of Big Data in mind; thus they are not applicable tout court in this new setting. This paper moves the first steps towards enabling the specification of reasoning tasks on Big Data with ASP. In particular we present our ongoing work in the direction of extending the well-known DLV system to interact in a plausible way with Big Data repositories.

Keywords: ASP, Datalog, Big Data

1 Introduction

Modern information systems are facing an unprecedented phenomenon: the massive production and storage of enormous amounts of data (Big Data). The need for processing Big Data repositories has recently implied a technological switch including the development of new hardware and software architectures [10, 8] to handle the exponentially growing quantity of data coming from network connected devices, large enterprise information systems, etc. Nonetheless, one of the most relevant challenges in this setting is to get real value from Big Data by modeling, understanding, and reasoning on the information present in large data stores [13], thus enabling the development of powerful decision-making systems and high-revenue applications.

The area of computing dedicated to representing and solving complex tasks using information is called knowledge representation and reasoning (KRR) [9]. A main goal of KRR is to introduce formalisms that simplify the task of designing and building complex applications. Among the mainstream approaches to KRR, logic-based formalisms are well-known for their expressiveness and powerful knowledge-modeling capabilities. In particular, Answer Set Programming (ASP) [3], that extends Datalog with powerful knowledge modeling constructs, is suitable for modeling both database-oriented applications and more complex combinatorial optimization tasks arising in decision-making [3]. However, ASP systems were not conceived having the challenges of Big Data in mind; thus they are not applicable tout court in this new setting.

Recently less expressive logic languages, like Datalog [16], or logic-programs with a different semantics [14], were implemented on top of Big Data platforms. However, no ASP system for Big Data is available at the moment (cfr. a recent survey [12]) and connecting ASP with mainstream technologies for Big Data is still an open problem.

This paper moves the first steps towards enabling the specification of reasoning tasks on Big Data with ASP. In particular we present our ongoing work in the direction of extending the well-known DLV system [11] (actually, its most recent version [1]) to interact in a plausible way with Big Data repositories. In our proposal DLV is connected to SQL-based data warehousing tools such as Hive via a translation component, that allows to demand the computation of space-demanding tasks/queries to well-assessed Big Data software, and leave to the standard ASP engine the burden of evaluating more computationally complex decision-making tasks over a selection of the original data.

2 Answer Set Programming

In this Section, we briefly recall syntax of the ASP language. For ASP semantics we refer the reader to [7].

A *term* is either a *simple term* or a *functional term*. A *simple term* is either a constant or a variable. If $t_1 \ldots t_n$ are terms and f is a function symbol of arity n, then $f(t_1, \ldots, t_n)$ is a *functional term*. If $t_1, \ldots, t_k$ are terms and p is a *predicate symbol* of arity k, then $p(t_1, \ldots, t_k)$ is an *atom*. A *literal* l is of the form a or *not* a, where a is an atom; in the former case l is *positive*, otherwise *negative*. A *rule* r is of the form $\alpha_1 | \cdots | \alpha_k$:– $\beta_1, \ldots, \beta_n, not\ \beta_{n+1}, \ldots, not\ \beta_m$. where $m \geq 0$, $k \geq 0$; $\alpha_1, \ldots, \alpha_k$ and $\beta_1, \ldots, \beta_m$ are atoms. We define $H(r) = \{\alpha_1, \ldots, \alpha_k\}$ (the *head* of r) and $B(r) = B^+(r) \cup B^-(r)$ (the *body* of r), where $B^+(r) = \{\beta_1, \ldots, \beta_n\}$ (the *positive body*) and $B^-(r) = \{not\ \beta_{n+1}, \ldots, not\ \beta_m\}$ (the *negative body*). If $H(r) = \emptyset$ then r is a *(strong) constraint*; if $B(r) = \emptyset$ and $|H(r)| = 1$ then r is a *fact*. A rule r is safe if each variable of r has an occurrence in $B^+(r)$. An ASP program is a finite set P of safe rules. A program (a rule, a literal) is said to be *ground* if it contains no variables. A predicate is defined

We remark that this definition of safety is specific for rules featuring only classical literals. For a complete definition we refer the reader to [5].

by a rule if the predicate occurs in the head of the rule. A predicate defined only by facts is an *EDB* predicate, the remaining predicates are *IDB* predicates. The set of all facts in P is denoted by $Facts(P)$; the set of instances of all *EDB* predicates in P is denoted by $EDB(P)$.

3 The DLV2 System

DLV2 [1] is the new version of the Answer Set Programming (ASP) system DLV. The system has been completely re-engineered: it now combines $\mathcal{I}$-DLV [4], a fully-compliant ASP-Core-2 grounder, with the well-assessed solver *wasp* [2]. Besides performance improvements w.r.t. to its predecessor, DLV2 is enriched with novel features such as support to annotations and directives that customize heuristics of the system and extend its solving capabilities. Moreover, the system offers some means to ease the interoperability with external sources of knowledge. In particular, by means of some $\mathcal{I}$-DLV features, it supports connections with relational and graph databases via explicit *directives* for importing/exporting data and calls to Python functions via *external atoms*. An accurate description of the system and the underlying techniques is out of the scope of this paper; we refer the interested reader to [4, 1]. Rather, in the following, we describe in more detail external atoms, since our proposal for integrating Big Data computation and ASP explicitly relies on them.

External Computation in DLV2 As anticipated above, the new DLV2 system, via its grounder $\mathcal{I}$-DLV, supports a special form for atoms, namely *external atoms*, geared towards external computations, whose extension is specified by means of external defined Python functions.

Formally, an external atom is of the form $\&p(t_0, \ldots, t_n; u_0, \ldots, u_m)$, where $n + m \geq 0$, $\&p$ is an *external predicate*, $t_0, \ldots, t_n$ are intended as *input terms*, and are separated from the *output terms* $u_0, \ldots, u_m$ by a semicolon (";"). In the following, we denote an external atom by $\&p(In; Out)$, where In and Out represent input and output terms, respectively.

An external literal is either *not* e or e, where e is an external atom, and the symbol *not* represents default negation. An external literal is safe if all input terms are safe, according to the safety definition in ASP-Core-2 standard [5]. External literals can appear only in the rule bodies, and each instance of an external predicate must appear with the same number of input and output terms throughout the whole program.

Given an external atom $\&p(In; Out)$ and a substitution σ, a ground instance of such external atom is obtained by applying σ to variables appearing in In and Out, obtaining $\sigma(\&p(In; Out)) = \&p(In_g; Out_g)$. The truth value of a ground external atom is given by the value $f_{\&p}(In_g, Out_g)$ of a decidable $n + m$-ary two-valued oracle function, where n and m are the lengths of In_g and Out_g, respectively. A negative ground external literal *not* e is *true*/*false* if e is *false*/*true*.

Intuitively, output terms are computed on the basis of the input ones, according to a semantics which is provided externally (i.e., from the outside of the logic program) by means of the definition of oracle functions written in Python. Basically, for each external predicate &*p* featuring n/m input/output terms, the user must define a Python function whose name is p, and having n/m input/output parameters. The function has to be compliant with Python version 3.

Example 1. As a simple example, let us consider the following rule, that makes use of an external predicate with two input and one output terms:

append(X, Y,Z) :– string(X), string(Y), &append_strings(X, Y;Z).

A program containing this rule must come along with the proper definition of *append_strings* within a Python function, as, for instance, the following:

```
def append_strings(X,Y): return str(X)+str(Y)
```

According to the given definition, as they are completely evaluated by $\mathcal{I}$-DLV as true or false, external predicates do not appear in the produced instantiation.

External atoms can be both functional and relational, i.e., they can return a single tuple or a set of tuples, as output. In Example 1, &*append_strings* is *functional*: the associated Python function returns a single value for each combination of the input values. In general, a functional external atom with $m > 0$ output terms must return a Python *sequence* containing m values. If $m = 1$, the output can be either as sequence containing a single value, or just a value, as in the example; if $m = 0$, the associated Python function must be boolean. A relational external atom with $m > 0$ is defined by a Python function that returns a sequence of m-sequences, where each inner sequence is composed by m values.

Example 2. The following rule uses a relational external atom:

prime_factor(X,Z) :– number(X), &compute_prime_factors(X;Z).

Intuitively, given a number X, the rule computes prime factors of X, demanding this task to a relational external atom, that receives as input the number X, and returns as output its factors. The semantics has to be provided via a Python function called *compute_prime_factors* returning a sequence of numbers each one representing a different factor of X.

4 Big DLV: ASP + Big Data

In this section we describe the main idea underlying our approach for integrating ASP computation, and in particular the DLV2 system, with Big Data sources. We first introduce a motivating example that will be used through the rest of the paper for illustrating the idea underlying our approach. Then, we provide some details about the usage of external atoms for our purposes.

4.1 KRR with Big Data

The following example showing a possible use case can be useful to grasp the intuition behind our approach.

`https://docs.python.org/3`

Let us consider the following scenario: Giovanni wants to go out for dinner and wants to invite a given number of people, possibly inviting friends of friends, in order to spend some funny and pleasant time. Invited people should be selected from a social network, choosing among the Giovanni's friendship net. In such social network subscribed people can add friends and mark some of these as close friends; moreover, the social network performs some stats on the degree of dislike among two people in the network. The following ASP program can be used to explore the friendship relations of such social network and then to provide Giovanni with suitable suggestions on people that could be invited.

$$
\begin{array}{ll}
& nfriends(10). \quad averageAge(25). \\
r_1 & possible\_friend(Y) \text{:-} close\_friend(giovanni, Y). \\
r_2 & possible\_friend(X) \text{:-} possible\_friend(Y), close\_friend(Y, X). \\
r_3 & suggested\_friend(Y, A) \text{:-} possible\_friend(Y), person(Y, A), A > 18. \\
r_4 & invite(X) \mid \text{-}invite(X) \text{:-} suggested\_friend(X). \\
r_5 & \text{:-} \#count\{X : invite(X)\}! = N, nfriends(N). \\
r_6 & \text{:-} \#sum\{A, X : suggested\_friend(X, A, \_), invite(X)\} < AVG * N, \\
& nfriends(N), averageAge(AVG). \\
r_7 & :\sim invite(X), suggested\_friend(X, \_), dislike(giovanni, X, D). \quad [D@1, X]
\end{array}
$$

The former two rules compute the transitive closure of the friendship relation of Giovanni, restricting the computation to close friends only; rule r_3 suggests a person Y if he is a possible friend and is older than 18; rule r_4 guesses if a suggested friend should be invited or not; rule r_5 ensures that the number of invited friends is exactly the desired one; r_6 imposes that the average age of the invited friends is not smaller than a given value; eventually, rule r_7 prefers solutions in which the total degree of dislike among Giovanni and invited people is minimized.

Intuitively, computing the transitive closure of the friendship relation in a social network could be very expensive when performed on a huge database. Thus, traditional main memory ASP systems cannot handle it; indeed, also the simple import of the friend relation is not feasible in practice. So, the idea is to delegate this heavy part of the computation to an external Big Data source. The remaining part that takes as input a heavily reduced part of the friendship, instead, can be conveniently expressed in a purely declarative way by means of ASP rules as reported above. We remark that from a computational perspective, this latter part encodes a NP-hard task that cannot be expressed by means of canonical RDB query languages such as SQL, Datalog, etc.

4.2 Interfacing DLV2 with Hive via External Atoms

In order to delegate the computation of data-intensive rules to Big Data tailored software, one can make use in the ASP program of a new external atom. Roughly, the external atom connects to a DB, may export some input facts to the DB, converts some given rules to queries, executes them on the DB and returns as output the extension of a specific predicate. In order to enable the external evaluation on a DB *db*, the ASP program should contain a rule r having in the body an external atom called *&bigasp*, that receives as input:

- *db* the name of the ODBC DSN (Data Source Name);
- *user* the name of the user who connects to the DB;
- *password* the password of that user;
- *rules* a string containing some Datalog rules that define the operations that will be performed on the DB;
- *output* a string representing the name of the relation to be imported in the ASP program;
- *input* [optional] a string containing a set of ASP facts that have to be exported to the DB.

During the evaluation, DLV2 invokes the external atom, imports the results of the evaluation and fills in the extension of the predicate *output* that has to appear as head in the rule r. Note that, this approach could be adopted to retrieve data from diverse Big Data sources.

Let us consider again our running example. We can delegate the computation of the transitive closure of the friendship relation to an external Big Data platform by replacing the first three rules in the program above with the following one:

$$
\begin{array}{l}
suggested\_friend(Y,A) :- \&bigasp(\text{“}my\_db\text{”}, \text{“}my\_user\text{”}, \text{“}my\_pass\text{”}, \text{“} \\
\quad possible\_friend(Y) :- close\_friend(giovanni, Y). \\
\quad possible\_friend(X) :- possible\_friend(Y), close\_friend(Y, X). \\
\quad suggested\_friend(Y, A) :- possible\_friend(Y), person(Y, A), A > 18.\text{”}, \\
\quad \text{“}suggested\_friend\text{”}; Y, A).
\end{array}
$$

Apart from connection parameters and the name of the output relation, the external atom takes as input the extracted rules; it invokes the machinery for enabling their evaluation on the external *my_db* and returns the results as a sequence of tuples representing the suggested friends with their age. Such tuples populate the extension of the *suggested_friend* relation so that the traditional ASP evaluation can continue.

5 System Architecture

We now describe an architecture where we indicate the software components that can be used to realize our idea. The general architecture of a framework for Big Data Analytics with ASP is composed by 3 macro-components as illustrated in Figure 1. In particular, the data layer of the system could rely on Hive, a data warehouse software project built on top of Hadoop for providing data summarization, query and analysis.

The choice of this tool is due to the fact that Hive is the mainstream for OLAP analysis over Big Data. Hive brings three main advantages: (i) it exploits

`http://hive.apache.org/`

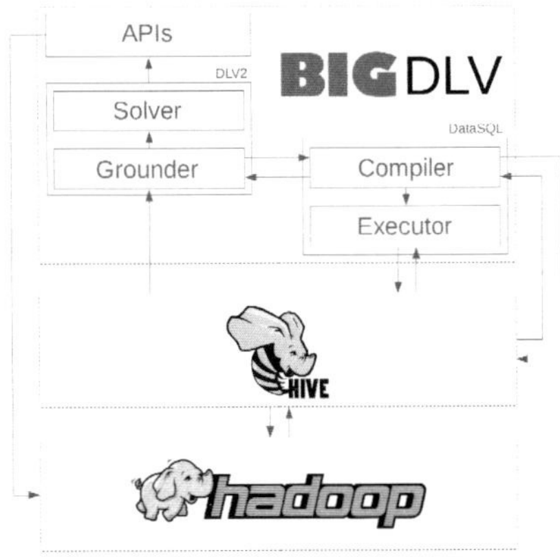

Fig. 1. General architecture of the framework for ASP reasoning over Big Data

the computational power of Hadoop clusters, (ii) it implements a standard relational model, that is equivalent to the data model supported by ASP, and (iii) it supports a querying language called H-QL, which is very close to the standard SQL. On top of Hive we find *BigDLV*, the core of our framework for Big Data Analytics. BigDLV should allow for reasoning in ASP over data stored and pre-processed within Hive. In particular, BigDLV should be able to extract extensions of input predicates from the underlying Big Data repository and, moreover, delegate parts of the computation to Hive. Figure 1 shows the internal architecture of BigDLV and focuses possible interactions with the underlying layers. This component encapsulates the DLV2 system which allows to define external atoms as discussed in Section 3: when an input program embeds a Datalog rule to be evaluated against the Hive repository, DLV2, by means of an external atom, invokes a Python component, called *DataSQL*, managing the interaction between DLV2 and Hive. DataSQL is in turn composed by two sub-modules, the *Compiler* and the *Executor*. The former compiles the rules received from DLV2 into an SQL query, while the latter runs the compiled query over Hive and retrieves the result. Results from Hive are first filtered out by the Executor and then returned back to DLV2. An end-user could ask the framework to store the final output of the whole evaluation process into the cluster. Note that, the Compiler module interacts directly with Hive in order to get information about table schemata matching the rule predicates. The implementation of the Compiler can follow the lines of [15] and thus supporting only stratified Datalog programs. Communication between DataSQL and Hive can be performed via *PyHive*, providing a collection of python DB-API interfaces for Hive.

https://github.com/dropbox/PyHive

https://www.python.org/dev/peps/pep-0249

6 Ongoing and Future Work

In this paper we described our idea for interfacing DLV2 with Big Data. Currently, we are implementing all the components mentioned in Section 4 and 5. Moreover we are developing a case of study that combines a Datalog sub-program modeling a heavy data-mining task (demanded to a Big Data platforms), with another component that models a computationally hard decision-making task (demanded to the ASP system). The case of study is part of the research project S^2BDW we are currently involved in and that focuses on a prognostic problem for foreseeing possible breaks on trains by analyzing data coming from sensors. Currently, we are focusing on applications in which the computation demanded to the external sources involves Big Data but returns an output which can be profitably handled in main memory. As a future work, we plan to better analyze the theoretical boundaries and limitations of our approach, in order to determine which kind of reasoning can be outsourced (e.g., going along the lines of [6]).

Acknowledgments. Work partially supported by MISE under project "Smarter Solutions in the Big Data World (S^2BDW)" (n. F/050389/01-02-03/X32).

References

1. Alviano, M., Calimeri, F., Dodaro, C., Fuscà, D., Leone, N., Perri, S., Ricca, F., Veltri, P., Zangari, J.: The ASP system DLV2. In: LPNMR. Lecture Notes in Computer Science, vol. 10377, pp. 215–221. Springer (2017)
2. Alviano, M., Dodaro, C., Leone, N., Ricca, F.: Advances in WASP. In: LPNMR. Lecture Notes in Computer Science, vol. 9345, pp. 40–54. Springer (2015)
3. Brewka, G., Eiter, T., Truszczynski, M.: Answer set programming at a glance. Commun. ACM **54**(12), 92–103 (2011)
4. Calimeri, F., Fuscà, D., Perri, S., Zangari, J.: I-DLV: the new intelligent grounder of DLV. Intelligenza Artificiale **11**(1), 5–20 (2017). https://doi.org/10.3233/IA-170104, `http://dx.doi.org/10.3233/IA-170104`
5. Calimeri, F., Ianni, G., Krennwallner, T., Ricca, F.: The answer set programming competition. AI Magazine **33**(4), 114 (2012)
6. Fan, W., Geerts, F., Libkin, L.: On scale independence for querying big data. In: PODS. pp. 51–62. ACM (2014)
7. Gelfond, M., Lifschitz, V.: The stable model semantics for logic programming. In: ICLP/SLP. vol. 88, pp. 1070–1080 (1988)
8. Ghemawat, S., Gobioff, H., Leung, S.: The google file system. In: SOSP. pp. 29–43. ACM (2003)
9. van Harmelen, F., Lifschitz, V., Porter, B.W. (eds.): Handbook of Knowledge Representation, Foundations of Artificial Intelligence, vol. 3. Elsevier (2008)
10. Harrison, G.: Next Generation Databases NoSQLand Big Data. Apress 2015 (2015)
11. Leone, N., Pfeifer, G., Faber, W., Eiter, T., Gottlob, G., Perri, S., Scarcello, F.: The DLV System for Knowledge Representation and Reasoning. ACM TOCL **7**(3), 499–562 (2006)
12. Lierler, Y., Maratea, M., Ricca, F.: Systems, engineering environments, and competitions. AI Magazine **37**(3), 45–52 (2016)

13. Sivarajah, U., Kamal, M.M., Irani, Z., Weerakkody, V.: Critical analysis of big data challenges and analytical methods. Journal of Business Research **70**, 263 – 286 (2017). https://doi.org/https://doi.org/10.1016/j.jbusres.2016.08.001
14. Tachmazidis, I., Antoniou, G., Faber, W.: Efficient computation of the well-founded semantics over big data. TPLP **14**(4-5), 445–459 (2014)
15. Terracina, G., Leone, N., Lio, V., Panetta, C.: Experimenting with recursive queries in database and logic programming systems. Theory and Practice of Logic Programming **8**(2), 129–165 (2008)
16. Yang, M., Shkapsky, A., Zaniolo, C.: Scaling up the performance of more powerful datalog systems on multicore machines. VLDB J. **26**(2), 229–248 (2017)

NewsVallum: Semantics-Aware Text and Image Processing for Fake News Detection system*

Giuliano Armano[1], Sebastiano Battiato[2], Davide Bennato[2], Ludovico Boratto[3], Salvatore M. Carta[1], Tommaso Di Noia[4], Eugenio Di Sciascio[4], Alessandro Ortis[2], Diego Reforgiato Recupero[1]

[1]Università degli studi di Cagliari
{salvatore,diego.reforgiato}@unica.it
[2]Università degli studi di Catania
battiato@dmi.unict.it, dbennato@unict.it, ortis@dmi.unict.it
[3]EURECAT, Centre Tecnològic de Catalunya
ludovico.boratto@acm.org
[4]Politecnico di Bari
{tommaso.dinoia,eugenio.disciascio}@poliba.it

Abstract. As a consequence of the social revolution we faced on the Web, news and information we daily enjoy may come from different and diverse sources which are not necessarily the traditional ones such as newspapers, either in their paper or online version, television, radio, etc. Everyone on the Web is allowed to produce and share news which can soon become viral if they follow the new media channels represented by social networks. This freedom in producing and sharing news comes with a counter-effect: the proliferation of fake news. Unfortunately, they can be very effective and may influence people and, more generally, the public opinion. We propose a combined approach of natural language and image processing that takes into account the semantics encoded within both text and images coming with news together with contextual information that may help in the classification of a news as fake or not.

1 Introduction

Over the past few years, a number of high-profile conspiracy theories and false stories have originated and spread on the Web. After the Boston Marathon bombings in 2013, a large number of tweets started to claim that the bombings were a “false flag” perpetrated by the United States government. Also, the GamerGate controversy started as a blogpost by a jaded ex-boyfriend that turned into a pseudo-political campaign of targeted online harassment. More recently, the Pizzagate conspiracy – a debunked theory connecting a restaurant

* Discussion Paper
SEBD 2018, June 24-27, 2018, Castellaneta Marina, Italy.

and members of the US Democratic Party to a child sex ring – led to a shooting in a Washington DC restaurant. These stories were all propagated via the use of "alternative" news sites like Infowars and "fringe" Web communities like 4chan. There are many reasons for the rise in alternative narratives, ranging from libelous (e.g., to harm the image of a particular person or group), political (e.g,. to influence voters), profit (e.g., to make money from advertising), or trolling. The barrier of entry for such alternative news sources has been greatly reduced by the Web and large social networks which offer the possibility to access to a growing amount of public content that is published worldwide every day [17]. Due to the negligible cost of distributing information over social media, fringe sites can quickly gain traction with large audiences. On the other hand, the growing impact of social media platforms allows any individual to public contents that are then spread globally. The entity of the diffusion of social media content is not related to its quality, but rather it is related to the content virality. However, the news shared on social platforms are not verified by users. As consequence, fake contents that stimulates the interest of people can be spread at large scale in very short time. Social media further changed the way we communicate online. Indeed, social posts contain very short text, often accompanied with a picture aimed to grab attention of users. Indeed, a social media post is more likely to get engagement if a photo accompanies it. Fake news presents itself as a content whose viral spread is possible thanks to the system of values it refers to. People tend to share content that expresses their own vision of the world – political, social, economic – usually without further checking. For this reason, we can imagine a process of checking the false content by referring to a series of metrics about the text and the content structure that could be used to identify the digital characteristics of a fake news.

2 Fake News Detection

The problem of detecting fake news is currently widely studied in literature [7] and there are sources that are known to spread fake news (e.g., both Wikipedia and FakeNewsWatch contain lists of fake-news websites). There are some experiments that try to identify fake news from a socio-structural point of view, such as the Hoaxy project (`https://hoaxy.iuni.iu.edu/`), which uses as an identification tool of false news the circulation of content among users through social media [26]. Conspiratorial narratives share several elements: the origin within particular social spaces (e.g., VKontakte, Reddit, 4Chan), the reference to an ideologically structured community (e.g., the no vax and alt-right groups), the use of deep fears (e.g., fears towards children). The conversation network topology is another element that in some cases reveals the content of the conversation itself, as shown in the Mapping Twitter Topic Network project.

Although academic research dedicated high efforts to fake news detection algorithms in the recent years, there is lack of solutions able to provide an on-demand, real time, news classification. Indeed, such a system requires a wide range of competences ranging from sociology, to combined image and Natural

Language Processing analysis, to big data management, Semantic Web, Machine Learning, etc. [14,11,16,25].

The amount of fake news is reaching crisis proportions and it is getting worse. Among the Vs that characterize Big Data (volume, variety, velocity), we have also the challenge of data veracity. Misinformation dynamics is where the big data concept of data veracity and the problem of fake news connect. Fake news is intentional misinformation and it is also dynamic.

Leveraging artificial intelligence is definitely a must to combat fake news. Artificial intelligence is able to learn behaviors based upon continually improving pattern recognition, so training a system to identify fake news based upon what sort of articles people have flagged as misinformation in the past is well within the reach of today's technology. Moreover, it is straightforward and very effective to apply machine learning tools of Big Data frameworks to come up with classification algorithms with the aim to spot fake news. In the context of fake news, tampered images represent a crucial role in reaching virality and allowing fake news to be shared at large scale. Although methods of multimedia forensics are able to detect tampered images [2,3,12,5], modern applications of AI can generate fake images depicting places, rooms, animals and even existing people. So far, both academic and industrial research laboratories built systems that can recognize faces and common objects in images with increasing accuracy. Now, similar methods are able to create realistic images. In this context, research efforts and development of recognition tools and systems for fake visual contents shared on the Web are needed [4,18]. Also, the exploitation of Natural Language Processing and Semantic Web technologies (lexical and semantic resources) and Cognitive Computation frameworks and tools (e.g., IBM Watson) is definitely a must. Those technologies allow going deeper toward the full comprehension of a given text [15]. They have already been successfully adopted in several artificial intelligence and natural language processing tasks and their combined usage has shown to outperform methods where they were used individually [16,22,24,13]. Their employment will provide huge benefits for the fake news recognition as well. Moreover, for the purposes of reaching the goal of fake news detection it is important to elaborate a scale of fake news complexity - from hoaxes to conspiracy theories - so as to isolate the digital elements that can help identifying the type of fake news.

2.1 The NewsVallum Approach

The proposed approach, we named **NewsVallum**, is expected to have high impact and to improve the state of the art on a wide range of research fields, ranging from applied artificial intelligence to the continuously disrupting field of the interaction between sociology and technology. An holistic approach is adopted, using the leading edge artificial intelligent techniques focused on image and text analysis. A joint approach to handle these two aspects that are foremost for understanding the characteristics of fake news is of paramount importance. In fact, people enjoy and share contents if they are in accordance with their vision of the world. As this subjective evaluation can be guided by both text and images, contents may be used to influence people towards a specific interpretation (this communicative process is called "framing").

As artificial intelligence is sometimes heralded as the new industrial revolution, a key motto of NewsVallum is to consider deep learning and reinforcement learning as the steam engine of this revolution, whereas data can be represented as its coal. A multimedia forensics approach is also used to make it possible to concentrate on news manipulation strategies not only at a technological level (i.e., using photo-editing programs), but also at a context level. In so doing, an analytic interpretation that goes beyond the level of technological manipulation is made, also concerning the contextualization of any given content. Another important characteristic of NewsVallum relies on the massive exploitation of sociological orientation and crowdsourcing. Here, the social dimension of fake news is used as theoretical reference to understand the consequences of the social processes concerning the main technological aspects related to the diffusion and circulation of fake contents. Moreover, the social dimension occurs also when the interpretation of contents is combined with multimedia forensics analysis strategies. This tends to compensate the lack of computational social science that typically characterizes research focused on fake news. In fact, being related to digital platforms, current research works have too often a strong technological bias and tend to forget the social dynamics of underlying the process. Crowdsourcing creates a collaboration between human analysis and computational approach, thus allowing to naturally focus on the human limits and on the technological constraints of fake contents. The NewsVallum approach targets two main goals. First of all, it is aimed at evaluating and assessing the reliability of information that is spread, published and shared through web platforms on a daily and also hourly basis. Indeed, so far the problem of automatic fake news classification has been tackled considering either text or images. In particular, the automatic classification of a piece of text as news has been tackled in [27] by applying a neural network and advanced text processing techniques. Authors in [20] highlighted the importance that images have in framing news stories and [19] studied how to characterize and identify fake images on Twitter during hurricane Sandy. To our knowledge, no proposals have been made able to classify a content as reliable or fake, which take into account the contribution of both text and images. Furthermore, NewsVallum aims to perform a real-time analysis of news, so that the procedures that will be devised and implemented could be used as web browser add-on. Providing the ability of issuing results in real time will be a crucial feature of the system, also due to the rapid spread that fake news have in social media. This first target will be the foundation for a yet more ambitious second target: a technology able to give a real time answer to common citizens needing an answer on the veracity of news found in social media and, in general, on the web. Through the exploitation of Linked Data technologies combined with personalized information access [1,6,?] the user is allowed to identify good and fake news as well as their sources. Recommendation systems fed by semantics-aware data have been proved to be very effective in the identification of items that can be of interest for users [9,10] also in mobile scenarios [23] by leveraging similarities and relatedness between entities in a knowledge graph [8]. Other than a proactive usage of data coming from Linked Data datasets, exploratory processes of Knowledge graphs [21] by the user may be helpful in finding the right information and identifying fake semantic associations.

2.2 Fake news detection and its sociological impact

NewsVallum targets both text and images together and this has also important sociological aspects and consequences for the following reasons.

The issue of fake news presents itself as the last stage of typical propaganda processes. The novelty lies in the introduction of the computational variable within the disinformation dynamics. According to the sociological theory of media construction of reality, media have a very important role in shaping our perception of the world. As long as mass media and social media keep spreading fake contents, the perception of the world could be modified accordingly, with enormous risks for democracy, security, and civil coexistence. The digital dimension of these dynamics makes these processes very complex, giving small chances to individuals in the task of finding truthful news and information. The properties of digital content such as persistence, replicability, scalability, searchability, greatly enhances the negative consequences that fake news can have on the society. This is the reason why, an innovative approach to the problem of disinformation is needed, able to combine advanced digital technologies (in particular, artificial intelligence, integrated analysis approaches, and multimedia forensics) with the goal of implementing a general framework able to give support in the task of understanding some of the social processes that underlie the current digital society. Only in this way it will be possible to develop a critical thinking positively biased by the underlying digital society. This result can be obtained by devising and implementing sophisticated technologies and approaches for fighting against a phenomenon that may have dangerous effects (on the medium and long run) on the whole society. The important and evolving requirements from the sociological point of view and the consequent technological challenges will be faced exploiting the recent revolutionary advances of AI domain. Indeed, there is evidence that modern artificial intelligence techniques (e.g. deep learning) are good at learning behaviors based on data, avoiding the influence of subjective (i.e., biased) opinions. These systems, which continuously improve the knowledge of patterns in the processed data, can be developed and trained for identifying fake news based on contents that people have flagged as misinformation in the past. Hence, this goal is well within the reach of today's technology.

Important goals that NewsVallum aims to reach for the technologies and algorithms developed in the approach are: i) simplicity, ii) scalability, as well as iii) versatility and reusability. The first goal can be attained considering that the employment of deep learning removes the need for feature engineering, replacing complex engineering-heavy pipelines with simple, end-to-end trainable models. Scalability will be addressed taking advantage of the Moore's law, as the proposed approaches are highly amenable to parallelization on GPUs. Versatility and reusability can be obtained as the deep learning models to be developed can be trained on additional data without restarting from scratch. This last feature is very important for the domain of fake news, in which continuous online learning is a preferred option.

Fake news detection is currently a topic of central interest at national and international level. At national level, one of the biggest Italian newspaper claims that 2017 was the year of fake news spread and even in 2018 several Italian newspapers discuss how fake news are fueling misinformation in politics, economics, and sport events. There is a specialized national police team entrusted with facing the problem, although it usually lacks of the powerful tools to deal with the problem. In the US, the spread of fake news has been seen as part of the rise of post-truth politics, in which the debate is framed by appeals to emotion disconnected from the details of policy. A study conducted by Stanford Graduate School of Education revealed difficulties of middle, high school and college students experienced in differentiating between advertisements and news articles where the information originated. The same study showed that 44% of all adults get their news from Facebook, and further investigations showed that nearly 40% of content by far-right Facebook pages and 19% of extreme left-leaning pages were false or misleading

3 Conclusion

The growing interest in fake news is motivated by the fact that people are typically not suited to distinguish between good information and fake news, in particular when the source of information is the Internet (and especially social media). In this context, the global nature of such an information-sharing environment allows fake news having a big impact in many fields, including politics, business, and health, at a worldwide scale. For these reasons, we expect that NewsVallum will find several practical applications that concern the verification of online contents. While providing services to detect, authenticate and check the reliability of online contents, the activities and research achievements related to NewsVallum would pursue and accelerate the technological and scientific progress in the field. Moreover, deep learning is currently considered a main research topic in the field of AI, as it creates the conditions for spreading the AI technology in various kinds of applications. NewsVallum is consistent with this trend, as it will give opportunities to young researchers for getting trained in this new and promising research topic. It is worth pointing out that the problem related with fake news, while affecting the information ecosystem, may also have negative impact on the democracy itself. In fact, fake contents may be used to generate hatred towards a social category, ruining the reputation of a political entity, and/or steering political elections with campaigns aimed at spreading false contents. Fake news is also an economic problem. Different economic stakeholders - no matter whether they are individuals, business companies or associations - perform decision-making by gathering information on different topics from digital sources, such as search engines or contents conveyed by social media. This is the reason why fake news, other than being an issue for the world of information, is also a problem for the world of business. In fact, in a society in which the speed of collecting and evaluating information is a strategic variable, fake news could lead to a wrong understanding of a particular socio-political scenario, with negative economic consequences. The expected impact of NewsVallum is to provide a set of tools to be used while assessing multimedia contents with the goal of unmasking fake news, so that political and/or economic decisions can be based on a proper evaluation of the data at hand.

References

1. Vito Walter Anelli, Tommaso Di Noia, Pasquale Lops, and Eugenio Di Sciascio. Feature factorization for top-n recommendation: From item rating to features relevance. In *Proceedings of the 1st Workshop on Intelligent Recommender Systems by Knowledge Transfer & Learning co-located with RecSys 2017*, pages 16–21, 2017.
2. Sebastiano Battiato, Giovanni Maria Farinella, Enrico Messina, and Giovanni Puglisi. Robust image alignment for tampering detection. *IEEE Transactions on Information Forensics and Security*, 7(4):1105–1117, 2012.
3. Sebastiano Battiato, Giovanni Maria Farinella, Giovanni Puglisi, and Daniele Ravì. Aligning codebooks for near duplicate image detection. *Multimedia Tools and Applications*, 72(2):1483–1506, 2014.
4. Sebastiano Battiato, Oliver Giudice, and Antonino Paratore. Multimedia forensics: discovering the history of multimedia contents. In *Proceedings of the 17th International Conference on Computer Systems and Technologies 2016*, pages 5–16, 2016.
5. Sebastiano Battiato and Giuseppe Messina. Digital forgery estimation into dct domain: A critical analysis. In *Proceedings of the First ACM Workshop on Multimedia in Forensics*, MiFor '09, pages 37–42, New York, NY, USA, 2009. ACM.
6. Vito Bellini, Vito Walter Anelli, Tommaso Di Noia, and Eugenio Di Sciascio. Autoencoding user ratings via knowledge graphs in recommendation scenarios. In *Proceedings of the 2Nd Workshop on Deep Learning for Recommender Systems*, DLRS 2017, pages 60–66, 2017.
7. Davide Bennato. The shift from public science communication to public relations. the vaxxed case. *JCOM*, 16(02):C02_en–2, 2017.
8. T. Di Noia, V.C. Ostuni, J. Rosati, P. Tomeo, E. Di Sciascio, R. Mirizzi, and C. Bartolini. Building a relatedness graph from linked open data: A case study in the it domain. *Expert Systems with Applications*, 44:354–366, 2016.
9. T. Di Noia, V.C. Ostuni, P. Tomeo, and E. Di Sciascio. Sprank: Semantic path-based ranking for top-n recommendations using linked open data. *ACM Transactions on Intelligent Systems and Technology*, 8(1), 2016.
10. Tommaso Di Noia, Vito Claudio Ostuni, Jessica Rosati, Paolo Tomeo, and Eugenio Di Sciascio. An analysis of users' propensity toward diversity in recommendations. In *Proceedings of the 8th ACM Conference on Recommender Systems*, RecSys '14, pages 285–288, 2014.
11. Amna Dridi and Diego Reforgiato Recupero. Leveraging semantics for sentiment polarity detection in social media. *International Journal of Machine Learning and Cybernetics*, 2017.
12. Fausto Galvan, Giovanni Puglisi, Arcangelo Ranieri Bruna, and Sebastiano Battiato. First quantization matrix estimation from double compressed jpeg images. *IEEE Transactions on Information Forensics and Security*, 9(8):1299–1310, 2014.

13. Aldo Gangemi, Valentina Presutti, and Diego Reforgiato Recupero. Frame-based detection of opinion holders and topics: A model and a tool. *IEEE Comp. Int. Mag.*, 9(1):20–30, 2014.
14. Aldo Gangemi, Valentina Presutti, Diego Reforgiato Recupero, Andrea Giovanni Nuzzolese, Francesco Draicchio, and Misael Mongiovì. Semantic web machine reading with FRED. *Semantic Web*, 8(6):873–893, 2017.
15. Aldo Gangemi, Valentina Presutti, Diego Reforgiato Recupero, Andrea Giovanni Nuzzolese, Francesco Draicchio, and Misael Mongiovì. Semantic web machine reading with fred. *Semantic Web*, 8(6):873–893, 2017.
16. Aldo Gangemi, Diego Reforgiato Recupero, Misael Mongiovì, Andrea Giovanni Nuzzolese, and Valentina Presutti. Identifying motifs for evaluating open knowledge extraction on the web. *Knowl.-Based Syst.*, 108:33–41, 2016.
17. Fabio Giglietto, Luca Rossi, and Davide Bennato. The open laboratory: Limits and possibilities of using facebook, twitter, and youtube as a research data source. *Journal of Technology in Human Services*, 30(3-4):145–159, 2012.
18. Oliver Giudice, Antonino Paratore, Marco Moltisanti, and Sebastiano Battiato. A classification engine for image ballistics of social data. In *International Conference on Image Analysis and Processing*, pages 625–636. Springer, 2017.
19. Aditi Gupta, Hemank Lamba, Ponnurangam Kumaraguru, and Anupam Joshi. Faking sandy: characterizing and identifying fake images on twitter during hurricane sandy. In *Proceedings of the 22nd international conference on World Wide Web*, pages 729–736. ACM, 2013.
20. Paul Messaris and Linus Abraham. The role of images in framing news stories. *Framing public life: Perspectives on media and our understanding of the social world*, pages 215–226, 2001.
21. Roberto Mirizzi, Azzurra Ragone, Tommaso Di Noia, and Eugenio Di Sciascio. Semantic wonder cloud: Exploratory search in dbpedia. In *Proceedings of the 10th International Conference on Current Trends in Web Engineering*, ICWE'10, pages 138–149, 2010.
22. Misael Mongiovì, Diego Reforgiato Recupero, Aldo Gangemi, Valentina Presutti, and Sergio Consoli. Merging open knowledge extracted from text with MERGILO. *Knowl.-Based Syst.*, 108:155–167, 2016.
23. Vito Claudio Ostuni, Giosia Gentile, Tommaso Di Noia, Roberto Mirizzi, Davide Romito, and Eugenio Di Sciascio. Mobile movie recommendations with linked data. In *Availability, Reliability, and Security in Information Systems and HCI - IFIP WG 8.4, 8.9, TC 5 International Cross-Domain Conference, CD-ARES 2013*, pages 400–415, 2013.
24. Diego Reforgiato Recupero, Valentina Presutti, Sergio Consoli, Aldo Gangemi, and Andrea Giovanni Nuzzolese. Sentilo: Frame-based sentiment analysis. *Cognitive Computation*, 7(2):211–225, 2015.
25. Diego Reforgiato Recupero, Sergio Consoli, Aldo Gangemi, Andrea Giovanni Nuzzolese, and Daria Spampinato. A semantic web based core engine to efficiently perform sentiment analysis. In *The Semantic Web: ESWC 2014 Satellite Events*, pages 245–248. Springer, 2014.
26. Chengcheng Shao, Giovanni Luca Ciampaglia, Alessandro Flammini, and Filippo Menczer. Hoaxy: A platform for tracking online misinformation. In *Proceedings of the 25th international conference companion on world wide web*, pages 745–750, 2016.
27. Marin Vuković, Krešimir Pripužić, and Hrvoje Belani. An intelligent automatic hoax detection system. In *International Conference on Knowledge-Based and Intelligent Information and Engineering Systems*, pages 318–325. Springer, 2009.

A Blockchain Infrastructure for the Semantic Web of Things

Michele Ruta*, Floriano Scioscia, Saverio Ieva,
Giovanna Capurso, Agnese Pinto, and Eugenio Di Sciascio

Polytechnic University of Bari, via E. Orabona 4, Bari (I-70125), Italy
name.surname@poliba.it

Abstract. The Semantic Web of Things (SWoT) improves the Internet of Things power by increasing resource representation capabilities through knowledge management and reasoning technologies adapted from the Semantic Web. This promotes information interoperability and decision autonomy. Nevertheless, trust and reliability issues remain basically unsolved. Large-scale, decentralized and dynamic infrastructures suffer from unpredictable volatility of nodes, which compromises resource availability. Trust and coordination are still difficult. Blockchain is increasingly used as a transactional data storage solution for distributed ledgers. It enables trustless collaboration by enforcing smart contracts and prevents data tampering by validating transactions through consensus protocols. This paper proposes a blockchain framework for SWoT contexts settled as a Service-Oriented Architecture. Nodes can exploit smart contracts for registration, discovery and selection of annotated services/resources. While semantic matchmaking enables relevant resource retrieval with logic-based ranking and explanation features, blockchain provides reliable transaction storage. A prototype has been developed by enhancing the standard *Hyperledger Iroha* framework. Application areas are discussed and experimental tests on a cluster of virtual nodes provide early insight on effectiveness, performance and scalability.

Keywords: Semantic Web of Things · Distributed transactional systems · Blockchain · Smart contracts · Service-Oriented Architectures · Semantic matchmaking

1 Introduction

The *Semantic Web of Things* (SWoT) [10] vision extends the Semantic Web initiative to the Internet of Things (IoT) by improving the representation capability of objects and environments through annotating them with semantically rich languages. Knowledge representation models and languages defined for the Semantic Web can provide the basic substrate for interoperable information modeling and sharing in the IoT. Machine understandability of adopted formalisms

* Corresponding author. Tel.: +39-339-635-4949; fax: +39-080-596-3410

allows applying automated inferences so that heterogeneous micro-devices, each conveying a small amount of information, can interact autonomously to provide high-level services to users, via decision support and task automation.

Anyway, IoT suffers from unpredictability of node and resource availability, due to the volatility of actors and appliances. This makes trust and coordination management difficult and these limits are inevitably inherited by the SWoT: their burden is particularly evident when reliable and trustworthy applications are needed. Blockchain technology is interesting from this perspective. In conventional distributed databases, a trusted intermediary is needed to guarantee irreversibility (*i.e.*, committed transactions cannot be altered or reverted) and prevent censorship (*i.e.*, all valid transactions are committed). *Blockchain* is a data structure and protocol for *trustless* distributed transactional systems: they avoid intermediaries by approving transactions through a distributed *consensus* protocol, which guarantees no single node –or small group of colluding nodes– can force the addition, removal or modification of data [2]. Blockchain could incorporate SWoT approaches providing interesting possibilities for large-scale distributed trustless systems. A SWoT blockchain basically amounts to a Service-Oriented Architecture (SOA) for regulating registration, discovery and selection operations. These tasks are intended as distributed and validated by consensus.

This paper proposes a framework for SWoT blockchain systems. A semantic-based resource discovery layer is integrated in a basic blockchain infrastructure, adding verifiable records for every single transaction. A distinguishing feature of the systems is *logic-based explanation* of discovery outcomes, grounded on non-standard inference services for semantic matchmaking [11]. The proposed system preserves fundamental blockchain features, also when size increases. Particularly, the effective and secure structure of the chain is capable of detecting erroneous or malicious changes on a transaction block, also in case of large amounts of volatile nodes. Annotations are registered as assets on the chain and non-standard inferences in [11] are executed by validating peers. The proposed framework has been implemented and tested on the *Hyperledger Iroha*[1] platform. It has been encapsulated in a cluster of *Docker*[2] containers to simulate a large SWoT infrastructure. Experiments on the framework assess the feasibility of the approach.

The remainder of the paper is reported hereafter. Section 2 recalls relevant background, while a functional and architectural description of the proposed framework is given in Section 3. Experimental results are provided in Section 4, followed by an overview of application areas for the approach in Section 5. Conclusion closes the paper.

2 Background

In what follows some relevant background is surveyed in order to make the paper self-contained.

[1] https://www.hyperledger.org/projects/iroha
[2] https://www.docker.com/

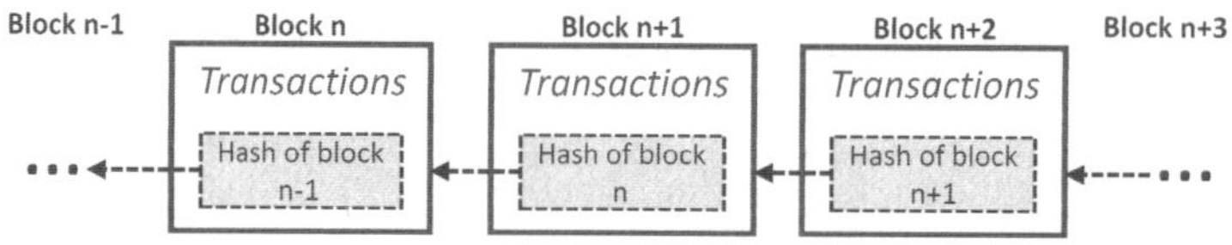

Fig. 1. Blockchain structure

2.1 Blockchain

The blockchain technology was born in 2009 with *Bitcoin*, an open source platform for electronic currency exploiting previous theoretical results on *Proof-of-Work* consensus algorithms [13]. Bitcoin relies on blockchain as a ledger of currency transfers. In a blockchain, transactions approved in a given time window are grouped in *blocks*. Figure 1 shows each block also contains a hash, computed from both the content of the block and the hash of the previous block. This forms a chain of blocks, preventing tampering even with old blocks without node agreement. Transactions are validated through consensus algorithms where all network nodes behave as peers, holding a copy of current blockchain status.

Many blockchain-based e-currencies have been proposed in latest years due to the worldwide success of Bitcoin. Furthermore, finance, industry and research communities have been increasingly experimenting with blockchain as a general-purpose distributed database enabling practical implementations of *Smart Contracts* (SCs) [12] *i.e.*, programs encoding and enforcing multi-party agreements and coordinated activities. While a trusted mediator is required in the original SC concept –restraining real-world deployments– blockchain consensus-based approach allows trustless collaboration of *Decentralized Autonomous Organizations* (DAOs) through parallel execution of SCs among network nodes. Every SC-enabled blockchain can thus be seen as a general-purpose application platform based on a distributed Virtual Machine (VM): emerging proposals include proprietary platforms (*e.g.*, *Ethereum*[3]) and standardization efforts, such as the *Hyperledger*[4] initiative steered by the Linux Foundation.

From a technical viewpoint, blockchain systems can be classified based on the following core design decisions:

– **Network access policy.** A blockchain network is *permissioned* if a white-list of allowed nodes exists and nodes are uniquely identified, or *permission-less* if any node can join at any time, even anonymously.

– **Consensus algorithm.** Permission-less systems require stricter consensus methods, such as Proof-of-Work, which is based on solving a cryptographic problem and guarantee data security unless a large portion of nodes is colluding to subvert the blockchain. Permissioned systems –where each node is accountable– may relax consensus constraints in order to reduce the computational load, by selecting simpler algorithms. State-machine replication protocols such as Byzantine Fault Tolerance (BFT) variants [13] are often adopted. The Iroha framework

[3] Ethereum Project: https://www.ethereum.org/

[4] Hyperledger: https://www.hyperledger.org/

adopted for the experiments of this paper uses a BFT consensus algorithm named *Sumeragi*.
– **Transaction model.** In typical blockchain systems, *assets* are registered and exchanged, so that at any time each node owns some assets in a given quantity. In the *Unspent Transaction Outputs* (UTXO) model, a transfer from A to B *consumes* (*i.e.*, deletes) records for A's spent assets and *produces* (*i.e.*, adds) new ones for B's received assets. In the *account-based* model, instead, every node has an account reporting all its assets, which is updated by transactions.
– **Smart contract language.** Blockchains can adopt any formalism for SC specification and execution, such as procedural (imperative) languages or logical (declarative) languages or automata [4]. Current proposals mostly adopt computationally complete programming languages, either existing (*e.g.*, Java in the *Iroha* framework of Hyperledger, exploited in this work) or created for the purpose (*e.g.*, Ethereum's *Solidity*).

Internet of Things (IoT) scenarios are expected to be among the main application areas in the near future. Blockchain applications in IoT contexts are mostly focused on supply chain [7] and Industry 4.0 [3]. The integration of Semantic Web technologies in blockchain has been discussed *e.g.*, in [3, 6], while [4] proposed *defeasible logics* for SC definition and implementation. Nevertheless, to the best of our knowledge this paper presents the first full blockchain framework integrating logic-based resource discovery.

2.2 Semantic Web of Things

Knowledge representation and reasoning in the SWoT are formally grounded on Description Logics (DLs), a family of logic languages in a decidable fragment of First Order Logic [1]. Basic DL syntax elements are: *concepts* (a.k.a. *classes*), standing for sets of objects; *roles* (a.k.a. *object properties*), linking pairs of objects in different concepts; *individuals* (a.k.a. *instances*), special named elements belonging to concepts. Each DL has a specific set of logical *constructors* for combining the above elements in concept and role *expressions*. Concept expressions can be used in *inclusion* (a.k.a. *subsumption*) and *definition* (a.k.a. *equivalence*) axioms, which model knowledge elicited for a given domain. A set of such axioms is called *Terminological Box (TBox)*, a.k.a. *ontology*. A set of individual axioms (a.k.a. *facts*) constitutes an *Assertion Box (ABox)*. TBox and ABox together make up a *Knowledge Base (KB)*.

The approach proposed in this paper leverages *semantic matchmaking*, *i.e.*, the retrieval of the most relevant resources for a given request, where both resources and requests are annotated with concept expressions w.r.t. a common ontology $\mathcal{T}$. Given a request R and a resource S, *subsumption* checks whether all features in R are included in S; *satisfiability* checks whether any constraint in R contradicts some specification in S. Unfortunately these classic inference services enable only a Boolean "full match or no match" approach. This is inadequate in complex scenarios, because full matches are rare and incompatibility is frequent when dealing with detailed resource descriptions. Therefore, non-standard inferences in [11] help to determine a semantic ranking of resources w.r.t. a request

and a logic-based explanation of outcomes:
– **Concept Contraction**: if request R and resource S are not compatible, Contraction determines which part of R is conflicting with S. If one retracts conflicting requirements in R, G (for *Give up*), a concept K (for *Keep*) is obtained, representing a contracted version of the original request, such that K and S are compatible w.r.t. $\mathcal{T}$. G represents "why" R and S clash.
– **Concept Abduction**: when R and S are compatible but S is not a full match for R, Abduction determines what should be hypothesized in S in order to completely satisfy R. The solution H (for *Hypothesis*) to Abduction is a concept representing "why" the subsumption relation does not hold. H can be interpreted as *what is requested in R and not specified in S*.
If R and S are incompatible, the matchmaking process uses Contraction to extract the compatible part K and then Abduction to obtain the required H_K for reaching a full match. Furthermore, *penalty functions* are computed based on the structure and number of elements in G and H_K [11], defining a well-founded *semantic distance* metric, which can be used to rank a set of resources by relevance (*i.e.*, semantic affinity) w.r.t. the request.

In SWoT contexts, computation resources of devices are strictly constrained and require careful software design. Adding more constructors makes DL languages more expressive, but leads to an increase in computational complexity of inference services, hence a tradeoff is needed. This paper refers to the moderately expressive *Attributive Language with unqualified Number restrictions* ($\mathcal{ALN}$) DL, which grants polynomial complexity to all the above standard and non-standard inferences.

3 Semantic-enhanced Blockchain for unpredictable scenarios

The proposed framework defines a semantic-based discovery layer built upon a standard blockchain system, retaining full backward compatibility.

3.1 Framework architecture

Figure 2 sketches the overall architecture, whose main features are reported hereafter.

- **Peer** agents registered in the blockchain are identified by their *public keys* and associated with *accounts*. Each agent can perform a semantic-based resource discovery in order to take ownership and transfer assets between accounts.
- **Assets** are annotated w.r.t. a domain ontology. They can represent physical or digital resources, as well as service instances. Peers can register assets through specific transactions, and annotations are stored in the blockchain.
- **Smart contracts** are enhanced by exploiting non-standard inference services described in Section 2.2. Particularly, each peer locally integrates an

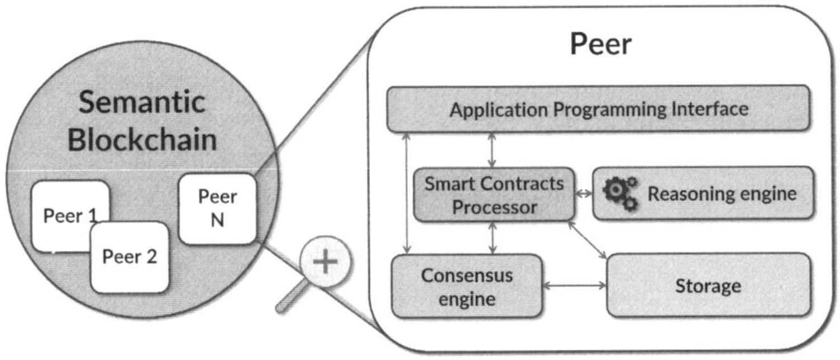

Fig. 2. Framework architecture

embedded matchmaking and reasoning engine, allowing semantic-based resource discovery [11].
- **Consensus engine** tracks and validates semantic-based transactions in a standard and transparent way.
- **Storage** for all transactions, including semantic ones, exploits *Merkle trees*, a data structure commonly adopted in blockchains for efficient detection of erroneous or malicious changes on a transaction block.

3.2 How to make smarter contracts: put semantics in the consensus protocol

The SWoT blockchain proposal is intended as a SOA enabling fundamental operations as registration, discovery, selection and final execution (payment). Such tasks are implemented as smart contracts, *i.e.*, their accomplishment is distributed and validation is reached by consensus. The distinguishing feature of the proposed approach w.r.t. basic blockchain infrastructures is the integration of advanced resource/service discovery grounded on semantic matchmaking. It allows computing a score measuring the semantic distance between the request and each available chain resource, both described w.r.t. the same domain ontology. This logic-based metric induces a relevance-ranked list of annotated elements w.r.t. the request. The non-standard inference services also provide a formal *explanation* of discovery outcomes, reinforcing user confidence in the discovery process. SOA primitives and corresponding SCs are outlined hereafter.

A. Resource registration. Multiple resource domains can coexist and be tracked in the same blockchain. Each domain is associated to a different ontology, providing the reference conceptual vocabulary for annotating resources. Resource instances are characterized by the following attributes:

- a Uniform Resource Identifier (URI) featuring the resource unambiguously (and possibly denoting its fruition endpoint, although this is not mandatory);

- a semantic annotation in Web Ontology Language (OWL 2)[5] describing the resource;
- the URI of the reference ontology, in order to cope with the co-existence of several resource domains in the same blockchain;
- a resource price: the framework supports any type of currency unit, pecuniary or otherwise (*e.g.*, in SWoT applications energy or time could be chosen).

By means of the `Registration` SC the owner node will register a resource as an asset on the blockchain storage, in order to make it available for discovery and usage.

B. Resource discovery. In order to search for a (set of) item(s), the requester randomly selects n peers and sends a multicast request specifying:

- URI of the reference ontology: this determines the resource domain, *i.e.*, the vocabulary used to express annotations of request and resources to be retrieved; the nodes receiving a request will not process resources annotated w.r.t. other ontologies in the semantic matchmaking;
- OWL semantic annotation of the request, specifying desired resource features and constraints;
- maximum price p_{max} the requester is willing to pay; resources with a price higher than this threshold will be skipped from matchmaking in order to reduce computational overhead;
- minimum semantic relevance threshold s_{min}, as a floating-point number in the $[0, 1]$ range, where 1 corresponds to a full match and 0 to a complete mismatch (both rare situations in realistic scenarios); after matchmaking, resources with a relevance score below this threshold will not be returned, as deemed irrelevant to the requester;
- maximum number of results r_{max} to be returned;
- requester's address.

The proposal adopts a *gossip-based* (a.k.a. *epidemic*) approach [5] to disseminate discovery requests and aggregate results as in Figure 3. This grants protocol simplicity and low computational overhead, which is a primary requirement in SWoT contexts. Nodes receiving the request execute semantic matchmaking of it with their own resources through an on-board matchmaking engine [11], implementing the non-standard inference services in Section 2.2. A list of at most r_{max} results satisfying both semantic relevance and price constraints is returned, ranked by relevance. Nodes also select other n random peers and forward the request. Nodes receiving forwarded requests behave in the same way, up to a search depth threshold m. Each queried node returns results directly to the original requester at the specified address.

C. Explanation. This is an optional step in a typical discovery process, invoked when a requester needs a justification of the matchmaking outcome. This

[5] OWL 2 Web Ontology Language Document Overview (Second Edition), W3C Recommendation 11 December 2012, http://www.w3.org/TR/owl2-overview/

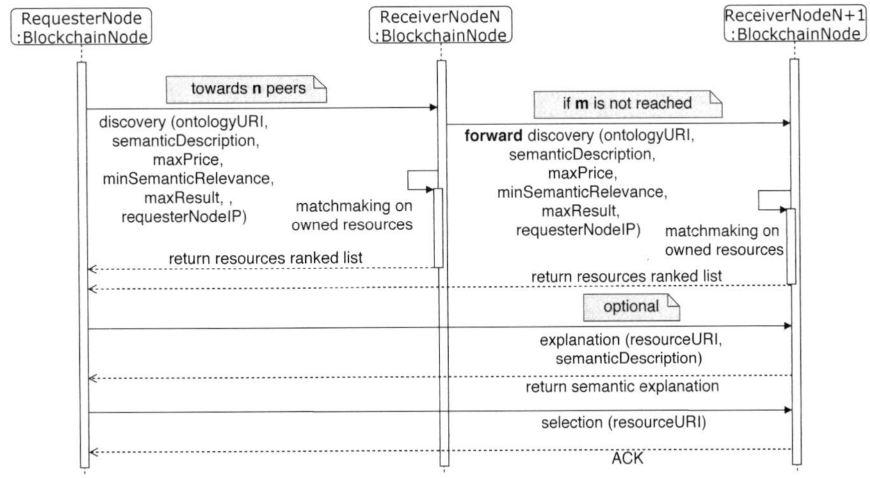

Fig. 3. Resource discovery and retrieval flow

can be useful, *e.g.*, to trigger a request refinement process [9], as it can make the requester aware of further features it did not include in its original request but it may be interested in. The requester node sends a unicast request containing: (i) the semantic annotation of the request; (ii) the URI of the discovered resource. The receiving node replies with the matchmaking outcome explanation, structured as: (i) semantic affinity score in the $[0, 1]$ interval; (ii) concept expressions of G and K from Concept Contraction and of H from Concept Abduction. G, K and H can be cached from the previous discovery step, if storage of the resource owner allows it.

D. Resource selection. After receiving all results –or just a subset, if the response delay of some nodes is greater than a fixed *timeout*– the requester selects the best resource(s) by means of `select` SC. A unicast message is delivered to the resource owner specifying the resource URI and a currency payment. The recipient answers with a properly usable resource representation: this depends on the actual kind of resource and meaning of the URI, *e.g.*, an interface endpoint to access a networked device or a further SC to be invoked. The proposal does not constrain resource fruition in any way, leaving application-specific details to the semantic annotation of the resources themselves.

The resource discovery and retrieval interaction sequence is shown in Figure 3. Each associated transaction is recorded on the blockchain for robustness, traceability and accountability purposes.

4 Performance assessment

In order to assess effectiveness and scalability of the proposed approach, an experimental evaluation campaign has been carried out starting from the *Iroha* framework from Hyperledger. The implemented prototype enhanced Iroha as in

what follows:
– the server API has been extended with support for semantic matchmaking;
– the SCs described in Section 3.2 have been implemented and the *Mini-ME* reasoning and matchmaking engine [11] has been integrated;
– *zlib*[6] compression library has been exploited to cope with the well-known verbosity of ontology languages as OWL.

In order to reach a quantitative performance analysis, small, medium and large scale chain scenarios have been considered, respectively with 50, 150 and 500 nodes. In each of them nodes have been split in two sets materially executing SC transactions with semantic-based discovery (see Section 3.2): *producers*, *i.e.*, providers of annotated resources, registered in the blockchain; *consumers*, *i.e.*, resource requesters.

The following experiment parameters have been set: (i) duration of 300 s; (ii) consumer/producer ratio of 0.1; (iii) 20 randomly-generated annotations per producer; (iv) each consumer sends a new randomly-generated request every 10 s; (v) each request can be forwarded to 4 nodes at most; (vi) a request is aborted if no match is found after 2 hops; (vii) the minimum threshold of semantic affinity is 0.9. Each scenario is executed several times by varying the following parameters: (i) the discovery timeout has been set to 2, 6 and 10 s; (ii) the explanation SC, described in Section 3.2, has been either enabled or disabled.

The experimental campaign has leveraged the adoption of *Docker* platform to deploy the testbed, by performing the following steps:
– the prototype has been compiled as a Docker image, to create all the scenarios;
– each node has been executed as a container instance of the compiled image;
– a Docker *Swarm mode* cluster has been deployed on 6 *VirtualBox* virtual machines running on a workstation[7], with an overlay network configured to allow communications among the Iroha nodes;
– the execution of experiments has been managed via the Docker API SDK[8].

The following performance metrics have been calculated: (i) average request processing time, both as all-out and split by task; (ii) average hit ratio per node, *i.e.*, percentage of requests with at least one resource satisfying the constraints within the given timeout. Experimental results are reported later on.

Time. Average turnaround times can be deemed as very low in experiments involving 50 and 150 nodes, as Figure 4 and Figure 5 show. the growth exhibits a linear trend, suggesting proper scaling. With 500 nodes, instead, absolute time reach the timeouts as depicted in Figure 6, due to the needed consensus about among a larger number of entities. Furthermore, in all the experiments the time of discovery process dominates the ones of explanation and selection phases. This could be due to the fact that matchmaking is the most computationally intensive task, despite the optimization of the adopted reasoning engine.

[6] http://zlib.net/
[7] Intel Xeon E5-2643 CPU at 3.30 GHz, 48 GB of RAM and Ubuntu 16.04 (64bit) operating system.
[8] https://github.com/spotify/docker-client

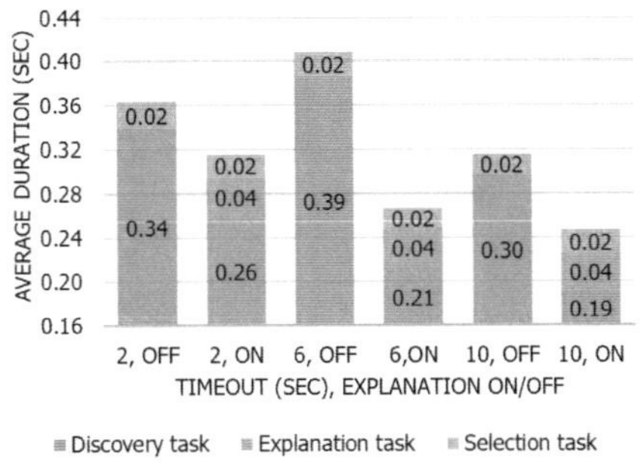

Fig. 4. Processing time for tasks on 50 nodes

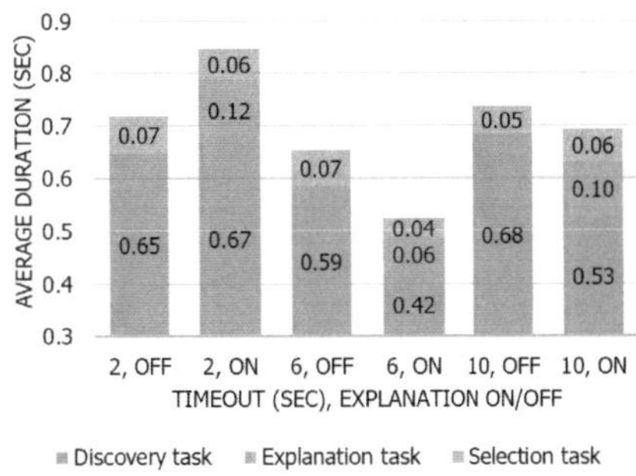

Fig. 5. Processing time for tasks on 150 nodes

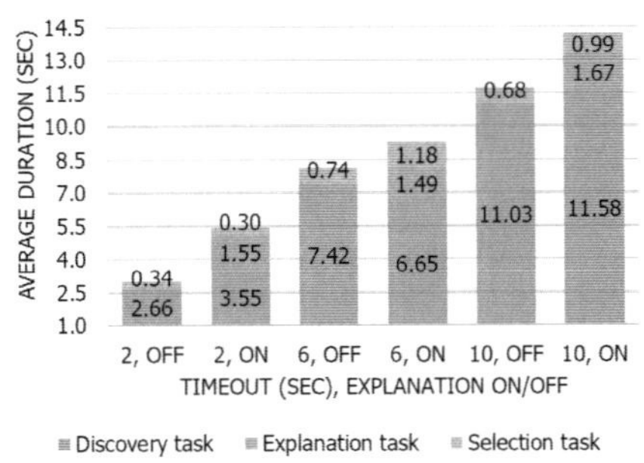

Fig. 6. Processing time for tasks on 500 nodes

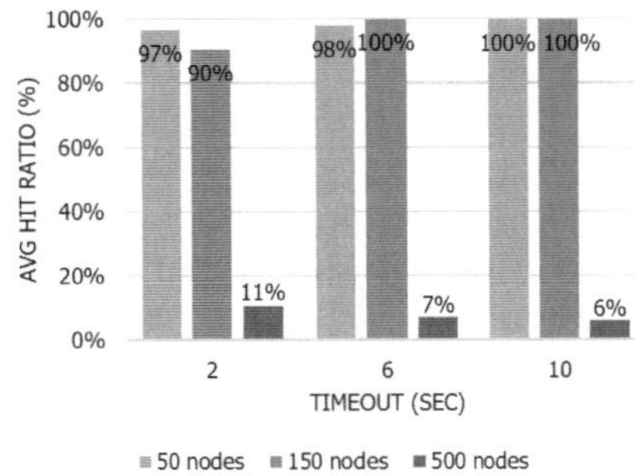

Fig. 7. Average hit ratio depending on timeout

Hit ratio. Figure 7 shows average results are closely related to the number of nodes. The best outcomes have been obtained in the small and medium scenarios with timeouts high enough. Conversely, in the 500 nodes case the average hit ratio is noticeably lower. The increased resource miss ratio is partially due to Docker Swarm deployment on a single host instead of adopting a more proper cluster computing environment: the large number of containers on the same host led to Docker resource contention issues affecting the CPU, file system and network load. Furthermore, the inherent complexity of consensus algorithms tends to increase at higher scales, leading to higher processing times and consequent increased probability of timeout expiration.

Early results supported the feasibility of the proposal, as performance is basically satisfactory for small-to-medium permissioned blockchains. Larger-scale scenarios could not be setup on the reference testbed due to the above limits with Docker Swarm deployment in a single-host environment. Testbed migration toward a computer cluster will be performed to re-evaluate semantic-enhanced blockchain performance in the same scenarios as well as to allow larger-scale simulations.

5 Applications

Semantic-enhanced blockchain systems enable discovery infrastructures for general-purpose machine-to-machine trustless marketplaces with minimal or no human intervention across multiple DAOs. This has several possible applications with potential transformation impact on relevant sectors.

– **Logistics.** Asset tracking and supply chain are among the most popular blockchain applications, due to the easy fit with existing industry standards. The simplest approaches rely on transactional ledgers for asset transfer [2]. Semantic-enhanced SC-based blockchains further allow any application logic to be implemented, and also support discoverable, composable and verifiable multi-step business processes in multi-party SOAs [8].

– **Industry 4.0**. IoT-based manufacturing benefits from blockchain technologies [2], granting not only a decentralized collaboration infrastructure, but also a ledger for process traceability of production and quality assurance. Semantic-based blockchain evolution can provide greater composition flexibility and rigorous process formalization.

– **Utility markets.** Energy, water and natural gas provisioning are increasingly relying on sensor networks, low-level digital control and high-level decision support. Semantic-enhanced blockchains can strongly support the *Smart Grid*, by providing both resource discovery and a robust ledger for contracts and payments, which are needed in large-scale peer-to-peer decentralized marketplaces.

– **Public sector.** Many public services can be made faster, cheaper and less error prone through process and data dematerialization. Blockchain technology can assist in the interfacing of the information systems of several independent branches and levels of the public administration. Furthermore, it plays the role of verifiable registry in property transfers as well as authentication and notary services. Semantic-based querying capabilities make information and functionalities more accessible to both citizens and decision-makers.

– **Financial services.** Traditional banks and finance institutions, private and public alike, are experimenting with blockchain technology to reduce operating costs of financial transactions management. Semantic-based approaches enable a marketplace of financial services, where atomic building blocks can be automatically discovered, compared and composed in order to provide the most suitable personalized solutions.

6 Conclusion

The paper proposed a framework redesigning resource discovery for SWoT scenarios thanks to an underlying blockchain infrastructure. Registration, discovery, selection and finalization tasks have been revisited as smart contracts with opportunistic and distributed execution, exploiting validation by consensus. Logic-based explanation of discovery outcomes is an important feature of the proposal, granted by non-standard inferences for request-resource matchmaking.

Future aims are basically directed to migrate the testbed toward a cluster of physical nodes, in order to remove bottlenecks biasing results and increase simulation scale. Development of case studies within the envisioned application areas is at an early stage and will be completed to fully validate benefits and possible limitations of the proposal in realistic settings.

Acknowledgements

This work was supported in part by Italian PON project ERHA (Enhanced Radiotherapy with HAdrons).

References

1. Baader, F., Calvanese, D., Mc Guinness, D., Nardi, D., Patel-Schneider, P.: The Description Logic Handbook. Cambridge University Press (2002)
2. Christidis, K., Devetsikiotis, M.: Blockchains and Smart Contracts for the Internet of Things. IEEE Access **4**, 2292–2303 (2016)
3. English, M., Auer, S., Domingue, J.: Block Chain Technologies & The Semantic Web: A Framework for Symbiotic Development. In: Lehmann, J., Thakkar, H., Halilaj, L., Asmat, R. (eds.) Computer Science Conference for University of Bonn Students. pp. 47–61 (2016)
4. Idelberger, F., Governatori, G., Riveret, R., Sartor, G.: Evaluation of logic-based smart contracts for blockchain systems. In: International Symposium on Rules and Rule Markup Languages for the Semantic Web. pp. 167–183. Springer (2016)
5. Jelasity, M., Montresor, A., Babaoglu, O.: Gossip-based aggregation in large dynamic networks. ACM Transactions on Computer Systems (TOCS) **23**(3), 219–252 (2005)
6. Kim, H.M., Laskowski, M.: Towards an Ontology-Driven Blockchain Design for Supply Chain Provenance (2016), https://ssrn.com/abstract=2828369
7. Korpela, K., Hallikas, J., Dahlberg, T.: Digital Supply Chain Transformation toward Blockchain Integration. In: Proceedings of the 50th Hawaii International Conference on System Sciences. pp. 4182–4191 (2017)
8. Norta, A.: Creation of smart-contracting collaborations for decentralized autonomous organizations. In: International Conference on Business Informatics Research. pp. 3–17. Springer (2015)
9. Ruta, M., Di Sciascio, E., Scioscia, F.: Concept Abduction and Contraction in Semantic-based P2P Environments. Web Intelligence and Agent Systems **9**(3), 179–207 (2011)
10. Scioscia, F., Ruta, M.: Building a Semantic Web of Things: issues and perspectives in information compression. In: Semantic Web Information Management (SWIM'09). In Proceedings of the 3rd IEEE International Conference on Semantic Computing (ICSC 2009). pp. 589–594. IEEE Computer Society (2009)
11. Scioscia, F., Ruta, M., Loseto, G., Gramegna, F., Ieva, S., Pinto, A., Di Sciascio, E.: A Mobile Matchmaker for the Ubiquitous Semantic Web. International Journal on Semantic Web and Information Systems (IJSWIS) **10**(4), 77–100 (2014)
12. Szabo, N.: Formalizing and securing relationships on public networks. First Monday **2**(9) (1997)
13. Vukolić, M.: The quest for scalable blockchain fabric: Proof-of-work vs. BFT replication. In: International Workshop on Open Problems in Network Security. pp. 112–125. Springer (2015)

Ethics-aware data governance (Vision Paper)

Letizia Tanca[1], Paolo Atzeni[3], Davide Azzalini[1], Ilaria Bartolini[2], Luca Cabibbo[3], Luca Calderoni[2], Paolo Ciaccia[2], Valter Crescenzi[3], Juan Carlos De Martin[6], Selina Fenoglietto[6], Donatella Firmani[3], Sergio Greco[4], Francesco Isgrò[5], Dario Maio[2], Davide Martinenghi[1], Maristella Matera[1], Paolo Merialdo[3], Cristian Molinaro[4], Marco Patella[2], Roberto Prevete[5], Elisa Quintarelli[1], Antonio Santangelo[6], Andrea Tagarelli[4], Guglielmo Tamburrini[5], and Riccardo Torlone[3]

[1]Politecnico di Milano, Italy, email: *first.last*@polimi.it
[2]Università di Bologna, Italy, email: *first.last*@unibo.it
[3]Università Roma Tre, Italy, email: *last*@uniroma3.it
[4]Università della Calabria, Italy, email: *last*@dimes.unical.it
[5]Università di Napoli Federico II, Italy, email: *last*@unina.it
[6]Politecnico di Torino, Italy, email: *last*@polito.it

Abstract. The number of datasets available to legal practitioners, policy makers, scientists, and many other categories of citizens is growing at an unprecedented rate. Ethics-aware data processing has become a pressing need, considering that data are often used within critical decision processes (e.g., staff evaluation, college admission, criminal sentencing). The goal of this paper is to propose a vision for the injection of ethical principles (fairness, non-discrimination, transparency, data protection, diversity, and human interpretability of results) into the data analysis lifecycle (source selection, data integration, and knowledge extraction) so as to make them first-class requirements. In our vision, a comprehensive checklist of ethical desiderata for data protection and processing needs to be developed, along with methods and techniques to ensure and verify that these ethically motivated requirements and related legal norms are fulfilled throughout the data selection and exploration processes. Ethical requirements can then be enforced at all the steps of knowledge extraction through a unified data modeling and analysis methodology relying on appropriate conceptual and technical tools.

1 Introduction

Traditional knowledge extraction (search, query, or data analysis) systems hardly pay any specific attention to ethically sensitive aspects and to the ethical and social problems their outcomes could bring about. However, such aspects are now becoming prominent, especially with regard to the protection of fundamental human rights and their underpinnings in normative ethics [14]. These demands are broadly reflected into codes of ethics, in the Responsible Research and Innovation (RRI) approach of the European Commission HORIZON 2020,

SEBD 2018, June 24-27, 2018, Castellaneta Marina, Italy. Copyright held by the authors.

in statements of the European Group on Ethics in Science and Technology (EGE, `https://ec.europa.eu/research/ege`) - with regard to research and innovation in the area of automated data selection and exploration processes - and also in legally binding regulations such as the EU General Data Protection Regulation (GDPR, `https://www.eugdpr.org`). More recently, computer scientists themselves - via professional organizations such as ACM and Informatics Europe - have been stressing the importance of raising, within their discipline, awareness with respect to ethical and societal issues regarding the use of data [18, 34]. Coherently with this broad ethical and legal framework, we propose a vision aiming to enhance and verify the protection and advocacy of these rights and values throughout each step of the knowledge extraction chain, thus providing all involved stakeholders with a set of novel computational methodologies and techniques to protect and promote fundamental ethical guarantees in data governance. Realizing this vision needs to be achieved in a principled way by analyzing the ethical challenges that must be addressed, by properly amalgamating and resolving contrasts between various ethical demands (e.g., transparency vs protection), and by developing an extensive list of ethical desiderata for data protection and processing. The resulting Ethical CheckList (ECL) will constitute the high-level specifications for any project embracing this vision.

Accordingly, a preliminary goal is to analyze and clarify the relevant meanings of ethically motivated desiderata about data processing. These notably include transparency, interpretability and understandability, in addition to non-discrimination (fairness), diversity protection and their ethical underpinnings. Moreover, the conceptual relationships between these desiderata and their mutual tensions needs to be analyzed, with the aim of identifying acceptable trade-offs for integrating ethical policies in data selection and exploration processes. This analysis may be used to identify ethically motivated specifications for the various models, technologies and tools to be delivered. With this, our vision will therefore contribute to establish higher social standards for transparency, privacy protection, fairness and non-discrimination in data governance.

The observation and enforcement of ethical principles in data management are achieved by considering the following steps of the analysis lifecycle: *i)* source selection, *ii)* data integration, and *iii)* knowledge extraction. Ensuring that the ECL is applied during all such phases allows all stakeholders to enact law regulations and ethical principles and verify that these are respected. Our vision will hence give birth to an ethical data analysis methodology and associated methodological and technical tools that will enforce the ECL specifications throughout the three above mentioned steps of the analysis lifecycle.

2 Methodology

Our vision's methodology builds on methods and tools for data management and on recent studies on data source selection, data integration, and knowledge extraction. The overall approach is to tackle problems that have a practical significance, providing general methods as well as concrete tools that demonstrate the approach. The relevant activities can be developed on two parallel tracks.

On one track, a new, ethics-aware, knowledge extraction lifecycle is carried on, where the experts in ethical, legal, and social disciplines work side-by-side with the computer scientists to *i)* identify the ethical requirements, *ii)* produce the desiderata checklist and *iii)* identify the most appropriate modeling tool(s) to combine them with the application requirements into a coherent framework. The other track is devoted to the study of novel methods for data source selection, integration, and knowledge extraction that comply with the identified ethical requirements. The two tracks are bridged by a conceptual model, based on the Context Dimension Model (CDM) of [2] described below, able to express the ethical requirements of the ECL by associating the various ethical dimensions (i.e., fairness, transparency, diversity, and data protection), along with their different inflections and levels of enforcement, with the knowledge extraction lifecycle activities. Providing a formal model of ethical requirements, to be adopted in each specific situation of use, will contribute to mitigate or remove possible biases from the considered data management methods. Since at present **no such integrated solutions for dealing with ethical issues in data management exist**, our vision will provide a methodological and technological breakthrough and a concrete answer to issues that the scientific community has started investigating in recent years [30, 25, 10] (`http://wp.sigmod.org/?p=1900`). Existing notable approaches, such as [27], consider scenarios in which there is no control on the knowledge extraction lifecycle, thus dealing with the specific, orthogonal goal of discovering bias in online information derived by third parties through the application of knowledge extraction techniques.

3 Ethical issues in the knowledge extraction lifecycle

We now elaborate on how the various issues arising in the knowledge extraction lifecycle are to be dealt with and how they advance the state of the art.

3.1 Source selection

Within this phase we focus on choosing the data source(s) appropriate for the target objectives in terms of quality and satisfaction of ethical requirements (such as trustability, personal rights protection, and fairness) taking into account the differences between categories and favoring the maximization of source diversity. Under this view, source selection is a novel data management problem, motivated by the recent proliferation of data. The research project more related to our goals is SourceSight [29], which proposes a system to interactively discover valuable sets of sources taking into account reliability and data quality, but without considering ethical issues. Along with institutional datasets, data from location-based services, and other kinds of open data, we also consider online social networks, which are nowadays the preferred communication means for information spread and opinion sharing. We address this problem by assessing the ethical requirements provided by the ECL in this phase, e.g., the bias/fairness/authority of the source population. To this end, we plan to design an iterative process in which the ECL is first assessed for each candidate source so as to select the most informative sources for the domain of interest. Innovative ways of labeling datasets with ethically- and socially-aware metadata are also needed, with the aim of detecting potential limits or flaws early on (e.g., gender imbalances, ethnic or class misrepresentation or underrepresentation).

3.2 Data integration

Within our vision, suitable tools assist the combination of data from different sources and the extraction of real-world entities. This issue are tackled, for data reconciliation, by leveraging existing record linkage methods and, for schema mapping, by tailoring ethically-aware integration views on the basis of the ethical context. Record linkage seeks to identify which objects refer to the same real-world entity, and is fundamental for data integration. Leveraging humans to compare records based on domain knowledge enables high-accuracy linkage in various domains [16]; however, unrestricted human access to data may not be suitable in the presence of sensitive information. For this reason, our goals include the prevention of sensitive informations leaks, and the collection of all the intermediate data transformation that yielded a given integration result, with the goal of enforcing the protection of user data and providing a transparent access to result generation. We also consider review methods for including the user in the data integration loop, for both data and schema reconciliation, so that high-quality integrated views and fine-grained feedbacks on the result can be provided. Merging conflicting information is critical for recent data integration research [9], especially when dealing with web sources and ethical aspects. Although specific source properties computed in the previous source selection step can help in the detection of fake values, the integration step can further contribute to this problem, empowering human experts with ubiquitous collaborative review tools (thus promoting fact-checking culture).

3.3 Knowledge extraction

We focus on various kinds of knowledge extraction methods: 1. Result personalization, 2. Information diffusion and influence propagation in social networks, 3. Explanation models enabling transparency and interpretability of results, 4. Privacy and security in knowledge extraction systems. Note that the research on topics 1. and 2. is related to the modification of existing techniques for knowledge extraction to *guarantee* that the process and results satisfy the appropriate ethical requirements, while topics 3. and 4. study techniques to *enforce and verify* that the ethical requirements be satisfied by the analysis process.
Result personalization. Personalization can be broadly defined as providing an overall customized, individualized user experience by taking into account the needs, preferences and characteristics of a user or group of users [12]. A data personalization method may re-rank the items in a collection to be shown to a user, focus only on items of interest, or recommend additional options. While personalization delivers relevant content, it also polarizes the perspectives and diminishes serendipity, whereas searching for relevant information on large datasets should provide results that are diverse enough [3] to ensure a fair coverage of the available alternatives. Methods that aim to qualify and quantify personalized experiences and their biasing effects have been overlooked in the literature.

Queries aiming to return only the more interesting results can either provide a ranking of objects (top-k queries) or consider some form of dominance to exclude sub-optimal choices (skyline queries [4]). Thanks to a recent contribution [6], free parameters (e.g., weights), are available to fine-tune the behavior of both kinds of query. For any specific dataset, one can characterize the parameter values that guarantee that the output satisfies the required ethical properties (e.g., preserving the distribution of a protected attribute). Research on such issues for ranking queries has provided preliminary results [36], but no study exists yet for skyline queries. Efficient methods are needed to determine such a set of parameter values, to study its stability wrt. a change in input data [31], and to provide metrics to choose among different parameter configurations. This requires analyzing the overhead incurred by methods providing such ethical guarantees, and studying the trade-off between the efficiency and the ethical level of the query process. Such techniques are also useful to ensure that the items of a query result are diverse enough, providing a balanced view of the result space.

The current user context has been adopted as a criterion for personalization by knowledge filtering. Design methods that support dynamic, context-based filtering of pertinent resources [22] facilitate the development of software that takes context into account. In the traditional software lifecycle, the CDM [2] represents the relevant dimensions of context (e.g., current location, situation of use, role of the user), along with a hierarchy of their possible values; any set of dimension values represents a possible context. Depending on the current context, only relevant data are provided to the user. This kind of personalization is naturally coupled with the ethical dimensions described above, also supporting user preferences and recommendations aware of both context and ethics [28].

Information diffusion and influence propagation in social networks. Online social networks (OSNs) are nowadays the preferred communication means for spreading information and sharing knowledge, such as advertising products/services, promoting ideas, sharing opinions. In this regard, influence maximization is central, i.e., to identify k initial influencers that maximize the spread of influence [33, 15]. An important but often overlooked aspect is that success of an information diffusion process might depend not only on the investment-budget (k), but also on the diversity of the initial influencers, as well as of the targets to be influenced. Members of an OSN present two kinds of diversity: *static*, which includes diversity of kind, socio-cultural aspects and other characteristics exogenous to the OSN; *dynamic*, which includes the knowledge, community experience, and shared information acquired over time. The various types of user diversity should be leveraged to push forward research on information diffusion and influence propagation along two main directions: *i)* diversity concerning the targets to be influenced and *ii)* diversity concerning the initial influencers. The former allows us to capture non-discrimination or fairness aspects in the outcome of the diffusion process; the latter enables modeling different triggering stimuli, which intuitively capture utilitarian aspects [10] in terms of marketing principles (e.g., diversification of users skills implies higher productivity). Addressing both fairness and utility opens to opportunities of ethics-preserving information diffusion, and can support the development of advanced methods around novel perspectives having ethical implications in OSN data analysis. One such perspective is related to the ever increasing phenomenon of fake-news/misinformation spread on the Web: bringing fairness and utility-oriented diversity aspects into fact-checking and misinformation debunking prompts us to develop sophisticated models to handle competitive influence propagation scenarios. There has been little work in diversity in information diffusion and influence propagation [1, 32, 13, 5]. Most of the existing notions of diversity have been developed around structural features of the network, or are based on user profile attributes, but no existing approach proposes diversity-aware solutions in influence propagation.

Explanation models enabling transparency and interpretability of results. Explanation models for results provided by big data transformations and machine learning (ML) systems are needed. The transparency requirement must be balanced with privacy preservation by identifying context-sensitive trade-offs. With the aim of supporting transparency in big data transformations, we consider techniques for data lineage, so as to trace the relationships between input and output data and to identify underlying processes. Data lineage (aka provenance) concerns data origin and transformation history, and enables transparency by supporting explanations of results and processes. However, it may also disclose private or confidential data, and the use of proprietary transformations [11]. Extending provenance techniques to Big Data poses new challenges and opportunities [35]. Providing explanations for ML systems that are often opaque to human beings is a challenge addressed in the emerging XAI (eXplainable AI) research area [20, 23]. In ML classifications, explanation requests are expressed as why-questions: Why were input data associated with class X? [17]. Answers may come in the form of I/O explanations (exhibiting prototypes of the output class) and inner explanations (additionally exhibiting salient components of both input and intermediate processing data). In I/O explanations one often exhibits a single prototype. In real-life, however, a single prototype may not be representative of the entire class, and discarded classification possibilities are important to interpret outcomes. Accordingly, state-of-art tools need to be extended by extracting multiple prototypes for both classification results and discarded classes for Deep Learning networks and other ML systems, e.g., via statistical methods like activation maximization [23] and sparse coding approaches [21]. Similarly, inner explanation tools need to be extended by identifying components of input and intermediate processing data contributing most to classification outcomes.

Privacy and security in knowledge extraction systems. Focusing on methods for data protection oriented to the preservation of privacy when releasing analysis results, we plan to study techniques for trading-off privacy budget for result accuracy. Aspects concerning privacy and security of personal data are increasingly relevant, as also testified by the GDPR, which unifies data protection laws across all European Union members. Several techniques have been developed so far for privacy protection. Differential privacy promises to enable general data analytics while protecting individual privacy, yet existing mechanisms do not support the wide variety of features and sources used in big-data analytics systems [19].

Data anonymization attempts to provide privacy while allowing general-purpose analysis, but recent de-anonymization results [24] proved that it cannot be relied upon. A further technique is homomorphic encryption, which makes it possible to perform certain operations on a ciphertext without decrypting it [26]. Homomorphic encryption techniques were recently coupled with a novel probabilistic data structure, the Spatial Bloom Filter (SBF) [7], designed to secure out location data. This data structure is suitable for any kind of set-based problem [8], and could be conveniently used in a number of applications. We focus on possible applications of the SBF for data protection. For instance, since an individual's interest may be seen as his own membership to a specific set, a promising application of the SBF is related to those services that rely on outsourced data reflecting people's interests for marketing actions and other commercial purposes. We focus on the study of methods for data protection oriented to the preservation of the privacy of individuals when releasing statistics. Indeed, aggregated data can be combined for inferring personal information, even if randomized.

4 Outlook

Embracing our vision will contribute to establish higher standards in democratic societies for transparency, privacy protection, fairness and non-discrimination in data governance. Trust building and public confidence will be fostered by supporting scrutiny without violating privacy, and by reducing the opaqueness of current data technologies. The resulting competencies and techniques will allow addressing the ethical issues in ethics-critical decision-making processes. On the whole, this vision will contribute to a more cognizant and responsible use of data, by promoting the ethics-aware development and use of technologies and systems for collecting, storing and processing data.

References

1. Q. Bao, W. K. Cheung, Y. Zhang. Incorporating structural diversity of neighbors in a diffusion model for social networks. *Web Intelligence* 2013: 431–438 (2013)
2. C. Bolchini, E. Quintarelli, L. Tanca. CARVE: Context-aware automatic view definition over relational databases. *Inf. Syst.* 38(1): 45-67 (2013)
3. I. Catallo et al. Top-k diversity queries over bounded regions. *TODS* 38(2): 10:1–10:44 (2013)
4. J. Chomicki, P. Ciaccia, N. Meneghetti. Skyline queries, front and back. *SIGMOD Record* 42(3): 6-18 (2013)
5. A. Caliò *et al.* Topology-driven Diversity for Targeted Influence Maximization with Application to User Engagement in Social Networks. *IEEE TKDE*, To appear
6. P. Ciaccia, D. Martinenghi. Reconciling Skyline and Ranking Queries. *PVLDB* 10(11): 1454-1465 (2017)
7. L. Calderoni, P. Palmieri, D. Maio. Location privacy without mutual trust: The Spatial Bloom Filter *Comput. Commun.*, vol. 68:. 4–16 (2015)
8. L. Calderoni, P. Palmieri, D. Maio. Probabilistic Properties of the Spatial Bloom Filters and Their Relevance to Cryptographic Protocols. *IEEE Transactions on Information Forensics and Security* 13(7): 1710–1721 (2018)

9. X.L. Dong, L. Berti-Equille, D. Srivastava. Data Fusion: Resolving Conflicts from Multiple Sources. *Handbook of Data Quality*. Springer, Berlin, Heidelberg (2013).
10. M. Drosou *et al.*. Diversity in big data: a review. *Big Data* 5(2): 73–84 (2017)
11. S. B. Davidson et al. On provenance and privacy. *ICDT* 2011: 3-10 (2011)
12. G. Koutrika. Data Personalization. In *Data Management in Pervasive Systems*, Springer Verlag, ISBN 978-3-319-20061-3: 213-234 (2015)
13. Y.-H. Fu, C.-Y. Huang, C.-T. Sun. Using global diversity and local topology features to identify influential network spreaders. *Physica A* 433(C):344–355 (2015)
14. L. Floridi, M. Taddeo. What is data ethics? *Phil. Trans. R. Soc.* A374:20160360. http://dx.doi.org/10.1098/rsta.2016.0360 (2016)
15. S. Galhotra *et al.* ASIM: A Scalable Algorithm for Influence Maximization under the Independent Cascade Model. *WWW* 2015: 35–36 (2015)
16. S. Galhotra *et al.* Robust Entity Resolution using Random Graphs. *SIGMOD* (2018)
17. D. Gunning. Explainable Artificial Intelligence (XAI). *Defense Advanced Research Projects Agency* (DARPA) (2017)
18. Informatics Europe & EUACM. When Computers Decide: European Recommendations on Machine-Learned Automated Decision Making (2018)
19. N. Johnson, J. P. Near, D. Song. Towards Practical Differential Privacy for SQL Queries. *PVLDB*, 11(5): 526–39 (2018)
20. Z.C. Lipton. The mythos of model interpretability. *arXiv*:1606.03490 (2017)
21. J. Mairal et al. Online learning for matrix factorization and sparse coding. *Journal of Machine Learning Research*, 11: 19-60 (2010)
22. K. Mens *et al.* Modeling and managing context-aware systems variability. *IEEE Software*, 34(6): 58–6 (2017)
23. G. Montavon *et al.* Methods for interpreting and understanding deep neural networks. *Digital Signal Processing* 73: 1-15 (2018)
24. A. Narayanan, S. Vitaly. Robust de-anonymization of large sparse datasets. *IEEE Symposium on Security and Privacy* (2008)
25. U. Pagallo. On the Principle of Privacy by Design and its Limits: Technology, Ethics and the Rule of Law. *European Data Protection* 2012: 331-346 (2012)
26. P. Paillier. Public-key cryptosystems based on composite degree residuosity classes. *Advances in CryptologyEUROCRYPT* (LNCS), vol. 1592: 223–238 (1999)
27. E. Pitoura *et al.* On Measuring Bias in Online Information. *SIGMOD Record* 46(4): 16-21 (2017)
28. E. Quintarelli, E. Rabosio, L.Tanca. Recommending New Items to Ephemeral Groups Using Contextual User Influence. *RecSys* 2016: 285-292 (2016)
29. T. Rekatsinas et al. SourceSight: Enabling Effective Source Selection. *SIGMOD* 2016: 2157-2160 (2016)
30. J. Stoyanovich, S. Abiteboul, G. Miklau. Data Responsibly: Fairness, Neutrality and Transparency in Data Analysis. *EDBT* 2016: 718-719 (2016)
31. M. Soliman et al. Ranking with uncertain scoring functions: semantics and sensitivity measures. *SIGMOD* 2011: 805-816 (2011)
32. F. Tang *et al.* Diversified social influence maximization. *ASONAM* 2014: 455–459 (2014)
33. Y. Tang, X. Xiao, Y. Shi. Influence maximization: near-optimal time complexity meets practical efficiency. *SIGMOD* 2014: 75–86 (2014)
34. USA ACM. Statement on the Importance of Preserving Personal Privacy - Foundational Privacy Principles and Practices. (2018)
35. J. Wang *et al.* Big data provenance: Challenges, state of the art and opportunities. *Big Data* 2015: 2509-2516 (2015)
36. M. Zehlike *et al.* FA*IR: A Fair Top-k Ranking Algorithm. *CIKM* 2017: 1569-1578 (2017)

Introducing Online Profile Learning in Crowdsourcing Task Routing
Discussion Paper

Silvana Castano[1], Alfio Ferrara[1], and Stefano Montanelli[1]

Università degli Studi di Milano
DI - Via Comelico, 39 - 20135 Milano
{silvana.castano,alfio.ferrara,stefano.montanelli}@unimi.it

Abstract. In this paper, we present an initial implementation with experimental results of online profile learning in Argo+, a framework for crowdsourcing task routing characterized by i) feature-based representation of both tasks and workers, and ii) learning techniques inspired to *Rocchio relevance feedback* for prediction of the most appropriate task to execute by a given worker.

1 Introduction

In the recent years, the crowdsourcing philosophy has gained a lot of attention and many crowdsourcing systems/platforms appeared on the web scene for satisfying the growing need of marketplaces where the offer of requesters providing jobs to execute can meet the work-force provided by the crowd. Humans have different knowledge and abilities, thus a crowd worker can be trustworthy on a certain task campaign that is coherent with her/his attitudes, as well as she/he can be inaccurate on another campaign with different topics and skill requirements not compliant with her/his attitudes. As a result, the capability to effectively discover and represent the profile of engaged crowd workers is becoming a strategic asset of emerging crowdsourcing marketplaces. The goal is to selectively choose a qualified and motivated crowd to recruit/involve in a given campaign according to the required knowledge/abilities based on the features of the tasks to execute. In this direction, the use of machine-learning techniques in crowdsourcing applications is being appearing in the recent literature for mining emerging worker skills from the analysis of executed tasks [6, 7, 12]. Online learning techniques based on (multi-armed) bandits algorithms have been also proposed for improving the quality of crowdsourcing results [8, 10, 14]. Online learning of worker skills is also concerned with the so-called *task routing* issue, that is the capability of a crowdsourcing system to assign a task to a worker

SEBD 2018, June 24-27, 2018, Castellaneta Marina, Italy.

based on the expectations to obtain a successful contribution from her/his answer. In the literature, popular solutions are characterized by the idea to rely on human factors for addressing task routing (e.g., [1, 9]).

In this paper, we present an initial implementation of online profile learning in Argo+, a framework for crowdsourcing task routing characterized by i) feature-based representation of both tasks and workers, and ii) learning techniques inspired to *Rocchio relevance feedback* for prediction of the most appropriate task to execute by a given worker. A detailed description of the Argo+ framework is provided in [5]. In the following, we focus on discussing the preliminary results obtained on a real crowdsourcing campaign, by comparing the performance of Argo+ against a baseline with conventional task routing techniques.

The paper il organized as follows. Section 2 presents the basic elements of the proposed Argo+ implementation. Experimental results are then discussed in Section 3. Concluding remarks are finally provided in Section 4.

2 Learning-based task routing

A crowdsourcing campaign is characterized by a crowd of workers $W = \{w_1, \ldots, w_k\}$ involved in the execution of a set of tasks $T = \{t_1, \ldots, t_n\}$. A **task** $t \in T$ is defined as $t = \langle id_t, a_t, m_t, d_t, F_t \rangle$, where id_t is the unique *task identifier*, a_t is the *task action*, m_t is the *task modality*, d_t is the *task description*, and F_t is the set of *task-features*. A task action a_t denotes the task target, namely the goal that needs to be satisfied through crowd execution (e.g., picture labeling, movie recognition, sentiment evaluation). A modality m_t represents the kind of worker answer required in task execution (e.g., creation, decision). A description d_t represents the task request given to each worker for illustrating what is demanded to her/him in the task execution. A set of task-features F_t manually associated with the task for providing a description of task requirements, namely a specification of the capabilities expected from a worker for being involved in the execution of the task t. For each feature $f \in F_t$, a *task-feature weight* $\omega(f)$ is associated to denote the relevance of f within the task-features F_t. A **worker** $w \in W$ is defined as $w = \langle id_w, F_w \rangle$, where id_w is the unique *worker identifier* and F_w is the **worker profile** expressed as a set of worker-features. A worker-feature $f \in F_w$ denotes a worker capability, either knowledge expertise or skill, and it is associated with a *worker-feature weight* $\omega(f)$ denoting the "degree" of expertise/ability associated with the worker.

2.1 Assigning tasks to workers

For enforcing task routing, Argo+ relies on a task classification procedure for aggregating the tasks T to execute into K classes, so that tasks with similar features F_t are associated with a same class. In the proposed implementation of Argo+, probabilistic topic modeling are exploited for task classification. The choice is motivated by the need to enforce a *soft aggregation* mechanism, where a task with a plurality of features can have multiple associated classes and it can be exploited by workers with different expertise, each one focused on a different class. In particular, the proposed solution is characterized by the use of Latent Dirichlet Allocation (LDA) [3] over the task-features, characterized by two discrete probability distributions, namely ϕ and θ. ϕ describes the probability distribution of task-features on classes. In particular, ϕ^k denotes the probability of each task-feature f of being associated with the kth class on the K possible classes. θ describes the probability distribution of classes on tasks. In particular, θ_t denotes the probability of the task t of belonging to each class k among the K possible classes. Finally, we denote θ_t^k the probability of the task t to be associated with the class k. The choice of K, namely the number of classes on which LDA works for task classification, is a configuration parameter and it is discussed in Section 3.

Consider a worker w and associated worker profile F_w. When w asks for a task t to execute, the probability distributions (ϕ, θ) created by task classification are exploited. Through ϕ, Argo+ calculates the maximum a posteriori estimation θ_w given the worker features F_w. This is done by using collapsed Gibbs sampling [13] to learn the latent assignment of features to classes given the observed features F_w. In particular, we repeatedly estimate the probability $p(f \mid \phi^k)$ of a feature f to be assigned to a class k and we exploit this to estimate the probability $p(k \mid w)$ of the class k to be the correct assignment for the worker w. This sampling process is repeated until convergence, so that for each class $k \in K$ we finally estimate:

$$\theta_w^k \propto \frac{\sum_{f \in F_w} \omega(f)_k}{\sum_{f \in F_w} \sum_{j \in K} \omega(f)_j}, \tag{1}$$

where $\omega(f)_i$ denotes the weight of features of type f that have been assigned to class i. Then, from the distribution θ_w, we select the class z and task t such that:

$$z = \arg\max_{z \in K} \theta_w^z. \tag{2}$$

$$t = \arg\max_{t \in T} \theta_t^z. \tag{3}$$

We stress that a task t is available for assignment until the number of task executions expected by the system is reached, then it is marked as finished and it is excluded from the assignment mechanism.

Example 1. Consider to enforce Argo+ on a system with task classification based on $K = 10$ and a set of thematic tags used as features both for tasks and workers. A worker w asks for a task to execute and the profile F_w is defined by the following features:

$F_w = \langle$ (web search, 0.85), (classification, 0.85), (smartphone, 0.51), (text, 0.34), ... $\rangle$

Starting from F_w, we exploit Equation 1 in order to classify the worker w with respect to the classes K. The resulting distribution θ_w is:

K	1	2	3	4	5	6	7	8	9	10
θ_w	0.07	0.57	0.02	0.08	0.06	0.02	0.02	0.04	0.02	0.07

From θ_w, we exploit Equation 2 to select the most relevant class for the worker profile, that is $k = 2$. The top-3 features associated with $k = 2$ in ϕ^2 are: classification, tweets, and web search, which motivates the relevance of the class with respect to the worker profile F_w. Given the class, it is now possible to exploit Equation 3 in order to select a task t for worker execution. The features F_t of the task selected for assignment to w are $F_w = \langle$ (web search, 1.0), (classification, 1.0), (smartphone, 1.0)$\rangle$

2.2 Learning worker profiles

Given a task t executed by a worker w, we need to assess the quality of the provided worker answer for deciding how to update the worker profile, and thus how to enforce learning. We call $\alpha(t)$ the *final task result* determined by the crowdsourcing system. We note that different solutions can be employed for determining $\alpha(t)$. Popular solutions are based on *majority voting* mechanisms where the final task result corresponds to the answer that obtained the majority of preferences by the involved workers. Alternative solutions are also possible, such as for example *statistics-based* techniques [4]. We say that a worker w provided a *successful contribution* to the task t when the worker answer coincides with (or is equivalent to) $\alpha(t)$. Otherwise, we say that a worker w provided an *unsuccessful contribution* to the task t. According to this, we define the *worker-task result* $\rho(w, t)$ as follows:

$$\rho(w,t) = \begin{cases} 1 \text{ if } w \textit{ provided succ. contrib.} \\ 0 \text{ otherwise} \end{cases}$$

For updating a worker profile, Argo+ relies on learning techniques inspired to the *Rocchio relevance feedback* [11]. When a worker w executes a task t, we associate the worker w with a new set of features $F'_w = F_w \cup F_t$. We denote $\omega(f)^w$ as the weight of the feature f in F_w (possibly being 0 if f was not in F_w) and $\omega(f)^t$ the weight of feature f in F_t (possibly being 0 if f was not in F_t). Then, the new weight $\omega(f)'$ for each feature in F'_w is updated as follows:

$$\omega(f)' = \gamma \cdot \omega(f)^w + (1 - \delta) \cdot \theta_t^z \cdot \rho(w,t) \cdot \omega(f)^t, \tag{4}$$

where γ is a dumping factor in [0,1] that determines how much of the original weight of the profile features contributes to the new weight, and z is the class chosen for the task assignment. The idea behind profile update is that when a worker profile feature is not included in the task features, its weight is reduced by a factor δ. In the other case, the new profile feature weight $\omega(f)'$ is computed as the weighted sum between the previous profile feature weight $\omega(f)^w$ and the task feature weight $\omega(f)^t$, which contribution is proportional to the relevance θ_t^z of the task t in the class z. The task feature weight $\omega(f)^t$ is forced to be equal to 0 when the worker does not provide a successful contribution on the task (resulting in a reduction of the corresponding profile feature weight).

Example 2. Consider the task assignment of Example 1. The worker w executed t and $\rho(w,t) = 1$. We update F_w by applying Equation 4. The updated worker profile F'_w is the following (the class-task relevance $\theta_t^2 = 0.77$):

$F_w = \langle$ (web search, 0.78), (classification, 0.78), (smartphone, 0.74), (text, 0.03), ... $\rangle$

We note that the three features of t affects the worker profile by changing the relative feature weights. Features web search and classification remain the most relevant, but the weight of smartphone that is a feature of t is increased. On the opposite, the feature text of F_w becomes remarkably less relevant in the new worker profile, due to the fact that it is not part of the task feature set F_t. After the profile update, Argo+ will exploit the new worker profile for the subsequent task assignments to w.

3 Experimental results

For evaluation, we present some preliminary experimental results based on the comparison of the proposed Argo+ implementation against a basic task routing mechanism called from now on baseline.

3.1 Experiment setup

Our experiment relies on a crowdsourcing campaign (named paintings) run through the Argo crowdsourcing system (i.e., the system version implementing baseline routing) between November and December 2018. The experiment involved 367 students from the Faculty of Arts and Literature at the University of Milan, who have been asked to examine a dataset of paintings in order to choose for each painting the correct author among a choice of six possible painters. The paintings dataset is composed by 948 paintings from 56 different authors spanning from the 13th century to the 20th century. Each task has been executed by more than one worker, for a total of 8,573 executions. The fact that the paintings dataset is featured by a correct answer for each task (i.e., the correct name of the painting author) makes it possible to easily evaluate the effectiveness of the work done by each worker (i.e., successful contribution) in terms of number of correct answers given to the tasks question.

To setup the experiment for evaluating Argo+, we compare the success rate of the baseline execution of paintings against the success rate obtained through two different executions of paintings in Argo+: i) one execution with a flat worker profile (called Argo+noprofile) where $\omega(f) = 0$ is initially defined for each feature (i.e., worker-feature), and ii) one execution with a custom worker profile (called Argo+profile) where $\omega(f) = 1$ for each feature on which the worker has declared a competence. Competences declared by workers have been collected through a self evaluation questionnaire about knowledge of painters and different periods in the art history. Task and worker features have been taken from Wikidata (`https://www.wikidata.org`) and they include the name of the author, the

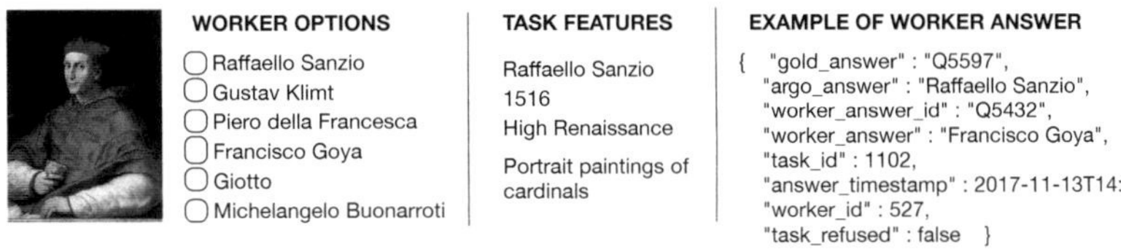

Fig. 1. Example of task with task feature and an example of (wrong) worker answer

year, and the Wikidata thematic categories available for a painting. An example of task and worker answer is given in Figure 1.

The goal of our experimental evaluation is to assess whether Argo+ improves the success rate with respect to baseline. In order to simulate the execution of Argo+noprofile and Argo+profile on exactly the same set of workers and answers used in baseline, our experiments are based on the idea to change the time-sequence of tasks executed by each worker in baseline according to the assignment schedule determined by Argo+. We aim at verifying whether the tasks successfully executed by a worker w are assigned to w before than others. Being the task answers the same for all the experiments, the overall success rate will be the same as well. However, if Argo+ performs better than baseline, we expect to execute correct tasks before. In other terms, we aim at verifying if Argo+ reaches a success rate better than baseline by taking into account the first r tasks assignments. In particular, we call r (*request timestamp*), the timestamp at which the crowdsourcing system receives the request for a task to execute by a worker, and we call $\sigma(r,\tau)$ the *success rate* of the system execution τ at the request timestamp r. A *system execution* is a stream of task answers, each one collected from a worker at a certain timestamp. In our evaluation, baseline is the reference system execution, while Argo+noprofile and Argo+profile represent alternative system executions of baseline where the time-sequence of task answers is changed according to the Argo+ routing mechanism. The success rate $\sigma(r,\tau)$ is defined as follows:

$$(a)\ \sigma(r,\tau) = \frac{1}{r}\sum_{i=1}^{r} \rho(w,t)^i \ ; \ (b)\ \sigma_R^\tau = \int_1^R \sigma(r,\tau)dr$$

where $\rho(w,t)^i$ in (a) is the worker-task result received by the system at the ith request timestamp in the execution τ and (b) measures the overall system performance of task routing with R representing the overall number of successfully executed tasks in a system execution τ (i.e., R is the sum of all the $\rho(w,t) = 1$ in τ). Given two different system executions ϵ and γ, the delta value $\delta_r(\gamma,\epsilon)$ represents how much the success rate of γ changes with respect to ϵ at time r. The delta value $\delta_r(\gamma,\epsilon)$ is defined as $\delta_r(\gamma,\epsilon) = \frac{\sigma(r,\gamma)}{\sigma(r,\epsilon)}$.

3.2 Considerations

Experiments have been performed with a number of classes $K = 30$ for task classification and a dumping factor $\gamma = 0.3$ for worker profile learning. The comparison of baseline against Argo+noprofile and Argo+profile on success rate $\sigma(r, \tau)$ and delta value $\delta(\gamma, \epsilon)$ are shown for the first 200 tasks requests in Figures 2(a) and 2(b), respectively. We observe that both Argo+noProfile and Argo+Profile suc-

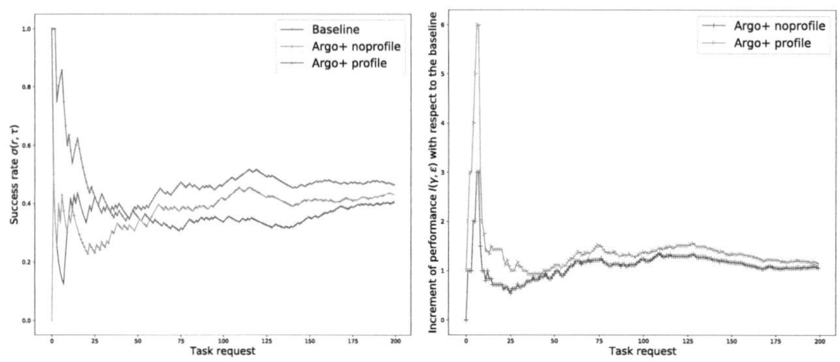

(a) (b)

Fig. 2. (a) success rate on executed tasks, (b) increment of performances with respect to baseline

ceed in improving the success rate of baseline, since successfully executed tasks are assigned to workers before other tasks in most cases. For the first 200 requests, the success rate of Argo+Profile is around 20% better than baseline. It is also interesting to note that, at the very beginning of the system execution ($r < 50$), the behavior of Argo+noProfile and Argo+Profile is very unstable since learning has insufficient information for recognizing the appropriate task class for each worker. However, Argo+ quickly learns the worker profile ($r \geq 50$) and this has a positive impact on the assignment of subsequent tasks. The performance of Argo+noProfile becomes similar to baseline after the 300th worker request. This is due to the fact that Argo+ first selects tasks that are highly relevant for the worker profile, while subsequent assignments are about residual tasks of the K classes for which the relevance for the worker profile is weaker.

Finally, we compare baseline and Argo+ through $\sigma_R^{\mathcal{T}}$ and we obtain that $\sigma_R^{\mathcal{T}} = 399.59$ for baseline, $\sigma_R^{\mathcal{T}} = 424.66$ for Argo+Profile, and $\sigma_R^{\mathcal{T}} = 399.61$ for Argo+noProfile. As a result, we observe that the use of a questionnaire for initializing the worker profile provides the best performance on the three considered system executions (see also Figure 2(b) on the increment value). However, after a small number of executions, the performance of the learning system without the initial set-up of the worker profile becomes similar to the one of the system execution initialized with the questionnaire. This confirms the intuition behind the use of flat profiles which argues that the auto-evaluation of worker skill/abilities could be misplaced with respect to the real worker expertise, and thus sometimes damaging the performance of the crowdsourcing system.

4 Concluding remarks

In this paper, we presented an implementation of profile learning techniques in Argo+ crowdsourcing framework [5] with some experimental results. Ongoing research activities are aimed i) to extend the experimentation for considering multiple kinds of tasks with different action, modality, and description, and ii) to improve the Argo+ framework to support worker profile management over different crowdsourcing campaigns with different task/worker features.

References

1. Amer-Yahia, S., Roy, S.B.: Human Factors in Crowdsourcing. PVLDB **9**(13), 1615–1618 (2016)
2. Arun, R., Suresh, V., Madhavan, C.V., Murthy, M.N.: On Finding the Natural Number of Topics with Latent Dirichlet Allocation: Some Observations. In: Proc. of the 14th PAKDD Conference. Hyderabad, India (2010)
3. Blei, D.M., Ng, A.Y., Jordan, M.I.: Latent dirichlet allocation. Journal of machine Learning research **3**(Jan), 993–1022 (2003)
4. Castano, S., Ferrara, A., Montanelli, S.: A Multi-Dimensional Approach to Crowd-Consensus Modeling and Evaluation. In: Proc. of the 34th ER Int. Conference. Stockholm, Sweden (2015)
5. Castano, S., Ferrara, A., Montanelli, S.: A Conceptual Framework for Crowdsourcing Task Assignment with Online Profile Learning. In: Submitted to the 37th ER Int. Conference. Xi'an, China (2018)
6. Gadiraju, U., Fetahu, B., Kawase, R.: Training Workers for Improving Performance in Crowdsourcing Microtasks. In: Proc. of the 10th EC-TEL. Toledo, Spain (2015)
7. Goncalves, J., Feldman, M., Hu, S., Kostakos, V., Bernstein, A.: Task Routing and Assignment in Crowdsourcing Based on Cognitive Abilities. In: Proc. of the 26th WWW Int. Conference. Perth, Australia (2017)
8. Jain, S., Narayanaswamy, B., Narahari, Y.: A Multiarmed Bandit Incentive Mechanism for Crowdsourcing Demand Response in Smart Grids. In: Proc. of the 28th AAAI Conference on Artificial Intelligence. pp. 721–727. Qulébec, Canada (2014)
9. Karger, D.R., Oh, S., Shah, D.: Budget-Optimal Task Allocation for Reliable Crowdsourcing Systems. Oper. Res. **62**(1), 1–24 (2014)
10. Liu, Y., Liu, M.: An Online Learning Approach to Improving the Quality of Crowd-Sourcing. IEEE Transactions on Networking **25**(4), 2166–2179 (2017)
11. Manning, C.D., Raghavan, P., Schütze, H.: Introduction to Information Retrieval, vol. 1. Cambridge university press Cambridge (2008)
12. Organisciak, P., Teevan, J., Dumais, S.T., Miller, R., Kalai, A.T.: A Crowd of Your Own: Crowdsourcing for On-Demand Personalization. In: Proc. of the 2nd AAAI HCOMP. Pittsburgh, USA (2014)
13. Porteous, I., Newman, D., Ihler, A., Asuncion, A., Smyth, P., Welling, M.: Fast Collapsed Gibbs Sampling for Latent Dirichlet Allocation. In: Proc. of the 14th ACM SIGKDD Int. Conference. pp. 569–577 (2008)
14. Tran-Thanh, L., Stein, S., Rogers, A., Jennings, N.R.: Efficient Crowdsourcing of Unknown Experts using Bounded Multi-armed Bandits. Artificial Intelligence **214**, 89–111 (2014)

On the interpretation of traces of low level events in business process logs
Extended abstract

Bettina Fazzinga[1], Sergio Flesca[2], Filippo Furfaro[2], Elio Masciari[3], and Luigi Pontieri[3]

[1] ICAR-CNR, Italy {fazzinga,masciari,pontieri}@icar.cnr.it
[2] DIMES, University of Calabria, Italy {flesca,furfaro}@dimes.unical.it

Abstract. We consider the scenario where the executions of different business processes are traced into a log, whose traces describe the process instances as sequences of low-level events (representing basic kinds of operations). In this context, we address the following problem: given a description of the processes' behaviors in terms of high-level activities (instead of low-level events), and in the presence of uncertainty in the mapping between events and activities, find all the interpretations of each trace Φ, in terms of the process model that Φ conforms to and of the sequence of activities that may have triggered the events in Φ. We describe the probabilistic framework presented in [7] supporting the extraction of a compact representation of Φ's interpretations, where each interpretation is associated with a probability score representing the probability of being the actual one.

Keywords: Business processes · Graph structure · Probabilistic conditioning.

1 Introduction

Thanks to the increasing diffusion of automated tracing systems, the analysis of log data describing executions of business processes has gained momentum with the growth of the Process Mining research field, which addresses the "*confrontation between event data and process models*" [1] through new process-aware data analysis tasks, such as: inducing a process model [2], quantifying "how much" a log and a model conform one to the other [14], and supporting advanced query-based process analytics [13, 6, 8, 9].

However, all the approaches and tools developed in this field require that each log event can be mapped to well-defined activities, corresponding to some high-level view of the process. As a matter of fact, this assumption often does not hold in practice: in the logs of many processes, the events just represent low-level operations, with no clear reference to the business activities that were carried out through these operations, as shown in the following example.

SEBD 2018, June 24-27, 2018, Castellaneta Marina, Italy.

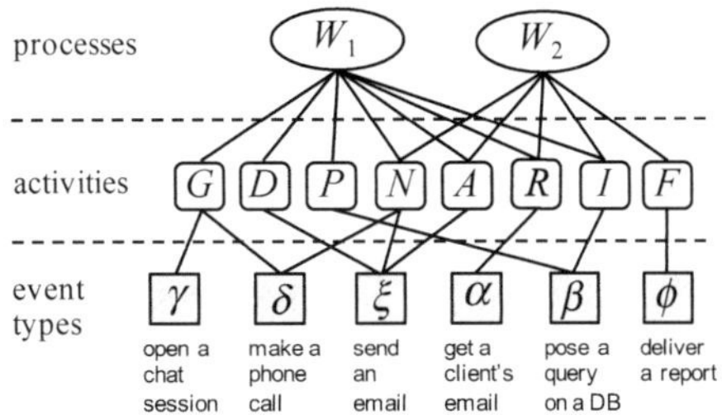

activity label	*activity description*
A	Send an alert to managers
D	Dispatch a contract proposal
F	Fix the issue
G	Get more information from the client
I	Retrieve data from the IS
N	Notify the request's outcome
P	Define a service package
R	Receive a request

Fig. 1. Running example: processes, activities and events (left), and activity descriptions (right). The graph on the left summarizes the possible mappings between activities and events, and process-activity relationships.

Example 1 (Running example). Consider the case of a phone company, where two business processes are carried out: a process W_1 for the activation of services, and an issue-management process W_2.

An abstract description of the behaviors of these processes is available in the form of loose process models, that specify which high-level activities compose each process, and several temporal constraints over the execution of the activities. The activities of processes W_1 and W_2 are shown in Figure 1 via process-activity links. In addition, assume that the following constraints are known to be satisfied by the two processes' instances: (i) every instance of either process starts and ends with an execution of activities R and N, respectively, and these activities cannot be executed multiple times in the instance; (ii) in every instance of W_1, any execution of activity P (resp. D) must be followed (resp. cannot be followed) by an execution of activity D (resp. P).

All these activities are performed by executing low-level operations (e.g., email exchanges, phone calls, database accesses). Figure 1 reports all the operations, regarded each as an event and denoted with a Greek letter, as well as their mapping to the high-level activities.

Notably, the event-activity mapping is many to many*: for example, activity G can produce an instance of either event δ or event γ, while an instance of event δ can be generated by the execution of either activity G or N. Thus, any execution of a process activity generates an instance of one of the events associated with the activity, and the sequence of all the event instances that are produced for an entire process instance is stored in the log as the* trace *of the process instance. For example, an instance of W_1 corresponding to the activity sequence $R\,I\,G\,P\,N$*

might be stored in the log in the form of a trace $\overline{\alpha}\ \overline{\beta}\ \overline{\gamma}\ \overline{\beta}\ \overline{\xi}$ *or of a trace* $\overline{\alpha}\ \overline{\beta}\ \overline{\delta}\ \overline{\beta}$ $\overline{\delta}$, *where* $\overline{\alpha}$ *(resp.* $\overline{\beta}$, $\overline{\gamma}$, *etc.) denotes an instance of event* α *(resp.* β, γ, *etc.).*

Assume that we want to interpret a trace $\Phi_{ex} = \overline{\alpha}\ \overline{\beta}\ \overline{\xi}\ \overline{\xi}$ *as an execution of either* W_1 *or* W_2, *that means replacing each event in* Φ_{ex} *with one of the activities that could have generated it, while ensuring that the resulting activity sequence complies with one of the process models. Only three of such activity sequences exist for* Φ_{ex}: $R\ I\ D\ N$, $R\ I\ A\ N$, *and* $R\ P\ D\ N$. *Indeed, the sequence* $R\ P\ A\ N$ *too complies with the event-activity mapping, but it is not a valid interpretation, since it does not conform to either* W_1 *(no occurrence of* D *appears in the sequence after that of* P*) or* W_2 *(*P *is not an activity of* W_2*).*

In the process management scenario like that illustrated above, we address the following problem, called *interpretation problem*: Given a log L, containing traces generated by an arbitrary number of business processes, and a set $\mathcal{W}$ of (partial) behavioral models for the processes, we want to interpret each trace $\Phi = e_1 \ldots e_m$ in L by establishing: 1) the process whose execution generated the sequence of events stored in Φ, and 2) for each low-level event e_i in Φ, which activity generated e_i as a result of its execution.

The need of bridging some abstraction gap between log events and process activities has been addressed by several recent works [11, 4, 3, 15, 12], However, these approaches cannot actually solve the interpretation problem stated above as: *(i)* they assume that all the given traces come from a single business process; and *(ii)* they return just one "optimal" interpretation for each trace. In fact, the problem stated here has been only considered in [5] and in [10] in simplified settings. Both these interpretation techniques have been considered as terms of comparison in the experimental evaluation of our approach performed in [7].

2 Our framework

In our context, an instance w of a *process* W is the execution of a sequence $A_1 \ldots A_m$ of *activities*; in turn, the execution of each activity A_i yields an instance e_i of an event E_i; hence, the trace describing w consists in the sequence $e_1 \ldots e_m$ of event instances. For any event e_i occurring in a trace, we assume that the starting time of its execution is stored in the log, and denote it as $e_i.t_s$. In the following, we assume given the sets $\mathcal{W}$, $\mathcal{A}$, $\mathcal{E}$ of (types of) processes, activities, and events, respectively.

We assume that every process $W \in \mathcal{W}$ is "regulated" by a "*composition rule*", that restricts the sequences of activities that are allowed to be executed when W is enacted. The set of composition rules of the processes in $\mathcal{W}$ will be denoted as $\mathcal{CR}$. More specifically, the composition rule associated with W is a tuple $\langle$*ActSet*, *StartAct*, *EndAct*, $\mathcal{IC}\rangle$, where:

- *ActSet* is the set of activities that are allowed to be executed in any instance of W;
- *StartAct* (resp. *EndAct*) $\subseteq$*ActSet* is the set of the starting (resp. ending) activities of W, which are the activities that are allowed to be executed at the beginning (resp. end) of any instance of W; and

- $\mathcal{IC}$ is a set of constraints of the form $A \Rightarrow_{\mathcal{T}} B$ (called *must-constraint*) or $A \Rightarrow_{\mathcal{T}} \neg B$ (called *not-constraint*), where A, $B \in \mathcal{A}$ and $\mathcal{T}$ is of the form '$\leq c$', where c is a constant.

Here, $A \Rightarrow_{\mathcal{T}} B$ (resp. $A \Rightarrow_{\mathcal{T}} \neg B$), that basically imposes that, within every instance of W, the beginning of an instance a of A always (resp. never) precedes the beginning of an instance b of B such that the width of the interval between the starting times of a and b satisfies $\mathcal{T}$. Omitting $\mathcal{T}$ is the same as specifying $\mathcal{T}$='$\leq \infty$'.

Example 2 (Running example (continued)). Continuing Example 1, it holds: $W_1.ActSet = \{G, D, P, N, A, R, I\}$, $W_2.ActSet = \{N, A, R, I, F\}$, $W_1.StartAct = W_2.StartAct = \{R\}$, $W_1.EndAct = W_2.EndAct = \{N\}$, $W_1.\mathcal{IC} = \{P \Rightarrow D, D \Rightarrow \neg P\}$, and $W_2.\mathcal{IC} = \emptyset$.

The solution of an instance $\Phi = e_1 \ldots e_m$ of the interpretation problem is called *interpretation for Φ consistent with $\mathcal{CR}$* (or, simply, *consistent* or *valid* interpretation, when Φ and $\mathcal{CR}$ are understood), and is a pair $\langle \sigma, W \rangle$, where:

- σ is called *sequence-interpretation* and is a sequence $A_1 \ldots A_m$ of activities, where $\forall j \in [1..m]$ $A_j \in$ *cand-act*(e_j) (where *cand-act*(e_j) is the set of activities whose execution is known to possibly generate an instance of e_j), meaning that each e_j is interpreted as the result of executing activity A_j;
- W is called *process-interpretation* and denotes a process, meaning that Φ is interpreted as generated by process W;
- σ conforms to the composition rule of W.

Example 3 (Running example (continued)). Consider trace $\Phi_1 = \overline{\alpha}\overline{\beta}\overline{\gamma}\overline{\xi}$, where $\overline{\alpha}$, $\overline{\beta}$, $\overline{\gamma}$, and $\overline{\xi}$ are instances of α, β, γ and ξ, respectively. The correspondence depicted in Figure 1 between the types of the events occurring in Φ_1 and the activities is encoded by: *cand-act*$(\alpha) = \{R\}$, *cand-act*$(\beta) = \{I, P\}$, *cand-act*$(\gamma) = \{G\}$ and *cand-act*$(\xi) = \{A, D, N\}$. On the basis of this *cand-act*$(\cdot)$, Φ_1 can be interpreted as the result of executing one of the following sequences of activities: $\sigma_1 = R\,I\,G\,A$, $\sigma_2 = R\,P\,G\,A$, $\sigma_3 = R\,I\,G\,D$, $\sigma_4 = R\,P\,G\,D$, $\sigma_5 = R\,P\,G\,N$, and $\sigma_6 = R\,I\,G\,N$. By also looking at the composition rules of the process models, we have that: (i) σ_1 is inconsistent with the composition rule of W_1, as $A \notin W_1 EndAct$, and also with W_2's composition rule, since both $G \notin W_2.ActSet$ and $A \notin W_2.EndAct$; (ii) σ_2 is inconsistent with the composition rule of W_1, since it violates $P \rightarrow D$ and it is $A \notin W_1.EndAct$, and it is inconsistent with also with the composition rule of W_2, since $G, P \notin ActSet$ and $A \notin W_2.EndAct$; (iii) σ_3 is inconsistent with the composition rules of both W_1 and W_2, since $D \notin W_1 EndAct$, $D \notin W_2.EndAct$ and $G \notin W_2.ActSet$; (iv) σ_4 is inconsistent with the composition rules of both W_1 and W_2, since $D \notin W_1 EndAct$ and $D \notin W_2.EndAct$ (also $G, P \notin W_2.ActSet$); (v) σ_5 is inconsistent with the composition rule of W_1, since it violates $P \rightarrow D$, and with W_2's composition rule, since $G \notin W_2.ActSet$; and (vi) σ_6 is consistent with the composition rule of W_1, and inconsistent with W_2's composition rule, since $G \notin W_2.ActSet$. Thus, we have only one consistent interpretation for Φ_1, that is $\langle \sigma_6, W_1 \rangle$. Consider now the trace $\Phi_2 = \overline{\alpha}\beta\overline{\xi\xi}$, which coincides with the trace Φ_{ex} of Example 1. As discussed in that example, the only consistent sequence-interpretations for Φ_2 are $\sigma_a = RIDN$, $\sigma_b = RPDN$, and $\sigma_c = RIAN$, leading to the following interpretations: $\langle\sigma_a, W_1\rangle$, $\langle\sigma_b, W_1\rangle$, $\langle\sigma_c, W_1\rangle$ and $\langle\sigma_c, W_2\rangle$.

As a matter of fact, an instance of the interpretation problem admitting multiple solutions. This situation is likely to happen frequently, for the following reasons: 1) the correspondence between events and activities is many to many, so that an event instance can be interpreted as the result of different activity executions; 2) the description of the process models provided by composition rules can be rather "loose", and hence there may be process instances consistent with the composition rules of different processes: that is, the execution of a sequence of activities can be interpreted as the execution of different processes.

The presence of this uncertainty suggests to address the interpretation problem in probabilistic terms: we model the correspondence between events and activities probabilistically. In this direction, we assume that the many-to-many correspondence between events and activities is modeled by a probability distribution function (pdf) $p^a(A|E)$ returning the *a-priori* probability that an instance of event E is generated by an execution of A. For instance, $p^a(A_1|E_1) = 0.75$ and $p^a(A_2|E_1) = 0.25$ means that any instance of event E_1 is generated by the execution of either A_1 or A_2, and that the former case is three times more probable than the latter. This pdf is said to be *a-priori* since it assigns probabilities to the activities, of which the event can be viewed as the low-level result, without looking at the context where the event instance happened. That is, it provides an interpretation for the events that occur in a trace without looking at the other events occurring in the same trace.

In the same spirit, we assume given a pdf $p^a(W)$ over $\mathcal{W}$, associating each $W \in \mathcal{W}$ with the *a-priori* probability that a trace in a log encodes an instance of W. For instance, given $\mathcal{W} = \{W_1, W_2\}$, $p^a(W_1) = p^a(W_2) = 0.5$ means that, in the absence of further knowledge, W_1 and W_2 are equi-probable interpretations of any trace.

Given the a-priori pdfs $p^a(A|E)$ and $p^a(W)$, we could employ a naïve way to solve the interpretation problem, that is the following: first, assume that the event instances in Φ are independent of one another; then, use the a-priori pdf $p^a(A|E)$ to probabilistically interpret each e_i in $\Phi = e_1 \dots e_m$ as an instance of an activity A_i, and the pdf $p^a(W)$ to probabilistically interpret the whole Φ as an instance of one of the processes, say W_j. As implied by the independence assumption, every sequence-interpretation $\sigma = A_1 \dots A_m$ obtained this way will be associated with the probability $p^a(\sigma) = \Pi_{i=1}^{m} p^a(A_i|E_i)$ (that is, the product of the a-priori probabilities of the event-to-activity mappings at each step), while the process-interpretation W_j will have probability $p^a(W_j)$. In turn, the interpretation $\langle\sigma, W_j\rangle$ will have probability $p^a(\langle\sigma, W_j\rangle) = p^a(\sigma) \cdot p^a(W_j)$. Unfortunately, this naïve approach is unlikely to provide reasonable results, as explained in the following example.

Example 4 (Running example (continued)). Assume that the a-priori probabilities of the activities are $p^a(R|\alpha) = 1$, $p^a(I|\beta) = p^a(P|\beta) = 0.5$, $p^a(G|\gamma) = 1$,

$p^a(G|\delta) = 0.4$, $p^a(N|\delta) = 0.6$, $p^a(A|\xi) = 0.2$, $p^a(D|\xi) = 0.5$, $p^a(N|\xi) = 0.3$, and $p^a(F|\phi) = 1$, and those of the the processes are $p^a(W_1) = 0.6$, $p^a(W_2) = 0.4$. Consider trace Φ_1. Every sequence-interpretation of Φ_1 is associated with a probability, implied by p^a and the independence assumption. In particular: $p^a(\sigma_1) = p^a(R|\alpha) \cdot p^a(I|\beta) \cdot p^a(G|\gamma) \cdot p^a(A|\xi) = 0.1$; $p^a(\sigma_2) = 0.1$; $p^a(\sigma_3) = p^a(\sigma_4) = 0.25$; $p^a(\sigma_5) = p^a(\sigma_6) = 0.15$. Moreover, owing to the values of $p^a(W_1)$ and $p^a(W_2)$, we can say that Φ_1 encodes an execution of W_1 with probability 0.6, and of W_2 with probability 0.4. In turn, the probabilities of any interpretation $\langle\sigma, W\rangle$ for Φ_1 (with $W \in \{W_1, W_2\}$ and $\sigma \in \{\sigma_1, \ldots, \sigma_6\}$) is $p^a(\langle\sigma, W\rangle) = p^a(\sigma) \cdot p^a(W)$. In particular: $p^a(\langle\sigma_1, W_1\rangle) = 0.1 \cdot 0.6 = 0.06$, $p^a(\langle\sigma_1, W_2\rangle) = 0.1 \cdot 0.4 = 0.04$, and so on. However, we know from our running example that there is only one interpretation consistent with the composition rules, that is $\langle\sigma_6, W_1\rangle$. Moreover, the sum of the probabilities of the consistent interpretations should be 1 (or, equivalently, every invalid interpretation should have zero probability), while, in this case, the a-priori probability of the only valid interpretation $\langle\sigma_6, W_1\rangle$ is $p^a(\sigma_6) \cdot p^a(W_1) = 0.09$, and the other interpretations (that are all invalid) have non-zero probability.

Example 4 shows that the naïve approach, relying only on the independence assumption and the a-priori pdfs for interpreting the traces, may yield wrong conclusions. In fact, to solve the interpretation problem, we resort to *probabilistic conditioning*, that is a well-known paradigm used in the general context of forcing integrity constraints over probabilistic databases where the assumption of independence between tuples is originally used. In our case, applying the conditioning paradigm means revising the a-priori pdf $p^a(\langle\sigma, W\rangle)$ over the interpretations into $p^a(\langle\sigma, W\rangle \,|\, \mathcal{CR})$. The latter returns either 0, if the interpretation $\langle\sigma, W\rangle$ is invalid, or the ratio of its a-priori probability to the sum of the a-priori probabilities of all the valid interpretations, otherwise.

The problem of conditioning a pdf is generally complex. In our scenario, we could revise $p^a(\langle\sigma, W\rangle)$ into $p^a(\langle\sigma, W\rangle \,|\, \mathcal{CR})$ by first enumerating all the interpretations of Φ, then discarding those not satisfying the composition rules, and finally revising the a-priori probabilities of the remaining ones. Unfortunately, this approach is often infeasible, as the interpretations to deal with are too many. For instance, if, for a trace of 50 event instances, two activities are on average compatible with each event of the trace, we have to consider 2^{50} sequence-interpretations.

Our main contribution is a framework for efficiently constructing a compact representation (called *cas-graph*) of the interpretations of an input trace Φ that are consistent with $\mathcal{CR}$, and of the conditioned pdf $p^a(\langle\sigma, W\rangle \,|\, \mathcal{CR})$.

2.1 Cas-graph

Figure 2 reports a simplified example of cas-graph, built over trace $\Phi_2 = \overline{\alpha}\beta\overline{\xi\xi}$ of our running example. The nodes of the cas-graph are of the form $\langle i$, *Act*, $W\rangle$, where i is the step of the trace over which the node has been built, *Act* is the activity of which e_i has been interpreted to be an execution, and W is the process of which Φ_2 has been interpreted to be an instance. The source nodes of the cas-graph are not built over trace steps, but they are only used as the nodes from which all the paths representing interpretations of Φ_2 as instances of a same process W start. This cas-graph represents the three interpretations $\langle\sigma_a, W_1\rangle$, $\langle\sigma_b, W_1\rangle$, $\langle\sigma_c, W_1\rangle$ (encoded by the three source-to-target paths originating from the source node over W_1), and the interpretation $\langle\sigma_c, W_2\rangle$ (encoded by the source-to-target path originating from the source node over W_2). Moreover, each source node n is assigned the conditioned probability that Φ is an instance of the process in n, whereas each edge $\langle n_{i-1}, n_i\rangle$ is assigned the conditioned probability that event e_i corresponds to an execution of the activity in n_i given that the event e_{i-1} corresponds to an execution of the activity in n_{i-1}. Basically, the probabilities of the two source nodes in Fig. 2 mean that Φ_2 is an execution of W_1 (resp. W_2) with probability 90% (resp. 10%). Moreover, the probabilities assigned to the edges encode the conditioned probabilities of the interpretations: the conditioned probabilities that $\langle\sigma_a, W_1\rangle$, $\langle\sigma_b, W_1\rangle$, $\langle\sigma_c, W_1\rangle$ and $\langle\sigma_c, W_2\rangle$ actually are the pairs ⟨ activity sequence, process ⟩ that generated Φ_2 can be obtained by multiplying the probabilities of the source nodes and of all the edges appearing along the paths that encode each of these interpretations (that is, $15\%(= 90\% \times 1 \times 58.3\% \times 28.6\% \times 1)$, 37.5%, 37.5% and 10%, respectively).

The nodes of a cas-graph are said to be *activity nodes*. Each activity node n is defined over an event e_i of Φ, and represents an interpretation of e_i as an instance of some activity A within the execution of some process W. In a cas-graph, an activity node is the successor of activity nodes encoding alternative interpretations of the previous event e_{i-1}, and its successors are activity nodes encoding alternative interpretations of the next event e_{i+1}.

The construction of the cas-graph is performed by considering the steps of Φ in order and, at each step, by progressively building the activity nodes over the current step. Specifically, constructing an activity node n over the current step requires checking whether the interpretation that it provides of the current step is consistent (according to $\mathcal{CR}$) with the interpretations of the past events encoded by the predecessors of n. Hence, in order to efficiently support this compatibility check, each activity node n also contains a compact description of what the interpretations of the previous steps impose on the interpretations of the future steps, due to the presence of $\mathcal{CR}$ (for the sake of simplicity, this

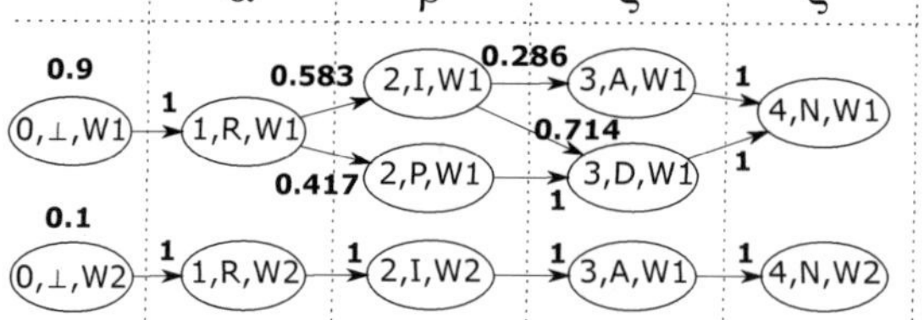

Fig. 2. A (simplified) example of cas-graph built over trace Φ_2 of our running example.

compact description was not reported in the nodes of the "simplified" cas-graph in Fig. 2). For more detail, we kindly refer the reader to [7].

3 Conclusion

We discussed the framework for efficiently interpreting business process logs composed of low-level events proposed in [7]. The proposed structure allows a compact representation of all the interpretations compatible with the constraints defined over the process models.

References

1. van der Aalst, W.M.P.: Process Mining: Discovery, Conformance and Enhancement of Business Processes. Springer (2011)
2. van der Aalst, W.M.P., Weijters, T., Maruster, L.: Workflow mining: Discovering process models from event logs. TKDE **16**(9), 1128–1142 (2004)
3. Baier, T., Mendling, J., Weske, M.: Bridging abstraction layers in process mining. Inf. Syst. **46**, 123–139 (2014)
4. Bose, R.P.J.C., van der Aalst, W.M.P.: Abstractions in process mining: A taxonomy of patterns. In: Proc. BPM. pp. 159–175 (2009)
5. Fazzinga, B., Flesca, S., Furfaro, F., Masciari, E., Pontieri, L.: A probabilistic unified framework for event abstraction and process detection from log data. In: Proc. CoopIS, ODBASE, and C&TC. pp. 320–328 (2015)
6. Fazzinga, B., Flesca, S., Furfaro, F., Masciari, E., Pontieri, L.: A compression-based framework for the efficient analysis of business process logs. In: Proc. SSDBM (2015)
7. Fazzinga, B., Flesca, S., Furfaro, F., Masciari, E., Pontieri, L.: Efficiently interpreting traces of low level events in business process logs. Inf. Syst. **73**, 1–24 (2018)
8. Fazzinga, B., Flesca, S., Furfaro, F., Masciari, E., Pontieri, L., Pulice, C.: A framework supporting the analysis of process logs stored in either relational or nosql dbmss. In: Proc. ISMIS. pp. 52–58 (2015)
9. Fazzinga, B., Flesca, S., Furfaro, F., Masciari, E., Pontieri, L., Pulice, C.: How, who and when: Enhancing business process warehouses by graph based queries. In: Proc. IDEAS. pp. 242–247 (2016)
10. Fazzinga, B., Flesca, S., Furfaro, F., Pontieri, L.: Online and offline classification of traces of event logs on the basis of security risks. J. of Intell. Inf. Syst. (2017)
11. Günther, C., Rozinat, A., van der Aalst, W.M.P.: Activity mining by global trace segmentation. In: Proc. Workshops BPM. pp. 128–139 (2009)
12. Mannhardt, F., de Leoni, M., Reijers, H.A., van der Aalst, W.M.P., Toussaint, P.J.: From low-level events to activities-a pattern-based approach. In: Proc. BPM. pp. 125–141 (2016)
13. Polyvyanyy, A., Ouyang, C., Barros, A., van der Aalst, W.M.: Process querying: Enabling business intelligence through query-based process analytics. Decision Supp. Syst. **100**, 41–56 (2017)
14. Rozinat, A., van der Aalst, W.M.P.: Conformance checking of processes based on monitoring real behavior. Inf. Syst. **33**(1), 64–95 (2008)
15. Tax, N., Sidorova, N., Haakma, R., van der Aalst, W.M.P.: Event abstraction for process mining using supervised learning techniques. In: Proc. IntelliSys 2016: Volume 1. pp. 251–269

How to Robustly Combine Judgements from Crowd Assessors with AWARE *

Marco Ferrante[1], Nicola Ferro[2], and Maria Maistro[2]

[1] Department of Mathematics, University of Padua, Padua, Italy
ferrante@math.unipd.it
[2] Department of Information Engineering, University of Padua, Padua, Italy
ferro@dei.unipd.it, maistro@dei.unipd.it

Abstract. We propose the *Assessor-driven Weighted Averages for Retrieval Evaluation (AWARE)* probabilistic framework, a novel methodology for dealing with multiple crowd assessors, who may be contradictory and/or noisy. By modeling relevance judgements and crowd assessors as sources of uncertainty, AWARE directly combines the performance measures computed on the ground-truth generated by the crowd assessors instead of adopting some classification technique to merge the labels produced by them. We propose several unsupervised estimators that instantiate the AWARE framework and we compare them with *Majority Vote (MV)* and *Expectation Maximization (EM)* showing that AWARE approaches improve both in correctly ranking systems and predicting their actual performance scores.

Keywords: crowdsourcing, unsupervised estimators, AWARE

1 Introduction

Ground-truth is central to the data processing area, as in top-k ranking in databases, information retrieval, natural language processing, video and image processing, information extraction and many others. Although ground-truth enables the scoring and comparison of algorithms with respect to human judgments, creating a dataset and, in particular, gathering relevance assessments is an extremely demanding activity, therefore there is an increasing interest for more effective and affordable ways of gathering assessments [3].

Crowdsourcing [4] has emerged as a viable option for ground-truth creation since it allows to cheaply collect multiple assessments for each task. However, it raises many questions regarding the quality of the collected assessments. Therefore, in order to obtain a ground-truth good enough to be used for evaluation purposes, the possibility of discarding the low quality assessors and/or combining them with more or less sophisticated algorithms has been considered.

* Extended abstract of [2].

The problem of merging multiple crowd assessors has been addressed mostly from a classification point of view, with traditional approaches which focus mainly on how to select assessors and/or discard low quality assessors and how to merge judgments from multiple assessors. We can consider this as a kind of "upstream" approach, because the aggregated ground-truth is created before systems are evaluated and performance scores are computed.

In this paper, we address the problem of ground-truth creation from a new angle, i.e. we investigate how to estimate performance measures in a way more robust to crowd assessors. In particular, we seek a better estimation of the true expected value of a performance measure, by leveraging its multiple observations, generated separately by the relevance judgements of each crowd assessor. We can consider this as as a kind of "downstream" approach, since the aggregation happens after performance measures have been computed.

The main intuition behind our approach is based on the idea that the choice of the "best" relevance judgments, operated ahead at the pool level, may have a diverse impact on different systems and on various performance measures. Indeed, systems rank the same documents differently and therefore the same correctly labelled or mis-labelled documents impact the performances of different systems in different ways. Therefore, we propose the *Assessor-driven Weighted Averages for Retrieval Evaluation (AWARE)* probabilistic framework, which allows us to combine multiple versions of a performance measure, computed from the ground-truth created by each crowd assessor, into a single composite measure, referred as the AWARE version of it. The AWARE framework specifies how performance measures have to be merged on the basis of the estimated crowd assessor accuracies and we propose several unsupervised estimators of such accuracies. The experimentation shows that AWARE approaches improve in terms of capability of correctly ranking systems and predicting their actual performance scores.

The paper is organized as follows: Section 2 introduces the AWARE framework; Section 3 gives an intuitive overview of several unsupervised estimators for determining the assessors accuracies; Section 4 carry out the experimental evaluation using TREC collections; finally, Section 5 draws some conclusions.

2 The AWARE Framework

In [1] we introduced the following definitions: let D and T be a *set of documents* and a *set of topics*, respectively; let $(REL, \preceq)$ be a totally ordered *set of relevance degrees*. For each pair $(t, d) \in T \times D$, the *ground-truth GT* is a map which assigns a relevance degree $rel \in REL$ to a document d with respect to a topic t.

In order to cope with and leverage crowd assessors, we assume that the relevance of a document is not deterministically known, but it is described by a probability distribution: instead of specifying a single value from REL as results of the relevance assessment, we model the uncertainty entailed in the assessment process as a whole distribution of possible values associated to each (t, d) pair. Furthermore, we assume that the ability of the crowd assessors is stochastically determined by a probability assigned to them, that we call their *accuracy*.

More precisely, we assume that there exists a probability space $(\Omega, \mathcal{F}, \mathbb{P})$, which provides the source of randomness and encompasses the judgements done by all the possible crowd assessors, on all the possible documents for any possible topic. Considering this space, we can extend the definition of the ground-truth as $GT : \Omega \times T \times D \to REL$. In this way, to any pair (t, d) we associate a random variable $GT(\cdot, t, d)$ with value on REL, whose distribution describes the relevance of the document d with respect to the topic t.

Let $\Lambda = \{W_1, \ldots, W_l\}$ be a finite set of crowd assessors and let us assume that there exists a random variable, $W : \Omega \times T \to \Lambda$, whose distribution identifies the ability of a single crowd assessor with respect to any given topic. We call $a_k(t) = \mathbb{P}[T = t, W = W_k]$ the *accuracy* of crowd assessor W_k in assessing topic t and we assume that $a_k(t)$ is determined by the expected ability she/he demonstrates in assessing all the possible documents for that topic.

The easiest way to jointly cope with these random objects, i.e. ground-truth and crowd assessors, is to consider their expectations. The expected relevance of document d for topic t, by the law of total expectation, is given by

$$\mathbb{E}\big[GT(t,d)\big] = \mathbb{E}\Big[\mathbb{E}\big[GT(t,d)\big|W\big]\Big] = \sum_{k=1}^{l} \mathbb{E}[GT(t,d)|W = W_k]\; a_k(t) \; .$$

Then for a performance measure $\mathrm{m}(\cdot)$, we can proceed in a similar way and define its AWARE version as its expectation with respect to $\mathbb{P}$:

$$\text{aware-m}\big(t, r_t\big) = \mathbb{E}\Big[\mu\big(\hat{r}_t\big)\Big] = \sum_{k=1}^{l} \mathbb{E}\big[\mu\big(\hat{r}_t\big)\big|W = W_k\big]\; a_k(t) \; ,$$

where μ is the scoring function associated to the performance measure $\mathrm{m}(\cdot)$ [1], and $\hat{r}_t$ is the judged run.

We estimate the first term by $\mu\big(\hat{r}_t^k\big)$, where $\hat{r}_t^k$ represents the judged run under the assessments done by the crowd assessor W_k. However, the estimation of the accuracies $a_k(t) = \mathbb{P}[T = t, W = W_k]$ is somehow more problematic. We therefore take a *random assessor* as a comparison point. In the case of binary relevance, i.e. when $REL = \{0, 1\}$, an assessor W_k is a *random assessor of parameter* $p \in [0, 1]$, if for any pair (t, d) the conditional random variables $GT(t, d)|W = W_k \sim Bin(1, p)$, where $Bin(1, p)$ denotes a Binomial random variable with parameter p, and are mutually independent.

A random assessor, of any possible parameter p, is the prototype of a "bad" or at least a "shallow" assessor, since p is the same for any possible pair (t, d). The basic idea that we will apply in the next section is that the farther a crowd assessor is from the random ones, the better she/he is and the higher her/his accuracy will be.

3 Estimating Crowd Assessor Accuracy

This sections aims at providing an intuitive overview of the proposed unsupervised estimators of the accuracy of a crowd assessor, more details can be found

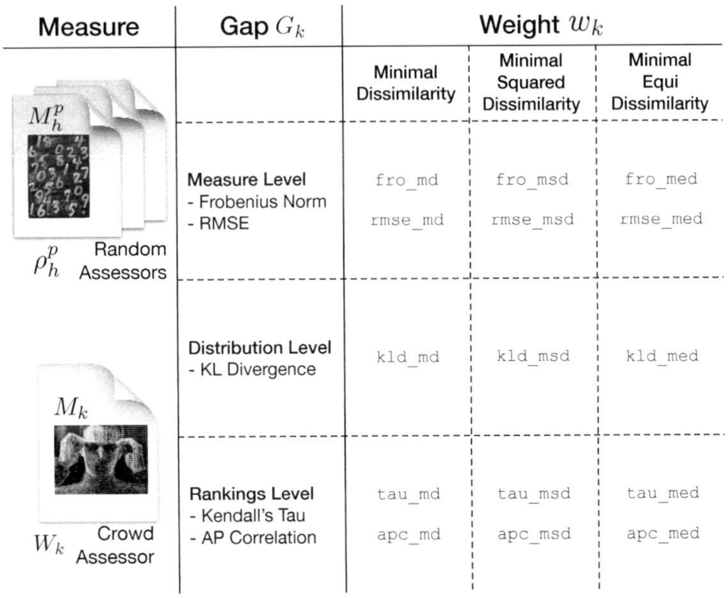

Fig. 1: Approach to determine the accuracy of a crowd assessor W_k with respect to a random assessors ρ_h^p.

in [2]. Figure 1 shows the main steps (granularity, gap and weight) we use to estimate the accuracy of a crowd assessor and the different estimators we can obtain by combining the various alternatives at each step. The idea is to compare the crowd assessor against a set of random assessors and how "different" this crowd assessor is from the random ones, i.e. how much better she/he is.

For each pool we generate, ρ_h^p, $h = 1, 2, \ldots, H$, a set of H random assessors of level p, i.e. which randomly evaluate as relevant the p per cent of the documents in the pool. We consider three different classes of random assessors: *uniform random assessor* with $p = 0.5$, *underestimating random assessor* with $p = 0.05$, and *overestimating random assessor* with $p = 0.95$. Each of these random assessors gives origin to an assessor measure M_h^p for a given performance measure $\mathrm{m}(\cdot)$.

Therefore, the intuitive idea described above boils down to determining some sort of "difference" between the measure M_k of a crowd assessor W_k and those M_h^p of the three random assessors ρ_h^p and turning this "difference" into an estimated accuracy a_t^k assigned to the crowd assessor W_k to compute the AWARE version of the performance measure $\mathrm{m}(\cdot)$. This is achieved in two main steps:

- *gap* G_k: this quantifies what "different" means. We consider three alternatives:
  - *measure level*: this operates directly on the assessor measures by computing either the Frobenius norm of their difference (labelled `fro`) or their *Root Mean Square Error (RMSE)* (labelled `rmse`);

   - *distribution level*: this works on the performance distributions estimated from the assessor measures by using *Kernel Density Estimation (KDE)* and computes the *Kullback-Leibler Divergence (KLD)* between them (labelled `kld`);
   - *rankings level*: this considers the system rankings induced by the assessor measures and compares them by using either the Kendall's tau correlation (labelled `tau`) or the AP correlation (labelled `apc`);
- *weight* w_t^k: this turns the gap computed in the previous step into an estimated accuracy to be assigned to a crowd assessor. In particular, we reason in terms of *dissimilarity* from random assessors since, for a crowd assessor W_k, being close to a random one ρ_h^p can be considered as an indicator of her/his poor quality. We have three alternatives:
   - *minimal dissimilarity* (labelled `md`): this computes a weight which is proportional to the minimum gap from one of the random assessors class, i.e. the closer to one of the random assessors, the smaller the weight;
   - *minimal squared dissimilarity* (labelled `msd`): this is similar to the previous case but uses the minimum squared gap;
   - *minimal equi-dissimilarity* (labelled `med`): this computes a weight which is proportional to the crowd assessor being equally distant from all three families of random assessors.

For each of the three random assessor classes, we generate a set of H replicates to cope with the uncertainty of the random generation process and to obtain better estimates. Therefore, for each crowd assessor W_k, we obtain a set of H estimates and we need to aggregate them into a single one; we compute a mean gap $\bar{G}_k$, averaging over the set of H gaps computed with respect to each random assessor ρ_h^p.

Finally, the described procedure produces an estimated accuracy a_t^k to be assigned to a crowd assessor W_k for each topic $t \in T$; this is what we call *topic-by-topic score granularity*, labelled `tpc`. However, we are also interested in the case when a single accuracy score is assigned to a crowd assessor W_k, i.e. when the a_t^k are the same for all the topics; this is what we call *single score granularity*, labelled `sgl`.

4 Experimental Evaluation

4.1 Experimental Setup

We use the TREC 21, 2012, Crowdsourcing [6] data sets developed in the *Text Relevance Assessing Task (TRAT)*. The TRAT required participating groups to simulate the relevance assessing role of the NIST for 10 of the TREC 08, 1999, Ad-hoc topics [9]. Participating groups had to submit a binary relevance judgements for every document in the judging pools of the ten topics. Two TREC Adhoc tracks used these 10 topics over the years: the TREC 08, 1999, Ad-hoc track [9] (labeled `T08`), and the TREC 13, 2004, Robust track [8] (labeled `T13`).

When it comes to the measures for evaluating the effectiveness of the different approaches, we adopt two criteria used in the TREC 22, 2013, Crowdsourcing track [7]: referred as *rank correlation* and *score accuracy*. We use *Average Precision (AP)* correlation [10] to compare the ranking of the systems produced for a given performance measure m(·), computed over the gold standard, with respect to the ranking produced for the same performance measure computed over the ground-truth, generated by one of the approaches under examination. In addition to correctly ranking systems, it is important that the performance scores are as accurate as possible. To this end, for a given performance measure m(·), we use the RMSE between the performance measure computed over the gold standard and the one computed over the ground-truth created by one of the approaches under examination.

When it comes to the assessor measures M_k and M_h^p, we consider *Average Precision (AP)*, *Normalized Discounted Cumulated Gain (nDCG)*, and *Expected Reciprocal Rank (ERR)*.

We consider three baselines, representing the state-of-the-art: the MV algorithm, labeled `mv`, and two variants of the EM algorithm: `emmv`, i.e. EM seeded by the pool generated by the MV algorithm, and `emneu`, i.e. EM initialized using the worker confusion matrix. Finally, we experiment also a fourth baseline labeled `uni`, representing AWARE in absence of any information, i.e. using uniform accuracies for all the merged crowd assessors.

4.2 Methodology

The goal of this section is to to investigate how the AWARE approaches and the state-of-the-art baselines behave with respect to different factors, and to compare the AWARE approaches against those baselines. To this end, we adopt a *General Linear Mixed Model (GLMM)* model for the three-way *ANalysis Of VAriance (ANOVA)* with repeated measures [5]. We are interested in determining whether a factor effect is significant, i.e. its *p*-value is less than 0.05, as well as in which proportion of the variance is due to it.

AP Correlation The ANOVA table – not reported due to space limit [2] – shows that `Measure` is a large size effect and it explains the largest share of variance; `Systems` is a large size effect as well and it is the second largest main effect; finally, also `Approach` is a large size effect but about 2 times smaller than `Measure` effect and 1.25 times smaller than `Systems` effect. Overall, this supports the intuition that led to the development of the AWARE framework: performance `Measures` and `Systems` effects do matter a lot when merging assessors and they should be taken into the play.

The Tukey HSD multiple comparison analysis reported in Figure 2a highlights the top group (dashed blue line), the group of approaches not significantly different from the `uni` baseline (dashed bright red line), the group of approaches not significantly different from `mv` (dashed dark red line), and the group of approaches not significantly different from `emmv` and `emneu` (dashed orange line). We can note how the top group is separated from the others while the `uni` and `mv` groups partially overlaps. In particular, we can see that the approaches significantly better than all the others are `sgl_tau_msd` (the top one), `sgl_apc_msd`,

Mean τ_{ap}	Approach	Group	
0.6759	sgl_tau_msd	X	Top Group
0.6709	sgl_apc_msd	XX	
0.6705	tpc_apc_msd	XXX	
0.6705	sgl_tau_md	XXX	
0.6696	sgl_tau_med	XXX	UNI Group
0.6683	tpc_apc_md	XXXX	
0.6679	sgl_apc_md	XXXX	
0.6675	sgl_apc_med	XXXXX	
0.6668	tpc_apc_med	XXXXXX	
0.6646	sgl_kld_med	XXXXXX	MV Group
0.6644	uni	XXXXX	
0.6644	tpc_kld_med	XXXXX	
0.6644	tpc_kld_md	XXXXX	
0.6644	tpc_kld_msd	XXXXX	
0.6636	sgl_fro_med	XXXX	
0.6627	sgl_fro_md	XXXXX	
0.6618	tpc_tau_msd	XXXXX	
0.6610	tpc_rmse_md	XXXX	
0.6610	tpc_fro_md	XXXX	
0.6607	sgl_rmse_med	XXX	
0.6603	sgl_kld_md	XXX	
0.6603	tpc_fro_med	XXX	
0.6603	tpc_rmse_med	XXX	
0.6592	mv	XXX	
0.6571	tpc_tau_md	XXX	
0.6562	sgl_fro_msd	XX	
0.6520	tpc_tau_med	XX	
0.6519	tpc_rmse_msd	XX	
0.6519	tpc_fro_msd	XX	
0.6471	sgl_rmse_md	X	
0.6471	sgl_kld_msd	X	
0.6184	sgl_rmse_msd	X	EM Group
0.6182	emmv	X	
0.6142	emneu	X	

(a) AP correlation

Mean RMSE	Approach	Group	
0.3953	sgl_rmse_med	X	Top Group
0.3955	tpc_rmse_med	X	
0.3955	tpc_fro_med	X	
0.4048	sgl_fro_med	XX	
0.4127	sgl_kld_md	XXX	
0.4219	sgl_fro_md	XXX	UNI Group
0.4287	tpc_rmse_md	XX	
0.4287	tpc_fro_md	XX	
0.4331	sgl_kld_msd	XXX	
0.4333	sgl_rmse_md	XXX	
0.4374	sgl_fro_msd	XXX	
0.4417	sgl_kld_med	XXXX	
0.4534	uni	XXXX	
0.4534	tpc_kld_med	XXXX	
0.4534	tpc_kld_md	XXXX	
0.4534	tpc_kld_msd	XXXX	
0.4534	sgl_apc_md	XXXX	
0.4540	sgl_apc_msd	XXXX	
0.4541	sgl_apc_med	XXXX	
0.4566	sgl_tau_md	XXXX	MV Group
0.4567	sgl_tau_med	XXXX	
0.4614	tpc_tau_med	XXX	
0.4615	sgl_tau_msd	XXX	
0.4640	tpc_apc_med	XXX	
0.4674	tpc_apc_md	XXX	
0.4728	tpc_tau_md	XXX	
0.4758	mv	XX	
0.4837	tpc_apc_msd	XX	
0.5021	tpc_tau_msd	X	
0.5498	tpc_fro_msd	X	
0.5498	tpc_rmse_msd	X	
0.5652	sgl_rmse_msd	X	
0.7068	emmv	X	EM Group
0.7333	emneu	X	

(b) RMSE

Fig. 2: Tukey HSD multiple comparison test for the `Approach` factor.

`tpc_apc_msd`, and `sgl_tau_md`, suggesting that the single score granularity is preferable to the topic-by-topic one and that the `tau` and `apc` gaps help to rank systems better. State-of-the-art approaches, namely `mv` (the best one in this group), `emmv`, and `emneu` are clearly separated from the top group. Finally, the AWARE `uni` baseline exhibits better performances than `mv`, even though it is not significantly different from it.

RMSE The ANOVA table – not reported due to space limit [2] – shows that the `Measure` factor is a large size effect with the greatest impact; `Approach` is a large size effect but, unlike the case of AP correlation, it is almost as important as `Measure`; finally, `Systems` is a large size effect but much smaller than the previous two. Overall, this further supports the intuition behind AWARE, but it also suggests that `Approaches` are much more prominent for the accurate estimation of the actual value of a performance measure, (assessed by the RMSE) than for ranking systems correctly (assessed by AP correlation).

The top group, reported in the Tukey HSD comparison of Figure 2b, consists of `sgl_rmse_med`, `tpc_rmse_med`, `tpc_fro_med` (the top ones with extremely close performances), `sgl_fro_med`, and `sgl_kld_md`; this suggests that there is more balance between single and topic-by-topic score granularities and that the gaps operating closer to the assessors measures (`fro`, `rmse`, `kld`) are more effective. State-of-the-art approaches are clearly distinct from the top group and, in this case, AWARE `uni` is significantly better than `mv` and the rest of them.

5 Conclusions and Future Work

In this paper, we presented the AWARE framework for robustly combining performance measures coming from multiple crowd assessors. The idea of AWARE stemmed from the observation of the potential impact of both performance measures and systems when it comes to correctly labeled/mis-labeled relevance judgements. Therefore, we proposed a probabilistic framework to take systems and performance measures into account during the estimation of the crowd assessors accuracies used to combine them. We then exemplified how to instantiate the proposed stochastic framework by introducing many unsupervised estimators of the accuracy of crowd assessors.

Finally, we conducted a thorough evaluation on TREC collections, comparing AWARE against state-of-the-art approaches and studying their influencing factors. The experimentation has provided multiple evidence supporting the intuition behind the AWARE framework. Moreover, it has shown that AWARE approaches perform better than state-of-the-art ones in terms of both ranking systems and correctly predicting their performance scores.

As future work we will investigate multi-feature estimators, i.e. estimators that take into account multiple performance measures at the same time to determine the accuracy of a crowd assessor, supervised estimators, i.e. estimators that leverage a gold standard instead of random assessors for determining the accuracy of a crowd assessor and extend the experiments to graded-relevance judgements.

References

1. Ferrante, M., Ferro, N., Maistro, M.: Towards a Formal Framework for Utility-oriented Measurements of Retrieval Effectiveness. In ICTIR, pp. 21–30, ACM, 2013.
2. Ferrante, M., Ferro, N., Maistro, M.: AWARE: Exploiting Evaluation Measures to Combine Multiple Assessors. In TOIS, 36(2), 20:1–20:38, 2017.
3. Halvey, M., Villa, R., Clough, P.: SIGIR 2014 Workshop on Gathering Efficient Assessments of Relevance (GEAR). In SIGIR, p. 1293, ACM, 2014.
4. Marcus, A., Parameswaran, A.: Crowdsourced Data Management: Industry and Academic Perspectives. In Foundations and Trends® in Databases, 6(1-2) pp. 1–16, Now Publishers, Inc, 2015.
5. Maxwell, S., Delaney, H.D.: Designing Experiments and Analyzing Data. A Model Comparison Perspective. Lawrence Erlbaum Associates, 2004.
6. Smucker, M.D., Kazai, G., Lease, M.: Overview of the TREC 2012 Crowdsourcing Track. In TREC, NIST, Special Publication 500-298, 2013.
7. Smucker, M.D., Kazai, G., Lease, M.: Overview of the TREC 2013 Crowdsourcing Track. In TREC, NIST, Special Publication 500-302, 2014.
8. Voorhees, E.M.: Overview of the TREC 2004 Robust Track. In TREC, NIST, Special Publication 500-261, 2004.
9. Voorhees, E.M., Harman, D.K.: Overview of the Eight Text REtrieval Conference (TREC-8). In TREC, pp. 1–24, NIST, Special Publication 500-246, 1999.
10. Yilmaz, E. and Aslam, J. A. and Robertson, S. E.: A New Rank Correlation Coefficient for Information Retrieval. In SIGIR, pp. 587–594, ACM, 2008.

Multidimensional Mining over Big Healthcare Data: A Big Data Analytics Framework

Mario Bochicchio[1], Alfredo Cuzzocrea[2], Lucia Vaira[1], Antonella Longo[1], Marco Zappatore[1]

[1]University of Salento, Lecce, Italy
{mario.bochicchio,lucia.vaira,
antonella.longo,marcosalvatore.zappatore}@unisalento.it
[2]University of Trieste and ICAR-CNR, Trieste, Italy
alfredo.cuzzocrea@dia.units.it

Abstract. Nowadays, a great deal of attention is being devoted to *big data analytics in complex healthcare environments*. *Fetal growth curves*, which are a classic case of *big healthcare data*, are used in prenatal medicine to early detect potential fetal growth problems, estimate the perinatal outcome and promptly treat possible complications. However, the currently adopted curves and the related diagnostic techniques have been criticized because of their poor precision. New techniques, based on the idea of *customized growth curves*, have been proposed in literature. In this perspective, the problem of *building customized or personalized fetal growth curves by means of big data techniques* is discussed in this paper. The proposed framework introduces the idea of *summarizing the massive amounts of (input) big data via multidimensional views* on top of which well-known *Data Mining methods* like *clustering* and *classification* are applied. This overall defines a *multidimensional mining approach*, targeted to *complex* healthcare environments. A preliminary analysis on the effectiveness of the framework is also proposed.

Keywords: Mining Big Data, Big Healthcare Data, Healthcare Systems.

1 Introduction

Big data analytics in complex healthcare environments (e.g., [13,14,15,16,17]) are of high interest at now, by following well-known principles of *big data management and mining* (e.g., [18,19,20]). Here, the main problem consists in devising models, techniques and algorithms focused to extract *useful knowledge* from enormous amounts of (big) data, with the goal of implementing so-called *big data intelligence*, i.e. deriving decisions, decision processes, guidelines and policies devoted to improve the target healthcare system (e.g., [13]). *Fetal growth curves*, which are a classic case of *big healthcare data*, are very important in prenatal medicine for fetal well-being evaluation. Indeed, they represent a mature and well-established practice to early detect potential fetal growth restriction, to estimate the perinatal outcome and promptly treat possible complications. The general idea underlying this test is very simple and effective: fetuses

SEBD 2018, June 24-27, 2018, Castellaneta Marina, Italy.

grow up showing a regular trend as a function of the gestational age. Therefore, their wellbeing can be assessed by tracking their sizes over the time and by comparing them with a reference growth curve known as "good". The implementation of the idea, based on ultrasounds pictures of the maternal abdomen, is quite simple, non-invasive and inexpensive.

In the clinical routine, fetal biometric parameters coming from this test are compared with a set of reference parameters, which are usually provided by the same test equipment. When results are too large or too small for the gestational age, they are classified as "potentially pathologic" and supplementary clinical tests are required/performed. A very problematic aspect in this practice is that several sets of fetal growth curves are reported in literature and the adoption of the right one is crucial to avoid errors (e.g., to avoid wrong classifications of fetuses as pathologic or non-pathologic) [5]. This is a hot topic for the obstetrics and gynecologist community [1], since the currently-adopted references lack of several mother-related aspects, such as ethnic group, food, drugs and smoke. Indeed, it has been recognized that these and other factors have a non-negligible influence on the actual growing trends of fetuses and, then, on the overall number of false-positives/negatives, and further unnecessary tests. In the current practice, failure rates as high as 46% are reported in literature [3], even considering the standard defined by the *World Health Organization* (WHO), so that, in several cases, it is hard to decide whether the fetus has to be considered pathologic or not. For this reason, *customized fetal growth charts* [1] have been proposed as an alternative to "literature-based" growth curves. The increasing acceptance of this best practice suggests for a new and ambitious perspective: the creation of an online service able to collect and analyze the world production of fetal growth data [2], in order to support obstetricians in the production of customized/personalized fetal growth curves. The clinical understanding of the phenomenon described by such a large amount of data is extremely intriguing, because of the underlying idea of finally grabbing a total understanding of the fetal growth processes. On the other hand, it is also challenging, due to both technical and medical reasons. These aspects are discussed in the remaining part of the paper. The main goal of the paper is that of assessing the feasibility of such online service. To this end, the paper proposes a *big data analytics framework for building customized or personalized fetal growth curves by means via innovative big data techniques*. The proposed framework introduces the idea of *summarizing the massive amounts of (input) big data via multidimensional views* [21] on top of which well-known *Data Mining methods* like *clustering* and *classification* are applied. This overall defines a *multidimensional mining approach*, targeted to *complex* healthcare environments. A preliminary analysis on the effectiveness of the framework is also proposed.

2 Building Customized Fetal Growth Curves by means of Big Data Analysis Techniques

In this Section, we provide the main contribution of our research, i.e. principles and definitions of a big data analytics framework for supporting multidimensional mining in complex healthcare environments. The idea of developing an online service to collect and analyze large datasets about maternal/fetal wellbeing and fetal growth, and supporting gynecologists and obstetricians in diagnoses of fetal growth restrictions has been considered valuable by several authors [1,3]. Actually, scaling this approach up to the worldwide production of fetal-maternal data could drive the medical community toward a deeper understanding of fetal pathologies, but several aspects have to be considered.

From a technical point of view, due to the volume of data to collect and analyze, the variety of descriptors associated to each mother/fetus and the velocity inherent to the phenomenon, Big Data techniques must be adopted. Indeed, every year there are about 160 millions of newborns in the world: on average this is equivalent to about 300 newborns per second. Considering that, according to international guidelines, for each healthy woman, about 10 clinical test (3 for growth tracking) are performed during pregnancy, and that for pathologic fetuses this number is significantly higher, the global production of data on the phenomenon can be estimated in a continuous stream of 1,000 – 10,000 new medical records per second, with an overall volume of 1 to 10 Petabytes per year. For the purposes of this paper, a more realistic scenario including 10% to 20% of fetal-growth data from at least two European countries is sufficient to test the proposed framework and tune it for further extension.

According to current methods adopted in the clinical practice for fetal-maternal wellbeing assessment, the main algorithms to analyze this stream would be based on: (*i*) *least-square method*, (*ii*) *multidimensional analysis*, (*iii*) clustering and classification techniques. The overall computational load is hard to estimate because of the problem is still under investigation, but *distributed approaches* and *parallelization techniques* are likely to be adopted. Moreover, the variety of data types (both structured and unstructured) is one of the main characteristics of this research field, because of the elements affecting fetal growth are not completely known and, every year, new variables come from the influence of new pathologies, medicines, therapies, pollutants etc. This heterogeneity is problematic to manage, but it is an important and unavoidable characteristic of the problem.

Referring to the algorithmic part, the possibility of constructing dynamic and customized fetal growth curves is mainly based on the following aspects:

- the application of *multidimensional analysis techniques*, which allow to both summarize the massive amounts of (input) big data via multidimensional and identify groups of patients (fetuses, in our case) who share similar growth patterns over the time;
- the possibility of searching for possible *correlation* of fetal growths vs parameters like ethnic group, maternal age, fetal gender, and so on.

The hypothesis is that fetuses at the same gestational age, with similar genetic make-up (e.g., ethnicity, familial aspects, and so forth) and in similar environmental conditions (e.g., food, smoke, drugs, and so forth), are subject to similar growth curves. This kind of fetuses will be referred, in the following of the paper as *Homogeneous Patient Groups* (HPG). This allows to identify patients who share common profiles in order to determine if a given fetus is potentially pathologic or not, when his/her growth parameters are different from those of the HPG to which he/she belongs. The membership to a specific group is established at run-time and a specific fetus can belong to one or more groups simultaneously, according to the analyzed features.

The diagnostic process is based on the following three main steps:

a) build the summarizing multidimensional view of the target experiment;
b) initially, the HPG of each mother/fetus is not known; it can be identified through anamnesis or specific tests and exams;
c) the wellbeing of each new fetus is assessed by comparing its actual sizes with the reference charts of the HPG identified by the previous step.

In terms of multidimensional analysis, patients can be represented as multidimensional points, and HPGs as regions, of a multidimensional space whose dimensions are all parameters affecting the fetal growth (ethnicity, maternal weight, height, familial aspects, foods, and so forth), and whose measures of analysis are the biometric parameters of the fetus. In this sense, step *b*) corresponds to identifying the patient's nearest HPG according to some distance measure, while step *c*) requires to compute the average size, the variance, and the corresponding percentile on a purposely defined (sufficiently-wide and updated) subset of elements of the same HPG. Moreover, HPGs can be periodically updated (e.g., every four to six months, considering that growth variations are not expected to emerge on shorter periods) by means of a suitable clustering algorithm. Considering that clustering algorithms are computationally intensive and cannot be repeated at the arrival of every new biometric fetal measure, a suitable classification algorithm must be exploited in order to decide to which precomputed clusters the new sample belong [10].

The innovative aspects of this method with respect to other approaches known in literature can be summarized as follows:

- HPGs are periodically updated rather than statically defined by means of standardized growth curves;
- reference growth curves are associated to each HPG (hundreds or thousands) rather than on few ethnic groups;
- fetal growth curves are continuously updated with the data coming from patients under examination, thus also revealing the long-term population trends in patient's growth.

3 Implementation, Preliminary Results and Discussion

We conducted some preliminary analysis to proof the effectiveness of our proposed framework, on the basis of real-life big healthcare data coming from a government/university research project. This Section describes the outcome of this task of our research.

In order to explore the implementation details of the proposed big data analytics framework for building customized fetal growth curves, we decided to collect and analyze an actual sample of fetal-maternal data coming from two facilities locate in the Apulia region in south Italy, namely: a university clinic, also involved in research about malformation and diabetes in pregnancy, and a general hospital. The facilities serve a basin of about 1.5 million citizens and assists more than 10,000 pregnant women per year. The sample, concerning about 500 pregnant women under assistance by 8 medical doctors, consists of a quite sparse table with about 2,500 records and 60 attributes grouped into 9 main categories (having obvious meaning):

- *Personal Data*;
- *Parity*;
- *Fetal Biometry*;
- *Diabetic Profile*;
- *Maternal Biometry*;
- *Familiarity*;
- *Glycemic Profile*;
- *Other Pathologies*;
- *Delivery Outcome*.

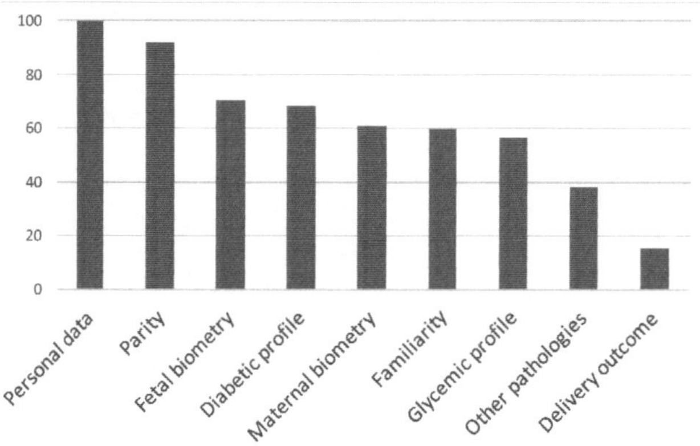

Fig. 1. Information Completeness.

For each category, the percentage of information completeness, defined as the number of not-null records over the total number of records, is represented in Fig. 1.

This collection permitted us to better understand the nature and the variability of data involved in maternal and fetal wellbeing monitoring. Moreover, it permitted us to define a set of *Dimensional Fact Models* (DFM) [23] able to describe a typical fetal-maternal test, along with its variable aspects. A simplified version of the main DFM is shown in Fig. 2.

According to the guidelines of the WHO on fetal growth curves, the available data sample has been also used to extract the reference curves for the target population to be analyzed. The process included a preliminary *normality distribution test* and a *linear regression*. This preliminary step was essential for a quantitative evaluation of the reduction of false positive/negative obtained with the new proposed method.

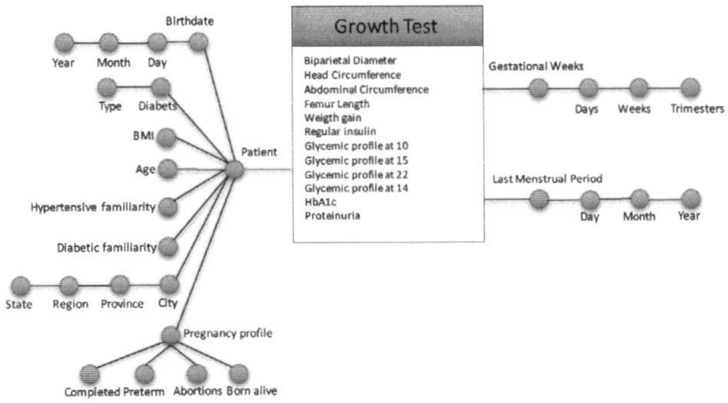

Fig. 2. DFM of a Fetal Maternal Test.

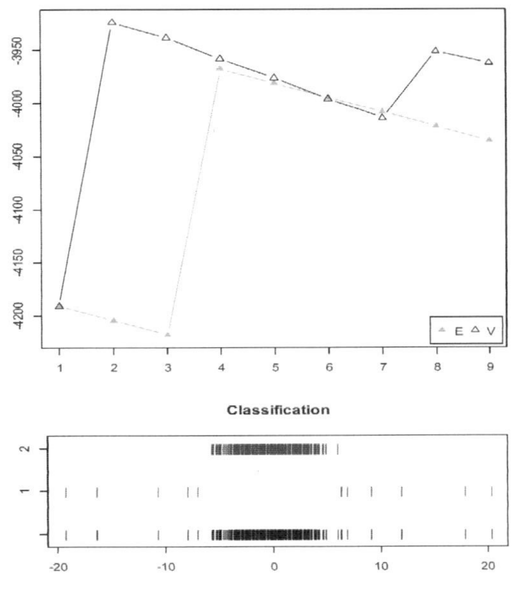

Fig. 3. Expectation Maximization Clustering Results.

For what concern the clustering analysis, the above-defined multidimensional model has been implemented on top of the OLAP server *Mondrian* [24] and two standard implementations of the density-based and EM clustering techniques have been provided by the *R environment* [25]. In our preliminary experimentation, we noticed that, while the EM algorithm converges on two overlapped clusters, no clear results come out from the density-based algorithm, probably due to the very non-homogeneous nature of the processed dataset. The results achieved by applying the EM algorithm are represented in Fig. 3 - up (Bayesian Information Criterion, used to estimate the number of clusters in the analyzed sample) and Fig. 3 - down (the original dataset and the two achieved clusters). Indeed, this approach can be improved by overcoming the well-known not-exciting performance of density-based clustering algorithms (e.g., [31]), for instance by adopting a kind of adaptive threshold like in [32].

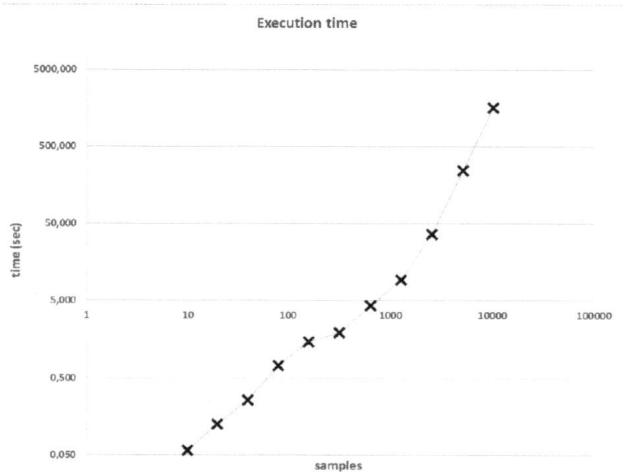

Fig. 4. EM Clustering: Execution Time vs. Sample Size.

Finally, in Fig. 4 it is reported the execution time of the adopted algorithm as a function of the problem size. This parameter is important to decide the maximum size of the clustered sample as well as how frequently it can be updated. The result shows that the execution time increases more than exponentially and that datasets of 5120 fetal sizes can be processed in about 4 minutes on a Pentium Core i5 @ 2.5 GHz, which is compatible with the discussed problem.

The application of these methodologies (i.e., multidimensional summarization and clustering analysis) confirms to us the effectiveness of our proposed framework in dealing with multidimensional mining in complex healthcare environments via big data analytics techniques.

4 Conclusions and Further Work

In this paper, we have introduced a big data analytics framework targeted to big healthcare data. The framework realizes a multidimensional mining approach for building customized or personalized fetal growth curves. The main idea consists in summarizing the massive amounts of (input) big data via multidimensional views on top of which well-known Data Mining methods like clustering and classification are applied. A preliminary analysis on the effectiveness of the framework has been also proposed.

Future work is mainly oriented towards extending our big data analytics framework by means of innovative computing metaphors such as *adaptiveness* (e.g., [29]) and *uncertainty* (e.g., [30]).

References

1. Gardosi J., Chang A., Kalyan B., Sahota D., Symonds E.M., "Customised antenatal growth charts", *Lancet 339(8788)*, pp. 283–287, 1992
2. Bochicchio M.A., Longo A., Vaira L., Malvasi A., Tinelli A., "Creating dynamic and customized fetal growth curves using cloud computing", in: *Proceedings of BIBE 2013*, pp. 1–4, 2013
3. Tinelli A. Bochicchio M.A., Vaira L., Malvasi A., "Ultrasonographic Fetal Growth Charts: An Informatic Approach by Quantitative Analysis of the Impact of Ethnicity on Diagnoses Based on a Preliminary Report on Salentinian Population", *BioMed Research International 2014 (1)*, Article ID 386124, 2014
4. Giorlandino M., Padula F., Cignini P., Mastrandrea M., Vigna R., Buscicchio G., Giorlandino C., "Reference interval for fetal biometry in Italian population", *Journal of Prenatal Medicine 3(4)*, pp. 62–68, 2009
5. Johnsen S.L., Wilsgaard T., Rasmussen S., Sollien R., Kiserud T., "Longitudinal reference charts for growth of the fetal head, abdomen and femur", *Eur J Obstet Gynecol Reprod Biol 127(2)*, pp. 172–185, 2006
6. Knorr-Held L., Best N. G., "A shared component model for detecting joint and selective clustering of two diseases", *Journal of the Royal Statistical Society 164(1)*, pp. 73–85, 2001
7. McLachlan G., Peel D., *"Finite Mixture Models"*, John Wiley & Sons, New York, USA, 2000
8. McLachlan G.J., Krishnan T., *"The EM Algorithm and Extensions"*, John Wiley & Sons, New York, USA, second edition, 2008
9. Bruno G., Cerquitelli T., Chiusano S., Xiao X., "A Clustering-Based Approach to Analyse Examinations for Diabetic Patients", in: *Proceedings of ICHI 2014*, pp 45–50, 2014
10. Pang-Ning T., Steinbach M., Kumar V., *"Introduction to Data Mining"*, Addison-Wesley, Boston, USA, 2006
11. Cerquitelli T., Chiusano S., Xiao X., "Exploiting clustering algorithms in a multiple-level fashion: A comparative study in the medical care scenario", *Expert Systems with Applications 55(1)*, pp. 297–312, 2016
12. Nithya N.S., Duraiswamy K., Gomathy P., "A Survey on Clustering Techniques in Medical Diagnosis", *International Journal of Computer Science Trends and Technology 1(2)*, pp. 17–22 , 2013
13. Sakr S., Elgammal A., "Towards a Comprehensive Data Analytics Framework for Smart Healthcare Services", *Big Data Research 4(1)*, pp. 44–58, 2016
14. Lee C., Kim T., Hyun S.J., "A data acquisition architecture for healthcare services in mobile sensor networks", in: *Proceedings of BigComp 2016*, pp. 439–442, 2016
15. Barkhordari N., Niamanesh M., "ScaDiPaSi: An Effective Scalable and Distributable MapReduce-Based Method to Find Patient Similarity on Huge Healthcare Networks", *Big Data Research 2(1)*, pp. 9–27, 2015
16. Mezghani E., Exposito E., Drira K., Da Silveira M., Pruski C., "A Semantic Big Data Platform for Integrating Heterogeneous Wearable Data in Healthcare", *Journal of Medical Systems 39(12)*, p. 185, 2015
17. Begoli E., Dunning T., Frasure C., "Real-Time Discovery Services over Large, Heterogeneous and Complex Healthcare Datasets Using Schema-Less, Column-Oriented Methods", in: *Proceedings of BigDataService 2016*, pp. 257–264, 2016

18. Cuzzocrea A., Saccà D., Ullman J.D., "Big data: a research agenda", in: *Proceedings of IDEAS 2013*, pp. 198–203, 2013
19. Cuzzocrea A., "Analytics over Big Data: Exploring the Convergence of Data Warehousing, OLAP and Data-Intensive Cloud Infrastructures", in: *Proceedings of COMPSAC 2013*, pp. 481–483, 2013
20. Yu B., Cuzzocrea A., Jeong D.H., Maydebura S., "On Managing Very Large Sensor-Network Data Using Bigtable", in: *Proceedings of CCGRID 2012*, pp. 918–922, 2012
21. Gray J., Chaudhuri S., Bosworth A., Layman A., Reichart D., Venkatrao M., Pellow F., Pirahesh H., "Data Cube: A Relational Aggregation Operator Generalizing Group-by, Cross-Tab, and Sub Totals", *Data Mining and Knowledge Discovery 1(1)*, pp. 29–53, 1997
22. Bailey T.L., "Fitting a mixture model by expectation maximization to discover motifs in biopolymers", in: *Proceedings of ISMB 1994*, pp. 28–36, 1994
23. Golfarelli M., Maio D., Rizzi S., "The Dimensional Fact Model: A Conceptual Model for Data Warehouses", *International Journal of Cooperative Information Systems 7(2-3)*, pp. 215–247, 1998
24. Mondrian – Pentaho Community, http://community.pentaho.com/projects/mondrian/, 2016
25. The R Project for Statistical Computing, https://www.r-project.org/, 2016
26. Agrawal D., Das S., El Abbadi A., "Big data and cloud computing: current state and future opportunities", in: *Proceedings of EDBT 2011*, pp. 530–533, 2011
27. Xia F., Yang L.T, Wang L., Vinel A., "Internet of things", *International Journal of Communication Systems 25(9)*, p. 1101, 2012
28. Dean J., Ghemawat S., "MapReduce: simplified data processing on large clusters", *Communications of the ACM 51(1)*, pp. 107–113, 2008
29. Cannataro M., Cuzzocrea A., Pugliese A., "XAHM: an adaptive hypermedia model based on XML", in: *Proceedings of SEKE 2002*, pp. 627–634, 2002
30. Cuzzocrea A., Kai-Sang Leung C., Kyle MacKinnon R., "Mining constrained frequent itemsets from distributed uncertain data", *Future Generation Computer Systems 37(1)*, pp. 117–126, 2014
31. Aliguliyev, R.M., "Performance Evaluation of Density-based Clustering Methods", *Information Sciences 179(20)*, pp. 3583–3602, 2009
32. Hassani M., Spaus P., Cuzzocrea A., Seidl T., "I-HASTREAM: Density-Based Hierarchical Clustering of Big Data Streams and Its Application to Big Graph Analytics Tools", in: *Proceedings of CCGrid 2016*, pp. 656–665, 2016

Counting Vehicles with Cameras

Luca Ciampi[1], Giuseppe Amato[1], Fabrizio Falchi[1], Claudio Gennaro[1], and Fausto Rabitti[1]

Institute of Information, Science and Technologies of the National Research Council of Italy (ISTI-CNR), via G. Moruzzi 1, 56124 Pisa, Italy

Abstract. This paper aims to develop a method that can accurately count vehicles from images of parking areas captured by smart cameras. To this end, we have proposed a deep learning-based approach for car detection that permits the input images to be of arbitrary perspectives, illumination, and occlusions. No other information about the scenes is needed, such as the position of the parking lots or the perspective maps. This solution is tested using Counting CNRPark-EXT, a new dataset created for this specific task and that is another contribution to our research. Our experiments show that our solution outperforms the state-of-the-art approaches.

Keywords: Counting · Convolutional Neural Networks · Machine Learning · Deep Learning

1 Introduction

This paper is motivated by the need to address the challenging real-world counting problem related to the estimation of the number of vehicles present in a park area, using images captured by smart cameras. The visual understanding of the collected images must face many challenges, perhaps common to all the counting tasks, like variations in scales and perspectives, the inter-object occlusions, the non-uniform illumination of the scene, and many others.

In order to address these challenges, we propose a deep learning-based approach that is able to accurately count cars in images *without* any extra information of the scenes, like the position of the parking lots or the perspective map. The latter aspect is a key feature since in this way our solution is directly applicable in unconstrained contexts.

To validate our approach, we also built a dataset, called *Counting CNRPark-EXT* dataset, collecting images from the parking lots in the campus of the National Research Council (CNR) in Pisa. The images are taken by nine different cameras in challenging conditions since they are captured from different perspectives, they present different illuminations and many occlusions. The result of the proposed methodology significantly outperforms the ones obtained using the state-of-the-art baseline methods.

2 Related Work

Objects counting has been tackled in computer vision by various techniques, especially for the estimation of the number of people in crowded scenes. Following the taxonomies adopted in [11] and [14] we can divide counting approaches into four main categories: counting by detection, counting by clustering, counting by regression and counting by density estimation.

Counting by *detection* is a supervised approach where a sliding window detector (i.e. a classifier that is slid over the entire image) previously trained is used to detect objects in the scene. This information is then used to count the number of objects. In the *monolithic* detection the classifier is trained in order to recognize the whole object we want to detect [7], while in the *part-based* detection we looking for specific parts of the object (such as head and shoulders for people detection) [9]. Finally, in the *shape-matching* detection, the classifier is about object shapes, for example composed of ellipses [15]. Even if these methods are quite simple to understand, they suffer in scenes with occlusions.

Counting by *clustering* tackles the counting problem in an unsupervised way. A clear advantage is that such an approach does not need to be trained and it is out of the box. However, the counting accuracy of such fully unsupervised methods is in general limited. The clustering by *self-similarities* technique relies on tracking simple image features and probabilistically group them into clusters, like in [1]. Then we can count clusters belonging to a certain category. The clustering by *motion similarities* approach relies instead on the assumption that a pair of points that appears to move together is likely to be part of the same individual, hence coherent feature trajectories can be grouped together to represent independently moving-entities, like in [13]. The main drawback in such a method is that it only works with continuous image frames and not with static images.

Counting by *regression* is a supervised method that tries to establish a direct mapping (linear or not) from the image features to the number of objects present in an image without explicit object detection or tracking. Since it does not rely on a specific classifier or model previously trained, it is more robust to occlusions and perspective distortions.

Finally, counting by *density estimation* is a supervised technique that extends in some way counting by regression approach, introduced in [8]. In this case, the (linear or not) mapping is between image features and a corresponding density map (i.e. a continuous-valued function), and not between features and the number of objects. Then we can calculate the integral over any region in the density map obtaining the count of objects within that region. This approach is robust to occlusions and perspective distortions because it does not rely on a specific classifier previously trained, just like counting by regression approach as well, but the key difference is that now we are exploiting a *pixel level mapping*: each pixel of the image is represented by a feature vector and mapped to a pixel of the corresponding density map. In some way, unlike in counting by regression, now we are incorporating spatial information in the learning process.

The extraction of suitable features is a crucial operation for all the four approaches that have been described. Since, in general, handcrafted features suffer a drop in accuracy when subjected to challenging situations (variances in illumination, perspective distortion, severe occlusion, etc.), most state-of-the-art counting methods employ deep-learning approaches, in particular exploiting Convolutional Neural Networks (CNNs), in order to extract suitable task-specific features automatically. Some works that use CNNs are [4] and [3] for crowd counting, and [12] for the vehicles counting task.

3 Dataset

A contribution of this paper is the creation of *"Counting CNRPark-EXT"*, a dataset of roughly 4,000 images containing more than 79,000 labeled cars. This dataset is based on the *CNRPark-EXT* dataset, presented in [2], a collection of roughly 150,000 bounding-box annotated images of vacant and occupied parking slots in the campus of the National Research Council (CNR). This dataset is challenging and describes most of the difficult situations that can be found in a real scenario: the images are captured by nine different cameras under various weather conditions, angles of view and light conditions. Furthermore, another challenging aspect is due to the presence of partial occlusion patterns in many scenes such as obstacles (trees, lampposts, other cars) and shadowed cars.

The *CNRPark-EXT* dataset is specifically designed for parking lot occupancy detection and it is not directly usable for the counting task, since each image, called *patch*, contains one single park space labeled according to the occupancy status of it, 0 for vacant and 1 for occupied. Since the purpose of this work is to count cars present in an image, the information needed to build the ground truth are full images (and not patches), the total number of vehicles considered in an entire scene, and, at least for some techniques, the locations of these vehicles. Therefore, starting from the *CNRPark-EXT* dataset, we summed up the occupancy status of the patches belonging to a same full image (note that a car space is occupied if and only if a car is present in the car space), obtaining the total number of cars considered in the whole scenes (i.e. obtaining a per-image ground truth). Only bounding boxes corresponding to occupied spaces are considered, identifying cars to be counted (i.e. obtaining a per-object ground truth). Table 1 reports the composition of *Counting CNRPark-EXT* dataset.

Table 1. Details of the dataset used in the experiments, with the various proposed subsets.

Subset	Number Images	Number Slots	Number Cars
All	4.081	144.965	79.307
Train	2.661	94.493	47.616
Validation	524	18.647	13.415
Test	896	31.825	18.276

4 A new vehicles counting solution using Mask R-CNN

Our solution is based on *Mask R-CNN* [6], a very popular deep convolutional neural network, employed in many detection systems. Unlike previous methods that tackle the localization problem by building a sliding-window detector, *Mask R-CNN* solves the problem by operating within the 'recognition using regions' paradigm [5], taking an image as input and producing as output labels for each detected object together with bounding boxes and masks localizing them. The authors differentiate between the convolutional backbone architecture, used for features extraction over an entire image, and the network head for bounding-box recognition (classification and regression) and mask prediction that is applied to each proposed region.

As a starting point, we considered a model of *Mask R-CNN* pre-trained on the COCO dataset [10], a large dataset composed of images describing complex everyday scenes of common objects in their natural context, categorized in 80 different categories. In order to count vehicles, we considered the detected objects belonging to the *car* and *truck* categories. Since this network is a generic objects detector, we specialize it to recognize the vehicles we want to count.

The first step has been the creation of a suitable labeled training set. In the case of Mask R-CNN, these labels correspond to masks and bounding boxes. As mentioned before, since the labels of our dataset are bounding boxes (perhaps not very accurate, since they localize parking lots and not the cars), we needed to add the masks on the vehicles to be detected in order to make *Counting CNRPark-EXT* dataset useful for our purposes. Mask creation is a very time-expensive operation - for each car in each image, we should associate the pixels that model the vehicles with a label. Since in the dataset we have hundreds of cars, this problem has been solved by taking advantage of the output of the pre-trained model of *Mask R-CNN.* Since this network produces in output accurate masks localizing objects, the idea is to save these masks automatically generated, parse them, and then manually add some of the remaining masks for the cars that were not detected.

First, we randomly selected a subset of our training set (about the 10%), fed the previous pre-trained Mask R-CNN model with these images, and saved the vertex coordinates of the polygons surrounding the masks localizing objects that the network produces in output along with the category associated with them. Next, a further analysis of these saved masks has been performed, changing the wrong associations between some objects labeled with categories that are not possible in our context (like *airplane* and *boat*), and that were instead vehicles we want to detect. In this way, we forced the network to learn to recognize these objects as cars and not as other wrong objects. Finally, we manually add some of the remaining masks localizing vehicles that were not automatically detected. At this point, we retrained the network using this new mask-labeled and task-specific dataset, frozen the weights of the backbone, and saving the new weights of the head after a few epochs. Figure 1 reports the pipeline of the described approach.

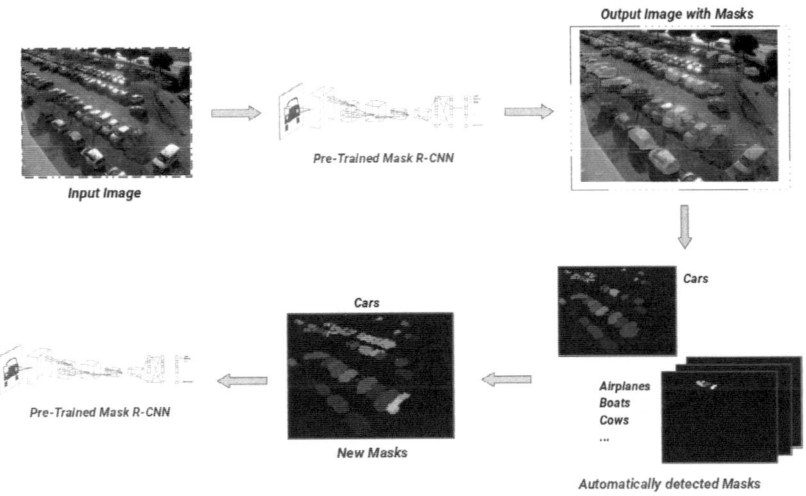

Fig. 1. Pipeline of our approach: we generate labels for the training set saving masks automatically generated by a pre-trained version of Mask R-CNN, parsing them and manually adding the missing ones. Then we use this annotated-dataset in order to re-train Mask R-CNN, specializing it in the detection of the vehicles we want to count.

5 Evaluation

In this section, we present the methodology and the results of the experimental evaluation. For testing purposes, we have used the test subset of the *Counting CNRPark-EXT* dataset.

Evaluation Metrics Following other counting benchmarks, we use Mean Absolute Error (*MAE*) and Root Mean Square Error (*RMSE*) as the metrics for comparing the performance of our solution against other counting approaches present in literature. MAE is defined as follows:

$$MAE = \frac{1}{N}\sum_{n=1}^{N}|c_n^{gt} - c_n^{pred}| \tag{1}$$

while RMSE is defined as:

$$RMSE = \sqrt{\frac{1}{N}\sum_{n=1}^{N}(c_n^{gt} - c_n^{pred})^2} \tag{2}$$

where N is the total number of test images, c_{gt} is the actual count, and c_{pred} is the predicted count of the n-th image. Note that as a result of the squaring of each difference, RMSE effectively penalizes large errors more heavily than small ones. Then RMSE should be more useful when large errors are particularly undesirable.

The above two metrics are indicative of quantifying the error of estimation of the objects count. However, as pointed out by [11], these metrics contain no information about the relation of the error and the total number of objects present in the image. To this end, another performance metric is taken into account, which is essentially a normalized MAE, that we call Mean Occupancy Error (*MOE*), because in this work quantifies the error in the evaluation of the occupancy of a car park, defined as:

$$MOE = \frac{1}{N} \sum_{n=1}^{N} \frac{|c_n^{gt} - c_n^{pred}|}{num\_slots_n} \tag{3}$$

where num_slots_n is the total number of parking lots in the current scene. In the next, this evaluation metric is expressed as a percentage.

Comparisons with the state of the art We have compared our vehicles counting solution against the method proposed in [2], a state-of-the-art approach for car parking occupancy detection, based on *mAlexNet*, a deep CNN specifically designed for smart cameras. This work represents an indirect method for counting cars in a car park, where the counting problem is cast as a classification problem: if a parking lot is occupied we increment the total number of cars, otherwise not.

The main drawback of such an approach is that the locations of the monitored objects of a scene must be known in advance. This technique fails if it is applied on a new camera added in the car park, just because it does not have the knowledge about where car slots are located: a preliminary annotation of the new camera and a new train of the network are then mandatory operations. So, this issue makes this car counting method not directly applicable in unconstrained contexts.

On the other hand, as already mentioned before, our counting approach is able to count vehicles without any extra information about the parking lots locations. Nevertheless, results using this classification approach applied to the *Counting CNRPark-EXT* dataset can be used as a baseline and as a basis of comparison.

Results The results of the experimental evaluation are reported in Table 2. Note that our solution not only outperforms the original pre-trained Mask-RCNN, but also it works better than the state-of-the-art approach using *mAlexNet*, considering all the three performance metrics.
Since counting errors could be due to different weather conditions (since different weather conditions might produce significant different illuminations of the scenes) and/or to different camera views (different camera views correspond to different perspectives), we perform a further analysis of the results by dividing them according to the number of cameras and to the weather condition they belong to. Figure 2 reports the errors scatter-plots of the errors. Note that, in general, our solution tends to underestimate the number of vehicles present in

Table 2. Results in terms of MAE, RMSE and MOE.

Method	MAE	RMSE	MOE
mAlexNet	1.34	2.83	4.17%
Mask R-CNN	1.56	2.89	5.23%
Re-trained Mask R-CNN	1.05	2.1	3.64%

the scene, but it responds well to perspective and illumination changes, having only a small performance decrease considering frames belonging to camera nine.

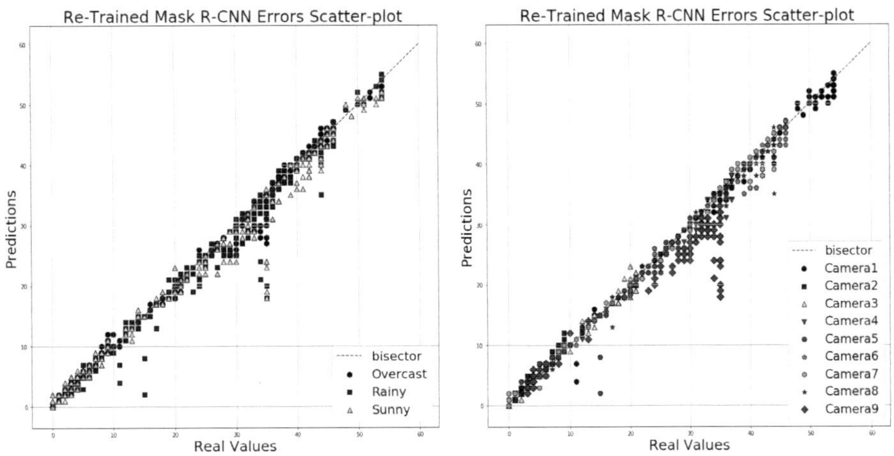

Fig. 2. Scatter-plots of the errors.

6 Conclusions

In this paper, we presented an efficient solution for counting vehicles in parking areas that exploit deep Convolutional Neural Networks (CNNs) to detect vehicles present in challenging scenes. Our proposed methodology does not require any manually entered information about the parking lots locations, allowing a simple 'plug-and-play' installation. The results outperform the ones obtained using the state-of-the-art baseline methods.

As a further contribution, we collected *Counting CNRPark-EXT*, a dataset containing images of real parking areas captured by nine cameras, with different weather conditions and perspective views.

References

1. Ahuja, N., Todorovic, S.: Extracting texels in 2.1 d natural textures. In: Computer Vision, 2007. ICCV 2007. IEEE 11th International Conference on. pp. 1–8. IEEE (2007)
2. Amato, G., Carrara, F., Falchi, F., Gennaro, C., Meghini, C., Vairo, C.: Deep learning for decentralized parking lot occupancy detection. Expert Systems with Applications **72**, 327–334 (2017)
3. Boominathan, L., Kruthiventi, S.S., Babu, R.V.: Crowdnet: A deep convolutional network for dense crowd counting. In: Proceedings of the 2016 ACM on Multimedia Conference. pp. 640–644. ACM (2016)
4. Ciregan, D., Meier, U., Schmidhuber, J.: Multi-column deep neural networks for image classification. In: Computer vision and pattern recognition (CVPR), 2012 IEEE conference on. pp. 3642–3649. IEEE (2012)
5. Gu, C., Lim, J.J., Arbeláez, P., Malik, J.: Recognition using regions. In: Computer Vision and Pattern Recognition, 2009. CVPR 2009. IEEE Conference on. pp. 1030–1037. IEEE (2009)
6. He, K., Gkioxari, G., Dollár, P., Girshick, R.: Mask r-cnn. In: Computer Vision (ICCV), 2017 IEEE International Conference on. pp. 2980–2988. IEEE (2017)
7. Leibe, B., Seemann, E., Schiele, B.: Pedestrian detection in crowded scenes. In: Computer Vision and Pattern Recognition, 2005. CVPR 2005. IEEE Computer Society Conference on. vol. 1, pp. 878–885. IEEE (2005)
8. Lempitsky, V., Zisserman, A.: Learning to count objects in images. In: Advances in neural information processing systems. pp. 1324–1332 (2010)
9. Li, M., Zhang, Z., Huang, K., Tan, T.: Estimating the number of people in crowded scenes by mid based foreground segmentation and head-shoulder detection. In: Pattern Recognition, 2008. ICPR 2008. 19th International Conference on. pp. 1–4. IEEE (2008)
10. Lin, T.Y., Maire, M., Belongie, S., Hays, J., Perona, P., Ramanan, D., Dollár, P., Zitnick, C.L.: Microsoft coco: Common objects in context. In: European conference on computer vision. pp. 740–755. Springer (2014)
11. Loy, C.C., Chen, K., Gong, S., Xiang, T.: Crowd counting and profiling: Methodology and evaluation. In: Modeling, Simulation and Visual Analysis of Crowds, pp. 347–382. Springer (2013)
12. Onoro-Rubio, D., López-Sastre, R.J.: Towards perspective-free object counting with deep learning. In: European Conference on Computer Vision. pp. 615–629. Springer (2016)
13. Rabaud, V., Belongie, S.: Counting crowded moving objects. In: Computer Vision and Pattern Recognition, 2006 IEEE Computer Society Conference on. vol. 1, pp. 705–711. IEEE (2006)
14. Sindagi, V.A., Patel, V.M.: A survey of recent advances in cnn-based single image crowd counting and density estimation. Pattern Recognition Letters (2017)
15. Zhao, T., Nevatia, R., Wu, B.: Segmentation and tracking of multiple humans in crowded environments. IEEE transactions on pattern analysis and machine intelligence **30**(7), 1198–1211 (2008)

An Attention-based Recurrent Neural Networks Framework for Health Data Analysis

Qiuling Suo[1], Fenglong Ma[1], Giovanni Canino, [2], Jing Gao, [1], Aidong Zhang[1], Agostino Gnasso, MD[3], Giuseppe Tradigo [2], Pierangelo Veltri [2]

[1]Department of Computer Science and Engineering, University at Buffalo, NY, USA
[2]Department of Surgical and Medical Sciences, Magna Graecia University, Catanzaro, Italy
[3]Metabolic Diseases Unit, Department of Clinical and Experimental Medicine, Mater Domini Hospital, Magna Graecia University, Catanzaro, Italy

(Extended Abstract of Recent Publication)

Abstract

In this paper we focus on prediction of health status of patients from the historical Electronic Health Records (EHR). We propose a multi-task framework that can monitor the multiple status of diagnoses. Patients' historical records are fed into a Recurrent Neural Network (RNN) which memorizes all the past visit information, and then a task-specific layer is trained to predict multiple diagnoses. Experimental results show that prediction accuracy is reliable if compared to widely used approaches [1]

1 Introduction

Disease monitoring is often limited by physician experience, test time, economic barriers and so on. The Electronic Health Record (EHR) is a valuable source for exploratory analysis to monitor diseases and assist clinical decision making. However, due to the complexity of EHR data, the efficient mining of EHRs is not trivial.

Recent work has made rapid progress in utilizing EHRs for predictive modeling tasks in healthcare, including predicting unplanned readmission [1], early prediction of chronic disease [3], adverse event detection [4] and monitoring disease progression [5]. The main idea here is to learn a good representation of a patient's historical health information, in order to improve the performance of the prediction for future risks.

In order to model the dependencies of diagnoses, deep leaning techniques, such as recurrent neural networks, can be employed. Recent work [10, 1, 8, 3, 9] shows that deep learning can significantly improve the prediction performance. To handle the temporality of multivariate sequences, dynamically modeling the

[1] An extended version of such a paper has been included in the proceedings of AMIA 2018, Washington DC[2]

sequential data is necessary. Recurrent neural networks (RNNs), in particular Long Short-Term Memory (LSTM) and Gated Recurrent Units (GRU), have achieved state-of-the-art performance in handling long-term dependencies and nonlinear dynamics.

In this paper, our goal is to predict the status of multiple diagnoses (or observations), with each diagnosis having multiple severity levels. We form our problem as multi-task learning, which first learns a shared representation from all the features, and then performs task-specific predictions. We propose an attention-based RNN model to monitor patient's longitudinal health information. First, we use an RNN to memorize all the information from historical visits, and then attention mechanisms to measure visit importance. Based on the latent representation, we train multiple classifiers and each focuses on the prediction of a specific task. We perform our model on two applications: predicting chronic states for bone health, and monitoring BloodTest values for cardiovascular disease.

2 Method

The basic component of our framework is gated recurrent unit, which is a state-of-the-art deep learning architecture for modelling long range sequences. To further improve its performance, we apply attention mechanisms to measure the importance of historical sequences. To predict the status of multiple diagnoses, we add a multi-task classification layer on top of the learned representations.

We implement our RNN with Gated Recurrent Units (GRU) [16], which has been shown to have comparable performance as Long-Short Term Memory (LSTM), while employing a simpler architecture.

RNN can remember the past information for future prediction. However, it is limited to only a few latest steps, with more impact from later ones, and may not be able to discover major influences from earlier timestamps. Therefore, we apply attention mechanisms to memorize the effect from long-time dependencies, which have gained success in many tasks.

Our task is to predict the status of multiple measurement results at the time $(t+1)$ given the historical records from x_1 to x_t. Figure 1 shows a high-level overview of the proposed model. Given the information from time 1 to t, the i-th visit's health record x_i is fed into an RNN network, which outputs a hidden state h_i as the representation of the i-th visit. Along with the set of hidden states $\{h_i\}_{i=1}^{t-1}$, we compute their relative importance α_t, and then obtain a *context* state c_t. From the context state c_t and the current hidden state h_t, we can obtain an *attentional hidden* state $\tilde{h}_t$, which is used to predict diagnoses in the $(t+1)$-th visit. For the prediction, we use M softmax classifiers, which correspond to the M different diagnoses, to predict the severity level for each diagnosis. The representation h_t contains the visit information of all the input features, and the task-specific classifier focuses on the prediction of each diagnosis.

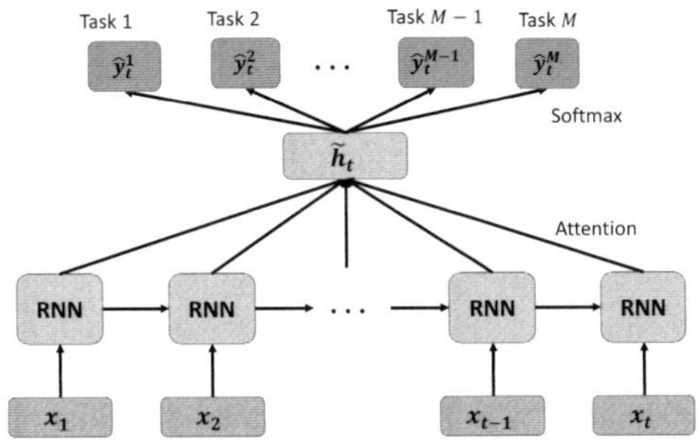

Fig. 1. Overview of the proposed model.

3 Experiments

We conduct experiments on two real-word datasets, and evaluate the performance of the proposed attention-based RNN models compared to other prediction methods.

Study of Osteoporotic Fractures Dataset. The study of osteoporotic fracture (SOF) [?] is the largest and most comprehensive study focused on bone diseases. It includes 20 years longitudinal data about osteoporosis of 9,704 Caucasian women aged 65 years and older. Potential risk factors and confounders belong to several groups such as demographics, family history, and lifestyle. We process people's bone health diagnoses of different areas using the bone mineral density (BMD) values by comparison with young healthy references [18], resulting in three BMD levels: normal, osteopenia and osteoporosis.

BloodTest Dataset. This dataset [20] contains multivariate blood tests of 3,000 patients affected by cardiovascular disease from the University Hospital of Catanzaro, Italy. For each patient, there are several blood tests during their in-hospital stay, such as hemoglobin, triglycerides, glucose, and calcium. As suggested by doctors, we pick 12 blood analytes variables which are important to cardiovascular. Each variable has a normal range provided by doctors. Knowing variable transitions in advance can alarm doctors to take actions before the abnormal occurs, in order to reduce the risk of diseases.

As a common issue of EHR, these datasets are irregularly sampled and sparse, so that data preprocessing is needed. For each person, we remove those visits without any monitored variables recorded, and remove patients with less than three visits. We use simple imputation to fill missing variables. For the SOF data, we fill the missing variables with the values in the previous visit. For the BloodTest data, we impute missing sequences (where a single variable is missing entirely) with a clinical normal value. The used datasets with statistics is shown in Table 1.

For each patient, we want to predict the diagnosis results of each visit based on his/her previous records. To validate the performance of the proposed models

Table 1. Statistics of datasets.

Dataset	SOF	BloodTests
Number of patients	5,318	2,055
Number of visits	22,313	18,758
Average number of visits per patient	4.19	9.13
Number of normal claims	25,145	221,642
Number of low abnormal claims	55,399	17,407
Number of high abnormal claims	31,021	79,837
Total number of features	42	17
Number of monitored diagnoses	5	17

in this diagnosis prediction task, we conduct experiments on two categories of methods: baselines and RNN-based models.

We set up two kinds of baselines. The first baseline is to use the median value of each monitored variable from V_1 to V_t to predict V_{t+1} for continuous variables. This is based on a heuristic assumption that the most frequent state is more likely to occur. For each patient, we use his/her most popular health status as the current status, regardless of time variations. The second baseline is a multi-task logistic regression (LR). To predict information at V_{t+1}, we feed the health records at V_t to a logistic regression model with multiple softmax classifiers. This can be viewed as a simplified model of Figure 1 without using RNNs and attention mechanism to learn latent states. This model only considers the effect from the previous one time step, rather than long time history.

Diagnosis Prediction Table 2 shows the accuracy of the proposed approaches in comparison with baselines on the two datasets. For each patient in the testing set, we predict the health conditions for the subsequent visits using his/her historical health records. For the SOF dataset, we predict the probability of BMD states of normal, osteopenia and osteoporosis for different measurements such as hip and femoral neck. For the BloodTest dataset, we predict the probability of each blood analyte falling into normal, low abnormal and high abnormal. The results are averaged over 5 random trials of 5-fold cross validation. *Avg.# Correct* represents the average number of correctly predicted claims of 5 random trials. *Accuracy* represents the ratio between correctly predicted claims and total number of claims to be predicted. For the two datasets, RNN_l, RNN_g and RNN_c can clearly outperform plain RNN. Since the prediction of RNN mostly depends on recent visits, it may not memorize all the past information. Through attention-mechanism, RNN_l, RNN_g and RNN_c can fully take all the previous visit information into consideration, assign different attention scores for past visits, and achieve better performance compared to RNN.

Visit Interpretation The attention mechanism can be used to understand the importance of historical visits to the current visit. As an example, here we analyze the concatenation-based attention mechanism on the SOF dataset. Figure 2 shows a case study for predicting the diagnoses in the sixth visit through the previous five visits.

Table 2. Prediction performance on two datasets.

2*Method	Osteoporosis fracture		Cardiovascular blood test	
(r)2-3 (r)4-5	Avg.# Correct	Accuracy	Avg.# Correct	Accuracy
Median	10,509	0.8209±0.0057	32,253	0.7616±0.0013
LR	10,125	0.7909±0.0069	34,836	0.8225±0.772
RNN	10,769	0.8412±0.0042	36,167	0.8540±0.0051
RNN_l	**10,822**	**0.8454±0.0031**	36,443	0.8605±0.0056
RNN_g	10,805	0.8440±0.0027	36,423	0.8600±0.0059
RNN_c	10,816	0.8449±0.0023	**36,560**	**0.8632±0.0051**

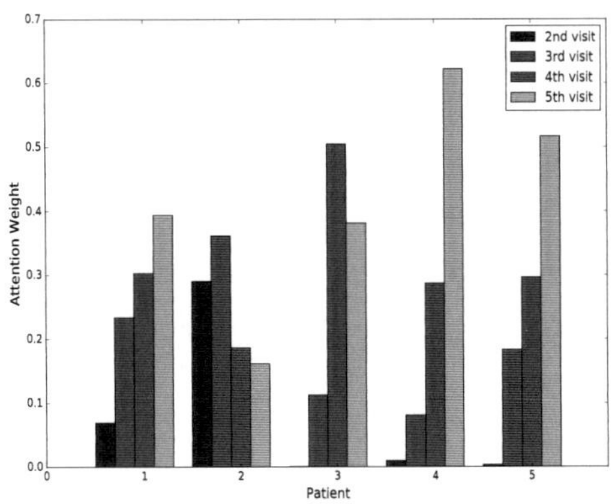

Fig. 2. Attention weights of five persons, each with four visits.

For chronic diseases, the last visit is often the most important since patients' health conditions change slowly. As in the figure, for the first, fourth and fifth patients, the importance of visit increases with time going on. However, this is not always the case due to the complexity of disease progression and impact from risk factors. Table 3 shows the variation of bone mineral density (BMD) diagnoses and attention scores of different visits of the second patient. In each visit, there are five different BMD diagnoses, and the values in the table indicate the severity of bone density loss. Although V_4 and V_5 are closer to V_6 in terms of time, V_2 and V_3 have the same condition as V_6. Thus health records of V_2 and V_3 are more important to V_6. We can see that the attention mechanism correctly assigns larger weights to V_2 and V_3. As for the BloodTest dataset, using attention mechanism to memorize all the past information is also important. An abnormal blood analyte can temporarily turn into normality via medicine, but it may fall back after some time. Therefore, interpreting visit importance through the attention mechanism can help to better monitor disease progression.

In diagnosis prediction, making decisions using very recent record is usually not enough, and it is important to lookup long term health information. To

Table 3. BMD diagnoses and attention scores of one patient with six visits on SOF dataset. 0 is normal, 1 is osteopenia, and 2 (osteoporosis) does not occur for this patient.

Diagnoses\Visits	V_2	V_3	V_4	V_5	V_6
Total hip	0	0	0	0	0
Femoral neck	1	1	0	0	1
Intertrochanteric	0	0	0	0	0
Trochanteric	0	0	0	0	0
Wards	1	1	1	1	1
Attention weights	0.290	0.361	0.187	0.162	–

understand the relationship between the length of patient medical history and the prediction performance, we select 1,000 patients from the BloodTest dataset with more than seven visits. Table 4 shows the accuracy of RNN_l in predicting the diagnoses from V_2 to V_7. We can see that with the number of visit increasing, the performance can often improve. We believe that it is due to the fact that RNN is able to learn better estimates of patient information as it memorizes longer health records.

Table 4. Prediction accuracy for V_2 to V_7 on BloodTest dataset.

Visit	Accuracy
V_2	0.8579
V_3	0.8624
V_4	0.8706
V_5	0.8792
V_6	0.8780
V_7	0.8735

Acknowledgement This work was supported in part by NSF IIS-1218393 and IIS-1514204, and by SISTABENE POR project as PIHGIS POR project.

References

1. Nguyen P, Tran T, Wickramasinghe N, Venkatesh S. Deepr: A convolutional net for medical records. IEEE Journal of Biomedical and Health Informatics. 2016 Dec 1.
2. Qiuling Suo, Fenglong Ma, Giovanni Canino, Jing Gao, Aidong Zhang, Pierangelo Veltri, Agostino Gnasso A Multi-task Framework for Monitoring Health Conditions via Attention-based Recurrent Neural Networks. AMIA 2017, American Medical Informatics Association Annual Symposium, Washington, DC, November 4-8, 2017.
3. Cheng Y, Wang F, Zhang P, Hu J. Risk prediction with electronic health records: A deep learning approach. In Proceedings of the 2016 SIAM International Conference on Data Mining 2016 Jun 30 (pp. 432-440). Society for Industrial and Applied Mathematics.

4. Ma F, Meng C, Xiao H, et al. Unsupervised Discovery of Drug Side-Effects from Heterogeneous Data Sources. In Proceedings of the 23rd ACM SIGKDD International Conference on Knowledge Discovery and Data Mining.
5. Wang X, Sontag D, Wang F. Unsupervised learning of disease progression models. In Proceedings of the 20th ACM SIGKDD international conference on Knowledge discovery and data mining 2014 Aug 24 (pp. 85-94). ACM.
6. Zhou J, Liu J, Narayan VA, Ye J. and Alzheimer's Disease Neuroimaging Initiative. Modeling disease progression via multi-task learning. NeuroImage. 2013 Sep 30;78:233-48.
7. Henriques R, Antunes C, Madeira SC. Generative modeling of repositories of health records for predictive tasks. Data Mining and Knowledge Discovery. 2015 Jul 1;29(4):999-1032.
8. Li H, Li X, Ramanathan M, Zhang A. Prediction and informative risk factor selection of bone diseases. IEEE/ACM Transactions on Computational Biology and Bioinformatics (TCBB). 2015 Jan 1;12(1):79-91.
9. Suo Q, Xue H, Gao J, Zhang A. Risk Factor Analysis Based on Deep Learning Models. In Proceedings of the 7th ACM International Conference on Bioinformatics, Computational Biology, and Health Informatics 2016 Oct 2 (pp. 394-403). ACM.
10. Che Z, Kale D, Li W, Bahadori MT, Liu Y. Deep computational phenotyping. In Proceedings of the 21th ACM SIGKDD International Conference on Knowledge Discovery and Data Mining 2015 Aug 10 (pp. 507-516). ACM.
11. Lipton ZC, Kale DC, Elkan C, Wetzell R. Learning to diagnose with LSTM recurrent neural networks. arXiv preprint arXiv:1511.03677. 2015 Nov 11.
12. Choi E, Bahadori MT, Sun J. Doctor ai: Predicting clinical events via recurrent neural networks. arXiv preprint arXiv:1511.05942. 2015 Nov 18.
13. Choi E, Bahadori MT, Sun J, Kulas J, Schuetz A, Stewart W. RETAIN: An Interpretable Predictive Model for Healthcare using Reverse Time Attention Mechanism. In Advances in Neural Information Processing Systems 2016 (pp. 3504-3512).
14. Choi E, Bahadori MT, Song L, Stewart WF, Sun J. GRAM: Graph-based Attention Model for Healthcare Representation Learning. arXiv preprint arXiv:1611.07012. 2016 Nov 21.
15. Ma F, Chitta R, Zhou J, et al. Dipole: Diagnosis Prediction in Healthcare via Attention-based Bidirectional Recurrent Neural Networks. In Proceedings of the 23rd ACM SIGKDD International Conference on Knowledge Discovery and Data Mining.
16. Chung J, Gulcehre C, Cho K, Bengio Y. Empirical evaluation of gated recurrent neural networks on sequence modeling. arXiv preprint arXiv:1412.3555. 2014 Dec 11.
17. Zeiler MD. ADADELTA: an adaptive learning rate method. arXiv preprint arXiv:1212.5701. 2012 Dec 22.
18. Bonnick SL. Bone densitometry in clinical practice. Totowa, NJ: Humana Press; 1998 Jun 24.
19. Luong MT, Pham H, Manning CD. Effective Approaches to Attention-based Neural Machine Translation. In Empirical Methods in Natural Language Processing. 2015 Aug.
20. Canino G, Guzzi PH, Tradigo G, Zhang A, Veltri P. On the analysis of diseases and their related geographical data. IEEE journal of biomedical and health informatics. 2015 Oct 30.
21. Bergstra J, Breuleux O, Bastien F, et al. Theano: A CPU and GPU math compiler in Python. In Proc. 9th Python in Science Conf 2010 Jun (pp. 1-7).

Let's Make it Dirty with BART!

Donatello Santoro[1], Patricia C. Arocena[2], Boris Glavic[3], Giansalvatore Mecca[1], Renée J. Miller[2], and Paolo Papotti[4]

[1]Università della Basilicata - Italy, [2]University of Toronto - Canada
[3]Illinois Inst. of Technology - USA, [4]Eurecom - France

(Discussion Paper)

Abstract. In the last few years many automatic or semi-automatic data-repairing algorithms have been proposed in order to improve the quality of a given database. Due to the richness of research proposals, it is important to conduct experimental evaluations to assess each tool's potential. BART is an open-source error-generation system conceived to support thorough experimental evaluations of these data-repairing systems. In this paper we discuss how generating errors in data is a complex problem, with several facets. We introduce the important notions of detectability and repairability of an error, that stand at the core of BART. Then, we show how, by changing the features of errors, it is possible to influence quite significantly the performance of the tools. Finally, we concretely put to work five data-repairing algorithms on dirty data of various kinds generated using BART, and discuss their performance.

1 Introduction

Data quality is a very important concern in data management. To date, many (disparate) automatic and semi-automatic data-cleaning algorithms have been proposed in the database community [13][12][8][5][6][4]. These algorithms come from different inspirations. Most of them are *constraint-based*: they assume that the target database comes with a set of data-quality rules – for example, functional dependencies (FDs) or conditional functional dependencies (CFDs) – and data is repaired to remove violations to these constraints. Others, on the contrary, do not rely on constraints, but rather on statistics-based approaches to identify suspect values or outliers and try to repair them.

Due to the richness of research proposals, it is important to conduct thorough and fair experimental evaluations to assess each tool's potential. In fact, other fields like *entity resolution*, *record linkage*, *schema mapping* and *data exchange* have worked to develop consolidated tools and benchmarks for empirically evaluating algorithms [14] [1] [3]. Thorough evaluation of data-cleaning systems requires systematic control over the amount of errors in a dataset, and over how hard these errors are to repair. Dirty datasets must be paired with a

SEBD 2018, June 24-27, 2018, Castellaneta Marina, Italy.

ground-truth clean dataset to enable evaluation of the quality of a repair produced by a cleaning algorithm. To support rigorous empirical evaluations, an error-generation system must be able to generate multiple dirty versions of a dataset with low user effort, and scale to large datasets.

Bart. BART [2][17] is the first error-generation tool explicitly conceived to support empirical evaluations of data-repairing algorithms as per the requirements outlined above. It takes as input a clean database and a set of data-quality rules, and injects errors into the database. Rules are expressed using the powerful language of *denial constraints* [15] and errors can be of several kinds, such as typos, duplicated values, nulls, and outliers. We show the major components of the system in Figure 1. A user interacts with BART by creating error-generation tasks, using a GUI or CL interface. These tasks are then interpreted by BART's error-generation engine to create dirty versions of a clean database.

The system provides the highest possible level of control over the error-generation process. Among other parameters, it allows users to choose the percentage of errors, whether they want a guarantee that errors are detectable using the given constraints, and even provides an estimate of how hard it will be to restore the database to its original clean state. BART is open-source: its codebase is available on GitHub and can be further extended by the community to develop new features and functionalities.

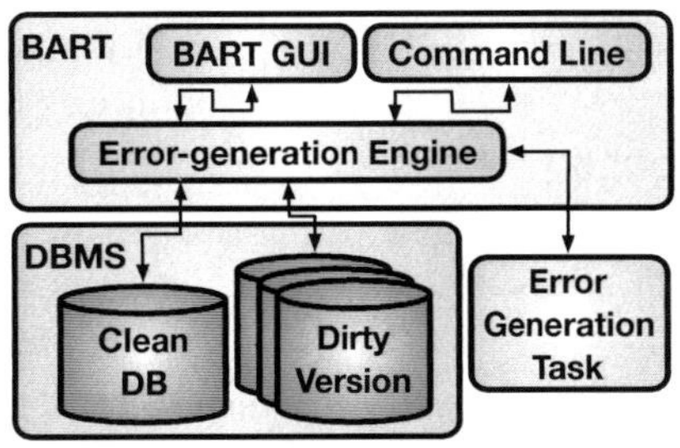

Fig. 1. BART System Overview

Evaluation Overview. The empirical evaluation convey three primary insights about the system.

(*i*) First, we will discuss how the fine-level control over the features of errors distinguishes BART from previous error-generating techniques used in evaluating data-repairing systems.

(*ii*) Then, we will discuss how the characteristics of errors may significantly influence the quality of repairs generated by a system.

(*iii*) Finally, we will demonstrate five different algorithms in action on dirty data generated using BART, to reveal new insights on their (relative) performance as the characteristics of the errors are varied by BART.

Overall, the attendees will learn how the availability of a tool like BART may help to level the field and raise the bar for evaluation standards in data cleaning.

The paper is organized as follows. Section 2 introduces the main motivation for the system, and the notions of detectability and repairability of errors. Sec-

BART: Benchmarking Algorithms for data Repairing and Translation
`https://github.com/dbunibas/BART`

Player Name	Season	Team	Stadium	Goals
t_1 : Giovinco	2013-14	Juventus	Juv.Stadium	3
t_2 : Giovinco	2014-15	Toronto	BMO Field	23
t_3 : Pirlo	2014-15	Juventus	Juv.Stadium	5
t_4 : Pirlo	2015-16	N.Y.City	Yankee St.	0
t_5 : Vidal	2014-15	Juventus	Juv.Stadium	8
t_6 : Vidal	2015-16	Bayern	Allianz Ar.	3

Fig. 2. Example Clean Database

tion 3 provides an overview of the system and of its main use cases. Finally, Section 4 discusses the empirical evaluation, and the main lessons that can be learned from it.

2 Concept and Motivation

Assume we are given a database about soccer players, shown in Figure 2, and we want to assess the performance of repair algorithms according to a few data-quality rules.

(*i*) A first FD stating that Name and Season are a key for the table: d_1 : Name, Season $\rightarrow$ Team, Stadium, Goals.

(*ii*) And, a second FD stating that Team implies Stadium: d_2 : Team $\rightarrow$ Stadium.

We specify these rules in BART using the language of *denial constraints*. Denial constraints are a very expressive language, capable of capturing most data-quality rules used for data-repairing, including FDs, CFDs, cleaning equality-generating dependencies, editing rules, fixing rules, and ordering constraints [13]. For the sake of simplicity, here we omit the technical details about the syntax and semantics of denial constraints, and show example data-quality rules in the more familiar syntax of FDs.

To evaluate data-repair systems, we proceed as follows.

(*i*) We start with a clean instance I, like the one in Figure 2, and the set of constraints $\Sigma = \{d_1, d_2\}$ discussed above.

(*ii*) We inject errors by applying a set of *cell changes*; each cell change $\mathsf{ch} = \langle t_i.A := v \rangle$ updates the value of attribute A in tuple t_i to a new value v, e.g, $\langle t_1.\mathsf{Season} := \mathsf{2011\text{-}12} \rangle$. By applying a set of cell changes $\mathcal{C}h$ to I, we obtain a new instance $I_d = \mathcal{C}h(I)$, named the *dirty* instance.

(*iii*) We run a data-repairing algorithm over I_d to obtain a repaired instance I_{rep}. We measure the quality of the algorithm using precision and recall. Intuitively, we count how many changes in $\mathcal{C}h$ have been restored to their original values in I_{rep}. Further details are in the full paper [2].

We want now to emphasize how different ways to change the cells of the clean instance may lead to errors that show completely different features when considered from the perspective of a data-repairing tool.

2.1 Detectability

When evaluating a constraint-based repair algorithm, we want to make sure the errors we inject are detectable by the system in question. After all, an error that cannot be detected, cannot be repaired. To reason about detectability, we need a notion for determining whether a cell change is involved in a constraint violation. Consider the following cell change: $\mathsf{ch}_1 = \langle t_1.\mathsf{Season} := \mathsf{2012\text{-}13} \rangle$ that updates tuple t_1 as follows:

Player Name	Season	Team	Stadium	Goals
t_1 : Giovinco	**2012-13**	Juventus	Juv.Stadium	3

This change does not introduce a violation to any of the constraints in Σ, i.e., after the cell change the modified database instances does fulfill all the constraints. Therefore, any data-repairing tool that relies on the constraints to detect dirtiness in the database will not be able to detect the change. We call this an *undetectable change.*

More formally, a cell change $\mathsf{ch} = \langle t_i.A := v \rangle$ in $\mathcal{C}h$ introduces a *detectable error* in I for constraint dc if: (i) cell $t_i.A$ is *involved in a violation* with dc in instance I_d, and (ii) cell $t_i.A$ was not involved in a violation with dc in instance I. Here "involved in a violation" is defined based on the fact that a constraint can be associated with a query that returns sets of cells that cause a violation. We call this type of queries *violation-detection* queries. A cell is involved in a violation with a constraint dc if it is in the result of the violation-detection query for dc [2]. For example, the violation-detection query for d_2 is $Q_{d_2}(i, i', t, a, a') = \mathsf{Player}(i, n, s, t, a, g),\ \mathsf{Player}(i', n', s', t, a', g'),\ a \neq a',\ i \neq i'$. This query returns the Team and Stadium attributes of pairs of Player tuples with the same team, but different stadiums. Using the tuple *id*'s, sets of cells involved in violations can be determined based on the result of this query.

BART allows users to control whether changes to the clean database are detectable when using the constraints in Σ. BART may be configured to generate random changes, that do not need to be detectable, or errors that are guaranteed to be detectable using the constraints. Note this requires BART to reason efficiently and holistically about a set of changes to ensure that they are detectable using a given set of constraints.

Interestingly, this latter requirement significantly increases the complexity of the error-generation process. In fact, generating a given number of errors in a clean database that are detectable using a set of constraints Σ is an NP-complete problem [2]. To deal with this complexity BART implements several novel optimizations [2] that balance the need for control over the nature of errors and scalability.

We assume every tuple has a unique identifier that per convention is the first attribute. Queries are expressed in a notation similar to Datalog.

2.2 Repairability

An alternative change that indeed introduces a detectable error is the following: $\mathsf{ch}_2 = \langle t_1.\mathsf{Season} := \mathsf{2014\text{-}15}\rangle$. After this update, tuples t_1 and t_2 violate FD d_1, which states that Name and Season are a key for the table:

Player Name	Season	Team	Stadium	Goals
t_1 : Giovinco	**2014-15**	Juventus	Juv.Stadium	3
t_2 : Giovinco	2014-15	Toronto	BMO Field	23

This change is easily detected using the constraints. Still, it is quite difficult for an automatic data-repairing algorithm to restore the database to its clean state. Notice, in fact, that after this change, the original value 2013-14 has been removed from the active domain of the dirty database. A correct repair cannot be found by any repair algorithm that uses the values in the database as the candidates for repair. BART uses the notion of *repairability* of an error to characterize this aspect. In the case above, it would assign repairability 0 to change ch_2. Different detectable changes may have quite different repairability values. As an example, consider now change $\mathsf{ch}_3 = \langle t_1.\mathsf{Stadium} := \mathsf{Delle\ Alpi}\rangle$. The change is detectable using FD d_2. In addition, the redundancy in the dirty database may be used to repair the database:

Player Name	Season	Team	Stadium	Goals
t_1 : Giovinco	2013-14	Juventus	**Delle Alpi**	3
t_3 : Pirlo	2014-15	Juventus	Juv.Stadium	5
t_5 : Vidal	2014-15	Juventus	Juv.Stadium	8

The new, dirty tuple t_1 is involved in two violations to d_2, one with t_3, another with t_5. In both cases, the change is in violation with Juv.Stadium. By a straightforward probabilistic argument, BART would calculate a 2/3 repairability for this error, and rank it as a medium-repairability error.

Errors may have higher repairability, even 1 in some cases. Consider, for example, an additional rule d_3: $\mathsf{Team}[Juventus], \mathsf{Season}[2013-14] \rightarrow \mathsf{Stadium}[Juv.Stadium]$. This CFD rule states unequivocably that Juventus has played its home games for season 2013–14 in the Juventus Stadium. Since this knowledge is part of the constraint, the dirty cell can easily be restored to its original, clean state.

2.3 Other Kinds of Errors

To conclude this discussion about the features of errors, we notice that the notions of detectability and repairability, that are centered around detecting violations to constraints, are not the only ones supported by BART.

Consider, for example, change $\mathsf{ch}_4 = \langle t_1.\mathsf{Goals} := 123\rangle$. This change is not detectable using the constraints. However, it might be detected by a statistics-based data-repairing algorithm, because it introduces an *outlier* into the distribution of values of the Goals attribute. BART can be configured in order to generate changes of this kind as well.

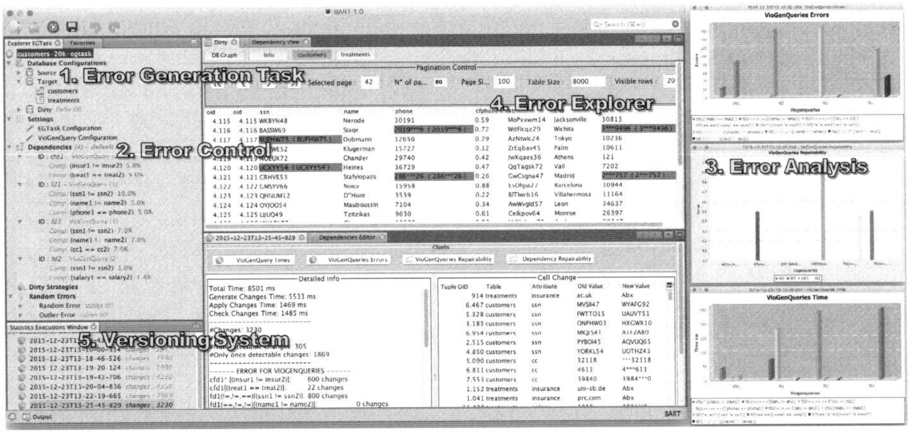

Fig. 3. User interface

3 Overview of the System

BART provides users with the graphical user interface shown in Figure 3 to handle error-generation tasks. An *error-generation task*, **E** is composed of four key elements: (*i*) a database schema S; (*ii*) a set Σ of denial constraints (DCs) encoding data quality rules over S; (*iii*) an instance I of S that is clean with respect to Σ; (*iv*) a set of configuration parameters Conf (shown in Figure 3.1) to control the error-generation process. These parameters specify, among other things, which relations can be changed, how many errors should be introduced, and how many of these errors should be detectable. They also let the user control the degree of repairability of the errors.

Based on this, BART supports several uses cases. The main one consists of generating a desired degree of detectable errors for each constraint. In addition, users may also specify a range of repairability values for each constraint; BART will estimate the repairability of changes, and only generate errors with estimated repairability within that range. In addition to detectable errors, BART may also generate random errors of several kinds: *typos* (e.g., 'databse'), *duplicated values*, *bogus* or *null values* (e.g., '999', '***'). Random errors may be freely mixed with constraint-induced ones. Finally, BART can introduce outliers in numerical attributes. BART provides sophisticated features to analyze the characteristics of errors that are introduced in the data. It generates charts to analyze the number of errors detected by each constraint, and their estimated repairability (shown in Figure 3.3). It also offers a versioning system, that allows users to generate different dirty databases for the given scenario, and compare the characteristics of their errors.

Finally, BART offers a flexible set of metrics to measure the quality of the repairs generated by a data-repairing tool. In fact, different algorithms can repair data in different ways. For example, some algorithms can produce repairs that mark dirty cells using a variable, while others always restore the dirty instance with a constant value. Different metrics have been proposed and are implemented in BART to uniformly evaluate these heterogenous changes in the data [4, 11].

4 Empirical Evaluation

We conduct [17] an empirical evaluation of several data-repairing algorithms over dirty data generated using BART.

We used two publicly available tools, Llunatic [11] and Nadeef [8], to run four rule-based data-repairing algorithms: (*i*) Greedy [5, 7]; (*ii*) Holistic [6]; (*iii*) Llunatic [10]; and (*iv*) Sampling [4]. In addition, we evaluated (*v*) SCARE [18], a statistics-based tool.

The tools were tested with several repair tasks, based on synthetic and real datasets, some of them constraint-based and some statistics-based. We briefly list them here: (*i*) Employees is a synthetic scenario in the full paper [2]; (*ii*) Customers is a synthetic scenario from Geerts et al. [10]; (*iii*) Tax is a synthetic scenario from Fan et al. [9]; (*iv*) Bus is a real-world scenario from Dallachiesa et al. [8]; and (*v*) Hospital is a real-world scenario used in several data-repairing papers (e.g., [8, 10]).

Datasets and constraints have been chosen to exhibit different characteristics. Some have high redundancy in their data. Others contain numerical attributes, and constraints containing ordering ($<$, $>$) comparisons. Some datasets have *master-data* [16] and CFDs, while others have only FDs. All these differences help to validate our techniques and the tools under exam.

Notice the purpose of the evaluation was not to assess the quality of the repair algorithms, rather to show how BART can be used to uncover new insights into the data-repairing process. Some important insights are the following.

Lesson 1: Data-repairing is not yet Mature. We expect that a wide degree of variability in quality among all algorithms will emerge from our evaluations. This variability does not clearly emerge from evaluations reported in the literature, suggesting there is no definitive data-repairing algorithm yet.

Lesson 2: Repairability Matters. We observe different trends with respect to repairability. Typically, repair algorithms return very good repairs when sufficient information is available (i.e., high repairability); however, their quality tends to degrade quickly as repairability decreases.

A key observation is that repairability has a strong correlation with the quality of the repairs. In this respect, we believe it nicely captures the *"hardness"* of the data-repairing problem and it helps in getting a concrete intuition of the power and the limits of existing solutions.

Lesson 3: We Need to Document Our Dirty Data. We may conclude that tools exhibit quite different performance on data-repairing problems of different nature, and the repairability is a natural proxy to characterize how *"difficult"* a data-repairing problem is.

In light of this and to level the field, we believe it is crucial to have at our disposal systematic error-generation tools and to properly document the characteristics of the dirty data used in empirical evaluations of data-repairing solutions. BART is a concrete step in this direction.

Lesson 4: Generating Errors is Hard. The problem of systematically generating errors, however, is not an easy one. We will show how different configurations of the error-generation task affect the overall scalability of the system, and discuss the main optimizations that BART relies on in order to tame the complexity of the process.

References

1. B. Alexe, W. Tan, and Y. Velegrakis. Comparing and Evaluating Mapping Systems with STBenchmark. *PVLDB*, 1(2):1468–1471, 2008.
2. P. C. Arocena, B. Glavic, G. Mecca, R. J. Miller, P. Papotti, and D. Santoro. Messing-Up with BART: Error Generation for Evaluating Data Cleaning Algorithms. *PVLDB*, 9(2):36–47, 2015.
3. M. Benedikt, G. Konstantinidis, G. Mecca, B. Motik, P. Papotti, D. Santoro, and E. Tsamoura. Benchmarking the chase. In *PODS*, pages 37–52. ACM, 2017.
4. G. Beskales, I. F. Ilyas, and L. Golab. Sampling the Repairs of Functional Dependency Violations under Hard Constraints. *PVLDB*, 3(1):197–207, 2010.
5. P. Bohannon, M. Flaster, W. Fan, and R. Rastogi. A Cost-Based Model and Effective Heuristic for Repairing Constraints by Value Modification. In *SIGMOD*, pages 143–154, 2005.
6. X. Chu, I. F. Ilyas, and P. Papotti. Holistic Data Cleaning: Putting Violations into Context. In *ICDE*, pages 458–469, 2013.
7. G. Cong, W. Fan, F. Geerts, X. Jia, and S. Ma. Improving Data Quality: Consistency and Accuracy. In *VLDB*, pages 315–326, 2007.
8. M. Dallachiesa, A. Ebaid, A. Eldawy, A. K. Elmagarmid, I. F. Ilyas, M. Ouzzani, and N. Tang. NADEEF: a Commodity Data Cleaning System. In *SIGMOD*, pages 541–552, 2013.
9. W. Fan, F. Geerts, X. Jia, and A. Kementsietsidis. Conditional Functional Dependencies for Capturing Data Inconsistencies. *ACM TODS*, 33, 2008.
10. F. Geerts, G. Mecca, P. Papotti, and D. Santoro. Mapping and Cleaning. In *ICDE*, pages 232–243, 2014.
11. F. Geerts, G. Mecca, P. Papotti, and D. Santoro. That's All Folks! LLUNATIC Goes Open Source. *PVLDB*, 7(13):1565–1568, 2014.
12. J. He, E. Veltri, D. Santoro, G. Li, G. Mecca, P. Papotti, and N. Tang. Interactive and deterministic data cleaning. In *SIGMOD*, pages 893–907, 2016.
13. I. F. Ilyas and X. Chu. Trends in cleaning relational data: Consistency and deduplication. *Foundations and Trends in Databases*, 5(4):281–393, 2015.
14. H. Köpcke, A. Thor, and E. Rahm. Evaluation of entity resolution approaches on real-world match problems. *VLDB*, 3(1-2):484–493, 2010.
15. A. Lopatenko and L. Bravo. Efficient Approximation Algorithms for Repairing Inconsistent Databases. In *ICDE*, pages 216–225, 2007.
16. D. Loshin. *Master Data Management*. Knowl. Integrity, Inc., 2009.
17. D. Santoro, P. C. Arocena, B. Glavic, G. Mecca, R. J. Miller, and P. Papotti. BART in action: Error generation and empirical evaluations of data-cleaning systems. In *SIGMOD*, pages 2161–2164, 2016.
18. M. Yakout, L. Berti-Équille, and A. K. Elmagarmid. Don't be SCAREd: Use SCalable Automatic REpairing with Maximal Likelihood and Bounded Changes. In *SIGMOD*, pages 553–564, 2013.

How Modern Deductive Database Systems Can Enhance Data Integration

Francesco Calimeri[1,2], Simona Perri[1], Giorgio Terracina[1], and Jessica Zangari[1]

[1] Department of Mathematics and Computer Science, University of Calabria, Rende, Italy
{calimeri,perri,terracina,zangari}@mat.unical.it
[2] DLVSystem Srl, Rende, Italy
calimeri@dlvsystem.com

Abstract. Data integration systems provide a transparent access to heterogeneous, possibly distributed, sources; deductive database and their extensions allow to easily address complex issues arising in data integration. However, the gap between state-of-the-art deductive databases and data integration systems is still to be closed. In this paper we focus on some recent advancements implemented in the $\mathcal{I}$-DLV system, and point out how these can facilitate the development of advanced data integration systems.

Keywords: Deductive DataBase, Data Integration, Instantiation, Answer Set Programming

1 Introduction

The task of an *information integration system* is to combine data residing at different sources, providing the user with a unified view called *global schema*. Users can formulate queries in a transparent and declarative way over the global schema: they do not need to be aware of details about the sources: the information integration system automatically retrieves relevant data from the sources, and suitably combines them to provide answers to user queries [16]. The global schema may also contain integrity constraints (such as key dependencies, inclusion dependencies, etc.).

Recent developments in IT, have made available a huge number of information sources, typically autonomous, heterogeneous and widely distributed. As a consequence, information integration has emerged as a crucial issue in several application domains, e.g., distributed databases, cooperative information systems, data warehousing, ontology-based data access, or on-demand computing. Deductive database systems in general, and Answer Set Programming (ASP) in particular, are powerful tools in this context, as demonstrated, for instance, by the approaches formalized in [3, 4, 17]. More generally, the adoption of logic-based systems allows to easily address complex problems like Consistent Query Answering (CQA) [22] and querying ontologies under inconsistencies [15]. The database community has spent many efforts in this area, and relevant research results have been obtained to clarify semantics, decidability and complexity of data-integration systems under different assumptions. However, filling the gap between deductive database systems and database integration tools is still an open challenge, and continuous improvements and extensions in ASP systems [9, 14] are certainly important contributions to reach this goal.

In this paper we discuss some of the most recent database oriented innovations in ASP as implemented in the $\mathcal{I}$-DLV system, and we point out how such improvements may enhance advanced data integration systems.

2 The $\mathcal{I}$-DLV System

The $\mathcal{I}$-DLV system [7] is a stand-alone modern ASP instantiator and deductive database engine, that has been also integrated as the grounding module of the renewed version of the popular system DLV [1]. The description of all the features of $\mathcal{I}$-DLV is out of the scope of this paper. In the following, we outline the major features having an important impact on $\mathcal{I}$-DLV as deductive database engine. For a comprehensive list of customizations and options, along with further details, we refer the reader to [7, 6] and to the online documentation [10].

2.1 Overview of evaluation features

$\mathcal{I}$-DLV supports the ASP-Core-2 [5] standard language; its high flexibility and extensible design ease the incorporation of optimization techniques, language updates and customizability. We provide next a brief overview of its instantiation process, focusing on peculiar optimizations whose synergic work, that can be driven at a fine-grained level from the user, is the key of $\mathcal{I}$-DLV efficiency.

Optimizations. The system adopts a bottom-up evaluation strategy based on a semi-naïve approach [27]. One of the most crucial and computationally expensive tasks is the grounding of each rule; it resembles the evaluation of the *relational joins* among positive body literals, and $\mathcal{I}$-DLV adopts a bunch of techniques to optimize it, many of which inspired by the database field and properly enhanced and readapted to $\mathcal{I}$-DLV purposes. Here we mention *body-reordering* criteria, *indexing* strategies and *decomposition rewritings* [8], along with additional fine-tuning optimizations acting to different extents on the evaluation process, with the general common aim of reducing the search space and improving overall performances [7].

- *Body-reordering* techniques aim at finding an optimal execution ordering for the join operations, by varying the order of literals in the rule bodies. Different orderings have been defined for $\mathcal{I}$-DLV; the one adopted by default has been specifically designed by considering the effects of each literal on the binding of variables [7].

– *Indexing* techniques, instead, are intended to optimize the retrieval of matching instances from the predicate extensions. $\mathcal{I}$-DLV defines a flexible indexing schema: any predicate argument can be indexed, allowing both single- and multiple-argument indices, and for each predicate different indexing data structures can be built "on-demand", only if needed, while instantiating a rule containing that predicate in its body.
– $\mathcal{I}$-DLV exploits also a heuristic-guided *decomposition rewriting* technique relying on hyper-tree decompositions that replaces long rules with sets of smaller ones, with the aim of transforming the input program into an equivalent one possibly evaluated more efficiently.
– Eventually, we cite a series of techniques falling into the category of *join optimizations*, such as "pushing down selections" and other join rewritings; they have diverse aims, such as decreasing the number of matches considered during rule instantiation, early recovering inconsistencies in the input program, or syntactically rewriting the input program with the twofold intent of easing the instantiation and improving performance.

Query answering in $\mathcal{I}$-DLV is empowered with the *magic-sets* technique [2]: when the input program features a query, it simulates a top-down computation by rewriting the input program for identifying the relevant subset of the instantiation which is sufficient for answering the query. Restrictions on the instantiation is obtained by means of additional "magic" predicates, whose extensions represent relevant atoms with respect to the query.

Customizability. $\mathcal{I}$-DLV provides a fine-grained control over the whole computational process, allowing for enabling/disabling each one of the many optimization techniques both via command-line options and inline annotations. More in detail, $\mathcal{I}$-DLV programs can be enriched by global and local annotations (i.e., on a per-rule basis), for customizing some machineries such as *body ordering* and *indexing*. For instance, the indexing schema of a specific atom in a rule can be constrained to satisfy some specific conditions, annotating the rule as follows: `%@rule_atom_indexed(@atom=a(X,Y,Z), @arguments={0,2}).` when instantiating the annotated rule, the atom $a(X, Y, Z)$ will be indexed, if possible, with a double-index on the first and third arguments.

Since its release, $\mathcal{I}$-DLV proved its reliability and efficiency as both ASP grounder and deductive database engine. Recently, in the latest ASP Competition [14] $\mathcal{I}$-DLV ranked both as first and second combined with an automatic solver selector [12] that inductively chooses the best solver depending on some inherent features of the instantiation produced, and with the state-of-the-art solver *clasp* [13], respectively. Moreover, $\mathcal{I}$-DLV performance results are promising also as deductive database system [7]. The system has been tested on the query-based set of problems from OpenRuleBench [20], an open set of resources featuring a suite of benchmarks for analyzing performance and scalability of different rule engines, and compared with the former DLV version and XSB [24], which was among the clear winners of the official OpenRuleBench runs [20] and is currently one of the most widespread logic programming and deductive database systems. Results show that not only $\mathcal{I}$-DLV behaves better than DLV, but it is definitely competitive against XSB. For a detailed description on such experiments we refer the reader to [7].

2.2 Interoperability Features

In this section we briefly illustrate mechanisms and tools of $\mathcal{I}$-DLV for *(i)* interoperability with external systems, *(ii)* accommodation of external sources of computation, and *(iii)* value invention/modification within logic programs. In particular, $\mathcal{I}$-DLV supports direct connection with relational databases and SPARQL enabled ontologies via explicit import/export *directives*, and access to external data via calls to Python scripts with *external atoms*.

RDBMS Data Access. $\mathcal{I}$-DLV can import relations from an RDBMS by means of an `#import_sql` directive. For instance, `#import_sql(DB, "user", "pass", "SELECT * FROM t", p)` can access database `DB` and import all tuples from table `t` into facts with predicate name `p`. Similarly, `#export_sql` directives are used to populate specific tables with the extension of a predicate.

Ontology-Based Data Access. Data can also be imported from *local* RDF/XML files and from *remote EndPoints* via SPARQL queries by means of directives of form: `#import_local_sparql("file","query",pred_name,pred_arity[,types]).` or `#import_remote_sparql("endpoint_url","query",pred_name,pred_arity[,types]).` where `query` is a SPARQL statement defining data to be imported and the optional `types` specifies the conversion for mapping data types to ASP-Core-2 terms. For the local import, `file` can be either a local or remote URL pointing to an RDF/XML file: in the latter case, the file is downloaded and treated as a local RDF/XML file; in any case, the ontology graph is built in memory. As for the remote import, the `endpoint_url` refers to a remote endpoint and building the graph is up to the remote server; this second option might be very convenient in case of large datasets.

Generic Data Access via Python scripts. Input programs can be enriched by external atoms of the form: $\&\mathtt{p}(\mathtt{i_1}, \ldots, \mathtt{i_n}; \mathtt{o_1}, \ldots, \mathtt{o_m})$, where `p` is the name of a Python function, $\mathtt{i_1}, \ldots, \mathtt{i_n}$ and $\mathtt{o_1}, \ldots, \mathtt{o_m}$ $(n, m \geq 0)$ are input and output terms, respectively. For each instantiation $\mathtt{i}'_1, \ldots, \mathtt{i}'_n$ of the input terms, function `p` is called with arguments $\mathtt{i}'_1, \ldots, \mathtt{i}'_n$, and returns a set of instantiations for $\mathtt{o_1}, \ldots, \mathtt{o_m}$. For instance, a single line of Python: `def rev(s): s[::-1]` is sufficient to define a function `rev` that reverses strings, and which can be used within a rule of the following form: $revWord(Y) \text{:-}\, word(X), \&\mathtt{rev}(\mathtt{X}; \mathtt{Y})$. External atoms give the user a powerful tool for significantly extending interoperability, granting access to virtually unlimited external data sources. Hence, additional import/-export features to specific semistructured or unstructured data sources can be externally defined by suitable Python scripts. Obviously, "native" support for interoperability should be preferred whenever available. In fact, it is intuitive to understand that native support allows much better performance; experiments

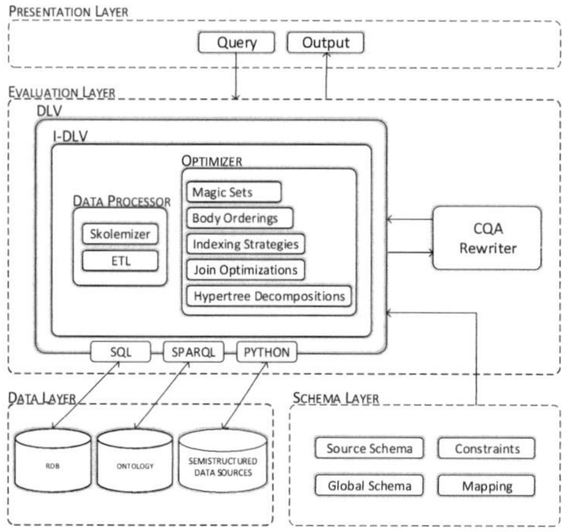

Fig. 1. Architecture of a data integration system based on $\mathcal{I}$-DLV.

reported in [6] give an idea of the effective gain on performance obtainable with a native support of SQL/SPARQL local import directives against the same directives implemented via Python scripts.

Value invention/modification. The availability of both external atoms and function symbols, included in the ASP-Core-2 compliance, allows to address very interesting issues from a database perspective. First of all, it is well known that function symbols allow to implement value invention by skolemization. This turns out to be a very useful feature when dealing with ontologies. Moreover, the generality of external atoms allows to include in logic rules data modification processes, typical of ETL workflows. In [26] we already described how external atoms may help data cleaning processes in a logic-based scenario.

3 Application of $\mathcal{I}$-DLV Features for Data Integration

The adoption of deductive database technology for data integration solutions is not new [16, 17, 25, 19, 23]; however, the recent developments on ASP described in this paper, allow a more concrete application of deductive systems in real-world applications requiring integration of heterogeneous data such as RDBMS, Ontologies and Semi-structured information sources. A general architecture for a modern integration system based on $\mathcal{I}$-DLV is presented in Figure 1, where both main architectural elements and specific $\mathcal{I}$-DLV functionalities oriented to data integration are highlighted; these will be described next by *layers*.

The *Data Layer*, which comprises the set of input information sources, can handle several kind of data types: *(i)* standard databases can be directly accessed through the `import_sql` directives included in $\mathcal{I}$-DLV; *(ii)* graph databases, RDF ontologies, and more generally SPARQL-enabled ontologies, can be accessed by the `import_local_sparql` and `import_remote_sparql` directives; *(iii)* interoperability with any other kind of input format can be granted by external atoms relying on suitable Python scripts.

The *Schema Layer* includes everything that describes the data integration context from a conceptual point of view, namely source and global schemas, mappings and constraints, in a way similar to what has been widely studied in the literature [16]. The support to this design phase could be provided by already available external graphical tools, such as the one presented in [11].

The *Evaluation Layer* includes everything that allows to transform input data, schemas, and queries into answers in an effective way. The core role is played by $\mathcal{I}$-DLV which, as previously pointed out, has been incorporated as the grounding module of the DLV system. Here we concentrate our attention on three main logical portions: the *Data Processor*, the *Optimizer*, and the *CQA Rewriter*.

The *Data Processor* highlights some of the advanced functionalities included in $\mathcal{I}$-DLV; in more detail, the general capabilities of Python-based external atoms put into play the possibility to include ETL processes inside the ASP engine. This is a particularly interesting innovation, since reasoning on deductive databases usually excluded ETL processes that were confined to external workflows. Moreover, ASP-Core-2 compliance of the $\mathcal{I}$-DLV language implies the possibility to exploit function symbols as predicate arguments; in a database oriented setting, this allows to easily simulate skolemization. This is a particularly interesting feature when ontologies are among the inputs; in fact, it is well known that, in particular cases, value invention in ontologies can be handled via skolemization. This opportunity significantly expands data integration potentialities of the system w.r.t. existing proposals. It is worth observing that, in a parallel project involving DLV, a more general extension of ASP supporting existentially quantified rule heads, and consequently more complex axioms in ontologies, named DLV$^{\exists}$, has been proposed [18]; however this language extension and the corresponding evaluation engine is not included in $\mathcal{I}$-DLV yet.

The *Optimizer* applies to the resulting ASP program all database oriented optimizations previously outlined, and included in $\mathcal{I}$-DLV. In more detail, magic sets, join optimizations, hypertree decompositions, body orderings and indexing strategies may altogether provide crucial speedup in query answering processes, thus allowing the adoption of the system in real application scenarios.

In order to complete the picture relative to the *Evaluation Layer*, it is worth observing that, if the global schema is equipped with constraints that must be satisfied during data integration, *Consistent Query Answering* techniques and optimizations such as the ones presented in [21, 22] can be applied. In Figure 1, this is represented as a functionality external to DLV since it is not included inside the engine yet. However, it would be straightforward to incorporate them inside the system since they are based on rewritings of ASP programs.

Finally, the *Presentation Layer* is devoted to allow users to compose queries and get the corresponding results. Again available external graphical tools [11] can support this phases.

4 Future Work

In this paper we briefly reported on the most recent advancements on the deductive system $\mathcal{I}$-DLV for database oriented features, and we have shown their application to a data integration setting. In particular, reported features clearly show that data integration is still a very active and promising research area, which is kept strongly alive by new challenges arising from ontologies, semi-structured and unstructured information sources. Given the positive results in terms of efficiency and extensibility we obtained for the $\mathcal{I}$-DLV system, first of all we plan to incorporate in $\mathcal{I}$-DLV the features already developed in parallel projects, such as the CQA rewriting and optimizations techniques and the support to existential rules introduced in DLV$^{\exists}$ for ontology querying. Moreover, we plan to explicitly implement connectors to different data formats. As a matter of facts, reasoning on top of big data is also part of ongoing projects in the research group.

References

1. Alviano, M., Calimeri, F., Dodaro, C., Fuscà, D., Leone, N., Perri, S., Ricca, F., Veltri, P., Zangari, J.: The ASP system DLV2. In: LPNMR. Lecture Notes in Computer Science, vol. 10377, pp. 215–221. Springer (2017)
2. Alviano, M., Faber, W., Greco, G., Leone, N.: Magic sets for disjunctive datalog programs. Artif. Intell. **187**, 156–192 (2012)
3. Arenas, M., Bertossi, L.E., Chomicki, J.: Specifying and Querying Database Repairs using Logic Programs with Exceptions. In: Larsen, H.L., Kacprzyk, J., Zadrozny, S., Andreasen, T., Christiansen, H. (eds.) Proceedings of the Fourth International Conference on Flexible Query Answering Systems (FQAS 2000) (2000)
4. Calì, A., Lembo, D., Rosati, R.: Query rewriting and answering under constraints in data integration systems. In: IJCAI. pp. 16–21. Morgan Kaufmann (2003)
5. Calimeri, F., Faber, W., Gebser, M., Ianni, G., Kaminski, R., Krennwallner, T., Leone, N., Ricca, F., Schaub, T.: Asp-core-2: Input language format. ASP Standardization Working Group, Tech. Rep (2012)
6. Calimeri, F., Fuscà, D., Perri, S., Zangari, J.: External computations and interoperability in the new DLV grounder. In: AI*IA. Lecture Notes in Computer Science, vol. 10640, pp. 172–185. Springer (2017)
7. Calimeri, F., Fuscà, D., Perri, S., Zangari, J.: I-DLV: the new intelligent grounder of DLV. Intelligenza Artificiale **11**(1), 5–20 (2017). https://doi.org/10.3233/IA-170104, http://dx.doi.org/10.3233/IA-170104
8. Calimeri, F., Fuscà, D., Perri, S., Zangari, J.: Optimizing answer set computation via heuristic-based decomposition. In: PADL. Lecture Notes in Computer Science, vol. 10702, pp. 135–151. Springer (2018)
9. Calimeri, F., Gebser, M., Maratea, M., Ricca, F.: Design and results of the fifth answer set programming competition. Artif. Intell. **231**, 151–181 (2016)
10. Calimeri, F., Perri, S., Fuscà, D., Zangari, J.: $\mathcal{I}$-DLV homepage (since 2016), https://github.com/DeMaCS-UNICAL/I-DLV/wiki
11. Febbraro, O., Grasso, G., Leone, N., Reale, K., Ricca, F.: Datalog development tools - (extended abstract). In: Datalog. Lecture Notes in Computer Science, vol. 7494, pp. 81–85. Springer (2012)

12. Fuscà, D., Calimeri, F., Zangari, J., Perri, S.: I-DLV+MS: preliminary report on an automatic ASP solver selector. In: RCRA@AI*IA. CEUR Workshop Proceedings, vol. 2011, pp. 26–32. CEUR-WS.org (2017)
13. Gebser, M., Kaminski, R., Kaufmann, B., Romero, J., Schaub, T.: Progress in clasp series 3. In: LPNMR. Lecture Notes in Computer Science, vol. 9345, pp. 368–383. Springer (2015)
14. Gebser, M., Maratea, M., Ricca, F.: The sixth answer set programming competition. J. Artif. Intell. Res. **60**, 41–95 (2017)
15. Lembo, D., Lenzerini, M., Rosati, R., Ruzzi, M., Savo, D.F.: Inconsistency-tolerant query answering in ontology-based data access. J. Web Sem. **33**, 3–29 (2015)
16. Lenzerini, M.: Data integration: A theoretical perspective. In: PODS. pp. 233–246. ACM (2002)
17. Leone, N., Gottlob, G., Rosati, R., Eiter, T., Faber, W., Fink, M., Greco, G., Ianni, G., Kałka, E., Lembo, D., Lenzerini, M., Lio, V., Nowicki, B., Ruzzi, M., Staniszkis, W., Terracina, G.: The INFOMIX System for Advanced Integration of Incomplete and Inconsistent Data. In: Proceedings of the 24th ACM SIGMOD International Conference on Management of Data (SIGMOD 2005). pp. 915–917. ACM Press, Baltimore, Maryland, USA (Jun 2005)
18. Leone, N., Manna, M., Terracina, G., Veltri, P.: Efficiently computable datalog$\exists$ programs. In: KR. AAAI Press (2012)
19. Leone, N., Ricca, F., Rubino, L.A., Terracina, G.: Efficient application of answer set programming for advanced data integration. In: PADL. Lecture Notes in Computer Science, vol. 5937, pp. 10–24. Springer (2010)
20. Liang, S., Fodor, P., Wan, H., Kifer, M.: OpenRuleBench: An Analysis of the Performance of Rule Engines. In: Proceedings of the 18th International Conference on World Wide Web, WWW 2009, Madrid, Spain, April 20-24, 2009. pp. 601–610. ACM (2009). https://doi.org/10.1145/1526709.1526790, http://doi.acm.org/10.1145/1526709.1526790
21. Manna, M., Ricca, F., Terracina, G.: Consistent query answering via ASP from different perspectives: Theory and practice. Theory and Practice of Logic Programming **13**(2), 277–252 (2013)
22. Manna, M., Ricca, F., Terracina, G.: Taming primary key violations to query large inconsistent data via ASP. TPLP **15**(4-5), 696–710 (2015). https://doi.org/10.1017/S1471068415000320, http://dx.doi.org/10.1017/S1471068415000320
23. Nardi, B., Reale, K., Ricca, F., Terracina, G.: An integrated environment for reasoning over ontologies via logic programming. In: RR. Lecture Notes in Computer Science, vol. 7994, pp. 253–258. Springer (2013)
24. Swift, T., Warren, D.S.: XSB: Extending Prolog with Tabled Logic Programming. Theory and Practice of Logic Programming **12**(1-2), 157–187 (2012). https://doi.org/10.1017/S1471068411000500, http://dx.doi.org/10.1017/S1471068411000500
25. Terracina, G., Leone, N., Lio, V., Panetta, C.: Experimenting with recursive queries in database and logic programming systems. Theory and Practice of Logic Programming **8**, 129–165 (2008)
26. Terracina, G., Martello, A., Leone, N.: Logic-based techniques for data cleaning: An application to the italian national healthcare system. In: LPNMR. Lecture Notes in Computer Science, vol. 8148, pp. 524–529. Springer (2013)
27. Ullman, J.D.: Principles of Database and Knowledge-Base Systems, Volume I. Computer Science Press (1988)

Towards Progressive Search-driven Entity Resolution

Alberto Pietrangelo[1], Giovanni Simonini[1*], Sonia Bergamaschi[1], Ioannis Koumarelas[2], and Felix Naumann[2]

[1] Università degli Studi di Modena e Reggio Emilia
181067@studenti.unimore.it; giovanni.simonini@unimore.it; sonia.bergamaschi@unimore.it

[2] Hasso Plattner Institute, University of Potsdam, Germany
ioannis.koumarelas@hpi.de; felix.naumann@hpi.de

Abstract. Keyword-search systems for databases aim to answer a user query composed of a few terms with a ranked list of records. They are powerful and easy-to-use data exploration tools for a wide range of contexts. For instance, given a product database gathered scraping e-commerce websites, these systems enable even non-technical users to explore the item set (e.g., to check whether it contains certain products or not, or to discover the price of an item). However, if the database contains dirty records (i.e., incomplete and duplicated records), a pre-processing step to clean the data is required. One fundamental data cleaning step is *Entity Resolution*, i.e., the task of identifying and fusing together all the records that refer to the same real-word entity. This task is typically executed on the whole data, independently of: *(i)* the portion of the entities that a user may indicate through keywords, and *(ii)* the order priority that a user might express through an *order by* clause.
This paper describes a first step to solve the problem of *progressive search-driven Entity Resolution*: resolving all the entities described by a user through a handful of keywords, progressively (according to an *order by* clause). We discuss the features of our method, named *SearchER* and showcase some examples of keyword queries on two real-world datasets obtained with a demonstrative prototype that we have built.

Keywords: Keyword search · Entity Resolution · Data Cleaning · Pay-as-you-go · Query-driven Data Integration

1 Introduction

Entity Resolution (ER) is a fundamental task for *data cleaning* and *integration* [8][7][11][4]: it aims to identify different representations of the same real-world entity in a given dataset. Typically, an ER workflow is composed of three

* Corresponding author

main sub-tasks: *blocking*, *matching*, and *resolution*. The listed steps may depend on other tasks themselves; e.g.: *blocking* may require *schema-alignment* for the *blocking rules definition*; the *match function* may require the generation of a labeled training set to properly train a *classifier*, etc. We adopt this simplification for the sake of the presentation. Blocking is typically employed to avoid the quadratic complexity of the naïve solution (which compares all possible pairs of records) [6]. Basically, blocking provides the set of *candidate pairs* that are actually compared through a *match function*, i.e., a binary function that takes as input two records r_1 and r_2 and answers the question "*do* r_1 *and* r_2 *refer to the same real-world entity?*"—we say that r_1 and r_2 are *matching* ($r_1 \equiv r_2$) if the answer is *yes*, *non-matching* ($r_1 \not\equiv r_2$) otherwise. Finally, a *resolve function* takes as input all the records referring to a single entity (i.e., a set of matching records) and returns a single *representative* record, resolving conflicts of matches (e.g., it may result that $r_1 \equiv r_2$, $r_2 \equiv r_3$, but $r_1 \not\equiv r_3$), and inconsistent attribute values (e.g., $r_1 \equiv r_2$, but some attributes have different values). This task is also known as *Data Fusion*.

The Challenge

When the computational resources and/or the time are critical components for ER [9], *progressive* ER aims to yield record pairs progressively, trying to maximize the *recall* in case of early termination [18][14][16]. Yet, these techniques are specifically designed to yield *any* match as soon as possible, without considering any indication of the user (i.e., the query); adapting them to the progressive search-driven problem, in a keyword search system [5], is not trivial. This can be particularly useful for data exploration [17]. Consider the following example.

Example: *Given a dirty dataset of e-commerce products gathered from several sources on the Web, say that a user wants to find all the entities (i.e., resolved records) referring to* `Apple iPhone 8` *smartphones, ordered by decreasing price. (This is represented in the keyword-based query in Query 1.) Furthermore, say that the user has a limited time budget for such a task and wants to retrieve as many entities as possible within that budget.*

Keywords:	`Apple iPhone 8`
Ordering:	`Price`
Sort:	`DESCENDING`

Query. 1. Keyword query issued to retrieve all the "Apple iPhone 8" in the database, ordered by decreasing price.

Employing a traditional *batch* approach to ER, i.e., resolving the whole dataset and then executing the query, might be quite expensive on real datasets composed of millions of entities. Even existing progressive ER approaches are useless with such a problem, since they aim to approximate the optimal order of the record comparisons on the basis of the matching likelihood of the record pairs—the matching likelihood is assessed through heuristics, such as the similarity of some attributes. Thus, to generate the final result for Query 1, they have to perform the whole ER process; this is because the most expensive `Apple iPhone 8` entity might correspond to records that have the lowest matching likelihood in the dataset.

Our approach

In this paper, we investigate the problem of the *progressive search-driven Entity Resolution*. We propose a first attempt to address this problem by envisioning an ER method, called *SearchER*, which enables users to express the *relevance* of the entities of their interest by means of a keyword query combined with the selection of an attribute that determines the ordering (descending or ascending).

From the user point of view, *SearchER* takes as input: *(i)* a dirty dataset, *(ii)* a blocking function, *(iii)* a user keyword query (which defines the entities of interest), *(iv)* an attribute for the ordering predicate, and *(v)* the ordering type (i.e., *ascending* or *descending*). Then, *SearchER* returns as output the solution for the user query, progressively. Under the hood *SearchER* exploits the blocking function to define the space of possible comparisons; then it identifies some initial candidate records to be resolved (i.e., those containing the keywords) and iteratively explores comparisons that involve these records. For ordering entities, *SearchER* considers not only the ordering attribute, but also the number of keywords that are associated to the entities. For example, considering Query 1, it may happen that an entity with a low price containing all the keywords is emitted before an entity with a high price, but that does not contain all the keywords. In other words, we assume that the keywords are more important than the ordering for the user. For this reason, we say that the final solution is *approximate*, since the final ordering might not be completely respected.

We also built a first experimental prototype of *SearchER* and tested it with some queries on two real-world datasets. This very preliminary result does not intend to show the efficacy of our method in general, yet it allows us to showcase that such an approach to ER is actually feasible and promising.

The reminder of this paper is organized as follows: Section 2 introduces the preliminaries; Section 3 describes the envisioned *SearchER* method; Section 4 reports our preliminary experiments on two real-world datasets; Section 5 describes main related work; finally, Section 6 concludes the paper and discusses the ongoing and future work.

2 Preliminaries

To perform ER, the naïve comparison of all possible pairs of records has a quadratic complexity, thus for scaling to large datasets *blocking* techniques are generally employed [6]: the records are indexed according to heuristics (called *blocking criteria*) into clusters (possibly overlapping) and the all-pair comparison is executed only within each cluster (a.k.a. *block*). Thus, the efficacy of blocking (i.e., how many matches are indexed in the blocks) strictly depends on the definition of the blocking criteria. Intuitively, large and overlapping blocks capture more matches than small and non-overlapping ones, but at the expense of efficiency.

An approach that has been shown to achieve high accuracy is *meta-blocking*, which operates on large and overlapping blocks, restructuring them to filter out non promising comparisons.

Meta-blocking relies on the assumption that the matching likelihood of any two records is analogous to their degree of co-occurrence in a block collection. This means that a block collection B has to be generated by a blocking method that yields redundancy-positive blocks, where the similarity of two records is proportional to the number of blocks they share.

Based on redundancy, which is common for blocking methods [12], meta-blocking represents the block collection as a *blocking graph*. This is an undirected weighted graph $\mathcal{G}_B(V_B, E_B)$, where V_B is the set of nodes, and E_B is the set of weighted edges. Every node $n_i \in V_B$ represents a record $r_i \in R$, while every edge $e_{i,j}$ represents a comparison $c_{i,j} \in B \subseteq R \times R$. A *weighting function* is employed to weight the edges, leveraging the co-occurrence patterns of records in B: each edge is assigned a weight that is derived exclusively from the (characteristics of the) blocks its adjacent records have in common. For example, the *ARCS* function sums the inverse cardinality of common blocks, assigning higher scores to pairs of records sharing smaller (i.e., more distinctive) blocks.

For the problem of progressive search-driven ER, we propose a revised and extended version of the blocking graph model, as explained in Section 3.

3 The SearchER Method

At its core, *SearchER* employs a *blocking function* to generate the block collection that is exploited for building blocking graph. In the following we describe the novel *node-weighting* and *edge-weighting* strategies employed by *SearchER* for building the blocking graph, and finally we describe how the blocking graph is employed by *SearchER* for the query evaluation.

Revised node weighting: The nodes are weighted according to the likelihood of appearing in the final solution. This introduces the concept of *Record-Relevance*; the intuition is explained with the following example:

Example: Consider Query 1, issued by a user that is looking for `iPhone` *entities and requires the results to be generated progressively, from the most expensive to the cheapest ones. Say that a record r_1 refers to entity ε_1 and has a high price. Say also that r_1 has many edges connecting it to many records with low prices, and that these edges have a high matching likelihood. So, it is likely that the final (resolved) price of ε_1 will not be high. This means that it is likely that ε_1 will not belong to the final solution. Hence, the Record-Relevance (i.e., the node-weight) of r_1 should be low.*

Record-Relevance computation: The Record-Relevance is assessed by adapting *tf-idf* [10], a widely employed information retrieval measure, in the following way: firstly, a weight is assigned to each node proportionally to the number of

In our preliminary experiment we employ *Token Blocking* [12], which considers each token as a blocking key, regardless of the attribute in which it appears.

keywords that the corresponding record contains (e.g., using tf-idf); secondly, a fraction of the weight (e.g., *fracweight/#neighbors*) is equally propagated to its neighbours.

Revised edge weighting: The weight of the edges captures the likelihood of *affecting* the final solution. The weighting schema considers both the matching likelihood of an edge (as in meta-blocking [15]), and its *Edge-Relevance.*

Example: Consider Query 1. Say that a record r_1 *is connected to only one record* r_2 *with its same price, and both belong to the real-world entity* ε_1 *(i.e.,* $r_1.year = r_2.year$ *and* $r_1 \equiv r_2$*). Then, performing the comparison of* r_1 *and* r_2 *will not change the rank of* ε_1*. Hence, the Edge-Relevance (i.e., the edge-weight) of the edge connecting* r_1 *and* r_2 *should be low.*

The *Edge-Relevance* also depends on the *resolve* function employed by the user. For the intuition consider the following example:

Example: Consider Query 1. Say that r_1 *(with a high price* $r_1.year$*) is connected to another record* r_2 *(with* $r_2.year \ll r_1.year$*). Then, the Record-Relevance of* r_1 *(and* r_2*) should change on the basis of the resolve function: if the resolve function assigns* `MAX`$(r_1.year, r_2.year)$ *as final price of the entity, it is more likely for* r_1 *(and* r_2*) to be part of the answer for Query 1; which is not true if the resolve function assigns* `MIN`$(r_1.year, r_2.year)$ *as final price.*

Edge-Relevance computation: The Edge-Relevance between two nodes is computed as the weight in a traditional blocking graph, normalized by the relative variation (e.g., $\Delta price = r_i.year - r_j.year$) of the attribute value that is employed for the ordering clause. The edge weight has to be stored also with a *sign* that indicates the direction of the variation: a positive value means that the value of the adjacent node r_i with the smaller id is greater than the other node r_j with a higher id (i.e., $i < j$)—this is just a convention, it could be the other way around. Thus, the edge weight can be interpreted differently on the basis of the *resolve* function (e.g., MIN/MAX price of the matching records).

Query evaluation: Processing a user's query, the blocking graph is not built in its entirety (i.e., considering all the records/nodes); instead, only the portion of the graph that is valuable for the query is considered. In fact, given a block collection, the *node-centric subgraph* of the blocking graph for any node r_i (i.e., the subgraph involving r_i and its neighbours only) can be efficiently built using algorithms described in [12] and [19]. Thus, *SearchER* considers only the node-centric subgraphs of the nodes that correspond to the records containing at least one of the given keywords, and merges subgraphs that share nodes. Notice that the resulting blocking graph can be disconnected.

When looking at the obtained blocking graph, we observe in preliminary experiments that for queries with a limited number of keywords (ideally the vast majority), many nodes tend to have the same weights. *SearchER* divides them into *levels* and resolves the records starting from the highest levels and sorts the comparisons within each level according to their edge-weights. As soon as a node is evaluated (i.e., all the comparisons involving it have been performed), the resulting entity is emitted.

4 Preliminary experimental results

We devised a prototype of *SearchER* that takes advantage of the proposed data model and performed preliminary experiments by issuing keyword queries on top of two well-known, real-world datasets (for which the ground-truth of the matching records is known). The first dataset is `CDDB` [13], which contains CD entities described with: name, artist, category, genre, and year fields along with the track titles. The second dataset is `CORA` [13], which contains computer science research articles described with: affiliation, author, location, title, venue and year.

In the following we report the results obtained for the following queries:

q1: "Rock"	issued on `CDDB`
q2: "Rock and Roll"	issued on `CDDB`
q3: "Genetic Algorithms Applications"	issued on `CORA`
q4: "Artificial Intelligence"	issued on `CORA`
q5: "Jazz Music"	issued on `CDDB`

Ordering: `Year`
Sort: `DESCENDING`

For each query, the entities are sorted by descending values of the attribute `year` for both the datasets. As *resolve* function we employed $MAX(r_i.year, r_j.year)$, yet very similar results have been obtained employing $MIN(r_i.year, r_j.year)$. In our evaluation we consider as baselines: *Standard Blocking* (SB) and *Sorted Neighbour* (SN), with the same configurations of [6]: the ER process is executed employing these methods, and then we performed the queries on top of the resolved entity set (using tf-idf for ranking the results). The results for $q1$, $q2$, $q3$ and $q4$ are shown in Figure 2: it reports the number of emitted entities that satisfy the corresponding query (y-axis), as function of the number of pairwise comparisons performed (x-axis).

The results show that *SearchER* starts emitting entities much earlier (in terms of compared pairs) than the other methods; this is because traditional blocking techniques have to wait until the last comparison in order to evaluate the user query. Surprisingly, we observe that for some queries ($q3$ and $q4$ in Figure 2c,d), the baselines cannot identify as many matches as *SearchER*. This is due to the underlying blocking techniques that fail to yield some of the candidates that are actually matches, and which are correctly identified as such in the blocking graph.

Similarly, for query $q5$, we report the number of entities found, in function of the number of comparisons (Figure 3a) and in function of the time (Figure 3b). Showing that the advantage of *SearchER* is evident also considering the execution w.r.t. execution time.

5 Related Work

Query Driven Approach—To avoid the ER evaluation on the whole dataset before answering any query, recent works proposed a *Query Driven Approach* (QDA) to ER [2][1], which aims to resolve only the portion of the entities in a dataset that are

We report that the proposed method provides an approximate solution: some of the emissions are not in the corrected order and a tolerance range has been considered.

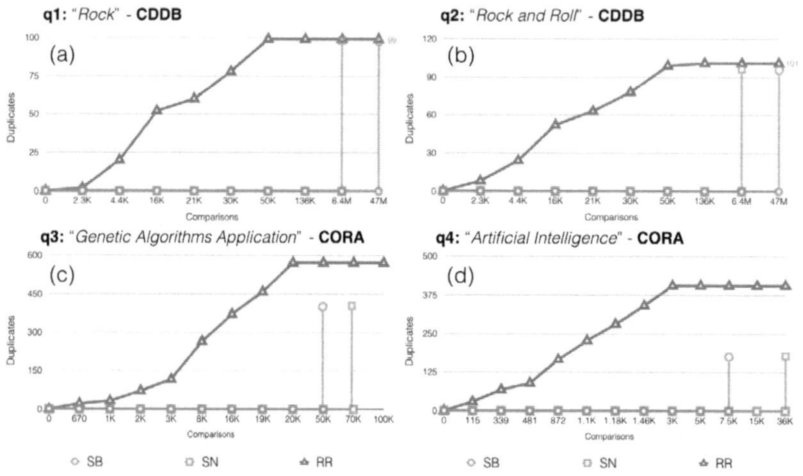

Fig. 2. Results for q1, q2, q3 and q4.

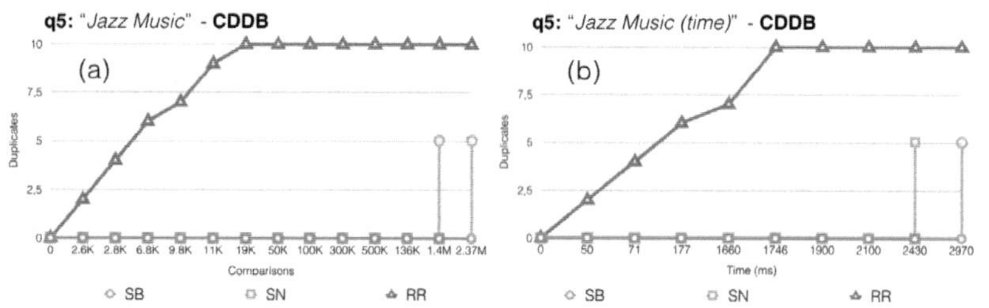

Fig. 3. Results for q5

actually relevant to the user, by exploiting `SPJ SQL` clauses. The `ORDER BY` clause is out of the scope of QDA.

Thus, Query 1, where the relevance ordering is expressed through an `ORDER BY` clause, will force QDA to resolve all the entities in the dataset and then sort them by price. Furthermore, QDA strictly relies on batch blocking, which is employed as initial step of the ER. Hence, adapting QDA to work in a pay-as-you-go fashion is not trivial.

6 Conclusion and Future Work

In this paper, we have presented a preliminary study of the problem of progressive search-driven Entity Resolution, namely the task of deduplicating records of a dirty dataset by following a user query that expresses: *(i)* the keywords representing the entities of interest (e.g., "Apple iPhone 8"); *(ii)* the ordering of interest (e.g., from the most expensive to the cheapest). We have proposed a first solution for solving this problem, and proposed an approximate method, called *SearchER*.

We believe that the proposed method paves the way for further investigation of the problem. In particular, we are currently devising a method to provide an exact solution for a wide range of *resolution function*; e.g., w.r.t. Query 1: *minimum/-maximum/user−defined−function*([*price*]) for determining the final price of an entity. We are also investigating how to exploit different blocking techniques (other than Standard Blocking and meta-blocking) and advanced similarity functions for the matching phase [3]. Finally, we will compare approximate solutions (such as *SearchER*) and exact solutions, to thoroughly study their characteristics and defining the trade-offs to guide practitioners.

References

1. Altwaijry, H., Kalashnikov, D.V., Mehrotra, S.: Query-driven approach to entity resolution. PVLDB **6**(14), 1846–1857 (2013)
2. Altwaijry, H., Kalashnikov, D.V., Mehrotra, S.: QDA: A query-driven approach to entity resolution. IEEE TKDE **29**(2), 402–417 (2017)
3. Benedetti, F., Beneventano, D., Bergamaschi, S., Simonini, G.: Computing inter-document similarity with context semantic analysis. Information Systems (2018)
4. Bergamaschi, S., Ferrari, D., Guerra, F., Simonini, G., Velegrakis, Y.: Providing insight into data source topics. J. Data Semantics **5**(4), 211–228 (2016)
5. Bergamaschi, S., Guerra, F., Simonini, G.: Keyword search over relational databases: Issues, approaches and open challenges. In: Bridging Between Information Retrieval and Databases. pp. 54–73 (2013)
6. Christen, P.: A survey of indexing techniques for scalable record linkage and deduplication. IEEE TKDE **24**(9), 1537–1555 (2012)
7. Dong, X.L., Srivastava, D.: Big Data Integration. Morgan & Claypool (2015)
8. Getoor, L., Machanavajjhala, A.: Entity resolution: Theory, practice & open challenges. PVLDB **5**(12), 2018–2019 (2012)
9. Madhavan, J., Cohen, S., Dong, X.L., Halevy, A.Y., Jeffery, S.R., Ko, D., Yu, C.: Web-scale data integration: You can afford to pay as you go. In: CIDR. pp. 342–350 (2007)
10. Manning, C.D., Raghavan, P., Schütze, H.: Introduction to information retrieval. Cambridge University Press (2008)
11. Naumann, F., Herschel, M.: An Introduction to Duplicate Detection. Synthesis Lectures on Data Management, Morgan & Claypool Publishers (2010)
12. Papadakis, G., Papastefanatos, G., Palpanas, T., Koubarakis, M.: Scaling entity resolution to large, heterogeneous data with enhanced meta-blocking. In: EDBT. pp. 221–232 (2016)
13. Papadakis, G., Svirsky, J., Gal, A., Palpanas, T.: Comparative analysis of approximate blocking techniques for entity resolution. PVLDB **9**(9), 684–695 (2016)
14. Papenbrock, T., Heise, A., Naumann, F.: Progressive duplicate detection. IEEE TKDE **27**(5), 1316–1329 (2015)
15. Simonini, G., Bergamaschi, S., Jagadish, H.V.: BLAST: a loosely schema-aware meta-blocking approach for entity resolution. PVLDB **9**(12), 1173–1184 (2016)
16. Simonini, G., Papadakis, G., Palpanas, T., Bergamaschi, S.: Schema-agnostic progressive entity resolution. In: IEEE ICDE. pp. 53–64 (2018)
17. Simonini, G., Zhu, S.: Big data exploration with faceted browsing. In: HPCS. pp. 541–544 (2015)
18. Whang, S.E., Marmaros, D., Garcia-Molina, H.: Pay-as-you-go entity resolution. IEEE TKDE **25**(5), 1111–1124 (2013)
19. Zhu, S., Fiameni, G., Simonini, G., Bergamaschi, S.: SOPJ: A scalable online provenance join for data integration. In: HPCS. pp. 79–85 (2017)

A Novel Accusation Model for Document Fingerprinting

Bettina Fazzinga[1], Sergio Flesca[2], Filippo Furfaro[2], and Elio Masciari[3]

[1] ICAR-CNR, Italy
{fazzinga,masciari,pontieri}@icar.cnr.it
[2] DIMES, University of Calabria, Italy
{flesca,furfaro}@dimes.unical.it

Abstract. Watermarking digital content is a very common approach leveraged by creators of copyrighted digital data to embed fingerprints into their data. The rationale of such operation is to mark each copy of the data in order to uniquely identify it. These watermarks are embedded in a suitable way to prevent their stripping or modification by users for illegal distribution of the copy. If a copy is illegally distributed by a pirate user (or a set of users referred as coalition) it can be identified by the distributor that can analyze the fingerprint and accuse as traitor the person in charge of that copy. Actions can then be taken against this user, to prevent further illegal distribution. Many approaches have been defined to obtain optimal fingerprinting code based on the well-known Tardos encoding. However, such approaches suffer a great limitation, i.e., when the fingerprinting code embedded in a document is too short, it is not useful for accusing a traitor in a trial, as the probability that s/he might be innocent is too high, nevertheless, the fingerprint code can be used to drive further investigation. To overcome this limitation, in this work we provide a simple yet powerful accusation scheme that can be applied for a widely used approach such phrase substitution[4] that prove itself to be effective in many real world applications when the length of the fingerprinting codes is too short to be used for accusing a traitor in a trial with the classical approaches.

1 Introduction

Protection of copyrighted contents is a crucial activity for digital content producers in order to avoid unauthorized use of the artifacts or worse in order to prevent sensible information to be stealth (e.g. private documents of an administrative board). A common solution is the unique identification of each copy by embedding some distinguishing features. This activity is usually known as *fingerprinting* (a.k.a. *watermarking*) and the embedded content is referred as *code*.

In order to make this process robust against possible malicious users attacks, it is mandatory to hide the positions where the code is embedded. Indeed, attacks can be performed by group of malicious users (referred in what follows as pirates), who compare their copies and identify the positions where they differ as a position of the embedded code. The latter is referred as coalition attack. If the coalition succeeds in this identification process, pirates can then arbitrarily change the code in these positions. For the purpose of designing proper protection strategies, we can assume however that they do not know the positions of the hidden code where the bits of their codes agreed and therefore they cannot alter these positions. This assumption is referred as the *marking condition*.

A (collusion resistant) fingerprinting code can be built by a randomized procedure to choose codewords (the code generation) and a tracing algorithm tailored for tracing one of the pirates based on all these codewords and the forged codeword read from the unauthorized copy made by the pirates.

Obviously, we should avoid two type of errors: 1) accusing an innocent user and 2) not accusing a pirate. In this respect, the tracing algorithm fails if it falsely accuses an innocent user or outputs no accused user at all. The above mentioned errors should occur with small probability.

This problem have been largely investigated in the literature and all the approaches proposed so far shares a common terminology that we introduce here in order to ease the reading of next sections.

More in detail, we briefly recall the following key terms:

- *Alphabet size.* The codewords are sequences over a fixed alphabet Σ. Usually, fingerprinting codes are built by leveraging the binary alphabet $\Sigma = \{0, 1\}$, however larger alphabets can be used thus the size Σ of the alphabet is an important parameter;
- *Codelength.* This parameter refers to the length of the codewords, usually denoted by n;
- *Number of users.* Usually denoted by N, it coincides with the number of codewords.
- *Pirate Coalition Size.* This parameter takes into account the actual size of the coalition that could be lower than the expected one (say it c), in such a case, the accusation algorithm should achieve a small error probability;
- *Error probability.* A code is ϵ-secure against a coalition of c pirates if the probability of the error of the accusation algorithm is at most ϵ for any set of at most c pirates performing an arbitrary pirate strategy to produce the forged codeword under the marking assumption;
- *Code rate.* The rate R of a fingerprinting code is computed as $R = \frac{log(N)}{n}$, where the logarithm is binary.

The goal of fingerprinting schemes is to find efficient and secure fingerprinting codes while taking into account the high cost of embedding every single digit of the code. This implies that fingerprinting codes should be short. However, in literature many proposal have been defined based on the seminal work of Tardos[9] that state many interesting theoretical results. Tardos fingerprinting is optimum as the code length that is sufficient to deal with n users, c pirates and an innocent safety guarantee bounded by ϵ is asymptotically minimum. Moreover, the accusation algorithm allows to detect traitors by looking only at the code they have been assigned to, disregarding both the codes assigned

Many fingerprinting algorithm guarantee a small probability of accusing an innocent even if the number of pirates is greater than the expected one. However, in that case, the probability of producing no accusation increases.

to other users and the type of attack that have been performed. It is worth noticing that in literature have been defined many other approaches that slightly outperforms Tardos scheme while having the same asymptotical complexity [7, 8]. Unfortunately, Tardos based fingerprinting are not effective in accusation processes when the leveraged code is too short. For instance, in the case that the code has to be embedded in a textual document by applying some modification of words, phrases or generally speaking tokens appearing in the text of the document as described in [2], and the document is about 20 pages long it is expected that the longest fingerprint that can be embedded is at most 200 bit long. In such a case, the Tardos accusation algorithm fails in accusing any user with a suitable probability of being guilty as in the case that the maximum coalition size is 2 and the desired probability of being guilty is 90% it requires a code of length at least 800 bits. This code length could be impractical in many scenarios.

In order to overcome the above mentioned limitations, new approaches have been proposed and one of the most interesting is *joint-decoding*. Joint-decoders compute the guilty probability for a *set* of users instead of a single one. A first proposal has been made in [6, 5], however those algorithms are tailored for small coalition and do not scale-up properly. This drawback occurs as the search space computation grows up exponentially w.r.t. the number of users (or the maximum expected number of users that we may conjecture that could form a coalition for spreading the pirated copy).

To ameliorate this problem, joint-decoding has been investigated from the theoretical viewpoint in order to define efficient approaches that work properly for real life situations. In this respect, a *Markov Chain Monte Carlo (MCMC)* based approach has been proposed in [1]. The proposed approach leverages Gibbs sampling for estimating the marginal probability that a user joined a coalition for generating a pirated copy. However, this approach turns to be ineffective for code length greater than 1024 bit due to the low quality of the probability estimation (as noted by the authors themselves).

The main limitation of the above mentioned Tardos based approaches is that they perform satisfactorily when dealing with image or video fingerprinting[3] while their use for textual documents turns to be ineffective. More in detail, textual document watermarking is prone to several types of attacks, even very simple ones like the so called *cut & paste* attack. This attack allows to completely strip the watermark and the corresponding fingerprinting code by simply extracting the text in the source document and inserting it in a brand new document. The latter cause the deletion of eventual watermark inserted in the source text. This type of attack causes the fingerprint of the pirated copy to be empty, thus avoiding any accuse to users by using Tardos based schemes.

In order to overcome such limitations, we propose a simpler but still effective accusation model based on *Metropolis-Hastings (MH)* sampling. Next sections are devoted to our proposal description.

1.1 Main Contributions

In this paper we address the fingerprinting code design by leveraging joint decoding strategies based on Metropolis-Hastings scheme. More in detail:

- we implemented an accusation scheme based on MH Joint-decoding, which is remarkably accurate even in condition where the code rate R is very low;

- we performed a deep experimental assessment of our approach that resulted quite effective w.r.t. the actual baseline for this kind of approaches.

2 Background on Tardos code construction and exploitation

2.1 Preliminaries

In this section, we briefly describe the fingerprinting scheme proposed in [10]. We first recall the basic assumption for this kind of encoding: pirates are not aware on the position where the code is embedded in the document, i.e. the marking condition is verified.

Definition 1 (Marking condition). *A fingerprint set of length m for n users over the alphabet Σ is an n by m matrix X over Σ. A coalition of users is a subset C of $\{1, \ldots, n\}$. A pirated copy $y \in \Sigma^m$ generated by a coalition C satisfies the marking condition w.r.t. a coalition C and fingerprint set X iff, for all positions $1 \leq i \leq m$, if all the values X_{ji} with $j \in C$ agree with some letter $s \in \Sigma$ then $y_i = s$.*

The following definition introduce some key notions about fingerprinting codes.

Definition 2 (Fingerprinting Code). *A fingerprint code of length m for n users over the alphabet Σ is a distribution over the pairs (X, σ), where X is fingerprint set of length m for n users and σ is an algorithm that takes a string $y \in \Sigma^m$ (the pirated copy) as input, and produces a subset $\sigma(y) \subseteq [n] = \{1, 2, \ldots, n\}$ (the set of accused users). For $\emptyset \neq C \subseteq [n]$, a C-strategy is an algorithm ρ that takes the submatrix of X formed by the rows with indexes in C as input, and produces a string $y = \rho(X) \in \Sigma^m$ as output. If for each X $y = \rho(X)$ satisfy the marking condition w.r.t. C and X we say that ρ satisfies the marking condition. We say that a fingerprint code is ϵ-secure against coalitions of size c, if for any coalition C of size $|C| \leq c$ and for any C-strategy ρ, the error probability*

$$P[\sigma(\rho(X)) = \emptyset \vee \sigma(\rho(X)) \subseteq C]$$

is at most ϵ.

2.2 Building the Code

Let n and c be positive integers, $0 < \epsilon < 1$ and let $k = \lceil log(1/\epsilon) \rceil$. We define the binary fingerprint code $F_{nc\epsilon}$ of length $m = 100c^2k$ for n users to be the following distribution over the pairs (X, σ).

(X, σ) is constructed in two phases. First, let p_i be independent, identically distributed random variables from $[t, 1-t]$ for all $1 \leq i \leq m$ obtained as follows. Let $t = \frac{1}{300c}$, $t' = \arcsin(\sqrt{t})$ and r_i be selected by picking uniformly at random a value in $[t', \pi/2 - t']$. p_i is choosen equal to $\sin^2 r_i$.

In the second phase, we select the code matrix X, by selecting each entry X_{ji} independently from the binary alphabet $\{0, 1\}$ with $P[X_{ji} = 1] = p_i$. Notice that independence of the entries X_{ji} holds only in the second phase. That is, two random variables X_{ji} and $X_{j'i}$ are positively correlated as both of them tend to be 1 if p_i is large.

When constructing the code log always denotes the natural logarithm.

2.3 Accusation Algorithm

The accusation algorithm σ is built by leveraging the values p_i and the matrix X, as follows. We define the n by m matrix U with entries

$$U_{ji} = \begin{cases} \sqrt{\frac{1-p_i}{p_i}} \; if X_{ji} = 1, \\ -\sqrt{\frac{p_i}{1-p_i}} \; if X_{ji} = 0 \end{cases}$$

Let σ accuse user j on the pirated copy $y \in \{0,1\}m$ as input if

$$\sum_{i=1}^{m} y_i U_{ji} > Z$$

where $Z = 20ck$ is a threshold parameter. In other words, $\sigma(y)$ consists of the indices j for which the jth entry of Uy^T exceeds Z.

2.4 Error and Code Length Bounds

The following two theorems bound the error probabilities of the codes $F_{nc\epsilon}$. Theorem 1 bounds the "soundness error" of accusing an innocent user, while Theorem 2 bounds the "completeness error" of not accusing any guilty one. For both theorems $n \geq c \geq 1$ and $0 < \epsilon < 1$ are arbitrary.

Theorem 1 (Soundeness). *Let (X, σ) be distributed according to $F_{nc\epsilon}$. Let $j \in [n]$ be an arbitrary user, let $C \subseteq [n]$ be a coalition of arbitrary size not containing j, and let ρ be any C-strategy. We have*

$$P[j \in \sigma(\rho(X)] < \epsilon.$$

Theorem 2 (Completeness). *Let (X, σ) be distributed according to $F_{nc\epsilon}$. Let $C \in [n]$ be a coalition of size $|C| \leq c$, and let ρ be any C-strategy satisfying the marking condition. We have*

$$P[C \cap \sigma(\rho(X)) = \emptyset] < \varepsilon^{c/4}.$$

Based on the two theorems above the following corollary holds.

Corollary 1. *The fingerprint code $F_{nc\frac{\epsilon}{n}}$ is ϵ-secure against coalitions of size c if $c \geq 4$. The length of this code is $O(c^2 log(n/\epsilon))$.*

3 A MH-sampler based Joint Decoder

In this section, we describe our encoding scheme, based on Metropolis-Hastings algorithm.

3.1 Metropolis-Hastings Samplers

Metropolis-Hastings (MH) algorithm aims at approximating a probability density function $F(x_1, \ldots, x_n)$, named target distribution, whose exact formulation is unknown, exploiting the knowledge of a computable function $P(x_1, \ldots, x_n)$, named proposal distribution, that is proportional to $F(x_1, \ldots, x_n)$. The result of an executions of a MH sampler is a sequence of samples. This sequence of samples, which is typically represented as an histogram, yields an approximation of $F(x_1, \ldots, x_n)$ as it is generated with the guarantee that the occurrences of each sample $s \in S$ are proportional to $P(x_1, \ldots, x_n)$ (thus to $F(x_1, \ldots, x_n)$). In a sense, S has a similar shape to F. A possible implementation of MH algorithm is reported below.

Algorithm 1 The MH sampler

Input: N output samples; B: number of samples for burn-in;
Output: a sequence of k accused users $P = [p_1, \ldots, p_k]$

$S = \emptyset$
generate an initial sample s
for $i = 0$ to $B + N$ **do**
    $s' \leftarrow s$
    perturb s'
    $jitter = random()$
    if $jitter \leq min(1, \frac{P(s')}{P(s)})$ **then**
        $s = s$
    if $k \geq B$ **then**
        Add s to S
return S

The algorithm works as follows. We first generate an initial sample s by random picking up from the n-dimensional domain of P. At each step i a new candidate sample s' is generated by random perturbation of s. The perturbation is performed by modifying each component of s in order to obtain a new point in the sampling space. In order to make the perturbation strategy effective, we need to have specific implementation for the context at hand, i.e., we need to take into account the semantic of each dimension for the sample being considered.

Once s' is computed, we compute the ratio $r = \frac{P(s')}{P(s)}$. The latter operation measures the variation of the target function F as it is proportional to P. Tus, r is leveraged for deciding if s' can be accepted as a new sample for F. If s' can be used it is queued to S. More in detail, this action is performed according to a probabilistic evaluation: we generate a random number $jitter \in [0, 1]$ and we decide to accept s' if and only if $jitter \leq min(1, \frac{P(s')}{P(s)})$. The latter implies that s' will be accepted if $F(s')$ value is greater than $F(s)$ otherwise we conditionally accept s' with a probability score whose value is as lower as $P(s')$ is lower than $P(s)$. If s' is not acceptable, we add s to S's queue. Intuitively enough, it means that the adopted sampling generates samples with higher P values (thus higher F values) while samples with low P values have few occurrences in S or are excluded at all.

It is worth noticing that MH algorithm generates $B + N$ samples where B and N are input parameters, namely the number of samples you may want to *burn* before collecting the actual samples is S and the expexted cardinality of S. We need to perform an initial burn-in for the first samples generated by MH as the initial samples tend to be highly correlated with the initial samples thus they could be generated according to a different distribution w.r.t. the target one. For practical use, the burn-in is effective when at least 1000 iterations have been performed.

3.2 A MH sampler for Joint Decoding

Algorithm 2 describes our accusation strategy based on MH sampling.

Algorithm 2 The MH accusation algorithm

Input: A pirated copy y, the code matrix X, the probability array p, an integer $accU$, an integer $cMaxS$

Output: a sequence of k accused users $P = [p_1, \ldots, p_k]$

```
cCoal = ∅, cPcoal = 0
ST = ∅
for i = 1 to burnIt + It do
    tCoal = cCoal
    if 0 < |tCoal| < cMaxS then
        tCoal = genericUpdate(tCoal)
    else
        if |tCoal| = 0 then
            tCoal = addUser(tCoal)
        else
            tCoal = remUser(tCoal)
    tPCoal = computeProb(tCoal, y)
    jitter = random()
    if jitter < min(1, tPCoal/cPcoal) then
        cCoal = tCoal, cPcoal = tPCoal
    if i > burnIt then
        update(ST, cCoal)
return bestPirates(ST, accU)
```

Herein: $cCoal$ is the current coalition, $cPcoal$ is the probability of the current coalition, $tCoal$ is the generated coalition and $tPCoal$ is the probability of the generated coalition. Finally, ST is the set of generated coalition (that could contain duplicated elements).

The algorithm works in two phases. The first phase initializes the coalition set by generating $burnIt$ coalitions that will be discarded as explained in previous section.

The second phase generates it coalition that are added to ST. Each new coalition is generated by applying the following operation to the current coalition:

1. a random user not yet included in the coalition is added to it if the length of the coalition in not maximum;
2. a random user is removed from the coalition (if at least one user is in the coalition);
3. a random user of the coalition is replaced with a random user not included in the coalition.

More in detail, function *genericUpdate* updates the coalition by applying one of the above mentioned operations. Function *addUser* implements the third operation while *remUser* implements the second modification strategy.
Function *computeProb(tCoal,y)* computes the probability that a pirated copy y has been generated by coalition $tCoal$ whose users hold the codes included in matrix X_{tCoal} as follows:

$$computeProb(tCoal, y) \ = {p_{Coal}}^{|tCoal|-1} \prod_{i=1}^{m} p(X_{tCoal}\left[i\right], y\left[i\right]) \qquad (1)$$

where $p\left(X_{tCoal}\left[i\right], y\left[i\right]\right)$ is defined as follows. $p\left(X_{tCoal}\left[i\right], y\left[i\right]\right) = \frac{1}{3}$, if $\exists h, k$ s.t. $X_{tCoal}[i][h] \neq X_{tCoal}[i][k]$ and if no such h, k exists, and otherwise

$$p\left(X_{tCoal}\left[i\right], y\left[i\right]\right) = \begin{cases} p_u, & \text{if } y\left[i\right] = -1 \quad (a) \\ (1-p_u)p[i], & \text{if } y\left[i\right] = 1 \text{ e } X_{tCoal}\left[i\right] = 1 \ (b) \\ p_u p[i], & \text{if } y\left[i\right] = 1 \text{ e } X_{tCoal}\left[i\right] = 0 \ (c) \\ p_u(1 - p\left[i\right]), & \text{if } y\left[i\right] = 0 \text{ e } X_{tCoal}\left[i\right] = 1 \ (d) \\ (1-p_u)(1 - p\left[i\right]), & \text{if } y\left[i\right] = 0 \text{ e } X_{tCoal}\left[i\right] = 0 \ (e) \end{cases} \qquad (2)$$

Specifically, the definition $computeProb(tCoal, y)$ assumes that the probability that $tCoal$ generates y is the combination of two different independent contributions:

- the fact that $|tCoal|$ users formed a coalition, and
- the probability that the user in $tCoal$ generated y

The first contribution is represented by the factor ${p_{Coal}}^{|tCoal|-1}$ in Equation (1), where p_{Coal} is the probability that two randomly picked users cooperate. The second contribution is represented by the product, for each bit i of the pirated copy y, of the probability that the users in $tCoal$ generated the i-th bit of y. The latter probability is assumed to be p_u if the i-th bit of y is unreadable (case (a) of Equation (2)), where p_u is a constant representing the probability that a bit of the code is accidentally discovered by the pirates which made it unreadable or swithced its value even in the case that they all share the same value for that bit. In cases $(b), (e)$ of Equation (2), the probability that the users in $tCoal$ generated the i-th bit of y is assumed proportional to the probability the the bit is not accidentally discovered and the probability that that value of the bit was generated by the Tardos code generator. Finally, in cases $(c), (d)$ of Equation (2) the probability that the users in $tCoal$ generated the i-th bit of y is assumed proportional to the probability the the bit is accidentally discovered and the probability that that value of the bit was generated by the Tardos code generator. Summarizing, given a generic bit of the pirated copy, the probability that a coalition generated that bit is equal to $\frac{1}{7}3$ if the corresponding bits of the coalition are different from one another, otherwise it is assigned the value p_u or $1 - p_u$ multiplied by the probability $p(i)$ (or $(1 - p(i))$ that it has been generated by the Tardos fingerprint generator.

4 Experiments

In this section, we will describe the extensive experimental evaluation that we performed in order to assess the validity of our joint-decoding technique. More in detail, we will first describe the dataset generation then we will describe the standard approach we compare to and finally, we will describe the performance metrics that we computed by our experiments.

4.1 Data Set Generation

Testing the accuracy of fingerprinting codes requires a deep experimental evaluation, thus, we generated a dataset composed of 1.296.000 test cases that have been obtained as described in the following.

The dataset generator takes as input the following parameters:

- N: is the number of users that are going to receive the target document;
- L: is the length of the code generated for each user;
- A: is the attack type (in our study we consider Random, Majority and Minority attacks that will be explained below);
- C: is the pirate coalition size;
- $Pchange$: is the probability that coalition users will change a bit. Each bit can be changed independently by other bits.

For each bit of the code, every attack perform a code hiding by setting it to -1 with $Pchange$ probability. After this step, if all the pirates have the same bit they emit this common bit. If a given bit is not the same for all the pirates the different attack types work as follows:

1. *Random*: the bit is set to 1 or 0 with the same probability $\frac{1}{2}$;
2. *Majority*: the bit is set to the value that occur in more than 50% of users. If the bit value occurrences are tied we apply Random strategy;
3. *Minority*: the bit is set to the value that occur in less than 50% of users. If the bit value occurrences are tied we apply Random strategy;

Once defined the possible attack types we can generate a test case instance by performing the steps below:

1. We generate the Tardos codes of length L for N users;
2. We generate a pirate coalition of size C;

3. We generate an attack of type A performed by the pirates in the coalition that produce a pirated copy y.

As mentioned above, we generated a huge amount of instances. More in detail:

- We used the code length in the set $\{100, 150, 200, 250, 300, 350\}$;
- Number of users in the set $\{50, 100, 150, 200, 250, 300\}$;
- $Pchange$ values $\{0.01, 0.03, 0.05, 0.07, 0.09\}$;
- Coalition size ranging from 1 to 8;
- Random, Majority and Minority attacks.

For each combination of the above values we generate 300 test cases, thus the total number of cases is $300 * 3 * 6 * 6 * 5 * 8 = 1.296.000$.

4.2 Term of comparison and accuracy measurement

In order to compare our results with a reliable baseline, in this section we compare the performance of WFinger with the Tardos accusation algorithm. However, since we consider very short codes the choice of an adeguate probability threshold for the Tardos algorithm is very hard. Indeed, for a code of 200 bits, assuming that the maximum coalition size is 3 and requiring a probability of accusing an innocent lower than 20% no user will be accused. Hence, we had to consider a slightly modified version of the Tardos accusation algorithm, which accuses the user having the gretest value of $\sum_{i=1}^{m} y_i U_{ji}$ (see Section 2.3).

Finally, in order to perform a fair comparison with this modified version of the Tardos accusation algorithm, we considered as accuracy measure for both WFinger and Tardos the accuracy at one (named Acc in the figures), that is the fraction of the experiments where the accused user (which is the first one returned by WFinger and Tardos, respectively) is a guilty user.

4.3 Effectiveness Results

In Fig. 1 we first report the accuracy values obtained by our algorithm (denoted in the following as *WFinger*) and the modified Tardos algorithm (denoted in the following as *Tardos*) by averaging the results on the three types of attack. Fig. 1(a),(b),(c) and (d) report, respectively, the accuracy w.r.t. the coalition size (a), the length of the code (b), the number of users (c) and the probability of changing a bit of the code (d). As a remarkable result, we observe that, on average, the accuracy of *WFinger* that is greater than *Tardos* by a 20%.

As regards the accuracy w.r.t. the coalition size (Fig. 1(a)), it is worth noticing that the accuracy of both algorithms decreases as the coalition dimension increases as expected. However, for *WFinger* it is over 80% until the coalition size is 6, while for *Tardos* this result is obtained only for coalition size lower than 3. The better accuracy of our approach is compelling also when the coalition size further increase to 7 or 8 pirates.

As regards the accuracy w.r.t. the length of the code (Fig. 1(b)), it is easy to see that, for code length greater than 100 bits the accuracy of *WFinger* is greater than 80% and

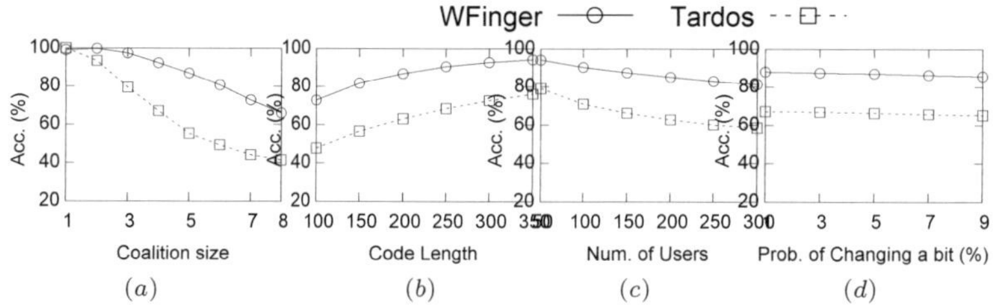

Fig. 1: Average Accuracy Results

for code length greater than 200 bits it is greater than 90%, while *Tardos* never reach an 80% accuracy.

As regards the accuracy w.r.t. the number of users (Fig. 1(c)), we can note that even for a huge number of users (greater than 250) the accuracy of *WFinger* is greater than 80% while *Tardos* never reach an 80% accuracy.

As regards the accuracy w.r.t. the probability of changing a bit of the code (Fig. 1(d)), we point out tha this analysis give an hint about the *robusteness* of our approach. More in detail, we introduce in our evaluation a parameter that states the possibility that a random bit of the code is accidentally changed. The probability of this event is very low, so we assign this parameter values lower than 10%. Also in this case *WFinger* (accuracy greater than 90%) performs better than *Tardos* (accuracy lower than 70%) for all probability values.

In order to provide a more detailed view of the obtained results, we report in Fig. 2, 3 and 4 the results obtained considering a single type of attack. It is easy to see that, also when considering a single type of attack, the accuracy of *WFinger* always overcome *Tardos* for every experimental setting.

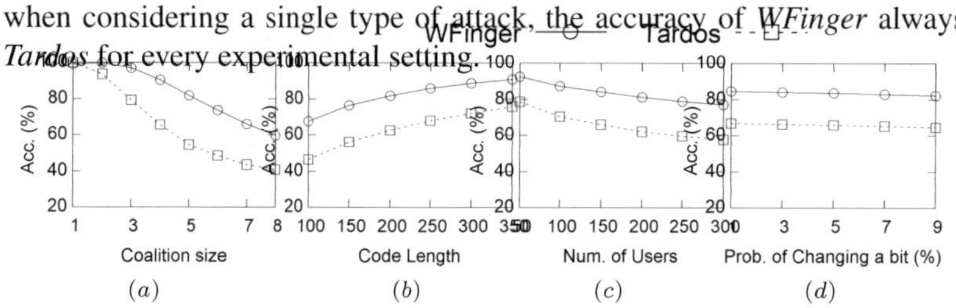

Fig. 2: Accuracy Results for the Random Attack

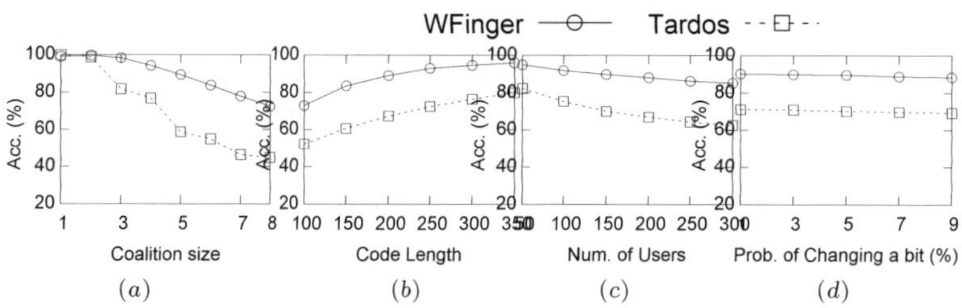

Fig. 3: Accuracy Results for the Majority Attack

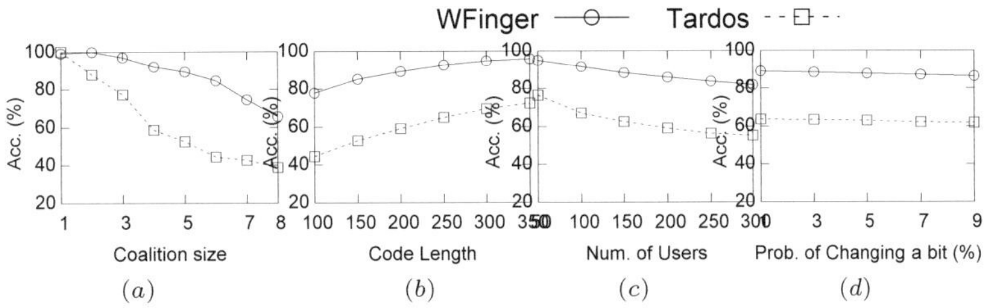

Fig. 4: Accuracy Results for the Minority Attack

5 Conclusion

In this paper we investigated the design of a fingerprinting code based on Metropolis-Hastings scheme. We implemented an encoding scheme that is quite accurate even if the code length is very short (300 bits). The deep experimental evaluation we performed, confirmed the validity of our approach in several stressing test bench.

References

1. Teddy Furon and Mathieu Desoubeaux. Tardos codes for real. In *2014 IEEE International Workshop on Information Forensics and Security, WIFS 2014, Atlanta, GA, USA, December 3-5, 2014*, pages 24–29, 2014.
2. Mohan S. Kankanhalli and K.F. Hau. Watermarking of electronic text documents. *Electronic Commerce Research*, 2(1):169–187, 2002.
3. A. Kot. Watermarking, data hiding and image forensic. In *2005 5th International Conference on Information Communications Signal Processing*, pages nil94–nil94, 2005.
4. S. H. Low, N. F. Maxemchuk, J. T. Brassil, and L. O'Gorman. Document marking and identification using both line and word shifting. In *INFOCOM '95. Fourteenth Annual Joint Conference of the IEEE Computer and Communications Societies. Bringing Information to People. Proceedings. IEEE*, pages 853–860 vol.2, 1995.
5. Koji Nuida. Short collusion-secure fingerprint codes against three pirates. In *Information Hiding - 12th International Conference, IH 2010, Calgary, AB, Canada, June 28-30, 2010, Revised Selected Papers*, pages 86–102, 2010.
6. Koji Nuida, Satoshi Fujitsu, Manabu Hagiwara, Takashi Kitagawa, Hajime Watanabe, Kazuto Ogawa, and Hideki Imai. An improvement of discrete tardos fingerprinting codes. *Des. Codes Cryptography*, 52(3):339–362, 2009.
7. Boris Skoric, Stefan Katzenbeisser, and Mehmet Utku Celik. Symmetric tardos fingerprinting codes for arbitrary alphabet sizes. *Des. Codes Cryptography*, 46(2):137–166, 2008.
8. Boris Skoric, T. U. Vladimirova, Mehmet Utku Celik, and Joop Talstra. Tardos fingerprinting is better than we thought. *IEEE Trans. Information Theory*, 54(8):3663–3676, 2008.
9. G. Tardos. Optimal probabilistic fingerprint codes. In *Conference Proceedings of the Annual ACM Symposium on Theory of Computing*, pages 116–125, 2003.
10. G. Tardos. Optimal probabilistic fingerprint codes. *Journal of the ACM*, 55(2), 2008.

Contrasting Fake Reviews in TripAdvisor (discussion paper)

Francesco Buccafurri[1], Michela Fazzolari[2], Gianluca Lax[1], and Marinella Petrocchi[2]

[1] DIIES, University Mediterranea of Reggio Calabria
Via Graziella, Località Feo di Vito
89122 Reggio Calabria, Italy
E-mail:{bucca,lax}@unirc.it
[2] Istituto di Informatica e Telematica - CNR
Via G. Moruzzi, 1
56124 Pisa, Italy
E-mail:{m.fazzolari,m.petrocchi}@iit.cnr.it

Abstract. Fake reviews are a concrete problem still affecting the reliability of systems like TripAdvisor, especially in the case of few reviews, thus in the first, most vulnerable, activity period of operators. In this work-in-progress paper, we present a model aimed to contrast this problem, based on a sort of normalization of scores given by users, to take into account the level of assurance of the reviews. This is done by considering two different dimensions, combined each other, which are the level of assurance of the identity of the review's author and the level of assurance of the occurrence of the evaluated experience. The paper presents a first validation of the approach conducted on real-life data, giving us very encouraging results.

Keywords reputation model, trust management, TripAdvisor.

1 Introduction

Over the last years, online reviews became very important since they reflect the customers' experience about a product or a service and nowadays constitute the basis on which the reputation of an organization is built. Online reviews have a great influence on the purchase decisions of other customers, who are increasingly relying on them [6].

Unfortunately, the confidence in such reviews is often misplaced, due to the fact that scammers are tempted to write fake information in exchange for some reward or to mislead consumers for obtaining business advantages [8]. These reviews are called *opinion spam* or *fake reviews* [4, 5].

The identification of fake reviews is not an easy task, since they can be identical to genuine ones. Nevertheless, several automatic techniques have been proposed in recent years. Fake reviews detection involves the identification of a set of features, linked with the content (review centric features) or with the review author (reviewer centric features).

Most of the existing machine learning approaches are not sufficiently effective in spotting fake reviews, nevertheless they are more reliable than manual detection. There exist several studies in the literature that rely on machine learning approaches and consider different set of review features [7, 10]. Further studies consider also reviewer centric features [9], which cannot be extracted from the text of a single review. In addition, graph-theory based approaches have been investigated to find relationships between reviews and their corresponding authors [3]. The spam detection techniques that combine reviews features and reviewers behaviors normally lead to better results [11].

In this work-in-progress paper we propose an approach different from the previous fake review detection approaches. Moreover, we introduce a reputation model and its preliminary experimental validation, designed to contrast the phenomenon of fake reviews in TripAdvisor. TripAdvisor is a very famous travel Website collecting reviews of travel-related contents. On the basis of these reviews, an aggregate score of each content is shown. Due to the economic value related to the effects of this system, and despite the efforts declared by TripAdvisor, the system is not immune from the problem of dishonest reviews, aimed either to fictitiously promote a given operator (i.e., self promoting attack) or to denigrate a competitor (i.e., slandering attack). Therefore, the noise occurring in the reviews derives not only from physiological subjectivity of the users [1]. Starting from a preliminary proposal [2], we define a model and a consequent methodology aimed to (partially) purify the system from the noise coming from fake reviews, in order to obtain more reliable *normalized* scores. This is done by considering two different dimensions, combined each other, which are the level of assurance of the identity of the review's author and the level of assurance of the occurrence of the evaluated experience.

It is worth noting that the approach here proposed is heuristic and any feature used to compute the trust is based on reasonable argumentations and ad hoc observations of the phenomenon, with no a specific validation of any single feature. Anyway, the paper is just aimed to give a general experimental validation of the whole approach and, thus, of the global combination of any feature.

The novel contributions, w.r.t. the initial proposal presented in [2], is that the model does not introduces new features required to TripAdvisor (in favor of the practical relevance of the proposal) and that this paper includes also an experimental validation of real-life TripAdvisor data.

The structure of the paper is the following. In the next section, we define the proposed reputation model. In Section 3, we describe the experiments carried out to validate our proposal. Finally, our conclusions are summarized in Section 4.

2 The Reputation Model

In this section, we describe our reputation model, whose components are listed in the following.

1. A set U of users, corresponding to the set of travelers, potentially covering all Web users.
2. A set S of service providers, corresponding to the set of restaurants, bars, hotels, and other operators registered to TripAdvisor.
3. For each service provider $s \in S$, a list of feedbacks $R(s)$ (which are the reviews), each corresponding to a transaction. A feedback $r_s \in R(S)$ for the service provider s is a tuple $\langle u, d, v, k, t, I \rangle$, where u is the author of the feedback, d is the time of the feedback, v is the time of the transaction, k is the score given by u on s (it is the aggregate score – also detailed into different dimensions), t is a text motivating k (it is the text included by the user to describe the experience) and I is the set of additional resources (it is the images posted by the user). Concerning u, we rely on the set of attributes which can be drawn from the system (and also by using external sources, like social-network sources).

The transaction corresponding to a feedback r_s is denoted by t_r. To implement the notion of certified reputation in this model, for a given feedback r_s, we need two basic measures, which are both numbers ranging in the interval $[0,1]$: (1) the trustworthiness of the identity of u, denoted by $trust(u)$, and (2) the trustworthiness of the transaction t_r, denoted by $trust(t_r)$.

The first measure $trust(u)$ is related to identity management issues and is a measure of the level of assurance of identity proofing given by the registration phase into the reputation system. Observe that we do not consider the level of assurance of the authentication phase, thus assuming that no attacks on accounts of users occur. This measure may take into account also external information associated with the digital identity of the user in the system (e.g., information coming from different sources as online social networks). We remark that the trustworthiness of the identity of u is directly related to misbehaving users, as any malicious activity is facilitated when the level of assurance of user identity is low. The trustworthiness of the transaction, denoted by $trust(t_r)$ is equally important. Indeed, fake reviews usually correspond to transactions that never occurred.

On the basis of the two measures above, we measure the trustworthiness $trust(r_s)$ of a feedback $r_s = \langle u, d, v, k, t, I \rangle$ associated with a transaction t_r, by the function $trust(r_s) = f(trust(u), trust(t_r))$ such that the higher $trust(u)$ and $trust(t_r)$, the higher $trust(r_s)$. In this paper, we experiment as first attempt a simple function f which is the linear combination of the two contributions. Once $trust(r_s)$ has been computed, the score k of the feedback r_s is *corrected* on the basis of the overall trustworthiness $trust(r_s)$ by means of a function $g(trust(r_s))$. This function is build is such a way that the score k is much closer to the average score obtained by the service provider s as the value $trust(r_s)$ is low.

Specifically, $g(k) = \frac{(\alpha+trust(r_s))\cdot k}{\sum_{r'_s \in R(S)}(\alpha+trust(r'_s))}$, where α is s suitable (small) offset to avoid null terms. This way, the mean computed over all the scores obtained by the operator s is just the mean weighted by trust values (shifted by α) of each review. Therefore, we obtain the *normalized* feedback r^*_s as $r^*_s = \langle u, d, v, g(k), t, I \rangle$.

Let us explain now how $trust(u)$, representing the level of assurance of identity the user u authoring the review, is computed. Of course, a significant part of the current weakness of the reputation system of TripAdvisor is based on the weakness of its digital identity management system.

Concerning $trust(u)$, we observe that the registration phase of TripAdvisor does not force the user to provide any non-self declared credential. Anyway, the possibility of registering via an existing Facebook profile is also allowed.

To compute the level of assurance of the identity, we consider in our model the following features (which are, in turn, numbers from 0 to 1).

- re (*reviewer experience*): it measures the seniority of the user in the system.
- tc (*text coherence*): it measures the coherence of the known information about the user (for example, the gender) and the text.
- rc (*review count*): it measures the number of reviews of the user. This feature is related to the fact that often fake reviews are done through accounts aimed to a specific goal (for example, for self-promotion or slandering attacks), so they are not reused massively, also to avoid the linkage with de-anonymizing information.
- fi (*Facebook identity*): it measures the level of assurance of the Facebook identity of the user (it is trivially 0 if the TripAdvisor account is not associated with a Facebook profile). Concerning this feature, we argue that a fake reviewer does not have any interest in allowing linkage of her/his TripAdvisor account with other (even fake) accounts, because probably tends to operate as much as possible in an anonymous way.

$trust(u)$ is then obtained as a linear combination of the above components.

To compute the level of assurance of the transaction $trust(t_r)$, we consider in our model the following features (which are, again, numbers from 0 to 1).

- dc (*data coherence*): it measures the coherence between the date of the review and the date of the transaction (this measure is based on the fact, according to our estimation, 50% of the reviews is done within 23 days, 75% within 34 days and 80% within 40).
- ip (*image proof*): it measures the degree of proof given by posted images that the transaction really occurred (trivially, no posted images corresponds to 0, the presence of images recognized as coherent with the other posted by the majority of users corresponds to the maximum value). Indeed, the standard behavior of a faker is to hide as much as possible any information that could be a potential risk for de-anonymization, also the publication of images, which is a typical action done by honest reviewers to give a proof of their claims.

– *rl* (*review locality*): it measures the presence of other reviews by the same user in the same location (city or region) if different from the place of residence corresponding to transactions experienced in the same period.
– *or* (*operator reaction*): it measures the presence of a reaction posted by the operator which is an outlier w.r.t. the standard behavior of the operator.

$trust(t_r)$ is also obtained as a linear combination of the above components.

3 Experiments

In this section, we describe the experiments carried out to validate the proposal: they are based on real-life reviews of restaurants extracted from the TripAdvisor site. First, we describe the data collection procedure and the error metrics used in the experiments. Then, we discuss how a score quantifying the (actual) quality of a restaurant has been computed (it is used as ground truth) and the method adopted to tune the weight of the reputation model parameters. Finally, we show the improvements obtained by our proposal in measuring the score of a restaurant.

3.1 Test Bed

For the study presented in this contribution, we consider data taken from TripAdvisor. Data were collected in January 2017, by developing an ad-hoc scraping software and by using the available API to crawl information. The web scraping process was performed by a Python script that navigated through the restaurants available on the Province of Lucca web page. The metadata related to a review, such as the language of the review, the rating, etc, were obtained by the available APIs. We also stored the reviewers' profiles, which include, when available, the age and country of origin.

At the end of the extraction phase, we obtained a dataset composed of 1.499 restaurants, 60.613 reviewers, and 107.556 reviews. Each review judges the quality of a restaurant by an integer *score* from 1 to 5.

In our experiments, we define the *bias* of a review w as $B^w = \frac{|s^w - GT^r|}{5}$, where s^w is the review score of the restaurant r, the operator $|x|$ denotes the absolute value of the number x, and Q^r (expected quality) is a real number in the interval $[1, 5]$ representing the quality of the restaurant r, which is computed as the average of the scores of that restaurant. B^w represents how much the review score is far from the score of the restaurant and it is normalized w.r.t. the maximum score (i.e., 5). For example, $B^w = 0$ means that the review score is coherent with the quality of the restaurant.

We define *review bias* of a restaurant r as

$$RB^r = \frac{\sum_{i=0}^{n} |B^{W_i}|}{n} \quad (1)$$

https://www.tripadvisor.com/Tourism-g187898-Lucca_Province_of_Lucca_Tuscany-Vacations.html where W_i is the i-th of the n reviews of the restaurant r. In words, it is used to quantify the amount of variation of the reviews of a restaurant w.r.t. the expected quality of that restaurant. For example, $RB^r = 0$ means that all review scores coincide and their value reflects the quality of r.

Given a reputation model t_u, we define its *error %*

$$E^u = \frac{\sum_{i=0}^{m} RB_i^r}{m} \cdot 100 \tag{2}$$

where m is the number of restaurants used in the reputation model and r_i is the i-th one. Clearly, it is the average of the review bias computed for all restaurants.

Finally, to compare the accuracy of two reputation models t_1 and t_2, we define the *improvement %* of t_1 (w.r.t. t_2) as $I_1 = \frac{E^1 - E^2}{E^1} \cdot 100$. Observe that the improvement can be negative in case the reputation model is less accurate than the compared one.

3.2 Parameter Setting

The reputation model presented in this paper uses only five of the parameters defined in Section 2, because they are the only ones evaluable from the collected dataset: two based on the identity of the reviewer and three based on the transaction. They assume a rate from 0 to 1 and how their rate is computed is now discussed.

- f_1 This parameter is related to the number of reviews done by the reviewer. We computed an average of 36 reviews for each reviewer and we assigned 1 to this parameter to reviewers with at least twice the average value. This values is linearly reduced to 0 for reviewers with only 1 review.
- f_2 This parameter is 1 if the reviewer signs in by Facebook, 0 otherwise.
- f_3 This parameter is 1 if the review contains at least an image, 0 otherwise.
- f_4 This parameter is related to length of the reviewer membership. As We have reviewers with activity up to 180 months, we assigned 1 to the rate of ID2 = 1 to reviewers with at least 90 months of activity. This values is linearly reduced to 0 for reviewers registered very recently (clearly, recently w.r.t. the period in which data have been collected)
- f_5 This parameter is related to the coherence between review date and visit date. We set $f_5 = 1$ if *time delta* < 15 days, else $f_5 = .75$ if *time delta* < 30 days, else $f_5 = .25$ if *time delta* < 45 days, 0 otherwise.

In the next experiment, we analyze the performance of our model in which a single parameter is considered. The result of this experiment is reported in Fig. 1.(a) and shows that some parameters are useful to improve the reputation model (namely, f_1, f_3, and f_4), others reduce its performance.

The next task is to combine all parameters and, for this purpose, we need to give a weight to each of them. Such weights are computed by applying a

Observe that this number includes many reviews that are not included in our dataset.

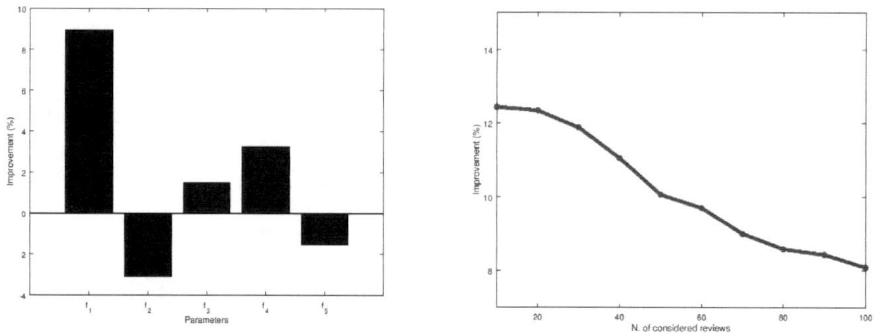

(a) Improvement of the reputation model enabling only one parameter at a time (b) Performance of the proposed reputation model

Fig. 1: Experiment results

multivariable regression model with the five parameters $f_1 \dots f_5$ which returned the following weights $w_1 = 0.6068$, $w_2 = 0.2520$, $w_3 = 0.0605$, $w_4 = 0.2864$, $w_5 = 0.5778$, where w_x is the weight of the parameter f_x with $1 \le x \le 5$. These weights will be used in the next experiment.

3.3 Validation

In this experiment, we measure the performance of the reputation model of TripAdvisor and the performance obtained by using the reputation model proposed in this paper, setting the parameter weight to the values obtained in Section 3.2. We measured the review bias for the first n reviews, with n ranging from 10 to 100: we limited the upper bound to 100 because, for higher values, the review bias is very low. In Fig. 1.(b), we report the improvement % of the proposed reputation model w.r.t. that of TripAdvisor. It is possible to see that our proposal always gives the best results: the improvement is higher when a restaurant has few reviews, that is when it is more vulnerable to fake reviews.

4 Conclusion

TripAdvisor, as well as many other reputation systems, suffers from self-promoting and slandering attacks typically performed by using fake accounts just created for this purpose, which post fake reviews not corresponding to real experiences. In this paper, we defined a new reputation model for the reviews of TripAdvisor. Our proposal aims at evaluate the dependability of a review on the basis of a level of assurance for both identity proofing and truth of the transaction. We validate our proposal by measuring the improvement obtained by enabling our reputation model on a real-life dataset reviews referring to restaurants of the Province of Lucca, Italy. Anyway, the paper is just aimed to give a general experimental validation of the whole approach and, thus, of the global combination of any feature. As a future work, a selective validation of the different features can be also performed.

Acknowledgment

This work has been partially supported by the project "Secure Citizen Remote Identification" (CUP J88C17000150006) and by the project "Stabilimento Virtuale" (CUP J38C17000100006), both funded by Regione Calabria - POR Calabria FESR-FSE 2014-2020 - Asse I and by the European Union under grants 675320 (NECS-Network of Excellence in Cybersecurity) and 700294 (C3ISP-Collaborative and Confidential Information Sharing and Analysis for Cyber Protection) and by Fondazione Cassa di Risparmio di Lucca that partially funds the ReviewLand project.

References

1. J. K. Ayeh, N. Au, and R. Law. Do We Believe in TripAdvisor? Examining Credibility Perceptions and Online Travelers' Attitude toward Using User-Generated Content. *Journal of Travel Research*, 52(4):437–452, 2013.
2. F. Buccafurri, G. Lax, S. Nicolazzo, and A. Nocera. A model implementing certified reputation and its application to tripadvisor. In *Availability, Reliability and Security (ARES), 2015 10th International Conference on*, pages 218–223. IEEE, 2015.
3. E. Choo, T. Yu, and M. Chi. Detecting opinion spammer groups through community discovery and sentiment analysis. In P. Samarati, editor, *Data and Applications Security and Privacy XXIX*, pages 170–187, Cham, 2015. Springer International Publishing.
4. M. Crawford, T. M. Khoshgoftaar, J. D. Prusa, A. N. Richter, and H. Al Najada. Survey of review spam detection using machine learning techniques. *Journal of Big Data*, 2(1):23, Oct 2015.
5. A. Heydari, M. a. Tavakoli, N. Salim, and Z. Heydari. Detection of review spam. *Expert Syst. Appl.*, 42(7):3634–3642, May 2015.
6. N. Jindal and B. Liu. Opinion spam and analysis. In *Proceedings of the 2008 International Conference on Web Search and Data Mining*, WSDM '08, pages 219–230, New York, NY, USA, 2008. ACM.
7. F. Li, M. Huang, Y. Yang, and X. Zhu. Learning to identify review spam. In *Proceedings of the Twenty-Second International Joint Conference on Artificial Intelligence - Volume Volume Three*, IJCAI'11, pages 2488–2493. AAAI Press, 2011.
8. B. Liu. *Sentiment Analysis and Opinion Mining*. Morgan & Claypool Publishers, 2012.
9. A. Mukherjee. Detecting deceptive opinion spam using linguistics, behavioral and statistical modeling. In *ACL*, 2015.
10. A. Mukherjee, B. Liu, and N. Glance. Spotting fake reviewer groups in consumer reviews. In *Proceedings of the 21st International Conference on World Wide Web*, WWW '12, pages 191–200, New York, NY, USA, 2012. ACM.
11. S. Rayana and L. Akoglu. Collective opinion spam detection using active inference. In *Proceedings of the 2016 SIAM International Conference on Data Mining*, pages 630–638, 2016.

Beyond Skyline and Ranking Queries: Restricted Skylines (Extended Abstract)

Paolo Ciaccia[1] and Davide Martinenghi[2]

[1]Università di Bologna, Italy, email: paolo.ciaccia@unibo.it
[2]Politecnico di Milano, Italy, email: davide.martinenghi@polimi.it

Abstract. Traditionally, skyline and ranking queries have been treated separately as alternative ways of discovering interesting data in potentially large datasets. While ranking queries adopt a specific scoring function to rank tuples, skyline queries return the set of non-dominated tuples and are independent of attribute scales and scoring functions. Ranking queries are thus less general, but cheaper to compute and widely used. In this paper, we integrate these two approaches under the unifying framework of *restricted skylines* by applying the notion of dominance to a set of scoring functions of interest.

1 Introduction

When simultaneously optimizing different criteria (e.g., the different attributes in a dataset), a problem known as *multi-objective optimization*, three approaches are prevalent [4]: *(1) ranking queries*, which focus on a scoring function expressing the relative importance of the different attributes; *(2) lexicographical queries*, which establish a strict priority among the attributes; *(3) skyline queries*, which return all the non-dominated objects (t dominates s iff t is no worse than s on all the attributes, and strictly better on at least one). As argued in the literature [4], each of these methods has pros and cons (also refer to Table 1).

Table 1: Pros and cons of multi-objective optimization approaches.

Evaluation criteria ↓ Queries →	Ranking	Lexicographic	Skyline
Simplicity of formulation	No	Yes	Yes
Overall view of interesting results	No	No	Yes
Control of result cardinality	Yes	Yes	No
Trade-off among attributes	Yes	No	No
Relative importance of attributes	Yes	Yes	No

Ranking queries heavily depend on the particular choice of weights in the scoring function, and thus fail to offer an overall view of the dataset. Lexicographic queries enforce a linear priority between attributes, thus even the smallest difference in the most important attribute cannot be compensated by the other attributes (a problem inherited by newer approaches, such as *p-skylines* [5]). Skyline queries provide a good overview of potentially interesting tuples, but may contain too many objects.

SEBD 2018, June 24-27, 2018, Castellaneta Marina, Italy.

Restricted skyline (R-skyline) queries, introduced in [2], consider arbitrary families of scoring functions (induced, e.g., by constraints on the weights), thus allowing greater flexibility than skylines and ranking queries. The linchpin of R-skylines is the novel concept of $\mathcal{F}$*-dominance*: t $\mathcal{F}$-dominates s when t is always better than or equal to s according to *all* the scoring functions in the family $\mathcal{F}$ (and strictly better for at least one scoring function in $\mathcal{F}$).

In this paper, we present a synthesis of the results in [2], where we introduced two R-skyline operators: ND, characterizing the set of non-$\mathcal{F}$-dominated tuples; PO, referring to the tuples that are potentially optimal, i.e., best according to some function in $\mathcal{F}$. R-skylines capture in a single framework all the practically relevant approaches to multi-objective optimization, traditionally dealt with separately, and enable the study of other scenarios of practical interest. For example, decision makers may encounter objectives in which the model parameters are characterized by complex preferences, perhaps coming from preference elicitation from a crowd (see, e.g., [3] and references therein for strategies for collecting preferences between tuples).

2 Restricted Skylines

We consider a relational schema $R(A_1, \ldots, A_d)$, with $d \geq 1$, where, w.l.o.g., each attribute value ranges in $[0, 1]$; we refer to an instance r over R.

The *skyline* of r, denoted $\textsc{Sky}(r)$, is equivalently defined *(i)* as the set of all *non-dominated* tuples (Eq. (1)), or *(ii)* as the set of *potentially optimal* tuples, i.e., those that are better than all the others according to at least one monotone scoring function [1] (Eq. (2)).

$$\textsc{Sky}(r) = \{t \in r \mid \nexists s \in r.\ s \prec t\} \tag{1}$$

$$\textsc{Sky}(r) = \{t \in r \mid \exists f \in \mathcal{M}.\ \forall s \in r.\ s \neq t \rightarrow f(t) < f(s)\} \tag{2}$$

where $s \prec t$ means "s dominates t", and $\mathcal{M}$ is the set of monotone scoring functions. While the former view is typically adopted for skylines, the latter is commonly applied to "top-k" queries (here with $k = 1$), i.e., those queries whose goal is to return the k best tuples according to a given scoring function.

We now introduce R-skylines, whose behavior is similar to $\textsc{Sky}$, but applied to a limited set of monotone scoring functions $\mathcal{F} \subseteq \mathcal{M}$. To this end, we say that t $\mathcal{F}$*-dominates* s, $s \neq t$, denoted by $t \prec_{\mathcal{F}} s$, iff $\forall f \in \mathcal{F}.\ f(t) \leq f(s)$.

Example 1. Consider the tuples $t = \langle 0.5, 0.5 \rangle$, $s = \langle 0, 1 \rangle$, the monotone scoring functions $f_1(x, y) = x + y$ and $f_2(x, y) = x + 2y$, and the set $\mathcal{F} = \{f_1, f_2\}$. We have $t \prec_{\mathcal{F}} s$, since $f_1(t) = f_1(s) = 1$ and $f_2(t) = 1.5 < f_2(s) = 2$. However, $t \not\prec_{\mathcal{M}} s$, since $\mathcal{M}$ includes $f_3(x, y) = 2x + y$, for which $f_3(t) = 1.5 > f_3(s) = 1$.

The *non-dominated restricted skyline* of r wrt. $\mathcal{F}$, denoted by $\textsc{nd}(r; \mathcal{F})$, is defined as the set of non-$\mathcal{F}$-dominated tuples:

$$\textsc{nd}(r; \mathcal{F}) = \{t \in r \mid \nexists s \in r.\ s \prec_{\mathcal{F}} t\}. \tag{3}$$

Here, as a convention, we consider lower values to be better than higher ones.

Note that the right-hand side of Eq. (3) is similar to that of Eq. (1), where $\prec$ has been replaced by $\prec_{\mathcal{F}}$. Observe that, clearly, $\prec_{\mathcal{M}}$ coincides with $\prec$.

The *potentially optimal restricted skyline* of r wrt. $\mathcal{F}$, denoted by $\text{PO}(r;\mathcal{F})$, returns the tuples that are best (top 1) according to some scoring function in $\mathcal{F}$.

$$\text{PO}(r;\mathcal{F})=\{t\in r \mid \exists f\in\mathcal{F}.\ \forall s\in r.\ s\neq t \rightarrow f(t)<f(s)\}. \quad (4)$$

The right-hand side of Eq. (4) is as in Eq. (2), with $\mathcal{F}$ instead of $\mathcal{M}$.

The following containment relationships between R-skylines and SKY hold:

$$\text{PO}(r;\mathcal{F}) \subseteq \text{ND}(r;\mathcal{F}) \subseteq \text{SKY}(r). \quad (5)$$

$$\text{PO}(r;\mathcal{M}) = \text{ND}(r;\mathcal{M}) = \text{SKY}(r). \quad (6)$$

The *$\mathcal{F}$-dominance region* $DR(t;\mathcal{F})$ of a tuple t under $\mathcal{F}$ is the set of all points in $[0,1]^d$ that are $\mathcal{F}$-dominated by t:

$$DR(t;\mathcal{F}) = \{s \in [0,1]^d \mid t \prec_{\mathcal{F}} s\}. \quad (7)$$

Such a region grows larger for smaller sets: $DR(t;\mathcal{F}_1) \supseteq DR(t;\mathcal{F}_2)$, if $\mathcal{F}_1 \subseteq \mathcal{F}_2$.

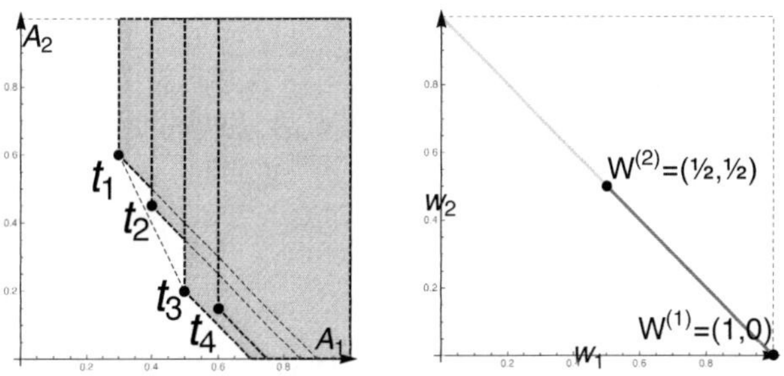

(a) Tuples from Example 2 in $[0,1]^d$, $d = 2$. $\mathcal{F}$-dominance regions in gray.

(b) Region of normalized weights such that $w_1 \geq w_2$ (in gray).

Fig. 1: Example 2 – tuples and weights in $[0,1]^d$, $d = 2$, $\mathcal{C} = \{w_1 \geq w_2\}$, $\mathcal{F} = \mathcal{L}_1^{\mathcal{C}}$, where $\mathcal{L}_1$ is the set of monotone scoring functions that are weighted sums of attribute values.

Example 2. Let $\mathcal{F}$ be the set of linear scoring functions $f(x,y) = w_1x+w_2y$ with $w_1 \geq w_2$ and let r consist of $t_1 = \langle 0.3, 0.6\rangle$, $t_2 = \langle 0.4, 0.45\rangle$, $t_3 = \langle 0.5, 0.2\rangle$, $t_4 = \langle 0.6, 0.15\rangle$ (Figure 1a). We have $\text{PO}(r;\mathcal{F}) = \{t_1, t_3\} \subseteq \text{ND}(r;\mathcal{F}) = \{t_1, t_2, t_3\} \subseteq \text{SKY}(r) = r$. Indeed, no tuple in r dominates any other tuple in r, and so $\text{SKY}(r) = r$. However, $t_3 \prec_{\mathcal{F}} t_4$, since $f(t_3) \leq f(t_4)$ holds for any $f \in \mathcal{F}$, as $w_1(0.5 - 0.6) \leq w_2(0.15 - 0.2)$ always holds when $w_1 \geq w_2$. Therefore $t_4 \notin \text{ND}(r;\mathcal{F})$. Figure 1a shows in gray the region of $[0,1]^d$ whose points (including tuple t_4) are $\mathcal{F}$-dominated by some tuple in r, i.e., $\cup_{t\in r} DR(t;\mathcal{F})$; Figure 1b shows in gray the region of normalized weights such that $w_1 \geq w_2$.

Finally, with linear scoring functions, as is well known [7], top-1 tuples can only lie in the boundary of the convex hull of the $\mathcal{F}$-dominated region, thus $t_2 \notin \text{PO}(r;\mathcal{F})$, since there is no function $f \in \mathcal{F}$ for which both $f(t_2) < f(t_1)$ and $f(t_2) < f(t_3)$, as there are no w_1, w_2 such that $w_1(0.4 - 0.3) < w_2(0.6 - 0.45)$, $w_1(0.4 - 0.5) < w_2(0.2 - 0.45)$, and $w_1 \geq w_2$ all hold.

3 Restricted Skylines and L_p Norms

A practically relevant case to consider is that of the *weighted* L_p norms, defined as follows, where $W = (w_1, \ldots, w_d) \in \mathcal{W}$ is a normalized weight vector, i.e., $\mathcal{W} \subseteq [0,1]^d$ and, for each $W = (w_1, \ldots, w_d) \in \mathcal{W}$, we have $\sum_{i=1}^{d} w_i = 1$:

$$L_p^W(t) = \left(\sum_{i=1}^{d} w_i t[A_i]^p\right)^{1/p}, \quad p \in \mathbb{N}. \tag{8}$$

We therefore turn our attention to the case in which the set of monotone scoring functions coincides with the family $\mathcal{L}_p$ of weighted L_p norms:

$$\mathcal{L}_p = \{L_p^W \mid W \in \mathcal{W}\}, \quad p \in \mathbb{N}. \tag{9}$$

The behaviors of ND and PO are very different under $\mathcal{L}_p$.

Theorem 1. *For every value of p and every r, $\text{ND}(r;\mathcal{L}_p) = \text{SKY}(r)$.*

Thus, any $\mathcal{L}_p$ family is "powerful enough" to reveal all skyline points with ND. However, this does not hold for PO, as indicated in the following theorems.

Theorem 2. *Let $p < p'$, with $p, p' \in \mathbb{N}$. Then, for every r, $\text{PO}(r;\mathcal{L}_p) \subseteq \text{PO}(r;\mathcal{L}_{p'})$.*

Theorem 3. *For each $p \in \mathbb{N}$, there exists r such that $\text{PO}(r;\mathcal{L}_p) \subset \text{SKY}(r)$.*

The results of Theorems 1, 2 and 3 suggest that, by imposing some constraints on the weights, one can use any $\mathcal{L}_p$ family to smoothly move from the skyline (no constraints) to top-1 queries (a single weight vector satisfies the constraints).

Checking $\mathcal{F}$-dominance for $\mathcal{L}_p$ norms with linear constraints on the weights can be done in PTIME. Let $\mathcal{L}_p^{\mathcal{C}}$ indicate the set $\mathcal{L}_p$ with linear constraints $\mathcal{C} = \{C_1, \ldots, C_c\}$ on weights, where $C_j = \sum_{i=1}^{d} a_{ji} w_i \leq k_j$ (for $j \in \{1, \ldots, c\}$).

Theorem 4 ($\mathcal{F}$-dominance test). *$t \prec_{\mathcal{L}_p^{\mathcal{C}}} s$ iff the following linear programming problem in the unknowns $W = (w_1, \ldots, w_d)$ has a non-negative solution:*

$$\begin{array}{lll}
\text{minimize} & \sum_{i=1}^{d} w_i (s[A_i]^p - t[A_i]^p) & \\
\text{subject to} & w_i \in [0,1] & i \in \{1, \ldots, d\} \\
 & \sum_{i=1}^{d} w_i = 1 & \\
 & \sum_{i=1}^{d} a_{ji} w_i \leq k_j & j \in \{1, \ldots, c\}.
\end{array} \tag{10}$$

Computing $\text{ND}(r; \mathcal{F})$ using Theorem 4 is likely to be time-consuming, since a different linear programming (LP) problem needs to be solved for each $\mathcal{F}$-dominance test. An alternative approach is to explicitly compute the $\mathcal{F}$-dominance regions of tuples, and then discard those tuples that belong to at least one of such regions. The advantage of this approach is that the computation of the $\mathcal{F}$-dominance region of a tuple t can be performed just once, thus independently of how many $\mathcal{F}$-dominance tests involve t.

In order to compute $DR(t; \mathcal{L}_p^{\mathcal{C}})$, we observe that the subset of $\mathcal{W}$ that satisfies $\mathcal{C}$, denoted $\mathcal{W}(\mathcal{C})$, is a convex polytope contained in the unit $(d-1)$-simplex.

Theorem 5 ($\mathcal{F}$-dominance region). *Let $W^{(1)}, \ldots, W^{(q)}$ be $\mathcal{W}(\mathcal{C})$'s vertices, with $W^{(\ell)} = (w_1^{(\ell)}, \ldots, w_d^{(\ell)})$ for $\ell \in \{1, \ldots, q\}$. The dominance region $DR(t; \mathcal{L}_p^{\mathcal{C}})$ of a tuple t under $\mathcal{L}_p^{\mathcal{C}}$ is the locus of points s defined by the q inequalities:*

$$\sum_{i=1}^{d} w_i^{(\ell)} s[A_i]^p \geq \sum_{i=1}^{d} w_i^{(\ell)} t[A_i]^p, \quad \ell \in \{1, \ldots, q\}. \tag{11}$$

Example 3. Let $d = 2$, $p = 1$, and consider tuples $t_1 = \langle 0.3, 0.6 \rangle$, $t_3 = \langle 0.5, 0.2 \rangle$, $t_4 = \langle 0.6, 0.15 \rangle$ from Example 2. For $\mathcal{C} = \{w_1 \geq w_2\}$ and considering that $w_1 + w_2 = 1$ and $0 \leq w_1, w_2 \leq 1$, the vertices of $\mathcal{W}(\mathcal{C})$ are $W^{(1)} = (1, 0)$ and $W^{(2)} = (0.5, 0.5)$. Figure 1a shows the tuples along with their $\mathcal{L}_1^{\mathcal{C}}$-dominance regions, while Figure 1b shows $\mathcal{W}(\mathcal{C})$. By Theorem 5, $DR(t_3; \mathcal{L}_1^{\mathcal{C}})$ is characterized by the system of inequalities:

$$\{s[A_1] \geq 0.5, \quad s[A_1] + s[A_2] \geq 0.7\}. \tag{12}$$

Tuple t_4 satisfies (12) and thus $t_3 \prec_{\mathcal{L}_1^{\mathcal{C}}} t_4$. For tuple t_1, the system becomes:

$$\{s[A_1] \geq 0.3, \quad s[A_1] + s[A_2] \geq 0.9\}. \tag{13}$$

Here, t_4 does not satisfy (13) and therefore $t_1 \not\prec_{\mathcal{L}_1^{\mathcal{C}}} t_4$.

As Example 3, Figure 1a and Inequalities (11) suggest, the "shape" of $DR(t; \mathcal{L}_p^{\mathcal{C}})$ (modulo cropping in the $[0, 1]^d$ hypercube) is independent of t, since the left-hand sides are the same and the right-hand sides are, for any given t, a constant. The only significant overhead introduced by this approach is the enumeration of the vertices of $\mathcal{W}(\mathcal{C})$. However, this has to be done just once for *all* tuples.

For any set $\mathcal{F}$, $\text{PO}(r; \mathcal{F})$ can be computed from $\text{ND}(r; \mathcal{F})$ by retaining only the tuples that are not $\mathcal{F}$-dominated by any "virtual" tuple obtained by combining other tuples in $\text{ND}(r; \mathcal{F})$. When $\mathcal{F} = \mathcal{L}_p^{\mathcal{C}}$, this is done by solving an LP problem.

Theorem 6 (PO test). *Let $\text{ND}(r; \mathcal{L}_p^{\mathcal{C}}) = \{t_1, t_2, \ldots, t_\sigma, t\}$. Then, $t \in \text{PO}(r; \mathcal{L}_p^{\mathcal{C}})$ iff there is no convex combination s of $t_1, \ldots, t_\sigma$ such that $s \prec_{\mathcal{L}_p^{\mathcal{C}}} t$, i.e., iff the following linear system in the unknowns $\alpha = (\alpha_1, \ldots, \alpha_\sigma)$ is unsatisfiable:*

$$\begin{aligned} \textstyle\sum_{i=1}^{d} w_i^{(\ell)} (\sum_{j=1}^{\sigma} \alpha_j t_j[A_i]^p) \leq \sum_{i=1}^{d} w_i^{(\ell)} t[A_i]^p \quad & \ell \in \{1, \ldots, q\} \\ \alpha_j \in [0, 1] \quad & j \in \{1, \ldots, \sigma\} \\ \textstyle\sum_{j=1}^{\sigma} \alpha_j = 1. & \end{aligned} \tag{14}$$

Algorithm 1: SVE1F for ND.

Input: *relation* r, *constraints* $\mathcal{C}$, *family* $\mathcal{F} = \mathcal{L}_p^{\mathcal{C}}$. Output: $\text{ND}(r;\mathcal{F})$.

1. **let** ND $:= \emptyset$; **let** $W^{(1)}, \ldots, W^{(q)}$ be the vertices of $\mathcal{W}(\mathcal{C})$
2. sort r using the coordinates of the centroid of $\mathcal{W}(\mathcal{C})$ as weights
3. **for each** s **in** r // *candidate $\mathcal{F}$-dominated tuple*
4.   compute left-hand sides of Inequalities (11)
5.   **for each** t **in** ND // *candidate $\mathcal{F}$-dominant tuple*
6.   **if** $t \prec s \vee t \prec_{\mathcal{F}} s$ **then continue** to line 3
7.   **let** ND $:=$ ND $\cup \{s\}$
8. **return** ND

Besides the $\mathcal{L}_p^{\mathcal{C}}$ family, Theorems 4, 5, and 6 also hold for *any* set $\mathcal{F}$ whose functions are weighted sums of monotone functions of single attributes and monotonic transforms thereof.

4 Algorithms and Experiments

We considered several algorithmic opportunities for the computation of ND.

- Appropriately sorting the dataset beforehand produces a topological sort with respect to the $\mathcal{F}$-dominance relation. With that, if tuple t precedes tuple s in the sorted relation, then $s \not\prec_{\mathcal{F}} t$.
- The $\mathcal{F}$-dominance test can be executed by either *i)* solving an LP problem as in Theorem 4 or *ii)* checking whether $t \in DR(s;\mathcal{F})$ as in Theorem 5 through vertex enumeration of the polytope $\mathcal{W}(\mathcal{C})$.
- We can either *i)* first compute SKY and then remove $\mathcal{F}$-dominated tuples (two phases), or *ii)* integrate dominance and $\mathcal{F}$-dominance tests (one phase).

The best choice is to use sorting, vertex enumeration and a single phase. The corresponding pseudocode is shown in Algorithm 1, called SVE1F. The main idea is to scan the tuples sortedly and to populate a current window ND of non-$\mathcal{F}$-dominated tuples. No tuple will ever be removed from ND, as no tuple can be $\mathcal{F}$-dominated by a tuple found later in the sorted relation. The vertices of the polytope $\mathcal{W}(\mathcal{C})$ are computed just once (line 1). Algorithm 1 interleaves dominance and $\mathcal{F}$-dominance tests, thus performing, for each new tuple s, a single pass over ND. Every candidate $\mathcal{F}$-dominated tuple s (line 3) is compared against every candidate $\mathcal{F}$-dominant tuple t (line 6) to decide whether s should be added to ND. The $\mathcal{F}$-dominance test of line 6 is done via Theorem 5 and, thus, it is useful to precompute the left-hand sides of Inequality (11) already at line 4.

For the computation of $\text{PO}(r;\mathcal{F})$, we start from the tuples in $\text{ND}(r;\mathcal{F})$ and, by Theorem 6, we discard any tuple t that is $\mathcal{F}$-dominated by a convex combination of tuples in $\text{ND}(r;\mathcal{F}) \setminus \{t\}$. However, directly checking $\mathcal{F}$-dominance via (14) may be prohibitively time consuming when $\sigma = |\text{ND}(r;\mathcal{F})| - 1$ is large. We therefore try, in Algorithm 2 (POND, i.e. PO via ND), to reduce as early as possible the set of candidate potentially optimal tuples (PO) by adopting the following heuristics: *i)* we start with a convex combination of only $\tilde{\sigma} = 2$ tuples (line 2), which will give rise to smaller, faster-to-solve systems (14) for testing $\mathcal{F}$-dominance; as long

Algorithm 2: POND for PO.

Input: *relation r, constraints $\mathcal{C}$, family $\mathcal{F} = \mathcal{L}_p^{\mathcal{C}}$.* Output: $\text{PO}(r;\mathcal{F})$.

1. **let** PO := $\text{ND}(r;\mathcal{F})$ // *via* SVE1F
2. **let** $\tilde{\sigma}$:= 2; **let** *lastRound* := **false**
3. **while**($\neg$*lastRound*)
4. **if** $\tilde{\sigma} \geq |\text{PO}| - 1$ **then** *lastRound* := **true**
5. **for each** t **in** PO in reverse order // *candidate $\mathcal{F}$-dominated tuple*
6. **if** $\exists s.\, s \prec_{\mathcal{F}} t$, s is convex comb. of the first $\min(\tilde{\sigma}, |\text{PO}|-1)$ tuples in $\text{PO}\setminus\{t\}$ **then let** $\text{PO}:=\text{PO}\setminus\{t\}$
7. **let** $\tilde{\sigma} := \tilde{\sigma} \cdot 2$
8. **return** PO

as $\tilde{\sigma} < |\text{PO}| - 1$, this condition is only sufficient for pruning, but not necessary; after each round, we double $\tilde{\sigma}$ (line 7); *ii)* we sortedly enumerate candidate $\mathcal{F}$-dominated tuples from PO in reverse order (line 5), as the worst tuples wrt. the ordering are the most likely to be $\mathcal{F}$-dominated; *iii)* using linear system (14), we check the existence of a convex combination of the *first* $\tilde{\sigma}$ tuples in PO (line 6), as they are the best wrt. the ordering and thus more likely to $\mathcal{F}$-dominate other tuples. In the last round (enabled by line 4) all the remaining tuples are checked against a convex combination of all the other tuples still in PO, which is now a necessary and sufficient condition for pruning, as in Theorem 6.

In [2], efficiency and effectiveness of the proposed algorithms have been measured on both real and synthetic scenarios with varying *i)* data distribution, *ii)* dataset size, *iii)* number of dimensions, and *iv)* number of constraints. With default settings (anticorrelated data, $N = 100K$ tuples, $d = 6$ dimensions, $\mathcal{F} = \mathcal{L}_1^{\mathcal{C}}$ family with $|\mathcal{C}| = 3$ constraints), our algorithms incur sub-second execution times. Such times increase as N increases, d increases and $|\mathcal{C}|$ decreases.

Both ND and PO reduce the size of the result wrt. SKY (Fig. 2a). For default values, their effectiveness is remarkable (9.8% of the SKY points are in ND and only 1% in PO). Somewhat surprisingly, computing ND via SVE1F may require much less time than computing SKY, because $\mathcal{F}$-dominance tests, albeit more costly than dominance tests, are more effective in pruning redundant tuples.

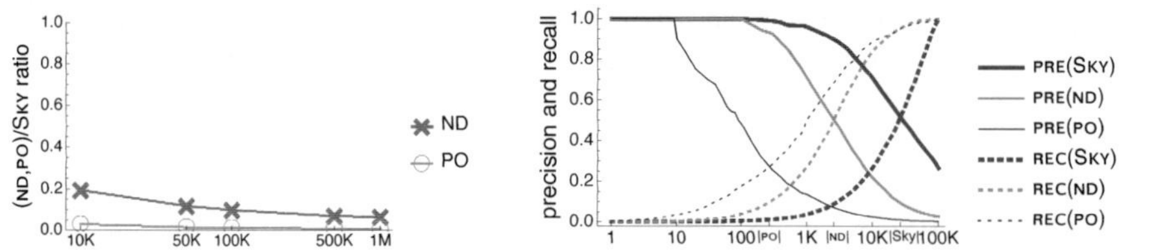

(a) $|\text{ND}|/|\text{SKY}|$ and $|\text{PO}|/|\text{SKY}|$ cardinality ratios as dataset size N varies.

(b) Precision and recall of top-k queries wrt. SKY, ND, and PO. Centroid of the $\mathcal{W}(\mathcal{C})$ as weight vector; $N = 100K$ tuples in the dataset.

Fig. 2: R-skylines vs. skyline and ranking queries (anticorrelated data with $d = 6$, $\mathcal{F} = \mathcal{L}_1^{\mathcal{C}}$, $|\mathcal{C}| = 3$).

Let $\mathcal{T}_k(r;f)$ indicate the set of top-k tuples in relation r wrt. a scoring function f. The *precision* of $\mathcal{T}_k(r;f)$ wrt. a set $\mathcal{S}$ is defined as $\text{PRE}(\mathcal{S}) =$

$|\mathcal{S} \cap \mathcal{T}_k(r; f)|/k$, whereas the *recall* is $\text{REC}(\mathcal{S}) = |\mathcal{S} \cap \mathcal{T}_k(r; f)|/|\mathcal{S}|$. Figure 2b shows precision and recall when f is the most representative weighted sum in $\mathcal{F}$ (i.e., f's weight vector is the centroid of $\mathcal{W}(\mathcal{C})$). Recall grows with k, while precision decreases. With standard parameter values, when $k = |\mathcal{S}|$ (and thus precision and recall are equal), REC(ND) is 50%, while REC(PO) is 38%. Retrieving the entire ND with a top-k query may however require to scan almost the entire dataset. As expected, top-k queries incur a small fraction of the execution time of `SVE1F` (below 7%).

5 Discussion

In this paper, we have presented a framework aiming to unify skyline and ranking queries. We have done so by introducing two R-skyline operators implementing the notions of non-dominated (ND) and potentially optimal (PO) tuples with respect to a set of scoring functions $\mathcal{F}$. The greater flexibility of these operators captures not only standard skyline and top-1 queries, but also constraints on the weights in the scoring functions, which are highly relevant in practice.

It is well known that choosing the "right" weights for a scoring function is a difficult task for users, since it is usually hard to predict the effects on ranking of changing one or more parameters. Replacing precise values with constraints on weights, as R-skylines do, is therefore a viable way to alleviate the problem.

We have shown that both ND and PO are very effective in focusing on tuples of interest, even in very large datasets. In practical cases, computing ND requires no more than a few seconds. For the more complex problem of computing PO, we have developed heuristics to reduce the number of LP problems to be solved.

Natural extensions of this framework include the notions of top-k query and k-skyband, with $k > 1$ [6].

References

1. J. Chomicki, P. Ciaccia, and N. Meneghetti. Skyline queries, front and back. *SIGMOD Record*, 42(3):6–18, 2013.
2. P. Ciaccia and D. Martinenghi. Reconciling skyline and ranking queries. *PVLDB*, 10(11):1454–1465, 2017.
3. E. Ciceri et al. Crowdsourcing for top-k query processing over uncertain data. *TKDE*, 28(1):41–53, 2016.
4. A. A. Freitas. A critical review of multi-objective optimization in data mining: a position paper. *SIGKDD Explorations*, 6(2):77–86, 2004.
5. D. Mindolin and J. Chomicki. Preference elicitation in prioritized skyline queries. *VLDB J.*, 20(2):157–182, 2011.
6. D. Papadias et al. Progressive skyline computation in database systems. *TODS*, 30(1):41–82, 2005.
7. M. A. Soliman et al. Ranking with uncertain scoring functions: semantics and sensitivity measures. In *SIGMOD*, pages 805–816, 2011.

Approximate Query Answering over Inconsistent Knowledge Bases

Sergio Greco, Cristian Molinaro, Irina Trubitsyna

DIMES, University of Calabria
{greco,cmolinaro,trubitsyna}@dimes.unical.it

Abstract. Consistent query answering is a principled approach for querying inconsistent knowledge bases. It relies on the central notion of *repair*, that is, a maximal consistent subset of the facts in the knowledge base. One drawback of this approach is that entire facts are deleted to resolve inconsistency, even if they may still contain useful "reliable" information.
To overcome this limitation, we propose an inconsistency-tolerant semantics for query answering based on a new notion of repair, allowing values within facts to be updated for restoring consistency. This more fine-grained repair primitive allows us to preserve more information in the knowledge base. We also introduce the notion of a *universal repair*, which is a compact representation of all repairs and can be computed in polynomial time. Then, we show that consistent query answering in our framework is intractable (coNP-complete). In light of this result, we develop a polynomial time approximation algorithm for computing a sound (but possibly incomplete) set of consistent query answers.

1 Introduction

Reasoning in the presence of inconsistent information is a problem that has attracted much interest in the last decades. Many inconsistency-tolerant semantics for query answering have been proposed, and most of them rely on the notions of *consistent query answer* and *repair*. A consistent answer to a query is a query answer that is entailed by every repair, where a repair is a "maximal" consistent subset of the facts of the knowledge base. Different maximality criteria have been investigated, but all the resulting notions of repair share the same drawback: a fact is either kept or deleted altogether, and deleting entire facts can cause loss of "reliable" information, as illustrated below.

Example 1. Consider the knowledge base (D, Σ)*, where* D *contains the following facts:*

works

john	cs	nyc
john	math	rome
mary	math	sidney

and Σ *is an ontology consisting of the following equality-generating dependency* σ*:*

$$\mathsf{works}(\mathsf{E}_1, \mathsf{D}, \mathsf{C}_1) \wedge \mathsf{works}(\mathsf{E}_2, \mathsf{D}, \mathsf{C}_2) \rightarrow \mathsf{C}_1 = \mathsf{C}_2.$$

SEBD 2018, June 24-27, 2018, Castellaneta Marina, Italy.

As an example, the fact works(john, cs, nyc) *states that* john *is an employee working in the* cs *department located in* nyc. *The dependency σ says that every department must be located in a single city. Clearly, the last two facts violate σ, so every repair would discard either of them.*

If we pose a query asking for the employees' name, the only consistent answer is john. *However, we might consider reliable the information on* mary *being an employee, as the only uncertainty concerns the* math *department and its city—roughly speaking, the information in the first column of the* works *table can be considered "clean".*

To overcome the drawback illustrated above, we propose a notion of repair based on updating values within facts. Update-based repairing allows for rectifying errors in facts without deleting them altogether, thereby preserving consistent values.

Example 2. Consider again the knowledge base of Example 1. Using value updates as the primitive to restore consistency, and assuming that the only uncertain values are math*'s cities, we get the following two repairs:*

john	cs	nyc
john	math	rome
mary	math	rome

john	cs	nyc
john	math	sidney
mary	math	sidney

If we ask again for the employees' name, both mary *and* john *are consistent answers.*

We show that consistent query answering in this setting is coNP-complete. Then, we show how to compute a "universal" repair, which compactly represents all repairs and can be used as a valuable tool to compute approximate query answers.

Example 3. A universal repair for the two repairs of Example 2 is reported below:

john	cs	nyc
john	math	$\perp_1$
mary	math	$\perp_1$

$\perp_1 = \text{rome} \vee \perp_1 = \text{sidney}$

where $\perp_1$ is a labeled null, and the "global" condition at the bottom restricts the admissible values for $\perp_1$, which are rome *and* sidney.

2 Related Work

Consistent query answering was first proposed in [1]. Query answering under various inconsistency-tolerant semantics for ontologies expressed in DL languages has been studied in several works (see, e.g., [13,14,3,4]), and in [17,18] for ontologies expressed by fragments of Datalog+/–. [4] have proposed an approach for the approximation of consistent query answers from above and from below. [7] proposed an approach based on three-valued logic to compute a sound but possibly incomplete set of consistent query answers. Different from our proposal, all the approaches above adopt the most common notion of repair, where whole facts are removed. This can cause loss of information, as illustrated in the toy scenario of Example 1—in real-life scenarios, it might well be the case that facts have much more attributes and only a few of them are involved in inconsistencies.

There have also been different proposals adopting a notion of repair that allows values to be updated [5,2,6]. Our repair strategy behaves similar to the one of [5] in that values on the right-hand side of functional dependencies (FDs) are updated. However, [5] focus on FDs only, while we consider more general EGDs, and they consider repairs that are minimal according to a specific cost model. [2] allow only numerical attributes to be updated, one primary key per relation is allowed, but keys are assumed to be satisfied by the original DB: thus, no repairing is possible w.r.t. keys, while we allow it, and we allow much more general constraints. Our repair strategy can be seen as an instantiation of the value-based family of policies proposed in [19], even though the two approaches differ in how multiple dependencies are handled, and while they focus on FDs only, we consider EGDs. [6] consider numerical databases and a different class of (aggregate) constraints. However, the main difference between this paper and the aforementioned ones is that none of them has investigated the approximate computation of consistent query answers.

Approximation algorithms providing sound but possibly incomplete query answers in the presence of nulls have been proposed in [11,15,16,9], but no dependencies are considered therein, and thus data is assumed to be consistent.

3 Preliminaries

We assume the existence of the following pairwise disjoint (countably infinite) sets: a set Const of *constants*, a set Var of *variables*, and a set Null of *labeled nulls*. Nulls are denoted by the symbol $\perp$ subscripted. A *term* is a constant, variable, or null. We also assume a set of *predicates*, disjoint from the aforementioned sets, with each predicate being associated with an *arity*, which is a non-negative integer.

An *atom* A is of the form $p(t_1, \ldots, t_n)$, where p is an n-ary predicate and the t_i's are terms. We write an atom also as $p(\mathbf{t})$, where $\mathbf{t}$ is a sequence of terms. An atom without variables is also called a *fact*. An *instance* is a finite set of facts. A *database* is an instance containing constants only.

A *homomorphism* is a mapping $h : \mathsf{Const} \cup \mathsf{Var} \cup \mathsf{Null} \to \mathsf{Const} \cup \mathsf{Var} \cup \mathsf{Null}$ that is the identity on Const. Homomorphisms are also applied to atoms and set of atoms in the natural fashion, that is, $h(p(t_1, \ldots, t_n)) = p(h(t_1), \ldots, h(t_n))$, and $h(S) = \{h(A) \mid A \in S\}$ for every set S of atoms. A *valuation* is a homomorphism ν whose image is Const, that is, $\nu(t) \in \mathsf{Const}$ for every $t \in \mathsf{Const} \cup \mathsf{Var} \cup \mathsf{Null}$.

Conditional instances. *Conditional instances* (also known as "conditional tables" [12,8]) are instances augmented with conditions restricting the set of admissible values for nulls. Let $\mathcal{E}$ be the set of all expressions, called *conditions*, that can be built using the standard logical connectives $\wedge$, $\vee$, $\neg$, $\Rightarrow$ and expressions of the form $t_i = t_j$, true, and false, where $t_i, t_j \in \mathsf{Const} \cup \mathsf{Null}$. We will also use $t_i \neq t_j$ as a shorthand for $\neg(t_i = t_j)$.We say that a valuation ν *satisfies* a condition ϕ, denoted $\nu \models \phi$, if its assignment of constants to nulls makes ϕ true. Formally, a *conditional instance* (CI) is a pair (I, Φ), where I is an instance and $\Phi \in \mathcal{E}$. The semantics of $C = (I, \Phi)$ is given by the set of its *possible worlds*, that is, the set of databases $pw(C) = \{\nu(I) \mid \nu \text{ is a valuation and } \nu \models \Phi\}$.

Equality generating dependencies. An *equality generating dependency* (EGD) σ is a first-order formula of the form $\forall \mathbf{x}\, \varphi(\mathbf{x}) \rightarrow x_i = x_j$, where $\varphi(\mathbf{x})$ is a conjunction of atoms (without labeled nulls) whose variables are exactly $\mathbf{x}$, and x_i and x_j are variables from $\mathbf{x}$. We call $\varphi(\mathbf{x})$ the *body* of σ, and call $x_i = x_j$ the *head* of σ. We will omit the universal quantification in front of dependencies and assume that all variables are universally quantified. With a slight abuse of notation, we sometimes treat a conjunction as the *set* of its atoms.

An instance I *satisfies* σ, denoted $I \models \sigma$, if whenever there exists a homomorphism h s.t. $h(\varphi(\mathbf{x})) \subseteq I$, then $h(x_i) = h(x_j)$. A instance I *satisfies* a set Σ of EGDs, denoted $I \models \Sigma$, if $I \models \sigma$ for every $\sigma \in \Sigma$.

Knowledge bases. A *knowledge base* (KB) is a pair (D, Σ), where D is a database and Σ is a finite set of EGDs. It is *consistent* if $D \models \Sigma$, otherwise it is *inconsistent*.

4 Repairing and Querying Inconsistent KBs

In this section, we present our notion of repair and analyze the computational complexity of two central problems: repair checking and consistent query answering.

We start by defining the EGDs we consider. Let Σ be a set of EGDs. An *argument* of Σ is an expression of the form $p[i]$, where p is an n-ary predicate appearing in Σ and $1 \leq i \leq n$.

Definition 1 (Argument and dependency graphs). *The* argument graph *of a set Σ of EGDs is a directed graph $G_\Sigma = (V, E)$, where V is the set of all arguments of Σ, and E contains a directed edge from $p[i]$ to $q[j]$ labeled σ iff there is an EGD $\sigma \in \Sigma$ such that:*

- *the body of σ contains an atom $p(t_1, \ldots, t_n)$ such that either t_i is a constant or t_i is a variable occurring more than once in the body of σ, and*
- *the body of σ contains an atom $q(u_1, \ldots, u_m)$ such that u_j is a variable also appearing in the head of σ.*

The dependency graph *of Σ is a directed graph $\Gamma_\Sigma = (\Sigma, \Omega)$, where Ω is the set $\{(\sigma_1, \sigma_2) \mid G_\Sigma = (V, E) \wedge (p([i], q[j], \sigma_1), (q[j], r[k], \sigma_2) \in E\}$. We say that Σ is* acyclic *if its dependency graph is acyclic.*

In the following, we write $\sigma_i < \sigma_j$ if $(\sigma_i, \sigma_j) \in \Omega$ or there is σ_k such that $\sigma_i < \sigma_k$ and $\sigma_k < \sigma_j$.

Example 4. Consider the following set of EGDs Σ:

$$\sigma_1\colon\ \mathsf{works}(\mathsf{X}, \mathsf{Y}_1, \mathsf{Z}_1) \wedge \mathsf{works}(\mathsf{X}, \mathsf{Y}_2, \mathsf{Z}_2) \rightarrow \mathsf{Y}_1 = \mathsf{Y}_2$$
$$\sigma_2\colon\ \mathsf{works}(\mathsf{X}_1, \mathsf{Y}, \mathsf{Z}_1) \wedge \mathsf{works}(\mathsf{X}_2, \mathsf{Y}, \mathsf{Z}_2) \rightarrow \mathsf{Z}_1 = \mathsf{Z}_2$$

Then, G_Σ has two edges: one from works[1] *to* works[2] *labeled σ_1, and another one from* works[2] *to* works[3] *labeled σ_2. Moreover, Γ_Σ has only the edge (σ_1, σ_2). Thus, Σ is acyclic and a topological sorting of EGDs is (σ_1, σ_2).*

In the rest of the paper we consider acyclic sets of EGDs only. Thus, from now on, Σ is understood to be acyclic. Before introducing our notion of repair, we provide some intuitions in the following example.

Example 5. Consider the database below and the set of EGDs of Example 4.

john	cs	rome
john	math	rome
mary	math	sidney

By enforcing σ_1 into the first two facts, either cs *or* math *can be chosen as* john*'s department. If the latter is chosen, then the database D' below is obtained.*

Suppose now that σ_2 is enforced into the last two facts of D'. Then, either rome *or* sidney *can be chosen as* math*'s city. If the former is chosen, then the database D'' below is obtained.*

$D' =$

john	math	rome
john	math	rome
mary	math	sidney

$D'' =$

john	math	rome
john	math	rome
mary	math	rome

No further dependency enforcement is applicable at this point and thus D'' is a repair.

When repairing inconsistent databases, conditional instances can be used to keep track of which values must be equal and which constants can be assigned to nulls. For instance, in Example 5 above, after the last dependency enforcement, we have to make sure that the last column contains the same city (which can be either rome or sidney).

Below we introduce the technical definitions, starting with a *repair step*.

Definition 2 (Repair step). *Let (I, Φ) be a CI, Σ a set of EGDs, and σ an EGD $\varphi(\mathbf{x}) \to x_i = x_j \in \Sigma$. Let h be a homomorphism s.t. $h(\varphi(\mathbf{x})) \subseteq h(I)$, $h \models \Phi$, and $h(x_i) \neq h(x_j)$.*

Moreover, let $\bot_m$ be a fresh null and (I', Φ') the CI obtained from (I, Φ) as follows:

1. *for each fact $p(u_1, ..., u_n)$ in I, if $\varphi(\mathbf{x})$ contains an atom $p(t_1, ..., t_n)$ s.t. $h(p(t_1, ..., t_n)) = h(p(u_1, ..., u_n))$, then for every $1 \leq k \leq n$, if $t_k \in \{x_i, x_j\}$,*
   - *replace u_k in $p(u_1, ..., u_n)$ with $\bot_m$;*
   - *if $u_k \in$ Null, replace every occurrence of u_k elsewhere with $\bot_m$;*
2. *Either $\Phi' = \Phi \wedge (\bot_m = h(x_i))$ or $\Phi' = \Phi \wedge (\bot_m = h(x_j))$.*

We say that $(I, \Phi) \xrightarrow{\sigma,h} (I', \Phi')$ is a repair step.

Intuitively, a repair step enforces an EGD that is not satisfied by the knowledge base.

A *repair sequence* of a knowledge base (D, Σ) is a (possibly empty) finite sequence of repair steps $C_i \xrightarrow{\sigma_i,h_i} C_{i+1}$ $(0 \leq i < m)$ such that $C_0 = (D, \mathsf{true})$ and $\sigma_i \in \Sigma$ for every i. We also say that the repair sequence is *from C_0 to C_m*. We call C_m the *result* of the repair sequence. Also, we say that the repair sequence is *maximal* if there does not exist a repair step of the form $C_m \xrightarrow{\sigma_m,h_m} C_{m+1}$.

It is easy to see that for each repair step $(I, \Phi) \xrightarrow{\sigma,h} (I', \Phi')$, if h' is a homomorphism s.t. $h' \models \Phi'$, then it assigns constants to nulls as dictated by Φ' (see item 2 of Definition 2).

Thus, all h' satisfying Φ' yield the same database $h'(I')$. For any conditional instance (I, Φ), we use the notation $\Phi(I)$ to denote the database derived from I by iteratively replacing nulls with constants or other nulls as dictated by Φ.

For ease of presentation, we assume that one can keep of a given fact f in the database during the repair process despite the value changes. Thus, we use $D[f,i]$ to denote the i-th term of a fact f in a database D. Given a repair sequence S from $C_0 = (D, \mathsf{true})$ to $C_m = (I_m, \Phi_m)$, we define the set of changes made by S as $update(S) = \{(f,i) \mid D[f,i] \neq \Phi_m(I_m)[f,i]\}$, where f is a fact of the database.

Example 6. Consider the database of Example 5 and the set of EGDs of Example 4. By enforcing first σ_1 using the first two facts, then σ_2 using the last two facts, and finally σ_2 using the first two facts, we get, respectively, the CIs C_1, C_2 and C_3 reported below:

C_1

john	$\bot_1$	rome
john	$\bot_1$	rome
mary	math	sidney

$\bot_1 = \mathsf{math}$

C_2

john	$\bot_1$	rome
john	$\bot_1$	$\bot_3$
mary	math	$\bot_3$

$\bot_1 = \mathsf{math} \wedge \bot_3 = \mathsf{sidney}$

C_3

john	$\bot_1$	$\bot_4$
john	$\bot_1$	$\bot_4$
mary	math	$\bot_4$

$\bot_1 = \mathsf{math} \wedge \bot_3 = \mathsf{sidney} \wedge \bot_4 = \mathsf{rome}$

No further repair steps are applicable at this point. Notice that $\bot_3 =$ sidney can be deleted from the condition of C_3 because it does not play a role anymore. A repair is obtained from C_3 by replacing every occurrence of $\bot_1$ with math*, and every occurrence of $\bot_4$ with* rome.

Definition 3 (Repair). *A* repair *for a knowledge base $K = (D, \Sigma)$ is a database $\Phi(J)$ such that there exists a maximal repair sequence S of K from (D, true) to (J, Φ) and $update(S)$ is minimal w.r.t. $\subseteq$.*

We use $repair(D, \Sigma)$ to denote the set of all repairs of a knowledge base (D, Σ). Every repair is indeed consistent [10].

The *consistent answers* to a query Q over a knowledge base (D, Σ) are defined in the standard way as follows: $Q(D, \Sigma) = \bigcap\{Q(D') \mid D' \in repair(D, \Sigma)\}$.

In the context of managing inconsistent knowledge bases, two fundamental problems are *repair checking* and *consistent query answering*, which are defined as follows. Let (D, Σ) be a knowledge base, D' a database, Q a query, and f a fact of constants. Then, the following two problems are defined: *repair checking*: decide whether $D' \in repair(D, \Sigma)$; *consistent query answering*: decide whether $f \in Q(D, \Sigma)$.

Repair checking is in PTIME while conjunctive query answering is coNP-complete in the data complexity [10].

[10] introduced the notion of a *universal repair*, which is a compact representation of all repairs for a given knowledge base, and can be computed in polynomial time. An example is provided below.

Example 7. Consider the database of Example 5 and the EGDs of Example 4. The following CI is a universal repair:

john	$\bot_1$	$\bot_5$
john	$\bot_1$	$\bot_5$
mary	math	$\bot_4$

$$(\bot_1 = \mathsf{cs} \wedge \bot_4 = \mathsf{sidney} \wedge \bot_5 = \mathsf{rome}) \vee$$
$$(\bot_1 = \mathsf{math} \wedge \bot_5 = \bot_4 \wedge (\bot_4 = \mathsf{rome} \vee \bot_4 = \mathsf{sidney}))$$

5 Approximation Algorithm

Since consistent query answering in intractable in our framework, [10] developed a polynomial time approximation algorithm to compute a sound (but possibly incomplete) set of consistent query answers. The basic idea is illustrated in the following example.

Example 8. Consider the knowledge base of Example 1 and the query asking for the pairs of departments located in different cities.

A universal repair, say U, is shown in Example 3. The first step of the approximation algorithm consists in assigning the "local condition" true *to every fact of U as follows:*

john	cs	nyc	true
john	math	$\perp_1$	true
mary	math	$\perp_1$	true

$\perp_1 = \text{rome} \vee \perp_1 = \text{sidney}$

Then, the "conditional evaluation" (cf. [8,10] for more details) of the query is performed—roughly speaking, it means that the query is evaluated using conditions that express how facts are derived. The result is the following set of facts associated with conditions:

cs	cs	true $\wedge$ true $\wedge$ nyc $\neq$ nyc
cs	math	true $\wedge$ true $\wedge$ nyc $\neq \perp_1$
math	cs	true $\wedge$ true $\wedge \perp_1 \neq$ nyc
math	math	true $\wedge$ true $\wedge \perp_1 \neq \perp_1$

Finally, conditions are evaluated in such a way that each of them yields one of the truth values true, false, unknown. *If the evaluation of a fact's condition yields* true, *then the fact is a consistent query answer. In the scenario above, the approximate consistent answers are* (cs, math) *and* (math, cs), *which are indeed consistent query answers.*

6 Conclusion

We proposed a framework for query answering over inconsistent KBs that is based on *(i)* a notion of repair that preserves more information than classical repair strategies, *(ii)* a compact representation of all repairs called universal repair, *(iii)* an approximation algorithm to compute under-approximations of consistent query answers.

As a direction for future work, we plan to investigate further approximation algorithms based on different conditions' evaluations. Another issue to be investigated is the generalization of our framework to more general classes of dependencies, such as TGDs or arbitrary EGDs.

References

1. Marcelo Arenas, Leopoldo E. Bertossi, and Jan Chomicki. Consistent query answers in inconsistent databases. In *Symposium on Principles of Database Systems (PODS)*, pages 68–79, 1999.

2. Leopoldo E. Bertossi, Loreto Bravo, Enrico Franconi, and Andrei Lopatenko. The complexity and approximation of fixing numerical attributes in databases under integrity constraints. *Information Systems*, 33(4-5):407–434, 2008.
3. Meghyn Bienvenu. On the complexity of consistent query answering in the presence of simple ontologies. In *AAAI Conference on Artificial Intelligence (AAAI)*, 2012.
4. Meghyn Bienvenu and Riccardo Rosati. Tractable approximations of consistent query answering for robust ontology-based data access. In *International Joint Conference on Artificial Intelligence (IJCAI)*, pages 775–781, 2013.
5. Philip Bohannon, Michael Flaster, Wenfei Fan, and Rajeev Rastogi. A cost-based model and effective heuristic for repairing constraints by value modification. In *International Conference on Management of Data (SIGMOD)*, pages 143–154, 2005.
6. Sergio Flesca, Filippo Furfaro, and Francesco Parisi. Querying and repairing inconsistent numerical databases. *ACM Transactions on Database Systems*, 35(2):14:1–14:50, 2010.
7. Filippo Furfaro, Sergio Greco, and Cristian Molinaro. A three-valued semantics for querying and repairing inconsistent databases. *Annals of Mathematics and Artificial Intelligence*, 51(2-4):167–193, 2007.
8. Gösta Grahne. *The Problem of Incomplete Information in Relational Databases*, volume 554 of *Lecture Notes in Computer Science*. Springer, 1991.
9. Sergio Greco, Cristian Molinaro, and Irina Trubitsyna. Computing approximate certain answers over incomplete databases. In *Alberto Mendelzon International Workshop (AMW)*, 2017.
10. Sergio Greco, Cristian Molinaro, and Irina Trubitsyna. Computing approximate query answers over inconsistent knowledge bases. In *International Joint Conference on Artificial Intelligence (IJCAI)*, pages 1838–1846, 2018.
11. Paolo Guagliardo and Leonid Libkin. Making SQL queries correct on incomplete databases: A feasibility study. In *Symposium on Principles of Database Systems (PODS)*, pages 211–223, 2016.
12. Tomasz Imielinski and Witold Lipski. Incomplete information in relational databases. *Journal of the ACM*, 31(4):761–791, 1984.
13. Domenico Lembo, Maurizio Lenzerini, Riccardo Rosati, Marco Ruzzi, and Domenico Fabio Savo. Inconsistency-tolerant semantics for description logics. In *International Conference on Web Reasoning and Rule Systems (RR)*, pages 103–117, 2010.
14. Domenico Lembo, Maurizio Lenzerini, Riccardo Rosati, Marco Ruzzi, and Domenico Fabio Savo. Inconsistency-tolerant query answering in ontology-based data access. *Journal of Web Semantics*, 33:3–29, 2015.
15. Leonid Libkin. How to define certain answers. In *International Joint Conference on Artificial Intelligence (IJCAI)*, pages 4282–4288, 2015.
16. Leonid Libkin. Certain answers as objects and knowledge. *Artificial Intelligence*, 232:1–19, 2016.
17. Thomas Lukasiewicz, Maria Vanina Martinez, Andreas Pieris, and Gerardo I. Simari. From classical to consistent query answering under existential rules. In *AAAI Conference on Artificial Intelligence (AAAI)*, pages 1546–1552, 2015.
18. Thomas Lukasiewicz, Maria Vanina Martinez, and Gerardo I. Simari. Inconsistency handling in Datalog+/– ontologies. In *European Conference on Artificial Intelligence (ECAI)*, pages 558–563, 2012.
19. Maria Vanina Martinez, Francesco Parisi, Andrea Pugliese, Gerardo I. Simari, and V. S. Subrahmanian. Policy-based inconsistency management in relational databases. *International Journal of Approximate Reasoning*, 55(2):501–528, 2014.

Complexity of Approximate Query Answering under Inconsistency in Datalog$^{\pm}$

Thomas Lukasiewicz[1], Enrico Malizia[2], and Cristian Molinaro[3]

[1] Department of Computer Science, University of Oxford, UK
thomas.lukasiewicz@cs.ox.ac.uk
[2] Department of Computer Science, University of Exeter, UK
e.malizia@exeter.ac.uk
[3] DIMES, University of Calabria, Italy
cmolinaro@dimes.unical.it

Abstract. Several semantics have been proposed to query inconsistent ontological knowledge bases, including the intersection of repairs and the intersection of closed repairs as two approximate inconsistency-tolerant semantics. In this paper, we analyze the complexity of conjunctive query answering under these two semantics for a wide range of Datalog$^{\pm}$ languages. We consider both the standard setting, where errors may only be in the database, and the generalized setting, where also the rules of a Datalog$^{\pm}$ knowledge base may be erroneous.

1 Introduction

Description logics (DLs) and existential rules from the context of Datalog$^{\pm}$ are popular ontology languages. In real-world ontology-based applications involving large amounts of data (such as ontology-based data extraction and/or integration), it is very likely that the data are inconsistent with the ontology, and thus inconsistency-tolerant semantics for ontology-based query answering are urgently needed.

Consistent query answering, first developed for relational databases [1] and then generalized as the AR semantics for several DLs [12], is the most widely accepted semantics for querying inconsistent ontologies. Query answering under the AR semantics is known to be a hard problem, even for very simple languages [12]. For this reason, several other semantics have been recently developed with the aim of approximating consistent query answering [12,2,17,4].

In particular, in [12], besides the AR semantics, three other inconsistency-tolerant query answering semantics are proposed, including the approximate *intersection of repairs (IAR)* semantics, in which an answer is considered to be valid, if it can be inferred from the intersection of the repairs (and the ontology). The *intersection of closed repairs (ICR)* [2] is another approximate semantics, in which an answer is valid, if it can be inferred from the intersection of the closure of the repairs (and the ontology).

The complexity of query answering under the AR semantics when the ontology is described using one of the central DLs is well-understood. The data and combined complexity were studied by [20] for a wide spectrum of DLs, while [2] identified cases

SEBD 2018, June 24-27, 2018, Castellaneta Marina, Italy.

for simple ontologies (within the *DL-Lite* family) for which tractable data complexity results can be obtained. In [17,19,16], the data and different types of combined complexity, respectively, of the AR semantics have been studied for ontologies described via existential rules and negative constraints. [3] analyzed the data and combined complexity of query answering under the AR and IAR semantics for different notions of maximal repairs over the language *DL-Lite*$_{\mathcal{R}}$. Recently, the AR semantics was extended to the *generalized repair* semantics (GAR) and its computational complexity analyzed [8]. In the GAR semantics, also ontological rules may be removed, and some database atoms and rules are assumed to be non-removable.

This paper continues this line of research and analyzes the complexity of inconsistency-tolerant query answering as follows:

- ▷ We consider different popular inconsistency-tolerant semantics, namely, the IAR and the ICR semantics, in both their standard and their generalized repair variants.
- ▷ We consider the most popular Datalog$^{\pm}$ languages: linear, guarded, sticky, and acyclic existential rules, along with "weak" generalizations, as well as full restrictions, and full (i.e., non-existential) rules in general.
- ▷ Our analysis concerns the data, fixed-program combined, bounded-arity combined, and combined complexity.

2 Datalog$^{\pm}$

We briefly recall some basics on existential rules from the context of Datalog$^{\pm}$ [6].

General. We assume a set $\mathbf{C}$ of *constants*, a set $\mathbf{N}$ of *labeled nulls*, and a set $\mathbf{V}$ of regular *variables*. A *term* t is a constant, null, or variable. We also assume a set of *predicates*, each associated with an arity, i.e., a non-negative integer. An *atom* has the form $p(t_1, \ldots, t_n)$, where p is an n-ary predicate, and $t_1, \ldots, t_n$ are terms. Conjunctions of atoms are often identified with the sets of their atoms. An *instance* I is a (possibly infinite) set of atoms $p(\mathbf{t})$, where $\mathbf{t}$ is a tuple of constants and nulls. A *database* D is a finite instance that contains only constants. A *homomorphism* is a substitution $h\colon \mathbf{C}\cup\mathbf{N}\cup\mathbf{V} \to \mathbf{C}\cup\mathbf{N}\cup\mathbf{V}$ that is the identity on $\mathbf{C}$ and that maps $\mathbf{N}$ to $\mathbf{C}\cup\mathbf{N}$. A *conjunctive query* (CQ) q has the form $\exists\mathbf{Y}\phi(\mathbf{X},\mathbf{Y})$, where $\phi(\mathbf{X},\mathbf{Y})$ is a conjunction of atoms without nulls. The *answer* to q over an instance I, denoted $q(I)$, is the set of all tuples $\mathbf{t}$ over $\mathbf{C}$ for which there is a homomorphism h such that $h(\phi(\mathbf{X},\mathbf{Y})) \subseteq I$ and $h(\mathbf{X}) = \mathbf{t}$. A *Boolean CQ* (BCQ) q is a CQ $\exists\mathbf{Y}\phi(\mathbf{Y})$, i.e., all variables are existentially quantified; q is *true* over I, denoted $I \models q$, if $q(I) \neq \emptyset$, i.e., there is a homomorphism h with $h(\phi(\mathbf{Y})) \subseteq I$.

Dependencies. A *tuple-generating dependency* (TGD) σ is a first-order formula $\forall\mathbf{X}\forall\mathbf{Y}\,\varphi(\mathbf{X},\mathbf{Y}) \to \exists\mathbf{Z}\,p(\mathbf{X},\mathbf{Z})$, where $\mathbf{X}\cup\mathbf{Y}\cup\mathbf{Z} \subseteq \mathbf{V}$, $\varphi(\mathbf{X},\mathbf{Y})$ is a conjunction of atoms, and $p(\mathbf{X},\mathbf{Z})$ is an atom, all without nulls. An instance I satisfies σ, written $I \models \sigma$, if the following holds: whenever there exists a homomorphism h such that $h(\varphi(\mathbf{X},\mathbf{Y})) \subseteq I$, then there exists $h' \supseteq h|_{\mathbf{X}}$, where $h|_{\mathbf{X}}$ is the restriction of h on $\mathbf{X}$, such that $h'(p(\mathbf{X},\mathbf{Z})) \in I$. A *negative constraint (NC)* ν is a first-order formula $\forall\mathbf{X}\,\varphi(\mathbf{X}) \to \bot$, where $\mathbf{X} \subseteq \mathbf{V}$, $\varphi(\mathbf{X})$ is a conjunction of atoms without nulls and $\bot$ denotes the truth constant *false*. An instance I satisfies ν, written $I \models \nu$, if there is no homomorphism h such that $h(\varphi(\mathbf{X})) \subseteq I$. Given a set Σ of TGDs and NCs, I satisfies

Σ, written $I \models \Sigma$, if I satisfies each TGD and NC of Σ. Given a class of TGDs $\mathbb{C}$, we denote by $\mathbb{C}_\perp$ the formalism obtained by combining $\mathbb{C}$ with arbitrary NCs. Finite sets of TGDs and NCs are also called *programs*, and TGDs are also called *existential rules*.

Knowledge Bases. A *knowledge base* is a pair (D, Σ), where D is a database, and Σ is a program. For programs Σ, Σ_T and Σ_{NC} are the subsets of Σ containing the TGDs and NCs of Σ, respectively. The set of *models* of $KB = (D, \Sigma)$, denoted $mods(KB)$, is the set of instances $\{I \mid I \supseteq D \wedge I \models \Sigma\}$. We say that KB is *consistent*, if $mods(KB) \neq \emptyset$, otherwise KB is *inconsistent*. The *answer* to a CQ q relative to KB is the set of tuples $ans(q, KB) = \bigcap\{q(I) \mid I \in mods(KB)\}$. The answer to a BCQ q is *true*, denoted $KB \models q$, if $ans(q, KB) \neq \emptyset$. The decision version of the *CQ answering* problem is as follows: given a knowledge base KB, a CQ q, and a tuple of constants $\mathbf{t}$, decide whether $\mathbf{t} \in ans(q, KB)$. Since CQ answering can be reduced in LOGSPACE to BCQ answering, we focus on BCQs. The *combined complexity* of BCQ answering considers the database, the set of dependencies, and the query as part of the input. The *bounded-arity combined* (or *ba-combined*) complexity assumes that the arity of the underlying schema is bounded by an integer constant. The *fixed-program combined* (or *fp-combined*) *complexity* considers the sets of TGDs and NCs as fixed; the *data complexity* also assumes the query fixed.

The Datalog$^\pm$ languages that we consider to guarantee decidability are among the most frequently analyzed in the literature, namely, linear (L) [6], guarded (G) [5], sticky (S) [7], and acyclic TGDs (A), along with their "weak" (proper) generalizations weakly guarded (WG) [5], weakly sticky (WS) [7], and weakly acyclic TGDs (WA) [9], as well as their "full" (proper) restrictions linear full (LF), guarded full (GF), sticky full (SF), and acyclic full TGDs (AF), respectively, and full (i.e., existential-free) TGDs (F) in general. We also recall the following further inclusions: L $\subset$ G, F $\subset$ WA $\subset$ WS, and F $\subset$ WG. We refer to, e.g., [8] for a more detailed overview and complexity results.

3 Approximate Inconsistency Semantics

We now recall three prominent inconsistency-tolerant semantics for ontology-based query answering, namely, the *ABox repair* (AR) semantics and its approximation by the *intersection of repairs* (IAR) and the *intersection of closed repairs* (ICR) semantics [12,2]; all three are based on the notion of *repair*, which is a maximal consistent subset of the given database. Furthermore, we newly define generalized repair variants [8] of the two intersection-based approximate repair semantics.

Classically, errors leading to inconsistencies are assumed to be only in the database, and not in the ontology. [8] have introduced the *generalized inconsistency semantics* allowing for errors also in the ontology, and for parts of the database and the ontology to be without errors. More specifically, for a knowledge base (D, Σ), the generalized semantics allows also (i) to minimally remove TGDs from Σ, and (ii) to partition both D and Σ into a hard and a soft part of non-removable and removable elements, respectively. The so partitioned database (resp., program) is called *flexible database* (resp., *program*).

A *flexible database* is a pair (D_h, D_s) of databases, called the *hard* and *soft database*, respectively. A *flexible program* is a pair (Σ_h, Σ_s) consisting of a finite set Σ_h of TGDs and NCs and a finite set Σ_s of TGDs, called the *hard* and *soft program*, respectively.

A *flexible knowledge base* is a pair $((D_h, D_s), (\Sigma_h, \Sigma_s))$, where (D_h, D_s) is a flexible database, and (Σ_h, Σ_s) is a flexible program. Note that a (standard) knowledge base (D, Σ) is a special case of a flexible one $((D_h, D_s), (\Sigma_h, \Sigma_s))$, where $D_h = \emptyset$, $D_s = D$, $\Sigma_h = \Sigma$, and $\Sigma_s = \emptyset$. Below, we provide definitions for flexible knowledge bases that generalize the ones for (standard) knowledge bases.

For knowledge bases $KB' = (D', \Sigma')$ and $KB'' = (D'', \Sigma'')$, we write $KB' \subseteq KB''$, if $D' \subseteq D''$ and $\Sigma' \subseteq \Sigma''$. A *selection* of a flexible knowledge base $((D_h, D_s), (\Sigma_h, \Sigma_s))$ is a knowledge base (D', Σ') such that $D_h \subseteq D' \subseteq (D_h \cup D_s)$ and $\Sigma_h \subseteq \Sigma' \subseteq (\Sigma_h \cup \Sigma_s)$. A *repair* of a flexible knowledge base FKB is an inclusion-maximal consistent selection of FKB. We denote by $Rep(FKB)$ the set of all repairs of FKB. Notice that for (standard) knowledge bases, a repair is usually defined as a maximal consistent subset of the database. However, when a flexible knowledge base models a standard one (i.e., $D_h = \emptyset$ and $\Sigma_s = \emptyset$), the definition above coincides with the classical one.

Example 1. Consider the flexible database (D_h, D_s) given by

$$D_h = \{Postdoc(p), Researcher(p), leaderOf(p', g')\} \text{ and } D_s = \{Prof(p), leaderOf(p, g)\},$$

asserting that p is a postdoc, a researcher, a professor, and the leader of the research group g, and that p' is the leader of g'. Consider also the flexible program (Σ_h, Σ_s) defined as

$$\begin{aligned} \Sigma_h = \{&Prof(X) &&\rightarrow Researcher(X), \\ &Postdoc(X) &&\rightarrow Researcher(X), \\ &Prof(X), Postdoc(X) &&\rightarrow \bot, \\ &leaderOf(X,Y) &&\rightarrow Group(Y)\}, \\ \Sigma_s = \{&leaderOf(X,Y) &&\rightarrow Prof(X)\}, \end{aligned}$$

expressing that professors and postdocs are researchers, professors and postdocs form disjoint sets, and *leaderOf* has *Prof* as domain and *Group* as range. It is easy to see that $mods(D, \Sigma) = \emptyset$, since p violates the disjointness constraint.

The flexible knowledge base $((D_h, D_s), (\Sigma_h, \Sigma_s))$ has two repairs (D', Σ') and (D'', Σ''):

$$\begin{aligned} D' &= D_h \cup \{leaderOf(p, g)\}, & \Sigma' &= \Sigma_h, \\ D'' &= D_h, & \Sigma'' &= \Sigma_h \cup \Sigma_s. \end{aligned}$$

In both, the atom $Prof(p)$ is removed; in the first one, also the rule $leaderOf(X, Y) \rightarrow Prof(X)$ is removed, while in the second one, the atom $leaderOf(p, g)$ is removed.

We now define the inconsistency-tolerant semantics considered. For a knowledge base $KB = (D, \Sigma)$, the *closure* $Cn(KB)$ of KB is the set of all ground atoms, built from constants in D and Σ, entailed by D and the TGDs of Σ. Let FKB be a flexible knowledge base, and let q be a BCQ.

- FKB entails q under the *generalized ABox repair* (GAR) *semantics*, if, for all $KB' \in Rep(FKB)$, $KB' \models q$.
- FKB entails q under the *generalized intersection of repairs* (GIAR) *semantics*, if $(D^*, \Sigma^*) \models q$, where $D^* = \bigcap\{D' \mid (D', \Sigma') \in Rep(FKB)\}$ and $\Sigma^* = \bigcap\{\Sigma' \mid (D', \Sigma') \in Rep(FKB)\}$.

	Data	*fp*-comb.	*ba*-comb.	Comb.
$\mathsf{L}_\bot, \mathsf{LF}_\bot, \mathsf{AF}_\bot$	in AC^{0+}	NP	Π_2^p	PSPACE
$\mathsf{S}_\bot, \mathsf{SF}_\bot$	in AC^{0+}	NP	Π_2^p	EXP
$\mathsf{F}_\bot, \mathsf{GF}_\bot$	co-NP	Θ_2^{P}	Π_2^p	EXP
$\mathsf{G}_\bot$	co-NP$^+$	Θ_2^{P}	EXP	2EXP
$\mathsf{A}_\bot$	in $\text{AC}^{0\star}$	NP	P^{NEXP}	P^{NEXP}
$\mathsf{WS}_\bot, \mathsf{WA}_\bot$	co-NP$^+$	Θ_2^{P}	2EXP	2EXP
$\mathsf{WG}_\bot$	EXP	EXP	EXP	2EXP

	Data	*fp*-comb.	*ba*-comb.	Comb.
$\mathsf{L}_\bot, \mathsf{LF}_\bot, \mathsf{AF}_\bot$	co-NP$^+$	Θ_2^{P}	Π_2^p	PSPACE
$\mathsf{S}_\bot, \mathsf{SF}_\bot$	co-NP$^+$	Θ_2^{P}	Π_2^p	EXP
$\mathsf{F}_\bot, \mathsf{GF}_\bot$	co-NP	Θ_2^{P}	Π_2^p	EXP
$\mathsf{G}_\bot$	co-NP$^+$	Θ_2^{P}	EXP	2EXP
$\mathsf{A}_\bot$	co-NP	Θ_2^{P}	P^{NEXP}	P^{NEXP}
$\mathsf{WS}_\bot, \mathsf{WA}_\bot$	co-NP$^+$	Θ_2^{P}	2EXP	2EXP
$\mathsf{WG}_\bot$	EXP	EXP	EXP	2EXP

Fig. 1. Complexity of *IAR* and *GIAR* (left) and of *ICR* and *GICR* (right) BCQ answering; all entries without "in" are completeness results. $^+$[19] for $\mathsf{L}_\bot$, $\mathsf{S}_\bot$, $\mathsf{G}_\bot$, $\mathsf{WS}_\bot$, and $\mathsf{WA}_\bot$. *[18].

- *FKB* entails q under the *generalized intersection of closed repairs* (GICR) *semantics*, if $(D_I, \Sigma^*) \models q$, where $D_I = \bigcap\{Cn(KB') \mid KB' \in Rep(FKB)\}$ and $\Sigma^* = \bigcap\{\Sigma' \mid (D', \Sigma') \in Rep(FKB)\}$.

In the definition above, observe that if *FKB* is a standard knowledge base, then $\Sigma^* = \Sigma$, and thus the definition above generalizes the AR, IAR, and ICR semantics for standard knowledge bases to the case of flexible knowledge bases. We talk of BCQ answering under the GAR, GIAR, and GICR semantics when flexible knowledge bases can be arbitrary, and we talk of BCQ answering under the AR, IAR, and ICR semantics when flexible knowledge bases model standard knowledge bases (i.e., $D_h = \emptyset$ and $\Sigma_s = \emptyset$).

4 Complexity Results

We give a precise picture of the complexity of BCQ answering from existential rules under the *IAR*, *ICR*, *GIAR*, and *GICR* semantics, which is summarized in Fig. 1.

4.1 Membership Results

IAR semantics. The following theorem proves all upper bounds equal to and above co-NP in Fig. 1, left side, excluding the Θ_2^{P} memberships.

Theorem 1. *If BCQ answering from databases under programs over some Datalog*$^\pm$ *language* L *is in* **C** *in the data (resp., fp-combined, ba-combined, and combined) complexity, then* IAR*-BCQ answering from databases under programs over* L *is in* co-$\text{NP}^{\mathbf{C}}$ *in the data (resp., fp-combined, ba-combined, and combined) complexity.*

Consider now the Datalog$^\pm$ fragments whose BCQ answering in the data complexity is in AC^0, i.e., $\mathsf{L}_\bot$, $\mathsf{S}_\bot$, $\mathsf{A}_\bot$, $\mathsf{LF}_\bot$, $\mathsf{AF}_\bot$, and $\mathsf{SF}_\bot$. In such cases, the following theorem states the upper bound in the *fp*-combined complexity.

Theorem 2. IAR*-BCQ answering for* $\mathsf{L}_\bot$*,* $\mathsf{S}_\bot$*, and* $\mathsf{A}_\bot$ *(and* $\mathsf{LF}_\bot$*,* $\mathsf{AF}_\bot$*, and* $\mathsf{SF}_\bot$*) is in* NP *in the fp-combined complexity.*

The following theorem proves all Θ_2^{P} upper bounds in Fig. 1, left side.

Theorem 3. IAR*-BCQ answering for* $\mathsf{WS}_\bot$ *and* $\mathsf{G}_\bot$ *(and* $\mathsf{WA}_\bot$*,* $\mathsf{F}_\bot$*, and* $\mathsf{GF}_\bot$*) is in* Θ_2^{P} *in the fp-combined complexity.*

ICR semantics. The following theorem proves all upper bounds in Fig. 1, right side, including the $\text{P}^{\text{NEXP}} = \text{co-NP}^{\text{NEXP}}$ membership for $\mathsf{A}_\perp$, excluding memberships in Θ_2^{P} and the combined complexity.

Theorem 4. *If BCQ answering from databases under programs over some Datalog$^\pm$ language L is in $\mathbf{C}$ in the data (resp., fp- and ba-combined) complexity, then ICR-BCQ answering from databases under programs over L is in* $\text{co-NP}^{\mathbf{C}}$ *in the data (resp., fp- and ba-combined) complexity.*

BCQ answering under the ICR semantics for all the considered Datalog$^\pm$ fragments but $\mathsf{WG}_\perp$ is in Θ_2^{P} in the *fp*-combined complexity.

Theorem 5. *ICR-BCQ answering for all the considered Datalog$^\pm$ fragments but* $\mathsf{WG}_\perp$ *is in Θ_2^{P} in the fp-combined complexity.*

As for the combined complexity, we get the following theorem.

Theorem 6. *If BCQ answering from databases under programs over some Datalog$^\pm$ language L is in the deterministic complexity class $\mathbf{C}$ in the combined complexity, then ICR-BCQ answering from databases under programs over L is in* $\text{PSPACE} \cdot \mathbf{C}$ *in the combined complexity.*

The membership results above can be extended to the generalized semantics case [15].

4.2 Hardness Results

As BCQ answering under the IAR and ICR semantics for Datalog$^\pm$ fragments L coincides with BCQ answering for L when there are no inconsistencies, we immediately obtain hardness for all NP, PSPACE, EXP, and 2EXP entries in Fig. 1.

IAR semantics. Hardness for co-NP of BCQ answering under the IAR semantics in the data complexity is shown by a reduction from deciding unsatisfiability of 3CNF formulas (UNSAT). It produces a knowledge base with a fixed $\mathsf{GF}_\perp$ program and fixed query. This proves all open co-NP-hardness results in Fig. 1, left side.

Theorem 7. *IAR-BCQ answering for* $\mathsf{GF}_\perp$ *(and* $\mathsf{F}_\perp$*) is* co-NP*-hard in the data complexity.*

We can show that IAR-BCQ answering for $\mathsf{A}_\perp$ is P^{NEXP}-hard in the *ba*-combined complexity, proving all P^{NEXP}-hardness results in Fig. 1, left side. Intuitively, the reduction for the P^{NEXP}-hardness proof in [8] for AR-BCQ answering for $\mathsf{A}_\perp$ in the *ba*-combined complexity is turned into a P^{NEXP}-hardness proof for IAR-BCQ answering in this case.

Theorem 8. *IAR-BCQ answering for* $\mathsf{A}_\perp$ *is* P^{NEXP}*-hard in the ba-combined complexity.*

BCQ answering under IAR semantics for $\mathsf{GF}_\perp$ (and thus also for $\mathsf{F}_\perp$, $\mathsf{G}_\perp$, $\mathsf{WA}_\perp$, and $\mathsf{WS}_\perp$) in the *fp*-combined complexity can be shown to be Θ_2^{P}-hard via a reduction from the Θ_2^{P}-complete problem COMP-SAT: Given two sets A and B of Boolean formulas, decide whether A contains more satisfiable formulas than B [13,14].

Theorem 9. *IAR-BCQ answering for* $\mathsf{GF}_\perp$ *(and* $\mathsf{F}_\perp$, $\mathsf{G}_\perp$, $\mathsf{WA}_\perp$, *and* $\mathsf{WS}_\perp$*) is* Θ_2^{P}-hard *in the fp-combined complexity.*

ICR semantics. ICR-BCQ answering in the data complexity is co-NP-hard by a reduction from UNSAT. This proves all open CO-NP-hardness results in Fig. 1, right side.

Theorem 10. *ICR-BCQ answering for* $\mathsf{LF}_\bot$, $\mathsf{AF}_\bot$, *and* $\mathsf{SF}_\bot$ *(and* $\mathsf{GF}_\bot$, $\mathsf{F}_\bot$, *and* $\mathsf{A}_\bot$*) is* CO-NP*-hard in the data complexity.*

BCQ answering under ICR semantics is Θ_2^{P}-hard in the *fp*-combined complexity, by a reduction from COMP-SAT, for all remaining entries in Fig. 1, right side, but for $\mathsf{WG}_\bot$.

Theorem 11. *ICR-BCQ answering in the fp-combined complexity is* Θ_2^{P}-hard *for all the considered Datalog*$^\pm$ *fragments.*

BCQ answering under the ICR semantics for $\mathsf{AF}_\bot$ (and thus also for $\mathsf{F}_\bot$) is Π_2^{P}-hard in the ba-combined complexity, by a reduction from $NQBF_{2,\forall}$, which is a variant of quantified Boolean formulas with two quantifiers starting with a universal one [10,21].

Theorem 12. *ICR-BCQ answering is* Π_2^{P}-hard *in the ba-combined complexity for* $\mathsf{AF}_\bot$ *(and* $\mathsf{F}_\bot$*).*

The following result shows that ICR-BCQ answering for $\mathsf{A}_\bot$ is $\mathrm{P}^{\mathrm{NEXP}}$-hard in the ba-combined complexity, proving all $\mathrm{P}^{\mathrm{NEXP}}$-hardness results in Fig. 1, right side.

Theorem 13. *ICR-BCQ answering for* $\mathsf{A}_\bot$ *is* $\mathrm{P}^{\mathrm{NEXP}}$*-hard in the ba-combined complexity.*

The following shows all Π_2^{P}-hardness results in Fig. 1, right side. The Π_2^{P}-hardness results in Fig. 1, left side, are proved similarly.

Theorem 14. *ICR-BCQ answering for* $\mathsf{L}_\bot$, $\mathsf{LF}_\bot$, $\mathsf{AF}_\bot$, $\mathsf{S}_\bot$, $\mathsf{SF}_\bot$, $\mathsf{F}_\bot$, *and* $\mathsf{GF}_\bot$ *is* Π_2^{P}*-hard in the ba-combined complexity.*

Also for the hardness results, it is possible to show that they extend to the generalized semantics case [15].

5 Summary and Outlook

We have given a precise picture of the complexity of BCQ answering under different approximate inconsistency-tolerant semantics for the most popular Datalog$^\pm$ languages and complexity measures. In addition to the standard setting, we have also considered the more general setting where also ontological rules may be removed.

Future research lines include considering other classes of existential rules and to define other semantics for inconsistency-tolerant ontological query answering. Another interesting direction for future work is to carry out a complexity analysis of the local generalized semantics [8]. Also, a more fine-grained way to analyze the complexity of query answering would be a non-uniform approach, looking at the complexity of a single ontology or a single ontology-mediated query (see, e.g., [11]).

Acknowledgements. This work was supported by The Alan Turing Institute under the UK EPSRC grant EP/N510129/1, and by the EPSRC grants EP/R013667/1, EP/L012138/1, and EP/M025268/1.

References

1. Marcelo Arenas, Leopoldo E. Bertossi, and Jan Chomicki. Consistent query answers in inconsistent databases. In *Proc. PODS*, pages 68–79, 1999.
2. Meghyn Bienvenu. On the complexity of consistent query answering in the presence of simple ontologies. In *Proc. AAAI*, pages 705–711, 2012.
3. Meghyn Bienvenu, Camille Bourgaux, and François Goasdoué. Querying inconsistent description logic knowledge bases under preferred repair semantics. In *Proc. AAAI*, pages 996–1002, 2014.
4. Meghyn Bienvenu and Riccardo Rosati. Tractable approximations of consistent query answering for robust ontology-based data access. In *Proc. IJCAI*, pages 775–781, 2013.
5. Andrea Calì, Georg Gottlob, and Michael Kifer. Taming the infinite chase: Query answering under expressive relational constraints. *J. Artif. Intell. Res.*, 48:115–174, 2013.
6. Andrea Calì, Georg Gottlob, and Thomas Lukasiewicz. A general Datalog-based framework for tractable query answering over ontologies. *J. Web Sem.*, 14:57–83, 2012.
7. Andrea Calì, Georg Gottlob, and Andreas Pieris. Towards more expressive ontology languages: The query answering problem. *Artif. Intell.*, 193:87–128, 2012.
8. Thomas Eiter, Thomas Lukasiewicz, and Livia Predoiu. Generalized consistent query answering under existential rules. In *Proc. KR*, pages 359–368, 2016.
9. Ronald Fagin, Phokion G. Kolaitis, Renée J. Miller, and Lucian Popa. Data exchange: semantics and query answering. *Theor. Comput. Sci.*, 336(1):89–124, 2005.
10. Gianluigi Greco, Enrico Malizia, Luigi Palopoli, and Francesco Scarcello. On the complexity of core, kernel, and bargaining set. *Artificial Intelligence*, 175(12–13):1877–1910, 2011.
11. André Hernich, Carsten Lutz, Fabio Papacchini, and Frank Wolter. Dichotomies in ontology-mediated querying with the guarded fragment. In *Proc. PODS*, pages 185–199, 2017.
12. Domenico Lembo, Maurizio Lenzerini, Riccardo Rosati, Marco Ruzzi, and Domenico Fabio Savo. Inconsistency-tolerant semantics for description logics. In *Proc. RR*, pages 103–117, 2010.
13. Thomas Lukasiewicz and Enrico Malizia. On the complexity of mCP-nets. In *Proc. AAAI*, pages 558–564, 2016.
14. Thomas Lukasiewicz and Enrico Malizia. A novel characterization of the complexity class Θ_k^P based on counting and comparison. *Theor. Comput. Sci.*, 694:21–33, 2017.
15. Thomas Lukasiewicz, Enrico Malizia, and Cristian Molinaro. Complexity of approximate query answering under inconsistency in datalog+/-. In *International Joint Conference on Artificial Intelligence (IJCAI)*, pages 1921–1927, 2018.
16. Thomas Lukasiewicz, Maria Vanina Martinez, Andreas Pieris, and Gerardo I. Simari. From classical to consistent query answering under existential rules. In *Proc. AAAI*, pages 1546–1552, 2015.
17. Thomas Lukasiewicz, Maria Vanina Martinez, and Gerardo I. Simari. Inconsistency handling in Datalog+/– ontologies. In *Proc. ECAI*, pages 558–563, 2012.
18. Thomas Lukasiewicz, Maria Vanina Martinez, and Gerardo I. Simari. Inconsistency-tolerant query rewriting for linear Datalog+/–. In *Proc. Datalog 2.0*, pages 123–134, 2012.
19. Thomas Lukasiewicz, Maria Vanina Martinez, and Gerardo I. Simari. Complexity of inconsistency-tolerant query answering in Datalog+/–. In *Proc. OTM*, pages 488–500, 2013.
20. Riccardo Rosati. On the complexity of dealing with inconsistency in description logic ontologies. In *Proc. IJCAI*, pages 1057–1062, 2011.
21. Marcus Schaefer. Graph Ramsey theory and the polynomial hierarchy. *Journal of Computer and System Sciences*, 62(2):290–322, 2001.

Dependency-based Query Result Approximation
(extended abstract)

Loredana Caruccio, Vincenzo Deufemia, and Giuseppe Polese

Department of Computer Science, University of Salerno,
via Giovanni Paolo II n.132, 84084 Fisciano (SA), Italy
{lcaruccio,deufemia,gpolese}@unisa.it

Abstract. Failing queries are database queries returning few o no results. It might be useful reformulating them in order to retrieve results that are close to those intended with original queries. In this paper, we introduce an approach for rewriting failing queries that are in the disjunctive normal form. In particular, the approach prescribes to replace some of the attributes of the failing queries with attributes semantically related to them by means of Relaxed Functional Dependencies (RFDs), which can be automatically discovered from data. The semantics of automatically discovered RFDs allow us to rank them in a way to provide an application order during the query rewriting process. Experiments show that such application order of RFDs yields a ranking of the approximate query answers meeting the expectations of the user.

Keywords: query rewriting, query relaxation, relaxed functional dependencies

1 Introduction

A common problem in query processing is coping with failing queries, that is, queries returning few or no answers. To this end, several techniques have been proposed to relax queries in order to make them return also approximate answers, so as to broaden the answer set. Manually relaxing failing queries is a time-consuming task, and if the query is over-relaxed, prohibitive costs are paid in terms of bandwidth per returned tuple. Thus, researchers have proposed automated approaches to query relaxation [15, 17–19], but the existing algorithms have several limitations, mostly due to a poor knowledge about the characteristics of the database instance under examination. To this end, automatic data profiling techniques are becoming available [1], which are capable of providing useful metadata concerning the characteristics of a database instance, including data dependencies, domain cardinalities, data quality constraints, and so on. They can be exploited for several purposes, including optimizations related to

SEBD 2018, June 24-27, 2018, Castellaneta Marina, Italy.

query processing, such as the optimization of query executions, rewriting queries and views upon schema evolutions [8], and so on.

In this paper we describe an approach exploiting Relaxed Functional Dependencies (RFDs) [5] to relax the results of failing queries [7]. In order to explain our approach, in what follows we provide a running example, which will be used throughout the paper.

	Make	Model	Price ($)	Location	Year	Start Production Year	Color	Mileage	Length (mm)	Power (kw)	EngineCC	Torque (Nm)	Consumption (US mpg) Urban/Extra Urban/Combined	Fuel
1	Ford	Focus 1.6tdci	6500	Pittsburgh (PA)	2007	2004	Red	60000	4342	80	1560	260	37.97/58.78/49.04	Diesel
2	Mazda	3 td	8000	Denver (CO)	2009	2009	Gray	45000	4580	80	1560	240	44.38/60.28/53.45	Diesel
3	Ford	Focus 1.6tdci	11000	San Diego (CA)	2010	2010	Blue	15000	4337	85	1560	270	52.29/69.19/61.86	Diesel
4	Ford	Focus 1.6i 16V	3000	Austin (TX)	2005	2004	Blue	48000	4342	73.8	1596	150	21.56/38.55/30.14	Gasoline
5	Volkswagen	Golf 1.6tdi	12000	Las Vegas (NV)	2008	2008	Black	70000	4199	77	1598	250	41.30/60.28/52.29	Diesel
6	Ford	Focus 1.6tdci	12300	Seattle (WA)	2011	2010	Gray	8000	4337	85	1560	270	52.29/69.19/61.86	Diesel
7	Volkswagen	Golf 1.6tdi	14000	Miami (FL)	2009	2008	Gray	50000	4199	77	1598	250	41.30/60.28/52.29	Diesel
8	Toyota	Avensis 1.8 16V SW	6000	New Orleans (LU)	2005	2003	Red	38000	4700	95	1794	170	25.06/40.55/32.64	Gasoline
9	Ford	Focus 1.6tdci	5000	Chicago (IL)	2006	2004	White	66000	4342	80	1560	260	37.97/58.78/49.04	Diesel
10	Ford	Fiesta 1.4 16V	7000	Charleston (SC)	2009	2008	Black	27000	3950	71	1388	125	31.39/51.12/41.30	Gasoline

Table 1. A sample of the car selling database.

Example 1. Let us consider the car selling database `CarDealerDB` of Table 1. There are several usage scenarios for this database. For instance, a user might search cars available for sale or examine detailed characteristics of some specific models.

Suppose the user is looking for a Ford `Focus` with a price around 8000$. Then s/he might enter the following query:

$Q \equiv$ `Model like '%Focus%' AND Price >= 7500 AND Price <= 8500`

By executing it on the `CarDealerDB` no tuples will be returned. However, some similar cars might have characteristics close to the requested one. Such similarities cannot be taken into account by the query, since we assume that no function is available for evaluating the similarity of categorical attributes. To this end, the approach we propose in this paper exploits automatically discovered RFDs to rewrite queries so as to enable them generate also approximate results. The semantics of RFDs enable us to derive ranking techniques that can be used to decide the application order of RFDs during the query rewriting process. To this end, we also provide experimental results proving that such application order yields approximating query answers meeting the expectations of the final user.

The paper is organized as follows. Section 2 discusses the related work, while Section 3 presents background information on RFDs. Then, we describe our query rewriting approach in Section 4 and discuss its empirical evaluation in Section 5. Finally, Section 6 concludes the paper.

2 Related Work

Approximation in query answering has been extensively studied in the recent years. Most of the early efforts were devoted to reduce response time by seeking approximate query answers. Some techniques performed data summaries, statistics or histograms to compute approximate answers [20]. The Aqua system focusses on the fast generation of approximate results, in order to improve efficiency [2]. The work in [21] introduces the problem of approximate data exchange, aiming to produce fast approximate answers, and successively exact answers.

The AIMQ query relaxation method removes some constraints from the query based on approximate functional dependencies [19]. It learns the attribute importance based on pre-extracted data, ranking the relevant answer tuples by using the similarities between an imprecise query and answer tuples. The AQRR method [15] is similar to AIMQ, but it exploits user preferences for deriving the attribute importance and to evaluate similarities between an imprecise query and answer tuples.

Muslea proposed a method adopting machine learning to learn rules from the database [17]. In particular, for each failed query, it will find the most similar rule for generating alternative queries. The query relaxation method proposed in [18] trains the system beforehand on portion of the data. The focus is on queries with conjunctions or disjunctions of atoms and the relaxation procedure is based on bayesian networks, targeting the approximation of domain knowledge. The approach is data driven, but a similar service can be achieved by exploiting schema information, and in particular integrity constraints, which in turn can be used to inform the user about the query failing conditions [13]. The approach proposed in [11] focuses on how to explain non-answer queries by pinpointing the constraint causing the empty result. The approach proposed in [9] allows to modify the query based on the notion of generalization, identifying the conditions under which a generalization is applicable. Koudas *et al.* [14] suggest alternative queries based on the "minimal" shift from the original one.

ORange is a system automatically assisting the user in the process of query refinement, aiming to satisfy a specific cardinality constraint [3]. The system exploits a similarity-aware a query refinement schema, which is also able to maximize its similarity w.r.t. to the original range query.

Finally, the framework proposed in [16] is able to relax queries in an interactive fashion, based on a process aiming to optimize a wide variety of application-dependent objective functions. In particular, given an initial query returning an empty-answer set, the framework dynamically computes and suggests alternative queries with fewer conditions than those initially requested, in order to help the user derive a query with a non-empty-answer.

3 Relaxed Functional Dependencies

In this section we will review the definition of relaxed functional dependency (RFD).

Consider a relational database schema $\mathcal{R}$ defined over a set of attributes $attr(\mathcal{R})$, derived as the union of attributes from the relation schemas composing $\mathcal{R}$. For an instance r of $\mathcal{R}$ and a tuple $t \in r$, we use $t[A]$ to denote the projection of t onto A; similarly, for a set X of attributes in $attr(\mathcal{R})$, $t[X]$ denotes the projection of t onto X.

Definition 1. Functional Dependency (FD). *An* FD *over $\mathcal{R}$ is a statement $X \to Y$ (X implies Y), with $X, Y \subseteq attr(\mathcal{R})$, such that, given an instance r of $\mathcal{R}$, $X \to Y$ is satisfied in r if and only if for every pair of tuples (t_1, t_2) in r, whenever $t_1[X] = t_2[X]$, then $t_1[Y] = t_2[Y]$.*

In the last part of the FD definition, we notice that the projections of two tuples over a subset of attributes are compared by means of the equality function. This is one of the two dimensions that have been modified in order to define RFDs, by enabling the use of tuple comparisons based on a *similarity constraint*. The latter, defined as $\phi_{\leq\alpha}$, can be expressed in terms of a similarity metric $\approx$, such that $a{\approx}b$ is true if a and b are "close" enough w.r.t. a predefined threshold (α). Examples of similarity metrics are the edit or the Jaro distance [10].

Another important characteristic of the FD definition is that it specifies a property of the database schema that must hold on every instance of it. This is the second dimension that has been modified to derive a general definition of RFD, which admits the possibility that the property might hold for a subset rather than all the tuples. The latter can be formally specified by means of a *condition* filtering the tuples on which the dependency applies, or by means a *coverage measure*. Given a database instance r of $\mathcal{R}$, and two sets of attributes $X, Y \subseteq attr(\mathcal{R})$, representing the Left-Hand-Side (LHS) and Right-Hand-Side (RHS), resp., of an RFD φ, a coverage measure Ψ on φ quantifies the amount of tuples in r violating or satisfying φ. It can be defined as a function $\Psi : dom_X \times dom_Y \to \mathbb{R}$, where dom_A is the domain of attribute A. As an example, the *confidence measure* evaluates the maximum number of tuples $r_1 \subseteq r$ such that φ holds in r_1 [12].

In what follows, we provide a formal definition of RFD.

Definition 2. Relaxed Functional Dependency (RFD). *Consider a relational database schema $\mathcal{R}$, and a relation schema $R = (A_1, \ldots, A_k)$ of $\mathcal{R}$. An* RFD *φ on $\mathcal{R}$ is denoted by*

$$\mathbb{D}_c : X_{\Phi_1} \xrightarrow{\Psi \geq \epsilon} Y_{\Phi_2} \tag{1}$$

where

- $c = (c_1, \ldots, c_k)$ is the set of conditions constraining the domain $\mathbb{D}$ on which φ applies;
- $X, Y \subseteq attr(R)$ with $X \cap Y = \emptyset$;
- Φ_1 (Φ_2, resp.) is a set of similarity constraints $\phi[X]$ ($\phi[Y]$, resp.).
- Ψ is a coverage measure defined on $\mathbb{D}_c$.
- ϵ is a threshold indicating the bound for the result of the coverage measure.

Given $r \subseteq \mathbb{D}_c$ a relation instance on R, r *satisfies* the RFD φ, denoted by $r \models \varphi$, if and only if: $\forall\ t_1, t_2 \in r$, if $\phi[X]$ indicates true for each constraint $\phi \in \Phi_1$, then *almost always* $\phi[Y]$ indicates true for each constraint $\phi \in \Phi_2$. Here, *almost always* means that $\Psi(\pi_X(r), \pi_Y(r)) \geq \epsilon$.

In other words, if $t_1[X]$ and $t_2[X]$ agree with the constraints specified by Φ_1, then $t_1[Y]$ and $t_2[Y]$ agree with the constraints specified by Φ_2 with a degree of certainty (measured by Ψ) greater than ϵ.

As an example, in a database of scientific publications it is likely to have the same address and affiliation for authors with the same name. Thus, an FD {Author} → {Address, Affiliation} might hold. However, these attributes might have been stored using different abbreviations. Thus, the following RFD might hold:

$$\mathbb{D}_{\text{TRUE}} : \mathsf{Author}_{\approx} \xrightarrow{\Psi_{err(0)}} \{\mathsf{Address}_{\approx}, \mathsf{Affiliation}_{\approx}\}$$

where $\approx$ is a string similarity function, and $\Psi_{err(0)}$ corresponds to the expression $\psi(X, Y) = 0$, where $\psi(X, Y)$ measures the number of tuples violating the RFD. However, authors might change affiliation during their life, or there might be homonimies, possibly caused by first name abbreviations. As a consequence, the previous RFD should tolerate possible exceptions. This can be modeled by introducing a different coverage measure into the RFD, making it conditional:

$$\mathbb{D}_{\text{TRUE}} : \mathsf{Author}_{\approx} \xrightarrow{\psi(Author, Address, Affiliation) \leq 0.02} \{\mathsf{Address}_{\approx}, \mathsf{Affiliation}_{\approx}\}$$

4 Methodology

Let us consider the car selling database (`CarDealerDB`) shown in Table 1. Among several usage scenarios for this database, let us consider one in which a user might search cars available for sale or examine detailed features for some specific car models. In particular, suppose the user is looking for a Ford `Focus` with a price around 8000$. Then s/he might enter the following query:

$Q \equiv$ `Model like '%Focus%' AND Price >= 7500 AND Price <= 8500`

By executing this query on `CarDealerDB` no tuples will be returned as result. However, some cars close to the query request might be returned, if we were capable of evaluating the similarity of categorical attributes. To this end, we propose an approach exploiting RFDs, in order to rewrite a query so as to enable it generate approximated results. The rewriting process consists in replacing attributes instantiated in the query with those related to them by means of RFDs. As an example, let us assume that the RFD

$$\mathbb{D}_{\text{TRUE}} : \mathsf{Model}_{\approx_t} \xrightarrow{\psi(Model, Length) \leq 0.1} \mathsf{Length}_{\approx_n}$$

holds on `CarDealerDB`, where $\approx_t$ and $\approx_n$ are proper text and numerical similarity functions, respectively. The RFD says that in 90% of cases, cars with similar models (categorical attribute) must have similar length (numeric attribute). We can therefore infer that, cars whose `Length` is similar to the `Focus` one are more suitable to be returned as result.

More generally, let us suppose that a query Q has a condition $X\ OP\ x$, where OP is a comparison operator, and the following RFD holds on the underlying database:

$$\mathbb{D}_{\text{TRUE}} : \mathsf{X}_{\approx_f} \xrightarrow{\psi(X,Y) \leq \epsilon} \mathsf{Y}_{\approx_g}$$

then we might rewrite Q in Q_1 OR ... OR Q_m, where Q_i is obtained from Q by replacing the condition $X\ OP\ x$ with a condition $Y \approx_g y_i$, where y_i is the value of Y for a tuple in which $X\ OP\ x$. Such process can be better formalized by using similarity subsets generated by inference algorithms for RFDs [6].

From the example in Table 1 it follows that cars with `Model like '%Focus%'` satisfy either `Length = 4337` or `Length = 4342`. Thus, Q can be rewritten into Q_1 OR Q_2, where:

$Q_1 \equiv$ `Length`$\geq$ `4337`$-\varepsilon_i$ `AND Length` $\leq$ `4337`$+\varepsilon_i$ `AND Price` $\geq$ `7500 AND Price` $\leq$ `8500`
$Q_2 \equiv$ `Length`$\geq$ `4342`$-\varepsilon_i$ `AND Length` $\leq$ `4342`$+\varepsilon_i$ `AND Price` $\geq$ `7500 AND Price` $\leq$ `8500`

When computing Q_1 and Q_2 for $\varepsilon_i = 250$, we get the tuple t_2 as result, which corresponds to a Mazda 3, since its Length is similar to the one of Focus, and the Price matches the one of the original query.

It is worth to note that the attribute X of the query Q can also be a portion of the LHS of some RFDs, e.g.,

$$\mathbb{D}_{\text{TRUE}} : \mathsf{A}_{\approx_{f_1}} \mathsf{X}_{\approx_{f_2}} \mathsf{B}_{\approx_{f_3}} \xrightarrow{\psi(A,X,B,Y)\leq\epsilon} \mathsf{Y}_{\approx_g}$$

In this case, supposing that A, B, Y are textual attributes, we relax Q by replacing $X\ OP\ x$ with a condition "($Y \approx_g y_1$ AND $A \approx_{f_1} a_1$ AND $B \approx_{f_3} b_1$) OR ... OR ($Y \approx_g y_n$ AND $A \approx_{f_1} a_n$ AND $B \approx_{f_3} b_n$)", where y_i is the value of Y for a tuple in which $X\ OP\ x$, $A\ OP\ a_i$, and $B\ OP\ b_i$. Thus, we do not consider the whole $Y \approx_g y$ category, but its subset consisting of the tuples having the values for A and B similar to one of the tuples where $X\ OP\ x$. For instance, since the following dependency

$$\mathbb{D}_{\text{TRUE}} : \mathsf{Model}_{\approx_{f_1}} \mathsf{Power}_{\approx_{f_2}} \mathsf{EngineCC}_{\approx_{f_3}} \xrightarrow{\psi(X,Y)\leq 0.05} \mathsf{Torque}_{\approx_g}$$

holds on the `CarDealearDB`, we can relax the condition `Model like '%Focus%'` with
((`Torque` $\geq$ `240` AND `Torque` $\leq$ `280`) AND (`EngineCC` $\geq$ `1530` AND `EngineCC` $\leq$ `1590`) AND (`Power` $\geq$ `75` AND `Power` $\leq$ `85`)) OR
((`Torque` $\geq$ `250` AND `Torque` $\leq$ `290`) AND (`EngineCC` $\geq$ `1530` AND `EngineCC` $\leq$ `1590`) AND (`Power` $\geq$ `80` AND `Power` $\leq$ `90`)) OR
((`Torque` $\geq$ `130` AND `Torque` $\leq$ `170`) AND (`EngineCC` $\geq$ `1566` AND `EngineCC` $\leq$ `1626`) AND (`Power` $\geq$ `68.8` AND `Power` $\leq$ `78.8`)).

However, in practice the rewriting process of the query might be accomplished according to different RFDs. Hence, we need to establish a priority in the application of the different RFDs during the relaxation process, so as to meet user preferences. To this end, we found out that current RFD discovery algorithms rank the extracted RFDs based on the coverage and similarity thresholds [6], and only extract non-trivial RFDs, discarding redundant ones. Thus, by following the same ranking order used in RFD discovery algorithms, we naturally meet user preferences, since it is expected that the user would prefer relaxing queries by first using RFDs with high coverage and high similarities.

Datasets	Precision	Recall
Breast-Cancer	0.85	0.92
Hepatitis	0.81	0.89
Lymphography	0.82	0.93

Table 2. Precision and recall obtained for the considered datasets.

5 Experimental Results

We evaluated the proposed approach on three different datasets. In particular, we considered the Breast-cancer, the Hepatitis, and the Lymphography datasets drawn from the UC Irvine Machine Learning repository [4].

In order to evaluate the performances of the proposed approach, we have defined 5 failing queries for each considered dataset. Successively, we have requested a domain expert to analyze the datasets and the queries in order to identify the ten tuples most similar to the target result of each query (ground truth). Finally, we have (*i*) applied the proposed approach to rewrite the five failing queries, (*ii*) run them on the considered dataset, and (*iii*) compared their results to the ground truth.

We measured the effectiveness of the proposed approach with precision and recall. Let A be the set of tuples obtained from the queries generated by the proposed approach and B the ground truth identified by the expert. Then, we computed the *precision* as $|A \cap B|/|A|$, while *recall* as $|A \cap B|/|B|$ [22]. The results of precision and recall for each dataset are shown in Table 2.

As we notice, we obtained high values for both measures, especially the recall. We can observe that the number of RFDs impacts on the quality of the resulting queries. This is due to the fact that ranking strategies used in current RFD discovery algorithms suffer from some noise when the datasets contain many RFDs.

6 Conclusions and Future Work

We have described an approach for rewriting failing queries that are in disjunctive normal form [7]. It relies on RFDs, which capture important constraints among attributes. Automatically extracted RFDs provide parameters enabling us to derive the priority by which they should be applied during the query relaxation process. We have experimentally verified that such priorities meet user expectations in terms of query results.

In the future we plan to define new ranking strategies for RFDs, in order to better refine their application order, and to further improve the performances of the proposed query rewriting technique. Moreover, we are currently investigating further query rewriting rules exploiting additional semantic properties of RFDs.

References

1. Abedjan, Z., Golab, L., Naumann, F.: Profiling relational data: a survey. The VLDB Journal **24**(4), 557–581 (2015)
2. Acharya, S., Gibbons, P.B., Poosala, V., Ramaswamy, S.: The Aqua approximate query answering system. In: SIGMOD. pp. 574–576 (1999)
3. Albarrak, A., Noboa, T., Khan, H.A., Sharaf, M.A., Zhou, X., Sadiq, S.: ORange: Objective-aware range query refinement. In: MDM. pp. 333–336 (2014)
4. Blake, C.L., Merz, C.J.: UCI repository of machine learning databases (1998), `http://www.ics.uci.edu/mlearn/MLRepository.html`
5. Caruccio, L., Deufemia, V., Polese, G.: Relaxed functional dependencies – A survey of approaches. IEEE TKDE **28**(1), 147–165 (2016)
6. Caruccio, L., Deufemia, V., Polese, G.: On the discovery of relaxed functional dependencies. In: IDEAS. pp. 53–61 (2016)
7. Caruccio, L., Deufemia, V., Polese, G.: Learning effective query management strategies from big data. In: ICMLA. pp. 643–648 (2017)
8. Caruccio, L., Polese, G., Tortora, G.: Synchronization of queries and views upon schema evolutions: A survey. ACM TODS **41**(2), 9:1–9:41 (2016)
9. Chaudhuri, S.: Generalization and a framework for query modification. In: ICDE. pp. 138–145 (1990)
10. Elmagarmid, A.K., Ipeirotis, P.G., Verykios, V.S.: Duplicate record detection: A survey. IEEE TKDE **19**(1), 1–16 (2007)
11. Huang, J., Chen, T., Doan, A., Naughton, J.F.: On the provenance of non-answers to queries over extracted data. In: PVLDB. pp. 736–747 (2008)
12. Huhtala, Y., Kärkkäinen, J., Porkka, P., Toivonen, H.: TANE: An efficient algorithm for discovering functional and approximate dependencies. The Computer Journal **42**(2), 100–111 (1999)
13. Janas, J.M.: On the feasibility of informative answers. In: Advances in Data Base Theory, pp. 397–414. Springer (1981)
14. Koudas, N., Li, C., Tung, A.K.H., Vernica, R.: Relaxing join and selection queries. In: VLDB. pp. 199–210 (2006)
15. Meng, X., Ma, Z.M., Yan, L.: Answering approximate queries over autonomous web databases. In: WWW. pp. 1021–1030 (2009)
16. Mottin, D., Marascu, A., Roy, S.B., Das, G., Palpanas, T., Velegrakis, Y.: A holistic and principled approach for the empty-answer problem. The VLDB Journal **25**(4), 597–622 (2016)
17. Muslea, I.: Machine learning for online query relaxation. In: KDD. pp. 246–255 (2004)
18. Muslea, I., Lee, T.: Online query relaxation via bayesian causal structures discovery. In: AAAI. pp. 831–836 (2005)
19. Nambiar, U., Kambhampati, S.: Mining approximate functional dependencies and concept similarities to answer imprecise queries. In: WebDB. pp. 73–78 (2004)
20. Poosala, V., Ganti, V.: Fast approximate query answering using precomputed statistics. In: ICDE. p. 252 (1999)
21. de Rougemont, M., Vieilleribiére, A.: Approximate data exchange. In: ICDT. pp. 44–58 (2007)
22. Salton, G.: Introduction to Modern Information Retrieval. McGraw-Hill (1983)

From Hypertree Width to Submodular Width and Data-dependent Structural Decompositions

Francesco Scarcello

DIMES, University of Calabria, 87036, Rende, Italy
scarcello@dimes.unical.it

Abstract. Identifying the frontier of tractability for conjunctive queries is a long-standing question in database theory. Recent advances in structural decomposition methods provide an important answer regarding the fixed-parameter tractability of conjunctive queries, and efficient algorithms based on decomposition methods have been implemented in database management systems. The paper shows that these techniques are useful not only for long and complex queries, but even for short and simple ones. Moreover, it sheds some light on some subtle issues that are not completely understood yet, and discuss open problems, such as the gap remaining between the theoretical fixed-parameter polynomial-time upper-bound and the running times required by actual algorithms used in practice.

1 Introduction

Conjunctive queries are defined through conjunctions of atoms (without negation), and are known to be equivalent to Select-Project-Join queries. The problem of evaluating such queries is NP-hard in general, but it is feasible in polynomial time on the class of acyclic queries (we omit "conjunctive," hereafter), which was the subject of many seminal research works since the early ages of database theory This class contains all queries Q whose associated query hypergraph $\mathcal{H}_Q$ is acyclic, where $\mathcal{H}_Q$ is a hypergraph having the variables of Q as its nodes, and the (sets of variables occurring in the) atoms of Q as its hyperedges.

In fact, queries arising from real applications are hardly precisely acyclic. Yet, they are often not very intricate and, in fact, tend to exhibit some limited degree of cyclicity, which suffices to retain most of the nice properties of acyclic ones. Therefore, several efforts have been spent to investigate invariants that are best suited to identify nearly-acyclic hypergraphs, leading to the definition of a number of so-called *(purely) structural decomposition-methods* [12,9], such as the *tree decompositions* [20] and, after some years, the *(generalized) hypertree* [7,8], *fractional hypertree* [15], *component hypertree* [11], and *greedy hypertree* [14,13] decompositions. These methods aim at transforming a given cyclic hypergraph into an acyclic one, by organising its edges (or its nodes) into a polynomial number of clusters, and by suitably arranging these clusters as a tree, called decomposition tree. The original problem instance can then be evaluated over such a tree of subproblems (in our case, subqueries), with a cost that is exponential with respect to a measure of the complexity of the subproblems, also called *width* of

SEBD 2018, June 24-27, 2018, Castellaneta Marina, Italy.

the decomposition, and polynomial if this width is bounded by some constant. For instance, according to the treewidth notion, the width of a decomposition is given by the maximum cardinality (minus one) of the set of variables occurring in the subqueries associated with the vertices of the decomposition tree. The (generalized) hypertree width considers instead the number of atoms occurring in each subproblem, in other terms, the number of hyperedges needed to cover the relevant variables in each vertex of the decomposition tree. The fractional hypertree width [15] is similar, but it is based on a fractional cover of such variables, instead of an integral one, as in the case of (plain) hypertree decompositions.

Besides the theoretical guarantees on the cost of evaluating class of queries having bounded (fractional) hypertree width, experimental evidence of the benefits gained from these structural decomposition methods in query optimization (and in the equivalent Constraint Satisfaction Problem) has been provided in the literature by a number of different authors and in different application domains, see, e.g., [5,6,1].

A yet more general width-concept is the *submodular width* [19], where the cost of a decomposition is determined by the worst possible submodular function of sets of variables of the given hypergraph. Recall that a set function f is submodular if, for every element x and any pair of sets S and T with $S \subseteq T$ and $x \notin T$, $f(S \cup \{x\}) - f(S) \geq f(T \cup \{x\}) - f(T)$ holds. That is, the marginal contribution of any element decreases when sets become larger. This powerful notion is strictly more general than all previous techniques, as there are classes of hypergraphs having bounded submodular width, but unbounded fractional hypertree width. However, having bounded submodular width (smw) does not guarantee a polynomial-time combined complexity as for hypertree decompositions, but just fixed-parameter tractability where the query hypergraph is used as a parameter. This means that we have a polynomial-time data complexity of the form $O(f_1(\mathcal{H}_Q) \cdot |\text{DB}|^{f_2(\text{smw})})$, where f_1 is an exponential function of the query size. Marx also proved that having bounded smw is in fact a necessary condition for the fixed-parameter tractability of conjunctive queries (unless the Exponential Time Hypothesis fails) [19]. Unfortunately, it is not clear how to recognise queries of bounded submodular width. It is worthwhile noting that, unlike the previous methods, the decompositions used to answer the query depend not only on the hypergraph $\mathcal{H}_Q$, but on the actual database DB, too. Nevertheless, the submodular width of $\mathcal{H}_Q$ depends only on $\mathcal{H}_Q$, which makes it an actual structural measure.

The primary aim of the paper is to shed light on the recent achievement in structural decomposition methods, in particular

- to make clear why the powerful notion of fractional hypertree width is not able to catch the precise complexity of a given query;
- to show, by using the case study of queries whose hypergraphs are simple cycles, that using data-dependent decompositions, as in the case of submodular width, provides better upper bounds on the cost of queries, and effective algorithms;
- to make evident that the benefits of such sophisticated notions occur not only in long and complex queries, but even in short and simple ones, occurring in most real-world applications;
- to give a hint of what is the submodular width of a query, and a hint of the problems that are still open in this area of research.

2 Hypertree decompositions and the AGM bound

Let $\mathcal{H}$ a hypergraph, and denote the set of its nodes by $nodes(\mathcal{H})$ and the set of its hyperedges by $edges(\mathcal{H})$. Formally, a *tree decomposition* [20] of $\mathcal{H}$ is a pair $\langle T, \chi \rangle$, where $T = (V, F)$ is a tree, and χ is a labelling function assigning to each vertex $p \in V$ a set of vertices $\chi(p) \subseteq nodes(\mathcal{H})$, such that the following three conditions are satisfied: (1) for each node b of $\mathcal{H}$, there exists $p \in V$ such that $b \in \chi(p)$; (2) for each hyperedge $h \in edges(\mathcal{H})$, there exists $p \in V$ such that $h \subseteq \chi(p)$; and (3) for each node b in $nodes(\mathcal{H})$, the set $\{p \in V \mid b \in \chi(p)\}$ induces a connected subtree of T. The *width* of $\langle T, \chi \rangle$ is the number $\max_{p \in V}(|\chi(p)| - 1)$. The *treewidth* of $\mathcal{H}$, denoted by $tw(\mathcal{H})$, is the minimum width over all its tree decompositions.

Hypertree Decompositions A *generalized hypertree decomposition* of a hypergraph $\mathcal{H}$ is a triple $HD = \langle T, \chi, \lambda \rangle$, called a *hypertree* for $\mathcal{H}$, where $\langle T, \chi \rangle$ is a tree decomposition of $\mathcal{H}$, and λ is a function labelling the vertices of T by sets of hyperedges of $\mathcal{H}$ such that, for each vertex p of T, $\chi(p) \subseteq \bigcup_{h \in \lambda(v)} h$. That is, all nodes in the χ labelling are covered by hyperedges in the λ labelling.

Consider a generalized hypertree decomposition HD=$\langle T, \chi, \lambda \rangle$. The cyclicity measure used in standard generalized hypertree decompositions, called generalized hypertree width and denoted by $ghw(\mathcal{H})$, is based on the cardinality of the set $\lambda(p)$ in charge of covering $\chi(p)$, for each vertex p of the decomposition tree. Contrasted with the treewidth, which is based on the cardinality of $\chi(p)$, it is clear that $ghw(\mathcal{H}) \leq tw(\mathcal{H})$ always holds. It has been observed that more general notions can be obtained by allowing the use of more general functions $f_{HD}(\cdot)$, to measure the weight $f_{HD}(p)$ of any vertex of T, and hence to define the width of a hypertree decomposition.

A *fractional hypertree decomposition* [15] of a hypergraph $\mathcal{H}$ is a pair $FHD = \langle HD, \gamma \rangle$, where $HD = \langle T, \chi, \lambda \rangle$ is a generalized hypertree decomposition of $\mathcal{H}$, and γ is a mapping associating each vertex p of T with a function $\gamma_p : \lambda(p) \mapsto \mathbb{R}$ mapping hyperedges to non-negative real numbers. For each vertex p in T, γ_p encodes a *fractional cover* of the nodes in $\chi(p)$: for each $v \in \chi(p)$, $\sum_{h \in \lambda(p), v \in h} \gamma_p(h) \geq 1$. Define $\rho(p) = \sum_{h \in \lambda(p)} \gamma_p(h)$. The *width* of FHD is the maximum of $\rho(p)$ over all vertices p in T. The *fractional hypertree width* of $\mathcal{H}$, denoted by $fhw(\mathcal{H})$, is the minimum width over all its fractional hypertree decompositions.[2]

Generalized hypertree width is obtained if in the definition of fractional hypertree decomposition we restrict the codomain of each γ_p to be integral. It is thus not surprising that there are hypergraphs where the fractional hypertree width is smaller than the (generalized) hypertree width.

The additional power of fractional covers in the decomposition vertices makes the problem intractable, in general. Indeed, for a given hypergraph $\mathcal{H}$ and for any fixed $w \geq 2$, computing a hypertree decomposition of width at most w (if any) is feasible in polynomial-time, while checking whether $\mathcal{H}$ has fractional hypertree width at most w is NP-hard [4]. However, there is a polynomial-time algorithm for deciding whether the fractional hypertree width is $f(w)$ for a function f in $O(w^3)$ [18].

[2] The equivalent (original) definition in [15] does not use the λ-labeling, so that γ_p weighs all hyperedges. Our definition is used, e.g., in [1].

Query evaluation Queries whose (fractional) hypertree width is bounded by some constant k can be answered in polynomial time. Given a query Q and a hypertree decomposition HD for the query hypergraph $\mathcal{H}_Q$, the query can be transformed into an acyclic query, based on the decomposition HD. Each vertex of the decomposition tree can be viewed as a subproblem to be solved: in our database context, such a vertex p is associated with a subquery Q_p whose atoms are the atoms in $\lambda(p)$, and whose set of output variables is $\chi(p)$. By computing the answers of these subqueries, we obtain an acyclic query equivalent to Q that can be evaluated easily, by standard techniques. Equivalently, we can see this transformation as a query plan for Q (where some atoms can appear multiple times with different projections, if necessary). The crucial observation here is that the maximum number of answers of the subquery Q_p associated with each vertex p is at most $|r_p|^{\rho(p)}$, where r_p is the largest database relation associated with the hyperedges in $\lambda(p)$ [15,3]. Moreover, such answers can be efficiently computed within this upper bound [1].

Tight Bounds The so-called AGM bound [3] states that, in fact, the upper bound on the number of solutions at each subproblem Q_p provided by the best fractional cover ρ^* is tight: there exists some database DB such that the number of answers of Q_p over this database meets the fractional cover upper bound. This result has been refined in [10], where a bound based on the so-called *coloring number* $C(Q_p)$ of such a query is defined, in order to take into account the output variables, as well as certain kinds of functional dependencies.

It follows that, whenever the fractional hypertree width of a query Q is w, and we have any fractional hypertree decomposition of width w, there always exists a database DB such that evaluating the subproblem Q_p at some vertex p of the decomposition tree requires $\Omega(N^w)$ time, where N is the size of the largest relation occurring in Q_p. Yet, from the results based on the submodular width, it turns out that we could do much better. How is that possible?

3 When worst cases are unachievable

In this section, we show that fractional hypertree decompositions do not provide a tight bound on the cost of evaluating conjunctive queries. This is not very clear, at a first sight, because of the results mentioned in the previous section. However, we see that even in very simple queries the worst cases predicted by fractional hypertree width are impossible to achieve.

Let us start with a hint of what happens. Consider a conjunctive query q with an associated hypergraph $\mathcal{H}_q$ having $\mathit{fhw}(\mathcal{H}_q) = k$, and let HD be a width-k fractional hypertree decomposition for q. Let v be a vertex of HD whose associated subproblem has a fractional cover of weight k. Then, there exists a database DB such that solving this subproblem takes at least $O(n^k)$ time. However, it is possible that there exists another decomposition HD' with no subproblem having such an evaluation cost over this specific database DB. In its turn, HD' will have a critical database DB$'$ for which some of its subproblems require $O(n^k)$ time. But DB$'$ is not necessarily a bad case for the previous decomposition HD. Therefore, it is possible that, for the given query q, for every database DB there is a fractional hypertree decomposition where any subproblem occurring in its vertices can be evaluated in less than $O(n^k)$ time.

As a case study of this phenomenon, we investigate the class of conjunctive queries whose associated hypergraphs are (simple) cycles. These queries have (fractional) hypertree width 2, but they can be actually evaluated in subquadratic time on any given database.

A simple example: the cycles First, consider the following simple cyclic query q_4, whose (hyper)graph G_4 is shown in Figure 1:

$$ans(\bar{X}) \leftarrow r_1(X_1, X_2) \wedge r_2(X_2, X_3) \wedge r_3(X_3, X_4) \wedge r_4(X_4, X_1).$$

Consider the decomposition of this graph in the center of Figure 1, which involves subproblems such as $r_1(X_1, X_2) \wedge r_2(X_2, X_3)$ and $r_3(X_3, X_4) \wedge r_4(X_4, X_1)$ having a fractional cover of weight 2. It follows that there exists a database DB_4 such that, e.g., the subquery $ans(X_1, X_2, X_3) \leftarrow r_1(X_1, X_2) \wedge r_2(X_2, X_3)$ has $O(N^2)$ answers, where for the sake of simplicity we assume that the relations are the same and that they have N tuples each.

Think now of how this worst-case bound can be achieved. First assume that r_i is a cartesian product of the domain of its variables: we have $N = |d(X_1)| \cdot |d(X_2)|$ so that $|d(X_1)| = N^{1/2}$. Because $ans(X_1, X_2, X_3)$ cannot be larger than the cartesian products of the domain of its variables, it follows that, in this case, $|ans(X_1, X_2, X_3)| \leq N^{3/2}$. In order to reach the worst-case bound of N^2, in DB_4 the attributes should have quite different domain sizes. In particular, we must have many values on the extremal variables of the chain X_1, X_2, X_3, that is, almost N values for X_1 and X_3, and a few values for X_2. For instance, X_2 may have just one skew value that is connected to all values for X_1 and X_3, so that $ans(X_1, X_2, X_3) = d(X_1) \times 1 \times d(X_3)$ and $|ans(X_1, X_2, X_3)| = N^2$. For completeness, note that if X_2 has many values, say almost N, than it should behave like a key, and the size of $ans(X_1, X_2, X_3)$ will be almost linear in N. Summing-up, to achieve the $O(N^2)$ worst-case bound on $ans(X_1, X_2, X_3)$, we should have $|d(X_2)| = \Delta$, with Δ much smaller than N. However, in this case we can use the decomposition shown on the right in Figure 1: note that the subproblems in the vertices of this decomposition have at most $N\Delta$ answers, achieved in the vertices in the middle where we have a cartesian product of the form $r_i \times d(X_2)$. The cost of evaluating q_4 over DB_4 using this decomposition is thus $O(N\Delta)$, which is smaller than the $O(N^2)$ cost predicted by fractional hypertree width.

We next show that the above reasoning can be generalized to any database, showing that *the quadratic fractional hypertree-width worst-case is not tight*, in particular such a query can be evaluated in $O(N^{3/2})$, that is, within the same bound as the triangle query.

A general bound for evaluating cycles Following the intuition described in the previous section, we next show that actually we can guarantee a subquadratic evaluation time for every conjunctive query having a cycle as its hypergraph and on any given database. A further ingredient to obtain a precise upper bound is to consider horizontal fragments of the relations, and possibly use different decompositions for evaluating the given query on different fragments. Therefore, not only we look for the best decomposition with regard to specific database, but also the best ones for different fragments of the database.

This bound is a slight improvement of the upper bound described in [16] and it is quite similar to the upper bound given in [2] for the special case of queries asking for length-k simple cycles in graphs, whose techniques are indeed used both in [16] and

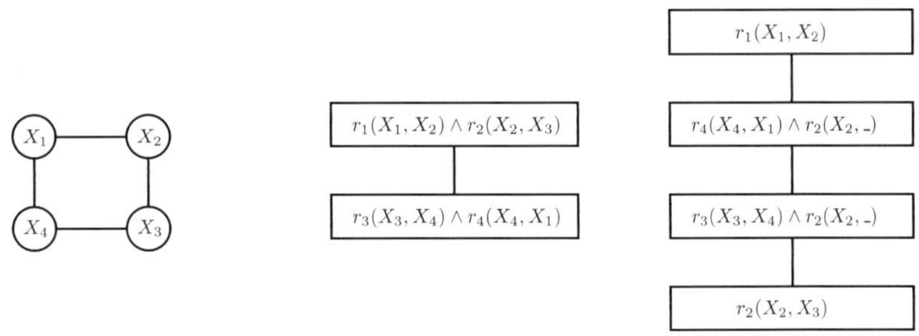

Fig. 1. The graph G_4 and two of its hypertree decompositions

in the present paper. Contrasted with this latter upper bound, our result is more general because it works with queries involving any combination of arbitrary binary relations, while the results on graphs assume only one relation (the edge relationship of the input graph).

Theorem 1. *Let $\mathcal{C}$ be any class of conjunctive queries whose associated hypergraphs are (simple) cycles. Then, the answers of any query in $\mathcal{C}$ having k atoms on a database of size N can be computed in $O((2/k)^{\frac{1}{\lceil k/2 \rceil}} \cdot N^{2-\frac{1}{\lceil k/2 \rceil}} + OUT)$, where OUT is the size of the output.*

Proof. Consider the following query $q_k \in \mathcal{C}$ over a database DB_k of size $\bar{N}$:

$$ans(\bar{X}) \leftarrow r_1(X_1, X_2) \wedge r_2(X_2, X_3) \wedge \cdots \wedge r_k(X_k, X_1),$$

where $r_1, \ldots, r_k$ are binary relation symbols, not necessarily distinct, and for each $i \in [k]$, r_i has N_i tuples. Its associated hypergraph G_k is a simple cycle having k vertices and k edges, and both $hw(G_k) = 2$ and $fhw(G_k) = 2$ holds.

Let $\delta > 0$ be a number that will be determined later. For each $i \in [k]$, let $r'_i \subseteq r_i$ be the (horizontal) fragment of r_i consisting of the tuples $\{\langle v, v' \rangle \in r_i \mid v$ *occurs in more than* δ *tuples in* $r_i\}$. Let q'_i be the variant of query q_k where the atom $r_i(X_i, X_{i+1})$ is replaced by $r'_i(X_i, X_{i+1})$, and consider a hypertree decomposition for q'_i of the form shown on the right in Figure 1, with X_i playing the role of X_2. Note that the number of tuples in the projection $r'_i(X_i, \_)$ occurring in the decomposition vertices is at most N_i/δ, so that q_i can be evaluated in $O(\bar{N}N_i/\delta + OUT_i)$. The OUT_i answers of this modified query are all those answers of q_k such that X_i is instantiated with any value of its domain having degree at least δ (if any). After the evaluation of all such modified queries, we get all the OUT_δ answers of q_k over DB_k where some variable takes a value having degree at least δ. The total time used for such computations is $O(\bar{N}\bar{N}/\delta + OUT_\delta)$. Note that, having these answers, each domain value having degree at least δ is no longer needed in any relation.

Then, we take care of the remaining fragment: consider the query q''_k: $ans''(\bar{X}) \leftarrow r''_1(X_1, X_2) \wedge r''_2(X_2, X_3) \wedge \cdots \wedge r''_k(X_k, X_1)$ over the database DB''_k with the relations $r''_i = r_i \setminus r'_i$, for each $i \in [k]$. We evaluate this query by using a tree decomposition of the form shown in the center of Figure 1 with two big vertices, each one covering half of the query. The width w of this decomposition is $\lceil k/2 \rceil$. Let r_s and r_t be the smallest relations in the database DB''_k, having number of tuples N_r and N_t, respectively. We can always choose the decomposition in such a way that r_s and r_t occur in different vertices. Consider now the evaluation of the subproblem comprising the relation r_s: because every value has degree at most δ, every tuple of r_s can have at most δ extensions to tuples in the subsequent relation in the subproblem, say r_z; the same happens for every tuple in r_z, and so on for all the atoms in this subproblem. The evaluation of these atoms takes $O(N_s\delta^{w-1})$ time and, similarly, we need $O(N_t\delta^{w-1})$ to evaluate the subproblem occurring in the other vertex of the decomposition, for a total cost of $O((N_s + N_t)\delta^{w-1})$. Because r_s and r_t are the smallest relations, it can be seen easily that $(N_s + N_t) \leq 2\bar{N}/k$, so that the total cost for evaluating q''_k over DB''_k using such a decomposition is $O(2\delta^{w-1}\bar{N}/k + \mathit{OUT}'')$, where OUT'' is the size of the output relation $ans''(\bar{X})$. By equating the cost of using the two kinds of decompositions, we can compute the value $\delta = (k/2\bar{N})^{1/w}$ that guarantees that we obtain the same evaluation cost for either kind of fragment and for every possible input database. With this value, the total cost for evaluating q_k on any given database DB_k of size $\bar{N}$ is $O((2/k)^{1/w}N^{2-1/w} + \mathit{OUT})$, where OUT is the size of the output relation $ans(\bar{X})$. □

4 Discussion and Open problems

Recent advances have shown that powerful structural decompositions such as the (fractional) hypertree width or the submodular width may lead to effective algorithms even for very simple queries, and not just for long and complex ones (possibly involving atoms with large arities), which have been the typical targets for these sophisticated techniques. Moreover, we have seen that the worst case upper bounds of the so-called purely structural decomposition methods, where the choice of the decomposition depends only on the query hypergraph, are not tight.

Contrasted with such methods, the notion of submodular width, which is based on data-dependent decompositions, is more powerful and in fact characterises the frontier of fixed-parameter tractability for conjunctive queries. The algorithm used in [19] is based on the computation of almost uniform horizontal fragments of all possible subproblems that can be evaluated in polynomial-time. Very roughly, uniform means here that, in each fragment and for any subset of variables of a subproblem, partial solutions over these variables extend to full solutions of the subproblem in a similar way. Whenever a subproblem does not meet this condition, it can be split in more subproblems leading to new fragments. The subproblems of each new instance associated with a fragment are kept locally consistent. That is, tuples that are not useful in that fragment are filtered out, and the procedure continues looking for new small, consistent and uniform subproblems to deal with. This procedure works in fixed-parameter polynomial time, where the parameter is the size of the query. Eventually, under the promise that the submodular width is below some fixed threshold w (which is used to define precisely the above process), there should exist some tree decomposition whose subproblems are among those that we have computed. Furthermore, whenever for an instance associated with some fragment its subproblems are not empty, because they are pairwise consistent we can conclude that the given query has some answer on the input database; otherwise, we conclude that there are no answers (see also [14] for such consistency properties).

Marx's algorithm is quite involved and its actual cost is quite high even for queries with a few variables. The PANDA algorithm described in [17] aims at obtaining a similar worst case bound, but is more suitable to effective implementations. However, because of its different uniformization procedure, its cost involves a $(\log n)^h$ factor, where

h is the number of atoms in the query, which is not allowed in fixed-parameter polynomial time algorithms (the parameter cannot occur as the exponent of a number that depends on the input size). In fact, it is still open whether or not such a bad factor can be avoided, so that an effective fixed-parameter polynomial time algorithm can be implemented. An algorithm for computing the submodular width of a given hypergraph is also missing, as well as a possible approximation of this notion. Furthermore, the frontier of polynomial-time tractability for conjunctive queries involving atoms of arbitrary arities is still unknown, and it is even unknown whether it can actually be charted or not.

References

1. Aberger, C.R., Lamb, A., Tu, S., Nötzli, A., Olukotun, K., Ré, C.: Emptyheaded: A relational engine for graph processing. ACM TODS **42**(4), 20:1–20:44 (2017).
2. Alon, N., Yuster, R., Zwick, U.: Finding and counting given length cycles. Algorithmica **17**(3), 209–223 (1997).
3. Atserias, A., Grohe, M., Marx, D.: Size bounds and query plans for relational joins. SIAM J. on Comp. **42**(4), 1737–1767 (2013)
4. Fischl, W., Gottlob, G., Pichler, R.: General and fractional hypertree decompositions: Hard and easy cases. In: Proc. of PODS'18 (2018)
5. Ghionna, L., Granata, L., Greco, G., Scarcello, F.: Hypertree decompositions for query optimization. In: Proc. of ICDE'07. pp. 36–45 (2007)
6. Ghionna, L., Greco, G., Scarcello, F.: H-DB: A Hybrid Quantitative-structural SQL Optimizer. In: Proc. of CIKM '11. pp. 2573–2576 (2011)
7. Gottlob, G., Leone, N., Scarcello, F.: Hypertree decompositions and tractable queries. JCSS **64**(3), 579–627 (2002)
8. Gottlob, G., Leone, N., Scarcello, F.: Robbers, marshals, and guards: Game theoretic and logical characterizations of hypertree width. JCSS **66**(4), 775–808 (2003)
9. Gottlob, G., Greco, G., Scarcello, F.: Treewidth and hypertree width. In: Tractability: Practical Approaches to Hard Problems, pp. 3–38. Cambridge University Press (2014).
10. Gottlob, G., Lee, S.T., Valiant, G., Valiant, P.: Size and Treewidth Bounds for Conjunctive Queries. J.ACM **59**(3), 1–35 (2012)
11. Gottlob, G., Miklós, Z., Schwentick, T.: Generalized hypertree decompositions: NP-hardness and tractable variants. J.ACM **56**(6), 30:1–30:32 (2009)
12. Greco, G., Leone, N., Scarcello, F., Terracina, G.: Structural decomposition methods: Key notions and database applications. In: A Comprehensive Guide Through the Italian Database Research Over the Last 25 Years., Studies in Big Data, vol. 31, pp. 253–267. Springer
13. Greco, G., Scarcello, F.: Greedy strategies and larger islands of tractability for conjunctive queries and constraint satisfaction problems. Inf. Comput. **252**, 201–220 (2017).
14. Greco, G., Scarcello, F.: The power of local consistency in conjunctive queries and constraint satisfaction problems. SIAM J. Comput. **46**(3), 1111–1145 (2017).
15. Grohe, M., Marx, D.: Constraint solving via fractional edge covers. ACM Trans. on Alg. **11**(1), 4:1–4:20 (2014)
16. Joglekar, M., Ré, C.: It's all a matter of degree - using degree information to optimize multiway joins. Theory Comput. Syst. **62**(4), 810–853 (2018).
17. Khamis, M.A., Ngo, H.Q., Suciu, D.: What do shannon-type inequalities, submodular width, and disjunctive datalog have to do with one another? In: Proc. of PODS 2017, pp. 429–444.
18. Marx, D.: Approximating fractional hypertree width. ACM T. on Alg. **6**(2), 29:1–17 (2010)
19. Marx, D.: Tractable hypergraph properties for constraint satisfaction and conjunctive queries. J.ACM **60**(6), 42:1–42:51 (2013)
20. Robertson, N., Seymour, P.: Graph minors. II. Algorithmic aspects of tree-width. J. of Alg. **7**(3), 309–322 (1986)

Formalization and Complexity of MongoDB Queries (Extended Abstract)*

Elena Botoeva, Diego Calvanese, Benjamin Cogrel, and Guohui Xiao

Faculty of Computer Science
Free University of Bozen-Bolzano, Italy
lastname@inf.unibz.it

Abstract. In this paper, we study MongoDB, a widely adopted but not formally understood database system managing JSON documents and equipped with a powerful query mechanism, called the aggregation framework. We define its formal abstraction MQuery, of which we study expressivity and computational complexity. We show the equivalence of MQuery and nested relational algebra, and obtain (tight) bounds in combined complexity, which range from LOGSPACE to alternating exponential-time with a polynomial number of alternations.

1 Introduction

JavaScript Object Notation (JSON) is currently adopted extensively as the de-facto standard format for representing nested data. JSON organizes data as semi-structured tree-shaped documents, with a minimalistic set of node types, and as such is commonly considered a lightweight alternative to XML. JSON documents can also be seen as complex values [7,1,15], in particular due to the presence of nested arrays. Consider, e.g., the document in Figure 1, containing personal information (such as name and birth-date) about Kristen Nygaard, and information about the awards he received, the latter stored inside an array.

Following its massive adoption by practitioners, recently JSON has also received attention in the database theory community. A powerful (Turing-complete, in its full generality) Datalog-like query language for JSON named JLogic is introduced in [8], where the expressive power and complexity of the full language and of significant fragments are studied. In [4], both JSON and its main schema language JSON Schema[1] are formalized, and their expressive power and the computational complexity of basic computational tasks, such as satisfiability and evaluation of expressions, are studied. Although some of the latter results apply to the simple *find* query language[2] of the widespread JSON-based document database system MongoDB, still little is known about the precise formal properties of the query languages for JSON with rich capabilities popular among practitioners, such as JSONiq [6] and SQL++ [12].

* SEBD 2018, June 24–27, 2018, Castellaneta Marina, Italy. Copyright held by the author(s). This is an abridged version of [3].

[1] http://json-schema.org/

[2] https://docs.mongodb.com/manual/crud/

```
{ "_id": 4,
  "awards": [
    { "award": "Rosing Prize", "year": 1999, "by": "Norwegian Data Association" },
    { "award": "Turing Award", "year": 2001, "by": "ACM" },
    { "award": "IEEE John von Neumann Medal", "year": 2001, "by": "IEEE" } ],
  "birth": "1926-08-27",
  "contribs": [ "OOP", "Simula" ],
  "death": "2002-08-10",
  "name": { "first": "Kristen", "last": "Nygaard" } }
```

Fig. 1. A sample JSON document in the `bios` collection.

Differently from XML, where XQuery is the official standard query language, embraced also by the developer community, so far there is no standard query language for JSON. However, in terms of adoption, the *MongoDB aggregation framework*[3] is currently the most prominent language providing rich querying capabilities over collections of JSON documents, and hence has become the de-facto standard language for JSON. This language is modeled on the flexible notion of a data processing pipeline, where a query consists of multiple stages, each defining a transformation using a specific operator, applied to the set of documents produced by the previous stage. As such, the language is very expressive and rich in features, but it has been developed in an ad-hoc manner, resulting in some counter-intuitive behavior.

We study the formal foundations and computational properties of the MongoDB aggregation framework, which has many similarities with well-known query languages for complex values, e.g., nested relational algebra (NRA) [14] and Core XQuery [11].

Our first contribution is a formalization of the JSON data model and of the aggregation framework query language, in which we deliberately abstract away some low-level features of MongoDB: we adopt set semantics (as opposed to bag or list semantics), and we abstract away from order within documents. Our formal language, which we call *MQuery*, includes the ***match***, ***unwind***, ***project***, ***group***, and ***lookup*** operators, roughly corresponding to the NRA operators select, unnest, project, nest, and left join, respectively. In our investigation, we consider various fragments of MQuery, which we denote by $\mathcal{M}^{\alpha}$, where α consists of the initials of the stages allowed in the fragment.

Our second contribution is a characterization of the expressive power of MQuery obtained by devising translations in both directions between (a suitably defined *well-typed* fragment of) MQuery and NRA, showing that the two languages are equivalent in expressive power. Our translations are compact (i.e., polynomial), hence complexity results between MQuery and NRA carry over.

Our third contribution is an investigation of the computational complexity of $\mathcal{M}^{\text{MUPGL}}$ and its fragments. We establish several tight bounds (in combined complexity), which range from LOGSPACE-complete for $\mathcal{M}^{\text{M}}$ to $\text{TA}[2^{n^{O(1)}}, n^{O(1)}]$-complete for MQuery itself. As a byproduct, we also establish a tight lower bound for the combined complexity of Boolean query evaluation in NRA.

In the following, we assume familiarity with nested relational algebra (NRA) [9,14].

[3] `https://docs.mongodb.com/manual/core/aggregation-pipeline/`

VALUE ::= LITERAL | OBJECT | ARRAY
OBJECT ::= {{ LIST<KEY : VALUE> }}
ARRAY ::= [LIST<VALUE>]

LIST<T> ::= ε | LIST^{+} <T>
LIST^{+} <T> ::= T | T , LIST^{+} <T>

Fig. 2. Syntax of JSON objects. We use double curly brackets to distinguish objects from sets.

2 JSON Documents

In this section, we propose a formalization of the syntax and the semantics of JSON documents. With respect to MongoDB, we abstract away the order of key-value pairs within a document.

A MongoDB database stores collections of documents, where a collection corresponds to a table in a (nested) relational database, and a document to a row in a table. We define the syntax of documents. *Literals* are atomic values, such as strings, numbers, and Booleans. A *JSON object* is a finite set of key-value pairs, where a *key* is a string and a *value* can be a literal, an object, or an array of values, constructed inductively according to the grammar in Figure 2 (where the terminals are '{{', '}}', '[', ']', ':', and ','). We require that the set of key-value pairs constituting a JSON object does not contain the same key twice. A *(MongoDB) document* is a JSON object not nested within any other object, with a special key '`_id`', used to identify the document. Figure 1 shows a document with keys `_id`, `awards`, `birth`, etc. Given a collection name C, a *(MongoDB) collection for* C is a finite set F_C of documents, each identified by its value of `_id`, i.e., each value of `_id` is unique in F_C. Given a set $\mathbb{C}$ of collection names, a *MongoDB database instance* D *(over* $\mathbb{C}$*)* is a set of collections, one for each name $C \in \mathbb{C}$. We write $D.C$ to denote the collection for name C.

We formalize JSON objects as finite *unordered, unranked, node-labeled, and edge-labeled trees* (see Figure 3 for the tree t_{KN} corresponding to the document in Figure 1, where we have additionally labeled nodes with n_i, to refer to them later). We assume three disjoint sets of labels: the sets K of *keys* and I of *indexes* (non-negative integers), used as edge-labels, and the set V of *literals*, containing the special elements $\mathbf{null}$, $\mathbf{true}$, and $\mathbf{false}$, and used as node labels. A *tree* is a tuple $(N, E, L_{\mathsf{n}}, L_{\mathsf{e}})$, where N is a set of nodes, E is the edge relation, $L_{\mathsf{n}} : N \to V \cup \{\text{'}\{\!\{\}\!\}\text{'}, \text{'}[\,]\text{'}\}$ is a node labeling function, and $L_{\mathsf{e}} : E \to K \cup I$ is an edge labeling function, such that *(i)* (N, E) forms a tree, *(ii)* a node labeled by a literal must be a leaf, *(iii)* all outgoing edges of a node labeled by '{{}}' must be labeled by keys, and *(iv)* all outgoing edges of a node labeled by '[ ]'

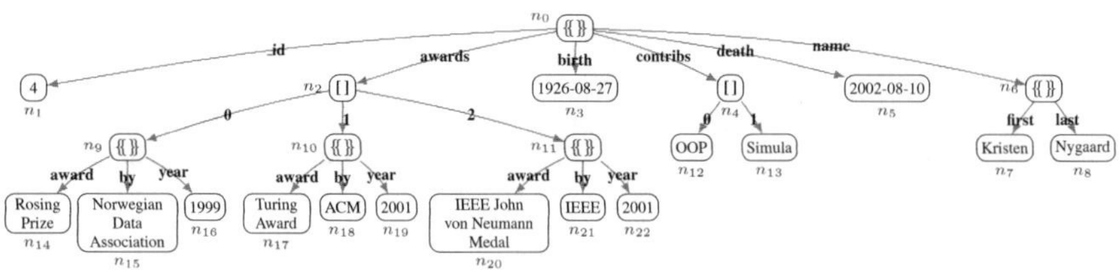

Fig. 3. The tree t_{KN} corresponding to the JSON document in Figure 1.

must be labeled by distinct indexes. The *type* of a node x in a tree t, denoted $\mathsf{type}(x, t)$, is defined as $\mathsf{literal}$ if $L_\mathsf{n}(x) \in V$, object if $L_\mathsf{n}(x) = \text{‘}\{\!\!\{\}\!\!\}\text{’}$, and array if $L_\mathsf{n}(x) = \text{‘[ ]’}$. $\mathsf{root}(t)$ denotes the root of t. A *forest* is a set of trees.

We define inductively the *value represented by* a node x in a tree t, denoted $\mathsf{value}(x, t)$: *(i)* $\mathsf{value}(x, t) = L_\mathsf{n}(x)$, if x is a leaf in t; *(ii)* let $x_1, \ldots, x_m$, be all children of x with $L_\mathsf{e}(x, x_i) = k_i$. Then $\mathsf{value}(x, t)$ is $\{\!\!\{k_1{:}\mathsf{value}(x_1, t), \ldots, k_m{:}\mathsf{value}(x_m, t)\}\!\!\}$ if $\mathsf{type}(x, t) = \mathsf{object}$, and $[\mathsf{value}(x_1, t), \ldots, \mathsf{value}(x_m, t)]$, if $\mathsf{type}(x, t) = \mathsf{array}$. The *JSON value represented by* t is then $\mathsf{value}(\mathsf{root}(t), t)$. Conversely, the *tree corresponding to a value* u, denoted $\mathsf{tree}(u)$, is defined as $(N, E, L_\mathsf{n}, L_\mathsf{e})$, where N is the set of all x_v such that v is an object, array, or literal value appearing in u, and for $x_v \in N$: *(i)* if v is a literal, then $L_\mathsf{n}(x_v) = v$ and x_v is a leaf; *(ii)* if $v = \{\!\!\{k_1{:}v_1, \ldots, k_m{:}v_m\}\!\!\}$ for $m \geq 0$, then $L_\mathsf{n}(x_v) = \text{‘}\{\!\!\{\}\!\!\}\text{’}$, and x_v has m children $x_{v_1}, \ldots, x_{v_m}$ with $L_\mathsf{e}(x_v, x_{v_i}) = k_i$; *(iii)* if $v = [v_1, \ldots, v_m]$ for $m \geq 0$, then $L_\mathsf{n}(x_v) = \text{‘[ ]’}$, and x_v has m children $x_{v_1}, \ldots, x_{v_m}$ with $L_\mathsf{e}(x_v, x_{v_i}) = i - 1$. In the following, when convenient, we blur the distinction between JSON values and the corresponding trees.

3 The MQuery Language

MongoDB is equipped with an expressive query mechanism provided by the *aggregation framework* (see [2] for its formal syntax. Our first contribution is a formalization of the core aspects of this query language, where we use set (as opposed to bag and list) semantics, and we deliberately abstract away some low-level features that either are not relevant for understanding the expressive power and computational properties of the language, or appear ad-hoc and possibly are remnants of experimental development. We call the resulting language *MQuery*.

An *MQuery* is a sequence of stages, also called a *pipeline*, applied to a collection name C, where each stage transforms a forest into another forest. The grammar of MQuery is given in Figure 4. In an MQuery, *paths*, which are (possibly empty) concatenations of keys, are used to access actual values in a tree, similarly to how attributes are used in relational algebra. We use ε to denote the empty path. For two paths p and p', we say that p' is a *(strict) prefix* of p, if $p = p'.p''$, for some (non-empty) path p''. MQuery allows for five types of *stages*:

- ***match*** μ_φ, which selects trees according to criterion φ. Such criterion is a Boolean combination of atomic conditions $p = v$, expressing the equality of a path p to a value v, or $\exists p$, expressing the existence of a path p. E.g., for $\varphi_1 = (\texttt{\_id}{=}4)$, $\varphi_2 = (\text{awards.award=”Turing Award”})$, and $\varphi_3 = (\text{name} = \{\!\!\{\text{first: ”Kristen”}\}\!\!\})$, μ_{φ_1} and μ_{φ_2} select t_{KN}, but μ_{φ_3} does not.

$\varphi ::= \mathbf{true} \mid p = v \mid \exists p \mid \neg\varphi \mid \varphi \vee \varphi \mid \varphi \wedge \varphi$	$P ::= p \mid p/d \mid p, P \mid p/d, P$
$d ::= v \mid p \mid [d, \ldots, d] \mid \beta \mid (\beta ?\, d{:}\, d)$	$G ::= p/p \mid p/p, G$
$\beta ::= \mathbf{true} \mid p = p \mid p = v \mid \exists p \mid \neg\beta \mid \beta \vee \beta \mid \beta \wedge \beta$	$A ::= p/p \mid p/p, A$
$s ::= \mu_\varphi \mid \omega_p \mid \rho_P \mid \gamma_{G:A} \mid \lambda_p^{p=C.p}$	$\text{MQuery} ::= C \triangleright s \triangleright \cdots \triangleright s$

Fig. 4. The MQuery language. Here, p denotes a path, v a value, C a collection name, φ a criterion, d a value definition, β a Boolean value definition, s a stage, P a list for project, G a list for grouping, and A a list for aggregation.

- ***unwind*** ω_p, which flattens an array reached through a path p in the input tree, and outputs a tree for each element of the array. E.g., ω_{awards} applied to t_{KN} produces three trees, which coincide on all key-value pairs, except for the `awards` key, whose values are nested objects such as, e.g., {{award: "Turing Award", year: 2001, by: "ACM"}}.
- ***project*** ρ_P, which modifies trees by projecting away paths, renaming paths, or introducing new paths. Here P is a sequence of elements of the form p or q/d, where p is a path to be kept, q is a new path whose value is defined by d, and among all such paths p and q, there is no pair p, p' where p is a prefix of p'. A *value definition* d can provide for q: *(i)* a constant v, *(ii)* the value reached through a path p (i.e., *renaming* path p to q), *(iii)* a new array defined through its values, *(iv)* the value of a Boolean expression β, or *(v)* a value computed through a conditional expression $(\beta ?\, d_1 \colon d_2)$. E.g., $\rho_{\text{bool}/(\text{birth}=\text{death}),\, \text{cond}/((\exists \text{awards})?\, \text{contribs}: \texttt{\_id}),\, \text{newArray}/[0,1]}$ applied to t_{KN} produces {{bool: **false**, cond: ["OOP", "Simula"], newArray: [0,1]}}.
- ***group*** $\gamma_{G:A}$, which groups trees according to a grouping condition G and aggregates values of interest according to A. Both G and A are (possibly empty) sequences of elements of the form p/p', where p' is a path in the input trees, and p a path in the output trees. Each different combination $\boldsymbol{v}$ of values in the input trees for the p's in G determines a group. For each such group there is a tree in the output with an `_id` whose value is constructed from $\boldsymbol{v}$ and the ps in G. The remaining keys in each output tree have as value an array constructed using the aggregation expression A. Consider, e.g., as input {{a: 1, b: "x"}}, {{a: 1, b: "y"}}, and {{a: 2, b: "z"}}. Then $\gamma_{\text{c}/\text{a}:\text{bs}/\text{b}}$ produces the two groups {{`_id`: {{c: 1}}, bs: ["x","y"]}} and {{`_id`: {{c: 2}}, bs: ["z"]}}.
- ***lookup*** $\lambda_p^{p_1=C.p_2}$, which joins input trees with trees in an external collection C, using a local path p_1 and a path p_2 in C to express the join condition, and stores the matching trees in an array under a path p. E.g., let C consist of {{`_id`: 1, a: 3}} and {{`_id`: 2, a: 4}}. Then $\lambda_{\text{docs}}^{\texttt{\_id}=C.\text{a}}$ evaluated over t_{KN} adds to it `docs`: [{{`_id`: 2, a: 4}}].

We consider various fragments $\mathcal{M}^{\alpha}$ of MQuery, where α consists of the initials of the allowed stages. E.g., $\mathcal{M}^{\text{MUPGL}}$ denotes MQuery itself, while $\mathcal{M}^{\text{MUPG}}$ disallows lookup.

For the formal semantics of MQuery, we first observe that a path p over a tree t is interpreted as the set of nodes reachable via p from the root of t, where the indexes of intermediate arrays encountered in the tree are skipped. Then, given a forest F and a stage s, we can define the forest $F \triangleright s$ (for a lookup stage, we also require an additional forest F' as parameter) obtained by applying s to F. We refer to [3] for details. The semantics of an MQuery is obtained by composing (via $\triangleright$) the answers of its stages.

Definition 1. *Let $\boldsymbol{q} = C \triangleright s_1 \triangleright \cdots \triangleright s_n$ be an MQuery. The* result of evaluating $\boldsymbol{q}$ *over a MongoDB instance D, denoted $ans_{\mathsf{mo}}(\boldsymbol{q}, D)$, is defined as F_n, where $F_0 = D.C$, and for $i \in \{1, \ldots, n\}$, $F_i = (F_{i-1} \triangleright s_i)$ if s_i is not a lookup stage, and $F_i = (F_{i-1} \triangleright s_i[D.C'])$ if s_i is a lookup stage referring to an external collection name C'.*

4 Expressivity of MQuery

In this section we characterize the expressivity of MQuery in terms of nested relational algebra (NRA), and we do so by developing translations between the two languages. To make it possible to compare MQuery and NRA, we need to define how MongoDB instances can be viewed as nested relations. In the case of a MongoDB instance with an irregular structure, there is no natural way to define such a relational view. This happens either when the type of a path in a tree is not defined, or when a path has different types in two trees in the instance. Therefore, in order to define a schema for the relational view, which is also independent of the actual MongoDB instances, we impose on them some form of regularity. This is done by introducing the notion of *type* τ of a tree, which is analogous to complex object types [11], and similar to JSON schema [13].

A forest F is of type τ if all its trees are of type τ, and it is *well-typed* if it is of some type τ. We can then associate to each type τ a relation schema $\mathsf{rschema}(\tau)$ in which, intuitively, attributes correspond to paths, and each nested relation corresponds to an array in τ. The names of sub-relations and of atomic attributes in $\mathsf{rschema}(\tau)$ are given by paths from the root in τ, and therefore are unique. And we can define the relational view $\mathsf{rel}(F)$, of a well-typed forest F.

To define the relational view of MongoDB instances, we introduce the notion of *(MongoDB) type constraints*, which are given by a set $\mathcal{S}$ of pairs (C, τ), one for each collection name C, where τ is a type. We say that a database D *satisfies* the constraints $\mathcal{S}$ if $D.C$ is of type τ, for each $(C, \tau) \in \mathcal{S}$. For a given $\mathcal{S}$, for each $(C, \tau) \in \mathcal{S}$, we refer to τ by τ_C. Moreover, we assume that in $\mathsf{rschema}(\tau_C)$, the relation name R_{τ_C} is actually C. Then, for a set $\mathcal{S}$ of type constraints and a MongoDB instance D satisfying $\mathcal{S}$, the *relational view* $\mathsf{rdb}_{\mathcal{S}}(D)$ of D with respect to $\mathcal{S}$ is the instance $\{\mathsf{rel}(D.C) \mid (C, \tau) \in \mathcal{S}\}$.

Finally, we define equivalence between MQueries and NRA queries. To this purpose, we also define equivalence between two kinds of answers: well-typed forests and nested relations. We say that a well-typed forest F is *equivalent* to a nested relation $\mathcal{R}$, denoted $F \simeq \mathcal{R}$, if $\mathsf{rel}(F) = \mathcal{R}$. An MQuery $\boldsymbol{q}$ is *equivalent to* an NRA query Q w.r.t. type constraints $\mathcal{S}$, denoted $\boldsymbol{q} \equiv_{\mathcal{S}} Q$, if $ans_{\mathsf{mo}}(\boldsymbol{q}, D) \simeq ans_{\mathsf{ra}}(Q, \mathsf{rdb}_{\mathcal{S}}(D))$, for each MongoDB instance D satisfying $\mathcal{S}$ (where $ans_{\mathsf{ra}}(Q, \mathcal{R})$ denotes the answer to the NRA query Q computed over the nested relation $\mathcal{R}$).

We are now ready to establish the correspondence between NRA and MQuery. On the one hand, we show that $\mathcal{M}^{\text{MUPGL}}$ captures NRA, while $\mathcal{M}^{\text{MUPG}}$ captures NRA over a single collection. In our translation from NRA to MQuery, we have to deal with the fact that an NRA query in general has a *tree* structure where the leaves are relation names, while an MQuery contains *one sequence* of stages. So, we have to show how to "linearize" tree-shaped NRA expressions into a MongoDB pipeline. More precisely, we can show that it is possible to combine two $\mathcal{M}^{\text{MUPG}}$ sequences $\boldsymbol{q}_1$ and $\boldsymbol{q}_2$ of stages into a single $\mathcal{M}^{\text{MUPG}}$ sequence $\mathsf{pipeline}(\boldsymbol{q}_1, \boldsymbol{q}_2)$, so that the results of $\boldsymbol{q}_1$ and $\boldsymbol{q}_2$ can be accessed from the result of $\mathsf{pipeline}(\boldsymbol{q}_1, \boldsymbol{q}_2)$ for further processing. Having defined $\mathsf{pipeline}(\boldsymbol{q}_1, \boldsymbol{q}_2)$, we are ready to show how to translate NRA to MQuery. For a singleton set $\mathcal{S} = \{(C, \tau_C)\}$ of type constraints for a collection name C and an NRA query Q over the relation name C (with schema $\mathsf{rschema}(\tau_C)$), we can define inductively on the structure of Q a pipeline $\mathsf{nra2mq}(Q)$, and then translate Q into the $\mathcal{M}^{\text{MUPG}}$ query $C \triangleright \mathsf{nra2mq}(Q)$. We obtain that $C \triangleright \mathsf{nra2mq}(Q) \equiv_{\mathcal{S}} Q$. This result can be generalized to NRA queries over multiple collections, by making use of *lookup*. We obtain:

Theorem 1. *$\mathcal{M}^{\text{MUPG}}$ captures NRA over a single collection, while $\mathcal{M}^{\text{MUPGL}}$ captures full NRA. Moreover there are polynomial translations from NRA to $\mathcal{M}^{\text{MUPG}}$/$\mathcal{M}^{\text{MUPGL}}$.*

To define a translation from MQuery to NRA we want to exploit the structure, i.e., the stages of MQueries. Hence, we define a translation $\mathsf{mq2nra}(s)$ from stages s to NRA expressions such that, for an MQuery $C \triangleright s_1 \triangleright \cdots \triangleright s_n$, the corresponding NRA query is defined as $C \circ \mathsf{mq2nra}(s_1) \circ \cdots \circ \mathsf{mq2nra}(s_n)$[4], where we identify the collection name C with the corresponding relation schema in the relational view. However, such a translation might not always be possible, since MQuery is capable of producing non well-typed forests, for which the relational view is not defined. Therefore, we restrict our attention to MQueries with stages preserving well-typedness. It is possible to check whether an MQuery satisfies this property.

The translation $\mathsf{mq2nra}(s)$, for well-typed stages s, is quite natural, although it requires some attention to properly capture the semantics of MQuery. It is given in [2].

Theorem 2. *Let S be a set of type constraints, $\boldsymbol{q}$ an MQuery $C \triangleright s_1 \triangleright \cdots \triangleright s_m$ in which each stage is well-typed for its input type, and $Q = C \circ \mathsf{mq2nra}(s_1) \circ \cdots \circ \mathsf{mq2nra}(s_m)$. Then $\boldsymbol{q} \equiv_S Q$. Moreover, the size of Q is polynomial in the size of $\boldsymbol{q}$ and S.*

5 Complexity of MQuery

We have studied the complexity of $\mathcal{M}^{\text{MUPGL}}$ and of some of its fragments, and have obtained the following results:
- What we consider the minimal fragment, namely $\mathcal{M}^{\text{M}}$, which allows only for match, is LOGSPACE-complete in combined complexity.
- Projection and grouping allow one to create exponentially large objects, but by representing intermediate results compactly as DAGs, one can still evaluate $\mathcal{M}^{\text{MPGL}}$ queries in PTIME. Specifically, $\mathcal{M}^{\text{MP}}$ is PTIME-hard in query complexity and $\mathcal{M}^{\text{MPGL}}$ is in PTIME in combined complexity.
- For $\mathcal{M}^{\text{MU}}$, the use of unwind causes loss of tractability in combined complexity, specifically it leads to NP-completeness, but the language remains LOGSPACE-complete in query complexity.
- Further adding project in $\mathcal{M}^{\text{MUP}}$, or lookup in $\mathcal{M}^{\text{MUL}}$, leads again to NP-harness even in query complexity, although $\mathcal{M}^{\text{MUPL}}$ stays NP-complete in combined complexity.
- In the presence of unwind, grouping provides another source of complexity, since it allows one to create doubly-exponentially large objects; indeed $\mathcal{M}^{\text{MUG}}$ is PSPACE-hard in query complexity.
- The full language $\mathcal{M}^{\text{MUPGL}}$ and also the $\mathcal{M}^{\text{MUPG}}$ fragment are complete for $\text{TA}[2^{n^{O(1)}}, n^{O(1)}]$ (i.e., exponential time with a polynomial number of alternations [5,10]) in combined complexity, and in AC^0 in data complexity.

The latter result provides also a tight $\text{TA}[2^{n^{O(1)}}, n^{O(1)}]$ bound for the combined complexity of Boolean query evaluation in NRA, whose exact complexity was open [11].

6 Conclusions and Future Work

We have carried out a first formal investigation on the foundations and computational properties of the MongoDB aggregation framework, currently the most widely adopted

[4] We follow the convention that $(f \circ g)(x) = g(f(x))$.

expressive query language for JSON. We proposed a clean abstraction for its five main operators, which we called MQuery. We have studied the expressivity of MQuery, establishing the equivalence between its well-typed fragment and NRA, by developing compact translations in both directions. This shows that, despite its design driven by practical requirements, the aggregation framework relies on solid foundations. Moreover, we analyzed the computational complexity of significant fragments of MQuery, obtaining several (tight) bounds. As a byproduct, we obtained also a tight bound for NRA.

We are currently working on applying our results to provide high-level access to MongoDB data sources by relying on the standard ontology-based data access (OBDA) paradigm [16]. We build on the translation from NRA to MQuery presented in Section 4.

Acknowledgements. This research has been partially supported by the projects OnProm and STyLoLa, respectively funded through the 2015 Call and the 2017 Interdisciplinary Call, both issued by the Research Committee of the Free University of Bozen-Bolzano.

References

1. S. Abiteboul and C. Beeri. The power of languages for the manipulation of complex values. *VLDBJ*, 4(4):727–794, 1995.
2. E. Botoeva, D. Calvanese, B. Cogrel, and G. Xiao. Expressivity and complexity of MongoDB (Extended version). CoRR Technical Report arXiv:1603.09291, 2017.
3. E. Botoeva, D. Calvanese, B. Cogrel, and G. Xiao. Expressivity and complexity of MongoDB queries. In *Proc. ICDT*, volume 98 of *LIPIcs*, pages 9:1–9:22, Dagstuhl, Germany, 2018.
4. P. Bourhis, J. L. Reutter, F. Suárez, and D. Vrgoč. JSON: Data model, query languages and schema specification. In *Proc. PODS*, pages 123–135, 2017.
5. A. K. Chandra, D. C. Kozen, and L. J. Stockmeyer. Alternation. *JACM*, 28(1):114–133, 1981.
6. D. Florescu and G. Fourny. JSONiq: The history of a query language. *IEEE Internet Computing*, 17(5):86–90, 2013.
7. S. Grumbach and V. Vianu. Tractable query languages for complex object databases. In *Proc. PODS*, pages 315–327, 1991.
8. J. Hidders, J. Paredaens, and J. Van den Bussche. J-Logic: Logical foundations for JSON querying. In *Proc. PODS*, pages 137–149, 2017.
9. G. Jaeschke and H.-J. Schek. Remarks on the algebra of non first normal form relations. In *Proc. PODS*, pages 124–138, 1982.
10. D. S. Johnson. A catalog of complexity classes. In *Handbook of Theoretical Computer Science*, volume A, chapter 2, pages 67–161. Elsevier, 1990.
11. C. Koch. On the complexity of nonrecursive XQuery and functional query languages on complex values. *ACM TODS*, 31(4):1215–1256, 2006.
12. K. W. Ong, Y. Papakonstantinou, and R. Vernoux. The SQL++ semi-structured data model and query language: A capabilities survey of SQL-on-Hadoop, NoSQL and NewSQL databases. CoRR Technical Report arXiv:1405.3631, 2017.
13. F. Pezoa, J. L. Reutter, F. Suarez, M. Ugarte, and D. Vrgoč. Foundations of JSON schema. In *Proc. WWW*, pages 263–273, 2016.
14. J. Van den Bussche. Simulation of the nested relational algebra by the flat relational algebra, with an application to the complexity of evaluating powerset algebra expressions. *TCS*, 254(1):363–377, 2001.
15. J. Van den Bussche and J. Paredaens. The expressive power of complex values in object-based data models. *Information and Computation*, 120(2):220–236, 1995.
16. G. Xiao, D. Calvanese, R. Kontchakov, D. Lembo, A. Poggi, R. Rosati, and M. Zakharyaschev. Ontology-based data access: A survey. In *Proc. IJCAI*. AAAI Press, 2018.

Ontology Population for Open-Source Intelligence (Discussion Paper)

Giulio Ganino, Domenico Lembo, Massimo Mecella, and Federico Scafoglieri

DIAG, Sapienza Università di Roma, Italy
{lembo, ganino, mecella, scafoglieri}@diag.uniroma1.it

Abstract. We present an approach based on GATE (General Architecture for Text Engineering) for the automatic population of ontologies from text documents. We describe some experimental results, which are encouraging in terms of extracted correct instances of the ontology. We then focus on a phase of our pipeline and discuss a variant thereof, which aims at reducing the manual effort needed to generate pre-defined dictionaries used in document annotation. Our additional experiments show promising results also in this case.

1 Introduction

Open-Source INTelligence (OSINT) is intelligence based on publicly available resources, such as news sites, blogs, forums, etc. OSINT is nowadays used in many application scenarios, like, for instance, security, market intelligence, or statistics. A major issue in using *Internet as a data source* is that Web data come mainly in the form of free text, thus with no structure and formal semantics. This therefore requires that two problems have to be faced, that is, how to derive structured information from unstructured text, and how to interpret the derived information according to a precise semantics.

Towards a comprehensive solution to this problem, in this paper we investigate how to populate a domain ontology with the information extracted from documents crawled from the Web. Ontologies are indeed nowadays recognized as the best means to represent domain knowledge at the conceptual level, and thus are particularly suited to define the concepts and relationships of interest for an application. Thus, structuring Web data according to the predicates and axioms defined in an ontology turns out to be particularly effective to our aims, even in the light of the reasoning abilities ontologies allow for [2]. It is worthwhile however to point out that we do not consider here the task of extracting (the intensional/schema level of) ontologies in an automatic way from text documents. Domain ontologies indeed have usually a very complex intensional structure, and their design is typically carried out manually, since automatic ontology construction approaches are in general not able to deal with all the needs of the specific application domain at hand [7, 1]. In this work we instead pursue an approach for information extraction from text that assumes that a domain ontology is already available, and that text should be mined to extract instances of ontology predicates.

To solve this task, *Named Entity Recognition* (NER) [3] can be initially adopted, but this approach is mainly focused on instantiating specific concepts (persons, places, or organizations), without considering relationships among them. *Relational Information Extraction* attempts in addition to identify and instantiate the relationships existing among concepts. We will adopt both approaches, by relying on open-source technologies.

Specifically, we make use of the GATE system[1], given its ability to customize the underlying architecture components and to incorporate other external components developed by third parties. Information extraction in GATE is carried out through different stages, each depending on the contingent needs of the user, who can either adopt existing dictionaries (a.k.a. Gazetteers) or create different extraction rule sets through the adoption of Java Annotation Patterns Engine (JAPE) language [4]. GATE has become popular in the last years, especially in relation to information extraction from English documents. To some extent, it also supports other languages, primarily thanks to the dictionaries created and then shared on the platform by its many users.

We have tested our techniques within the XASMOS and RoMA projects, involving the Leonardo company and the Sapienza research center on Cyber Intelligence and Information Security. In the projects, we have considered the case study "Mafia Capitale", from the name of an important inquiry of 2015 that received a lot of attention by the Italian media, and thus turned out to be a valid testbed (for both number of available Web documents and significance of the domain). For this work, we have created specific dictionaries and JAPE rules for the Italian language to instantiate, with the information acquired from text documents, an ontology designed for our case study. We present the case study successfully applied to more than 2600 documents crawled from the Web.

We have experienced that some of the tasks we conducted, such as dictionary or JAPE rule definition, are rather domain specific and time-consuming. We investigated how to refine our approach so that the time needed for these tasks is reduced and the solution adopted can be more easily reused in different contexts. In particular, after describing our approach and the use case, we propose a general technique for dictionary construction, which relies on the extraction of gazetteers lists from the open KB Wikidata[2].

This paper is an extended abstract of [6].

2 Background

Natural Language Processing (NLP). NLP aims at solving problems related to the automatic generation and understanding of human language [9]. The process carried out by NLP is made up of several steps:

- *Tokenization*: This task breaks down the raw text in tokens, which can be words, spaces or dots.
- *Part of Speech (POS)*: This phase aims at labeling each word with a unique tag indicating its syntactic role, i.e. Noun, Verb, or Pronoun.
- *Named Entity Recognition (NER)*: NER labels atomic elements in a sentence into categories (such as "Person" or "Location") through the application of specific rules or statistical machine learning techniques [8].

[1] `https://gate.ac.uk/`

[2] `https://www.wikidata.org/`

- *Semantic Role Labelling (SRL)*: SRL gives a semantic role to a syntactic constituent of a sentence, and add further labels to words in the documents. SRL aims at understanding the meaning of an entire sentence starting from the meaning of each word taken in isolation and the relationship existing among the words [11].

General Architecture for Text Engineering (GATE). GATE, is an architecture, a framework and a development environment for Language Engineering (LE) [5]. It has a component-based model, allowing for easy combination of Processing Resources (PRs), thereby facilitating comparison of alternative configurations of the system or different implementations of the same module (e.g., different parsers). GATE comprises a core library and a set of reusable LE modules, which perform basic language processing tasks, such as POS and semantic tagging. This provides a good starting point for new applications. The modules used in this work are described in Section 3.

Ontologies. An ontology is a formal description of an abstract, simplified view of a certain portion of the world [7]. Ontologies can be naturally used to represent knowledge on the web, where they are mainly adopted to add semantics to data. This also enables the usage of the reasoning mechanisms ontologies are equipped with [2]. The importance of ontologies to interpret and structure Web data is testified also by the standardization effort carried out by the W3C, which led to the definition of OWL[3].

As usual in ontologies, OWL distinguishes between *intensional* and *extensional* knowledge. Intensional knowledge is given in terms of logical axioms involving Classes (a.k.a. concepts) and properties, which are of two types, ObjectProperties (a.k.a. binary relationships or roles) and DataProperties (a.k.a. attributes). Classes denote sets of objects, ObjectProperties denote binary relations between objects, whereas DataProperties denote binary relations between objects and values from predefined datatypes. Person, livesIn and personAge are examples, of Class, ObjectProperty, and DataProperty, respectively. At the extensional level, an OWL ontology is a set of assertions about its instances. For example, ClassAssertion(Person John) indicates that the individual John is an instance of Person, whereas ObjectPropertyAssertion(livesIn John NY) specifies that the pair of individuals (John, NY) is an instance of livesIn.

3 Approach

Our approach comprises two phases: *Semantic Annotation* and *Ontology Population*.

Semantic annotation. In this stage we create annotations, i.e., metadata that indicate properties of the text contained in the analyzed documents. At the end of this phase, the annotations will allow us to identify those entities that are indeed instances of the classes and properties of the ontology given as input to our pipeline. In our GATE-based approach, this phase relies on several PRs, which are available as GATE plugin-ins, possibly provided by third-party organizations[4]. Such resources are described below.

1. *GATE Unicode Tokeniser*: this is a PR of the GATE core library used to split the text in *Tokens* and *SpaceTokens*, where the latter denote spaces among single terms, whereas the former are numbers, punctuations, symbols, and words.

[3] Ontology Web Language (`https://www.w3.org/TR/owl2-primer/`)

[4] `https://gate.ac.uk/gate/doc/plugins.html`

2. *RegEx Sentence Splitter*: it is another PR of the GATE core library. It is used to divide documents into *sentences*. It is essentially language-independent, and thus can be used as is for very many languages, including Italian. It is implemented in Java, and is based on regular expressions that define syntactic rules for sentence identification. At the end of this phase two new annotations are added to the document, i.e., *Sentences* and *Splits*, the latter indicating separation between sentences.
3. *TreeTagger POS*[5]: it is a component for document annotation with POS and lemma information, developed at University of Stuttgart. It is a Markov Model tagger which makes use of a decision tree.
4. *Gazetteer* [4]: this GATE built-in component annotates the documents on the basis of a set of lists of words, such as names of cities or organisations, or abbreviations for types of companies (e.g., ltd., Corp., Inc.). Each list can be associated with so-called major and minor types. These types correspond to categories, such that minor types are more specific than the corresponding major types. If the document contains a string matching with an element of a Gazetteer list, the component annotates the string with the major and minor type of this list. In case the string has more than one match, major and minor types of all the matching lists are added.
5. *JAPE Transducer*: this component is used to import user-written JAPE rules into the GATE platform. A JAPE program is constituted by a set of pattern/action rules, such that the left-hand side of a rule consists of an annotation pattern description, and the right-hand side consists of an annotation manipulation statement. The JAPE language allows to recognize regular expressions among the annotations produced from the PRs that run before the JAPE Transducer. Once the expression is found, a further annotation referring to the searched patterns/entities is added to the document [4].

Ontology population. It is the process of inserting instances into a domain ontology. To this aim we used three PRs, two of which are JAPE-based modules that essentially convert annotations created in the semantic annotation phase so that they are compatible with the format used by the third PR, called *OwlExporter*[6], which is the PR that concretely extracts ontology instances in the form of OWL assertions from the annotated text [6]. The OwlExporter manages two ontologies: a domain specific ontology, like the one we developed for our use case, and a domain-independent NLP ontology, which contains concepts commonly used in LE, like paragraphs, sentences, or noun phrases [10].

4 Case Study

We used Web Content Extractor[7] to retrieve articles concerning the "Mafia Capitale" inquiry and appeared on the Web portals of some major Italian newspapers between June 16, 2015, and February 29, 2016. The crawling phase generated 2657 articles.

We have then defined a domain ontology to represent some aspects of interest for the domain at hand. Our ontology is defined on a alphabet of 21 Classes, 9 ObjectProperties and 14 DataProperties. We have then manually created specific Gazetteer lists and JAPE

[5] `http://www.cis.uni-muenchen.de/~schmid/tools/TreeTagger`
[6] `http://www.semanticsoftware.info/owlexporter`
[7] `http://www.newprosoft.com/web-content-extractor.htm`

Table 1. Results of test #1

Words	Annotations	CA	OPA	Correct	Missing	Precision	Recall
6.084	414	404	10	403	98	97%	78%

rules for document annotation through the GATE PRs described in Section 3. We remark that the both Gazetteer lists and JAPE rules are specific for the Italian language.

To evaluate our approach, we carried out two tests, both performed on a MacBook Pro 9.2, with Intel Core i7 2,90 GHz and 8GB RAM. In the first test, we have chosen 10 documents, in a random way, among those produced by the crawling phase, and have asked a domain expert to annotate them, to identify all and only the instances of the ontology predicates that can be extracted by these documents. We have then compared the annotations produced by our pipeline with the annotations of the domain expert, by computing the *Precision* (P) and the *Recall* (R). We remind that $P = C/(C+S)$, where $C+S$ is the number of annotations produced through our pipeline, some of which are indeed correct (C), if compared with the annotations identified by the expert, whereas others are spurious (S) (i.e., false positive), whereas $R = C/(C+M)$, where M denotes the annotations missed by our pipeline, with respect to those identified by the expert (i.e., false negative). The results of this first test are given in Table 1, where *Words* indicates the number of words contained in the analyzed documents, *Annotations* is the total number of annotations produced by our pipeline, i.e., $C+S$, *CA* and *OPA*, denote the number of Class and ObjectProperty assertions extracted, respectively (to keep the expert annotation task simple, we did not consider DataProperty annotations).

We got excellent Precision and good Recall, a significant number of class assertions, but few ObjectProperty assertions. As for the precision, the errors we obtained were only due to the wrong annotations associated to the word "Marino", which is both a city and the last name of a Rome ex-mayor, since our JAPE rules were not able to disambiguate this situation. We notice however, that such kind of problem can be solved by adding other PRs to our pipeline, like the Pronomial Coreference (PC)[8], which provides an annotation on pronouns that refer to already annotated entities. This PR is currently available in GATE only for the English language, and some extension is needed to make it work also for the Italian.

The value we obtained for the Recall is mainly affected by the fact that we were not able to identify many ObjectProperty assertions. Whereas for this aspect there is much space for improvement, e.g., by adding further JAPE rules, we believe that the usage of the PC mentioned above can be helpfull also to increase the Recall, since many links between entities can be discovered by correctly annotating pronouns.

In the second test we have processed in our pipeline all the 2657 articles produced by the crawling phase. The results are shown in Table 2, where also the overall running time needed to process all documents is given. In the table, *DPA* denotes the number of DataProperty assertions we were able to extract. Due to the large number of documents used in this test, we could not measure overall precision and recall, but we mainly used this test to evaluate the impact of our approach on a large text corpus. Our results are

[8] `https://gate.ac.uk/sale/tao/splitch6.html#sec:annie:pronom-coref`

Table 2. Results of test #2

Words	CA	OPA	DPA	Exec.time (sec.)
1.285.290	38.452	419	99.145	1.948,88 ($\sim$30 mins)

encouraging, in particular for the number of CA and DPA extracted. Furthermore, to get an idea of the quality of the result, we measured the precision on the 1% of the data in the output (involving a domain expert) and we have got a value of 94%.

5 Simplifying Gazetteer Lists Generation

As said in Section 3, the Gazetteer PR annotates the documents on the basis of a set of lists of words, used to find occurrences of these words in the text, (e.g., for the NER task). In our use case, it was crucial to create all the Gazetteer lists we used, because all the articles we analyzed are in Italian, and when we started our project no reusable support for Gazetteer lists for this language was available. To create the lists related to the domain entities of "Mafia Capitale", we use two methods:

- based on *Open Data Sources (ODS)*: Lists have been downloaded (and then manually refined) from open data Web sites. In particular, we did this for the first and last name of individuals belonging to a specific category, e.g., the members of the Government of the city of Rome. To this aim we have downloaded specific lists of interest from, e.g., OpenPolitici[9], for the lists of Politicians currently in charge, and also from other data sources, such as DBpedia.
- based on *Human-Knowledge (HK)*: When we could not find a specific list in an open data source, we resorted to a completely manual construction of the dictionary, by exploiting personal knowledge on the topic and web searches. This has been in particular done to construct lists of words that identify certain categories (e.g., containing all phrases used to mean "Lawyer").

The construction of such lists through this approach was non-trivial and required a significant amount of time. We thus investigated alternative methods for Gazetteer lists generation that could reduce the manual effort required, and could be easily replicable in different domains, thus augmenting the generality of our approach. To this aim, we focused on Wikidata as an informative source for Gazetteer lists production.

Wikidata is a collaboratively edited knowledge base, which organizes a large amount of data in a structured way according to a general reference ontology. It is an openly accessible resource, following the Semantic Web standards for exporting, interconnecting and querying data, which can be edited and read by both machine and humans. We have downloaded a Wikidata RDF dump (specifically we used the version of March 3, 2017), and have loaded it on a graph database management system with RDF/SPARQL support, namely Blazegraph[10]. This has enabled us to access Wikidata information

[9] http://politici.openpolis.it/
[10] https://www.blazegraph.com/

Table 3. Annotations through Gazetteer lists based on ODS/HK vs. those based on Wikidata

List	Entries	Annotations	Spurious Ann.	Missing Ann.	Precision	Recall
First Names ODS	8913	322	83	0	74%	100%
First Names Wikidata	2517	262	31	5	88%	98%
Criminal Organizations HK	25	37	21	0	43%	100%
Criminal Organizations Wikidata	68	20	18	14	10%	12%
Criminal Organizations Wikidata Mod.	273	30	24	10	20%	37%
Politicians ODS	1083	11	0	40	100%	22%
Politicians Wikidata	7778	17	0	34	100%	33%
Journalists ODS	369	4	0	4	100%	50%
Journalists Wikidata	3727	8	0	0	100%	100%
Political Parties ODS	131	23	0	2	100%	92%
Political Parties Wikidata	447	4	0	21	100%	16%
Political Parties Wikidata Mod.	1293	26	7	6	73%	76%

through standard SPARQL queries. By virtue of this approach it is possible to avoid tedious and time-consuming development of ad hoc solutions for each wanted Gazetteer list. Indeed, once the setup of the system is completed, a user just needs to define and execute a set of SPARQL queries to obtain the lists of interest. Such queries are specified taking into account the lists to populate, the Wikidata ontology structure, and its data model. The result of each SPARQL query is a CSV file, which has to be simply renamed into a `.lst` file to be processed by the Gazetteer PR.

To compare the two approaches, we considered five lists containing Italian Politicians, Journalists, First Names, Criminal Organizations, and Political Parties, respectively. Each list has been produced and used in two versions, i.e., ODS/HK based and Wikidata based. The comparison has been done on 15 articles and followed the same criteria of the first test described in Section 4: a hand-based annotation aimed at identifying entities in the five chosen lists has been done by a domain expert; then, the articles have been annotated through the Gazetteer PR by using the two different sets of lists generated by the two approaches. The results are shown in Table 3.

From an analysis of the lists created by Wikidata we noticed that they contain various entries with typos and flaws, which was expected to some extent. Our experiments however show that the Precision value for annotations with the Wikidata lists is the same or better than Precision with ODS/HK lists in all cases but the Criminal Organizations one. For several Wikidata lists, also the Recall is close to the one measured for the corresponding ODS/HK list. For the cases of Criminal Organizations and Political Parties we instead initially got very low values for the Recall. This was mainly due to problems with uppercase/lowercase letters (since GATE is case sensitive). We thus refined the two lists by adding for each term the three versions: all uppercase letters, all lowercase letters, and capitalized words. In Table 3 these new lists are denoted as *Wikidata Mod.* We can observe that with this fix the value of Recall become greater than that of the original Wikidata lists, and has reached acceptable levels. However, for the *Political Parties Wikidata Mod.* list this approach has generated a decrease of Precision. This has been caused by the introduction of new entries, e.g., the word *si* (which is the lowercase version of the acronym SI, an Italian Political Party). This word is indeed used in Italian as reflexive pronoun, thus leading to some wrong annotations. Although the decrease of Precision, we notice that the modification of the Political Parties list increase the Recall of 60%.

From the data present in Table 3, we can conclude that our experiments have been quite successful, since the Wikidata based approach has adequate values in terms of number of annotations, Precision and Recall. Realistically, these values keep unchanged when the number of analysed articles increases. We believe that this confirms that resorting to Wikidata for producing lists to be used by the Gazetteer PR allows for both time savings and good results.

6 Conclusions

Future improvements of our approach include the insertion of the PC component discussed in Section 4 in our pipeline. Also, we are working on further refinement of our solution in order to simplify some of the phases that now require a manual intervention, in the spirit of the work done on Gazetteer lists described in Section 5. In particular, we are currently investigating a way to streamline the definition of JAPE rules.

Acknowledgments. This work has been partly supported by Leonardo Company in the context of the *XASMOS* initiative, and by the Italian project *RoMA* (SCN_00064). Giulio Ganino has been supported by the FILAS grant *Laboratori teorico-sperimentali a supporto delle applicazioni spaziali delle industrie laziali* (FILAS-RU-2014-1058).

References

1. N. Antonioli, F. Castanò, S. Coletta, S. Grossi, D. Lembo, M. Lenzerini, A. Poggi, E. Virardi, and P. Castracane. Ontology-based data management for the Italian public debt. In *Proc. of FOIS '14*, pages 372–385, 2014.
2. F. Baader, D. Calvanese, D. McGuinness, D. Nardi, and P. F. Patel-Schneider, editors. *The Description Logic Handbook: Theory, Implementation and Applications*. Cambridge University Press, 2nd edition, 2007.
3. R. Collobert, J. Weston, L. Bottou, M. Karlen, K. Kavukcuoglu, and P. Kuksa. Natural language processing (almost) from scratch. *J. Mach. Learn. Res.*, 12:2493–2537, Nov. 2011.
4. H. Cunningham. *Developing Language Processing Components with GATE Version 8*. University of Sheffield Department of Computer Science, 2014.
5. H. Cunningham, D. Maynard, K. Bontcheva, and V. Tablan. GATE: A Framework and Graphical Development Environment for Robust NLP Tools and Applications. In *Proc. of ACL'02*, 2002.
6. G. Ganino, D. Lembo, M. Mecella, and F. Scafoglieri. Ontology population for open-source intelligence: a GATE-based solution, 2018. Submitted to an Int. Journal.
7. N. Guarino. Formal ontology in information systems. In *Proc. of FOIS '98*, Frontiers in Artificial Intelligence, pages 3–15. IOS Press, 1998.
8. M. Johnson, S. Khudanpur, M. Ostendorf, and R. Rosenfeld. *Mathematical Foundations of Speech and Language Processing*. Springer New York, 2004.
9. R. Navigli. Word sense disambiguation: a survey. *ACM COMPUTING SURVEYS*, 41(2):1–69, 2009.
10. R. Witte, N. Khamis, and J. Rilling. Flexible ontology population from text: The OwlExporter. In *Proc. of LREC'10*, may 2010.
11. H. Zhao, X. Zhang, and C. Kit. Integrative semantic dependency parsing via efficient large-scale feature selection. *J. of Artificial Intelligence Research*, 46:203–233, 2013.

An IoT-enabled Framework for Context-aware Role-based Access Control

Giorgio Delzanno, Giovanna Guerrini

DIBRIS, University of Genova, Italy

Abstract. We present a framework for enforcing the application of context-aware Role-based Access Control policies based on an Internet of Things eco-system inspired by the Google's Physical Web. In this setting we are interested in capturing three contextual dimensions, namely who-where-when, and using these information to restrict access to shared resources. Formally, the framework consists of features types, an automata-based model of time-sensitive roles, context-aware permission rules, and an IoT infrastructure based on Eddystone Beacons for validating a policy against the current state of users.

1 Introduction

In modern distributed systems based on the Internet of Things (IoT), security layers of software applications must be tightly integrated with the underlying system/network infrastructure. The integration is needed in order to increase the privacy of user data, to ensure availability of access control configuration services, and to integrate edge and fog components in the, possibly seamless, eco-system that governs information assurance. In particular, devices at the edges of an IoT system can be employed as active parts of location-based and time-dependent access control policies enforcement mechanisms. Furthermore, a tighter integration between the security layer and distributed infrastructures could provide better provenance on data and information flows.

According to this idea, in this paper we present a framework for enforcing the application of geo-referenced Role Based Access Control (RBAC) policies [5] based on an IoT infrastructure inspired by the Google's Physical Web paradigm [4,6,7,8,9,11,12,13,14,15]. The Google's Physical Web project enables smartphone users to interact with physical objects and locations through the use of beacon technology. Beacons are low cost radio transmitters that typically transmit a unique ID on a regular interval, e.g., 100-1000ms, in a range of approximatively 30 meters. Bluetooth-enabled devices can detect a beacon and receive its corresponding identifier, following the so-called lighthouse metaphor. Smartphone applications can use such IDs to signal their physical presence in

SEBD 2018, June 24-27, 2018, Castellaneta Marina, Italy.

the beacon vicinity to a remote server and the limited transmission range of these transmitters provides precise users localization. The Physical Web is particularly useful for indoor scenarios equipped with low cost devices such as beacon transmitters. This technology can be applied to set up non-invasive and precise localization methods, with easily configurable privacy protection layers (e.g., associations between user IMEI's and beacon identifiers, etc), to generate location-based provenance meta-data, and to ensure a tight integration between access control policies, physical spaces, and policy enforcement mechanisms.

Our framework consists of features types, context-aware permission rules, and an IoT infrastructure for validating a policy against the current state of users. In this setting, we are interested in capturing three contextual dimensions, namely who-where-when, and use these information to restrict access to shared resources. Users are assigned to stateful roles. A role must be considered as a slowly changing condition of users, whereas a state represents time-dependent a behavior associated with a specific role (e.g. typically a faculty member can act as instructor, mentor, course attendee, etc). Similarly, locations have time-dependent states that capture possible different usages of the same physical space (e.g. a room can be used for meetings, seminars, courses, etc). Our time model is based on deterministic finite-state automata inspired by logical specification languages for the linear time flow. Access control rules are defined on top of role and location states. Therefore, they can be used to define complex (i.e. automata-based) time-dependent access policies.

We illustrate the main ideas underlying the specification language of context-aware control access policies using an example. Consider a campus which physical spaces are organized in buildings, floors, and rooms. A room may have several usages, e.g., meeting room, seminar room, lecture room. The usage depends on a predefined time schedule. The same room can have different usages in different time slots. Users can assume different roles, e.g., student, teacher, mentor. Furthermore, users perform actions like consulting and updating records related to attendance at a given lecture, finding information on teachers, retrieving statistics, etc. Permission rules formalize access control policies to public and private data. Permissions are context-aware in that access to specific data can be constrained by the physical location of the user. Permission rules have to specify properties such as: a student can update its attendance record only when she/he gets access to the system from a classroom, teachers can get statistics on student attendance anywhere, students can get information of teacher presence anywhere in the department building, etc. This scenario can be nicely formalized by introducing a time-dependent stateful model for roles and locations. The timed model is based on a linear flow of time represented as an automata with a total transition function (i.e., automata that have a lasso shape). Roles and locations have an associated labeling function dependent of time that determines the dynamics in each role specialization and in the usage of physical spaces. Validation is defined against permission rules associated to user operations by considering a notion of state based on the current user location and the system time.

The main novelty of our proposal w.r.t. classical approaches like GeoRBAC [5], TRBAC [1] or proximity frameworks like PROX [10] is the combination of an automata-based specification of context-aware access control model with an IoT validation infrastructure that can be automatically reconfigured by encoding a policy into a relational data model and a corresponding control program for policy enforcement.

A prototype of the system is currently under evaluation in our University with the aim of providing an automated support for the management of typical Academic Campus services like registration of attendance to lectures and meetings, rooms and lectures allocations, etc. Specifically, lecture attendance is often a problem for the performance of academic degrees (especially bachelor). Intermediate tests are often used as a way to encourage students to actively attend lectures and take exams. The platform provides (physical) web services and mobile applications for the registration and analysis of lecture/meeting attendance. Beacons are used to detect, in almost real-time, the presence of a student in a lecture room. Our specification language can then be used to formally configure access control to private data ensuring that users can modify their own record only when they are physically present in a given room authenticated in the system with their own smartphones. Furthermore, the same architecture can be applied in every scenario that requires a verified list of attendees, for example in the case of meetings in which it is mandatory to generate on-the-fly reports or collect results of several voting during the same meeting.

A prototype of the system has been developed using the Node.js server-side technology and Android for dedicated mobile app interfaces. The internal structure of Node.js allows the system to handle a large number of connections in a short period of time reducing potential risks of denial of service failures and attacks. Furthermore, Android OS provides natively support for beacons, for secure network connectivity, and for protecting device resources. In our system private data are exposed to the server only after obtaining permissions from the users. The system has been tested in a real scenario in the Database course of the Computer Science Bachelor degree at the University of Genova (more than 120 students).

In the paper, we present the specification language, the validation mechanism, system requirements, design principles, and implementation choices of the proposed architecture. The remainder of the paper is organized as follows. Sections 2 and 3 specify the model, in terms of policy specification language and enforcement. Section 4 focuses on infrastructure and system requirements. Section 5 discusses software related issues (architecture, data model, and prototype solutions) while Section 6 concludes.

2 Time Flow, Roles, Locations and Operations

Based on models for georeferenced and temporal access control languages [1,2,3,5], in our model both roles and locations are assigned a time-dependent notion of state. First of all, our notion of context is based on three dimensions: who, where, and when. In other words we assume that the IoT infrastructure can provide precise information on current location and role (state) of each user in the window with granularity associated to the time model selected in the specific policy. To formalize these ideas, we first define our model of time.

Linear Time Model In this paper we consider a linear time model defined via a finite automata $A_T = \langle P, succ\rangle$, such that P is a finite set of time points and $succ : P \rightarrow P$ is a total function that defines the successor $succ(p)$ of any point $p \in P$. In other words, A_T is an automata that can only consist of an initial finite suffix entering into a finite and simple loop. The automata A_T will be used to model different time granularities, e.g., possibly repeated time/days slots during a week, months, etc.

Roles We define roles using feature types, i.e., a partially ordered set of entities. More specifically, the set of roles is defined by a finite set *Role* equipped with a binary relation $\sqsubseteq$ such that $\langle Role, \sqsubseteq\rangle$ forms a lattice, i.e., *Role* has top and bottom element, and every subset of elements in *Role* admits a least upper bound and a greatest lower bound. The $\sqsubseteq$ relation can be viewed as a hierarchy relation (specialization) that can be used to build role hierarchies. For instance, $bachelorstudent \sqsubseteq student$ Every role $r \in Role$ comes with a finite set of possible states $State_r$ and a labeling function $\rho_r : P \rightarrow State_r$ that associates a given state to every time point. The labeling function must be compatible with $\sqsubseteq$ in that if $R_1 \sqsubseteq R_2$ the R_1 inherits all permits of R_2. In our model permits are associated with states, thus compatibility requires that if $R_1 \sqsubseteq R_2$, then $State_{R_2} \subseteq State_{R_1}$, i.e., state containment is contravariant w.r.t. role specialization.

Locations The set of physical spaces *Location* is a finite set equipped with a binary relation $\sqsubseteq$ such that $\langle Location, \sqsubseteq\rangle$ forms a lattice. Every $l \in Location$ comes with a finite set of possible states $State_l$ and a labeling function $\rho_l : P \rightarrow State_l$ that associates a given state with every time point. Similarly to roles, the location labeling function must be compatible with the hierarchy relation, i.e., if $L_1 \sqsubseteq L_2$, then $State_{L_2} \subseteq State_{L_1}$, i.e., state containment is contravariant w.r.t. location specificity (i.e. specific users may have enlarged permissions in fixed locations inside a building).

Operations Operations are defined by a finite set of labels *Ops*.

Example 1. As an example, consider a linear time automata A_T with states $\{0, 1, 2, 3, 4\}$ s.t. $succ(i) = i + 1\ mod\ 5$ s.t. $1 = Mon$, $2 = Tue$, etc. Now let us consider the set

$$Role = \{Student, Teacher\}$$
$$State_{student} = \{Attendant, Mentor\}$$
$$State_{teacher} = \{Teacher\}$$

where we omit top and bottom elements for simplicity. We assume here that users can be either students or teachers that access with two types of resources. Now we assume that $\rho_{Student}(i) = Attendant$ for $i \in \{0, \ldots, 3\}$, and $\rho_{Student}(4) = Mentor$. Furthermore,

$$Location = \{Building, Floor, Room1, Room2\}$$

s.t. $Room \sqsubseteq Floor \sqsubseteq Building$,

$$State_{Room1} = State_{Room2} = \{Meeting, Course, Floor, Building\}$$
$$State_{Floor} = \{Floor, Building\}$$
$$State_{Building} = \{Building\}$$

where we omit top and bottom elements for simplicity. Furthermore, $\rho_{Room1}(i) = Course$ for $i \in \{0, \ldots, 3\}$, and $\rho_{Room1}(4) = Meeting$, $\rho_{Room2}(i) = Meeting$ for $i \in \{0, \ldots, 4\}$.

Finally, we consider the following set of operations

$$Ops = \{GetRecord, UpdateRecord, FindTeacher, GetStatistics\}$$

The get/update record actions correspond to read/write operations on database containing student activity reports, such as course attendance data, mentoring activities, etc, that require certified time accountability, e.g., courses in which attendance is mandatory for a given percentage of hours. FindTeacher allows users to check for the presence of a teacher during specific time window and in specific locations. GetStatistics corresponds to read operations on aggregate data such as course attendance.

3 Access Control Rules and Policy Enforcement

Based on the previous sections, we are now ready to introduce our notion of permissions in order to define context-aware access control rules.

Definition 1 (Permission). *A permission rule is a tuple*

$$p = \langle Op, RoleState, LocationState \rangle$$

where $Op \in Ops$*,* $RoleState$ *is a role state in* $\bigcup_{r \in Role} State_r$*, and* $LocationState$ *is in* $\bigcup_{l \in Location} State_l$*.*

To clarify the meaning of permission rules, we need to introduce users, sessions, and then a validation mechanism.

Let Id be a denumerable set of user identifiers. Every user has an associated labeling function *session* that associates to the user an instance role. Permissions are then defined by rules associated to role and location states. More precisely, we introduce a notion of current state of a user via a state function defined as follows. For $u \in Id$, $state(u, t) = loc$, where we assume that loc is an instance of $Locations$.

Definition 2 (Validation of an operation). *User u can perform operation Op at time t if and only if there exists a permission rule $p = \langle Op, RS, LS \rangle$ s.t.*

- $state(u, t) = loc$,
- $session(u) = role$,
- *for every* $R \in Role$ *s.t.* $role \in R$ *we have that* $\rho_R(t) = RS$
- *for every* $L \in Location$ *s.t.* $loc \in L$ *we have that* $\rho_L(t) = LS$.

Example 2. We list below some examples of permissions.

- $p_1 = \langle UpdateRecord, Attendant, Course \rangle$ s.t. students can update their attendance records from the room of a course only.
- $p_2 = \langle UpdateRecord, Mentor, Meeting \rangle$ s.t. mentors can update their mentor accounting records from a meeting room only.
- $p_3 = \langle GetStatistics, Teacher, Building \rangle$: teachers can consult the student records anywhere in a building.
- $p_4 = \langle FindTeacher, Mentor, Building \rangle$: only mentors are allowed to use the service to locate a teacher in a building.

4 IoT Infrastructure

A prototype of the context-aware access control validation mechanism has been implemented using a IoT infrastructure based on the combination of beacons, wi-fi network technology, mobile, web, and database management components a typical scenario of the Physical Web paradigm proposed by Google. Our operative scenario is a typical example of an Academic Campus and we assume that each classroom is equipped with at least one beacon configured with a unique identifier consisting of three subfields called UUID, MajorID, and MinorID. In our experimental setup we adopted Estimote beacons. For lecture rooms for at most 180 students a fix beacon turned out to be sufficient to detect all enabled smartphones. We also assume that rooms of staff members are equipped with beacons to inform students of their presences in the building and office-hour updates. Finally, we assume that each room provides wi-fi access to students, e.g., via Eduroam (`https://www.eduroam.org/`) access points. A (Web) server must be installed either on an external cloud provider or on a local server. In both cases it must be reachable from the local network, i.e., the firewall configuration must provide access to Web APIs needed by the smartphone and Web applications.

The platform is based on a combination of hardware and software solutions that must be deployed in physical spaces like lecture and meeting rooms in an academic campus. The infrastructure and system requirements can be summarized as follows.

1. The system should provide *precise indoor localization* of users via their smartphones. The required precision must be in the order of a few tens of meters (i.e., to cover a lecture room).

2. *Registration* of user presence must be done in *real-time*. The server must be reachable from every lecture room.
3. *Rooms* must be viewed as *geofences*. Only users inside a given room should be able to update data with georeferenced permissions.
4. The system should be *resistant to server failures*, e.g., by using multiple server instances on different machines.
5. Logged *data must be stored persistently* in a data storage system. Data storage must be accessible to the application and administrators, only.
6. *Users must be informed* that the server makes use of localization data.
7. *Users must give their permission* for releasing data stored in the device (IMEI).
8. *Data* stored in the server *should not be released to third parties.*
9. Users must be *uniquely identified via official credentials* such as the matriculation (staff) number assigned by the central administration.
10. User devices must be *identified uniquely using IMEIs*. Every user must associate a unique device (IMEI) to the corresponding personal identifier.
11. *Data* exchanged with the users must be *encrypted and sent on secure channels.*
12. To *limit the budget*, hardware and software infrastructures must be composed by *low cost devices*, standard networking services provided in academic environments (e.g. server on virtual machines), open-source software and development frameworks for server-side and mobile applications.

To meet all the above requirements, we need to satisfy constraints both at the physical level (infrastructure and hardware) and at the software level (networking and platform).

5 Software Platform Architecture

The software platform consists of an app with different views depending from the current user (e.g., students, teacher, administrator), a Web application, and a persistency server as described in the next sections. The server provides secure APIs (secure TCP) for accepting user requests and for sending notifications. Persistent data are stored in a MySQL server accessible only from the server. The Web application allows staff members to create and modify user profiles, visualize historical data and statistics for both classrooms and individual students. Although responsive, this functionality must be viewed as an access point designed for a traditional (non mobile) browser. *Role* and *Location* are modeled using relational schemes. The state machines that defines *RoleStates* and *LocationStates* is stored as a relation containing a key for the time points, and states for each role instance. Thus validation of user state can be reduced to a query in the record associated to the current time point. Machine time is mapped to virtual time used in the access control specification by using a mapping function that is selected by the administrator. The mapping models the granularity of the considered time model (e.g, it extracts current day and hour from machine

Matricula	IMEI
3471890	980000832471652
3471891	990000551621881
3471895	990000144425624

Table 1. Association between student ID and IMEI

	9-11	11-13
Mon	CS1 (room 1)	Seminar (room 1)
Tue	CS2 (room 1)	Seminar (room 2)
Wed	CS1 (room 1)	Seminar (room 2)
Thu	CS2 (room 1)	Seminar (room 2)
Fri	CS3 (room 1)	Tutoring (room 2)

Table 2. Weekly Room Allocation Plan

time or sim.). This provides an alignment between machine time and automata time used in the enforcement step.

As an example, assume that Alice Smith is enrolled in the first year of a Computer Science Bachelor degree. Alice has student ID 3471890 and the association between her identifier and the IMEI of her smartphone (and of other two students) is shown in Table 1. The association between beacons identifiers and rooms is shown in Table 3. According the permission rule $p_1 = \langle UpdateRecord, Attendant, Course\rangle$ and $p_2 = \langle UpdateRecord, Mentor, Meeting\rangle$ attendance and tutoring hours registration for Alice Smith is synchronized in accordance to the data in Table 2 and Table 3 and the current location of Alice and time. Timing is based on the server time in order to avoid manipulation of timestamps sent with user requests. Registration in all other cases (different location, times) is forbidden.

The middleware underlying the platform has been implemented combining different technologies. The server has been implemented using the Node.js IoT framework, an efficient server-side development framework based on Javascript and on the npm eco-system. Node.js provides very efficient packages for handling secure TCP connections, Web servers, and applications. Node.js server-side libraries are optimized for network intensive applications even when executed on single host or cluster. Indeed, Node.js allows to handle a large number of connections in a short period of time reducing potential risks of denial of service (this is very useful in our context since the system has to handle hundreds of requests in a few minutes). This property is due to the internal structure of the Node.js event-driven engine. Requests are not handled using multiple threads as in the Apache server model since the Node.js engine is based on an event loop that executes callbacks sequentially. Callbacks are picked from multiple priorities FIFO queues. Furthermore, thread pool implemented using the C++ libuv concurrency library supports the execution of asynchronous callbacks. Differently from server architectures based on multiple threads, in Node.js the response to connection requests require few system resources since they basically require

Physical space	beaconID
room 1	101
room 2	102

Table 3. Association between rooms and beacons

the emission of events whose synchronous effect is that of enqueuing callback invocations in the I/O queue. This choice mitigates the risk of classical denial of service attacks based on a high number of simultaneous requests that could congest the server by exhausting system resources (e.g., creation of new threads to scale up the server).

The prototypes of the mobile applications have been developed in the Android OS. Android OS provides native support for beacons (e.g., using OS notification management or beacon SDKs like Estimote SDK). It also provides secure network connections and access control policy management that protects private data. Private data are exposed to the server only after obtaining permissions from the owner. The authentication mechanism built on top of associations between user and device identifier relies on secure network connections (secure TCP sockets) between the smartphone application and the server. A smartphone app, configured to detect beacons using libraries like the Estimote SDK, is provided in two different versions: students and teachers. The *student app* provides sign-up, sign-in, and sign-out and a wide range of functionalities. The sign-up service associates the smartphone IMEI to the unique student enrollment number and to his contact details. After the first user registration, sign-in is automatically enabled whenever the app is activated by the user. Indeed, the server can retrieve the IMEI of the smartphone from the initial connection request issued by the app. Thus, the silent authentication stage is based on the association between the user identifier and the registered IMEI. Upon authentication, students can register their attendance to a given lecture in a given time-slot. The lectures schedule of each student is indeed synchronized, server-side, with the lectures and rooms allocations plan, for each enrollment year. Thanks to this synchronization, attendance is enabled only in specific time-slots and in physical spaces. In addition the app provides user interfaces for visualizing the historical data stored in the persistence server (profile, attendance log) and interfaces to visualize, via a calendar widget, lecture plans (according to the corresponding study plan), seminars, and other events registered by staff members.

Using protocols similar to those adopted for the student view, the *teacher app* provides a user interface for visualizing statistics on students attendance, lectures and events calendar. The aggregated number of presences provides indications for each course trend: it is indeed possible to understand if the number of students attending at the beginning of the course decreases significantly or remains stable during the semester. It is also possible to check if there are days or time-slots with a significant decrease in attendance and consequently try to implement strategies to avoid such drop out. The app also provides a control widget for the notification of presence in office-hours. Staff members can create, modify, and delete events that will be notified to users and visualized in their calendar view. Furthermore, they can access the room allocation service that is moderated by a dedicated administrator.

6 Conclusions and Future Work

The Google's Physical Web project – center stage at the Google IO developer conference in 2016– was conceived to enable smartphone users to interact with physical objects and locations through the use of beacon technology. The Google Physical Web architecture has been supported with physical devices such as Estimote beacons and client API's. Beacons are low cost radio transmitters that typically transmit a unique ID on a regular interval, e.g. 100-1000ms, in a range of approximatively 30 meters. Bluetooth-enabled devices can detect a beacon and receive its corresponding identifier, following the so-called lighthouse metaphor. Smartphone applications can use such ID to signal their physical presence in the beacon vicinity to a remote server and the limited transmission range of these transmitters provides precise users localization. The typical application domain of physical web is that of proximity marketing [8]. In this context, beacons are located nearby specific products and smartphone applications, enabled to detect beacons, redirect the user towards web sites with details on the products, brand, coupons, special offers, etc. Beacons have been applied in other domains like indoor localization [6,7,9,11,15], crowdsensing in public transportation [4], tourism [13], usage of physical spaces [12]. The main novelty of our physical web application comes from the use of beacons as enabling-technology to enforce context-aware access control policies. As a future work, we plan to extend both the specification language and the compilation of permission rules into an enforcement eco-system (devices, apps, data model, control program) and to study more applicative scenarios both in academic environment as well as in the enterprise domain.

Acknowledgments The authors would like to thank Claudio Orlando for his contribution to the prototype implementation.

References

1. E. Bertino, P. A.. Bonatti, and E. Ferrari. TRBAC: A temporal role-based access control model. *ACM Trans. Inf. Syst. Secur.*, 4(3):191–233, 2001.
2. E. Bertino, B. Catania, E. Ferrari, and P. Perlasca. A logical framework for reasoning about access control models. *ACM Trans. Inf. Syst. Secur.*, 6(1):71–127, 2003.
3. E. Bertino and E. Ferrari. Information security. In *The Practical Handbook of Internet Computing*. 2004.
4. D. Cianciulli, G. Canfora, and E. Zimeo. Beacon-based context-aware architecture for crowd sensing public transportation scheduling and user habits. In *The 8th International Conference on Ambient Systems, Networks and Technologies (ANT 2017) / The 7th International Conference on Sustainable Energy Information Technology (SEIT 2017)*, pages 1110–1115, 2017.

5. M. L. Damiani, E. Bertino, B. Catania, and P. Perlasca. GEO-RBAC: A spatially aware RBAC. *ACM Trans. Inf. Syst. Secur.*, 10(1):2, 2007.
6. W. He, P.-H. Ho, and J. Tapolcai. Beacon deployment for unambiguous positioning. *IEEE Internet of Things Journal*, 4(5):1370–1379, 2017.
7. J.-H. Huh and K. Seo. An indoor location-based control system using bluetooth beacons for IoT systems. *Sensors*, 17(12):2917, 2017.
8. K. Eun Jeon, J. She, P. Soonsawad, and P. Chet Ng. BLE beacons for internet of things applications: Survey, challenges, and opportunities. *IEEE Internet of Things Journal*, 5(2):811–828, 2018.
9. T. Kaulich, T. Heine, and A. Kirsch. Indoor localisation with beacons for a user-friendly mobile tour guide. *KI*, 31(3):239–248, 2017.
10. M. S. Kirkpatrick, M. L. Damiani, and E. Bertino. Prox-RBAC: A proximity-based spatially aware RBAC. In *19th ACM SIGSPATIAL International Symposium on Advances in Geographic Information Systems, ACM-GIS 2011*, pages 339–348, 2011.
11. A. Mackey and P. Spachos. Performance evaluation of beacons for indoor localization in smart buildings. In *2017 IEEE Global Conference on Signal and Information Processing, GlobalSIP 2017*, pages 823–827, 2017.
12. R. Purta and A.n Striegel. Estimating dining hall usage using bluetooth low energy beacons. In *ACM International Joint Conference on Pervasive and Ubiquitous Computing and ACM International Symposium on Wearable Computers, UbiComp/ISWC 2017*, pages 518–523, 2017.
13. G. Sato, G. Hirakawa, and Y. Shibata. Push typed tourist information system based on beacon and augumented reality technologies. In *31st IEEE International Conference on Advanced Information Networking and Applications, AINA 2017*, pages 298–303, 2017.
14. A. Weisling and A. Xambó. Beacon: Exploring physicality in digital performance. In *Proceedings of the Twelfth International Conference on Tangible, Embedded, and Embodied Interaction, TEI 2018*, pages 586–591, 2018.
15. J. Zhu, K. Zeng, K.-H. Kim, and P. Mohapatra. Improving crowd-sourced wi-fi localization systems using bluetooth beacons. In *9th Annual IEEE Communications Society Conference on Sensor, Mesh and Ad Hoc Communications and Networks, SECON 2012* , pages 290–298, 2012.

Lessons Learned and Research Agenda for Big Data Integration of Product Specifications (Discussion Paper)

Luciano Barbosa[1], Valter Crescenzi[2], Xin Luna Dong[3], Paolo Merialdo[2], Federico Piai[2], Disheng Qiu[4], Yanyan Shen[5], and Divesh Srivastava[6]

[1] Universidade Federal de Pernambuco luciano@cin.ufpe.br
[2] Roma Tre University {name.surname}@inf.uniroma3.it
[3] Amazon lunadong@amazon.com
[4] Wanderio disheng@wanderio.com
[5] Shanghai Jiao Tong University shenyy@sjtu.edu.cn
[6] AT&T Labs – Research divesh@research.att.com

Abstract. The product domain represents a challenging scenario for developing and evaluating big data integration solutions: the number of sources providing product specifications is very large, and ever increasing over time. The volume of available data is impressive, and these data keep changing very frequently. In this paper, we present ongoing efforts, challenges and our research agenda to address big data integration for product specifications.

1 Introduction

This paper describes our recent experiences dealing with the issue of extracting and integrating data from product specification pages on the Web, the challenges that we encountered and opportunities we leveraged. We provide an overview on our ongoing research activities on this problem, we discuss the lessons that we have learned from our experience, and illustrate open problems and future directions.

Integrating data from the product domain represents a challenging issue, presenting most of the difficulties associated with big data solutions at the web scale. Thousands of websites contain an impressive number of product pages. Each page provides information about a single product: usually general product specifications (typically technical and physical features), and some source-specific data, such as, price and customers' reviews.

Integrating product data might enable many valuable applications, such as data driven market analysis, question answering, and price comparison. However, data integration at the web-scale raises intriguing *challenges* due to the volume, variety, velocity, and veracity of data [3].

- In this context, the *volume* of data refers not only to the large number of products but, even more importantly, to the number of sources. In order to achieve coverage and diversity, we need to process a very large number of sources across the entire web, not just a small number of pre-selected sources.
- The *variety* of data is directly influenced by the number of sources and arises at many different levels, affecting every task of our pipeline. At the product category level, websites, especially the head ones, organize products according to such a vast plethora of categorization strategies that it gets very difficult, if not impossible, to reconcile them into a unified taxonomy. At the product description level, heterogeneities are related to attributes and values, which are published according to different granularities (e.g., physical dimensions in one field vs three separate fields for width, length, height), formats (e.g., centimeters vs inches) and representations (e.g., the color of a product as a feature vs distinct products for different colors).
- The *Velocity* of data concerns the rate of appearance and disappearance of pages in sources as well as the rate of appearance and disappearance of web sources. Also, while some attributes (such as technical and physical features) are quite stable over time, the contents of the individual pages can change daily, for example for prices and reviews.
- The *Veracity* of data deals with honest mistakes that can occur in web pages, but also with deceits, that is, deliberate attempts to confuse or cheat (e.g., providing imprecise or erroneous product characteristics).

2 End-to-End Data Integration Pipeline

To address the above challenges, we are working on an end-to-end data integration solution for product specification pages. For simplicity of presentation, we describe our approach as a linear pipeline, as depicted in Figure 1, where tasks are performed in sequence and independent of one another. However, there might be feedback loops between the tasks, as intermediate results can indeed influence the performance and the behavior of the preceding tasks and of the end to end solution.

In our vision, the information need is expressed by an input set of sample pages. We observe that products are typically organized in *categories*, and hence we expect that the sample pages refer to products from the categories of interest. Our approach is inspired by the Open Information Extraction [4] paradigm: the schema for the target data is not specified in advance, and the categories of the target products do not refer to a predefined product taxonomy, but they are rather inferred from data in the product pages of the input sample and in the product pages that are gathered from the Web along a progressive and iterative process.

Every task produces output to feed the successive task in the pipeline, but intermediate results could find other compelling application scenarios as well. To this end, we advocate that the pipeline must include an empirical evaluation benchmark for every task.

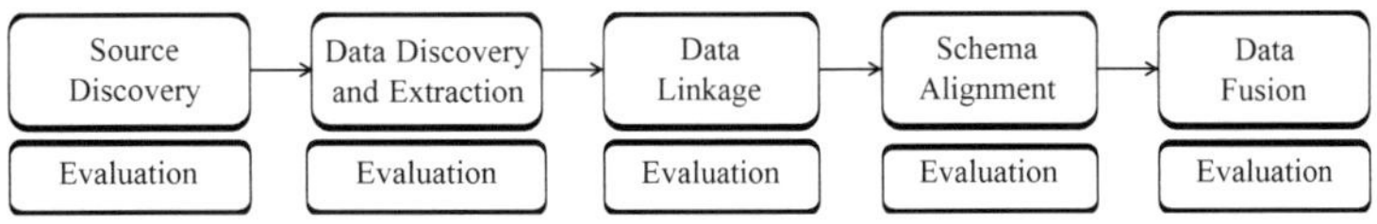

Fig. 1. Our end-to-end big data integration pipeline for product specifications.

Source discovery aims at efficiently finding and crawling product websites in order to gather pages that refer to the products of interest. One might believe that discovering product websites is a minor task, as a relatively small number of *head sources* can offer enough data for most of the products. For example, amazon.com already provides data about an impressive number of products. However, valuable information is actually published by an enormous number of *tail sources* [1, 2], i.e., sources that each provide a small number of product entities. These tail sources are important because they improve coverage. They can often offer *tail entities*, i.e., products that are present in a small number of sources, as well as *tail attributes*, i.e., product properties that are present in a small number of entities. Also, tail sources ofter refer to *tail categories*, i.e., small niche categories of products. Finally, *tail sources* contribute to information diversity, as they provide values that depend on the local source, such as, product reviews and price.

Data discovery and extraction has the objective of processing the pages harvested in the previous task in order to locate and extract product attribute names and their values. As we mentioned above, we do not rely on a predefined schema, but rather extract attributes bottom-up, with the goal of discovering not just *head attributes*, but also *tail attributes* that cannot always be described in advance.

Data linkage seeks to cluster pages from different sources that refer to the same products. It is worth observing that in the traditional data integration pipeline, schema alignment is performed before record linkage [3]. Unfortunately, with a very large number of sources, such a traditional approach becomes infeasible because of the huge variety and heterogeneity among attributes. We propose then to perform data linkage before schema alignment as we can take advantage of the opportunity that products are named entities, and hence a product specification page usually publishes the product identifier.

Schema alignment addresses the challenge of semantic ambiguity and aims to reconcile the attributes offered by different sources, that is, to understand which attributes have the same meaning and which ones do not, as well as identify value transformations to normalize different representations of the same attribute values. Since we do not rely on a global schema given in advance, correspondences among attributes are established bottom-up leveraging the results of the previous data extraction and data linkage phases.

Data fusion tackles the issue of reconciling conflicting values that may occur for attributes from different sources. Data fusion aims at evaluating the trustworthiness of data, deciding the true value for each data item, and the accuracy of the sources. To address these challenges, data fusion techniques rely on data redundancy, which further motivates the need to process many sources.

2.1 Our approach: redundancy as a friend

Our approach to develop the above pipeline aims at taking advantage of the *opportunity* that products are named entities, and hence a product specification page usually publishes the product identifier. Web sources that deliver product specification pages publish product identifiers mainly for economic reasons: websites need to expose the product identifiers to let them be indexed by shopping agents and available to customers who search products for comparing prices or consulting specifications. Large e-commerce marketplaces strongly encourage sellers and retailers to publish product identifiers, as they improve efficiency both for the internal management of data and for the exchange of data with search engines like Google and Bing.

The presence of identifiers allows us to drive the pipeline from source discovery to data integration by leveraging the opportunity of *redundancy of information at the global level*, and the *homogeneity of information at the local level*.

- At the global level, we observe that head (popular) products are present in several head (large) sources as well as in many tail (small) sources. Therefore, we expect that identifiers of head products are spread across many sources. Further, many head products in a category will often co-occur in multiple sources.
- At the local level, we observe that the structure and the semantics of information, within each source, tend to be regular. Hence, we expect the product specification and product identifiers presented in a given page are published according to the same structure for every page in the same source.

Figure 2 illustrates the key intuitions underlying our approach from source discovery to data integration to meet the goal of *effectively* and *efficiently* dealing with head and tail sources, hence including all pages of head and tail entities. Starting from known head entities in head sources, we take advantage of homogeneity of information at the local level to extract product specifications and identifiers for tail entities in head sources (even head sources offer many tail entities). Then, we exploit the presence of head entities across sources: searching head identifiers, we discover tail sources (even tail sources offer a few head entities). Again, we exploit homogeneity of information at the local level to extract identifiers and specifications for tail entities in tail sources.

---

eBay, Amazon, Google Shop explicitly require sellers to publish the id for many product categories. For example, see eBay's rules:
http://for-business.ebay.com/product-identifiers-what-they-are-and-why-they-are-important.

Based on our *Redundancy as a friend* approach, we developed a focused crawler, Dexter [6], to discover and crawl product web sites offering product pages for the input categories. Dexter starts from a seed set of product pages, and iteratively discovers and crawls new sources, from which extracts products specifications. Then, we developed a big data linkage approach specifically tailored for product pages that takes advantage of the redundancy of information at a global level, and homogeneity of structure and semantic at the individual source level [5].

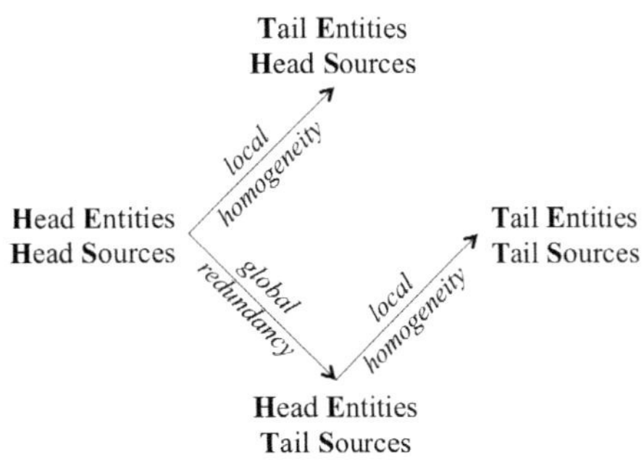

Fig. 2. Our approach.

3 Lessons Learned and Research Agenda

In an experimental evaluation performed between Sept 2014 and Feb 2015, we have trained the focused Dexter crawler [6] to gather product pages from 10 coarse categories: camera, cutlery, headphone, monitor, notebook, shoes, software, sunglasses, toilet accessories, televisions. The crawler discovered 3.5k websites, for a total of 1.9M pages. Each website contributed to provide pages for the different categories, and pages were grouped into 7,145 clusters, corresponding to the local categories exposed by the websites (on average every websites has 2 local categories). The dataset is publicly available on-line.

Building a Benchmark Product Dataset – We compared the contents of our dataset with pages in Common Crawl, an open repository of web crawl data. About 68% of the sources discovered by our approach were not present in Common Crawl. Only 20% of our sources contained fewer pages than the same sources in Common Crawl, and a very small fraction of the pages in these sources were product pages: on a sample set of 12 websites where Common Crawl presented

Note that the on-line version (https://github.com/disheng/DEXTER) is an extension of the dataset presented in [6].
http://commoncrawl.org/

more pages than in our dataset, we evaluated that only 0.8% of the pages were product pages.

These results suggest the critical need for the community to build a suitable benchmark product dataset to conduct big data research. Our dataset can be considered a first step in this direction. Another important step would be that of maintaining the dataset over time, as discussed next.

Maintaining the Benchmark Product Dataset: Addressing the Velocity Challenge – In March 2018, we have checked all the URLs of the pages of the dataset. We have observed that just 30% of the original pages and 37% of the original sources are still valid (we consider a source valid if it contains at least one working URL). We also performed an extraction of the product specifications. We obtained complete specification from just 20% of the pages.

These numbers clearly indicate that the velocity dimension affects all the tasks of the pipeline. Developing solutions to collect snapshots over regular time intervals and perform data integration over time can open intriguing research directions. While some activities, such as checking the appearance/disappearance of sources can be done on monthly basis, others, such as crawling web sites to check appearance/disappearance of pages and changes in the pages should be performed more frequently. To this end, the development of efficient incremental solutions for source discovery and web crawling represent interesting research directions.

As our experiments emphasize, data extraction rules are brittle over time. The development of wrappers resilient to changes in the pages has always been a primary goal in data extraction research. A dataset with multiple snapshots over a long interval of time, as the one that we have advocated above, could serve as a benchmark for data extraction solutions.

Harnessing Velocity – We observe that while velocity represents a challenge, it could also become an opportunity. We observe that analyzing changes in the pages could help improve our data extraction and data linkage techniques.

For example, one of the main challenges of the product identifier extraction step is to eliminate identifiers that refer to suggested and related products, instead of the main product of the page. Examining the same product page over time may help us to more easily separate out the former part, since those may change faster over time than the description of the product in the page.

Schema Alignment – We are currently working on the development of techniques to perform schema alignment for our product domain. The main difficulties that we have to face are due to the heterogeneity at the schema and at the instance level, due to the large number of independent sources.

To give a concrete example of the heterogeneity at the schema level, consider the dataset collected using the Dexter crawler, described earlier in this section. The specifications extracted from these sources contain more than $86k$ distinct attribute names (after normalization by lowercasing and removal of non alphanumeric characters). Most of the attribute names (about $85k$) are present in less than 3% of the sources, while only 80 attribute names occur in 10% of the sources, with the most popular attribute name occurring in just 38% sources.

The solution that we are investigating exploits data linkage to cluster attributes that share the same values. Since heterogeneity occurs also at the instance level, we aim at progressively finding correspondences between the cluster resolving increasingly complex matches between values with different representations.

Addressing the Veracity Challenge and Data Fusion – Analyzing the sources of our dataset we noticed that some clusters contain product pages from different categories. In some cases, the errors are in the sources: some websites adopt unexpected (or even completely wrong) criteria as, for example, classifying monitors under a laptop category or vice-versa; other websites aggregate products and related accessories (which represent another category of products). In other cases, the errors are due to wrong classifications by the system.

To overcome these issues we want to investigate different solutions. First, we believe that introducing feedbacks in our pipeline could significantly improve data quality, especially for precision. For example, alternating source discovery and data linkage we could select better identifiers to feed to Search for source discovery, thus increasing the precision, with respect to the target category, of the sources. Similarly, results from schema alignment could help improve the precision of linkage, as pages whose attributes do not align are unlikely to represent the same product. Another promising direction to improve precision without penalizing recall is to study solutions to exploit humans in the loop. In particular, we aim at developing and evaluating techniques based on active learning and crowdsourcing to continuously train the classifiers with effective and updated training sets.

We have observed many inconsistencies between values of a product attribute across sources. Existing data fusion techniques [2, 3] can help to resolve these inconsistencies when they are due to honest mistakes, possibly in combination with extraction errors. However, the product domain also exhibits inconsistencies due to deceit, where sources may deliberately provide imprecise or erroneous product characteristics. Identifying and effectively addressing such inconsistencies at web scale is an important direction of future work.

Beyond Source Homogeneity – Our approach to data extraction is based on the assumption that pages are structurally homogeneous at the local source level. This is a valid assumption for a vast majority of websites, but there are exceptions. For example, some websites that publish used products have a weak template and leave the seller the freedom to publish the product specification without any structural imposition. For some application scenarios, one can simply drop these sources. If on the contrary they are important, data extraction should be performed by solutions that do not rely on the template.

Beyond Product Specifications – So far we have considered the extraction of the identifiers and of the specifications. However important data that complete the product description are price and reviews. Challenging issues for the extraction of price are to distinguish the price of the principal product in the page from the prices of other products, such as suggested products, similar products, and the actual price from discounts or list price. Reviews represent important information in many applications. An interesting problem is how to combine structured data from the specification with the unstructured data of the reviews.

References

1. Dalvi, N., Machanavajjhala, A., Pang, B.: An analysis of structured data on the web. Proceedings of the VLDB Endowment **5**(7), 680–691 (2012)
2. Dong, X.L.: How far are we from collecting the knowledge in the world? In: Keynote at 19th International Workshop on Web and Databases. ACM (2016)
3. Dong, X.L., Srivastava, D.: Big data integration, vol. 7. Morgan & Claypool Publishers (2015)
4. Etzioni, O., Banko, M., Soderland, S., Weld, D.S.: Open information extraction from the web. Communications of the ACM **51**(12), 68–74 (2008)
5. Qiu, D., Barbosa, L., Crescenzi, V., Merialdo, P., Srivastava, D.: Big data linkage for product specification pages. In: Proceedings of the 2018 ACM SIGMOD International Conference on Management of data. ACM (2018)
6. Qiu, D., Barbosa, L., Dong, X.L., Shen, Y., Srivastava, D.: Dexter: large-scale discovery and extraction of product specifications on the web. Proceedings of the VLDB Endowment **8**(13), 2194–2205 (2015)

Wind Speed Forecasting via Structured Output Learning

Annalisa Appice[1,2](✉), Antonietta Lanza[1], and Donato Malerba[1,2]

[1] Dipartimento di Informatica, Università degli Studi di Bari Aldo Moro via Orabona, 4 - 70126 Bari - Italy
[2] Consorzio Interuniversitario Nazionale per l'Informatica - CINI
annalisa.appice@uniba.it, antonietta.lanza@uniba.it, donato.malerba@uniba.it

Abstract. In the context of the wind energy management, the study of time series data by means of a predictability analysis can be very helpful. For example, accurate wind speed forecasts are necessary to schedule dispatchable generation and tariffs in the day-ahead electricity market. This paper examines the use of structured output learning, in order to model historical wind speed data and yield accurate forecasts of the wind speed on the day-ahead (24 h) horizon. The proposed method is based on a multi-resolution analysis of the historical data, which are represented at multiple scales in both space and time. Handling multi-resolution wind speed data allows us to leverage the knowledge hidden in both the spatial and temporal variability of the shared information, in order to identify spatio-temporal aided patterns that contribute to yield accurate wind speed forecasts. In an assessment, using benchmark data, we show that the multi-resolution structured output learning is able to determine more accurate forecasts than the state-of-the-art structured output models.

1 Introduction

Nowadays power and energy systems with wind energy being as integral system have been successful. The benefit of clean wind energy also brings the challenge of forecasting wind power for optimal management of electricity grids. However, the variable nature of wind speed [17] poses operational challenges for wind power integration into modern power systems. As the wind variability occurs in time, as well as in space scales, the profiles of the available power of wind sources depend on the geographic location, the season (or time of the year), the time of the day and other physical parameters.

In this paper, the wind speed forecasting task is addressed by considering wind speed data measured every 10 minutes along day-ahead time horizons. We propose a specific time series approach that applies artificial intelligence,

SEBD 2018, June 24-27, 2018, Castellaneta Marina, Italy.

in order to learn a forecasting model from the historical data only. A peculiar contribution is the consideration of multi-resolution representations of historical data, in order to handle the variability of the wind speed information at the space and time scales. Our purpose is the investigation of the implications of learning multi-resolution data on the accuracy of the forecasting operation. Specifically, we formulate the day-ahead forecasting task as a structured output predictive learning problem [4]. A multi-target model is considered, in order to learn a single model that predicts multiple output variables at the same time – one variable for each time point over the 24-ahead horizon. The decision of learning an output structured model is supported by various studies which have repeatedly proved that multi-target models are typically easier to interpret, perform better, and overfit less than single-target predictions [4, 29, 7].

Neighboring and windowing mechanisms are adopted, in order to represent the historical data at various scales in both space and time, respectively. These mechanisms are combined with the standard deviation operator that is used to quantify the spatial and/or temporal variability of the data. This multi-resolution representation of the wind speed variability contributes to define new input variables, as well as new output variables. In this way, we are able to learn a multi-target model that accounts for the variability of measurements at different sites and times. The viability of the proposed method is assessed in the structured output learning by comparing the accuracy of traditional multi-target models to the accuracy of multi-resolution multi-target models in a benchmark scenario. The sensitivity of the accuracy of the proposed forecasting model learned is evaluated along the size of the scale. Finally, the accuracy gained in by taking into account appropriate patterns of the data variability is explored.

The paper is organized as follows. In the next Section, we briefly report the state-of-the-art of the time series analysis for the problem of wind speed forecasting. In Section 3, we describe the basics of this study. In Section 4, we present the multi-resolution structured output learning phase proposed here. In Section 5 we describe the benchmark dataset considered for the empirical evaluation and illustrate the relevant results. Finally, Section 6 draws some conclusions and outlines some future work.

2 Related work

In the literature, different forecasting horizons have been investigated: long-term (from one day to one week ahead), medium-term (from 6 h to one day ahead), short-term (from 30 min to 6 h ahead) and very short-term (few seconds to 30 min ahead) [28, 11]. On the other hand, various approaches have been developed for wind speed forecasting in renewable energy systems. In particular, three main predictive categories are described in the literature [6, 30, 3]: the physical [1, 15], the time series [27, 8, 20, 13, 18, 22, 21, 2, 5] and the hybrid [16, 10, 12] approaches. The physical approach describes a physical relationship between wind speed, atmospheric conditions, local topography and the output from the wind power turbine. The time series approach consists of time series forecasts, which are based on the historical data (the wind speed collected at a specific site), while neglect commonly the meteorological data. Finally, the hybrid approach applies a combination of physical and time series models.

By focusing the attention on the time series approach (which is the most popular in practice and also the subject of this paper), a wide plethora of time-series methods employ a general class of statistical models, that is, the Auto-Regressive Moving Average (ARMA) or Auto-Regressive Integrated Moving Average (ARIMA), in order to estimate future observations of a wind farm through a linear combination of the past data. The recent literature [26, 13, 19] has shown that these auto-regressive models are very well suited to capture short range correlations. Hence, they have been used extensively in a variety of (very) short-term forecasting applications (less than 6 hours). Recent studies have also proved that auto-regressive models can be profitably extended, in order to account for spatial characteristics of time series data and gain in accuracy [23–25]. In alternative, the time series approach also involves the use of artificial intelligence techniques, which are commonly well suited to produce accurate prediction in medium-term and long-term forecasting applications. Examples of artificial intelligence wind speed forecasting methods apply Neural Networks [9], Support Vector Machine [31], Regression Trees [18], K-Nearest Neighborhood [5] and Cluster analysis [22, 21].

By investing in artificial intelligence, this paper explores the use of the structured output learning in a medium-term wind speed forecasting application (24 h ahead). We note that the benefits of structured output learning in time series forecasting have been recently assessed in [7] considering the problem of deriving 24 h ahead solar radiation forecasts. Differently from this seminal study, that has modeled the spatial "correlation" of the solar radiation, in order to define new "input" variables only, we leverage here the power of a model of both the spatial and temporal "variability" of the wind speed, in order to define new "input" and "output" variables, which contribute to yield accurate 24 h ahead forecasts of the wind speed.

3 Basics

Premises Without loss of generality, the applicative scenario we consider in this work is described by the following four premises. First, the spatial location of a wind farm is modeled by means of 2-D point coordinates (e.g. latitude and longitude). Second, the spatial locations of the wind farms are known, distinct and invariant. Third, wind farms transmit measurements of the wind speed and they are synchronized in the transmission time. Finally, transmission time points are equally spaced in time.

Learning task Based upon these premises, the task we intend to perform is to forecast wind speed at each farm of the grid. The forecasting model is that learned from the input historical data of the wind speed, as they are collected

Multi-dimensional representations of geographic space can be equally dealt.

from a grid of wind farms, every 10 minutes, over $m+1$ consecutive days. We also consider additional input information, which models the wind speed variability at the spatial, temporal and spatio-temporal scales. The output of the learning phase is a structured output predictive model that allows us to yield fine-grained forecasts for the next day (24 hours) at 10 minutes intervals, based on the input historical wind speed data as they are measured at 10 minutes over the past m days.

Input and output variables Formally, let k_i be the i-th farm, (X_i, Y_i) are the geographic coordinates of k_i. Let us consider the historical wind speed data, measured from k_i, over days $1, \ldots, m, m+1$. They are transformed into a training example, that is represented by vectors $\mathbf{x_i}$, $\mathbf{x_i^S}$, $\mathbf{x_i^T}$ and $\mathbf{x_i^{ST}}$, which cover the role of independent input variables, and vectors $\mathbf{y_i}$, $\mathbf{y_i^S}$, $\mathbf{y_i^T}$ and $\mathbf{y_i^{ST}}$, which cover the role of dependent output (or target) variables, respectively. We note that the input variables are calculated over days $1, \ldots, m$, while the output variables are calculated over day $m+1$. These input and output variable vectors are formally described in the following.

Vector $\mathbf{x_i}$ is defined as follows:

$$\mathbf{x_i} = (x_{i_1}, \ldots, x_{i_{144}}, x_{i_{145}}, \ldots, x_{i_{288}}, \ldots, x_{i_{144m}}), \tag{1}$$

where x_{i_t} denotes the wind speed measured from k_i at time t with $t = 1, \ldots, 144m$ (i.e. every day is divided into 144, ten minutes spaced, time points so that t denotes the time point that occurs every 10 minutes at days $1, \ldots, m$). Similarly, vector $\mathbf{y_i}$ is defined as follows:

$$\mathbf{y_i} = (y_{i_{144m+1}}, \ldots, y_{i_{144(m+1)}}), \tag{2}$$

where y_{i_t} represents the wind speed measured from k_i at time t with $t = 144m+1, \ldots, 144(m+1)$ (every 10 minutes at day $m+1$).

By applying the standard deviation operator in combination with the neighboring and/or windowing mechanisms, we are able to define new data vectors that represent the variability of the multi-resolution wind speed data considered at spatial, temporal and spatio-temporal scales. In particular, the spatial scale is defined by the neighboring mechanism, the temporal scale is defined by the windowing mechanism, while the spatio-temporal scale is define by combining the neighboring and windowing mechanisms.

Given radius R, applying the neighboring mechanism to k_i, a circular neighborhood of k_i is constructed. This is a set of wind farms k_j so that $d(k_i, k_j) \leq R$ where $d(\cdot, \cdot)$ denotes the geographic distance. Considering the spatial scale defined by this neighboring mechanism, we define vectors $\mathbf{x_i^S}$ and $\mathbf{y_i^S}$, which represent farm k_i at the space scale with radius R over days $1 \ldots, m$ and day $m+1$, respectively. Procedurally,

$$\begin{aligned}\mathbf{x_i^S} &= (x^S_{i_1}, \ldots, x^S_{i_{144}}, x^S_{i_{145}}, \ldots, x^S_{i_{288}}, \ldots, x^S_{i_{144m}}),\\ \mathbf{y_i^S} &= (y^S_{i_{144m+1}}, \ldots, y^S_{i_{144(m+1)}})\end{aligned} \tag{3}$$

where:

$$x^S_{i_t} = stdev(\{x_{j_t}|d(k_i,k_j) \leq R\})\ with\ t = 1\ldots,144m,$$
$$y^S_{i_t} = stdev(\{y_{j_t}|d(k_i,k_j) \leq R\})\ with\ t = 144m+1\ldots,144(m+1). \quad (4)$$

Given length L so that L is a factor of 144, the windowing mechanism transforms the sequence of consecutive time points $t_1,\ldots,t_{144(m+1)}$ into the sequence of $\frac{144}{L}(m+1)$ consecutive time windows so that:

$$windowing[1\ldots144(m+1)] =$$
$$= \underbrace{W_1[1\to L], W_2[L+1\to 2L],\ldots,W_{\frac{144}{L}}[(\frac{144}{L}-1)L+1\to 144]}_{day\ 1}, \underbrace{\ldots}_{day\ 2},\ldots,\underbrace{\ldots}_{day\ m},$$
$$\underbrace{W_{\frac{144}{L}m+1}[t_{\frac{144}{L}m}+1\to t_{\frac{144}{L}m+L}],\ldots,W_{\frac{144}{L}(m+1)}[t_{\frac{144}{L}m}+(\frac{144}{L}-1)L+1\to t_{\frac{144}{L}(m+1)}]}_{day\ m+1}, \quad (5)$$

where each each window covers L consecutive time points. Considering the temporal scale defined by this windowing mechanism, we can define vectors $\mathbf{x_i^T}$ and $\mathbf{y_i^T}$, which represent farm k_i at the time scale with length L over days $1\ldots,m$ and day $m+1$, respectively. Procedurally,

$$\mathbf{x_i^T} = (x^T_{i_1},\ldots,x^T_{i_{\frac{144}{L}}},x^T_{i_{\frac{144}{L}+1}},\ldots,x^T_{i_{\frac{144}{L}2}}\ldots x^T_{i_{\frac{144}{L}(m-1)+1}},\ldots,x^T_{i_{\frac{144}{L}m}}),$$
$$\mathbf{y_i^T} = (y^T_{i_{\frac{144}{L}m+1}},\ldots,y^T_{i_{\frac{144}{L}(m+1)}}) \quad (6)$$

where:

$$x^T_{i_t} = stdev(\{x_{i_r}|r\in W_t\})\ with\ t = 1,\ldots,\frac{144}{L}m,$$
$$y^T_{i_t} = stdev(\{y_{i_r}|r\in W_t\})\ with\ t = \frac{144}{L}m+1,\ldots,\frac{144}{L}(m+1). \quad (7)$$

Finally, given radius R and length L, we define vectors $\mathbf{x_i^{ST}}$ and $\mathbf{y_i^{ST}}$, which represent farm k_i at the space scale with radius R and the time scale with length L over days $1,\ldots,m$ and day $m+1$, respectively. Procedurally,

$$\mathbf{x_i^{ST}} = (x^{ST}_{i_1},\ldots,x^{ST}_{i_{\frac{144}{L}}},x^{ST}_{i_{\frac{144}{L}+1}},\ldots,x^{ST}_{i_{\frac{144}{L}2}}\ldots x^{ST}_{i_{\frac{144}{L}(m-1)+1}},\ldots,x^{ST}_{i_{\frac{144}{L}m}})$$
$$\mathbf{y_i^{ST}} = (y^{ST}_{i_{\frac{144}{L}m+1}},\ldots,y^{ST}_{i_{\frac{144}{L}(m+1)}}) \quad (8)$$

where:

$$x^{ST}_{i_t} = stdev(\{x_{j_r}|d(k_i,k_j)\leq R\ and\ r\in W_t\})\ with\ t = 1,\ldots,\frac{L}{144}m,$$
$$y^{ST}_{i_t} = stdev(\{y_{j_r}|d(k_i,k_j)\leq R\ and\ r\in W_t\})\ with\ t = \frac{144}{L}m+1,\ldots,\frac{144}{L}(m+1). \quad (9)$$

4 Multi-Resolution Structured learning - MuReS

Let us consider a wind farm grid $\mathcal{K}$, which is composed of N wind farms $k_1, k_2, \ldots, k_N$, and a historical dataset $\mathcal{D}$, which comprises wind speed measurements collected from $\mathcal{K}$ over $m+1$ days. Adopting the notation introduced in Section 3, $\mathcal{D}$ is spanned over an independent input space $\mathbf{X} \times \mathbf{X^S} \times \mathbf{X^T} \times \mathbf{X^{TS}}$ and a dependent output space $\mathbf{Y} \times \mathbf{Y^S} \times \mathbf{Y^T} \times \mathbf{Y^{TS}}$. The structured predictive model f^{+ST} can be learned from $\mathcal{D}$ so that:

$$f^{+ST}\colon \mathbf{X} \times \mathbf{X^S} \times \mathbf{X^T} \times \mathbf{X^{TS}} \rightarrow \mathbf{Y} \times \mathbf{Y^S} \times \mathbf{Y^T} \times \mathbf{Y^{TS}}, \tag{10}$$

This predictive model is a "multi-resolution" upgrade of the traditional structured output predictive model [4, 29]. We note that the output space of $f^{+ST}(\cdot)$ yields 24 h forecasts of the fine-grained wind speed ($\mathbf{Y}$), as well as 24 h ahead forecasts of the winds speed variability at the space and time scales considered ($\mathbf{Y^S}$, $\mathbf{Y^T}$ and $\mathbf{Y^{TS}}$). However, this study aims at yielding accurate fine-grained forecasts of wind speed; hence the empirical study will explore the accuracy of model $f^{+ST}(\cdot)$ along $\mathbf{Y}$ only.

In this study, predictive model $f^{+ST}(\cdot)$ is learned as a tree, i.e. a hierarchy of clusters (Predictive Clustering Trees (PCTs)): the top node corresponds to one cluster containing all the data, which is recursively partitioned into smaller clusters while moving down the tree. CLUS, including PCTs for multi-target regression [14], is available at clus.sourceforge.net.

5 Experimental study

The experiments are carried out using real world data publicly provided by the DOE/NREL/ALLIANCE3 (http://www.nrel.gov/). The data (see Figure 1) consist of wind speed measurements from 1326 different locations at 80m of height in the Eastern region of the US. The data were collected in 10 minutes intervals during the year of 2004. This wind farm grid was able to produce 580 GW, and each farm produces between 100 MW and 600 MW. For the evaluation of the results, we consider the root mean squared error (RMSE), computed over the grid at each time point, as an indicator of the predictive performance. We derive twelve (training and testing) datasets, which are constructed as follows: for every month, days 1-11 defines a training dataset that is processed to learn the forecasting model (with $m = 10$), while days 15-25 defines the testing set used to evaluate the performance of the forecasting model learned on the corresponding training dataset. The 24 h ahead forecasting errors, averaged on the twelve datasets, are analyzed. For this empirical evaluation, the multi-resolution information is modeled at the spatial scale with radius $R = 10$ km or $R = 50$ km, as

The traditional structured output predictive model $f\colon \mathbf{X} \rightarrow \mathbf{Y}$ can be simply learned in this scenario by neglecting the information on the data variability.

The information on the wind speed variability is included in the output learning setting as a constraint to improve the predictive ability of the forecasting model learned.

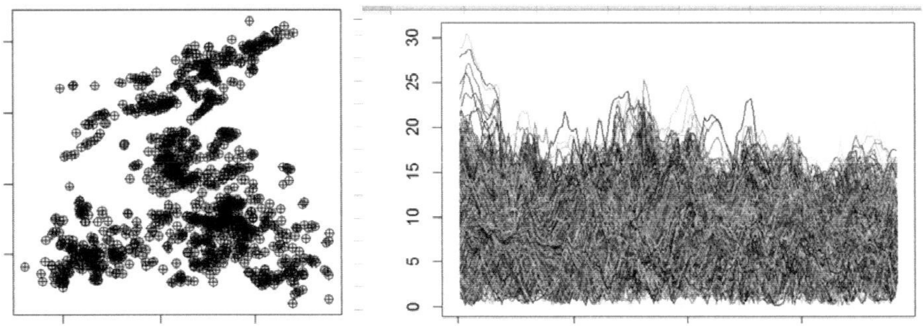

Fig. 1. Wind speed data

well as at the temporal scale with length $L = 1$ hour (6 consecutive time points) or $L = 3$ hours (18 consecutive time points). The performance of the standard deviation operator is compared to that of the sum and mean operators. Finally, the forecasting performance of the multi-resolution structured output predictive model ($f^{+ST}(\cdot)$) is compared to the performance of the baseline structured output predictive model ($f(\cdot)$).

Evaluating scale size We start by analyzing the performance of the multi-resolution structured output predictive models learned by MuReS along the size of the space (R) and time (L) scales. We run MuReS with the standard deviation operator computed over neighborhoods with radius $R = 10$km or $R = 50$km and windows with length $L = 1$h or $L = 3$h. Average RMSE results are plot in Figure 2. They show that the accuracy of the forecasting model is more sensitive to the time scale than to the spatial scale. In any case, the decrease in the forecasting accurcy performance, due to a large scale in the temporal resolution, starts being observed starting from forecasts produced 12 hours far from the current time point. Therefore, selecting the appropriate scale size is a crucial issue to yield accurate long-term forecasts. Based on these preliminary results, we select $R = 10$km and $T = 1$h for the remaining of this study.

Evaluating multi-resolution operator We proceed by exploring the performance of the multi-resolution structured output predictive models learned by MuReS along the selection of the multi-resolution operator used to model the wind speed variability. Considering $R = 10$km and $T = 1$h, we compare the forecasting accuracy achieved when the data variability model is computed through the standard deviation operator to the accuracy achieved when the variability model is computed through the sum or mean operators. Average RMSE results are plot in Figure 3. Results empirically support the effectiveness of our choice of resorting to the standard deviation as the most appropriate second order statistic to model the wind speed variability in both space and time. It actually contributes to gain in forecasting accuracy in this peculiar application.

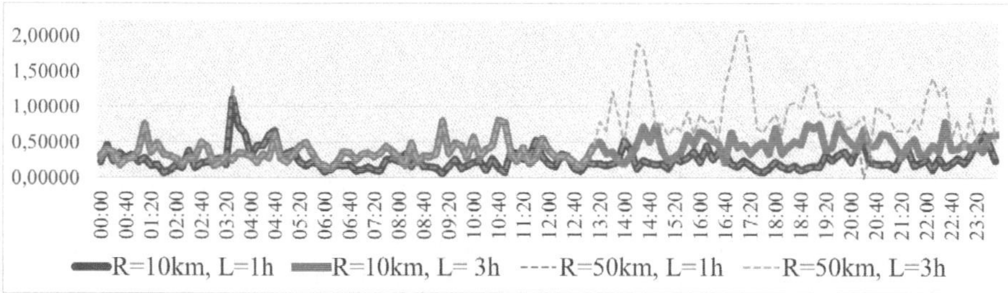

Fig. 2. Multi-resolution structured output predictive models ($R = 10, 50$km, $L = 1, 3$h): testing RMSE (averaged on twelve testing datasets - axis Y) plotted with respect to 10 minutes-spaced time points (over 24 h ahead horizon - axis X).

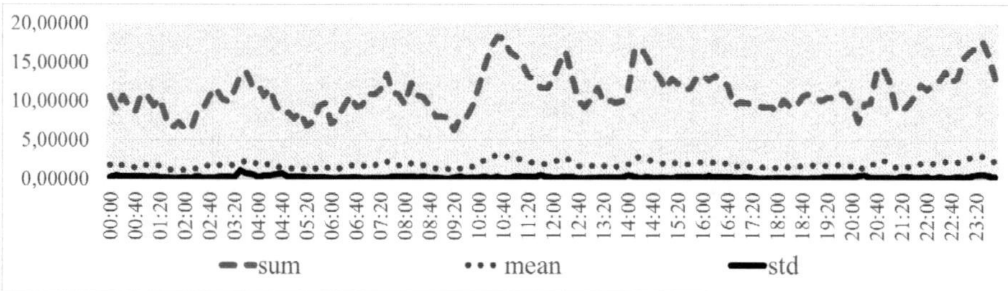

Fig. 3. Multi-resolution structured output predictive models (multi-resolution operator analysis - sum, mean and standard deviation): testing RMSE (averaged on twelve testing datasets - axis Y) plotted with respect to 10 minutes-spaced time points (over 24 h ahead horizon - axis X).

Evaluating multi-resolution learning schema We complete this study by comparing the performance of the multi-resolution structured output predictive models learned by MuReS with $R = 10$km, $L = 1$h and the standard deviation as multi-resolution operator to the performance of the baseline structured output predictive models learned neglecting data variability at space and time scales. Average RMSE results are plot in Figure 4. These results show empirically the viability of the main idea inspiring this study: the accuracy of the structured output predictive learning in the wind speed forecasting can be greatly improved by augmenting both the input and output spaces of the learning problem with multi-resolution information modeling the data variability of the wind speed observed at both space and time scales.

6 Conclusion

This paper studies the problem of the medium-term (24 h ahead) wind speed forecasting by considering different dimensions of analysis: data variability, spa-

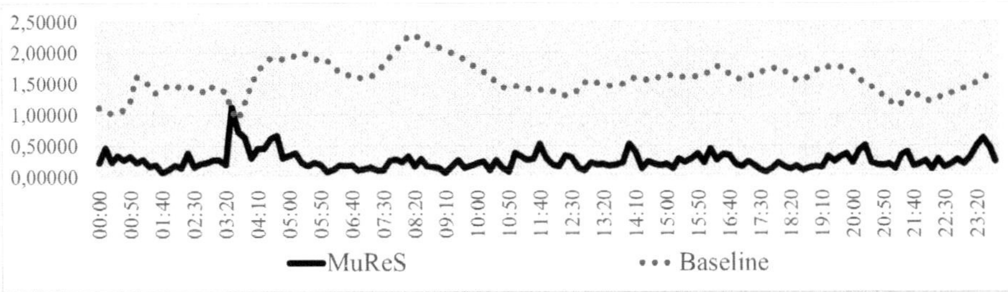

Fig. 4. Multi-resolution structured output predictive models (multi-resolution analysis - multi-resolution structured output model (MuReS) vs structured output model (Baseline): testing RMSE (averaged on twelve testing datasets - axis Y) plotted with respect to 10 minutes-spaced time points (over 24 h ahead horizon - axis X).

tial and temporal resolution, structured output learning, aiming to investigate the relevant implications for the dealing with the multi-resolution representation of the data variability for the problem at hand. Results in a benchmark dataset clearly show that accounting for the data variability at space and time scales allows us to learn output prediction models, which are much more accurate than traditional models that neglect the multi-resolution information. Moreover, experimental results confirm that the standard deviation is an appropriate multi-resolution operator of the data variability to be taken into account in this specific application. Finally, defining the size of the scale (particularly in the time scale) can be crucial issue to guarantee accurate long-term forecasts. As future work, we intend to explore the implications of these models of the data variability in statistical time series models (e.g Arima or Var). We also plan to investigate more sophisticated incremental learning methods that are able to update the forecasting model as new historical data are collected, in order to fit the learned models to drifting data.

7 Acknowledgments

Authors thank Enrico Laboragine for his support in developing the algorithm presented and running the experiments. This work was partially supported by the EU-funded project TOREADOR (ICT-16-2015, Grant Agreement A. no. 688797), as well as by the University of Bari Aldo Moro - funded ATENEO Project 2014 on "Mining of network data" and ATENEO Project 2015 on "Models and Methods to Mine Complex and Large Data".

References

1. W. Albert, S. Chi, and C. J.H. An improved grey-based approach for electricity demand forecasting. *Electric Power Systems Research*, 67:217–224, 2003.

2. V. Almeida and J. Gama. Collaborative wind power forecast. In *3rd International Conference on Adaptive and Intelligent Systems ICAIS 2014*, volume 8779 of *LNCS*, pages 162–171. Springer, 2014.
3. D. Ambach and P. Vetter. Wind speed and power forecasting - a review and incorporating asymmetric loss. In *2016 Second International Symposium on Stochastic Models in Reliability Engineering, Life Science and Operations Management (SMRLO)*, pages 115–123, 2016.
4. A. Appice and S. Dzeroski. Stepwise induction of multi-target model trees. In J. N. Kok, J. Koronacki, R. L. de Mántaras, S. Matwin, D. Mladenic, and A. Skowron, editors, *Machine Learning: ECML 2007, 18th European Conference on Machine Learning, Warsaw, Poland, September 17-21, 2007, Proceedings*, volume 4701 of *Lecture Notes in Computer Science*, pages 502–509. Springer, 2007.
5. A. Appice, S. Pravilovic, A. Lanza, and D. Malerba. Very short-term wind speed forecasting using spatio-temporal lazy learning. In N. Japkowicz and S. Matwin, editors, *Discovery Science - 18th International Conference, DS 2015, Banff, AB, Canada, October 4-6, 2015, Proceedings*, volume 9356 of *Lecture Notes in Computer Science*, pages 9–16. Springer, 2015.
6. M. Bhaskar, A. Jain, and N. V. Srinath. Wind speed forecasting: Present status. In *2010 International Conference on Power System Technology*, pages 1–6, 2010.
7. M. Ceci, R. Corizzo, F. Fumarola, D. Malerba, and A. Rashkovska. Predictive modeling of PV energy production: How to set up the learning task for a better prediction? *IEEE Trans. Industrial Informatics*, 13(3):956–966, 2017.
8. S. Fan, J. Liao, R. Yokoyama, L. Chen, and W.-J. Lee. Forecasting the wind generation using a two-stage network based on meteorological information. *IEEE Transactions on Energy Conversion*, 24(2):474–482, 2009.
9. U. B. Filik and T. Filik. Wind speed prediction using artificial neural networks based on multiple local measurements in eskisehir. *Energy Procedia*, 107:264 – 269, 2017. 3rd International Conference on Energy and Environment Research, ICEER 2016, 7-11 September 2016, Barcelona, Spain.
10. G. Giebel, J. Badger, I. M. Perez, P. Louka, and G. Kallos. Short-term forecasting using advanced physical modelling-the results of the anemos project. results from mesoscale, microscale and cfd modelling. In *Proc. of the European Wind Energy Conference 2006*, 2006.
11. G. Giebel, R. Brownsword, G. Kariniotakis, M. Denhard, and C. Draxl. *The State-Of-The-Art in Short-Term Prediction of Wind Power: A Literature Overview, 2nd edition.* ANEMOS.plus, 2011. Project funded by the European Commission under the 6th Framework Program, Priority 6.1: Sustainable Energy Systems.
12. Z. Hui, L. Bin, and Z. Zhuo-qun. Short-term wind speed forecasting simulation research based on arima-lssvm combination method. In *ICMREE) 2011*, volume 1, pages 583–586, 2011.
13. R. G. Kavasseri and K. Seetharaman. Day-ahead wind speed forecasting using f-arima models. *Renewable Energy*, 34(5):1388 – 1393, 2009.
14. D. Kocev, C. Vens, J. Struyf, and S. Dzeroski. Tree ensembles for predicting structured outputs. *Pattern Recognition*, 46(3):817–833, 2013.
15. M. Lange and U. Focken. New developments in wind energy forecasting. In *Power and Energy Society General Meeting - Conversion and Delivery of Electrical Energy in the 21st Century, 2008 IEEE*, pages 1–8, 2008.
16. M. Negnevitsky, P. Johnson, and S. Santoso. Short term wind power forecasting using hybrid intelligent systems. In *Power Engineering Society General Meeting, 2007. IEEE*, pages 1–4, 2007.

17. M. Negnevitsky, P. Mandal, and A. K. Srivastava. An overview of forecasting problems and techniques in power systems. In *2009 IEEE Power Energy Society General Meeting*, pages 1–4, 2009.
18. O. Ohashi and L. Torgo. Wind speed forecasting using spatio-temporal indicators. In *ECAI 2012 - PAIS-2012) System Demonstrations Track*, volume 242 of *Frontiers in Artificial Intelligence and Applications*, pages 975–980. IOS Press, 2012.
19. J. Palomares-Salas, J. De la Rosa, J. Ramiro, J. Melgar, A. Aguera, and A. Moreno. Arima vs. neural networks for wind speed forecasting. In *IEEE International Conference on Computational Intelligence for Measurement Systems and Applications, CIMSA 2009*, pages 129–133, 2009.
20. C. Potter and M. Negnevitsky. Very short-term wind forecasting for tasmanian power generation. *IEEE Transactions on Power Systems*, 21(2):965–972, 2006.
21. S. Pravilovic, A. Appice, A. Lanza, and D. Malerba. Mining cluster-based models of time series for wind power prediction. In S. Greco and A. Picariello, editors, *22nd Italian Symposium on Advanced Database Systems, SEBD 2014, Sorrento Coast, Italy, June 16-18, 2014.*, pages 9–20, 2014.
22. S. Pravilovic, A. Appice, A. Lanza, and D. Malerba. Wind power forecasting using time series cluster analysis. In *17th International Conference on Discovery Science, DS 2014*, volume 8777, pages 276–287. Springer, 2014.
23. S. Pravilovic, A. Appice, and D. Malerba. An intelligent technique for forecasting spatially correlated time series. In *13th International Conference of the Italian Association for Artificial Intelligence, AI*IA 2013*, volume 8249 of *LNCS*, pages 457–468. Springer, 2013.
24. S. Pravilovic, A. Appice, and D. Malerba. Integrating cluster analysis to the ARIMA model for forecasting geosensor data. In *21st International Symposium on Foundations of Intelligent Systems, ISMIS 2014*, volume 8502 of *LNCS*, pages 234–243. Springer, 2014.
25. S. Pravilovic, M. Bilancia, A. Appice, and D. Malerba. Using multiple time series analysis for geosensor data forecasting. *Inf. Sci.*, 380:31–52, 2017.
26. J. Shi, X. Qu, and S. Zeng. Short-term wind power generation forecasting: Direct versus indirect arima-based approaches. *International Journal of Green Energy*, 8(1):100–112, 2011.
27. G. Sideratos and N. Hatziargyriou. An advanced statistical method for wind power forecasting. *Power Systems, IEEE Transactions on*, 22(1):258–265, 2007.
28. S. S. Soman, H. Zareipour, O. Malik, and P. Mandal. A review of wind power and wind speed forecasting methods with different time horizons. In *North American Power Symposium 2010*, pages 1–8, 2010.
29. D. Stojanova, M. Ceci, A. Appice, D. Malerba, and S. Dzeroski. Dealing with spatial autocorrelation when learning predictive clustering trees. *Ecological Informatics*, 13:22–39, 2013.
30. X. Wang, P. Guo, and X. Huang. A review of wind power forecasting models. *Energy Procedia*, 12(0):770 – 778, 2011.
31. J. Zhou, J. Shi, and G. Li. Fine tuning support vector machines for short-term wind speed forecasting. *Energy Conversion and Management*, 52(4):1990 – 1998, 2011.

Ensemble Learning for Multi-type Classification in Heterogeneous Networks (Discussion Paper)

Francesco Serafino, Gianvito Pio, and Michelangelo Ceci

University of Bari, Dept. of Computer Science, Via Orabona, 4, 70125 Bari (Italy)

Abstract. In the literature, several methods have been proposed for the analysis of network data, but they usually focus on homogeneous networks. More recently, the complexity of real scenarios has impelled researchers to design classification and clustering methods able to work also on heterogeneous networks, which consist of different types of objects and links. However, they often make assumptions on the structure of the network that are too restrictive or do not exploit different forms of network correlation and autocorrelation. Moreover, when several nodes of the network have missing values, standard methods can lead to either building incomplete classification models or to discarding relevant dependencies (correlation or autocorrelation). In this discussion paper, we describe an ensemble learning approach for multi-type classification that we proposed recently, which is able to exploit *i)* the possible presence of correlation and autocorrelation phenomena, and *ii)* the classification of instances (with missing values) of other node types in the network. Experiments performed on real-world datasets show that the proposed method is able to significantly outperform state-of-the-art algorithms.

1 Introduction

In the real world we can easily find objects which appear to be connected to each other, thus forming complex networks. Connections among these objects can represent different types of relationships, which can be found in several fields, including biology, epidemiology, geography, finance, etc. Most of the works in the literature about mining networked data focus on homogeneous networks, where all the objects are of the same type (and can, accordingly, be represented by a predefined set of features/characteristics) and the links among them describe a single type of relationship. A common example of a homogeneous network is that of social networks: objects represent people and links represent the friendship relationships. However, real scenarios are more complex due to the presence of multiple types of objects that are connected through different types of links, forming heterogeneous networks. For example, in well-known databases about movies (e.g., IMDb) we have movies, actors, users, tags, etc. In the bio-medical domain, databases contain genes, proteins, tissues, pathways and diseases. In all these cases, objects of different types establish different types of relationships.

Consequently, recent works have proposed new data mining methods that work on heterogeneous information networks. For example, in [15] and [16] the

SEBD 2018, June 24-27, 2018, Castellaneta Marina, Italy.

authors propose new clustering solutions, whereas in [6] and [7] the authors propose classification/prediction methods. Other methods that were initially proposed for relational data can be almost directly applied for the analysis of heterogeneous information networks [9]. However, existing methods suffer from one or more of the following limitations: *i)* they impose strict restrictions on the structure of the network, which must be know apriori; *ii)* they are not able to take into account (and possibly exploit) one of the main peculiarities of network data, i.e. the presence of different forms of *autocorrelation* [1, 14], according to which two connected nodes in the network tend to share some properties; *iii)* they are not able to consider the possible presence of missing values for some attributes, which can lead to either learning incomplete classification models or to discarding possibly relevant dependencies; *iv)* they are not able to classify objects of different types, where each type can have a different set of labels.

In this discussion paper, we describe the approach proposed in [13], which is able to work on heterogeneous networks with arbitrary structures and is able to capture both correlation and autocorrelation phenomena which involve the target objects (i.e., objects which are the main subject of the classification task). Moreover, we exploit the same strategy to predict possibly relevant missing values belonging to other objects, appearing strongly related to the target objects. Methodologically, we extend the method Mr-SBC [2], in order to also capture network autocorrelation phenomena, handle relevant missing values and perform multi-type classification. These last three issues are tackled by resorting to a combined bagging-boosting ensemble learning solution able to exploit information conveyed by objects (also of the same type) directly or indirectly connected to the main subject(s) of the classification task. Specifically, we propose two extensions of the Mr-SBC algorithm: ***i)* ST-MrSBC (Self-Training MrSBC)**, which is able to capture possible autocorrelation phenomena by resorting to a variant of the self-training method; ***ii)* MT-MrSBC (Multi-Type MrSBC)**, which iteratively analyzes objects of multiple types, in order to predict possible missing values, belonging either to the target type of the main classification task or to other object types that are strongly related to the main classification task. We consider the network classification task according to the *within-network* setting [4]: objects for which the class is known are linked to objects for which the class must be estimated [10] (which can be either the subject of the main classification task or other objects related to the main classification task). This semi-supervised setting, which allows the classification phase to take advantage of both labeled and unlabeled examples, leads to smoother predictions [3]. In multi-type classification, we add an additional mechanism to smooth the prediction function: capturing relationships among objects of different types, i.e, capturing correlations among labels of objects of different types.

2 Problem Statement and Background

Before describing the proposed method, in the following we introduce the notation used. We work on heterogeneous networks, which we formally define as

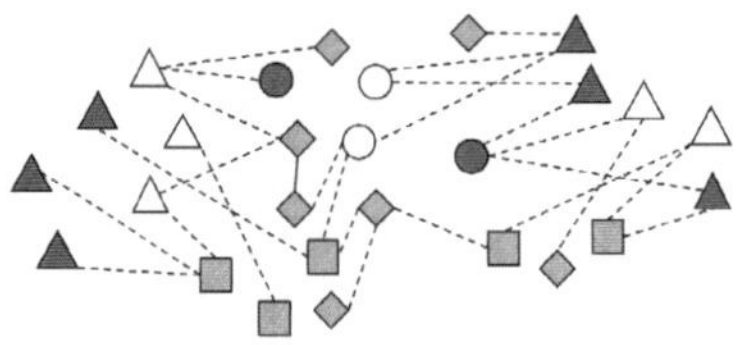

Fig. 1. An example of a heterogeneous network. The shape indicates the type of nodes: triangles and circles are nodes of target types (primary or secondary), and can be labeled (green) or unlabeled (white). Gray nodes belong to task-relevant types.

$G = (V, E)$, where V is the set of nodes and E is the set of edges among nodes. Both nodes and edges can be of different types. Moreover:
• Each node type T_p implicitly defines a subset of nodes $V_p \subseteq V$.
• Each node $v' \in V$ is associated with a node type $t_v(v') \in \mathcal{T}$, where $\mathcal{T}$ is the finite set $\{T_p\}$ of all the possible types of nodes in the network.
• A node type T_p defines a set of attributes $\mathcal{X}_p = \{X_{p,1}, X_{p,2}, \ldots, X_{p,m_p}\}$.
• An edge type R_j defines a subset of edges $E_j \subseteq (V_p \times V_q) \subseteq E$, where V_p and V_q are not necessarily based on different types.
• An edge e between two nodes v' and v'' is associated with an edge type $R_j \in \mathcal{R}$, where $\mathcal{R}$ is the finite set $\{R_j\}$ of possible edge types in the network.

In the considered task, we define a role for each node type: $\mathcal{T}_t$ (primary targets), which are considered as the targets of the main classification task; $\mathcal{T}_{st}$ (secondary targets), which are strongly related to the main classification task, for which a prediction of missing values is considered relevant; $\mathcal{T}_{tr}$ (task-relevant), which are the other node types. An example is reported in Figure 1. Only nodes of target (primary and secondary) types are actually classified, on the basis of all the nodes. However, we are actually interested in the maximization of the prediction accuracy only of objects of the primary target types.

3 The proposed ensemble learning method

In this section we describe the two solutions ST-MrSBC and MT-MrSBC. Both take as input a partially labeled heterogeneous network and work iteratively. At each iteration, they build an ensemble of Mr-SBC [2] classifiers from different subsets of labeled nodes (either known or predicted in the previous iterations), whose combination of the output will possibly lead to a stronger model.

Following the idea in [12] (for multi-label classification tasks), MT-MrSBC shuffles all the target types. This is motivated by the fact that a predefined ordering of the analysis of target types can negatively affect the classification accuracy, since a wrong decision can inhibit the exploitation of relevant dependencies and, consequently, can possibly enforce the exploitation of irrelevant/wrong dependencies. In the literature, this phenomenon is also observed in random-scan Gibbs sampling, as opposed to systematic-scan Gibbs sampling [8].

Once the order of analysis has been defined, MT-MrSBC samples a subset of nodes of the first target type and builds a weak (since built from a subset

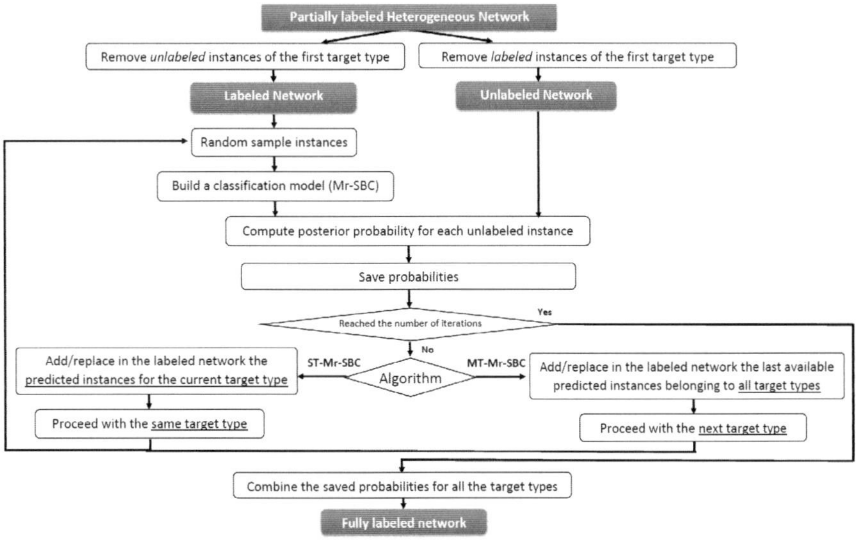

Fig. 2. High-level description of ST-MrSBC and MT-MrSBC.

of instances) predictive model through Mr-SBC. This predictive model is applied to classify unlabeled nodes which are then added to the labeled network. The obtained probabilities are also stored for the final combination of the outputs. Then, we select a new target type and repeat the process. Note that, at this stage, predictions performed for the previous target types are available to Mr-SBC when building a prediction model for the new target. Target types are shuffled again every time they are all processed. The number of iterations is limited by a user-defined threshold and the outputs obtained for each target type over all the iterations are combined to obtain the final (strong) predictive model. ST-MrSBC uses a similar process, but works on a single target type. Therefore, it exploits predictions obtained on the same target type in the previous iterations. The main difference with respect to the standard self-training is in the construction of the labeled network when a new iteration starts. Specifically, ST-MrSBC builds an ensemble of weak classifiers from different subsets of labeled nodes, instead of considering only the output of the last iteration.

Construction of labeled and unlabeled networks

At each iteration, we select the target attribute of the next target type and build two separate networks: the first contains only labeled nodes, and the second contains only unlabeled nodes. These networks are built by considering the complete network and by removing unlabeled and labeled nodes, respectively. This means that all the nodes of other target types, as well as nodes of task-relevant types, are included in both networks. While the network of labeled nodes, for each target type, changes at different iterations, the network of unlabeled nodes remains stable and the algorithm classifies the same nodes several times.

The way nodes are considered as training instances at each iteration is random. In fact, the algorithm randomly selects, according to a uniform distribution, a given percentage *perc* of labeled nodes from the labeled network. Note that, at a given iteration, the labeled network could contain also nodes that were initially unlabeled but that were classified during a previous iteration. In the case of ST-MrSBC, the last available predictions will regard the same target type, whereas in the case of MT-MrSBC, the last available predictions will regard all the target types (primary and secondary). This behavior is coherent with the assumption that predictions performed on other target types (primary or secondary) can help in the predictions of the label of nodes of the current target type. This implies that, at the next iteration, the algorithm will take into account some labels predicted at the previous iterations. This choice is, apparently, in contrast with most of the self-training approaches, which usually select the most reliable predictions for the next iterations. However, *1)* this solution does not necessarily lead to better results with respect to a random selection [5], and *2)* we do not use predictions as "hard" constraints, but in the next iterations we are able to retract decisions that are not coherent with the new state of the network.

Estimation of probabilities

At the end of each iteration, we build a classification model through Mr-SBC for the current target type from the network of labeled nodes. We remind that Mr-SBC is a naïve Bayes classifier which relies on a set of first-order rules induced from data stored in the tables of a relational database (see [2] for details).

For each unlabeled node v', the identified classification model is exploited to compute the posterior probability (which takes into account both network correlation and network autocorrelation) and its label $\psi_t(v')$, according to the following equation based on the Bayes' theorem:

$$\psi_t(v') = argmax_{Y_c} P(Y_c|R_{v'}) = argmax_c P(Y_c) \cdot P(R_{v'}|Y_c)/P(R_{v'}), \quad (1)$$

where Y_c is a possible class value of the target attribute y, and $R_{v'} \subseteq R_D$ is the subset of first-order rules, identified by Mr-SBC, covering the object v'.

The labeled nodes are then added to the labeled network for the subsequent iterations, as described before. The probabilities are exploited at the end of the entire process. In fact, after the last iteration, the final classifier combines the probabilities computed during all the iterations: for each target type T_t and for each node v', the method computes the final probability as the average of the probabilities computed over the ensemble in the following way:

$$\psi_t(v') = argmax_c \frac{1}{z} \sum_{k=1}^{z} P(Y_c|R_{v'k}) = argmax_c \frac{1}{z} \sum_{k=1}^{z} \frac{P(Y_c)P(R_{v'k}|Y_c)}{P(R_{v'k})}, \quad (2)$$

where z is the number of iterations, i.e., the number of classifiers in the ensemble, for each target type (the total number of iterations is $z \cdot |L_t|$) and $R_{v'k}$ is the set of rules identified from the labeled network at the k-th iteration. The rationale behind the combination in Equation (2) is twofold: *a)* the predictions obtained at each iteration are based on different training sets, which may focus on different properties of the concept to be learned; *b)* the predictions are made more stable.

Dataset	#Nodes	#Edges	Primary targets	Secondary targets
MOVIE	2,051	59,532	movies	users
NBA	36,593	63,924	teams	players
YELP	1,387,596	1,371,060	business - users	N/A
IMDB	212,039	342,161	movies	users
STACK	92,800	114,385	posts	users

Table 1. Quantitative information about the considered datasets

4 Experiments

We performed our experiments on five heterogeneous networks: MOVIE, NBA, YELP, IMDB and STACK. Some quantitative information about these datasets can be found in Table 4, while additional information can be found in [13].
In order to evaluate the different variants of the ensemble learning solutions we propose, we compared them with the original version of Mr-SBC. This allows us to evaluate the contribution of each aspect of our method, i.e., the iterative nature of the ensemble-based self-training approach (introduced in **ST-MrSBC**) and the multi-type classification of both primary and secondary targets (implemented in **MT-MrSBC**). Moreover, we evaluate the performance of MT-MrSBC by considering both a lexicographic (**LexicographicMT-MrSBC**) and a random ordering (**RandomMT-MrSBC**) of target types.

In order to perform a comparison with other systems, we also ran the experiments with four competitor methods. In particular, we considered *i)* the relational version of the nearest neighbour algorithm (**RelIBK**), *ii)* the SVM-based algorithm SMO (**RelSMO**), *iii)* the algorithm **GNetMine** [7], which is natively able to work on heterogeneous networks, and *iv)* the algorithm **HENPC** [11], recently proposed to solve the multi-type classification task in heterogeneous networks. However, RelIBK, RelSMO and HENPC were not able to finish within 3 days of execution, while GNetMine was not able to compute the results for Yelp dataset, since the system went out of memory (on a server with 32GB of RAM). In these cases, we ran the experiments on a reduced set of nodes (about $1,000$ nodes for each target type) of the datasets IMDB, STACK and YELP.

As regards the parameter setting of ST-MrSBC and MT-MrSBC, we considered a random sampling of 20% of nodes for each classifier in the ensemble and the number of iterations for each target type z ranging from 1 to 50.

We collected all the classification accuracy values and performed the Nemenyi post-hoc tests on single datasets, on all the datasets and on the reduced datasets for the comparative evaluation. The result of the statistical tests are depicted in Figure 3. In particular, we can observe that for the datasets NBA and for the target type *users* of the dataset Yelp, the improvement provided by LexicographicMT-MrSBC and RandomMT-MrSBC over the competitors is statistically significant at p-value= 0.05. Focusing on LexicographicMT-MrSBC, we observe two specular and interesting cases: for the dataset IMDB it provides the best result, while for the target type *Business* of the dataset Yelp it appears to be the worst approach. This instability is again caused by the static ordering on the target types. Indeed, in the first case, the exploitation of the dependency *movies* $\rightarrow$ *users* (which is surely strong, if we observe the result) led LexicographicMT-MrSBC to obtain a better result with respect to RandomMT-MrSBC, which alternatively (and randomly) exploited the dependencies *movies* $\rightarrow$ *users* and *users* $\rightarrow$ *movies* (which appears weak). On the contrary, in the second case, the static (unlucky) choice of the dependency to be exploited brought LexicographicMT-MrSBC to the bottom of the ranking.

Finally, the results obtained by our comparative evaluation (Figure 3 - last chart) shows that the improvement provided by the proposed method is able to give Mr-SBC the advantage of outperforming the competitors Indeed, the original Mr-SBC is not able to outperform the considered competitors, while the ensemble learning (ST-MrSBC) leads to outperform all the competitors (although not statistically w.r.t. HENPC and RelIBk). The advantage comes from the combination of capturing label dependencies between multiple types and of the ensemble learning approach (MT-MrSBC), which improves the accuracy.

Overall, we can conclude that the application of the proposed method, which is able to capture both correlation and autocorrelation phenomena, as well as to predict missing values, by exploiting the same classification method adopted for primary targets, can lead to better, more stable predictions when applied to real-world data organized in heterogeneous networks.

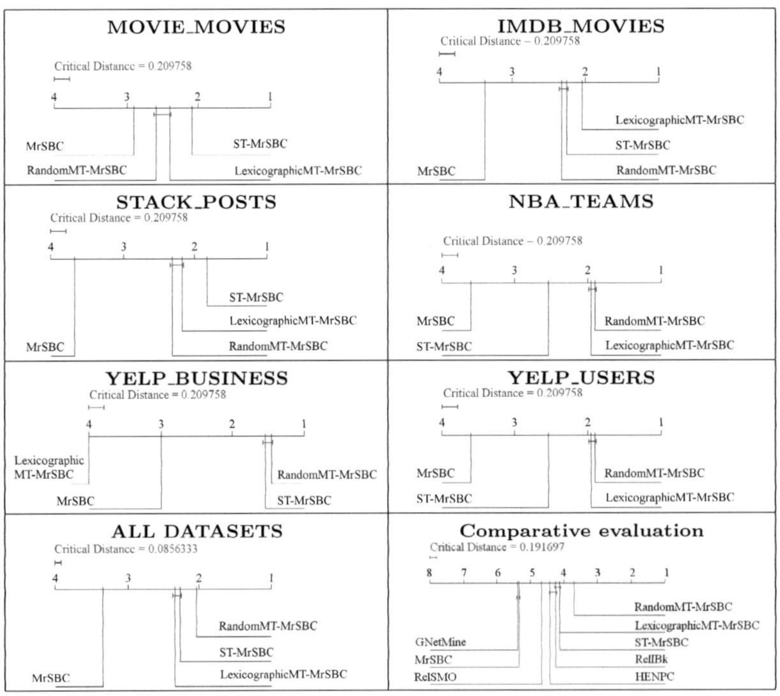

Fig. 3. Results of the Nemenyi post-hoc test on the average accuracy. Better algorithms are positioned on the right-hand side, and those that do not significantly differ in performance (at p-value $= 0.05$) are connected with a line.

5 Conclusions

In this paper, we proposed an extension of the system Mr-SBC which works on heterogeneous networks and that is able to solve multi-type classification tasks, by capturing both correlation and autocorrelation phenomena. Experiments performed on real datasets show that both the proposed variants are able to significantly outperform the original Mr-SBC, especially with a random ordering of the target types, as well as four other well-known competitor algorithms.

As future work, we plan to study the sensitivity to the sampling size and the possibility to select only a subset of labeled nodes for the next iteration.

Acknowledgments

We would like to acknowledge the European project MAESTRA - Learning from Massive, Incompletely annotated, and Structured Data (ICT-2013-612944).

References

1. P. Angin and J. Neville. A shrinkage approach for modeling non-stationary relational autocorrelation. In *ICDM*, pages 707–712. IEEE Computer Society, 2008.
2. M. Ceci, A. Appice, and D. Malerba. Mr-SBC: a multi-relational naive bayes classifier. In *PKDD 2003*, pages 95–106. Springer, 2003.
3. O. Chapelle, B. Schölkopf, and A. Zien. *Semi-Supervised Learning*. The MIT Press, 2nd edition, 2010.
4. C. Desrosiers and G. Karypis. Within-network classification using local structure similarity. In *ECML PKDD '09*, pages 260–275, Berlin, 2009. Springer-Verlag.
5. Y. Guo, X. Niu, and H. Zhang. An extensive empirical study on semi-supervised learning. In *ICDM*, pages 186–195. IEEE, 2010.
6. M. Ji, J. Han, and M. Danilevsky. Ranking-based classification of heterogeneous information networks. In *SIGKDD '11*, pages 1298–1306, NY, USA, 2011. ACM.
7. M. Ji, Y. Sun, M. Danilevsky, J. Han, and J. Gao. Graph regularized transductive classification on heterogeneous information networks. In *ECML PKDD 2010*, volume 6321 of *LNCS*, pages 570–586. Springer Berlin, 2010.
8. J. S. Liu. *Monte Carlo Strategies in Scientific Computing*. Springer Publishing Company, Incorporated, 2008.
9. C. Loglisci, M. Ceci, and D. Malerba. Relational mining for discovering changes in evolving networks. *Neurocomputing*, 150:265–288, 2015.
10. S. A. Macskassy and F. Provost. Classification in networked data: A toolkit and a univariate case study. *J. Mach. Learn. Res.*, 8:935–983, May 2007.
11. G. Pio, F. Serafino, D. Malerba, and M. Ceci. Multi-type clustering and classification from heterogeneous networks. *Inf. Sci.*, 425:107–126, 2018.
12. J. Read, B. Pfahringer, G. Holmes, and E. Frank. Classifier chains for multi-label classification. *Machine Learning*, 85(3):333–359, 2011.
13. F. Serafino, G. Pio, and M. Ceci. Ensemble learning for multi-type classification in heterogeneous networks (doi: 10.1109/tkde.2018.2822307). *IEEE TKDE*, 2018.
14. D. Stojanova, M. Ceci, A. Appice, and S. Dzeroski. Network regression with predictive clustering trees. *Data Min. Knowl. Discov.*, 25(2):378–413, 2012.
15. Y. Sun, J. Han, P. Zhao, Z. Yin, H. Cheng, and T. Wu. Rankclus: integrating clustering with ranking for heterogeneous information network analysis. In *EDBT '09*, pages 565–576, New York, NY, USA, 2009. ACM.
16. Y. Sun, Y. Yu, and J. Han. Ranking-based clustering of heterogeneous information networks with star network schema. In *ACM SIGKDD*, pages 797–806, 2009.

Discussion Paper
Deriving Local Explanations for Black Box Models

Eliana Pastor and Elena Baralis

Politecnico di Torino, Italy
{eliana.pastor, elena.baralis}@polito.it

Abstract. Many high performance machine learning methods produce black box models, which do not disclose their internal working that yields the prediction. We propose a novel explanation method that explains the predictions of any classifier by analyzing the prediction change obtained by omitting relevant subsets of attribute values. Our method overcomes the exponential time complexity of previous works by learning a local model in the neighborhood of the prediction to explain. Preliminary experiments show that, despite the approximation introduced by the local model, the explanations provided by our method are effective in detecting also correlation among attributes. Our method is model-agnostic. Hence, experts can compare explanations and local behaviors of the predictions for the same instance made by different classifiers.

Keywords: Interpretability · Prediction Explanation · Local model.

1 Introduction

The application of machine learning algorithms is becoming pervasive in every aspect of our society. Since classification models could greatly affect people lives, understanding how a classification model works or why a decision is made is gaining more and more importance. Accuracy and interpretability of a machine learning model are frequently considered as a trade-off: the greater is the accuracy of a model, the lower is its understandability. The experts often favor accuracy over interpretability. However, an accurate model does not imply a trustworthy one.

Given the importance of interpretability, we propose a novel explanation method that explains the predictions made on single instances by any classifier. This methodology is model-agnostic. Hence, it is applicable to any classification method without making any assumption on its internal logic. The explanation highlights the feature values of a particular instance that are relevant for the prediction made by a specific classifier. The explanation is based on the knowledge of the local behavior of the model, captured by an interpretable local model.

The paper is organized as follows. Section 2 describes related work. Section 3 introduces the proposed technique, while Section 4 describes some preliminary experiments that show the effectiveness of our method. Finally, Section 5 draws conclusions and outlines future works.

2 Related Work

Many algorithms have been proposed for improving the interpretability of already existing classification models. We can identify two main approaches: model-dependent solutions and model-agnostic ones.

Model-dependent solutions are applicable only for specific classification models. Ad hoc solutions have been proposed for improving the understandability of neural networks [2, 20], Naive Bayes models [16], Support Vector Machines (SVM) [3, 6, 13], and random forest models [5, 12, 15]. These methods only address some specific classification algorithms. The explanation of how the models work is presented by means of different techniques, e.g. rules [2, 3, 12, 15], visualizations [6, 20], nomograms [13, 16], global feature importance [5]. Thus, no comparison among different techniques in terms of model interpretability is possible.

Model-agnostic or model-independent solutions treat the machine learning model as a black box. Some solutions try to explain the original model globally. As an example, the algorithm TREPAN approximates a generic model f learning a classification tree on the predictions of f [7]. It can be argued that the interpretable but simple decision tree could not be able to mimic the complexity of the whole model.

Other approaches propose a general method for explaining individual predictions, i.e. why particular decisions are made. Ribeiro et al. [18] introduce a model-agnostic method for explaining individual prediction by learning an interpretable and linear model in the locality of the prediction to be explained. However, the linear approximation may not be faithful if the model is highly non-linear even in the locality of the prediction [18].

Several works study how a prediction changes if parts of the input components are omitted. Fong and Vedaldi apply this approach for images' classification, approximating the elimination of parts of an image with meaningful perturbations [11]. Lemaire et al. [14] and Robnik-Šikonja and Kononenko [19] consider how each attribute value is relevant for the prediction for tabular data, by omitting one attribute value at a time. Štrumbelj et al. study also the omission of more attribute values together, thus also addressing the attribute interaction [22]. However, they compute the omission effect for the power set of the attributes. Hence, the method is affected by an exponential time complexity. A first solution for overcoming this problem is based on a sampling-based approximation [21]. The sampling is quasi-random and adaptive and it is based on a greedy approach, considering data characteristics, as the feature variance. We overcome the problem of the exponential time complexity by exploiting local properties of the original model to be explained.

3 Deriving Local Explanations

We propose a novel method to explain individual predictions of any classification model. Our method highlights the relevance of each attribute value in an instance for the prediction of its class label. The classification model is treated as a black box. Given the prediction that we want to explain, we "remove" one or more attribute values at a time and we measure how the prediction changes. If the prediction output changes, it means that the considered attributes are relevant for the prediction of the instance. The relevance of the attributes can be estimated as a difference of prediction probabilities with respect to a particular target class. The larger the difference, the more the omitted attribute values are relevant for the prediction.
With respect to previous approaches [14, 19, 22], we propose a novel methodology based on a local and interpretable model learned in the neighborhood of the prediction that we want to explain. The local model is provided by an associative classifier and highlights the subsets of feature values that are relevant for the prediction. Our explanation method is characterized by the following features.

- Only the relevant attribute subsets provided by the local model are considered, instead of the complete power set of all attribute combinations. Hence, our approach overcomes the exponential time complexity. Furthermore, the local approximation is based on the behavior of the original model.
- The local model is rule-based and it returns the association between subsets of feature values and class. The rules, being understandable, provide preliminary insight of why a particular decision is made by the considered model. This allows a qualitative understanding of the original model behavior.

Fig. 1: Steps of the explanation method.

In Figure 1, the steps of the explanation method are outlined. Considering the original model as a black box, we learn a local model in the locality of the prediction to be explained, the big white cross. We obtain from the local model a set of relevant rules that indicate the relevant subsets of feature values. Only these subsets are then used for estimating the contribution of each attribute value.

Let be f a generic trained classification model whose predictions we want to explain. f can be produced by any classifier because the proposed explanation method is model-agnostic. Given an instance x, our technique requires that, for each class c, the model f returns the class probability, $p(y{=}c\,|\,x)$, i.e. the probability that x belongs to class c. Many classification algorithms, the probabilistic classifiers (e.g. Naive Bayes, artificial neural networks), naturally provide class probabilities. When class probabilities are not available, we firstly apply post-modeling methods, the probability calibration methods, to obtain posterior probabilities [17].

3.1 Capturing the Locality by means of K Neighbors

Our goal is to understand the subsets of feature values that are relevant for the prediction of a particular instance x. We train a local interpretable model able to directly produce the relevant subsets. The interpretable model is trained only in the locality of x. The local training data is computed considering the K instances in the training set that are nearest to the instance x that we want to explain.

The choice of parameter K is important because it affects the generated model. To estimate K, we exploit techniques proposed for estimating the parameter K of the K-Nearest Neighbors classifier [10]. As future work, we will study a heuristic algorithm that automatically selects an optimal K for the particular prediction to be explained.

Once the K neighbors of the instance x are selected, they are labeled by the model f, whose prediction we want to explain.

3.2 Extracting Local Rules

The K labelled neighbors of instance x are used for training the local model. The local model provides the feature values that are relevant for the prediction. We use a rule-based classifier, more specifically an associative classifier. This kind of classifiers extracts classification rules from the training data. Association rules are in the form $A \rightarrow B$, where A is a set of items, and B, if the rules are used for classification purposes, is a class label [1]. These rules are denoted as CARs. An item is a pair (*attribute, value*). CARs highlight the subsets of feature values that are associated with the class label. In our implementation, as rule-based system we use the classifier L^3, *Live and Let Live*, an associative classifier that is based on a lazy pruning approach [4]. L^3 is trained with the K neighbors of the instance x that we want to explain. This local model is used for obtaining the *local rules*. From the local rules we retrieve the set of (*attribute=value*) pairs that are considered relevant for the classification task in the locality of the instance x to be explained.

3.3 Computation and Visualization of Attribute Contributions

The relevant feature subsets provided by the selected CARs drive the estimate of the feature contributions. We estimate the contributions of each attribute value by means of the definitions of *prediction difference* and *interaction contribution* proposed in [22]. We modify the original definitions to consider the relevant subset instead of the complete power set. These contributions represent the influence of each feature value in the determination of the class, for the prediction on a single instance x of the model f. The larger the value of its contribution, the more the corresponding attribute value determines the class. A positive contribution means that the attribute value has a positive influence in determining the class. A negative one, instead, means that the attribute value speaks against the prediction for that particular target class. The estimation of the contributions considers the subsets of attributes highlighted by the local model. The contributions of each attribute value can be visualized through a bar plot representation, following the visualization method proposed by Kononenko et al. [19]. The visualization allows the final users to understand in a simple and uniform way the motivation driving the prediction for instance x made by model f. An example of visualization is presented in the last step of Figure 1.

4 Preliminary Results

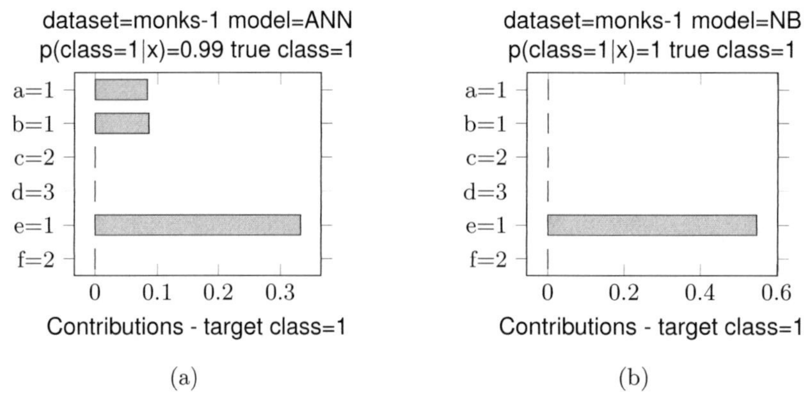

Fig. 2: Comparison of explanations of a particular instance of the *monks-1* data set. Explanation of (a) the neural network prediction and (b) the Naive Bayes prediction.

In this section, preliminary outcomes of our explanation method are presented and discussed. The considered data set is the artificial data set *Monk1* [9]. The data set is composed by 6 discrete attributes a,b,c,d,e,f and the class label can take value 1 or 0. Being artificial, the relationship between the attributes and the class value is known. The class is 1 if a=b or if e=1, 0 otherwise. Thus, it is possible to verify the results of our explanation methods, comparing explanations with the true relations among attributes.

To build the models and perform classification, we exploit the Python-based Orange 2.7 Data Mining Library [8].

As a first example, we train a multilayered feed-forward artificial neural network (ANN) using the *Monk1* data set. Let x = (a=1, b=1, c=2, d=3, e=1, f=2) be the instance that we want to explain. We know that the "true class" is 1 because *e=1* and *a=b*. Thus, *e* and both *a* and *b* in this case are important for the prediction. The ANN correctly predicts the class label as 1 with probability $p(class{=}1|x)$ equal to 0.99. To estimate what are the relevant subsets of feature values for the ANN for this particular instance, we train the associative classifier L^3 in the locality of instance x. In these experiments, the parameter K is set to the square root of the number of instances of the training data set [10]. For the support and confidence thresholds, we use L^3 default values, in particular 1% and 50% respectively. Preliminary experiments of sensitivity for these thresholds show that the results of the local model are stable if the values of support and confidence are changed in the neighborhood of the default values. The local model returns the following CARs:

$$\{e = 1\} \rightarrow class = 1$$
$$\{a = 1,\ b = 1\} \longrightarrow class = 1$$

Hence, if *e=1* the instance is assigned to the class 1 or also if *a* and *b* are both equal to 1. These relations, based on our knowledge of the *Monk1* data set, should indeed determine the class. The local behavior captures the true explanation. Once this relevant subset is defined, we can compute the contribution of each attribute value to the prediction [22]. The result is shown in Figure 2a. The largest contribution is given by term *e=1*, followed by the terms *a* and *b*.

If we explain the prediction for the same instance and still with respect to class 1, made by another model, we may obtain a different result. The explanation should capture how the model behaves in the locality of the instance. Different models work differently. This difference may be on the predicted class label, but also on the feature values that drive the prediction.

Consider the explanation of the same instance x and still built with respect to class 1, but classified by the Naive Bayes classifier. The local model returns a single relevant rule:

$$\{e = 1\} \rightarrow class = 1$$

Only attribute *e* equal to 1 is considered relevant for class 1. The resulting contributions are shown in Figure 2b. The Naive Bayes classifier assigns correctly the instance x to class 1, but only because *e=1*. The local model and the explanation highlight that the Naive Bayes classifier has not learned the association that if *a=b* then *class=1*. The Naive Bayes classifier, because of its assumption of independence between features, is not able to learn the importance that *a* and *b* have together. Hence, the local model and the explanation in this case successfully reflect the model behavior.

Despite the approximation introduced by considering only relevant subsets, in our preliminary tests we obtain explanations comparable to the results in previous works, in which the complete power set of attribute values is taken into consideration [22].

We can compare the predictions of the same instance made by different classifiers by simply comparing the attribute value contributions and local rules. The comparison allows experts to inspect the local behavior of different classifiers. Based on their prior knowledge, they can decide which prediction to trust. It is important to notice that these considerations can be made by domain experts regardless of the intrinsic interpretability of the model. Being our method model-agnostic, the explanations are presented in the same way for all classifiers, ranging from the naturally interpretable, as decision trees, to the black box ones, as the neural networks.

5 Conclusions and Future Work

We propose a novel model-agnostic explanation method that explains the individual predictions of any classifier. The original classification model is treated as a black box. We omit subsets of attribute values and we measure how the prediction changes. We overcome the exponential time complexity that derives from the computation of the power set of the feature values by learning a local model. The local model is an associative classifier that is learned in the locality of the instance whose prediction is to be explained. It returns the subsets of feature values that are relevant for that particular prediction: only these subsets are omitted.

Preliminary tests show that our technique is able to capture the diverse internal logic of different classification techniques. Accuracy and interpretability in this way can no longer be considered as a trade-off. The experts can choose accurate models but also verify if these models can be trusted. Hence, our explanation method helps users in the selection of the best classification approach.

As future work we plan to (*i*) evaluate the approximation error introduced by considering only the relevant subsets highlighted by the local model and (*ii*) define a technique to automatically detect an appropriate value of K, the number of neighbors to be considered in the local model, to adapt its value to different data distributions.

References

1. Agrawal, R., Imieliński, T., Swami, A.: Mining association rules between sets of items in large databases. SIGMOD Rec. **22**(2), 207–216 (Jun 1993)
2. Andrews, R., Diederich, J., Tickle, A.B.: Survey and critique of techniques for extracting rules from trained artificial neural networks. Knowledge-based systems **8**(6), 373–389 (1995)
3. Barakat, N., Bradley, A.P.: Rule extraction from support vector machines: a review. Neurocomputing **74**(1-3), 178–190 (2010)
4. Baralis, E., Chiusano, S., Garza, P.: A lazy approach to associative classification. IEEE Transactions on Knowledge and Data Engineering **20**(2), 156–171 (2008)

5. Breiman, L.: Random forests. Machine learning **45**(1), 5–32 (2001)
6. Caragea, D., Cook, D., Honavar, V.G.: Gaining insights into support vector machine pattern classifiers using projection-based tour methods. In: Proceedings of the Seventh ACM SIGKDD International Conference on Knowledge Discovery and Data Mining. pp. 251–256. KDD '01, ACM, New York, NY, USA (2001)
7. Craven, M., Shavlik, J.W.: Extracting tree-structured representations of trained networks. In: Advances in neural information processing systems. pp. 24–30 (1996)
8. Demšar, J., Curk, T., Erjavec, A., Gorup, Č., Hočevar, T., Milutinovič, M., Možina, M., Polajnar, M., Toplak, M., Starič, A., et al.: Orange: data mining toolbox in python. The Journal of Machine Learning Research **14**(1), 2349–2353 (2013)
9. Dheeru, D., Karra Taniskidou, E.: UCI machine learning repository (2017), http://archive.ics.uci.edu/ml
10. Duda, R.O., Hart, P.E., Stork, D.G.: Pattern classification. John Wiley & Sons (2012)
11. Fong, R., Vedaldi, A.: Interpretable explanations of black boxes by meaningful perturbation. arXiv preprint arXiv:1704.03296 (2017)
12. Hara, S., Hayashi, K.: Making tree ensembles interpretable. arXiv preprint arXiv:1606.05390 (2016)
13. Jakulin, A., Možina, M., Demšar, J., Bratko, I., Zupan, B.: Nomograms for visualizing support vector machines. In: Proceedings of the eleventh ACM SIGKDD international conference on Knowledge discovery in data mining. pp. 108–117. ACM (2005)
14. Lemaire, V., Feraud, R., Voisine, N.: Contact personalization using a score understanding method. In: 2008 IEEE International Joint Conference on Neural Networks (IEEE World Congress on Computational Intelligence). pp. 649–654 (June 2008)
15. Mashayekhi, M., Gras, R.: Rule extraction from random forest: the rf+ hc methods. In: Canadian Conference on Artificial Intelligence. pp. 223–237. Springer (2015)
16. Možina, M., Demšar, J., Kattan, M., Zupan, B.: Nomograms for visualization of naive bayesian classifier. In: European Conference on Principles of Data Mining and Knowledge Discovery. pp. 337–348. Springer (2004)
17. Niculescu-Mizil, A., Caruana, R.: Predicting good probabilities with supervised learning. In: Proceedings of the 22nd international conference on Machine learning. pp. 625–632. ACM (2005)
18. Ribeiro, M.T., Singh, S., Guestrin, C.: "Why Should I Trust You?": Explaining the Predictions of Any Classifier. In: Proceedings of the 22Nd ACM SIGKDD International Conference on Knowledge Discovery and Data Mining. pp. 1135–1144. KDD '16, ACM, New York, NY, USA (2016)
19. Robnik-Šikonja, M., Kononenko, I.: Explaining classifications for individual instances. IEEE Transactions on Knowledge and Data Engineering **20**(5), 589–600 (May 2008)
20. Tzeng, F.Y., Ma, K.L.: Opening the black box-data driven visualization of neural networks. In: Visualization, 2005. VIS 05. IEEE. pp. 383–390. IEEE (2005)
21. Štrumbelj, E., Kononenko, I.: An efficient explanation of individual classifications using game theory. J. Mach. Learn. Res. **11**, 1–18 (Mar 2010)
22. Štrumbelj, E., Kononenko, I., Robnik Šikonja, M.: Explaining instance classifications with interactions of subsets of feature values. Data Knowl. Eng. **68**(10), 886–904 (Oct 2009)

Querying RDF Data Cubes through Natural Language
[Discussion Paper]

Maurizio Atzori[1], Giuseppe M. Mazzeo[2*], and Carlo Zaniolo[3]

[1] Math/CS Department
University of Cagliari, Italy
atzori@unica.it
[2] Facebook Inc.
Menlo Park, USA
mazzeo@cs.ucla.edu
[3] University of California
Los Angeles, USA
zaniolo@cs.ucla.edu

Abstract. In this discussion paper we present QA^3, a question answering (QA) system over RDF cubes. The system first tags chunks of text with elements of the knowledge base (KB), and then leverages the well-defined structure of data cubes to create the SPARQL query from the tags. For each class of questions with the same structure a SPARQL template is defined. The correct template is chosen by using a set of regex-like patterns, based on both syntactical and semantic features of the tokens extracted from the question. Preliminary results are encouraging and suggest a number of improvements. Over the 50 questions of the QALD-6 challenge, QA^3 can process 44 questions, with 0.59 precision and and 0.62 recall, remarkably improving the state of the art in natural language question answering over data cubes.

1 Introduction

Governments of several countries recently started to publish information about the public expenses using the RDF data model [2], in order to improve transparency. The need to publish statistical data, which concerns not only Governments but also many other organizations, has pushed the definition of a specific RDF-based model, namely, the RDF data cube model [4], whose current version was published in January 2014. The availability of data of public interest from different sources has thus favored the creation of projects, such as Linked-Spending [1], that collect statistical data from several organizations, making

* This work has been done when Dr. Mazzeo was working at University of California, Los Angeles (USA)

them available as an RDF KB, according to the Linked Data principles. However, while RDF data can be efficiently queried using the powerful SPARQL language, only technical users can benefit from their potential by extracting human-understandable information. The problem of providing a user-friendly interface that enables non-technical users to query RDF knowledge bases has been widely investigated during the last few years. Some of the existing approaches are the following. *Exploratory browsing* enables users to navigate the RDF graph by starting from an entity (node) and then moving to other entities by following properties (edges). Although users do not need to know beforehand the names of properties, this approach is effective only for exploring the graph in the proximity of the initial entity, and it is not suitable for aggregate queries. *Faceted search* supports top-down searches: starting with the whole dataset as potential results of the search, the user can progressively restrict the results by adding constraints on the properties of the current result set [10]. This approach was recently applied to the RDF data cubes [15], following the long tradition of graphical user interfaces for OLAP analysis, based on charts representing different kind of aggregations of the underlying data. Another user-friendly system for querying RDF data is SWiPE [6], which enables users to type the constraints directly in the fields of the infobox of WikiPedia pages. While this paradigm is very effective for finding list of entities with specific properties, its generalization to the RDF data cubes is not trivial. *Natural language interfaces* let the user type any question in natural language and translate it into a SPARQL query. The current state-of-the-art system is Xser [18], which was able to yield F-scores equal to 0.72 and 0.63 in the 2014 and 2015 QALD challenges [3], respectively. Although its accuracy is not very high, Xser largely won over the other participating systems. This witnesses the fact that translating natural language questions into SPARQL queries is a really hard task. The difficulty of this task can be reduced by using a *controlled natural language* (CNL), i.e., a language which is is generated by a restricted grammar [9,14,16]. While the accuracy of these systems is very high, some effort is required for following the language that can be recognized. None of the previously proposed systems, however, has been specialized for question answering over RDF data cubes.

Question answering over RDF cubes is, indeed, a brand new challenge, which raises issues different from those of question answering on a "general" KBs [11]. In fact, questions in this context are very specific, i.e., oriented towards extracting statistical information. For these questions a very accurate interpretation of specific features of the typical OLAP queries, such as different kind of aggregations or constraints on dimensions, is crucial, and misinterpretations can not be tolerated. In fact, while a partial interpretation of a general question might yield an acceptable answer, in an aggregation query misinterpreting a constraint is likely to result in a totally wrong answer.

In this discussion paper we present QA^3 (pronounced as *QA cube*), a question answering system for RDF data cubes [5]. An overview of QA^3 is presented in Section 2, and preliminary experimental results are reported in Section 3. We finally conclude the paper with Section 4.

2 An overview of QA^3

QA^3 translates questions posed in natural language into SPARQL queries, assuming that the answer to the questions can be provided using one of the RDF data cubes "known" by the system. Given a KB containing datasets stored using the RDF data cube model [4], QA^3 works in three steps:

- the question is tagged with elements of the KB, belonging to the same dataset. This step also detects which dataset is the most appropriate to answer the question;
- the question is tokenized, using Stanford parser [13], and the annotations are augmented using the tags obtained from the previous step. The sequence of tokens is then matched against some regex-like patterns, each associated with a SPARQL template;
- the chosen template is filled with the actual clauses (constraints, filters, etc.) by using the tags and the structure of dataset.

In the following each step is described in more detail.

2.1 Tagging questions with elements of the KB

Given a string Q representing a question, for each dataset D we try to match the literals in D against chunks of Q. Before performing the matching, the strings are normalized, by removing the stop words and performing lemmatization. The result of the matching between Q and the dataset D can be represented as set of pairs $\langle C, T \rangle$, where C is a chunk of Q and T is a set of triples in D. Each matching is associated with a quality measure, which is based on the percentage of Q that is covered by tagged chunks. Some other advanced ranking methods (such as [7]) could be used to further improvements in case of multiple candidates. We notice that related work [8] extracts connected subgraphs given keywords instead of triples, although we connect them later constraining them to a sparql template (see later). The quality measure (% of Q) enables the system to choose the dataset which most likely has to be used to provide an answer to the question.

2.2 Finding the SPARQL query template

The domain in which QA^3 operates is quite structured, especially compared to that of general question answering (e.g., DBpedia). As a consequence, the meaningful questions (i.e., questions that can be answered using the available KB) are likely to have a SPARQL translation which follow a limited set of well defined *templates*. For instance, if the user wants to know how much his city spent for public works in 2015, the question has to contain all the elements needed to detect the dataset to be used, the measure to aggregate and the aggregation function, and the constraints to be applied to restrict the computation on the observations in which the user is interested. This question, like a wide range of similar questions, can be answered by using the following SPARQL query template, based on the RDF cube dictionary [4]:

```
SELECT sum(xsd:decimal(?measure)) {
   ?observation qb:dataset <dataset> .
   ?observation <measure> ?measure .
   <constraints>
}
```

where `<dataset>` and `<measure>` have to be replaced with the correct URIs, and `<constraints>` has to be replaced with a set of triples specifying the constraints for the variable `?observation`, representing the observations.

In order to leverage the typical homogeneity of the structures of these questions, we implemented a system, working of a set of SPARQL templates, that automatically detects the template to be used to provide an answer. To this end, each template is associated with one (or possibly more) regular expressions built on the tokens of the questions. The tokens are obtained using the Stanford parser [13], which tokenizes the question and annotates each token with its lemma, its POS (part of speech) tag, and its NER (named entity recognition) tag. The annotations are augmented with the elements of the knowledge base (dataset, measure, dimension, attribute, literal) obtained at the previous step, and with a tag representing a possible aggregate function. For the latter, a specific (small) dictionary has been defined, using the words that are used most often to name aggregation functions (e.g., sum, total, average, maximum, etc.).

Thus, for each token we have the following features: (1) the POS tag, (2) the lemma, (3) the word (i.e., the original text), (4) the NER tag, (5) the KB tag (S: dataset, M: measure, D: dimension, A: attribute, E: entity, L: literal, O: none), and (6) the aggregation tag (S: sum, A: average, M: max, N: min, O: none).

The patterns used to match the tokens are defined as 7-tuples, where the i-th element represents the possible set of values for the i-th feature of the token (the features are assumed to follow the order in which they are listed above). For instance, the pattern `WP|WDT,_,_,_,!E` matches with tokens having `WP` or `WDT` as POS tag, any lemma, word, NER tag (_), and the token must not be annotated as entity (`E`). The features that are not explicitly specified in the pattern (in this case the aggregation tag), are allowed to take any value (_ is implicitly assumed).

Patterns can be followed by a `#` symbol and by a string that represents a label name, that can be used to get the actual token/s that matched the pattern. These simple patterns can be used to build more complex regular expressions. We describe them by means of an example:

```
{_}* WP|WDT {_,_,_,_,O,O}* _,_,_,_,O,!O#1 {_,_,_,_,M|S#2}* {_}*
```

Each pattern of the expression above must match subsequent chunks of the whole question. The interpretation of the patterns appearing in the expression is the following:

- any sequence of tokens ({_}*);
- a token with the POS tag `WP` or `WDT`;
- any sequence of tokens, whatever their POS tag, lemma, word, and NER are (_), without any specific KB annotation and without any specific aggregation function (`O`);
- a token with any POS tag, any lemma, any word, and any NER, without any specific KB annotation (`O`) and with a specific aggregation function (`!O`). This token is assigned the label *1* (`#1`);
- any sequence of tokens with any POS tag, any lemma, any word, and any NER, with a KB annotation that can be a measure (`M`) or a dataset (`S`). The type of tag for the aggregation function is not specified, which means it can be anything (in practice, it will be none). These tokens are assigned the label *2* (`#2`);
- any sequence of tokens ({_}*).

This expression can be matched against several questions, such as: "What is the total aid to the Anti Corruption Commission in the Maldives in 2015?". In general, that expression matches questions asking for the computation of an aggregation function, which is represented by the token with label *1* computed over a measure, which is represented by the token with label *2*. The measure could also be implicitly denoted by the name of the dataset (e.g., when the dataset is about a specific measure of a set of observations - *expenditures of town of Cary*). These questions can be translated into a SPARQL query with the following structure:

```
select <groupByVar>
   <aggregationFunction##1>(xsd:decimal(?measure)) {
      ?observation qb:dataSet <dataset> .
      ?observation <measure##2> ?measure .
      <constraints>
   } <groupByClause>
```

where `<aggregationFunction##1>` has to be replaced by the actual aggregation function, which can be derived using the token annotated with label *1*, `<dataset>` must be replaced with the URI of the dataset found in the previous step, `<measure##2>` must be replaced with the actual measure, using tokens labeled with *2*. Finally, `<constraint>`, `<groupByVar>` and `<groupByClause>` must be replaced with the actual variable/clause (possibly empty), that are derived using the KB tagging, as described in the following.

We remark that this strategy for deriving the SPARQL template is quite general and the definition of new templates is quite simple. Although capturing all the natural language questions is not possible through a finite set of patterns, we found that very few expressions are enough to cover most of the questions posed in a typical form (see Section 3).

2.3 Filling out contraints and group-by

The most interesting part is the construction of the constraints and the group-by clauses. In order to construct the constraints, we observe that (i) if a literal is tagged, then it must be connected to the observation through an attribute, which is also reported in the annotation, and (ii) if an entity is tagged, then it must be connected to the observation through a dimension. The dimension could be explicitly tagged in the question, but it can be also derived by maintaining an index that maps every entity e to the dimensions which can take e as value. The substring `<constraints>` of the template can be thus replaced with a string representing the triples obtained as described above. Regarding the group-by variable and clause, we observe that a question requiring their use has to contain an attribute or dimension which is not bound to a value (literal or entity, respectively). Therefore, we can try to find those tokens that are tagged with a dimension/attribute X to which no value is associated. We then replace `<groupByVar>` with a variable identifier, say `?gbvar`, and `?observation` is connected to `?gbvar` using the URI of X, and the `<groupByClause>` placeholder is replaced with `group by ?gbvar`. If no such attribute/dimension X can be found, both `<gbvar>` and `<groupby>` are replaced by the empty string.

3 Experimental results

QA^3 participated in the task 3 of QALD-6 challenge [3], where it was able to process 44 questions over the 50 available ones. The recall and precision over the 44 processed questions are 0.62 and 0.59 respectively, which correspond to F-score 0.6. The global F-score, assuming F-score 0 over the 6 unprocessed questions, is 0.53. In more details, over the 44 processed questions, QA^3 provides a correct answer (F-score 1) to 25 questions, a partial answer (F-score strictly between 0 and 1) to 3 questions, and a wrong answer (F-score 0) to 16 questions. The correct dataset can be found for 42 questions. For 30 of these questions the full set of correct annotations is found. Finally, for 25 of the questions with correct annotations QA^3 generates the SPARQL query that provides the correct results. A set of 6 pairs expression/template is currently being used, in order to detect the correct SPARQL template to be used for each question. These experimental results refer to our first version of QA^3, that we later improved and deeply discussed in [5] and made freely available.

A direct comparison against other systems has been independently performed by the QALD 6 Challenge [3], as reported in Fig. 1. The best performer in this comparison is a special version of the SPARKLIS system [9] tailored to statistical questions, a system that does not accept natural language questions. Instead, as explained in the next section it uses a faceted search approach, and its performance is, therefore, dependant on the level of expertise the user has (values for expert and beginner are shown). To the best of our knowledge, the

see the two modules `https://github.com/atzori/qa3tagger` (ad-hoc tagger) and `https://github.com/gmmazzeo/qa3` (template-based sparql generation)

System	Processed	Recall	Precision	F1 (processed)	F1 Global (overall)
SPARKLIS (used by an expert)	50	0.94	0.96	0.95	0.95
SPARKLIS (used by a beginner)	50	0.76	0.88	0.82	0.82
QA3 (initial tuning)	**44**	**0.62**	**0.59**	**0.60**	**0.53**
CubeQA	49	0.41	0.49	0.45	0.44

Fig. 1. Comparison against other QA systems, as reported by the QALD-6 independent competition

only two systems that answer free natural language questions over RDF cubes are CubeQA [12], described in the next section, and our QA^3. Compared to the state-of-the-art CubeQA, we get a remarkable improvement of $0.62/0.41 = 51\%$ in recall, 20% in precision. This is in part given by the ability of QA^3 to self-evaluate the confidence of a computed answer (thanks to the score measure of the tagger), and also by the good expressivity of the template/pattern system.

We also remark that F1 and F1 Global, i.e., the F1 measure computed over all questions (not only those for which the system provides an answer) are respectively 33% and 20% higher than those of CubeQA. These results show that QA^3 provides a sensible improvement over the state of the art.

In terms of running time, the most expensive part is performed by the search for the correct dataset. Our in-memory tagging algorithm takes about $100ms$ to annotate a question for a given dataset. Current version of QA^3 takes therefore $100ms{*}50 \approx 5s$ to check for the best candidate dataset and annotate the question with triples necessary to find and fill in the correct SPARQL query template (real times ranging from 2s to 7s). While reasonable, this exhaustive approach would not scale well in case of thousands of datasets. We consider current results very encouraging, and we plan to improve QA^3 by using 1) a heuristic-based approach for the dataset search, 2) word embeddings for semantic relatedness instead of lemma-based term matching, and 3) a machine-learning approach for SPARQL template generation.

4 Conclusions

In this discussion paper we have presented QA^3, a system that can answer natural language questions about statistical data by finding the appropriate LinkedSpending [1] dataset and computing a correct SPARQL query. It works on different kind of typical statistical questions. The system has been implemented, opensourced on GitHub and also freely available online at `http://qa3.link/`.

During the discussion, questions taken from the QALD-6 challenge [3] will be lively employed, but the attendees will be also welcome to suggest other questions. Future work will explore the use of machine learning to generate the regex-like patterns and related privacy issues [17] related with the use of statistical data.

Acknowledgments

This research was supported in part by a 2015 Google Faculty Research Award, NIH 1 U54GM 114833-01 (BD2K) and Sardegna Ricerche (*project OKgraph*, Capitale Umano Alta Qualificazione, CRP 120).

References

1. LinkedSpending project. `http://linkedspending.aksw.org/`.
2. Linking Open Data cloud diagram. `http://lod-cloud.net/`.
3. Question Answering over Linked Data (QALD). `http://qald.sebastianwalter.org/`.
4. The RDF Data Cube Vocabulary. `https://www.w3.org/TR/vocab-data-cube/`.
5. M. Atzori, G. M. Mazzeo, and C. Zaniolo. QA^3: a Natural Language Approach to Question Answering over RDF Data Cubes. *Semantic Web Journal*, 2018.
6. M. Atzori and C. Zaniolo. Swipe: searching wikipedia by example. In *Proc. of the 21st Int. World Wide Web Conf., WWW 2012 (Companion Volume)*, pages 309–312, 2012.
7. A. Dessi and M. Atzori. A machine-learning approach to ranking RDF properties. *Future Generation Computer Systems*, 54:366–377, 2016.
8. S. Elbassuoni and R. Blanco. Keyword search over rdf graphs. In *Proceedings of the 20th ACM CIKM '11*, pages 237–242. ACM, 2011.
9. S. Ferré. Sparklis: An expressive query builder for sparql endpoints with guidance in natural language. *Semantic Web*, 7(1):95–104, 2016.
10. R. Hahn, C. Bizer, C. Sahnwaldt, C. Herta, S. Robinson, M. Bürgle, H. Düwiger, and U. Scheel. Faceted wikipedia search. In *Proc. of 13th Int. Conf. of Business Information Systems, BIS 2010*, pages 1–11, 2010.
11. K. Höffner and J. Lehmann. Towards question answering on statistical linked data. In *Proc. of the 10th Int. Conf. on Semantic Systems, SEMANTICS*, 2014.
12. K. Höffner, J. Lehmann, and R. Usbeck. Cubeqa - question answering on RDF data cubes. In *The Semantic Web - ISWC 2016 - 15th International Semantic Web Conference, Kobe, Japan, October 17-21, 2016, Proceedings, Part I*, pages 325–340, 2016.
13. D. Klein and C. D. Manning. Accurate unlexicalized parsing. In *41st Annual Meeting of the Association for Computational Linguistics*, pages 423–430, 2003.
14. A. Marginean. Gfmed: Question answering over biomedical linked data with grammatical framework. In *Working Notes for CLEF 2014 Conference*, pages 1224–1235, 2014.
15. M. Martin, K. Abicht, C. Stadler, A. N. Ngomo, T. Soru, and S. Auer. Cubeviz: Exploration and visualization of statistical linked data. In *Proc. of the 24th Int. World Wide Web Conf., WWW 2015 (Companion Volume)*, pages 219–222, 2015.
16. G. M. Mazzeo and C. Zaniolo. Answering controlled natural language questions on RDF knowledge bases. In *Proc. of the 19th International Conference on Extending Database Technology, EDBT 2016*, pages 608–611, 2016.
17. D. Pedreschi, F. Bonchi, F. Turini, V. Verykios, M. Atzori, B. Malin, B. Moelans, and Y. Saygin. *Privacy protection: Regulations and technologies, opportunities and threats.* Springer, 2008.
18. K. Xu, Y. Feng, S. Huang, and D. Zhao. Question answering via phrasal semantic parsing. In *Proc. of 6th Int. Conf. of the CLEF Association, CLEF 2015*, pages 414–426, 2015.

Context Aware Source Selection for Linked Data

Barbara Catania, Giovanna Guerrini, and Beyza Yaman

University of Genoa, Italy
{firstname.name@dibris.unige.it}

Abstract. The traditional Web is evolving into the Web of Data, which gathers huge collections of structured data over distributed, heterogeneous data sources. *Live queries* are needed to get current information out of this global data space. In live query processing, *source selection* allows the identification of the sources that most likely contain relevant content. Due to the semantic heterogeneity of the Web of Data, however, it is not always easy to assess relevancy. *Context* information might help in interpreting the user's information needs. In this paper, we discuss how context information can be exploited to improve source selection.

1 Introduction

In the last decade, significant efforts have been devoted to the development of the Web of Data, i.e., a Web in which not only documents, but also data, can be first class citizens. A huge amount of Linked Data has been published to construct a global data space based on open standards [7]. However, it is still difficult to benefit from data in the Web of Data in an effective way. Typical systems operating on Linked Data collect (crawl) and pre-process (index) large amounts of data, and evaluate queries against a centralized repository. Given that crawling and indexing are time-consuming operations, data in the centralized index may be out of date at query execution time. On the other hand, an ideal query answering system for *live querying* [6] should return current answers in a reasonable amount of time, even on corpora as large as the Web.

Since in the Linked Data context there is a large number of small size sources, the main problems in processing queries in live query systems become (*i*) finding the sources containing triples that can contribute to the overall query answer, (*ii*) efficiently fetching triples from these sources, possibly in a parallel way. The first process is referred to as *source selection* [6] and requires knowledge of the data source content, with the aim of returning a ranked list of sources, ordered by relevance. Lightweight data summaries for determining relevant sources during query evaluation have been proposed and are exploited for this task [11]. Such data summaries are approximate multidimensional index structures that store descriptions of the content of data sources.

The diversity of publishers, however, results in data fulfilling an information need being stored in many different sources and described in many different ways. The semantic enrichment of data, indeed, does not solve the problem of identifying relevant information with respect to a given domain, rather causes a shift of heterogeneity issues from the syntactic to the semantic level. By exploiting a more abstract notion of *context*, we can better interpret the request and devise the most relevant sources for the user's information needs.

Context may capture different properties of data, users or user-data interactions, and may come from data themselves, the querying device (e.g., ambient information) as well as from the execution environment (e.g., history of previous queries) [1, 5]. Despite the different additional information it can capture and rely on, matching data not only with respect to the user request but also with respect to a reference context associated with such request can help in determining the portion of the entire information that is most relevant to the user. Contexts have been used, e.g., in offering personalized services and recommendations and improving data selection [2, 8, 10], however, surprisingly, as far as we know, no approach has been defined yet exploiting context information for improving the linked data source selection process.

This paper goes in this direction and faces the problem of effective and efficient source selection for Linked Data, with the aim of proposing techniques that automatically discover sources providing most relevant answers, by exploiting a *domain-dependent context hierarchy* (as part of the more general framework envisioned in [3, 4]). In this paper, we consider RDF data sources and SPARQL queries and present: (*i*) two distinct extended data summaries enabling context-aware source selection (Section 2); (*ii*) an instantiation of the approach with a specific context taxonomy (Section 3); (*iii*) a preliminary experimental evaluation of the proposed structures on such instantiation (Section 4). Future work directions are discussed in Section 5.

2 Extended Data Summaries for Context-Aware Source Selection

In this section, we first briefly introduce the data summary our approach relies on, i.e., QTree [6], and the two extensions we propose to enable context-aware source selection. Both approaches rely on: (*i*) a context taxonomy $(\mathcal{C}, \preceq)$, where $\mathcal{C}$ is the set of contexts and $\preceq$ is a subconcept relationship among them; (*ii*) a distance function $d : \mathcal{C} \times \mathcal{C} \to [0, 1]$ measuring the distance between contexts in the taxonomy; (*iii*) a function γ for associating contexts with triples and queries. $(\mathcal{C}, \preceq)$ and γ can come with data or be (semi)automatically extracted from them while d is data independent and is provided as an input parameter for the proposed techniques. Additional details on the proposed approaches can be found in [12].

2.1 Data Summaries: QTree

Data summaries [6, 11] have been proposed as an approach for efficiently determining which sources may contribute answers to a query in live distributed query

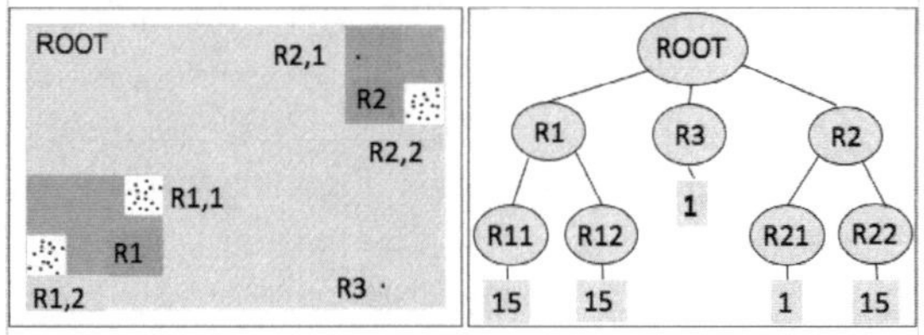

(a) Data points and regions (b) Region hierarchy and buckets

Fig. 1: 2-dimensional QTree [6]

systems. They describe the data provided by the sources in a summarized form. We specifically refer to the QTree indexing structure [6] which is a combination of R-trees and multidimensional histograms. The first step is to transform the RDF triples provided by the source into numerical points in a 3-dimensional space. Hash functions are applied to the individual components of RDF triples (i.e., *subject*, *predicate*, *object*) to obtain 3 numerical values for each triple. The employed hash functions, relying on a prefix-hashing approach, are such that triples with similar content are assigned close points in the multidimensional space, so that they are clustered close to each other. This 3-dimensional space is then indexed by a hierarchical data structure (the QTree, shown in Fig.1.b) in which nodes represent multidimensional regions, through minimal bounding boxes (MBBs). The region of a node always covers all the regions of its children. Fig.1.a) illustrates the 2-dimensional data points and regions indexed by the QTree. (A 2-dimensional space is used for the sake of simplicity.)

The leaves of the QTree (referred to as *buckets*) keep statistical information about the data items contained in the respective region. In Fig.1.b) leaves contain the number of points within the corresponding region. To summarize the sources, the number of triples contributed by the source is maintained inside the bucket as a set of pairs $\langle source, number\_of\_triples \rangle$. This set is kept ordered on the first component, so that sources contributing the highest number of triples appear first. Thus, the bucket corresponding to a region R contains a list of pairs: $\langle s, card(\{t | hash(t) \in R, origin(t) = s\}) \rangle$ for each source s containing at least one triple which is hashed to a point in region R. $origin(t)$ denotes the data source (a RDF set of triples available on the Web) containing t, obtained by dereferencing the subject of t.

When a SPARQL query is executed, each basic graph pattern (BGP) is converted into a set of coordinates by applying the hash functions to the pattern elements. BGPs containing variables are represented by regions spanning the whole range of hash values for the respective dimension. Then, the buckets containing sources contributing to the query are discovered by looking for overlapping MBBs in the QTree. Buckets returned by each BGP search are then intersected to identify joins. Sources contained in the resulting buckets are ranked based on an estimation of the *number of triples* contributing to the query result (computed taking into account the bucket region and the size of the intersection between bucket and query regions).

2.2 Context-Aware Source Selection via QTree

The first approach we propose does not modify QTree internal nodes and exploits context information in the ranking phase only. Indeed, each source in a bucket is associated not only with the number of triples contributed by the source inside the bucket but also with the set of related contexts. Thus, buckets now contain sets of triples $\langle source, set\_of\_contexts, number\_of\_triples \rangle$. More specifically, the bucket corresponding to a region R contains a set of triples $\langle s, \bigcup_{t|hash(t) \in R, origin(t)=s} \gamma(t), card(\{t|hash(t) \in R, origin(t) = s\}), \rangle$ for each source s containing at least one triple which is hashed to a point in region R.

We assume now that a SPARQL query comes together with a reference context. The query representation and the index search do not change but, once the intersecting buckets are discovered and the contained sources retrieved, they are ranked according to: (*i*) *context distance*, computed as the aggregate (based on either AVG, MIN, or MAX function) of the distances d in the context taxonomy between any context associated with the source and the query context; (*ii*) *number of triples*, defined as in Subsection 2.1. These two indicators are normalized between $[0, 1]$ and combined in a linear way.

2.3 Modelling the Context as a Fourth Dimension

The second, alternative, approach models the context as a fourth dimension of the data space (in addition to subject, predicate, and object), thus extending the QTree data structure. This leads to an increase of the dimensionality of the data summary but this increases the pruning potential as well and, thus, potentially, the effectiveness of the indexing structure.

Each context is mapped to a number, so that close numbers reflect similar contexts. This is achieved by an appropriate node numbering in the tree corresponding to the context taxonomy. This way, similar data will still be clustered into the same bucket. Thus, *hash* function, first applied to triples and returning a point in the 3D space, is now extended, leading to function $hash_4$, so that a quadruple consisting of a triple t plus one of its contexts in $\gamma(t)$ is hashed to a point in the 4D space. The structure of internal nodes does not change with respect to the original QTree, while 4D QTree buckets keep list of pairs $\langle source, context \rangle$ with the number of triples they contribute to a bucket. Thus, assuming R is the 4D region associated with a bucket, the bucket contains a set of pairs $\langle \langle s, c \rangle, card(\{t|hash_4(\langle t, c \rangle) \in R, c \in \gamma(t)\}) \rangle$.

Queries and the associated contexts are mapped to four dimensional regions, similarly to what happens for BGPs in the original QTree, but taking into account the context as fourth component. Index search now selects buckets that intersect a region representing *BGP+context* instead of only BGP. Ranking is performed similarly to what we discussed in Section 2.2 but ranking each $\langle source, context \rangle$ pair in a bucket separately.

3 Context-Modeling Using SKOS

Different context models [1, ?] lead to different instantiations of the proposed approaches. In the following, as a concrete example, we discuss *context modeling* by means of a SKOS concept taxonomy.

SKOS. SKOS (Simple Knowledge Organization System) is a W3C recommendation for defining, publishing, and sharing concepts over the Web and it is used for knowledge organization. Concepts are entity categories identified by URIs. Though not providing semantic and reasoning capabilities as powerful as ontologies, concepts enhance the potential of search capabilities. Moreover, mappings between concepts from different concept schemes and in diverse data sources, and a hierarchical organization of concepts, are provided. The fundamental element of SKOS is the (`skos:Concept`) class, which instances, identified by URIs, represent domain concepts. Properties (`skos:broader`) and (`skos:narrower`) are one the inverse of the other and are used to assert a generalization/specialization relationship between two concepts [9]. For instance, the RDF triple (`:Palace skos:broader :TouristAttraction`) states that the touristic attraction concept is broader (i.e., more general) than the palace concept. SKOS is foreseen to be applied for associating concepts (i.e., resources of type (`skos:Concept`)) with resources through the (`dct:subject`) property.

Context modeling through SKOS. We model each context as a SKOS concept. In order to create a domain dependent context taxonomy, we started from a portion of DBpedia English SKOS concepts and related hierarchical relationships, as a *seed*. The portion consists of a subtree of the tree rooted at the concept `Tourist_attractions_in_Europe`. Starting from English DBPedia, resources related to contexts in the seed taxonomy through the `dct:subject` predicate, as well as triples describing them, are retrieved (via SPARQL queries posed to endpoints) and become part of our dataset (and they are associated with the corresponding concept as a context). Then, (`owl:sameAs`) links both at the instance and at the concept level are exploited for retrieving further concepts and instances.

The set of collected SKOS concepts is finally organized into a taxonomy $(\mathcal{C}, \preceq)$, containing 1632 nodes (SKOS concepts), related by the (`skos:broader`) relationship. Nodes are then numbered through a visit of the tree, and the generated numbers are used for hashing. Distance d between two contexts is defined as the length of the shortest path connecting them in the taxonomy, normalized between 0 and 1. Contexts for triples (function γ) are defined as the contexts associated with their subjects or objects. The resulting dataset contains 1.086.874 triples, from 13.466 RDF sources.

https://www.w3.org/TR/skos-reference/

Index	# generated buckets/maximum # buckets	Index Size	Hash interval
QTree	8.092/25.000	31,3 MB	[0 – 2000]
Ext QTree	8.092/25.000	64,8 MB	[0 – 2000]
4D QTree	50.000/50.000	188.4 MB	[0 – 2000]

Table 1: QTree details

4 Experimental Results

The experiments were performed on a machine with CPU Intel Core i3-2350M 2.30GHz, 6 GB of RAM size, running 64-bit Windows 7 Professional. Applications were developed in Java HotSpot(TM) 64-Bit Server VM under Java SE 1.8. Starting from the dataset described in Section 3, we created Qtree, Ext QTree, and 4D QTree, according to the values pointed out in Table 1. Notice that the maximum number of buckets (a parameter of the creation process) is higher for 4D QTree since the number of tuples to be indexed is higher in this case.

In this paper, we report experimental results related to the execution of *star-shaped queries*, sets of triple patterns sharing the same variable at the subject position. Star-shaped queries with a variable number of joins, ranging from 0 to 7, were randomly generated, guaranteeing at least one result on the considered dataset. For each number of join, 10 queries have been created, each associated with a random context. Each query was executed 10 times.

Selectivity and Performance. Fig. 2 compares QTree, Ext QTree, and 4D QTree with respect to the number of returned buckets, sources, and execution time. From Fig.2.a we note that, thanks to context information which is indexed together with triples, 4D QTree filters out more buckets during BGP search than 3D approaches. The same number of buckets is always returned by QTree and Ext QTree, since the two data structures differ only for information contained at the bucket level. On the other hand, 4D QTree returns a higher number of buckets as result for the join execution (Fig.2.b) since, as shown in Table 1, setting the maximum number of buckets to 50.000 does not guarantee a good data distribution among buckets (the number of created buckets coincide with the maximum value), many bucket regions intersect, and are returned as result. The number of sources returned by 4D QTree is however much lower compared with QTree and Ext QTree (Fig.2.c), thanks to context filtering during index search. For what concerns average execution time (in milliseconds, Fig.2.d), as expected, it coincides for QTree and Ext QTree and is often higher for 4D QTree, due to the higher number of intersections among buckets to be performed.

Context Accuracy. Accuracy is computed as the average distance between the contexts returned as results by Ext QTree and 4D QTree index searches and the context associated with the query. In the Ext QTree, since each source is associated with a set of contexts, we first compute an aggregate distance for

Experiments related to *path-shaped queries* are not reported due to space constraints.

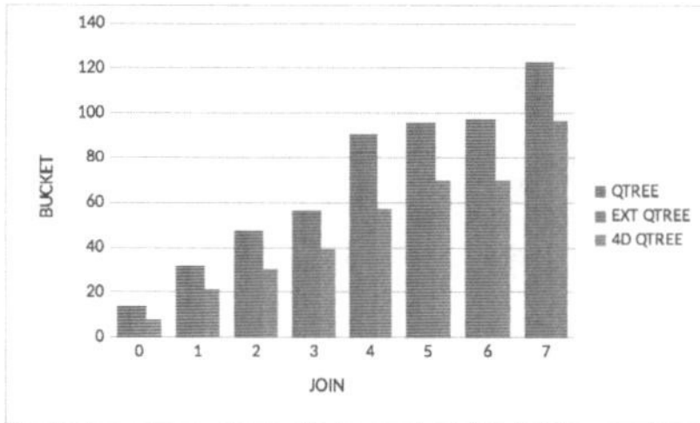

(a) Avg num. of returned buckets by BGP search

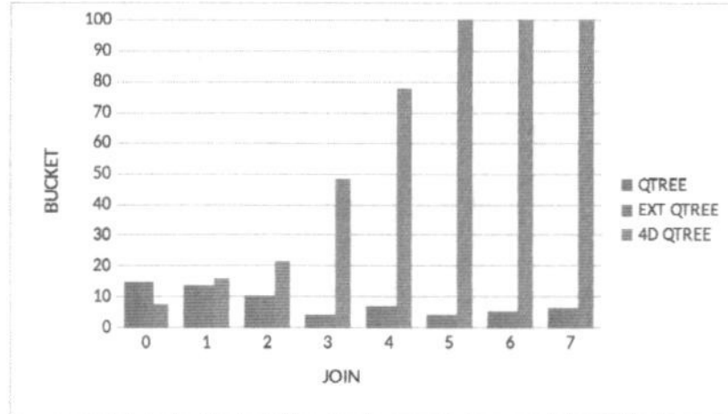

(b) Avg num. of join buckets

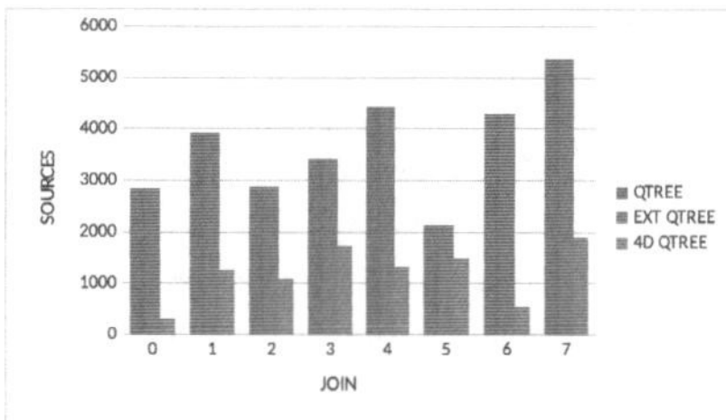

(c) Avg num. of returned sources

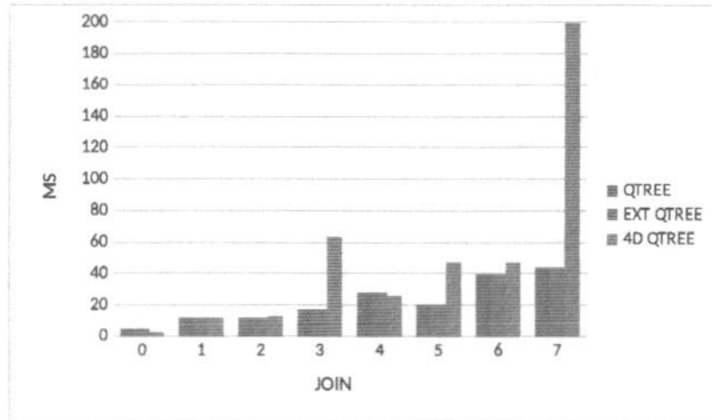

(d) Avg execution time

Fig. 2: Returned buckets, sources and execution time

each source (based on either AVG or MIN function) and then we average all them. Fig.3 shows that 4D QTree average context distance is always lower than the Ext QTree average context distance, when using AVG (Fig.3.a). Combined with Fig.2, this means that 4D QTree always retrieves less sources with a more relevant context, on average, than Ext QTree. When considering MIN (Fig.3.b), Ext QTree performs better than 4D QTree, since each data source returned by Ext QTree is associated with all its related contexts, including that leading to the minimum distance. This is not necessarily true with 4D QTree.

Impact of Ranking. We considered various ranking functions differing in the weights used in the linear combination. Aggregate context distances in Ext QTree are computed using the MIN aggregate function. The performed experiments, not reported here for space constraints, show that 4D QTree average ranking values computed for all the returned sources are lower than the corresponding Ext QTree ranking values. This is coherent with the previously presented results. When we consider the first k ranked sources, 4D QTree ranking values are higher than corresponding Ext QTree ones. Thus, 4D QTree is able to select, among all the returned ones, "better" sources than the Ext QTree.

5 Conclusions and Future Work

In this paper, we proposed two approaches exploiting *context* information in increasing source selection effectiveness and efficiency. This way of exploiting

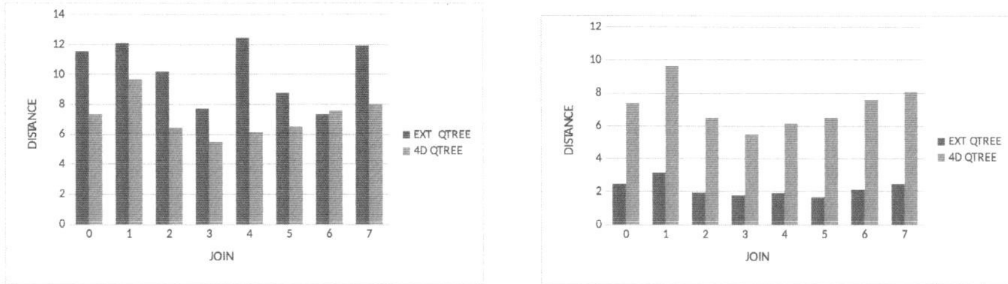

(a) Average Distance (b) Average Min. Distance

Fig. 3: Context result accuracy

context is, to the best of our knowledge, novel. Experimental results show that the proposed context-based data summaries succeed in selecting the most relevant data sources with respect to the query and the associated context, with a reasonable overhead. Future work includes the design of algorithms supporting top-k search in QTree and the extension of the proposed data structures with data source quality information, with the aim of selecting not only relevant but also accurate answers, by preferring trusted sources.

References

1. C. Bettini et Al. A survey of context modelling and reasoning techniques. *Pervasive and Mobile Computing* 6(2):161–180, 2010.f
2. C. Bolchini et Al. A data-oriented survey of context models. *ACM Sigmod Record*, 36(4):19–26, 2007.
3. B. Catania et Al. Wearable queries: Adapting common retrieval needs to data and users. In *DBRank*, 2013.
4. B. Catania, G. Guerrini, and B. Yaman. Context-dependent quality-aware source selection for live queries on linked data. In *EDBT*, 2016.
5. C. Ghidini and F. Giunchiglia. Local Models Semantics, or contextual reasoning=locality+compatibility. *Artif. Intell.* 127(2):221–259, 2001.
6. A. Harth et Al. Data summaries for on-demand Queries over Linked Data. In *WWW*, 2010.
7. T. Heath and C. Bizer. Linked data: Evolving the web into a global data space. *Synthesis lectures on the semantic web: theory and technology*, 1(1):1–136, 2011.
8. R. Meusel et Al. Towards automatic topical classification of lod datasets. In *CEUR Workshop Proceedings. Vol. 1409*, 2015.
9. A. Miles et Al. Skos core: simple knowledge organisation for the web. In *International Conference on Dublin Core and Metadata Applications*, pages 3–10, 2005.
10. T. Rekatsinas et Al. Finding quality in quantity: The challenge of discovering valuable sources for integration. In *CIDR*, 2015.
11. J. Umbrich et Al. Comparing Data Summaries for Processing Live Queries over Linked Data. *World Wide Web*, 14(5-6):495–544, 2011.
12. B. Yaman. *"Exploiting Context-Dependent Quality Metadata for Linked Data Source Selection"*. PhD thesis, 2018.

Using Ontology-based Data Summarization to Develop Semantics-aware Recommender Systems*

Vito Walter Anelli[1], Tommaso Di Noia[1], Andrea Maurino[2], Matteo Palmonari[2], Anisa Rula[2]

[1] Polytechnic University of Bari, Via Orabona, 4, 70125 Bari, Italy
firstname.lastname@poliba.it
[2] University of Milano-Bicocca, Piazza dell'Ateneo Nuovo, 1, 20126 Milano, Italy
firstname.lastname@unimib.it

Abstract. In the current information-centric era, recommender systems are gaining momentum as tools able to assist users in daily decision-making tasks. Within the recommendation process, Linked Data have been already proposed as a valuable source of information to enhance the predictive power of recommender systems but an open issues is still related to feature selection of the most relevant subset of data in the whole semantic web. In this paper, we show how ontology-based (linked) data summarization can drive the selection of properties/features useful to a recommender system. In particular, we compare a fully automated feature selection method based on ontology-based data summaries with more classical ones, and we evaluate the performance of these methods in terms of accuracy and aggregate diversity of a recommender system exploiting the top-k selected features.

1 Introduction

Semantics-aware Recommender Systems (RSs) exploiting information held in knowledge graphs, as the ones available as Linked Data (LD), represent one of the most interesting and challenging application scenarios for LD [6]. A high number of solutions and tools have been proposed in the last years showing the effectiveness of adopting LD as knowledge sources to feed a recommendation engine (see [5] and references therein for an overview). Nevertheless, how to automatically select the "best" subset of a LD dataset to feed a LD-based RS without affecting the performance of the recommendation algorithm is still an open issue. Notice that the selection of the top-k features to use in a RSs means to discover which properties in a LD-dataset (e.g., DBpedia) encode the knowledge useful in the recommendation task and which ones are just noise [20]. In most of the approaches proposed so far, usually, the FS process is performed by human experts that manually choose properties resulting more "suitable" for a given scenario. Over the years, many algorithms and techniques for feature selection , e.g., Information Gain, Information Gain Ratio, Chi Squared Test and Principal Component Analysis, have been proposed with reference to machine learning tasks but they do not consider a characteristic which makes unique LD: they come with semantics attached.

The main objective of this paper is to investigate how ontology-based data summarization [28] can be used as a new and semantic-oriented feature selection technique for

* Discussion Paper. An extended version of this work has been presented at [7].
SEBD 2018, June 24-27, 2018, Castellaneta Marina, Italy. Copyright held by the author(s).

LD-based RSs. We define a feature selection method that automatically extracts the top-k properties that are deemed to be more important to evaluate similarity between instances of a given class on top of data summaries built with the help of an ontology. We perform an experimental evaluation on three well-known datasets in the RS domain (*Movielens*, *LastFM*, *LibraryThing*) in order to analyze how the choice of a particular FS technique may influence the performance of recommendation algorithms in terms of typical accuracy and diversity metrics. Experimental results show that information provided in ontology-based data summaries selects features that achieve comparable, or, in most of the cases, better performance than state-of-the-art, semantic-agnostic analytical methods such as Information Gain [19]. We believe that these results are interesting also because of practical reasons. LD summaries are published on-line and summary-based FS can be performed even without acquiring the entire dataset and efficiently (on top of summary information). The use of frequency associated with schema patterns in a FS approach was initially tested in a previous work[24].

The paper is organized as follows: in Section 2, we introduce the ontology-based data summarization approach used in this work, while in Section 3, we describe the feature selection and recommendation methods. Section 4 is devoted to the explanation and discussion of the experimental results. Section 5 briefly reviews related literature for schema and data summarization as well as on recommender systems while Section 6 discuss conclusions and future work.

2 Ontology-driven Linked Data Summarization

While relevance-oriented data summarization approaches are aimed at finding subsets of a dataset or an ontology that are estimated to be more relevant for the users [30], vocabulary-oriented approaches are aimed at profiling a dataset, by describing the usage of vocabularies/ontologies used in the dataset. The summaries returned by these approaches are complete, i.e., they provide statistics about every element of the vocabulary/ontology used in the dataset [28]. Statistics captured by these summaries that can be useful for the feature selection process are the ones concerning the usage of properties for a certain class of items to recommend.

Patterns and frequency. In our approach we use pattern-based summaries extracted using the ABSTAT framework. Pattern-based summaries describe the content of a dataset using schema patterns having the form $\langle C, P, D\rangle$, where C and D, are types (either classes or datatypes) and P is a property. For example, the pattern $\langle$`dbo:Film, dbo:starring, dbo:Actor`$\rangle$ tells that films exist in the dataset, in which star some actors. Differently from similar pattern-based summaries [17], ABSTAT uses the subclass relations in the data ontology, represented in a *Type Graph*, to extract only *minimal type patterns* from relational assertions, i.e, the patterns that are more type-wise specific according to the ontology. A pattern $\langle C, P, D\rangle$ is a minimal type pattern for a relational assertion $\langle a, P, b\rangle$ according to a type graph $\mathcal{G}$ iff C and D are the types of a and b respectively, which are minimal in $\mathcal{G}$. In a pattern $\langle C, P, D\rangle$, C and D are referred to as *source* and *target* types respectively. A minimal type pattern $\langle$`dbo:Film, dbo:starring, dbo:Actor`$\rangle$ (simply referred to as *pattern* in the following) tells that there exist entities that have `dbo:Film` and `dbo:Actor` as minimal

ABSTAT summaries for several datasets can be explored at `http://abstat.disco.unimib.it`

If no ontology is specified, all types are minimal and patterns are extracted like in frameworks that do not adopt minimalization types which are connected through the property P. Non minimal patterns can be inferred from minimal patterns and the type graph. Therefore, they can be excluded as redundant without information loss, making summaries more compact [28]. Each pattern $\langle C, P, D\rangle$ is associated with a *frequency*, which reports the number of relational assertions $\langle a, P, b\rangle$ from which the pattern has been extracted.

Local cardinality descriptors. For this work, we have extended ABSTAT to extract *local cardinality descriptors*, i.e., cardinality descriptors of RDF properties, which are specific to the patterns in which the properties occur. To define these descriptors, we first introduce the concept of restricted property extensions. The *extension* of a property P restricted to a pattern $\langle C, P, D\rangle$ is the set of pairs $\langle x, y\rangle$ such that the relational assertion $\langle x, P, y\rangle$ is part of the dataset and $\langle C, P, D\rangle$ is a minimal-type pattern for $\langle x, P, y\rangle$. Given a pattern π with a property P, we can define the functions (that return the closest integer):

$minS(\pi)$, $maxS(\pi)$, $avgS(\pi)$: denoting respectively the minimum, maximum and average number of distinct subjects associated to unique objects in the extension of P restricted to π;

$minO(\pi)$, $maxO(\pi)$, $avgO(\pi)$: denoting respectively the minimum, maximum and average number of distinct objects associated to unique subjects in the extension of P restricted to π.

ABSTAT can also compute global cardinality descriptors by adjusting the above mentioned definition so as to consider unrestricted property extensions. Local cardinality descriptors carry information about the semantics of properties as used with specific types of resources (in specific patterns) and can be helpful for selecting features used to compute the similarity between resources. For example, to compute similarity for movies, one would like to discard properties that occur in patterns π with `dbo:Film` as source type and $avgS(\pi) = 1$. We remark that the values of local cardinality descriptors for patterns with a property P may differ from values of global cardinality descriptors for P. Some examples of local cardinality descriptors can be found in the faceted-search interface (ABSTATBrowse). In conclusion, ABSTAT takes a linked dataset and - if specified - one or more ontologies as input, and returns a summary that consists of: a type graph, a set of patterns, their frequency, local an global cardinality descriptors.

3 Semantics-aware Feature Selection

Feature selection is the process of selecting a subset of relevant attributes in a dataset. Thanks to the feature selection process it is possible to improve the prediction performance, and to give a better understanding of the process that generates the data [12]. There are three typical measures of feature selection (i) "**filters**", statistical measures to assign a score to each feature (here the feature selection process is a preprocessing step and can be independent from learning[11]); (ii) "**wrapper**" where the learning system is used as a black box to score subsets of features [14]; (iii) **embedded methods** that perform the selection within the process of training [12]. In the following, we discuss two approaches used for the feature selection task: the first operates on the summarization of the datasets and the second operates on the instances of the datasets.

Feature Selection with Ontology-based Summaries. As described in Section 2, the ABSTAT framework provides two useful statistics: the pattern frequency and the cardinality descriptors that are used in the feature selection process as described in Figure 1. The

`http://abstat.disco.unimib.it/browse`

process starts by considering all patterns $\Pi = \{\pi_1, \pi_2, \ldots, \pi_n\}$ of a given class C occurring as a source type. The example in Figure 1 shows a subset of Π with `dbo:Film` as source type. The first step of our approach (*FILTERBY*) filters out properties based on the local cardinality descriptors. In particular, it filters only properties for which the average number of distinct subjects associated with unique objects is more than one ($avgS > 1$). The second step of the process (*SELECTDISTINCTP*) selects all properties of the patterns in Π by applying the maximum of the pattern frequency (# in the Figure). Then, the properties are ranked (*ORDERBY*) in a descending order on pattern frequency and then k properties (*TOPK*) are selected (k=2).

In some datasets, such as DBpedia, properties may use redundant information by using same properties with different namespaces, e.g., `dbo:starring` and `dbp:starring`. For this reason, in such case, a pre-processing step for removing replicated properties to avoid redundant ones is requested (see Section 4).

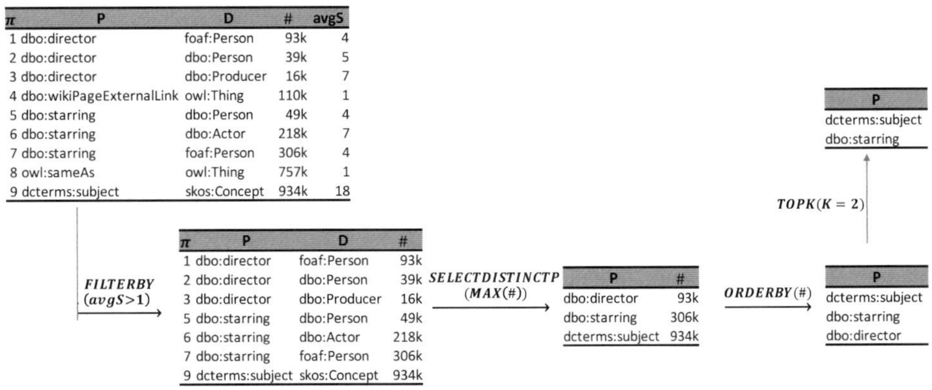

Fig. 1: Feature selection with ABSTAT with source type `dbo:Film`

Feature Selection with State-of-the-art Techniques. In this work we consider RDF properties as features, so among the different feature selection techniques available in the literature, we initially selected *Information Gain*, *Information Gain Ratio*, *Chi-squared test* and *Principal Component Analysis* as their computation can be adapted to categorical features as LD and we then evaluated their effect over the recommendation results. The features selected from each technique have been used as an input of the recommendation algorithm that uses the Jaccard index as similarity measure. In order to identify the best technique among the one we selected, they have been evaluated by using Information Gain (IG), Gain Ration and Chi Squared Test. At the end, IG[19] resulted as the best performing one. Then features are ranked according to their IG value and the top-k ones are returned.

Feature pre-processing. LD datasets usually have a quite large feature set that can be very sparse depending on the knowledge domain. For instance, taking into account the movies available in *Movielens*, properties as `dbp:artDirection` or `dbp:precededBy` are very specific and have a lot of missing values. On the other hand, properties as `dbo:wikiPageExternalLink` or `owl:sameAs` always have different and unique values, so they are not informative for a recommendation task.

For the sake of conciseness we do not report all the results here. Results obtained with other FS techniques can be found at `http://ow.ly/zAA530d0wu0`

For this reason, before starting the feature selection process with IG, we reduced *redundant* or *irrelevant* features. The pre-processing step has been done following [23]: we fixed a threshold $t_m = t_d = 97\%$ both for missing values and for distinct values and, then, we discarded features for which we had more than t_m of missing values and more than t_d of distinct values.

Recommendation Method. We implemented a content-based recommender system using an item-based nearest neighbors algorithm as in [20], where the similarity is computed by means of Jaccard's index (widely adopted for categorical features). In this work, the neighborhood of a resource includes all the nodes in the graph reachable starting from the resource i (respectively j) following the properties selected by the feature selection phase. The neighbors are thus one-hop features. The similarity values are then used to recommend to each user the items which result most similar to the ones she has liked in the past. Ratings are predicted as a normalized sum of neighbors ratings, weighted by their similarity values [21].

4 Experimental Evaluation

Datasets. The evaluation has been carried out on the three well-known datasets belonging to different domains, i.e. movies(Movielens 1M), books (LibraryThing), and music (`Last.fm`). The datasets contains, respectively, 1,000,209, 626,000 and 92,834 ratings. Movielens 1M and LibraryThing provide explicit ratings over 1-5 and 1-10 scales whereas `Last.fm` [3] provides users listening counts.

Measures. For evaluating the quality of our recommendation algorithm we are interested in measuring its performances in terms of accuracy of the predicted results and diversity. To evaluate recommendation **accuracy**, we used *Precision* (Precision@N) and *Mean Reciprocal Rank* (MRR). Precision@N is a metric denoting the fraction of relevant items in the Top-N recommendations. MRR computes the average reciprocal rank of the first relevant recommended item [26]. A good recommender system should provide recommendations equally distributed among the items, otherwise, even if accurate, they indicate a low degree of personalization [1]. To evaluate **aggregate diversity**, we considered *catalog coverage* (the percentage of recommended items in the catalog) and *aggregate entropy* [1]. Please note that here we are considering a global diversity rather than a personalized one [8].

Implementation. We tried different ranking and filtering functions to study their effect on feature selection. For lack of space we include the best combination from those proposed in section 3, **AbsOccAvgS**, that considers as input of *FILTERBY* the $avgS$ and *SELECTDISTINCTP* the maximum of the pattern frequency. Both for ABSTAT and IG we considered both the **Onlydbp** configuration in which, if among the first N features selected there are both `dbo:` and `dbp:` feature we consider only the `dbp:` one. Conversely in **Onlydbo** we take into account only the `dbo:` one.

ABSTAT Baseline. As a baseline for ABSTAT-based feature selection we use TF-IDF as is a well-known measure to identify most relevant terms (properties in this case) for a document (a class in this case). We adopt *TF-IDF* in our context where by document we refer to a set of patterns having the same subject-type and by term we refer to a property. *TF-IDF* is based on the number of properties occurring in a document (*TF*) and the logarithm of the ratio between the total number of documents and the ones containing the property (*IDF*).

`http://ir.ii.uam.es/hetrec2011/datasets.html`

	Precision@10		MRR@10		catalogCoverage@10		aggrEntropy@10	
Top K features	**5**	**20**	**5**	**20**	**5**	**20**	**5**	**20**
dbo.IG	.0841	.1076	.2961	.3390	.3372	.5226	7.94	8.44
dbo.AbsOccAvgS	**.1066**	.1067	**.3388**	.3402	.5344	.5208	8.68	8.51
dbo.TfIdf	.0823	.0856	.2994	.3123	.3520	.3908	7.83	7.99
dbp.IG	.0688	.1046	.2134	.3336	.2799	.5065	6.54	8.31
dbp.AbsOccAvgS	**.1065**	**.1059**	.3408	.3360	.5426	.5105	8.64	8.31
dbp.TfIdf	.0549	.0745	.1924	.2687	.2530	.3575	6.33	7.41

Table 1: Experimental results on the Movielens dataset.

	Precision@10		MRR@10		catalogCoverage@10		aggrEntropy@10	
Top K features	**5**	**20**	**5**	**20**	**5**	**20**	**5**	**20**
dbo.IG	.0571	.0579	.2346	.2274	.3988	.4037	10.47	10.44
dbo.AbsOccAvgS	.0561	.0593	.2328	.2329	.3982	.4030	10.54	10.48
dbo.TfIdf	.0579	.0605	.2374	.2477	.4086	.3991	10.55	10.20
dbp.IG	.0586	.0586	.2350	.2299	.4027	.4043	10.49	10.40
dbp.AbsOccAvgS	.0623	.0612	.2467	.2342	.3943	.4043	10.42	10.45
dbp.TfIdf	.0215	.0132	.1608	.1218	.1314	.2696	8.81	9.96

Table 2: Experimental results on the LastFM dataset.

	Precision@10		MRR@10		catalogCoverage@10		aggrEntropy@10	
Top K features	**5**	**20**	**5**	**20**	**5**	**20**	**5**	**20**
dbo.IG	.0411	.1319	.1989	.4083	.4425	.5053	11.06	11.20
dbo.AbsOccAvgS	.1283	.1292	.3986	.4063	.4915	.4949	11.14	11.14
dbo.TfIdf	.1024	.1132	.3064	.3554	.4026	.4508	10.76	10.96
dbp.IG	.0678	.1319	.2553	.4083	.4364	.5053	10.83	11.20
dbp.AbsOccAvgS	**.1319**	**.1316**	**.4026**	**.4113**	.4926	.5055	11.14	11.20
dbp.TfIdf	.0790	.1170	.2371	.3572	.3894	.4698	10.69	11.04

Table 3: Experimental results on the LibraryThing dataset.

Results Tables 1, 2, 3 show the experimental results obtained on, respectively, *Movielens*, *Last.FM* and *LibraryThing* datasets in terms of **Precision**, **MRR**, **catalogCoverage**, and **aggrEntropy**. Results are computed over lists of top-10 items recommended by the RS. We conducted experiments using top-k selected features for different k, i.e., $k = 5, 10, 15, 20$, and all configurations but we report only results for $k = 5, 20$ and best configurations . We highlight in bold only the values for which there is a statistical significant difference. For *Lastfm* dataset the differences are not statistical significant so the two methods are equivalent in selecting features.

Discussion. As an overall result, ABSTAT-based FS leads to the best results in terms of accuracy and diversity for both the movie and books domains while IG leads to better results (although not statistically significant) for music.

Specifically, considering the results on Movielens (Table 1), ABSTAT produces better accuracy with respect to IG in all the configurations both with 5 and 20 features. In terms of aggregate diversity, i.e. itemCoverage and aggrEntropy, ABSTAT is still the best choice, overcoming IG in almost all the situations. On Lastfm (Table 2) there are no particular differences, and hence the choice of the method seems irrelevant: both summarization-based and statistical methods are comparable. Eventually, on LibraryThing (Table 3), ABSTAT strongly beats IG in almost all the configurations. In particular, it gets more than twice of the precision and MRR respect to IG in top-5 features scenario. Summing up, ABSTAT beats IG in almost all the configurations on the two datasets Movielens and LibraryThing, while they act in the same way on the Lastfm dataset.

In order to investigate the reasons behind the different behaviors depending on the selected knowledge domain, we measured: (i) the number of minimal patterns and (ii) the average number of triples per resource and the corresponding variance. Regarding the former we may say that a higher number of minimal patterns means a richer and more diverse

The interested reader can find results for all values of k and configurations on GitHub: `http://ow.ly/zAA530d0wu0`

ontological representation of the knowledge domain. As for the latter, a high variance in the number of triples associated to resources is a clue of an unbalanced representation of the items to recommend. Hence, items with a higher number of triples associated result "more popular" in the knowledge graph compared to those with only a few. This may reflect in the rising of a stronger content popularity bias while computing the recommendation results. If we look at the values represented in Table 4 we may assert that a higher

Domain	Number of Minimal Patterns	Average Number of Triples	Variance
Movies	57757	74,015	549,313
Books	41684	44,966	169,478
Music	40481	80,502	981,509

Table 4: Ontological and data dimensions of the three datasets

sparsity in the knowledge graph data may give chance to statistical methods to beat ontological ones. In other words, it seems that the higher the sparsity of the knowledge graph at the data level, the lower the influence of the ontological schema in the selection of the most informative features to build a pure content-based recommendation engine.

5 Related Work

Summarization. Different approaches have been proposed for schema and data summarization[28]. Several data profiling approaches are aimed to describe linked data by reporting statistics about the usage of the vocabularies, types and properties. SchemeEx extracts interesting measures , by considering the co-occurrence of types and properties [15]. Linked Open Vocabularies, RDFStats [16] and LODStats [2] provide such statistics. In contrast, ABSTAT represents connections between types using schema patterns, for which it also provides cardinality descriptors. does not include cardinality descriptors for properties or patterns. TermPicker extracts [25] patterns consisting in triples $\langle S, E, O\rangle$, where S and O are *sets* of types and E is a set of predicates. Instead, ABSTAT and Loupe extract patterns each consisting in a triple $\langle C, P, D\rangle$ where C and D are types and P a property. TermPicker summaries do not describe cardinality and are extracted from RDF data without considering relationships between types. According to [18], which proposes a method to define and discover classes of cardinality constraints with some preliminary results, current approaches focus only on mining keys or pseudo-keys (e.g., [27]). We discover richer statistics about property cardinality like the above mentioned work, and in addition we compute cardinality descriptors for properties occurring in specific schema patterns.

Recommender Systems. One of the first approaches for using LD in a recommender system was proposed by Heitmann and Hayes[13]. A system for recommending artists and music using DBpedia was presented in [22]. The task of cross-domain recommendation leveraging DBpedia as a knowledge-based framework was addressed in [10], while in [29] the authors present a semantics-aware approach to deal with cold-start situations. In [9] the authors use a a hybrid graph-based algorithm built upon DBpedia and collaborative information. To the best of our knowledge, the only approaches proposing an automatic selection of LD features are [19, 24]. Finally, we observe that even approaches that do not perform automatic FS like [19, 4, 9] used (hand-crafted) FS to improve their performance.

6 Conclusions

In this work we investigated the role of ontology-based data summarization for feature selection in recommendation tasks. Here we compare results coming from ABSTAT, a

http://lov.okfn.org/

schema summarization tool, with classical methods for feature selection and we show that the former are allowed to compute better predictions not just in terms of precision of the recommended items but also considering other dimensions such as diversity. Experiments have been carried out in three different knowledge domains thus showing the effectiveness of a feature selection based on schema summarization over classical techniques such as Information Gain.

References

1. G. Adomavicius and Y. Kwon. Improving aggregate recommendation diversity using ranking-based techniques. *IEEE Trans. on Knowl. and Data Eng.*, 24(5), 2012.
2. S. Auer, J. Demter, M. Martin, and J. Lehmann. LODStats - An Extensible Framework for High-Performance Dataset Analytics. In *EKAW (2)*, 2012.
3. I. Cantador, P. Brusilovsky, and T. Kuflik. 2nd workshop on information heterogeneity and fusion in recommender systems (hetrec 2011). In *RecSys*. ACM, 2011.
4. M. de Gemmis, P. Lops, C. Musto, F. Narducci, and G. Semeraro. Semantics-aware content-based recommender systems. In *Recommender Systems Handbook*. 2015.
5. T. Di Noia. Knowledge-enabled recommender systems: Models, challenges, solutions. In *Proceedings of the 3rd International Workshop on Knowledge Discovery on the WEB, Cagliari, Italy, September 11-12, 2017.*, 2017.
6. T. Di Noia, I. Cantador, and V. C. Ostuni. Linked open data-enabled recommender systems: ESWC 2014 challenge on book recommendation. In *Semantic Web Evaluation Challenge - SemWebEval 2014 at ESWC 2014, Anissaras, Crete, Greece, May 25-29, 2014, Revised Selected Papers*, pages 129–143, 2014.
7. T. Di Noia, C. Magarelli, A. Maurino, M. Palmonari, and A. Rula. Using ontology-based data summarization to develop semantics-aware recommender systems. In *The Semantic Web - 15th International Conference, ESWC 2018, Heraklion, Crete, Greece, June 3-7, 2018, Proceedings*, pages 128–144, 2018.
8. T. Di Noia, V. Ostuni, J. Rosati, P. Tomeo, and E. Di Sciascio. An analysis of users' propensity toward diversity in recommendations. In *RecSys 2014 - Proceedings of the 8th ACM Conference on Recommender Systems*, pages 285–288. Association for Computing Machinery, Inc, 2014.
9. T. Di Noia, V. C. Ostuni, P. Tomeo, and E. Di Sciascio. Sprank: Semantic path-based ranking for top-*N* recommendations using linked open data. *ACM TIST*, 8(1):9:1–9:34, 2016.
10. I. Fernández-Tobías, I. Cantador, M. Kaminskas, and F. Ricci. A generic semantic-based framework for cross-domain recommendation. In *2nd Workshop on Information Heterogeneity and Fusion in Recommender Systems*, 2011.
11. X. Geng, T.-Y. Liu, T. Qin, and H. Li. Feature selection for ranking. In *SIGIR*. ACM, 2007.
12. I. Guyon and A. Elisseeff. An introduction to variable and feature selection. *Journal of Machine Learning Research*, 3, 2003.
13. B. Heitmann and C. Hayes. Using linked data to build open, collaborative recommender systems. In *AAAI Spring Symposium: Linked Data Meets Artificial Intelligence*, 2010.
14. R. Kohavi and G. H. John. Wrappers for feature subset selection. *Artificial Intelligence*, 97(1-2), 1997.
15. M. Konrath, T. Gottron, S. Staab, and A. Scherp. Schemex - efficient construction of a data catalogue by stream-based indexing of linked data. *Web Semant.*, 16, 2012.
16. A. Langegger and W. Wöß. RDFStats - an extensible RDF statistics generator and library. In *DEXA Workshops*, pages 79–83. IEEE, 2009.
17. N. Mihindukulasooriya, M. Poveda Villalon, R. Garcia-Castro, and A. Gomez-Perez. Loupe - An Online Tool for Inspecting Datasets in the Linked Data Cloud. In *ISWC Posters & Demonstrations*, 2015.
18. E. Muñoz. On learnability of constraints from RDF data. In *ESWC*. Springer, 2016.
19. C. Musto, P. Lops, P. Basile, M. de Gemmis, and G. Semeraro. Semantics-aware graph-based recommender systems exploiting linked open data. In *UMAP*, 2016.
20. P. Nguyen, P. Tomeo, T. Di Noia, and E. Di Sciascio. An evaluation of SimRank and Personalized PageRank to build a recommender system for the web of data. In *WWW '15 Companion*, pages 1477–1482. ACM, 2015.
21. X. Ning, C. Desrosiers, and G. Karypis. A comprehensive survey of neighborhood-based recommendation methods. In *Recommender Systems Handbook*, pages 37–76. 2015.
22. A. Passant. Dbrec: Music Recommendations Using DBpedia. In *9th ISWC*, pages 209–224. Springer-Verlag, 2010.
23. H. Paulheim and J. Fümkranz. Unsupervised generation of data mining features from linked open data. In *WIMS*, 2012.
24. A. Ragone, P. Tomeo, C. Magarelli, T. Di Noia, M. Palmonari, A. Maurino, and E. Di Sciascio. Schema-summarization in linked-data-based feature selection for recommender systems. In *Proceedings of the Symposium on Applied Computing, SAC 2017, Marrakech, Morocco, April 3-7, 2017*, pages 330–335, 2017.
25. J. Schaible, T. Gottron, and A. Scherp. Termpicker: Enabling the reuse of vocabulary terms by exploiting data from the linked open data cloud. In *The Semantic Web. Latest Advances and New Domains - 13th International Conference, ESWC 2016, Heraklion, Crete, Greece, May 29 - June 2, 2016, Proceedings*, pages 101–117, 2016.
26. Y. Shi, A. Karatzoglou, L. Baltrunas, M. Larson, N. Oliver, and A. Hanjalic. CLiMF: learning to maximize reciprocal rank with collaborative less-is-more filtering. In *RecSys*. ACM, 2012.
27. T. Soru, E. Marx, and A. N. Ngomo. ROCKER: A refinement operator for key discovery. In *WWW*. ACM, 2015.
28. B. Spahiu, R. Porrini, M. Palmonari, A. Rula, and A. Maurino. ABSTAT: ontology-driven linked data summaries with pattern minimalization. In *2nd Workshop on Summarizing and Presenting Entities and Ontologies, co-located with ESWC.*, 2016.
29. P. Tomeo, I. Fernández-Tobías, I. Cantador, and T. Di Noia. Addressing the cold start with positive-only feedback through semantic-based recommendations. *International Journal of Uncertainty, Fuzziness and Knowledge-Based Systems*, 25(Supplement-2):57–78, 2017.
30. G. Troullinou, H. Kondylakis, E. Daskalaki, and D. Plexousakis. RDF Digest: Efficient Summarization of RDF/S KBs. In *ESWC*, 2015.

Processing SPARQL Queries on Deep Web sources

Andrea Calí[1,4], Tommaso Di Noia[2], Thomas W. Lynch[3,1], and Azzurra Ragone[5]

[1]Dept of Comp. Sci. and Inf. Syst. Birkbeck, Univ. of London, UK
[2]SisInf Lab Politecnico di Bari, Italy
[3]Reasoning Technology Ltd, UK
[4]Oxford-Man Inst. of Quantitative Finance University of Oxford, UK
[5] Independent Researcher
andrea@dcs.bbk.ac.uk, tommaso.dinoia@poliba.it,
thomas.lynch@reasoningtechnology.com, azzurra.ragone@gmail.com

Abstract. The Deep Web is constituted by data accessible through dynamic Web pages requested through a Web interface. While Deep Web data sources have been usually modelled as relational in the literature, in many cases it is useful to export Deep Web data as Linked Data sets. In this context, processing queries poses some algorithmic challenges due to the inherent limitations of Deep Web sources which, requiring some inputs to be queried, function as services. In this paper we present a framework and a system to export Deep Web data as Linked Data sets. Further, we characterise a class of SPARQL queries that are executable directly, in spite of the limitations.

1 Introduction

The *Deep Web* (also known as *Hidden Web*) [9, 6, 3] is constituted by structured data that are available as dynamically generated Web pages, generated upon queries usually posed through HTML forms. The Deep Web content cannot be indexed by search engines and is therefore not immediately searchable or accessible. The Deep Web is separated from the so-called *Surface Web*, the latter being the set of ordinary, static Web pages. It is also known that the Deep Web is orders of magnitude larger than the Surface Web [8]. Deep Web data are normally structured and of great value; however, the limitations in accessing them make them hard to search and query. Integrating Deep Web sources as a single database poses several challenges. Normally in this approach, which allows for processing structured queries [3] as well as keyword queries [5], sources are federated into a single schema. Normally, in this approach one deals with known sources, which contain data related to a single domain of interest. Deep Web sources have been naturally modelled as relational tables that can be queried only

SEBD 2018, June 24-27, 2018, Castellaneta Marina, Italy.

according to so-called *access patterns* (or *access limitations*); more specifically, certain attributes are to be *selected* in the query in order to get an answer — such a selection corresponds to filling the corresponding attribute in the form with a value.

New ways of exposing structured data have recently emerged, which allow the composition of services for the creation of new integrated applications (mash-ups [11]) and knowledge spaces. Among the various technical proposals and approaches for data publication on the Web which survived to the present days, the two most relevant ones are: RESTful services [7] and Linked Data (LD) [2]. RESTful services provide an agile way of exposing data in a request/response fashion over HTTP, and has been widely adopted by programmers thanks to its easiness of implementation [1]. In this context, data are usually returned in XML or JSON documents after the invocation of a service. Among the issues related to the pure RESTful approach we mention the following:

- There is no explicit semantics attached to the returned data.
- There is no unique query language to invoke services. Each service exposes its own API, and APIs considerably differ from each other even when they refer to the same knowledge domain.
- The integration of different data sources is difficult and is often implemented ad-hoc.

On the other hand, the Linked Data approach is based on the idea that data can be delivered on the Web together with their explicit semantics, expressed by means of common vocabularies. Following the Linked Data principles, datasets should be made accessible through a SPARQL endpoint. Moreover, by using federated queries an agent is able to automatically integrate data coming from different sources thus creating a data space at a Web scale. Unfortunately, also the Linked Data approach comes with its drawbacks, among which we may mention:

- The effort in setting up a SPARQL endpoint is bigger than that of adopting a RESTful approach from service providers. Normally it is much easier to find a JSON-based service than a LD-based one.
- Programmers are usually more familiar with JSON services than with SPARQL endpoints.
- Service providers are usually not interested in exposing all the data they have; instead, they normally want to expose only a small portion of their data.

Based on the above points we can see that, while from the practical point of view the RESTful approach is the most efficient, if we look at the *knowledge* point of view the Linked Data paradigm represents a more suitable solution.

Actually, with JSON-LD this issue could be solved but this format is not widely adopted yet.

https://www.w3.org/DesignIssues/LinkedData.html

https://www.w3.org/TR/sparql11-federated-query/

Following the above observations, we built the PoLDo prototype system, which is able to export existing RESTful services, even third-party ones, as a SPARQL endpoint, thus making the underlying Deep Data sources part of the Linked Data cloud. Thanks to a configurable query planner, PoLDo is able to break down a SPARQL query into a sequence of RESTful service invocations and to orchestrate different services to provide a correct answer to the posed query. Starting from the data it retrieves from services, PoLDo builds a temporary RDF dataset used to compute the result set for the original SPARQL query.

In PoLDo, we expose Deep Web sources as services according to the aforementioned intrinsic restrictions. Rather than limiting ourselves to relational Deep Web sources, we model sources as Linked Data with access limitations, that is, SPARQL access points that are only accessible with queries that contain a certain fixed, ground (variable-free) pattern. This poses the problem of determining whether a query can be evaluated over a set of sources (in the form of SPARQL endpoints), while returning the *complete* answers, in the presence of the access limitations. For other queries, we can only expect to get partial answers.

2 Modelling and Querying

In this section we present a model for Linked Data sources that expose Deep Web data, with their inherent limitations. We characterise a class of queries that can be evaluated non-recursively on the data, while returning the complete set of answers (as if they were evaluated in the absence of limitations).

We first show how Deep Web sources are represented as relational data.

When dealing with databases with access limitations the relations can be expressed using the proper access modes. In the case of RESTful services we have the two access mode i and o (for *input* and *output* respectively) stating that for all the tuples $r(c_1, \ldots, c_n) \in \mathcal{DB}$ we have some of the arguments of r mapped to the inputs of the service and some to its outputs. Following [4], we denote access modes as superscript of the relation. As an example, a simple service can be expressed by a relation r_1 defined as $r_1^{oio}(C_1, C_2, C_3)$, where C_2 is an input parameter and C_1, C_3 are output parameters. Let us assume we have also another service $r_2^{ioo}(C_3, C_4, C_5)$, where C_3 is an input parameter and C_4, C_5 are output parameters. Notice that we use the same name for parameters that are compatible, that is, have as instance values (constants) of the same type; this is expressed by the notion of *abstract domain* in Deep Web [3], that is a domain specifying the class the objects it represents (e.g. telephone number, person's name etc.) rather than the concrete domain (string, integer etc.). The annotations that specify input and output parameters are also called *access patterns*. Access limitation affect the computation of the result of a query as not all data, in the forms of facts of the form $r_1(c_1, c_2, c_3)$ where c_1, c_2, c_3 are constants, may be accessible. Consider the conjunctive query q_1 defined as

$$q_1(X) \leftarrow r_1^{oio}(Y, a_2, X), r_2^{ioo}(X, a_4, Z)$$

. This query can be processed by executing the services corresponding to the relations r_1 and r_2 from left to right. Indeed, by invoking the first service with input

c_1 we obtain as output a set of pairs of constants of the type $\langle c_1, c_3\rangle$, each instantiating Y and X respectively, as a consequence of the fact that $r_1(c_1, a_2, c_3) \in \mathcal{DB}$. For each such pair, the second value c_3 is then used as input to invoke the service corresponding to r_2, thus obtaining as output a new set of pairs of the form $\langle c_4, c_5\rangle$. Among these pairs, due to the selection with a_4 on the second atom of the query, we are interested only in those such that $c_4 = a_4$. So this kind of query is *executable* and retrieves a *complete* answer that contains all solutions to the query over $\mathcal{DB}$. Notice that if the query is not executable, in some cases it can be executed from left to right by reordering the subgoals (atoms) [4]. This kind of queries are called *feasible* (or *orderable*). Feasible queries can be evaluated so as to return the *complete answer* to the query. If we had in addition the relation r_3 (and associated service) defined as $r_3^{oio}(C_5, C_4, C_6)$ and a query

$$q_2(X) \leftarrow r_1^{oio}(Y, a_2, X), r_2^{ioo}(X, a_4, Z), r_3^{oio}(Z, U, W),$$

we may not be able to compute all the answers. For example, the instance $\{r_1(d_1, d_2, d_3), r_2(d_3, d_4, d_5), r_3(d_5, d_4', d_6)\}$ will provide the answer $\langle d_3\rangle$ for q_2, but such answer cannot be retrieved due to the limitations. In general, the answers $q(D)$ to a query q on a database D (as computed if the data sources had no access limitations) is a superset of the answers $\mathrm{ans}(q, I, D)$ that can be actually retrieved through the access patterns, that is $\mathrm{ans}(q, I, D) \subseteq q(D)$, where I is a set of *initial constants* available to start the extraction of data from the sources.

When considering Linked Data sets, the limitations of the HTML forms (or others beyond the relational formalism) are reflected naturally as we explain below. We refer to the formalisation of SPARQL in [10].

Data are in the form of *triple patterns* of the form $\langle s, p, o\rangle \in (\mathbf{I} \cup B) \times \mathbf{I} \times (\mathbf{I} \cup B \cup \mathbf{L})$, where B is the set of blank nodes. We assume to have a partial relation ρ on predicates, where $\rho(p_1, p_2)$ means that p_1 and p_2 have compatible domains; this can be specified by the `rdfs:domain` of an `rdf:Property`, but we are not going to expose this in detail in this preliminary paper. The fact that two predicates have compatible domains reflects the notion of abstract domain in Deep Web.

Basic graph patterns (BGPs) are sets of *triple graph patterns* of the form $t \in (\mathbf{I} \cup \mathbf{L} \cup \mathbf{V}) \times (\mathbf{I} \cup \mathbf{V}) \times (\mathbf{I} \cup \mathbf{L} \cup \mathbf{V})$ where $\mathbf{I}$, $\mathbf{V}$ and $\mathbf{L}$ are the sets of IRIs, variables and labels, respectively.

In the context of integrating set of Deep Web data sources and answering queries posed on a set of such sources as if it was a single database, we assume to have a schema $\mathcal{S} = \{S_1, \ldots, S_n\}$ of Deep Web sources. Each source S_i, with $1 \leqslant i \leqslant n$, is an access point that has associated a set Λ_i of triple patterns that are called *input triple patterns (ITPs)*. Intuitively, in order to query a source, we need to use a SPARQL query that provides constants for the object (the

Analogously to [3], in a "traditional" data integration setting, we assume that we are integrating a set of known sources related to a domain of interest. We do not address here the problem of automatic discovery of sources, nor the problem of designing a global schema that offers a seamless model of the underlying data. Instead, we take the union of the sources as our database.

third element in the corresponding triple) of *all* such patterns. This reflects the structure of Deep Web sources when represented as relational tables. More specifically, to query a source S_i, we need a query that contains all input triple patterns Λ_i for S_i, with the third element (the object) instantiated to a value.

To start our exposition, we assume that queries are of the form $q = P_1 \text{ AND } P_2 \text{ AND } \ldots \text{ AND } P_n$, where, for all i s.t. $1 \leqslant i \leqslant n$, each P_i is a graph pattern query to be evaluated on S_i. We do not differentiate here between SELECT and CONSTRUCT query types. Now, we formalise the limitations on sources and we establish a criterion for determining queries that can be evaluated so that all answers are computed.

We consider a schema $\mathcal{S} = \{S_1, \ldots, S_n\}$ of Deep Web sources with access limitations $\Lambda = \{\Lambda_1, \ldots, \Lambda_n\}$. For each S_i, $1 \leqslant i \leqslant n$, Λ_i is a set of input triple patterns (ITPs) of the form $\lambda = \langle V_s, p, V_o \rangle \in \mathbf{V} \times \mathbf{I} \times \mathbf{V}$. Let $\mathcal{D} = \{D_1, \ldots, D_n\}$ be an instance for the schema $\mathcal{S}$, where D_i is the instance of S_i, , for all i s.t. $1 \leqslant i \leqslant n$.

Definition 1.

(a) *A triple pattern t* instantiates *an ITP* $\lambda = \langle V_s, p - V_o \rangle$ *if* $\alpha = \mu(\lambda)$ *such that* μ *is a mapping and* $\mu(V_o) \in \mathbf{I} \times \mathbf{L}$*. Notice that in this case* $\mu(p) = p$*.*
(b) *A source S with a set* Λ *of input triple patterns can be accessed with a BGP P if for each* $\lambda \in \Lambda$*, there is* $\alpha \in P$ *such that* α *instantiates* λ*.*

3 Processing Queries

We now focus on queries that can be executed on an instance $\mathcal{D}$ according to the access patterns

Definition 2. *Let* t_1, t_2 *be triple graph patterns defined as* $t_1 = \langle W_1, p_1, V \rangle, t_2 = \langle W_2, p_1, V \rangle$*, with* $\{W_1, W_2\} \subseteq \mathbf{I} \cup \mathbf{L} \cup \mathbf{V}$ *and* $V \in \mathbf{V}$*.*

(a) *We say that* t_1 feeds t_2 *if* $\rho(p_1, p_2)$*, that is,* p_1 *and* p_2 *are compatible (notice that both triple graph patterns have the same variable as third element).*
(b) *We say that* t_1 *and* t_2 match *if* $p_1 = p_2$*.*

We now identify a class of queries of the form $q = P_1 \text{ AND } P_2 \text{ AND } \ldots \text{ AND } P_n$ that are executable from left to right, after ordering the graph patternss P_i, on an instance $\mathcal{D}$ for a schema $\mathcal{S}$; we call such queries *orderable* in accordance with the relational terminology for queries under access limitations.

Definition 3. *Let q be a query of the form* $q = P_1 \text{ AND } P_2 \text{ AND } \ldots \text{ AND } P_n$*, posed on a schema* $\mathcal{S}$ *as previously defined. q is said to be* orderable *if* $P_1, \ldots, P_n$ *can be ordered as* $P_{i_1}, \ldots, P_{i_n}$ *such that:*

(a) *For every ITP* $\lambda \in \Lambda_{i_1}$*, there is* $\alpha \in P_{i_1}$ *such that* α *instantiates* λ*;*
(b) *For all j such that* $1 \leqslant j \leqslant n$*, for every ITP* $\lambda \in \Lambda_{i_j}$*, either*
(i) *there is* $\alpha \in P_{i_j}$ *such that* α *instantiates* λ*;*

(ii) there are $\beta \in P_{i_j}$ and $\gamma \in P_{i_\ell}$, witha $1 \leqslant \ell \leqslant i_j - 1$, such that (1) γ feeds β; (2) β and λ match.

Notice that this definition is analogous to the same one in the context of relational data under access limitations.

Proposition 1. *Every orderable query on a schema $\mathcal{S}$ of the form $q = P_1$ AND P_2 AND ... AND P_n can be executed on an instance $\mathcal{D}$, after suitably ordering $P_1, \ldots, P_n$, from left to right so that all answers $q(\mathcal{D})$ are retrieved.*

Proof (sketch). We know q can be ordered as in Definition 3; let us assume w.l.o.g. then that it is already ordered. It is easily seen that P_1 can be immediately evaluated on D_1. Then, for each j such that $2 \leqslant j \leqslant n$, P_j can be evaluated on D_j according to Λ_j because every ITPs λ of Λ_j is either *(1)* instantiated by some BGP in P_j or *(2)* instantiated by a triple pattern β', obtained from $\gamma \in P_\ell$, $1 \leqslant \ell \leqslant j-1$ (as per Definition 3) by replacing its third element with the values of the third element of $\mu(\gamma)$, where $\gamma \in P_\ell$, for every mapping μ resulting from the evaluation of P_ℓ on D_ℓ.

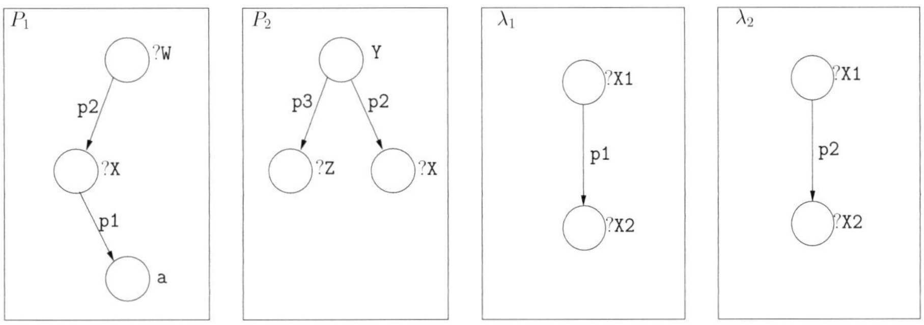

Fig. 1. Figure for Example 1

Example 1. Consider the query P_1 AND P_2, where P_1, P_2 are as in Figure 1 (we omit variables that appear only once), on a schema $\mathcal{S} = \{S_1, S_2\}$ with $\Lambda_1 = \{\lambda_1\}$, $\Lambda_2 = \{\lambda_2\}$, where λ_1, λ_2 are again as in Figure 1. The query q is processed by evaluating P_1 on S_1 directly and then, for all values v obtained by mapping ?X in the evaluation of P_1, by evaluating P_2' (see figure), obtained by replacing ?X with v in P_2.

4 PoLDo

In this section we briefly present the architecture of PoLDo, a prototype that processes queries over distributed Deep Web sources that are exposed as Linked Data sets.

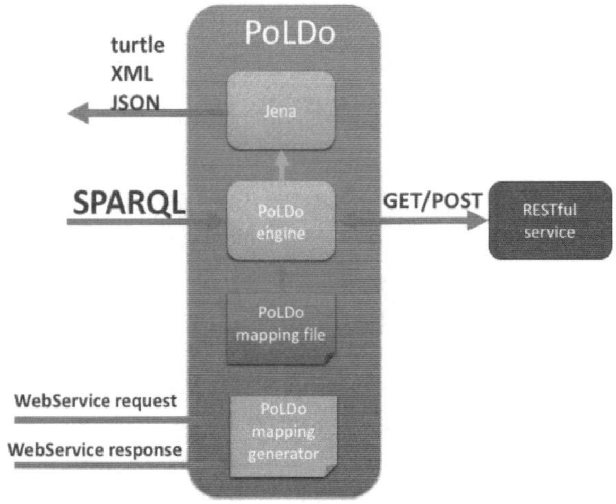

Fig. 2. A high level view for the architecture of PoLDo

The high level architecture of PoLDo is shown in Figure 2. The engine is responsible of getting the SPARQL query and breaking it down to a sequence of RESTful calls to a remote service. The transformation is made possible thanks to a mapping file that maps Linked Data URIs to the elements of the signature of the remote call. While querying the remote service, PoLDo feeds an RDF local triple store (Jena Fuseki, in its current implementation) which is in charge of processing the actual SPARQL query. More specifically, in our system we have the following components and models.

PoLDo **engine** The engine accepts the SPARQL query and extracts all the constants from the graph template in the WHERE clause. Then, by using the algorithm sketched in Section 3 , it uses the constants to query the external service and to get the data that will be used to create a local RDF representation of the data space. Thanks to the information encoded in the PoLDo mapping file, the engine is able to feed a local repository of RDF triples. The engine is also capable to exploit external services to get extracted resources' URI from mapped API services, that often return data related to the resource but not the URI.

Jena The Jena Model is used to save a Linked Data version of the data which are incrementally retrieved from the RESTful service. The availability of a third-party RDF model makes PoLDo able to support the full specification of SPARQL query language. Furthermore, it is able to return the data in all the formats supported by the query engine Jena ARQ.

PoLDo **Mapping Generator** The Mapping Generator is responsible for the generation of the mapping file. Given a RESTful service, it works in four steps. It analyzes request (HTTP GET) and response (JSON or XML) given to and by a web service, then extracts all the inputs and outputs. The user is then allowed to manually assign a class of membership to resources. The Mapping Generator queries the ontologies (DBpedia and LOV, in our first experimentation) and recommend how to link resources. After user confirmation, the final mapping file is generated and can to be used by the engine.

`PoLDo` **mapping file** This file contains information about how to map the URIs of the SPARQL query to inputs and outputs of the services. It also describes the access patterns as represented in Section 2 as well as their mutual relations (that is which triple graph patterns feed each other).

References

1. Vito Walter Anelli, Vito Bellini, Andrea Calì, Giuseppe De Santis, Tommaso Di Noia, and Eugenio Di Sciascio. Querying deep web data sources as linked data. In *Proceedings of the 7th International Conference on Web Intelligence, Mining and Semantics, WIMS 2017, Amantea, Italy, June 19-22, 2017*, pages 32:1–32:7, 2017.
2. Christian Bizer, Tom Heath, and Tim Berners-Lee. Linked data – the story so far. *Int. J. Semantic Web Inf. Syst*, 5(3):1–22, 2009.
3. Andrea Calì and Davide Martinenghi. Querying data under access limitations. In *Proc. of ICDE*, pages 50–59, 2008.
4. Andrea Calì and Davide Martinenghi. Querying the deep web. In *Proc. of EDBT 2010*, pages 724–727, 2010.
5. Andrea Calì, Davide Martinenghi, and Riccardo Torlone. Keyword queries over the deep web. In *Proc. of ER 2016*, pages 260–268, 2016.
6. Kevin Chen-Chuan Chang, Bin He, and Zhen Zhang. Toward large scale integration: Building a metaquerier over databases on the web. In *Proc. of CIDR*, pages 44–55, 2005.
7. Roy T. Fielding and Richard N. Taylor. Principled Design of the Modern Web Architecture. *ACM Transactions on Internet Technology*, 2(2):115–150, 2002.
8. Govind Kabra, Zhen Zhang, and Kevin Chen-Chuan Chang. Dewex: An exploration facility for enabling the deep web integration. In *Proc. of ICDE*, pages 1511–1512, 2007.
9. Jayant Madhavan, Loredana Afanasiev, Lyublena Antova, and Alon Y. Halevy. Harnessing the deep web: Present and future. In *Proc. of CIDR*, 2009.
10. Jorge Pérez, Marcelo Arenas, and Claudio Gutiérrez. Semantics and complexity of SPARQL. *ACM Trans. on Database Systems*, 34(3):16:1–16:45, 2009.
11. Ahmet Soylu, Felix Mödritscher, Fridolin Wild, Patrick De Causmaecker, and Piet Desmet. Mashups by orchestration and widgetbased personal environments: Key challenges, solution strategies, and an application. *Program*, 46(4):383–428, 2012.

A Similarity Function for Multi-Level and Multi-Dimensional Itemsets

Matteo Francia, Matteo Golfarelli, and Stefano Rizzi

DISI, University of Bologna, Italy

Abstract. The key objective of frequent itemsets (FIs) mining is uncovering relevant patterns from a transactional dataset. In particular we are interested in multi-dimensional and multi-level transactions, i.e., ones that include different points of view about the same event and are described at different levels of detail. In the context of a work aimed at devising original techniques for summarizing and visualizing this kind of itemsets, in this paper we extend the definition of itemset containment to the multi-dimensional and multi-level scenario, and we propose a new similarity function for itemsets, enabling a more effective grouping. The most innovative aspect of our similarity function is that it takes into account both the extensional and intensional natures of itemsets.

Keywords: Frequent itemset mining, Itemset summaries

1 Introduction

The key objective of frequent itemsets (FIs) mining is uncovering relevant patterns from a transactional dataset [2]. Since its initial formulation on transactions of uniform and flat items, where a transaction corresponds to a set of products bought together by a customer, FIs mining has been applied to different types of data. In particular, in this work we consider *multi-dimensional* and *multi-level* data [8]. A multi-dimensional transaction represents an event from different points of views, which we call *features*. In a multi-level transaction feature values are described using hierarchies with different levels of detail. A typical application is that of user profiling: each transaction describes a user by means of several features related for instance to where she lives, where she works, how much she earns; each feature values can be described at different, hierarchically-organized levels (e.g., she lives close to Macy's, which is in the Garment district, which is part of Manhattan). In this context, a FI describes a profile of a group of people sharing the same features/behavior.

The exponential nature of FIs [2] makes it difficult for data scientists and domain experts to visualize and explore their information content. Increasing the frequency threshold (i.e., the minimum itemset support) just decreases the number of FIs possibly leading to missing useful information; so, it is recognized that more effective approach is that of providing FI *summaries* to assist decision

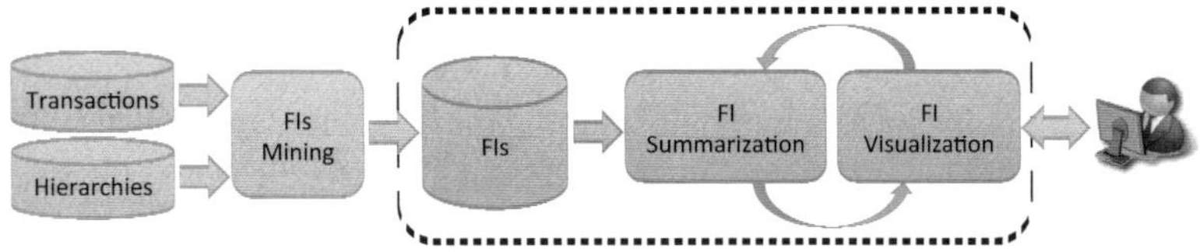

Fig. 1. A functional architecture of a framework to summarize and visualize FIs

makers in getting insights over data [14]. Summarization differs from FIs mining since the latter searches, within a set of transactions, those itemset that are frequently present disregarding redundancy. Conversely, summarization is an optimization problem that addresses the extraction of the minimum number of FIs that represent an entire population while maximizing the overall diversity of the representatives. The two techniques are complementary to enhance and simplify FIs analysis: the adoption of summarization on top of FIs mining makes the choice of a frequency threshold less critical and enables the discovery of both specific and general patterns. Though several FI summarization approaches have been proposed in the literature (e.g., [1,12,5]), they do not consider the multi-level and multi-dimensional natures of FIs. A third approach to make FI analysis more effective is the use of advanced visualizations. Interactive visual interfaces and visual data mining approaches can unveil hidden information, simplify the process of understanding, and allow users to focus their attention on what is important. Although some visual representations for FIs have been proposed in the literature [13,9,4], to the best of our knowledge no approaches for visualizing FIs summaries have been proposed so far.

To fill this gap, we are currently working on a framework addressing the summarization and visualization of multi-level and multi-dimensional FIs. As shown in Figure 1, our approach is independent of the algorithm applied for generating the FIs taken in input [11,3]. The summarization and the visualization components work jointly to give users the relevant information; the user can iteratively create and visualize new summaries that better meet her needs by tuning a set of parameters. In the context of this framework, here we extend the definitions of FIs and itemset containment to the multi-dimensional and multi-level scenario, and we propose a new similarity function for FIs that enables more effective groupings. The most innovative aspect of our similarity function is that it takes into account both the extensional and intensional natures of FIs. The intensional nature is considered in *feature-based similarity*: the higher the number of features (i.e., semantics) shared by two FIs, the higher their similarity; the extensional nature is considered in *support-based similarity*: the higher the percentage of transactions supporting both FIs, the higher their similarity. Adopting this two-faceted similarity function, agglomerative clustering algorithms [7] can then be leveraged to summarize FIs.

The paper is organized as follows. After providing the formal definitions of multi-dimensional and multi-level FIs in Section 2, in Section 3 we propose our similarity function. Finally, in Section 4 we discuss the research perspectives.

2 Itemsets

The itemsets we consider are multi-level, which implies the presence of a hierarchy of concepts. The type of hierarchies we consider are those defined in classic multi-dimensional modeling [6].

Definition 1 (Hierarchy). *A* hierarchy H *is defined by (i) a set* L_H *of categorical* levels, *(ii) a* domain $Dom(l)$ *including a set of* values *for each level* $l \in L_H$ *(all domains are disjoint), (iii) a* roll-up *partial order* $\succeq_H$ *of* L_H*, and (iv) a* part-of *partial order* $\geq_H$ *of* $\bigcup_{l \in L_H} Dom(l)$. *Exactly one level* $dim(H) \in L_H$*, called* dimension*, is such that* $dim(H) \succeq_H l$ *for each other* $l \in L_H$*. The part-of partial order is such that, for each couple of levels* l *and* l' *such that* $l \succeq_H l'$*, for each value* $v \in Dom(l)$ *there is exactly one value* $v' \in l'$ *such that* $v \geq_H v'$.

The itemsets we consider are also multi-dimensional, i.e., they refer to different features (e.g., worksIn) each related to a specific hierarchy (e.g., Location). A feature defines the semantics carried by an item at a specific hierarchical level. This can be formalized as follows:

Definition 2 (Domain Schema). *A* domain schema *is a triple* $\mathcal{D} = (\mathcal{H}, \mathcal{F}, \mu)$ *where: (1)* $\mathcal{H}$ *is a set of hierarchies; (2)* $\mathcal{F}$ *is a set of* features*; and (3)* μ *is a function mapping each feature onto one hierarchy.*

Example 1. As a working example we will use the Profiling domain schema, which describes the customers who regularly visit a mall and features the two hierarchies depicted in Figure 2. The first one is rooted in the Location dimension and has two branches: the first one describes locations from the geographical point of view (with reference to New York City), the second one based on their features. In the roll-up partial order we have, for instance, Neighborhood $\succeq_{\text{Location}}$ Borough; in the part-of partial order, we have Harlem $\geq_{\text{Location}}$ Manhattan. The second hierarchy describes incomes in terms of their ranges. The features of Profiling are worksIn, frequents, and earns; specifically,

$$\mu(\text{worksIn}) = \mu(\text{frequents}) = \text{Location}, \ \mu(\text{earns}) = \text{Income}$$

Itemsets are non-redundant sets of items, i.e., two items in an itemset cannot be defined on values related in the part-of partial order (e.g., GreenwichVillage and Manhattan). Finally, transactions are itemsets whose items are all defined on dimension values (e.g., Macy's).

Definition 3 (Itemset and Transaction). *Given domain schema* $\mathcal{D} = (\mathcal{H}, \mathcal{F}, \mu)$*, an* item *of* $\mathcal{D}$ *is a couple* $i = (f, v)$ *where* $f \in \mathcal{F}$*,* $v \in Dom(l)$*, and* l *is a level of hierarchy* $\mu(f)$*. An* itemset I *of* $\mathcal{D}$ *is a set of distinct items of* $\mathcal{D}$ *where, for each* $i, i' \in I$*, with* $i = (f, v)$ *and* $i' = (f, v')$*, it is* $v \not\geq_{\mu(f)} v'$ *and* $v' \not\geq_{\mu(f)} v$*. A* transaction *is an itemset only including items defined over dimensions of* $\mathcal{H}$.

Example 2. Examples of itemset I and transaction T of Profiling are

$$I = \{(\text{worksIn}, \text{Harlem}), (\text{frequents}, \text{Museum}), (\text{earns}, \text{High})\}$$
$$T = \{(\text{worksIn}, \text{CityCollege}), (\text{frequents}, \text{WhitneyMuseum}), (\text{earns}, \text{35to60})\}$$

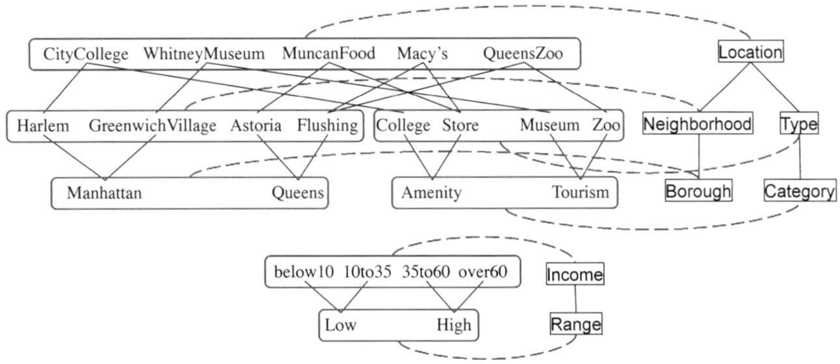

Fig. 2. Hierarchies (right) and values (left) for the Profiling domain schema; in red, the level-domain mappings

Working with multi-dimensional and multi-level items requires to extend the classic definition of *containment* between itemsets, which generalizes set containment taking hierarchies into account.

Definition 4 (Itemset Containment). *Given two itemsets I and I', we say that I is* contained *in I' (denoted $I \sqsubseteq I'$) iff for each item $i \in I$, $i = (f, v)$, there is an item $i' \in I'$, $i' = (f, v')$ such that $v' \geq_{\mu(f)} v$.*

Let $\mathcal{I}$ denote the set of all items of a schema domain. It can be easily verified that the containment relationship is reflexive, antisymmetric, and transitive, and that for each pair of itemsets in $\mathcal{I}$ there are a least upper bound and a greatest lower bound; so $\sqsubseteq$ induces a lattice on $2^{\mathcal{I}}$. The top element of the lattice is the empty itemset, the bottom element is $\mathcal{I}$. Given two itemsets I and I', we denote with $lub(I, I')$ and $glb(I, I')$ their least upper bound and greatest lower bound.

Example 3. Figure 3 shows a small portion of the containment lattice for Profiling; for simplicity we restrict to features frequents and earns and denote items by their value only. For instance, for frequents it is $\{\text{Amenity}\} \sqsubseteq \{\text{College}, \text{Store}\}$ and $\{\text{Amenity}\} \sqsubseteq \{\text{College}\}$. Besides, it is

$$lub(\{\text{CityCollege}\}, \{\text{College}, \text{Store}\}) = \{\text{CityCollege}, \text{Store}\}$$
$$glb(\{\text{CityCollege}\}, \{\text{College}, \text{Store}\}) = \{\text{College}\}$$

Transaction T is said to *support* itemset I iff $I \sqsubseteq T$. With reference to Example 2, T supports I. Given a set of transactions $\mathcal{T}$, the set of transactions that support I is denoted by $\mathcal{T}_I \subseteq \mathcal{T}$. This allows us to introduce a relevant numerical property of itemsets, namely, their *support*.

Definition 5 (Itemset Support). *Given itemset I, its support $sup(I)$ within a set of transactions $\mathcal{T}$ is defined as*

$$sup(I) = \frac{|\mathcal{T}_I|}{|\mathcal{T}|}$$

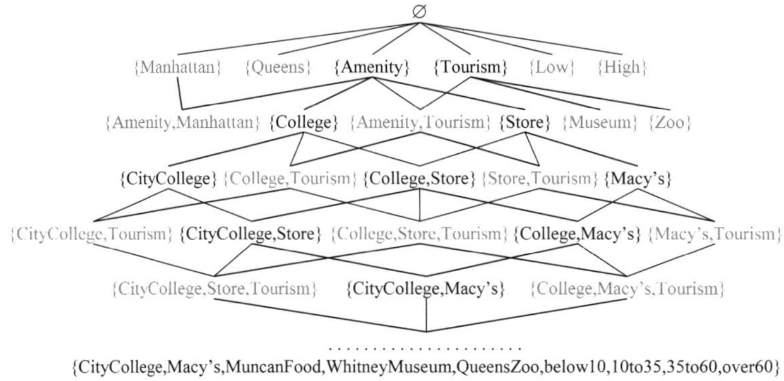

Fig. 3. A portion of the containment for Profiling, including containment arcs; itemsets in gray are not completely expanded

Itemset I is said to be *frequent* if it is greater or equal to a given threshold. Note that, since the containment relationship induces a lattice on the set $2^{\mathcal{I}}$ of all possible itemsets, it also induces a partial order over the set $\mathcal{F} \subseteq 2^{\mathcal{I}}$ of FIs. Thus, from now on we will say that $\mathcal{F}$ is a POS (Partially Ordered Set).

3 Itemset Similarity

We argue that itemset similarity is a two-faceted concept: (1) according to *feature-based* similarity, the higher the number of features (i.e., semantics) shared by two FIs, the higher their similarity; and (2) feature-based similarity is useless if two FIs include two distinct groups of transactions, thus, it is complemented by *support-based* similarity in which the higher the percentage of transactions supporting both FIs, the higher their similarity. These two aspects of similarity are not necessarily correlated; for example, support-based similarity can be low even if feature-based similarity is high when non-shared features are rare and supported by a small fraction of transactions.

In a multi-level and multi-dimensional domain, computing feature-based similarity is not just a matter of finding the subset of common items between two FIs, but it is also related to the informative value they carry in terms of level of detail. Intuitively, we consider an FI to be more *relevant* than another if it includes a larger number of distinct features; in turn, the relevance of a feature increases with the level of detail at which it is expressed.

Definition 6 (Itemset Relevance). *Given itemset I, its* relevance *is defined as*

$$rel(I) = \sum_{f \in Feat(I)} \left(rel(f) + \sum_{l \in Lev_f(I)} rel(l) \right)$$

where $Feat(I)$ is the set of distinct features of the items in I, $Lev_f(I)$ is the set of levels of the values coupled with feature f in the items of I, $rel(f)$ is the relevance of f, and $rel(l)$ is the relevance of level l. Conventionally, $rel(\varnothing) = 0$.

We finally introduce the similarity between two FIs as a linear combination of a support-based and a feature-based similarity.

Definition 7 (Itemset Similarity). *Given a set of transactions $\mathcal{T}$, a POS of FIs $\mathcal{F}$, two FIs I and I' supported by $\mathcal{T}$, and a coefficient $\lambda \in [0..1]$, the* similarity *of I and I' is defined as*

$$sim(I, I') = \lambda sim_{sup}(I, I') + (1 - \lambda) sim_{rel}(I, I')$$

where

$$sim_{sup}(I, I') = \frac{sup(glb(I, I'))}{sup(I) + sup(I') - sup(glb(I, I'))}$$

$$sim_{rel}(I, I') = \begin{cases} \frac{rel(lub(I,I'))}{rel(glb(I,I'))}, & \text{if } lub(I, I'), glb(I, I') \in \mathcal{F} \\ 0, & \text{otherwise} \end{cases}$$

Both sim_{sup} and sim_{rel} range in $[0..1]$ and can be intuitively explained as follows: sim_{sup} is the ratio between the number of transactions supporting both FIs I and I' and the number of transactions supporting either I or I'; sim_{rel} is the ratio between the relevance of the features common to I and I' and the relevance of the union of the features of I and I'. Clearly, since the lub and glb operators are commutative, it is always $sim(I, I') = sim(I', I)$.

Example 4. With reference to the hierarchies defined in Figure 2, we assume that (i) all features are equally relevant ($rel(f) = 1$ for all f), and (ii) relevance increases by 0.1 for each level of detail. Given FIs $I = \{$(frequents, College), (worksIn, Store)$\}$ and $I' = \{$(frequents, College), (frequents, Store)$\}$, it is

$L = lub(I, I') = \{$(frequents, College), (frequents, Store), (worksIn, Store)$\}$
$G = glb(I, I') = \{$(frequents, College)$\}$

Assuming for instance that $sup(I) = 0.3, sup(I') = 0.4, sup(L) = 0.2, sup(G) = 0.5$, and $\lambda = 0.5$, then $sim(I, I') = 0.44$.

4 Discussion

In this paper we have proposed an original similarity measure for multi-dimensional and multi-level FIs, to be used for enabling the creation of concise and valuable summaries of sets of FIs. Though for space reasons we cannot fully detail how summaries are defined and visualized in our approach, in this section we give an informal explanation.

First of all, since our goal is to support interactive exploration and navigation of FIs, we organize summaries in a hierarchical fashion so that they can be analyzed at different levels of detail. So we build a hierarchical clustering of the set of all FIs using an agglomerative algorithm; any (complete and disjoint) "cut" of the resulting dendrogram is a summary.

In a summary each cluster is represented by a single FI; specifically, the representative of cluster c is the most specific FI in c, i.e., such that $I \sqsubseteq rep(c), \forall I \in c$. With reference to this, we note that the strategy commonly used in the literature picks as a cluster representative its most general FI [5]; however, this strategy often lacks in properly characterizing clusters since it easily yields very low relevance as the cluster cohesion decreases, which may entail one or more features appearing in some of the cluster FIs to be missing from the representative. Conversely, when using our strategy, all the features appearing in at least one FI of the cluster are included in the representative.

As to the agglomerative clustering algorithm we adopt, it is basically a greedy algorithm that progressively merges couples of clusters starting from singletons and until one single cluster is obtained. Remarkably, the POS of FIs induced by our definition of itemset containment allows the search space to be significantly pruned. Indeed, our preliminary tests show that the POS obtained when a feature is described using a linear hierarchy of n levels is several orders of magnitude smaller than the one we would get if those n levels were flat. Another relevant improvement we get in terms of computational complexity depends on an interesting property of our similarity function. It can be proved that, in domains where the relevance of the levels of a hierarchy increases with the level of detail (i.e., $rel(l) \geq rel(l')$ if $l \succeq_H l'$), similarity is antimonotonic along the itemset containment relationship. As a consequence, at each step of our agglomerative algorithm we can just estimate the similarity between FIs that are *directly* contained into one another, thus avoiding a large number of useless computations.

Finally, to visualize summaries we adopt treemaps, a popular method for visualizing large hierarchical data sets by mapping hierarchical concepts into 2D areas [10]. Figure 4 shows a treemap in which the visualization area is partitioned into nested rectangles, each corresponding to a cluster of FIs whose area is proportional to the cluster cardinality; colors code both the predominant feature (i.e., the one with the highest relevance within the cluster FIs) of the cluster representative (hue) and its support (saturation). So, for instance, the top right pink rectangle describes a cluster that (i) includes 97 FIs with support ranging from 0.14 to 0.58 and relevance ranging from 1.00 to 3.60; (ii) has 10 child clusters in the dendrogram; and (iii) has a representative (namely, {(earns, avg30), (livesIn, close), (livesIn, collina_BO), (worksIn, Bologna), (worksIn, close)}) whose predominant feature is livesIn. On this visualization the user can then apply classical OLAP operators (roll-up, drill-down, slice-and-dice) to navigate the dendrogram so as to flexibly explore the set of FIs at different abstraction levels and focusing on the more relevant FIs.

References

1. Afrati, F.N., Gionis, A., Mannila, H.: Approximating a collection of frequent sets. In: Proc. SIGKDD. pp. 12–19. Seattle, USA (2004)

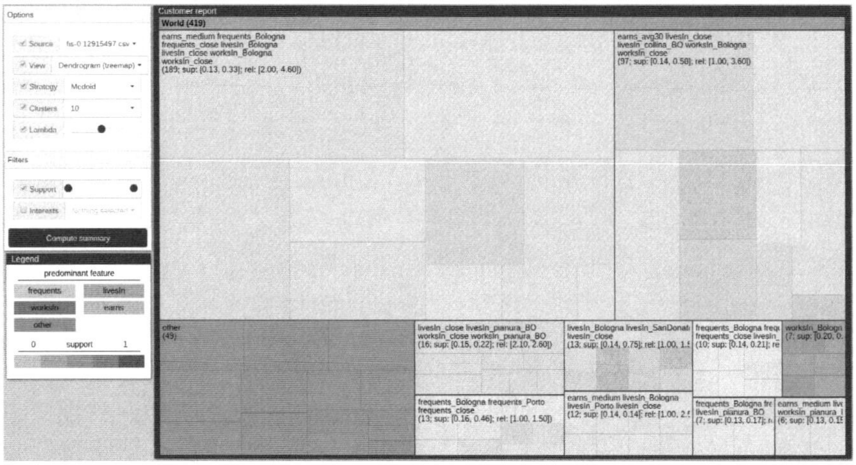

Fig. 4. Visualization of summaries

2. Agrawal, R., Srikant, R.: Fast algorithms for mining association rules in large databases. In: Proc. VLDB. pp. 487–499. Santiago, Chile (1994)
3. Baralis, E., Cagliero, L., Cerquitelli, T., D'Elia, V., Garza, P.: Support driven opportunistic aggregation for generalized itemset extraction. In: Proc. IS. pp. 102–107. London, UK (2010)
4. Bothorel, G., Serrurier, M., Hurter, C.: Visualization of frequent itemsets with nested circular layout and bundling algorithm. In: Proc. ISVC. pp. 396–405. Rethymnon, Greece (2013)
5. Chandola, V., Kumar, V.: Summarization — compressing data into an informative representation. Knowl. Inf. Syst. 12(3), 355–378 (2007)
6. Golfarelli, M., Rizzi, S.: Data warehouse design: Modern principles and methodologies. McGraw-Hill (2009)
7. Guha, S., Rastogi, R., Shim, K.: CURE: an efficient clustering algorithm for large databases. In: Proc. SIGMOD. pp. 73–84. Washington, USA. (1998)
8. Han, J., Fu, Y.: Mining multiple-level association rules in large databases. IEEE Trans. Knowl. Data Eng. 11(5), 798–804 (1999)
9. Leung, C.K., Carmichael, C.L.: FpViz: a visualizer for frequent pattern mining. In: Proc. SIGKDD. pp. 30–39. Paris, France (2009)
10. Shneiderman, B.: Tree visualization with tree-maps: 2-d space-filling approach. ACM Trans. Graph. 11(1), 92–99 (1992)
11. Srikant, R., Agrawal, R.: Mining generalized association rules. In: Proc. VLDB. pp. 407–419. Zurich, Switzerland (1995)
12. Wang, J., Karypis, G.: On efficiently summarizing categorical databases. Knowl. Inf. Syst. 9(1), 19–37 (2006)
13. Yan, X., Cheng, H., Han, J., Xin, D.: Summarizing itemset patterns: a profile-based approach. In: Proc. SIGKDD. pp. 314–323. Chicago, USA (2005)
14. Zhang, S., Jin, Z., Lu, J.: Summary queries for frequent itemsets mining. Journal of Systems and Software 83(3), 405–411 (2010)

Enabling big data exploration in dynamic contexts

Ada Bagozi, Devis Bianchini, Valeria De Antonellis, Alessandro Marini, Davide Ragazzi

Dept. of Information Engineering University of Brescia
Via Branze, 38 - 25123 Brescia (Italy)

Abstract. According to the Industry 4.0 vision, big data management is among the new challenges for the factory of the future. While many approaches have been developed to investigate data analysis, data visualisation, data collection and management, the impact of big data exploration is still under-estimated. In this paper, we propose an approach for big data exploration in a dynamic context of interconnected systems, such as the Industry 4.0 domain. The approach relies on three main pillars: (i) a multi-dimensional model, that is suited for supporting the iterative and multi-step exploration of big data; (ii) novel data summarisation techniques, based on clustering; (iii) a model of relevance, aimed to focus the attention on relevant data only.

Keyword: big data exploration, data summarisation, data relevance, Industry 4.0, smart manufacturing

1 Introduction

Big data management challenges raised from the abundance of real time data in Cyber-Physical Systems (CPS), enabled by the widespread diffusion of IoT technologies [1]. Data is emerging as a new industrial asset, to implement advanced functions like state detection, health assessment, as well as *manufacturing servitization* [2]. In this context, many approaches have addressed issues related to data collection and storage, analysis and visualisation. Nevertheless, big data exploration issues are still under-estimated. These issues are very relevant with reference to the principle of "human-in-the-loop" for Industry 4.0 applications [3], where operators are in charge of taking decisions in unknown situations, based on their long-term experience. Operators must be supported in managing the high volume of collected data in order to identify relevant insights on which these decisions will be based.

In this paper, we discuss the ingredients to enable exploration of real time data in a dynamic context of interconnected systems, where large amounts of data must be incrementally collected, organized and analysed on-the-fly. Such

SEBD 2018, June 24-27, 2018, Castellaneta Marina, Italy. Copyright held by the authors.

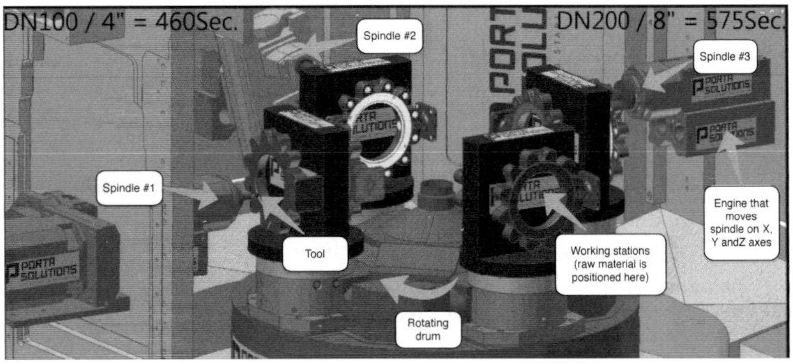

Fig. 1. The multi-spindle machine used for the case study.

ingredients have been already described in [10], where additional details about the proposed model and techniques, as well as an extended comparison with the state of the art, can be found. The approach relies on three main pillars: (i) a multi-dimensional model, to support the iterative and multi-step exploration of big data; (ii) novel data summarisation techniques, based on clustering; (iii) a model of relevance, aimed to focus the attention on relevant data only. The novel contribution of our approach relies on the clustering-based data relevance evaluation and its use in combination with the multi-dimensional model, in order to foster big data exploration. In fact, multi-dimensional data modeling, where information is organised according to dimensions, either flat or hierarchically organized, may ease data exploration [4]. Furthermore, data summarisation techniques enable aggregated views over high volume of data. Finally, data relevance evaluation helps operators to identify data of interest, also when exploration requirements are not well specified or must be iteratively refined based on collected data.

The paper is organised as follows: in Section 2 we will motivate the approach with the help of a smart factory case study and we highlight differences with respect to related work; in Section 3 we will provide a general overview of the approach; the architecture of a framework built on top of the proposed techniques and models will be presented in Section 4 and preliminary experiments in the case study will be described in Section 5; finally, Section 6 closes the paper.

2 Motivations and challenges

2.1 Smart factory case study

Let's consider an Original Equipment Manufacturer (OEM) producing multi-spindle machines. As shown in Figure 1, spindles work independently each other on the raw material, that is positioned on a rotating drum.
Each spindle is mounted on a unit moved by an electrical engine to perform X, Y and Z movements. The spindle rotation is impressed by an electrical engine

and its rotation speed is controlled by the machine control. Spindles use different tools (that are selected according to the instructions specified within the Part Program) in order to complete different steps in the manufacturing cycle. For each spindle, the velocity of the three axes (X, Y and Z), the electrical current absorbed by each engine, the value of rpm for the spindle and the percentage of power absorbed by the spindle engine (charge coefficient) are measured. Hereafter, with term *features* we will refer to the measured quantities. The aim is to monitor the axle hardening of each spindle and the tool wear. Axle hardening is monitored by observing changes in the values of energy consumption (spindle engine charge coefficient) for similar rpm. By detecting differences in energy consumption while using different tools, spindle hardening can be identified as the possible anomaly during the manufacturing operations. If the increase in energy consumption is related only to the usage of a specific tool, this has been recognised as a symptom of tool wear. We collected real data from three machines, each one equipped with three spindles and different tools. On each spindle, we monitored the eight features listed above.

2.2 Related work

In the considered motivating scenario, experience of human operators still plays a fundamental role. Data exploration must be performed in near real time and during incremental data collection. In [5] Exploratory Computing is defined as a multi-step process, going beyond traditional exploratory data analysis and Data Mining techniques. In our approach, we aim at performing a step forward by describing a combined use of multi-dimensional model, data summarisation and relevance evaluation techniques to foster exploration while dealing with disruptive characteristics of big data (e.g., mainly volume and velocity). The innovation we introduced, compared to On Line Analytical Processing [6] and faceted search [7], relies on the combined use of data summarisation and relevance evaluation techniques within a multi-dimensional model specifically designed for incremental big data organisation. In [4] OLAP-based exploration for multi-dimensional data is discussed, but no data relevance techniques are proposed. Similarly, authors in [8] propose the application of query approximation techniques for data that are incrementally collected, without providing a way of guiding target users towards data of interest. In [9] an approach to issue range queries over structured data is described. Semantic windows group data according to specific criteria (e.g., all data in a given time interval, all data in the same geographical area), while sampling techniques are applied to support users in query resolution. No incremental collection and organisation of data are performed. The three pillars we will introduce in the following (clustering, data relevance and multi-dimensional modeling) have been combined to foster exploration of huge amounts of data incrementally collected from dynamic systems.

3 Approach overview

Data summarisation. The characteristics of big data, namely, volume, velocity and variety, pose non trivial issues for data collection and organisation. High volume calls for techniques and tools to provide a compact view over the large amount of collected data. Furthermore, we deal with data streams, in which data is collected in a fast and incremental way. We address these issues by applying incremental clustering techniques. Clusters offer a two-fold advantage: (a) they give an overall view over a set of measures, using a reduced amount of information; (b) they allow to depict the behaviour of the system better than single records, that might be affected by noise and false outliers, in order to observe a given physical phenomenon. Clustering is performed in two steps: (i) in the first one, a variant of Clustream algorithm [11] is applied, that incrementally processes incoming data to obtain a *set of syntheses*, that provide a lossless representation of measures; (ii) in the second step, syntheses are clustered, in order to minimise the distance between their centroids within the same cluster and to maximise the distance between centroids across different clusters. Clusters give a balanced view of the observed physical phenomenon, grouping together syntheses corresponding to the same working status. The two-steps clustering algorithm enables an incremental procedure specifically developed to face data streams. Considering Δt as the time interval in which measures are grouped in syntheses, that in turn are clustered, every Δt seconds a new clusters set SC is generated, built on top of the previous iterations.

Clustering-based data relevance evaluation. Relevance-based techniques are used to focus exploration on relevant clusters only. In literature, data relevance is defined as the distance from an expected status. In our case, the expected status corresponds to the normal working conditions of monitored Cyber Physical Systems. The expected status can be tagged by human operators while observing the monitored system. Let's denote with $\hat{SC} = \{\hat{C}_1, \hat{C}_2, \ldots, \hat{C}_n\}$ the clusters set identified during normal working conditions, and with $SC = \{C_1, C_2, \ldots, C_m\}$ the current clusters set, where n and m do not necessarily coincide. Relevant data are recognised when SC differs from $\hat{SC}$. Therefore, the proposed relevance techniques are based on clusters set distance between SC and $\hat{SC}$, denoted with $\Delta(SC, \hat{SC})$, and enable to detect clusters movements, clusters contraction/expansion, changes in the number of clusters. We refer to [10] for details on $\Delta(SC, \hat{SC})$ computation.

Multi-dimensional model for data exploration. The multi-dimensional model is shown in Figure 2, using the hypercube representation, where axes represent exploration dimensions and nodes represent clusters sets computed on measures. Multi-dimensional modeling may help to organise clustered data according to different perspectives, compliant with operators' requirements. Among the dimensions, we always consider feature spaces, time and operational parameters. With *feature spaces* we refer to monitored phenomena (e.g., axle hardening, tool wear) observed by measuring a set of features. Time is of paramount importance, since the data summarisation procedure and data relevance techniques are strictly related to the time dimension. Operational parameters represent domain-specific settings or variables: for example, the working mode (G0, fast movement

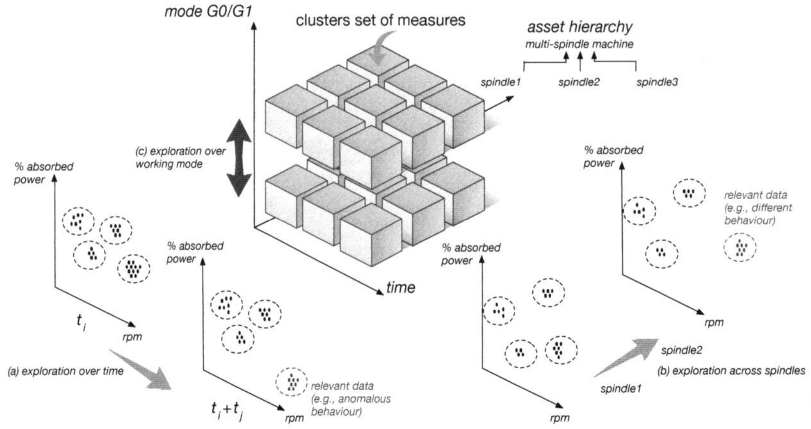

Fig. 2. The multi-dimensional data model for big data exploration.

of the spindle to catch the tool, or G1, slow movement of the spindle during the manufacturing), the tool used during manufacturing, the monitored system, the manufactured product. Dimensions may present hierarchies: for example, tools can be aggregated into tool types, monitored system follows the asset hierarchy (enterprise, shop floor, machine, components).

Exploration scenarios. Data relevance is used to identify dimensions over which summarised data changed, thus denoting an unexpected behaviour of the monitored system. Nevertheless, data relevance evaluation performed over all available dimensions may bring to high computational requirements. Therefore, *exploration scenarios* are proposed to constrain relevance evaluation over a subset of available dimensions, to prevent useless comparisons. In Figure 2, some examples of exploration scenarios are highlighted. Exploration for anomaly detection (a) detects anomalies by observing if collected data of a specific spindle changes and gets closer/overtakes physical limits of breakage. This exploration scenario constrains exploration over the time dimension and within the same monitored system. Exploration for performance comparison (b) focuses comparison between spindles working in the same conditions. Other exploration scenarios are defined to avoid erroneous comparisons. For example, let's consider the exploration over working mode (c) as shown in Figure 2: a comparison of system behaviour across G0 and G1 modes does not make sense. Modeling exploration scenarios, in order to abstract from their implementation, will be further investigated in future work.

4 IDEAaS Architecture

The approach described in this paper has been implemented within the IDEAaS (Interactive Data Exploration As a Service) framework, whose architecture is

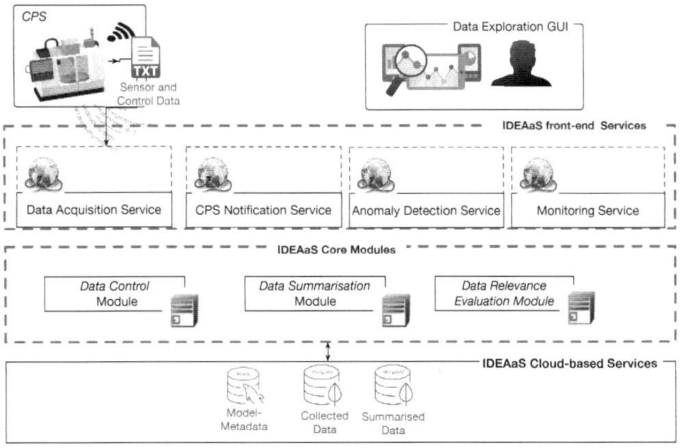

Fig. 3. The functional architecture of the IDEAaS framework.

shown in Figure 3. In the IDEAaS modular architecture, modules are distinguished in IDEAaS Core Modules (that include Data Control, Data Summarisation and Data Relevance Evaluation) and IDEAaS front-end Services, exposed both as web services and as standalone modules. Among these services, Data Acquisition Service is in charge of storing data collected from CPS. As shown in Figure 3, data coming from the physical system, properly collected through sensors and IoT technologies, is sent to the Data Acquisition Service to be processed. This service operates in order to minimise time spent for data acquisition. Specifically, data collected is first saved as JSON documents in a MongoDB NoSQL database (*Collected Data*), minimising any other operation, namely data control and cleaning and data clustering that are performed in parallel. Dimensions of the multi-dimensional model are stored as metadata into the *Model-MetaData* relational database. On collected data, summarisation and relevance evaluation techniques are applied. Resulting clusters sets are stored as JSON documents within *Summarised Data* database (also using MongoDB technology). The CPS Notification Service is in charge of notifying to target operators data of interest according to the relevance evaluation techniques. Data relevance can be used to serve different purposes, ranging from anomaly detection to performance monitoring of CPS, for which specific services will be designed in the future. On top of CPS Notification Service, a Data Exploration GUI will be developed as well, to allow operators to interact with the system and explore collected data. The IDEAaS architecture is implemented in Java, on top of a Glassfish Server Open Source Edition 4.

5 Preliminary experiments

We tested the efficiency and effectiveness of our approach in providing summarised data for exploration purposes, given the acquisition rate of records in

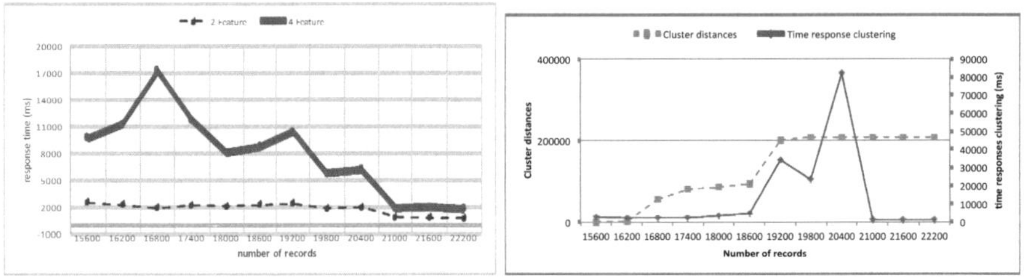

(a) (b)

Fig. 4. Tests on efficiency of clustering and hypercube generation (a) and on the effectiveness of the model of relevance, introducing a variation in collected records (b).

Working Days	Spindle 1		Spindle 2		Spindle 3	
	rpm decreas	energy consumption increase	rpm decreas	energy consumption increase	rpm decreas	energy consumption increase
01/08/2016 (operates normally)	/	/	/	/	/	/
02/08/2016	/	/	/	/	15%	16%
03/08/2016	20%	20%	/	/	29%	29%
04/08/2016	30%	30%	/	/	/	/
05/08/2016	40%	40%	20%	20%	/	/
06/08/2016	/	/	30%	30%	/	/
07/08/2016	/	/	20%	20%	/	/

(a)

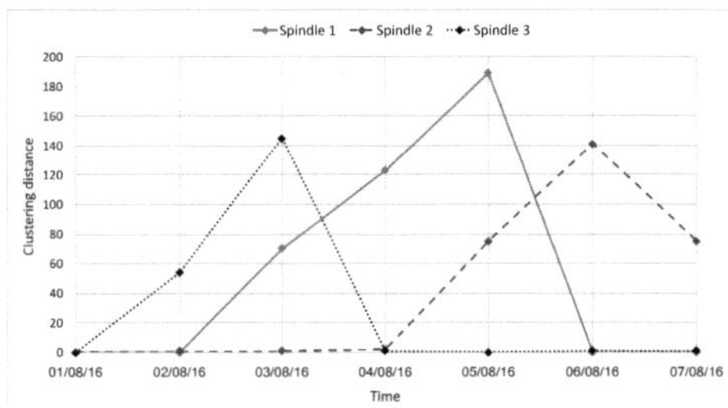

(b)

Fig. 5. Introduced variation in collected records that simulates spindle hardening (a) and evidences of the relevance evaluation techniques to identify changed records (b).

the considered case study. We collected 140 millions of records from the three machines. All records present a timestamp and have been collected every 200ms (5 records per second). We run experiments on an Intel Core i7-6700HQ, CPU 2.60 GHz, 4 cores, 8 logical cores, RAM 16GB. Collected records of measures have been saved within MongoDB as JSON documents grouped into collections. Documents present a simple structure, with at most one level of depth, and collections have been organised considering the time as main dimension, in order to speed up both data storage and data extraction for clustering, that is applied on slots of records on a time interval Δt. This enabled to storage all 140 millions of records in 1 hour and 14 minutes, with an acquisition rate of ~31,531 records per second. We tested clustering and hypercube generation on real data considering average values on 2 and 3 features (Figure 4a). The worse response time corresponds to the case where we performed clustering and relevance evaluation when no previous syntheses have been generated. Also in that case, IDEAaS framework was able to process ~15,600 records in 11.5 seconds (processing rate of ~1,356 records per second). Through the tasks of syntheses generation and clustering, the processed set of records is reduced to 7,2% on average. As shown in Figure 4b, we observed a variation in distance between clusters sets at the cost of decreasing the processing time to ~255 records per second, that is still acceptable. To test effectiveness of the IDEAaS framework in detecting working anomalies, we introduced unexpected working states to simulate spindle hardering by increasing energy consumption and decreasing rpm on a subset of collected data, as shown in Figure 5a. Experimental results depicted in Figure 5b show the clustering distance between clusters sets calculated at the time t and those calculated in case of normal working conditions. The figure shows how the techniques of the IDEAaS framework allow to timely identify the unexpected situations induced in the system under observation.

6 Concluding remarks

In this paper, we discussed the ingredients to enable exploration of real time data incrementally collected, organized and analysed on-the-fly. Our approach combines: (i) a multi-dimensional model, that is suited for supporting the iterative and multi-step nature of data exploration; (ii) efficient data summarisation techniques, based on clustering; (iii) a model of relevance, to focus the attention on relevant data only. Future efforts will be devoted to the parallelisation of clustering and relevance evaluation by relying on data organisation in the multi-dimensional model, to the development of data visualisation techniques and to the definition of different data exploration scenarios.

References

1. L. Monostori, Cyber-physical production systems: Roots, expectations and R&D challenges, in: Proc. of the 47th Conf. on Manufacturing Systems, 2014, pp. 9–13.
2. J. Lee, B. Bagheri, H. Kao, A Cyber-Physical Systems architecture for Industry 4.0-based manufacturing systems, Manufacturing Letters 3 (2015) 18–23.
3. F. Longo, L. Nicoletti, A. Padovano, Smart operators in industry 4.0: A human-centered approach to enhance operators capabilities and competencies within the new start factory context, Computers & Industrial Engineering 113 (2017) 144–159.
4. N. Kamat, P. Jayachandran, K. Tunga, A. Nandi, Distributed and Interactive Cube Exploration, in: Proc. of 30th Int. Conf. on Data Engineering (ICDE 2014), 2014.
5. M. Buoncristiano, G. Mecca, E. Quintarelli, Roveri, D. Santoro, L. Tanca, Database Challenges for Exploratory Computing, SIGMOD Record 44 (2) (2015) 17–22.
6. M. Golfarelli, S. Rizzi, Data Warehouse Design: Modern Principles and Methodologies, McGraw-Hill, 2009.
7. D. Tunkelang, Faceted Search (Synthesis Lectures on Information Concepts, Retrieval and Services), Morgan and Claypool Publishers, 2009.
8. A. Wasay, M. Athanassoulis, S. Idreos, Queriosity: Automated Data Exploration, in: Proc. of the IEEE International Congress on Big Data, 2015.
9. A. Kalinin, U. Cetintemel, S. Zdonik, Interactive data exploration using semantic windows, in: Proc. of the ACM SIGMOD 2014, pp. 505–516.
10. A. Bagozi, D. Bianchini, V. De Antonellis, A. Marini, D. Ragazzi, Summarisation and Relevance Evaluation Techniques for Big Data Exploration: the Smart Factory case study, in: Proc. of 29th Int. Conference on Advanced Information Systems Engineering (CAISE 2017), 2017, pp. 264–279.
11. C. Aggarwal, J. Han, J. Wang, P. Yu, A framework for clustering evolving data streams, in: Proc. of 29th Int. Conf. on Very Large Data Bases, 2003, pp. 81–92.

Design and evaluation of a genomics variant analysis pipeline using GATK Spark tools

Nicholas Tucci[1], Jacek Cała[2], Jannetta Steyn[2], and Paolo Missier[2]

[1] Dipartimento di Ingegneria Elettronica, Università Roma Tre, Roma, Italy
[2] School of Computing, Newcastle University, UK

Abstract. Scalable and efficient processing of genome sequence data, i.e. for variant discovery, is key to the mainstream adoption of High Throughput technology for disease prevention and for clinical use. Achieving scalability, however, requires a significant effort to enable the parallel execution of the analysis tools that make up the pipelines. This is facilitated by the new Spark versions of the well-known GATK toolkit, which offer a black-box approach by transparently exploiting the underlying Map Reduce architecture. In this paper we report on our experience implementing a standard variant discovery pipeline using GATK 4.0 with Docker-based deployment over a cluster. We provide a preliminary performance analysis, comparing the processing times and cost to those of the new Microsoft Genomics Services.

Keywords: Next Generation Sequencing, distributed processing, Spark, cluster computing, genomics, variant analysis

1 Introduction

The ability to efficiently analyse human genomes is a key component of the emerging vision for preventive, predictive, and personalised medicine [2]. Genome analysis aims to discover genetic variants that help diagnose genetic diseases in clinical practice, or predict risk factors e.g. for certain types of cancer [9]. A single exome contains about 10-15GB of data (encoded as a compressed FastQ file), while a whole genome totals up to 1TB. Depending on the specific kind of analysis, state of the art variant discovery and interpretation processes may take up to 10 hours to process a single exome. As whole-genome sequencing at population scale becomes economically affordable, personalised medicine will therefore increasingly require scalable variant analysis solutions.

With some variations, variant discovery consists of a pipeline where data flows through a number of well-understood steps, from the raw reads off the sequencing machine, to a list of functionally annotated variants that can be interpreted by a clinician. A number of algorithms, often implemented as open

SEBD 2018, June 24-27, 2018, Castellaneta Marina, Italy.

source and publicly available programs, are normally employed to implement each of the steps. A notable example is the GATK suite of programs from the Broad Institute [10], which forms the basis for the study presented in this paper, and is described more in detail below.

The most promising approach for improving the efficiency of the pipeline is to try and exploit the latent parallelism that may be available in some of the data as well as in the algorithms. In particular, there is increasing evidence that Hadoop-based implementations of deep genomic pipelines deployed on a cloud-based cluster can outperform equivalent pipelines that require HPC resources [8]. In our own work [1] we have shown that a workflow-based implementation that runs on a public cloud infrastructure (Azure) scales better than a script-based HPC version, while providing better cost control. The prevalent approach to achieve parallelism at the level of the single program (see Sec. 1.2) involves partitioning the input to the program in such a way that multiple instances can be executed in parallel, one on each partition, with a merge step at the end. Clearly, this *split-and-merge* pattern only works when the data chunks can be processed independently of one another. In such a case, existing tools can be *wrapped* as part of the pattern, without modification. Recently, however, a new generation of GATK programs have been released (4.0, in beta version at the time of writing), which re-implement a number of the algorithms as Spark programs. In this approach, the task of achieving parallelism is essentially delegated to the Spark infrastructure in combination with HDFS for dataset partitioning.

In this paper we present an initial analysis of the new GATK facilities. We have implemented the reference GATK pipeline in Spark, using the new 4.0 programs when possible, and by wrapping the programs that have not been ported to Spark. In the rest of the paper we describe this hybrid approach, report on the effort involved in deploying the pipeline both on a single-node Spark configuration and on a cluster, and present an initial performance evaluation on the Azure cloud for a variety of Spark settings, VM configurations, and cluster sizes.

When variant discovery pipelines are used for research purposes, transparency and control over pipeline composition are important factors to consider, especially in view of the rapid advances in the tools. An example of open-source platform is the Genome Variant Investigation Platform (GenomeVIP) [5], which employs GATK in addition to a number of other third party tools. On the other end of the spectrum, "black box" variant discovery services are now being offered, notably the new Microsoft Azure Genomics Services. Thanks to a grant from Microsoft, we were able to compare the GATK Spark approach with the new Microsoft Azure Genomics Services. We conclude that the Genomics Services are currently both faster and more cost-effective, when the Spark pipeline is deployed on the Azure cloud and the Spark processing times are translated into commercial rates. These results are preliminary, however, as GATK Spark tools are still in beta at the time of writing.

1.1 The Variant analysis pipeline

We begin by describing the target pipeline in some detail. The pipeline is roughly aligned with the GATK Best Practices guidelines and incorporates the latest GATK 4.0 Spark tools. Broadly speaking, it consists of three main phases, as indicated in Fig. 1, namely *Pre-processing*, *Variant Discovery*, and *Call Set Refinement*. The pre-processing phase takes the input raw exome dataset, in the FASTQ format, it aligns its content (unmapped reads of gene base pairs) against a reference genome like h19 or h38, using the well-known BWA aligner [3], and it marks any duplicates, i.e., by flagging up multiple paired reads that are mapped to the same start and end positions. These reads often originate erroneously from DNA preparation methods. They will cause biases that skew variant calling and hence should be removed, in order to avoid them in downstream analysis. The BQSR (Base Quality Score Recalibration) step then assigns confidence values to each of the aligned reads, taking into account possible sequencing errors. Finally, Variant Calling, performed using the GATK Haplotype Caller, identifies both single-nucleotide polymorphisms (SNPs) as well as insertion/deletion mutations (Indels).

Multiple variant files (gVCF), one for each sample, are then bundled together for the next phase, *Variant Discovery*. The specific steps include producing raw SNP and Indel VCF files, building recalibration models for those SNPs and Indels and refining the genotypes, that is, filtering out genotypes with low estimated accuracy. The final phase, *Variant Annotation*, is not part of the Best Practices and thus may be implemented using a variety of third party tools. We used Annovar, a well-known tool for functionally annotating genetic variants detected from diverse genomes [11]. As mentioned later, pre-processing time dominates the entire processing time and thus our performance analysis ignores phases two and three. However, in the following we highlight some of the implementation challenges for these steps.

1.2 Related work

SparkSeq [12] is a general-purpose library for genomic cloud computing built on top of Spark. Its strengths are its generality and extensibility, as it can be used to build customised analysis pipelines (in Scala). It appears that the library is built from the ground up, i.e., without leveraging existing implementations such as GATK.

In contrast, a general big data platform for genome data analysis, called Gesall, that uses a wrapper approach to reuse existing tools without change is presented in [6]. Gesall leverages the potential parallelism that is available from some of the existing tools, for instance BWA, by partitioning its input (SAM and BAM files) and then managing the parallel execution of multiple BWA instances.

`https://software.broadinstitute.org/gatk/best-practices/`

`https://software.broadinstitute.org/gatk/documentation/article.php?id=11081`

`https://software.broadinstitute.org/gatk/documentation/article.php?id=2805`

Making this work, however, requires a heavy stack of new MapReduce-based software to be injected between the data layer (HDFS) and the native tools.

A similar approach, namely to segment input data sets and then feed them to multiple instances of the tools, is presented in [6]. The distinctive element of the resulting framework is to perform load balancing by dividing chromosomal regions according to the number of reads mapped to each chromosome, as opposed to natural chromosome boundaries. This equalizes the size of each data chunk and, in addition to in-memory data management, achieves substantial speedup over a functionally equivalent but naively implemented Hadoop MapReduce based solution. The advantages of in-memory processing for efficient genome analysis have also been demonstrated recently in other ad hoc frameworks [4]. Yet another parallel version of a genomics pipeline that operates by partitioning the input data files is described in [7]. In this instance, however, some of the tools have been re-implemented (as opposed to simply wrapped) to explicitly leverage the embarrassingly parallel steps of the pipeline.

In contrast to these efforts, in our experiments we aim to show the potential of the tool re-implementation approach offered by the GATK 4.x tool suite, which are being incrementally ported to the Spark architecture.

2 Spark hybrid pipeline implementation

As mentioned, the main motivation for undertaking this work has been to experiment with a Spark implementation of the GATK Best Practices pipeline, based on the recent release of GATK 4.0. Not only are these tools natively built for Spark, but also, compared to the previous version (GATK 3.8), they are also better integrated with each other, for instance to avoid writing intermediate files to disk and increase efficiency.

At the time of writing, however, these new versions of the tools are limited to the pre-processing phase: `BwaAndMarkDuplicatesPipelineSpark`, `BQSRPipelineSpark` and `HaplotypeCallerSpark` (Fig. 1). Thus, the implementation necessarily required a hybrid approach, whereby pre-processing used the new Spark tools, while for the rest of the pipeline we used a wrapper method. For this, Spark offers a transformation called `Pipe`, which "pipes each partition of the RDD through a shell command, e.g. a Perl or bash script. RDD elements are written to the process's stdin and lines output to its stdout are returned as an RDD of strings". Thus, `Pipe` allows Bash scripts to execute from within Spark, but not efficiently, as pipelining across the steps requires the content of intermediate RDDs to be written out to files and then be read back in. Looking at Fig. 1, it should be clear that the variant discovery phase is a potential bottleneck, as it must process the entire batch of samples, with no parallelism available. However, as it turns out its processing time is negligible compared to that of pre-processing.

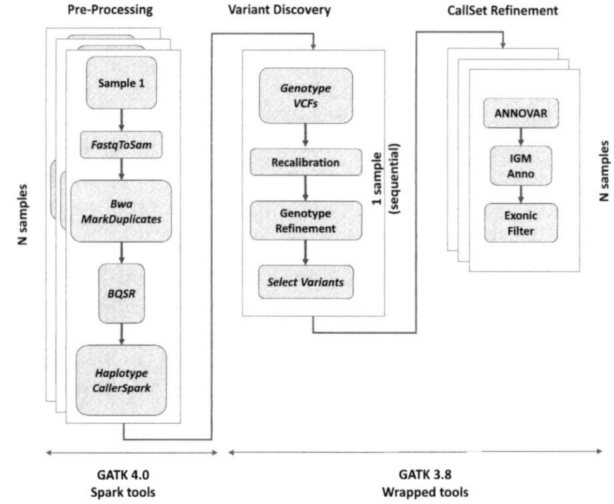

Fig. 1. Multi-sample Variant processing pipeline

2.1 Single node deployment

The hybrid native Spark/wrapper approach works well for a single-node deployment, as the entire pipeline can be launched using a single bash script that encapsulates the communication with the Spark driver. For a batch of N samples, the `spark-submit` command spawns one iteration per sample for the pre-processing (`BwaAndMarkDuplicatesPipelineSpark`, `BQSRPipelineSpark`, and `HaplotypeCallerSpark`), followed by a single `VariantDiscovery` for the entire batch and N calls of `CallsetRefinement`. The results produced by the execution have been validated against those obtained from our more established, workflow-based pipeline as described in [1].

2.2 Cluster deployment

In theory, Spark is designed to facilitate the seamless scaling out of applications over a cluster, with virtually no change to the code. The pre-processing phase of our pipeline would benefit the most from distribution, as it consists of native Spark applications as explained earlier. In reality, the deployment of a complex multi-tool pipeline like the one described requires substantial additional effort, mainly due to the requirement for Spark tools to read input and reference datasets from a HDFS data layer.

Commercial solutions such as Microsoft Azure *HDInsight* provide a preconfigured environment ready to execute Spark in cluster mode. This comes at a substantial cost, however (about twice the cost of an un-configured set of VMs). We therefore undertook the challenge of a manual Spark cluster configuration.

In this section we report on our experience realising a distributed version of the pipeline using a virtualisation approach, based on *Docker Swarm* technology. Our conclusion is that while Swarm greatly simplifies deployment, manual effort is still required especially to satisfy the data access requirements of the various components, and limitations are incurred for the fragments of the pipeline that are implemented using the wrapper method as explained earlier. Also, a distributed deployment is not always beneficial due to the additional communication overhead associated with a distributed execution, as we show in Sec. 3.

Swarm extends Docker by providing seamless and automated distribution of Docker containers over a cluster of VMs. A *swarm* is a group of machines *nodes*, that run Docker containers and are joined into a cluster. The usual Docker commands are executed on a cluster by a Swarm Manager.

Swarm managers may employ several strategies to run containers, such as "emptiest node", which fills the least utilized machines with containers, or "global", which ensures that each machine gets exactly one instance of the specified container. Swarm managers are the only machines in a swarm that can execute user commands, or authorize other machines to join the swarm as workers. Workers only provide capacity and do not have the authority to tell any other machine what it can or cannot do. In this context, a *service* is an image for an application that resides in a container and that is deployed over a swarm.

We have used Docker Swarm to deploy both Spark and HDFS over a cluster of nodes, using Docker Hub and Docker Images provided by Big Data Europe, as follows. The first step is to create a Swarm, which in our test cluster consists of three nodes: a Swarm Manager and two Swarm Workers as shown in Fig. 2. As both Spark and HDFS adopt Master-Slave architecture, the masters (Spark Master and HDFS Namenode) are deployed on the Swarm Manager. The Slaves (Spark workers and HDFS Data nodes) are deployed globally, that is, one replica is allocated to each node in the Swarm, including the Swarm Manager node. The Docker containers that host these images are connected through a dedicated overlay network.

Shared data, including all input samples, reference databases, GATK libraries, etc., reside on HDFS and are therefore naturally distributed and replicated over the Data nodes across the cluster. For the most part, this achieves location transparency as tools need only access the data through Spark HDFS drivers (readers and writers). There are two exceptions, however. Firstly, non-Spark tools expect data to be accessible on a local file system. This is achieved by mounting HDFS Data nodes as virtual Docker volumes so they are accessible from within a Docker container. Secondly, the reference genome had to be replicated to each local Worker file system (see *reference image* in Fig. 2). This is achieved by encapsulating the dataset itself as a Docker Image container, which is then automatically deployed by Swarm using the "global" Swarm mode, as indicated above. One advantage of this encapsulation approach is that it makes it easier to upgrade the reference genome, eg from h19 to h38.p1, the most recent.

`https://docs.docker.com/engine/swarm/`

`https://www.big-data-europe.eu/`

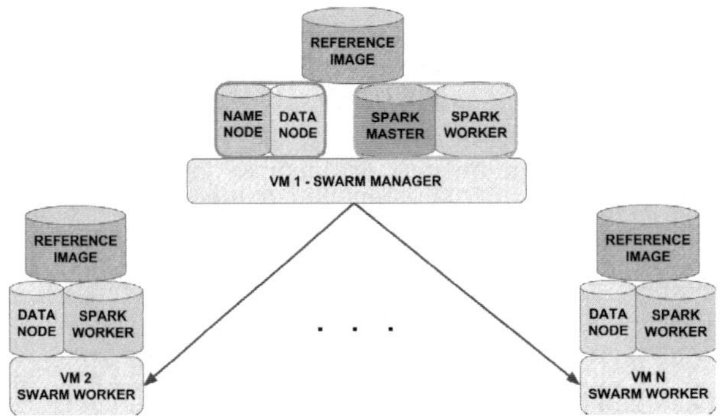

Fig. 2. Virtualised Spark and HDFS cluster deployment using Docker Swarm

2.3 Cluster mode pipeline execution

A key observation, already made earlier, is that none of the non-Spark programs that make up the pipeline can be distributed. This is the case for the initial step, `FastqToSam`, as well as for all the steps after pre-processing, which are necessarily executed on the Spark Master container. As the processing time is linear in the number of samples, this justifies allocating a larger VM to the Spark Master.

With this in mind, execution on a cluster consists of four main steps, controlled by a master bash script. These are summarised in Fig. 3. The first step, `FastqToSam`, is non-Spark and produces local uBAM files, which then needs to be distributed across the HDFS nodes (step 2) to be made available to the Spark pre-processing tools (step 3). As explained, these tools communicate through HDFS files and at the time of writing are not easy to integrate more deeply, i.e., by sharing intermediate datasets using Spark process memory. Finally, step 4 consists of the execution of non-Spark tools, again on the Spark Master. This requires that outputs that reside on HDFS be moved back to the local file system.

In summary, the deployment may benefit from a partial porting of GATK tools to Spark, however non-GATK tools that escape this porting effort represent bottlenecks. Firstly, because they run in centralised mode, and secondly because of the different file infrastructure they require. Also, Spark tools appear to be designed in isolation, without attempting to eliminate intermediate data passing through HDFS reads and writes.

3 Experimental evaluation

In this section we report on preliminary results on the performance of the pipeline. For these experiments we used 6 exomes, from anonymised patients obtained from the Institute of Genetic Medicine at Newcastle University. These samples come with naturally slightly different sizes. Our samples sizes are in the

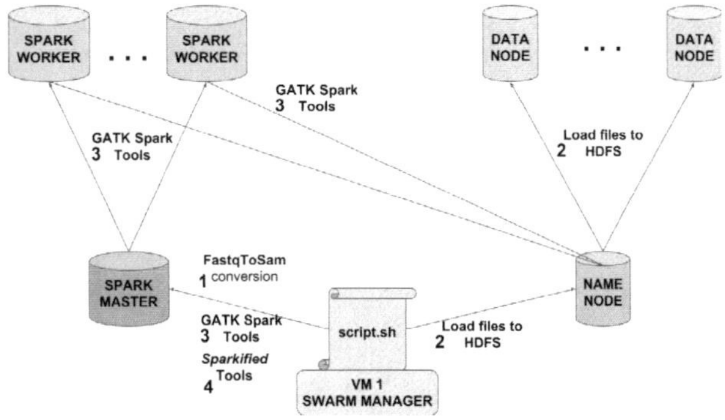

Fig. 3. Pipeline execution flow in cluster mode

range 10.8GB-15.9GB, with average 13.5GB (compressed). Using these samples, we analysed the runtime of the pipeline implementation described in Sec. 2, comparing the deployment modes described in the previous section, namely a single-node Spark model, known as "pseudo-cluster" mode, with a cluster mode configuration with up to four nodes. In both cases, all nodes are identical virtual machines on the Azure cloud with 8 cores, 55GB RAM. Our experiments aim to compare the effect of various Spark settings for each of these configurations.

We focused exclusively on the pre-processing phase, where the bulk of the processing occurs. Specifically, BWA alignment and duplicate marking (denoted BWA/MD in the following) accounts for 38% of the processing time, Base Quality Score Recalibration Processing (BQSRP) for 11%, and variant calling using the Haplotype Caller (HC) 39%. The rest of the pipeline, which only accounts for 12% of the processing, was not considered further in these experiments.

Four settings were used to tune the Spark configuration, indicated in the charts as X/Y/W/Z, where X is the driver process memory, Y the number of executors, W the number of cores allocated to each executor, and Z the memory allocated to each executor.

Charts 4(a) and 4(b) show the processing for two configurations: 20/2/4/16 and 20/4/2/8 respectively, for each of the six samples (ordered by size) and with a breakdown for each pre-processing tool. Both charts show a slight increase in processing time as the sample size increases (with an unexplained anomaly on the 13GB sample in both cases). These times are not significantly affected by the differences in configuration. Indeed, if we normalise the processing time by the input size, we observe very similar figures across the two configurations and for each tool, as shown in Fig. 5(a). Specifically, for the two configurations BWA/MD, BQSRP, and HC report an average of 19.3 vs 18.4 minutes/GB, 5.6 vs 5.3 minutes, and 20.2 vs 19.14 minutes, respectively.

For a deeper analysis on the effect of Spark settings, we then ran the pipeline on one single representative sample (PFC 0028, 14.2GB) on two additional settings, 10/4/2/8, and 10/8/1/6. Fig. 5(b) shows the results, with processing times

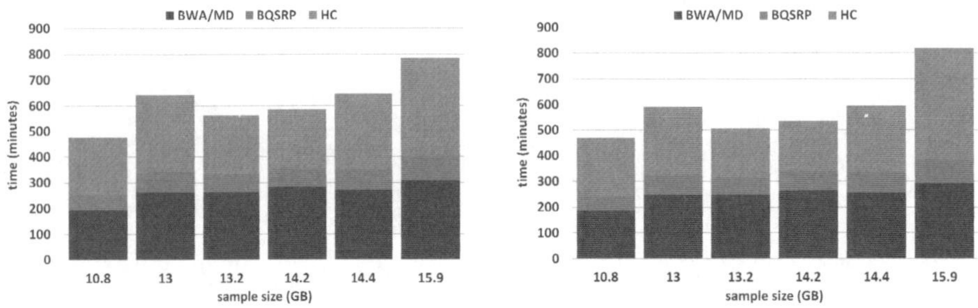

(a) Configuration 20/2/4/16

(b) Configuration 20/4/2/8

Fig. 4. Pre-processing steps for single node deployment configurations

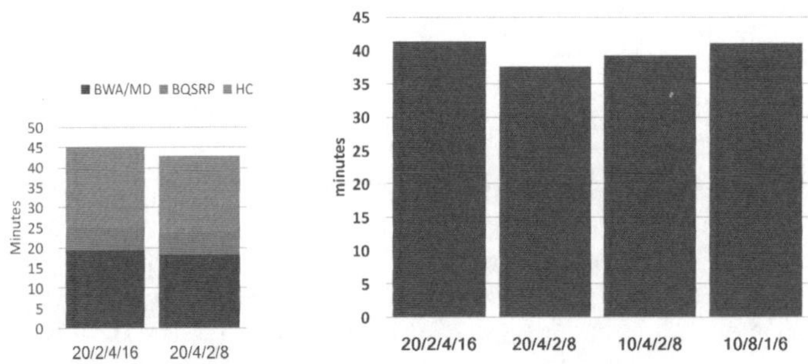

(a) Average time/GB for two configurations

(b) Pre-processing time/GB (all three steps) across four configurations for the same sample

Fig. 5. Normalised pre-processing processing time/GB

normalised by sample size for ease of comparison with the previous chart. Again, there is no indication that these four settings are critical in affecting the processing times.

More significant is the difference in processing time achieved by adding resources to the VMs. Fig. 6(a) shows a nearly ideal speedup as we double the number of cores (with a constant 55GB RAM per 8 cores, i.e. 110GB for 16 cores). It seems, however, that the Spark tools do not benefit from a larger VM beyond 16 cores. Note that the chart in Fig. 6(a) does not include the processing time for HC, as this took an unusually long time to run on a 16 cores configuration. This was due to an issue with a low-level library on the HC implementation, which was not resolved at the time of writing.

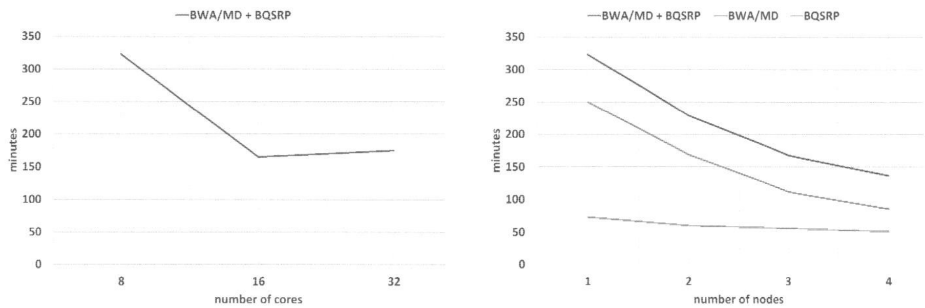

(a) single node (55GB RAM/core) (b) 8 cores/55GB RAM cluster mode

Fig. 6. Speedup of scaling-up and -out for the BWA/MD + BQSRP steps.

As expected, running Spark in the cluster mode shows a speedup as we increase the number of nodes, as shown in Fig. 6(b). However, we also note that scaling out, that is, by adding nodes, may incur an overhead that makes it less efficient than scaling up (i.e. adding cores and memory to a single node configuration). For instance, 2 nodes with 8 cores each process at 229 minutes, while a single node with 16 cores takes 165 minutes. This overhead is less noticeable when using 32 cores, which as we noted earlier does not improve processing time on a single host (175 minutes, Fig. 6(a)), while a 4x8 nodes cluster takes 137 minutes, a further improvement over the other configurations.

3.1 Comparing with Microsoft Genomics Services

Thanks to a grant from Microsoft Azure Research, we were able to process our patient samples using the new Microsoft Genomics Services. These services execute precisely the pre-processing steps of the pipeline, making it easier to compare with our results. The processing time for our reference PFC 0028 sample is an impressive 77 minutes (compare with the best time of 446 minutes on a single node, obtained from the figures in Fig. 6(a)) to which the average HC processing time has been added). However, at the time of writing these services were only offered as a *black box* that runs on a single, high-end virtual machine of undisclosed specifications. In terms of pricing, the current charges for using Genomics Services are £0.217 / GB, which translates to about £18.61 for processing our six samples. For comparison, the cost of processing the same samples using our pipeline with a 8 cores, 55GB configuration is estimated at £28.

4 Conclusions

We have presented an experimental evaluation of the design effort involved in implementing a genomics variant discovery pipeline using the recently released GATK Spark tools from the Broad Institute, and a performance analysis based on a single node and small cluster configuration. Our analysis is preliminary, as the GATK 4.x tools are still very recent, non-GATK tools or those that have not yet been ported represent bottlenecks. Firstly, because they run in centralised mode, and secondly because of the different file infrastructure they require. Also, Spark tools appear to be designed in isolation, without attempting to eliminate intermediate data passing through HDFS reads and writes.

Compared with the processing times reported for the Microsoft Azure Genomics Services, it appears that using Spark with the recent beta version of GATK tools is currently not economically competitive and thus is not recommended for operational use in clinical settings. This may change, however, as the GATK Spark tools mature. On the plus side, our implementation offers complete control over the evolution of the pipeline over time, a key requirement especially in a genetic research setting.

Acknowledgments

The authors are grateful to Microsoft for the Azure for Research grant that made it possible to experiment with Azure Genomics Services.

References

1. Cala, J., Marei, E., Yu, Y., Takeda, K., Missier, P.: Scalable and Efficient Whole-exome Data Processing Using Workflows on the Cloud. Future Generation Computer Systems, Special Issue: Big Data in the Cloud **65**(Special Issue: Big Data in the Cloud) (2016), `http://dx.doi.org/10.1016/j.future.2016.01.001`
2. Hood, L., Friend, S.H.: Predictive, personalized, preventive, participatory (P4) cancer medicine. Nature reviews Clinical oncology **8**(3), 184 (2011), `http://dx.doi.org/10.1038/nrclinonc.2010.227`
3. Li, H., Durbin, R.: Fast and accurate long-read alignment with Burrows-Wheeler transform. Bioinformatics (Oxford, England) **26**(5), 589–95 (mar 2010). https://doi.org/10.1093/bioinformatics/btp698, `http://www.pubmedcentral.nih.gov/articlerender.fcgi?artid=2828108{&}tool=pmcentrez{&}rendertype=abstract`

4. Li, X., Tan, G., Wang, B., Sun, N.: High-performance genomic analysis framework with in-memory computing. SIGPLAN Not. **53**(1), 317–328 (Feb 2018). https://doi.org/10.1145/3200691.3178511, `http://doi.acm.org/10.1145/3200691.3178511`
5. Mashl, R.J., Scott, A.D., Huang, K.l., Wyczalkowski, M.A., Yoon, C.J., Niu, B., DeNardo, E., Yellapantula, V.D., Handsaker, R.E., Chen, K., Koboldt, D.C., Ye, K., Feny, D., Raphael, B.J., Wendl, M.C., Ding, L.: Genomevip: a cloud platform for genomic variant discovery and interpretation. Genome Research **27**(8), 1450–1459 (2017). https://doi.org/10.1101/gr.211656.116, `http://genome.cshlp.org/content/27/8/1450.abstract`
6. Mushtaq, H., Al-Ars, Z.: Cluster-based Apache Spark implementation of the GATK DNA analysis pipeline. In: Bioinformatics and Biomedicine (BIBM), 2015 IEEE International Conference on. pp. 1471–1477. IEEE (2015)
7. Roy, A., Diao, Y., Evani, U., Abhyankar, A., Howarth, C., Le Priol, R., Bloom, T.: Massively parallel processing of whole genome sequence data: an in-depth performance study. In: Proceedings of the 2017 ACM International Conference on Management of Data. pp. 187–202. ACM (2017)
8. Siretskiy, A., Sundqvist, T., Voznesenskiy, M., Spjuth, O.: A quantitative assessment of the Hadoop framework for analyzing massively parallel DNA sequencing data. GigaScience **4**, 26 (2015). https://doi.org/10.1186/s13742-015-0058-5
9. Tian, Q., Price, N.D., Hood, L.: Systems cancer medicine: towards realization of predictive, preventive, personalized and participatory (P4) medicine. Journal of Internal Medicine (271) (2012)
10. Van der Auwera, G.A., Carneiro, M.O., Hartl, C., Poplin, R., Del Angel, G., Levy-Moonshine, A., Jordan, T., Shakir, K., Roazen, D., Thibault, J.: From FastQ data to highconfidence variant calls: the genome analysis toolkit best practices pipeline. Current protocols in bioinformatics pp. 10–11 (2013)
11. Wang, K., Li, M., Hakonarson, H.: Annovar: functional annotation of genetic variants from high-throughput sequencing data. Nucleic Acids Research **38**(16), e164 (2010). https://doi.org/10.1093/nar/gkq603, `http://dx.doi.org/10.1093/nar/gkq603`
12. Wiewiorka, M.S., Messina, A., Pacholewska, A., Maffioletti, S., Gawrysiak, P., Okoniewski, M.J.: SparkSeq: fast, scalable and cloud-ready tool for the interactive genomic data analysis with nucleotide precision. Bioinformatics (Oxford, England) **30**(18), 2652–2653 (sep 2014). https://doi.org/10.1093/bioinformatics/btu343

Cliques are Too Strict for Representing Communities: Finding Large k-plexes in Real Networks

Alessio Conte[2], Donatella Firmani[1], Caterina Mordente[3], Maurizio Patrignani[1], and Riccardo Torlone[1]

[1] Roma Tre University, donatella.firmani@uniroma3.it, {patrigna,torlone}@dia.uniroma3.it
[2] National Institute of Informatics, Japan, conte@nii.ac.jp
[3] Be Think Solve Execute, c.mordente@be-tse.it

Abstract. k-plexes are a formal yet flexible way of defining communities in networks. They generalize the notion of cliques and are more appropriate in most real cases: while a node of a clique C is connected to all other nodes of C, a node of a k-plex may miss up to k connections. Unfortunately, computing all maximal k-plexes is a gruesome task and state-of-the-art algorithms can only process small-size networks. In this paper we propose a new approach for enumerating large k-plexes in networks that speeds up the search by several orders of magnitude, leveraging on efficient techniques for the computation of maximal cliques.

1 Introduction

In the vast majority of networks representing real-world scenarios the distribution of edges is not uniform and it is often possible to clearly distinguish groups of nodes that are highly connected. The automatic detection of these groups, often called *communities*, helps to discover fundamental properties of large networks in a variety of different domains. For this reason this problem has been largely investigated [14]. A *clique* is a set of nodes in a network with all possible edges among them, and is a formal and strict way of defining a community. So strict, in fact, that cliques are generally thought to be too rigid to be used in practice [17]. A more appropriate notion in many practical cases is the *k-plex*: a set of nodes such that each of them has edges with all the others, with the possible exception of up to k missing neighbors (including itself). So, for example, for $k = 1$, k-plexes are cliques, for $k = 2$, each node may miss one edge, etc. Hence, k-plexes are a simple and intuitive generalization of cliques.

The problem of finding k-plexes arises in social network analysis [4], but it has wider applicability in several important areas employing graph-based data mining [19]. Unfortunately, the detection of all maximal k-plexes is unpractical being hindered by two main problems: (i) maximal k-plexes are even more numerous than maximal cliques, even if most k-plexes are small and not significant; (ii) the most efficient algorithms in the literature, such as [6], can only be used on small-size graphs: our experiments shows that the largest networks we were able to analyze with such algorithms have a few hundred nodes. In this paper we propose a solution to the first issue that is also a solution to the second one. Namely, if we restrict the search to *large* k-plexes, which are the most meaningful in practice, we can devise efficient algorithms to detect them.

Indeed, computing all maximal k-plexes does not make sense when the purpose is that of detecting communities. In this respect, it is useful to focus on the relationship between s, the size of a k-plex, and k itself. Starting from $k = 1$, which corresponds to cliques, if we increase the value of k, we obtain progressively sparser communities that are clearly less interesting in practice. (For $s \leq k$, a k-plex can be composed of isolated nodes, and there exist many disconnected k-plexes for $s < 2k$.) In this framework, our strategy for finding large k-plexes relies on two main observations. First, the complexity of the problem can be reduced in the vast majority of cases on the basis of certain properties of large k-plexes that can be efficiently checked and that allows us to filter out a large portion of the network before starting their search. The second consideration is that, differently to what happens for k-plexes, the state-of-the-art techniques to compute all maximal cliques are able to scale up to millions of nodes by decomposing the network into small blocks [12]. Unfortunately, the decomposition approach cannot be easily adapted to the detection of k-plexes. However, we demonstrate that we can find **all k-plexes non-smaller than** m by looking in the neighborhood of cliques of a size that depends on k and m. The knowledge of cliques in a network provides a hint for finding all the significant k-plexes.

Structure of this paper. Section 2 contains an informal overview of our approach. Detailed description of our algorithms and their theoretical basis can be found in [10]. Main experimental results of [10] are reported in Section 3. Finally, Sections 4 and 5 contain related work and our concluding remarks.

2 Overview

Our approach is based on two main ideas: (i) before starting the search of k-plexes, we can filter out a relevant portion of the network in which necessary conditions for the presence of large k-plexes do not hold, and (ii) in large networks, cliques can drive the search of k-plexes. While the first point provides an effective way to simplify the problem at hand, the second can lead to an efficient strategy for finding k-plexes. Let us elaborate on these ideas starting with the problem of finding all k-plexes of *maximum* size. Assume that we have computed all the maximal cliques of a network and let ω be the size of the maximum clique. Then, a maximum k-plex has size at least ω, since cliques are also k-plexes. For

We recall that the problem of enumerating maximal k-plexes is NP-Hard.

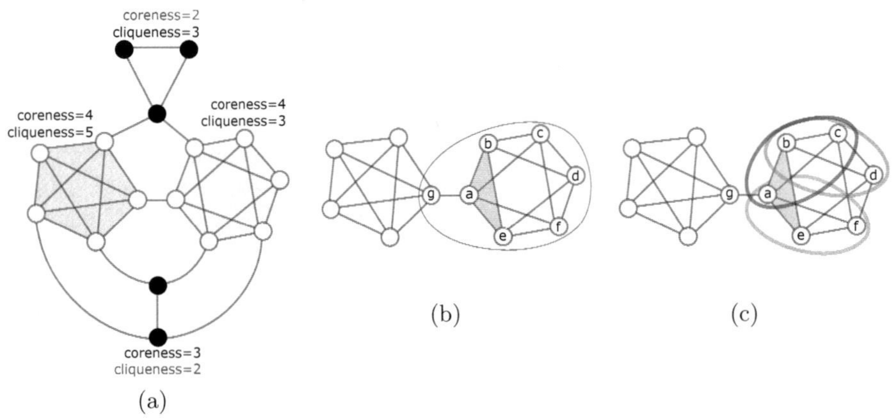

Fig. 1: An example network.

example, suppose we are searching for k-plexes in the network in Fig. 1a, which we will use as a running example in this section: we have that $\omega = 5$, since the maximum clique (the blue subgraph on the left hand side) involves five nodes.

Filtering. At this point, we observe that two filtering criteria can be applied.

1. CORENESS. Our first intuition follows from the very definition of k-plex: all the nodes of a k-plex of size m must have degree non-smaller than $m - k$. If we know that the size of a maximum k-plex is at least ω, this means that we can iteratively filter out any node that has degree lower than $\omega - k$. This corresponds to computing the *coreness* of all the nodes of the network (Lemma 2 of [10]), a process that can be executed in linear time [5]. For example, suppose we are searching for 2-plexes in the running example of Fig. 1a for which $\omega = 5$: we can filter out the three black nodes on the top of the picture since they have coreness 2, which is less than $\omega - k = 3$. In larger networks, this criterion allows us to cut up to 99% of the nodes.
2. CLIQUENESS. The second intuition is that any node of a k-plex of size m must be included in a clique of a size that depends on m. This is confirmed by Corollary 5.5 of [10] stating that any node of a k-plex larger or equal to m is included in a clique of size at least $\lceil m/k \rceil$. Then, if the size of the maximum k-plex is at least ω, we can cut out all nodes that do not belong to any clique of size at least $\lceil \omega/k \rceil$. For example, if we are searching for 2-plexes in the network depicted in Fig. 1a, we can filter out all nodes that do not belong to cliques of size at least $\lceil 5/2 \rceil = 3$, that is, the pair of black nodes in the bottom of the network. In large instances in our experiments this criterion, can be tested efficiently and is able to cut up to 98% of the nodes.

Even if some nodes can be filtered out both because their low cliqueness and low coreness, the network in Fig. 1a shows that the two filtering criteria are indeed independent. When both criteria are applied, the size of the network is reduced of magnitude and standard k-plexes algorithms may become feasible.

Once we have found the largest k-plexes, we may be interested into searching smaller ones. We have noted in the introduction that an exhaustive search does

Graph	n	density	ω	type
jazz	198	$1.41 \cdot 10^{-1}$	30	collaboration
grQc	5.241	$1.05 \cdot 10^{-3}$	44	collaboration
geom	6.158	$6.28 \cdot 10^{-4}$	22	collaboration
advogato	7.418	$1.75 \cdot 10^{-3}$	19	collaboration
hepPh	12.006	$1.64 \cdot 10^{-3}$	239	collaboration
astroPh	18.771	$1.12 \cdot 10^{-3}$	57	collaboration
newm	22.015	$2.42 \cdot 10^{-4}$	3	collaboration
mathSci	391.529	$1.14 \cdot 10^{-5}$	25	collaboration
dblp	511.163	$1.43 \cdot 10^{-5}$	115	collaboration
patents	3.8 M	$2.32 \cdot 10^{-6}$	11	citation

Table 1: Real-world networks in our experiments. Networks are sorted by size n.

not make much sense, since very small k-plexes are not significant, to the point that they may be even disconnected or composed by a set of isolated nodes. Hence, the second problem we tackle is to find all maximal k-plexes in the network of size bigger than a threshold m.

Local search. As mentioned above, our idea is to start from cliques, which are k-plexes but not necessarily maximal, and possibly enlarge them to find maximal k-plexes. Building on the cliqueness criterion, which ensures that each node of a k-plex C of size s is included into a clique of size at least $\lceil s/k \rceil$, we start from each of such cliques K. If we set $m \geq k^2$, we have that $|K| \geq \lceil s/k \rceil > k$, which implies that any other node of C must be adjacent to at least one node of K (in other words, K is a *dominating set* of C). Hence, we can search for C restricting to a block including K and all its adjacent nodes. For example, suppose you are searching for all maximal 2-plexes of size at least 5 in the network in Fig. 1a. Consider any clique of size at least $\lceil s/k \rceil = \lceil 5/2 \rceil = 3$, for example the clique $K = \{a, b, e\}$ (yellow triangle in Fig. 1b). The nodes of any k-plex of size at least 5 containing K are adjacent to K (surrounded nodes of Fig. 1b). We further reduce the size of the block by proving that C can be obtained by considering only nodes belonging to K and to other cliques of size at least $\lceil s/k \rceil$ intersecting with K (Lemma 5 of [10]). For example, the rightmost 2-plex of size 6 of Fig. 1a is all contained into the clique $\{a, b, e\}$ and three other cliques of size 3 intersecting with K (surrounded nodes of Fig. 1c). This gives rise to an efficient searching algorithm that decomposes the network into **blocks** each composed of one clique as the core, and all intersecting cliques as the boundary. Each block can be separately processed, possibly in a distributed environment.

3 Experiments

In this section, we compare our and previous algorithms over different real-world networks, and show the advantages and limitations of our approach. We use the algorithm in [12] for enumerating all the maximal cliques of the input graph G, and the algorithm in [6] for enumerating all the maximal k-plexes of the targeted graph **block**. Our code is publicly available [1]. We considered a mix of

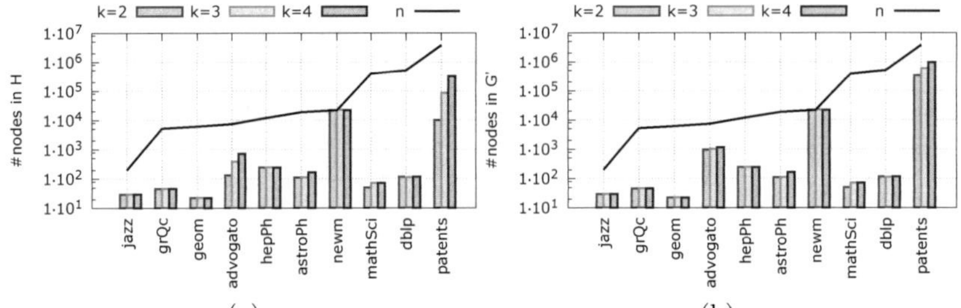

(a) (b)

Fig. 2: (a) Number of nodes (log scale) in the sub-graph H, setting $m = \omega$. (b) Number of nodes (log scale) surviving the CORENESS criterion.

real-world networks with various sizes and characteristics. All our networks are publicly available on the LASAGNE meta-repository [2], and come from different human activities. The networks considered in our experiments, together with their number of nodes (n), density, maximum clique size (ω), and their type, are listed in Table 1 We compare the execution of our methods for enumerating *large* k-plexes, with the most recent method for enumerating *all* k-plexes of the input graph [6]. All our executions have a reasonable 6 hours timeout, after which they are interrupted.

Filtering. In Figure 2a, we show the number of nodes in the residual sub-graph H, resulting from the application of CORENESS and CLIQUENESS criteria. We use different values of k and $m = \omega$, i.e, the maximum clique size. As frame of comparison, we show the number of nodes in G (i.e., n). The figure shows that, except for `newm` where $\omega = 3$, the sub-graph H is order of magnitudes smaller than G. Notably, for different networks (`jazz`, `geom`, `hephPh`, `newm`, and `dblp`), H is left with only the nodes of the maximum k-plex. In such lucky cases we can even skip the execution of the enumeration step. Since the sub-graph produced by a given k is included in the sub-graph produces by $k + 1$, is not surprising that higher values of k yield more nodes in H. (Remember that for $k = n$ we have $G = H$.) However, for most instances, the sub-graph is small with respect to G (thus allowing for faster enumeration of k-plexes) for different values of k. Finally, our criteria have little impact on the `newm` network, because its maximum clique size is only 3. Figure 2b reports the number of nodes of G residual after the CORENESS criterion, applied separately. For the considered networks, most nodes are filtered out by CORENESS. Then, the structures that are too connected to be filtered by CORENESS but too small to play a role in the search for k-plexes non-smaller than ω, are filtered out by CLIQUENESS. Such an additional CLIQUENESS step has bigger impact in `advogato` and `patents`.

Maximum k-plexes. In Table 2, we show running times for different steps of our algorithm `max_plexes`(G, k) for finding the **maximum k-plex**, compared to the time required for enumerating all k-plexes (column "FULL ENUM"), over the same input graph. For this experiment, we set $k = 2$ and report in column

GRAPH	FULL ENUM	OUR APPROACH		
		CORE	CLIQUE	ENUM
`jazz`	2 h	0,008 s	0,091 s	no need
`grQc`	> 6h	0,001 s	0,026 s	1,99 s
`geom`	> 6h	0,001 s	0,086 s	no need
`advogato`	> 6h	0,003 s	0,234 s	1 h 45 m
`hepPh`	> 6h	0,001 s	0,421 s	no need
`astroPh`	> 6h	0,046 s	0,892 s	2,92 s
`newm`	> 6h	0,22 s	0,167 s	> 6h
`mathSci`	> 6h	0,009 s	2,535 s	0,11 s
`dblp`	> 6h	0,005 s	4,336 s	no need
`patents`	> 6h	1,148 s	63,258 s	> 6h

Table 2: Running time for finding all the largest 2-plexes.

- CORE: running time of CORENESS criterion, and computing a sub-graph G';
- CLIQUE: running time of CLIQUENESS criterion over G', and computing H;
- ENUM: the execution time of the enumeration step over H.

The time for computing our criteria has little impact on the overall running time, which is dominated by the enumeration of 2-plexes of the residual sub-graph when necessary. As a consequence, in all the networks where H is left with only the nodes of the maximum clique, which is in turn also the maximum 2-plex, the computation of our algorithm ends successfully after fractions of seconds. For such networks, we write "no need" in the "ENUM" column. As frame of comparison, full enumeration of 2-plexes (i.e., as in [6]) requires hours even on our smallest network (`jazz`), and times out on the other networks. Whenever the enumeration step is necessary, its running time ranges from fractions of seconds (most networks) to 2 h, proportionally to the size of H (see Figure 2a for comparison). The only two instances that require more than 6 h are indeed `nemw` and `patents`, that correspond to the top two largest filtered sub-graphs. We observed that the results for higher values of k, namely $k = 3$ and $k = 4$, are similar. This is because the sub-graph H produced with higher valued of k contains only few more nodes than the sub-graph produced with $k = 2$.

Large k-plexes. In Table 3, we show the overall running time of our algorithm `large_plexes`(G, k, m) for finding **all k-plexes non-smaller than** m on different networks in our dataset. For this experiment, we use different values of k and set $m = 0.8\omega_k$, where ω_k is the maximum k-plex size, as computed by `max_plexes`(G, k). The time required for enumerating all k-plexes (column "FULL ENUM") of such networks is always larger than our timeout (6 hours). The table also show the number of k-plexes returned (column "FOUND"). All the networks considered contain less than a dozen k-plex non-smaller than $0.8\omega_k$, which are quickly found by our algorithm in most cases. Note that in this experiment CORENESS and CLIQUENESS are applied with $m = 0.8\omega_k$, which is possibly different from the threshold than in Figure 2a (i.e., when $0.8\omega_k \geq \omega$).

GRAPH	k	FULL ENUM	OUR APPROACH	
			TIME	#FOUND
grQc	2	> 6h	4,65 s	3
	4	> 6h	2,7 s	1
astroPh	2	> 6h	5 h 44 m	10
	4	> 6h	> 6h	-
mathSci	2	> 6h	2,75 s	7
	4	> 6h	> 6h	7

Table 3: Time for finding all k-plexes larger than 80% of the maximum clique.

4 Related Works

In the field of network analysis, dense substructures in graphs (aka dense subgraphs) are associated with communities, or more in general sets of closely related elements [14, 17]. The problem of finding these substructures has been extensively studied for decades, and continues to be the object of cutting edge research. The simplest and most rigorous definition of dense subgraph is the clique, i.e., a subgraph in which all nodes are pairwise connected. Many algorithms for finding all maximal cliques have been developed, most of them being inspired to the Bron-Kerbosh algorithm [7], such as [13, 18] or to the more recent paradigm of *reverse search* [3], such as [15, 9, 11]. McClosky [16] performs a thorough study to devise exact algorithms for finding the largest k-plex, and heuristics for finding lower upper bounds on its size, exploiting co-k-plexes (i.e., k-plexes on the complement graph) and graph coloring techniques. The usability of the algrorithms for finding the largest k-plex is however limited to small networks, as the running time exceeds the hour for graphs with hundreds of nodes. Cohen et al. [8] give a generic framework for enumerating all maximal subgraphs with respect to hereditary and connected hereditary graph properties, i.e., properties that are closed with respect to induced subgraphs and connected induced subgraphs, respectively. Berlowitz et al. [6] apply the framework in [8], together with insights on the k-plex problem, to produce efficient algorithms for the enumeration of maximal k-plexes and maximal connected k-plexes, which are respectively hereditary and connected hereditary. Other quasi clique models include the one defined by Zhai et al. [19], that is a k-plex with additional connectivity constraint, and more that can be found in this survey [17].

5 Conclusions

We have proposed a novel approach to the enumeration of large k-plexes, a formal and meaningful way to define interesting communities in real-world networks that generalizes the notion of clique. In the future, we intend to further extend the applicability of our approach and tackle the problem of computing large k-plexes on real world networks with millions of nodes. Our future work also includes experimenting with a variety of networks coming from different domains, such as (but not limited to) biological networks, web graphs, and product co-purchasing networks.

Bibliography

[1] http://patrignani.dia.uniroma3.it/large-k-plexes. [Online; accessed Feb-2017].

[2] http://lasagne-unifi.sourceforge.net. [Online; accessed Feb-2017].

[3] D. Avis and K. Fukuda. Reverse search for enumeration. *Discrete Applied Mathematics*, 65(1-3):21 – 46, 1996.

[4] B. Balasundaram, S. Butenko, and I. V. Hicks. Clique relaxations in social network analysis: The maximum k-plex problem. *Oper. Res.*, 59(1):133–142, Jan. 2011.

[5] V. Batagelj and M. Zaversnik. An o(m) algorithm for cores decomposition of networks. *CoRR*, cs.DS/0310049, 2003.

[6] D. Berlowitz, S. Cohen, and B. Kimelfeld. Efficient enumeration of maximal k-plexes. In *SIGMOD*, SIGMOD '15, pages 431–444. ACM, 2015.

[7] C. Bron and J. Kerbosch. Finding all cliques of an undirected graph (algorithm 457). *Commun. ACM*, 16(9):575–576, 1973.

[8] S. Cohen, B. Kimelfeld, and Y. Sagiv. Generating all maximal induced subgraphs for hereditary and connected-hereditary graph properties. *Journal of Computer and System Sciences*, 74(7):1147 – 1159, 2008.

[9] C. Comin and R. Rizzi. An improved upper bound on maximal clique listing via rectangular fast matrix multiplication. *CoRR*, abs/1506.01082, 2015.

[10] A. Conte, D. Firmani, C. Mordente, M. Patrignani, and R. Torlone. Fast enumeration of large k-plexes. In *KDD*, pages 115–124. ACM, 2017.

[11] A. Conte, R. Grossi, A. Marino, and L. Versari. Sublinear-space bounded-delay enumeration for massive network analytics: Maximal cliques. In *ICALP*, pages 148:1–148:15, 2016.

[12] A. Conte, R. D. Virgilio, A. Maccioni, M. Patrignani, and R. Torlone. Finding all maximal cliques in very large social networks. In *EDBT*, pages 173–184, 2016.

[13] D. Eppstein and D. Strash. Listing all maximal cliques in large sparse real-world graphs. In *SEA*, pages 364–375, 2011.

[14] S. Fortunato. Community detection in graphs. *Physics reports*, 486(3):75–174, 2010.

[15] K. Makino and T. Uno. New algorithms for enumerating all maximal cliques. In *SWAT*, pages 260–272, 2004.

[16] B. McClosky and I. V. Hicks. Combinatorial algorithms for the maximum k-plex problem. *J. Comb. Optim.*, 23(1):29–49, 2012.

[17] J. Pattillo, N. Youssef, and S. Butenko. *Clique Relaxation Models in Social Network Analysis*, pages 143–162. Springer New York, New York, NY, 2012.

[18] E. Tomita, A. Tanaka, and H. Takahashi. The worst-case time complexity for generating all maximal cliques and computational experiments. *Theor. Comput. Sci.*, 363(1):28–42, 2006.

[19] H. Zhai, M. Haraguchi, Y. Okubo, and E. Tomita. A fast and complete algorithm for enumerating pseudo-cliques in large graphs. *International Journal of Data Science and Analytics*, 2(3-4):145–158, 2016.

Temporal Recurrent Activation Networks

Giuseppe Manco, Giuseppe Pirrò, and Ettore Ritacco

ICAR - CNR, via Pietro Bucci 7/11C, 87036 Arcavacata di Rende (CS), ITALY,
{name.surname@icar.cnr.it}

Abstract. We tackle the problem of predicting whether a target user (or group of users) will be active within an event stream before a time horizon. Our solution, called PATH, leverages recurrent neural networks to learn an embedding of the past events. The embedding allows to capture influence and susceptibility between users and places closer (the representation of) users that frequently get active in different event streams within a small time interval. We conduct an experimental evaluation on real world data and compare our approach with related work.

1 Introduction

There is an increasing amount of streaming data in the form of sequences of events characterized by the time in which they occur and their mark. This general model has instantiations in many contexts, from sequences of tweets characterized by a (re)tweet time and identity of the (re)tweeter and/or the topic of the tweet, to sequences of locations characterized by the time and location of each check-in. We focus on influence-based activation networks, that is, event sequences where the occurrence of an event can boost or prevent the occurrence of another event. Understanding the structural properties of these networks can provide insights on the complex patterns that govern the underlying evolution process and help to forecast future events. The problem of inferring the topical, temporal and network properties characterizing an observed set of events is complicated by the fact that, typically, the factors governing the influence of activations and their dependency from times are hidden. Indeed, we only observe activation times and related marks, (e.g. retweet time) while, activations can depend on several factors including the stimulus provided by the ego-network of a user or his attention/propensity towards specific themes. The goal of this paper is to introduce PATH (Predict User Activation from a Horizon), which focuses on scenarios where there is the need to *predict whether a target user (or group of users) will be active before a time horizon* T_h. PATH can be used, for instance, in market campaigns where target users are the potential influencers that if active, before T_h, can contribute to further spread an advertisement and trigger the activation of influencees that can consider a given product/service. PATH learns

SEBD 2018, June 24-27, 2018, Castellaneta Marina, Italy.

an embedding of the past event history via Recurrent Neural Networks that also cater for the diffusion memory. The embedding allows to capture influence and susceptibility between users and places closer (the representation of) users that frequently get active in different streams within a small time interval.

Related Work. We conceptually separate related research into: (i) approaches like DeepCas [9] and DeepHawkes [2] that tackle the problem of predicting the length that a cascade will reach within a timeframe or its incremental popularity; (ii) approaches like Du et al. [4] and Neural Hawkes Process (NHP) [10] model and predict time event markers and time; (iii) approaches based on Survival Factorization (SF) [1] that leverage influence and susceptibility for time and event predictions; (iv) other approaches that do not use neural networks (e.g., [5, 3, 12]). `PATH` adopts a different departure point from these approaches: it focuses on predicting the activation of (groups of) users before a time horizon. Differently from (i) `PATH` considers time and uses an embedding to capture both influence and susceptibility between users and predict future activations. Moreover, (i) focuses on the prediction of cumulative values only (e.g., cascade size). Differently from (ii), we do not assume that time and event are independent. Besides, (ii) focuses on predicting event types (e.g., popular users), which is not enough in the scenarios targeted by `PATH` (e.g., targeted market campaigns) where one is interested in predicting the behavior of specific users and not their types. A for (iii), it fails in capturing the cumulative effect of history while `PATH` captures by using an embedding. As for (iv), the main difference is that `PATH` can automatically learn (via neural networks) an embedding representing influence/susceptibility.

The contributions of the paper are as follows: **(i)** `PATH`, a classification-based approach based on recurrent neural networks allowing to model the likelihood of observing an event as a combined result of the influence of other events; **(ii)** an experimental evaluation and a comparison with related work.

The remainder of the paper is organized as follows. We introduce the problem in Section 2. We present `PATH` in Section 3. We compare our approach with related research in Section 4. We conclude and sketch future work in Section 5.

2 Problem Definition

We focus on network of individuals who react to solicitations along a timeline. An activation network can be viewed as an instance of a marked point processes on the timeline, defined as a set $X = \{(t_h, s_h)\}_{1 \leq h \leq m}$. Here, $t_h \in \mathbb{R}_+$ denotes the events of the point process, and $s_h \in \mathbb{M}$ denote the marks in the measurable space $\mathbb{M}$. Relative to activation networks, the specification of s_h occurs by means of the realizations u_h, c_h and $\mathbf{x}_h$, where $u_h \in \mathcal{V}$ (with $|\mathcal{V}| = N$) represent individuals, $c_h \in \mathcal{I}$ (with $|\mathcal{I}| = M$) represent solicitations and $\mathbf{x}_h$ is side information which characterizes of the reaction of the entity, described as an instance relative to a feature space of interest. For example, $\mathcal{V}$ can represent users who are engaged in online discussions $\mathcal{I}$, and the tuple $(t_h, (u_h, c_h, \mathbf{x}_h))$ represents the contribution of u_h to discussion c_h with the post $\mathbf{x}_h$. It is convenient to view the process as a set of *cascades*: that is, for each $c \in \mathcal{I}$ we can consider the subset $\mathcal{H}^c =$

$\{(t, u, \mathbf{x}) | (t, (u, c, \mathbf{x})) \in X\}$ of elements marked by c, with $m_c = |\mathcal{H}^c|$. Also, $\mathbf{t}^c$ and $\mathcal{U}^c$ represent the projections on the first and second column of $\mathcal{H}^c$. We also denote by $\mathcal{H}^c_{<t}$ (resp. $\mathcal{H}^c_{\leq t}$) the set of events $e_i \in \mathcal{H}^c$ such that $t_i < t$ (resp., $t_i \leq t$). The terms $\mathbf{t}^c_{<t}$ and $\mathcal{U}^c_{<t}$ can be defined accordingly. The relationship $u \prec_c v$ denotes that both u and v are active in $\mathcal{H}^c$ and there are some events relative to u and v such that u precedes v in some events. Finally, $\mathcal{C} = \{\mathcal{H}^1, \cdots \mathcal{H}^M\}$ denote a collection of M cascades over $\mathcal{V}$ and $\mathcal{I}$.

Modeling diffusion. We start from the observation that what is likely to happen in the future (viz. which user will be active and when) depends on what happened in the past (viz. the chain of previously active users). One important point to take into account is the susceptibility of users, that is, the extent to which they are influenced by specific previously activated users. Our model should be flexible enough to reflect both *exciting* and *inhibitory* effects. While the former boosts the likelihood of observing u active in c, the latter actually could prevent it to do so. Given a cascade $\mathcal{H}^c$, a timestamp $t \geq 0$ and a user $u \notin \mathcal{U}^c_{<t}$, the goal is to obtain an estimate of the density function $f(t, u|\mathcal{H}^c_{<t})$, which can be used to model the following evolution scenario: *given a time horizon T^c_h; how likely is it that u will become active in c within T^c_h?*

The challenge, at this point, is how to concretely formulate the density f. We can decouple its specification as follows:

$$f(t, u|\mathcal{H}^c_{<t}) = g(t|u, \mathcal{H}^c_{<t}) \cdot h(u|\mathcal{H}^c_{<t}), \tag{2.1}$$

where the first component represents the likelihood that u becomes active within t, given the current history, and the second component represents the likelihood that u activates (independent of the time) as a reaction to the current history.

As for $\mathcal{H}^c_{<t}$, explicit information includes features like the sequence of user activations, their activation times, the relative activation speed, and possibly the topic of the cascade. Nevertheless, our assumption is that $\mathcal{H}^c_{<t}$ can also encode latent information including susceptibility and influence between users that can be derived, for instance, from neighborhood information in a network (e.g., follower/followee relations in Twitter) or user behaviors (e.g., users that retweet after a certain set of other influential user (re)tweet). This is exactly what we want to unveil in our modeling.

Embedding history. We want to learn and embedding of users in a latent K-dimensional space such that users in the same cascade are closer in the embedding, and users within different cascades are distant. We make usage of two matrices $\mathbf{S} = [\mathbf{s}_1, \ldots, \mathbf{s}_N], \mathbf{A} = [\mathbf{a}_1, \ldots, \mathbf{a}_N] \in \mathbb{R}^{N \times K}$ that represent the susceptibility and influence, respectively. Matrices are computed by relying on the standard network architecture borrowed from the `word2vec` paradigm [11]:

$$\mathbf{a}_v = \mathbf{W}_e \mathbf{v} \qquad \mathbf{s}_u = \mathbf{V}_e \mathbf{u}$$

Here, $\mathbf{u}, \mathbf{v}$ represents the one-hot encodings of u and v. The matrices $\mathbf{W}_e, \mathbf{V}_e$ represent the embeddings, obtained by minimizing an adapted form of contrastive loss [6] that penalizes the distance of users within the same cascades and the closeness of users in different cascades.

Capturing the diffusion memory. To encode temporal relationship within $\mathcal{H}^c_{<t}$ we use recurrent neural networks (RNNs) An RNN is a recursive structure that, at the current step, gets as input the previous network state (the outputs form the hidden units) along with the current input to compute a new state. The following picture provides an overview of a simple RNN cast to our context. At each step k, we feed into the network an event $e_k \in \mathcal{H}^c$ that encodes the current user (u_k) and its activation time (t_k). The learned hidden state (h_k) represents the non-linear dependency between these components and past events, which can be used to model $f(t_k, u_k|\mathcal{H}^c_{<t_k})$. In the following, we adopt the LSTM instantiation of the RNN framework [7]. The idea of an LSTM unit is to reliably transmitting important information many time steps into the future. At every time step, the unit modifies the internal status by deciding which part to keep or replace with new information coming from the current input. We use the shortcut $\mathbf{h}_k = \text{LSTM}(\mathbf{z}_k, \mathbf{h}_{k-1})$ to denote a functional architecture that elaborates an input $\mathbf{z}_k$ and outputs the updated state.

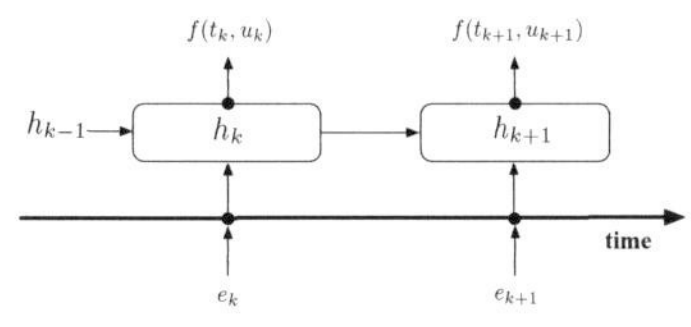

3 PATH: Predicting User Activation from a Horizon

We now introduce `PATH` (Predicting User Activation from a Horizon), which focuses on simplifying $f(t, u|\mathcal{H}^c_{<t})$ as the binary response function $\mathbb{I}(t \leq T_h|u, \mathcal{H}^c_{<t})$ that denotes whether u becomes active in c within T_h. We focus on events $e_k \in \mathcal{H}^c$ where where the features of interest $\mathbf{x}_k$ are limited to the time delay $\delta_k = t_k - t_{k-1}$ relative to the previous activation within the cascade. This allows us to capture the property that cascades may have intrinsically different diffusion speeds causing some of them to concentrate users' activations in a short timeframe while others in a more extended interval. Given a partially observed cascade $\mathcal{H}^c_{<t_l}$ (with $t_l < T^c_h$ representing the timespan of the observation window), our objective is to predict, for a given entity $u \notin \mathcal{U}_{t_l}$, whether $u \in \mathcal{U}_{T^c_h}$.

In order to uncover all the characteristics of the activations within cascades, we consider a model built on all possible prefixes of the available cascades. Notice that, in our reconstruction, we do not consider the first element within the cascade, which we assume becomes "spontaneously" active. Finally, for each $u \notin \mathcal{U}^c$, we associate the cascades $\mathcal{H}^c_{\leq t_j} \cup \{(t_j, u, \delta_j)\}$ (with $1 \leq j \leq m_c - 1$) and $\mathcal{H}^c \cup \{(T^c_h, u_i, (T^c_h - t_{m_c}))\}$ with negative labels. Again, the intuition is that, since u is not active no partial cascade provides the sufficient intensity to activate u within the given time horizon. Adding negative examples in the data preparation represent an effective data augmentation process, which enlarges the training data by inferring new inputs in the training set. This is crucial to let the approach better fine tune separation between active and inactive users, as well as better characterize the true activation time of active users. Let $\mathcal{T}_\mathcal{C}$

denote the set of all pairs partial sequence/associated label that can be built from the above discussion. Our idea is to exploit the embedding and LSTM tools described in the previous section to solve the supervised problem at hand. Figure 1 illustrates the basic architecture of the model. Given a pair $\langle \mathcal{H}_i, y_i \rangle \in \mathcal{T}_C$ with $|\mathcal{H}|=n$ and by considering $e_k = (t_k, u_k, \delta_k) \in \mathcal{H}$ (with $1 \leq k \leq n$), the architecture of the network can be captured by the following equations:

$$\mathbf{a}_k = \mathbf{W}_e \mathbf{u}_k \tag{3.1}$$

$$\mathbf{h}_k = \text{LSTM}\left([\mathbf{a}_k, t_k, \delta_k], \mathbf{h}_{k-1}\right) \tag{3.2}$$

$$\hat{y}_i = \sigma\left(\mathbf{W}_o \mathbf{h}_n\right) \tag{3.3}$$

$$\tilde{y}_i = \exp\left\{ - \left\| \mathbf{a}_n - \sum_{k=1}^{n-1} \mathbf{a}_k \right\|^2 \right\} \tag{3.4}$$

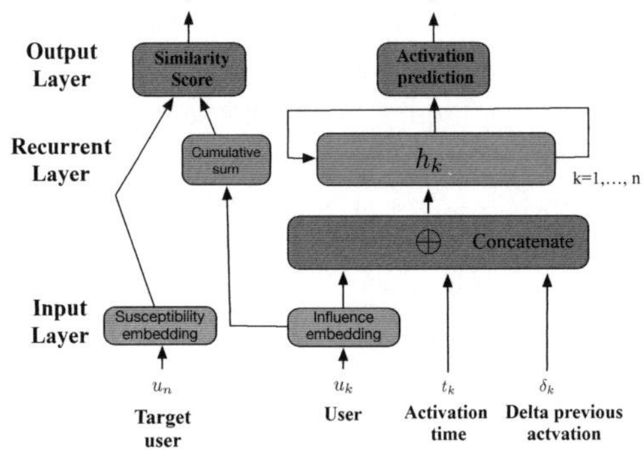

Fig. 1: Overview of PATH.

Here, $\hat{y}_i$ represents the probability that y_i is positive, as provided by the network: that is, it encodes the probability that u_n becomes active within t_n; $\tilde{y}_i$ encodes the affinity between u_n and all users preceding it within $\mathcal{H}_i$. The distance $\|\mathbf{a}_n - \sum_{k=1}^{n-1} \mathbf{a}_k\|$ plays a crucial role here: since the target user is on the tail of the cascade, the embedding should emphasize the similarities with the predecessors that trigger an activation, and by the converse minimize the similarities with those ones which do not trigger it. The loss is a combination of cross-entropy and the embedding loss previously described:

$$\mathcal{L} = \sum_{\substack{\langle \mathcal{H}, y \rangle \in \mathcal{T}_C \\ |\mathcal{H}|=n}} \left\{ y \left(\gamma \log(\hat{y}) + \beta \log \tilde{y} \right) + (1-y) \left(\gamma \log(1-\hat{y}) + \beta \log(1-\tilde{y}) \right) \right\} \tag{3.5}$$

where γ and β are weights balancing cross-entropy and embedding.

4 Experiments

We validate our approach by analysing the algorithm on real-life datasets. In particular, we analyse the capability of the algorithm at predicting the activation time of users within an information cascade. The implementation we use in the experiments can be found at `https://github.com/gmanco/PATH`.

Datasets. We evaluated the prediction capability of PATH by exploiting two real-world datasets containing propagation cascades crawled from the timelines of `Twitter`[2] and `Flixster`.[3] In particular, `Twitter` includes ~32K nodes with ~9K cascades while `Flixster` includes ~2K nodes with ~5K cascades.

[2] http://www.twitter.com/

[3] http://www.flixster.com/

The information propagation mechanism on `Twitter` is expressed by retweeting, in other words a chain of repetitions and transmissions of a tweet from a set of users to their neighbors in a recursive process. Each activation corresponds to a retweet. An activation in `Flixster` happens when a user rates a movie, while a cascade is composed by all the activations related to the same movie. The two datasets differ essentially for the following characteristics: `Twitter` includes a larger number of users and shorter delays than `Flixster`. In addition, retweets intuitively highlight two relevant aspects, namely the importance of the topic and the single influence of the individual from which the retweet is performed. By contrast, movie ratings are more likely to exhibit a cumulative effect: popular movies are more likely to be considered than unpopular ones.

Evaluation Methodology. We evaluate `PATH` against two baseline models, both relying on Survival Analysis [8]. The first instantiation implements a Cox proportional hazard model (*CoxPh* in the following). We implement the model using the `lifelines`[4] package and extract, for each event $e_k \in \mathcal{H}^c$, the following features: (1) size of the prefix; (2) last activation time; (3) average delay for each active user so far; (4) number of neighbors in the history, and (5) coverage percentage of them within the history; (6) the activation time of the most recent neighbor, if any; (7) correlation between the activation of the current user an its neighbors within the history, computed in previous cascades. This model represents an intuitive baseline where features are manually engineered and include a mix of external information (coming from the underlying network neighborhood) and information derived from the cascade itself. The second instantiation is given by the *Survival Factorization* (*SF* in the following) framework described in [1]. The comparison is important since *SF* relies on the same guiding ideas of `PATH` (influence/susceptibility) with the difference that there is no cumulative effect of $\mathcal{H}^c_{<t_k}$, but instead an influential user has to be detected for each activation.

To evaluate the approaches we proceed as follows: given training and test sets $\mathcal{C}_{train}$ and $\mathcal{C}_{test}$, we train the model on $\mathcal{C}_{train}$ and measure the accuracy of the predictions on $\mathcal{C}_{test}$. The two sets are obtained by randomly splitting the original dataset by ensuring that there is no overlap among the cascades of the two sets, but there is no entity in the test that has not been observed in the training. For the evaluation, we chronologically split each cascade $c \in \mathcal{C}_{test}$ into c_1 and c_2 such that, for each $u \in c_1$ and $v \in c_2$, we have that $u \prec_c v$. Next, we pick a random subsample $c_3 \subseteq \mathcal{V} - \mathcal{U}^c$. Then, given a target horizon T^c_h, we measure *TP*, *FP*, *TN* and *FN* by feeding the models on c_1 and then predicting the activation within T^c_h for each element in $c_2 \cup c_3$. The choice of T^c_h can follow different strategies; Fixed horizon (Fixed horizon (FH): setting T^h_c as the maximum observed activation time $T^{test}_h = \max\{t | t \in \mathbf{t}^c, c \in \mathcal{C}_{test}\}$; Variable horizon (**VH**): varying T^c_h from the smallest to the largest activation time and computing the activation probabilities associated to each possible value; Actual Time (**AT**): a particular case of the VH strategy, where $T^c_h \triangleq T^{u,c}_h$ is relative to the true activation time in c of each user $u \in c_2 \cup c_3$.

[4] see `http://lifelines.readthedocs.io` for details.

We plot the ROC and the F-Measure curves relative to the above alternatives and report the AUC and F values. For *PATH*, the encoding of sequences as described in section 3 already presumes that users are evaluated on intermediate timestamps prior to their actual activation. Thus, VH and AT roughly coincide in this case. Since both *CoxPh* and *SF* are capable of inferring, for each $(u, \mathcal{H})$ pair, the probability $S_u(t|\mathcal{H})$, the comparison with `PATH` is done by computing $1 - S_u(\tilde{t}|\mathcal{H})$ where $\tilde{t}$ is the horizon timestamp. The parameter space for `PATH` was explored by grid-search, measuring the loss on a separate portion of the training set by 5-fold cross-validation. We report 5 different instantiations, which differ from the number of cells in the LSTM (32/64), the dimensionality of the embedding (32/64) and the batch size in the training (128/256/512). Concerning *SF*, the number of factors was set to 16 for both datasets.

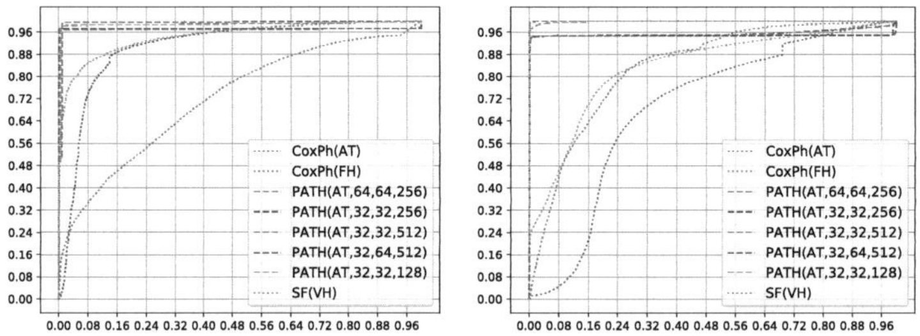

(a) `Flixster` (b) `Twitter`

Fig. 2: ROC Curves for `PATH`,*CoxPh* and *SF* on both datasets.

Evaluation Results. Figure 2 reports the ROC curves where we observe that `PATH` outperforms the baselines and in particular exhibits a very good accuracy on all configurations. This is especially true on `Flixster`, where by the converse *SF* does not seem capable of correctly correlating previous activations times. The cumulative influence effect is evident here, as a natural consequence of the underlying domain where cascading effects are more likely as a consequence of a "word of mouth" process. On `Twitter`, where the activation is more likely due to the influence of a single user (as testified by the good performance of *SF*), `PATH` still achieves the best scores, thus proving the capability of the recurrent layer to adapt the influence to a single user. By analyzing Fig. 3, which displays the F-measure curve for varying values of the threshold on the probabilities, we can observe that, contrary to the baselines, higher thresholds do not cause a significant drop of the recall. The only exception is *CoxPh* (FH), which seems more stable on `Flixster`. This is a clear sign that the probabilities associated with active and inactive users in `PATH` differ substantially, and in particular active events are associated with significantly higher probabilities than inactive events.

5 Concluding Remarks and Future Work

We focused on the problem of predicting user activations in a given time horizon and show that the embedding of the user activation history, where users that

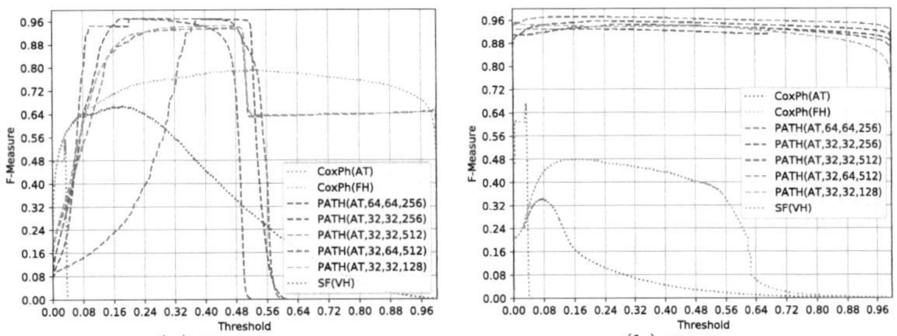

(a) `Flixster` (b) `Twitter`

Fig. 3: F-Measure curves for `PATH`,*CoxPh* and *SF* on both datasets.

become active on the same cascades are placed close, can be effectively learned via recurrent neural networks. Experiments performed on real datasets show the effectiveness of the approach in accurately predicting next activations. It is natural to wonder whether it is possible to cast the intuitions behind our approach in a generative setting, to predict both which user is likely to become active, and the time segment upon which s/he will become active.

References

1. N. Barbieri, G. Manco, and E. Ritacco. Survival factorization on diffusion networks. In *PKDD*, pages 684–700, 2017.
2. Q. Cao et al. Deephawkes: Bridging the gap between prediction and understanding of information cascades. In *CIKM*, pages 1149–1158, 2017.
3. Peng Cui, Shifei Jin, Linyun Yu, Fei Wang, Wenwu Zhu, and Shiqiang Yang. Cascading outbreak prediction in networks: a data-driven approach. In *KDD*, pages 901–909. ACM, 2013.
4. N. Du, H. Dai, R. Trivedi, U. Upadhyay, M. Gomez-Rodriguez, and L. Song. Recurrent marked temporal point processes: Embedding event history to vector. In *KDD*, pages 1555–1564, 2016.
5. A. Guille and H. Hacid. A predictive model for the temporal dynamics of information diffusion in online social networks. In *WWW*, pages 1145–1152, 2012.
6. R. Hadsell, S. Chopra., and Y. LeCun. Dimensionality reduction by learning an invariant mapping. In *CVPR*, pages 1735–1742, 2006.
7. S. Hochreiter and J. Schmidhuber. Long short-term memory. *Neural Computation*, 9(8):1735–1780, 1997.
8. J.D. Kalbfleisch and L.P. Ross. *The Statistical Analysis of Failure Time Data*. Wiley Series in Probability and Statistics, 2002.
9. C. Li, J. Ma, X. Guo, and Q. Mei. Deepcas: An end-to-end predictor of information cascades. In *WWW*, pages 577–586, 2017.
10. H Mei and J.M. Eisner. The neural hawkes process: A neurally self-modulating multivariate point process. In *NIPS*, pages 6757–6767, 2017.
11. T. Mikolov, I. Sutskever, K. Chen, G. Corrado, and J. Dean. Distributed representations of words and phrases and their compositionality. In *NIPS*, 2013.
12. L. Yu, P. Cui, F. Wang, C. Song, and S. Yang. From micro to macro: Uncovering and predicting information cascading process with behavioral dynamics. In *ICDM*, pages 559–568, 2015.

Graph Databases Benchmarking on the Italian Business Register

Nicola Ferro[1] and Luca Sinico[2]

[1] Department of Information Engineering, University of Padua, Italy
ferro@dei.unipd.it
[2] Infocamere, Italy
luca.sinico@infocamere.it

Abstract. In this paper, we develop a benchmark for graph database systems based on the real data of the Italian Business Register, consisting of about 10 million entities and 5 million relationships among them. We evaluate three state-of-the-art open source graph database systems – ArangoDB, Neo4J, and OrientDB – and we compare them to a well-known relational database management system, namely PostgreSQL. We found out that the strong points of graph databases are: the purposely designed storage techniques, which let them have good performance on graph datasets; and the purposely designed query languages, which go beyond the standard SQL and manage the typical problems that arise when graphs are explored. However, we have seen that the main performance increments have been obtained when heavy graph situations are queried; for simpler situations and queries, a relational database performs equally well.

1 Introduction

Graph databases [3, 2] are becoming a more and more adopted data model and technology. Common use cases for graph databases are social graphs, recommender systems, business relationships, network impact analysis, geospatial applications such as maps and route planning for rail or logistics, telecommunication or energy distribution networks, fraud detection, and many more.

The success of graph databases in such fields is due not only to their data model, which naturally model the domain of interest, but also to their query functionalities and their graph processing APIs which allow us to express queries and operations on graphs more easily than, e.g., the SQL language.

In this paper, we focus on the application of graph databases to the case of the Italian Business Register[3] ("Registro Imprese"), i.e. the register of company details (name, articles of association, directors, headquarters, ...), their share

SEBD 2018, June 24-27, 2018, Castellaneta Marina, Italy.

[3] http://www.registroimprese.it/

holders, their subsidiaries, and all subsequent events that occurred after registration – for instance, amendments to the articles of association and company roles, relocations, liquidations, insolvency procedures, and so on.

The Italian Business Register thus provides a complete picture of the legal position of each company and is a key archive for drawing up indicators of economic and business development. Its main function is to ensure an organic system of legal disclosure for companies, ensuring the provision of timely information throughout the country. The Italian Business Register is thus intrinsically a graph of relationship among Italian companies. This work has been conducted in the context of a joint project with InfoCamere s.c.p.a., the company which manages the Italian Business Register. We aim at comparing graph database systems, also with respect to traditional relational systems, to determine the best solutions to develop an innovative application to search and access the Italian Business Register. Therefore, we studied and tested three of the most important open source graph databases – ArangoDB[4], Neo4j[5], OrientDB[6] – and we also compared them to a well-known relational database, namely PostgreSQL[7]. We used a real dataset, i.e. the data of the Italian companies and their equity participations, constituted by, roughly, 6 million companies, 4 million persons and 5 million relationships among them.

The paper is organized as follows: Section 2 briefly summarizes related works; Section 3 describes the compared graph databases; Section 4 introduces the domain of interest and the experimental setup; Section 5 reports the conducted experiments and their results; finally, Section 6 wraps up the discussion and outlooks possible future works.

2 Related Works

In recent years there have been several efforts to evaluate graph databases and develop benchmarks for this purpose. [10] compared Neo4J to the MySQL[8] relational database management system by using synthetic data. [5] used synthetic data to evaluate traversal operations for different graph database systems, among which Neo4J, OrientDB, and DEX (now Sparksee, commercial)[9]. [7] used both synthetic data and real data from the Amazon's co-purchasing network to evaluate several systems, among which Neo4J, OrientDB, DEX/Sparksee, and InfiniteGraph[10] (commercial). [6] used synthetic data to evaluate Neo4J, OrientDB, and DEX/Sparksee according to different workloads – load, traversal, and intensive. [8] compared a wide range of graph and relational database systems using synthetic data against specific test cases, namely Single Source Short-

[4] `https://www.arangodb.com/`
[5] `https://neo4j.com/`
[6] `https://orientdb.com/`
[7] `https://postgresql.org/`
[8] `https://www.mysql.com/`
[9] `http://sparsity-technologies.com/`
[10] `http://www.objectivity.com/products/infinitegraph/`

est Paths (SSSP) problem, Shiloach-Vishkin connected components algorithm, and PageRank. [1] used two real datasets, namely Wiki-Talk and Slashdot, to evaluate Neo4J, OrientDB and other systems. Finally, [9] used the *Linked Data Benchmark Council* (LDBC)[11] *Social Network Benchmak* (SNB) to evaluate Neo4J, PostgreSQL and other systems. Note that LDBC develops also another benchmark, i.e. the *Semantic Publishing Benchmark* (SPB).

Our work differs from the state-of-the-art because it relies on real data, instead of synthetic ones as many of the works above, and explores a new domain, i.e. the business register, which is not covered by previous works.

3 Property Graph Databases

A *property graph* [4] is a directed graph were both nodes and edges can contain *properties* which, typically are, key-value pairs. Moreover, both nodes and edges are typed, allowing for semantic enrichment of the data.

We compared the graph databases described in the following sections. Table 1 summarizes and compares the main features of the analyzed graph databases.

ArangoDB ArangoDB is an open-source NoSQL multi-model database management system supporting three data models, namely graphs, key/value pairs, and documents. It is a schema-free DBMS, implemented in C/C++ and JavaScript, and supports several operating systems (Linux, OS X, Windows, Raspbian and Solaris).

ArangoDB represents documents in a proprietary *JavaScript Object Notation (JSON)* binary format, called *VelocyPack*, which is a platform-independent serialization format. It manages two kinds of documents, i.e. nodes and edges. It has its own proprietary and declarative query language – *ArangoDB Query Language (AQL)*, which offers aggregate, ordering, filtering, and sub-querying, and graph-traversal functions, especially suitable to express how graphs have to be explored, e.g. breadth or depth-first, how many times to visit a node or an edge, whether to avoid duplicates and cycles.

Neo4j Neo4j is an open-source NoSQL graph database implemented in Java and Scala, portable across many operating systems. Its data model consists of node objects, which can be labeled, connected by named and directed edge objects, where both nodes and edges can act as containers of properties. Neo4j stores graph data in different files for each part of the graph – nodes, relationships, labels, and properties – specifically arranged to facilitate graph traversals.

Cypher is the proprietary and declarative query language provided by Neo4j. It is designed for working with graph data and defines the structure of the patterns to be searched or created over the graph data. It allows for a sort of graphical specification of queries or search patterns by means of an ASCII art like drawing.

[11] `http://www.ldbcouncil.org/`

Feature	ArangoDB	Neo4j	OrientDB	PostgreSQL
Category	NoSQL	NoSQL	NoSQL	Relational
Initial release	2012	2007	2010	1996
Database Model	Graph Document Key-Value	Graph	Graph Document Key-Value Object	Relational Object
Graph model	Property graph	Property graph	Property graph	–
Native graph	Yes	Yes	Yes	–
Index-free adjacency	No	Yes	∼Yes	–
Implementation	C++ JavaScript	Java Scala	Java	C
Indices	Yes, secondary	Yes, secondary	Yes, secondary	Yes, secondary
Transactions (Single instance)	Yes, ACID	Yes, ACID	Yes, ACID	Yes, ACID
Data scheme	Schema-less	Schema-less	Schema-less Schema-ful	Schema-ful
Referential integrity	∼Yes (edges)	Yes (edges)	∼Yes (edges)	Yes
Data typing	Yes	Yes	Yes	Yes
Query Language	AQL	Cypher	SQL "extended"	SQL
Stored procedures	AQL JavaScript	Java	SQL JavaScript Groovy	PL/pgSQL PL/Tcl PL/Perl PL/Python
Graph functions	Yes	Yes	Yes	No
Drivers	JavaScript Java PHP Python Perl .Net ...	Java C/C++ JavaScript PHP Ruby Python ...	Java JDBC JavaScript PHP Ruby Python ...	C/C++ JDBC PHP Ruby Python ODBC ...
Access methods	RESTful HTTP	RESTful HTTP Java API	RESTful HTTP Java API Binary	JDBC C API
Triggers	∼Yes (via FOXX Queues)	∼Yes (via Event Handler)	∼Yes (Hooks)	Yes
Concurrency	Yes	Yes	Yes	Yes
User concepts	Yes	Yes	Yes	Yes
Durability	Yes	Yes	Yes	Yes
Community license	Apache v2	GPL v3	Apache v2	BSD
Replication conflict resolution	Master/Master Master/Agent	Master/Slave	Master/Master Master/Slave	Master/Slave
Data sharding	Yes	No	Yes	No
Caching	Data Query results	Data Query plans	Data Query results	Data Query plans

Table 1. Feature matrix

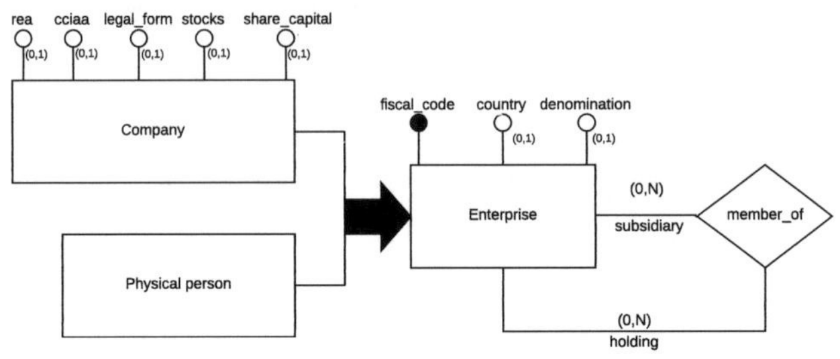

Fig. 1. ER schema of the simplified Italian Business Register.

OrientDB OrientDB, initially born as an object-oriented database, is now an open-source multi-model database management system, supporting alternative paradigms, namely objects, documents, key/value pairs, and graphs. It is developed in Java and multi-platform. It relies on its object-oriented nature to model graphs as node and edge elements together with their properties.

OrientDB comes with a sort of dialect of the SQL query language, which provides specific extension for graph traversal and pattern specification.

4 Experimental Setup

4.1 Use Case

InfoCamere[12] is the IT company of the Italian Chambers of Commerce. By developing up-to-date and innovative IT solutions and services, it connects the Chambers of Commerce and their databases through a network that is also accessible to the public via the Internet. Thanks to InfoCamere, businesses, Public Authorities, trade associations, professional bodies and simple citizens both in Italy and abroad can easily access updated and official information and economic data on all businesses registered and operating in Italy. The Italian Chambers of Commerce are public bodies entrusted to serve Italian businesses through over 300 branch offices located throughout the country. InfoCamere helps them in pursuing their goals in the interest of the business community, especially through the provision of the Italian Business Register and services over it.

[12] https://www.infocamere.it/

We use a simplified version of the Italian Business Registers, whose *Entity–Relationship (ER)* schema is shown in Figure 1. There are two entities, namely *companies* and *physical persons*, whose attributes are:

- `fiscal_code`: a unique identifier;
- `rea`: an identification code for linking to the REA register (Repertorio Economico Amministrativo);
- `cciaa`: the identifier of the Chamber of Commerce where the company is registered;
- `type`: either company or physical person;
- `denomination`: the business name for companies or the name for persons;
- `country`: the registration country for companies, e.g. foreign companies with branches in Italy or the birth country for persons;
- `legal_form`: a code representing the legal nature of a company, e.g. sole proprietorship;
- `share_capital`: the amount of company's share capital;
- `stocks`: the number of financial stocks.

The recursive relationship distinguishes between two roles: the `subsidiary` and the `holding` company.

The dataset is a snapshot of the Italian Business Register at October 2016, consisting of about 10.5 million companies and physical persons and about 5 million relationships among them.

4.2 Queries

According to the requirements for developing advanced services on the Italian Business Registry, there are two typologies of queries that need to be answered, e.g. for supporting antitrust, investigations, financial organizations, loans and so on:

- *how is a company composed?*
  - retrieve the companies which own equity shares of a given company, i.e. the *holding companies*;
  - retrieve the companies directly connected to a given company regardless of type of participation, i.e. both *subsidiaries* and *holdings*;
  - retrieve the list and level of all the direct and indirect subsidiaries of a given company, e.g. shell companies;
- *how are companies linked?*
  - retrieve the list of the companies which are shared subsidiaries of two given companies;
  - retrieve the list of the companies which are shared holdings of two given companies;
  - get the shortest path between two given companies.

Each query is performed on three types of workloads: *small-weight* (also referenced as Small), *medium-weight* (Medium), and *large-weight* (Large) workload for that query. For example, for the "Subsidiaries and holdings of a company" query, the light situation is given by a company that has few (units) subsidiaries and holdings; the medium case is given by a company with a good number (hundreds) of subsidiaries and holdings; the heavy case is given by a company that has a very large number (thousands) of subsidiaries and holdings.

We used the query language provided by each database to implement the queries: AQL for ArangoDB; Cypher or the Java API in the case of complex queries for Neo4j; its extended SQL for OrientDB; and SQL for PostgreSQL.

4.3 Configuration

All tests have been done during an internship at InfoCamere. We set up a virtual instance of a RedHat Linux server with the following characteristics: AMD Opteron 6276, x86_64, dual-core, single-thread per core, 64bit, 2.3GHz; 6GB DRAM; 100GB HDD; Red Hat Enterprise Linux Server release 6.8 (Santiago); OpenJDK 1.8.0_101 64-Bit Server VM (Java version 8u101).

We used the following versions of the tested databases: ArangoDB 3.0.10; Neo4J 3.0.6; OrientDB 2.2.11; and, PostgreSQL 9.6.1.

We performed a cache warm-up; we repeated each query 20 times, reporting averaged values and confidence intervals; after each query, we re-started the database and warmed-up the cache again.

5 Evaluation

5.1 How is a Company Composed?

In this section we report the performance of the queries corresponding to the use cases aimed at defining how a company is composed.

Holdings of a company Figure 2 shows, on the left, the typical subgraph for the holdings of a company and, on the right, the performance of the different systems in the three workloads, where we have 4 resulting nodes in the small case, 418 nodes in the medium case, and 6067 nodes in the large case.

From Figure 2.(b), it emerges that the best performing system is ArangoDB while the worst one is Neo4J; OrientDB and PostgreSQL are very similar and about one order of magnitude slower than ArangoDB. In terms of stability, i.e. low variance among query performance, PostgreSQL is the top performing system, closely followed by ArangoDB.

Subsidiaries and holdings of a company Figure 3 shows, on the left, the typical subgraph for the subsidiaries and holdings of a company and, on the right, the performance of the different systems in the three workloads, where we

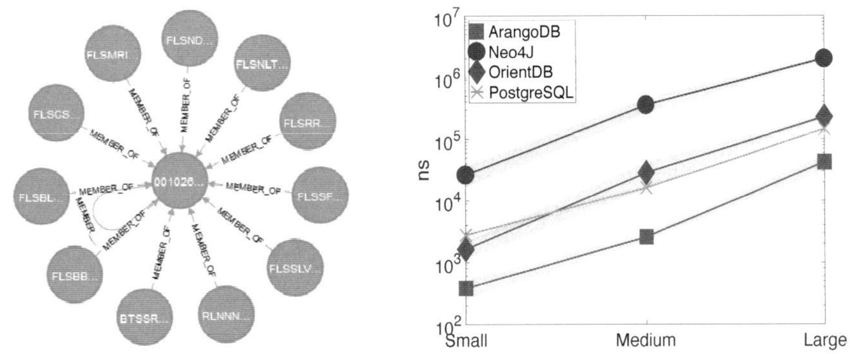

(a) Typical graph pattern. (b) Execution time.

Fig. 2. Holdings of a company.

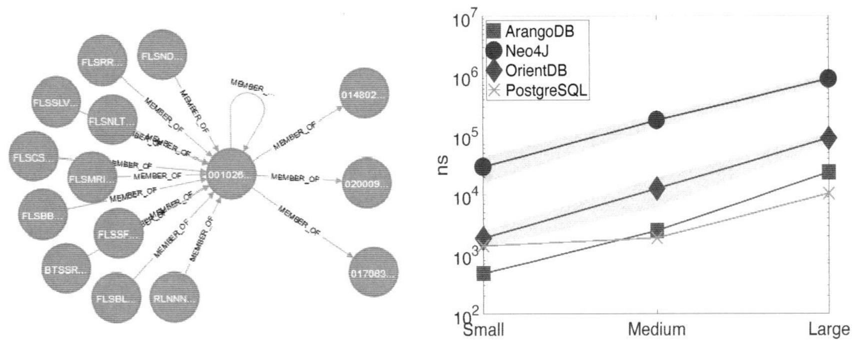

(a) Typical graph pattern. (b) Execution time.

Fig. 3. Subsidiaries and holdings of a company.

have 5 resulting nodes in the small case, 120 nodes in the medium case, and 1815 nodes in the large case.

As before, ArangoDB is the top performing system while Neo4J is the worst one. However, PostgreSQL is very competitive and better than ArangoDB in the medium and large cases. OrientDB performs roughly an order of magnitude slower than ArangoDB. In terms of variance, both ArangoDB and PostgreSQL are quite stable while OrientDB and Neo4J exhibit quite less stability.

Direct and indirect subsidiaries of a company Figure 4 shows, on the left, the typical subgraph for the direct and indirect subsidiaries of a company and, on the right, the performance of the different systems in the three workloads, where we have 12 resulting nodes in the small case, 76 nodes in the medium case, and 14037 nodes in the large case. Note that a challenging aspect of this query is a kind of "global uniqueness", i.e. the need to avoid duplicate records and to traverse the same nodes more than once.

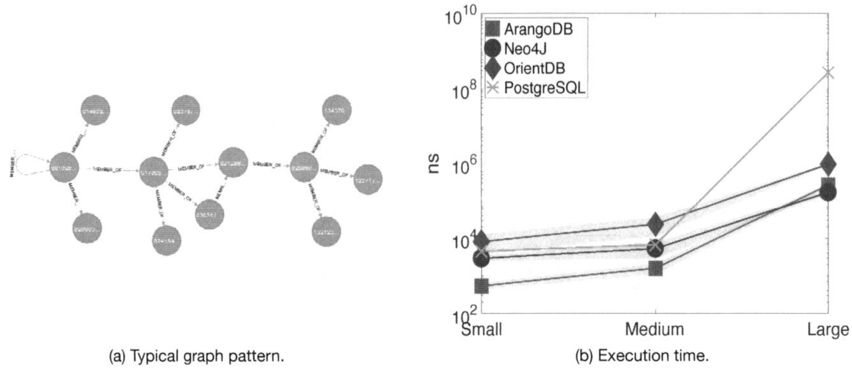

Fig. 4. Direct and indirect subsidiaries of a company.

We can observe that ArangoDB is still the top performing systems but the gap between systems is somehow smaller in this more complex case, being just about one order of magnitude for the small and medium cases. In these two cases, PostgreSQL is still very competitive with respect to graph databases while its performance greatly deteriorates in the large case, about three orders of magnitude slower. This is probably due to the way in which "global uniqueness" is imposed, i.e. only at a posteriori and not while traversing the graph. From the variance point of view, PostgreSQL is the most stable system closely followed by ArangoDB while, as in the previous cases, Neo4J and OrientDB are somehow less stable.

5.2 How are Companies Linked?

In this section we report the performance of the queries corresponding to the use cases aimed at defining how companies are linked among them.

Companies which are shared subsidiaries of two companies Figure 5 shows, on the left, the typical subgraph for the shared subsidiaries of two companies and, on the right, the performance of the different systems in the three workloads, where we have 6 resulting nodes in the small case, 84 nodes in the medium case, and 8728 nodes in the large case.

ArangoDB is again the top performing systems and the gap between systems is somehow small, being just about one order of magnitude for the small and medium cases. In these two cases, PostgreSQL is still very competitive with respect to graph databases while its performance greatly deteriorates in the large case, about four orders of magnitude slower. As before, from the variance point of view, PostgreSQL is the most stable system closely followed by ArangoDB while Neo4J and OrientDB are somehow less stable.

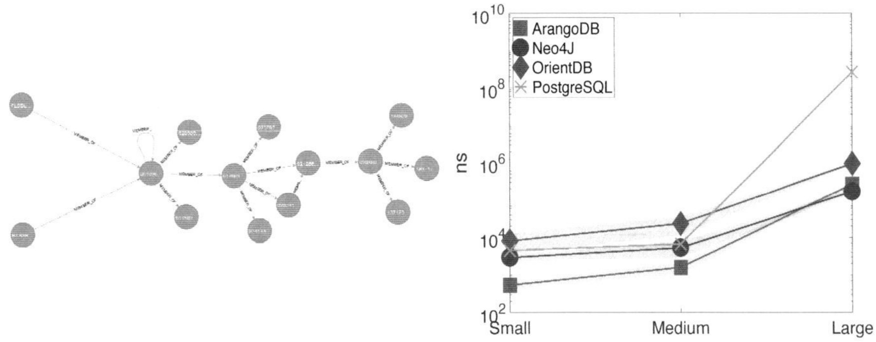

(a) Typical graph pattern. (b) Execution time.

Fig. 5. Companies which are shared subsidiaries of two companies.

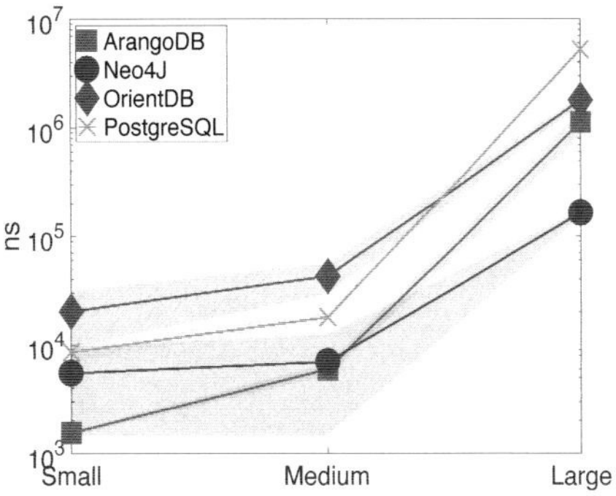

(a) Execution time.

Fig. 6. Companies which are shared holdings of two companies. The typical graph pattern is the same as in Figure 5.(a) but with reversed edges.

Companies which are shared holdings of two companies Figure 6 shows, on the left, the typical subgraph for the shared holdings of two companies and, on the right, the performance of the different systems in the three workloads, where we have 26 resulting nodes in the small case, 140 nodes in the medium case, and 19548 nodes in the large case.

This query is basically the same as the previous one but just with reversed direction of the edges. With respect to the previous query case, we can observe that there is a swap between ArangoDB, the top performing system in the small and medium cases, and Neo4j in the large case, where Neo4J is the best system. Moreover, in the small and medium cases, the variance in performance is greatly increased for both Neo4J and OrientDB. PostgreSQL somehow performs as in the previous query case, even if it improves in the large case being just about one order of magnitude slower.

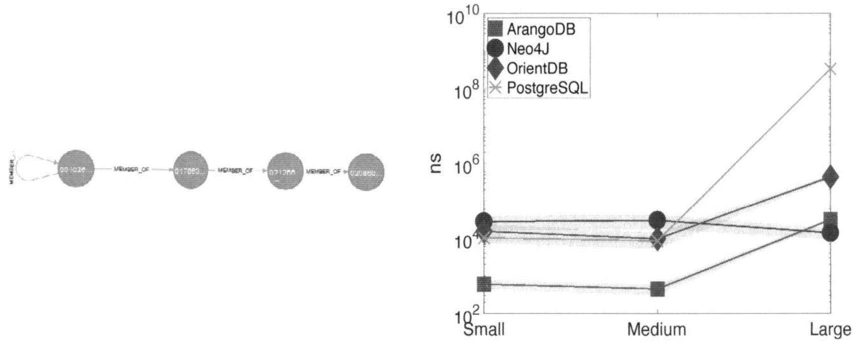

(a) Typical graph pattern.

(b) Execution time.

Fig. 7. Shortest path between two companies.

Shortest path between two companies Figure 7 shows, on the left, the typical subgraph for the shortest path between two companies and, on the right, the performance of the different systems in the three workloads, where we have a path made of 4 edges in the small case, 8 edges in the medium case, and 17 edges in the large case.

ArangoDB is again the top performing systems and the gap between systems is somehow small, being just about one order of magnitude for the small and medium cases. In these two cases, PostgreSQL is also very competitive with respect to graph databases while its performance greatly deteriorates in the large case, about three orders of magnitude slower. It is interesting to note that ArangoDB and Neo4J have very close performance in the large case and that the Neo4J performances are almost constant across the three cases. Finally, from the variance point of view, PostgreSQL is the most stable system closely followed by ArangoDB while Neo4J and OrientDB are somehow less stable.

5.3 Overall Considerations

By looking at the charts, it emerges that ArangoDB generally performs better than all the others, especially for the small and medium cases. For the large case, Neo4j works on par with ArangoDB or even better in all the queries that requires somehow heavier graph processing.

Furthermore, Neo4j and OrientDB have often quite close performance, especially for small and medium cases; for the large case, instead, there is no clear winner.

Overall, PostgreSQL typically performs well and it is competitive in the small and medium cases or when light graph processing is required, i.e. when just directly connected nodes are involved. On the other hand, it takes more time than the others when it has to process bigger amounts of data and/or more complex graph structures.

6 Conclusions and Future Work

We evaluated the performance of three state-of-the-art open source graph database systems – ArangoDB, Neo4J, and OrientDB – and one relational database management system – PostgreSQL. We developed a benchmark using the real data of the Italian Business Register, considering six types of queries involving more or less complex graph patterns, and accounting for three workloads – light, medium, and large. To the best of our knowledge, this is the first benchmark for graph databases using real business register data.

We found that ArangoDB is almost always the top-performing system, especially in the small and medium cases, followed by Neo4J and OrientDB for which there is no clear winner. When we consider the large workload case, ArangoDB and Neo4J get closer and, sometimes, the latter performs better. When it comes to PostgreSQL it is competitive for the small and medium cases but its performance deteriorate in the case of large workloads and more complex graph structures. In terms of performance stability, PostgreSQL is the most stable system, i.e. the one with lowest variance, closely followed by ArangoDB while Neo4J and OrientDB show a greater variance.

Future work will be about the release to the Chambers of Commerce and other users the application which uses the graph database technology, and will further inspect how to extract other valuable information from the graph data.

References

1. Abul-Basher, Z., Chignell, M.H., Godfrey, P., Yakovets, N.: TGDB: Towards a Benchmark for Graph Databases. In CASCON 2016. pp. 257–267. ACM Press, New York, USA (2016)
2. Angles, R., Arenas, M., Barceló, P., Hogan, A., Reutter, J., Vrgoč, D.: Foundations of Modern Query Languages for Graph Databases. ACM CSUR 50(5), 68:1–68:40 (2017)
3. Angles, R., Gutierrez, C.: Survey of Graph Database Models. ACM CSUR 40(1), 1:1–1:39 (2008)
4. Angles, R., Gutierrez, C.: An introduction to Graph Data Management. arXiv.org, Databases (cs.DB) arXiv:1801.00036 (2017)
5. Ciglan, M., Averbuch, A., Hluchy, L.: Benchmarking Traversal Operations over Graph Databases. In ICDEW 2012. pp. 186–189. IEEE Computer Society (2012)
6. Jouili, S., Vansteenberghe, V.: An empirical comparison of graph databases. In: SocialCom 2013. pp. 708–7015. IEEE Computer Society (2013)
7. Kolomičenko, V., Svoboda, M., Holubová, I.: Experimental Comparison of Graph Databases. In: IIWAS 2013. pp. 115–124. ACM Press, New York, USA (2013)
8. McColl, R., Ediger, D., Poovey, J., Campbell, D., Bader, D.A.: A Performance Evaluation of Open Source Graph Databases. In: PPAA 2014. pp. 11–17. ACM Press (2014)
9. Pacaci, A., Zhou, A., Lin, J., Tamer Özsu, M.: Do We Need Specialized Graph Databases?: Benchmarking Real-Time Social Networking Applications. In GRADES 2017. pp. 12:1–12:7. ACM Press (2017)
10. Vicknair, C., Macias, M., Zhao, Z., Nan, X., Chen, Y., Wilkins, D.: A Comparison of a Graph Database and a Relational Database. In: ACM SE 2010. pp. 42:1–42:6. ACM Press (2010)

GraphDBLP Released: Querying the Computer Scientists Network as a Graph

Mirko Cesarini[1,2], Fabio Mercorio[1,2], Mario Mezzanzanica[1,2], Vincenzo Moscato[3], and Antonio Picariello[3]

[1] Dept. of Statistics and Quantitative Methods, Univ. of Milano-Bicocca, Italy
[2] CRISP Research Centre, Univ. of Milano-Bicocca, Italy
[3] Dept. of Electrical Engineering and Information Technology (DIETI), Univ. of Naples-Federico II, Naples, Italy

(discussion paper)

Abstract. In this paper we introduce GraphDBLP, a tool that models the DBLP bibliography as a graph, and enriches the DBLP data through semantic keyword similarities computed via word-embedding. GraphDBLP has been implemented on top of the Neo4j graph-database, and it can be queried through the Cypher query language. We also provide three meaningful queries for exploring the DBLP community to (i) investigate author profiles by analysing their publication records; (ii) identify the most prolific authors on a given topic,and (iii) perform social network analyses over the whole community. GraphDBLP is available on Github. To date, it contains 5+ million nodes and 24+ million relationships, enabling users to explore the DBLP data by referencing more than 3.3 million publications, 1.7 million authors and more than 5 thousand publication venues. Thanks to the use of word-embedding, more than 7.5 thousand keywords and related similarity values were collected.

1 Introduction and Related Work

Academic researchers and their interactions can be seen as a network, which includes different topics, interests, research products published, and venues, too. The discovery of researchers' similarities, the estimation of these similarities, the identification of the authors that mostly contribute to a given topic, and the identification of similarities between different topics are important tasks with a practical significance in many fields, as in the case of community mining [16, 9], social networking [7, 18], and influence analysis as well [21, 3]. The idea behind GraphDBLP - firstly presented in [13] - is to organise the computer scientist network as a graph, using state-of-the-art word embedding algorithm to discover similarities between researchers, and to deploy the derived knowledge within a tool that anyone can use and improve over time.

To this end, GraphDBLP uses the DBLP [11] bibliography as a baseline. Several works have discussed the problems arising from analysing and monitoring the computer science community, such as expert-finding [15, 5], community detection [20, 3], community mining [10, 23], and keyword extraction [6]. Focusing on DBLP, the DBConnect project [23] aimed at exploiting random walks on the DBLP data model, measures

SEBD 2018, June 24-27, 2018, Castellaneta Marina, Italy.

the closeness between any two entities, to discover the community structure of the data, and to recommend collaborations. The FacetedDBLP [6] tool performs a high-quality selection and review of DBLP keywords. At that point, then the user can search publications using these refined keywords as a starting point. On the other hand, DBLP has also been at the basis of several studies and tools, as in [8], which used DBLP to analyse a pre-selected list of conferences/journals in a specific research field, and to understand how the community evolved over time in terms of topics and research collaborations. In [15], instead, DBLP was used to learn the academic ranking of experts according to a specific topic. Finally, in [3], DBLP evaluated the influence of relationships among communities in dynamic social networks.

However, though all these approaches and projects are effective and provide a substantial contribution, they have only focused on a specific and pre-defined task. On the other hand, modelling the DBLP data as a graph would allow applying graph-based algorithms (graph-traversal, shortest-path, clustering coefficient, etc) to enrich the DBLP data through new relationships. Indeed, DBLP contents can be also analysed from a semantic perspective through word embedding, which enables semantic similarities among contents to be modelled and extracted. GraphDBLP also shares with the methods and tools discussed above most of the *community mining* purposes and features. However, it has some distinctive elements that deserve to be discussed.

(i) GraphDBLP computes (a) similarity metrics among *venues* [1] and (b) metrics by weighting the *authors*' scientific production w.r.t to topics (namely, keywords). The former (a) is computed by focusing on the authorship networks; The latter (b) focuses on an author's publication records, estimating the weight of a keyword among all the author's publications (i.e., the *score)* and the author's prolificness on the whole DBLP community that is working on that keyword (i.e, the *relevance*). Hence, several interesting analyses may be computed e.g., investigation of author activities, comparison of author profiles of identification of influential authors;

(ii) GraphDBLP employs a language model (namely, word2vec) for the lexicon used in the titles of the papers to build-up a map of keyword similarities. The keyword similarity information is obtained (or updated) by automatically processing the DBLP data (rather than by using external dictionaries or taxonomies). These data are valuable as they improve the results of the analyses (e.g., "AI" recognised as similar to "Artificial Intelligence" with a score of 87% by learning lexical variants where they appear);

(iii) Knowledge retrieved from DBLP is represented as a graph, upon which Social Network Analysis (SNA) and graph-traversal queries can be performed;

(iv) GraphDBLP is implemented on top of an open-source graph database management system (i.e., Neo4j) and the whole source code for obtaining the GraphDBLP dataset has been made publicly available, so that anyone might contribute to the improvement of the graph instance of DBLP.

To date, our system allows performing community mining over 3.3M+ publications, 1.7M+ authors, 5K+ venues (including conferences and journals) and 7.5K+ keywords extracted from DBLP data through word embedding. The multi-graph generated

[1] In this work, venues include conferences and journals

is composed of $5,173,049$ nodes and $24,753,736$ relationships. GraphDBLP has been released in 2018 and publicly available on GitHub [2].

2 GraphDBLP at a Glance

In essence, GraphDBLP is a tool that allows users to perform graph-based queries on the DBLP data and some derived knowledge from it through:
(i) Venue similarities computed on the basis of the author communities;
(ii) Keywords similarities identified through word embeddings on keywords inherited from the FacetedDBLP project;
(iii) Authors research topics computed by analysing the publication records of each author. It also estimates the weight of a given keyword in the author publications (i.e., the *score)* as well as the global prolificness of the author in the whole DBLP community working on that keyword (i.e, the *relevance*).

The data model of GraphDBLP is depicted in Fig. 1 using the four building blocks of the Neo4j graph-database, which are labels, nodes, relationships, and properties. Information that can be directly inferred from the DBLP dataset includes the labels *Venues*, *Authors*, and *Publications*. Since the graph-based model supports entity hierarchies (in contrast with the relational model), a publication can be either an *Article* or an *InProc* or both [3]. Information about the *Keyword* label comes from the FacetedDBLP project keywords, while the *Keyword_Sim* represents additional keywords that have been found in the DBLP titles. Similarly, the solid lines in Fig. 1 represent relationships that can be derived from the DBLP and FacetedDBLP files. The dotted lines represent relationships created by reasoning over the DBLP graph, which are: (i) SIMILARITY, (ii) SIMILAR_TO, and (iii) HAS_RESEARCH_TOPIC. From a formal point of view, we modeled our graph-database as a directed multi-graph[4] as follows.

Definition 1 (Directed labelled multigraph). *A* Directed labelled multigraph *G is a tuple* $(N, E, L_N, L_E, P, \iota, \nu, \xi, \sigma, \varsigma)$ *composed of the following elements:*

N is a finite set of nodes*; E is a finite set of* edges*; L_N is a finite set of* node labels*; L_E is a finite set of* edge labels*; P is a finite set of* property labels*; ι is the* incidence *function that assigns to an edge $e \in E$ a pair of nodes $u_1, u_2 \in N$; ν is the* node labelling function $\nu : N \to L_N$ *that assigns a label $l \in L_N$ to a node $u \in N$; ξ is the* edge labelling function $\xi : E \to L_E$ *that assigns a label $l \in L_E$ to each edge $e \in E$; σ is the* edge property function $\sigma : E \times L_E \times P \to D$ *that assigns a value $v \in D$ to the property named $p \in P$ for the edge $e \in E$ with label $l \in L_E$. Notice that D can be numbers, boolean, or strings; ς is the* node property function $\varsigma : N \times P \to D$ *that assigns a value $v \in D$ to the property $p \in P$ for the node $u \in N$.*

Note that the incidence function is needed for connecting a pair of nodes through an edge, leaving the edge labelling function in charge of specifying which labels affect

[2] `fabiomercorio.github.io/GraphDBLP/`

[3] Though the same result could be achieved adding a property on the node, the use of multiple labels allows one to immediately access to the nodes with the desired label

[4] A multi-graph is a graph where multiple edges between two nodes are permitted and might be specified through labels. Our notation was inspired by [4]

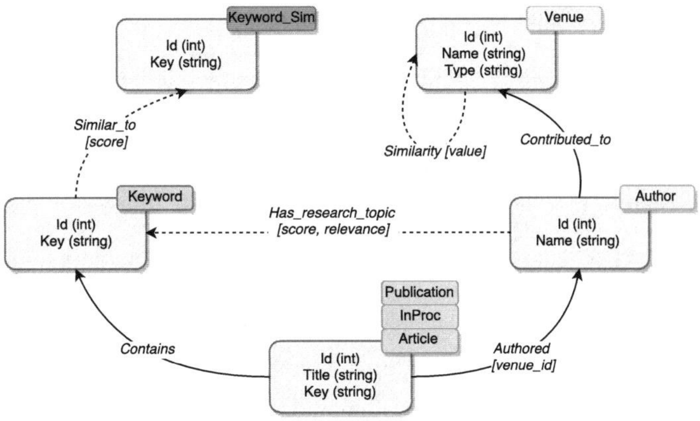

Fig. 1: The DBLP Graph Data Model

the node connections. The directed labelled multigraph is the formalism Neo4j uses to model a graph-store. Specifically, Neo4j is a property graph database, which means it can model attributed, labelled, directed multi-graphs. It is composed of four building blocks that one can easily map on the Def. 1, see [13] for details.

In the following we briefly describe how the additional knowledge has been derived from DBLP (i.e., the *dotted* relations of Fig. 1).

Building the SIMILARITY relation. The SIMILARITY relation estimates similarity between two venues based on the collaboration network that publishes there. Specifically, a *collaboration network* consists of a network of authors that publish on specific venues (i.e., the CONTRIBUTED_TO relation of Fig.1). In this way, we can compute the similarities between two venues v_1 and v_2 based on the authors that they have in common. We decided to employ the Jaccard index computed on authors. Let A_v be the set of authors that contributed to venue v, the Jaccard Index between two venues v_i and v_j. Notice that the similarity between venues (they can be either journals or conferences) does not rely on keywords or on citations, but on the collaboration network that contributed to those venues. This is an important characteristic of our approach as it aims at discovering the implicit behaviour of authors, rather than the explicit, which emerges from the citations.

Building SIMILAR_TO relation. Research keywords are an important element that enables the differentiation of research communities. Since DBLP does not explicitly provide neither topics nor abstracts of the stored publications, we decided to exploit the words of publication titles to derive research keywords. To this end, we used the Faceted-DBLP project, which uses GrowBag graphs for identifying computer-science specific keywords [6]. Then, for each title, we computed a list of top-k most similar keywords through word embedding.

Specifically, vector representation of words maps each word of a given lexicon to a unique vector in the corresponding N-dimensional space. In our context, each word can be considered as the title of a research product. Here, an important contribution has been given by the Word2Vec algorithm [14], that computes the vector representations of words by looking at the context where these words are used. Intuitively, given a word w and its context k (i.e., m words in the neighborhood of w), it uses the context k as a feature for predicting the word w.After the Word2vec training on the lexicon, words with similar meaning are mapped to a similar position in the vector space. For example, "model_checking" and "formal_verification" are close to each other.

In GraphDBLP, as the first step, each title is pre-processed according to the following pipeline: (i) html tag removal, (ii) html entities and symbol replacement, (iii) tokenization (punctuation is removed and space used to tokenise), (iv) lower case reduction, and (v) stop words removal. Then, each pre-processed title is added to the list of words W 3-gram model. Then, a N=500 vector representation of preprocessed titles is generated, and the similarities between each GraphDBLP keyword is stored within a Hash-table that assigns a list of similar n-gram to each GraphDBLP keyword.

Building the HAS_RESEARCH_KEYWORD relation. Here we describe how the research topics were computed for each author. To this end, we closely look at the authors (A), publications (P) and keywords (K) nodes of our model depicted in Fig. 1. This subgraph can be seen as a tripartite graph model (author-publication-keyword), as shown in Fig. 2a, where author a_1 has authored a publication p_1 that, in turn, contains a keyword k_1, and so on. Given an author $a \in A$, we can compute three distinct elements.
(-) Research Keywords as the list of keywords used by an author in publications. In the example above, the a_2 research keywords list is $[k_1, k_2, k_2, k_3, k_4, k_4]$;
(-) Research Keywords Score gives an estimate of the weight of each keyword in the research publications of a given author. In the example above, focusing on author a_2, keywords k_2 and k_4 have a score of $1/3$ each, while keywords $k1$ and k_3 have a score of $1/6$ each. Notice that the numerator of this value could be computed as the number of all distinct shortest paths starting from an author a_i and reaching the keyword k_j.
(-) Research Keywords Relevance gives an estimate of the prolificness of the author a_i on the research community working on a given keyword. For a given author, keyword pair, this value is computed as the ratio between the number of publications authored by a_i having the keyword k_j, and the total number of publications containing k_j.

Fig. 2b shows the author's relevance computed for each HAS_RESEARCH_TOPIC relationship. In this way, we can compute the HAS_RESEARCH_TOPIC relation and both the *score* and *relevance* for each author,keyword pair. Notice that these two attributes give two distinct views on the research publication records of an author. The score gives a rough estimate of how a given keyword ranks in the publication records of the author, whereas the relevance attribute estimates the extent to which the author contributed to keyword k, by taking into account all the publications concerning that keyword.

3 GraphDBLP Usage and Examples

GraphDBLP can be downloaded freely from GitHub. It provides three built-in queries, though any graph-based queries can be performed by using the Cypher Query Language. Here, we introduce how these queries works and what is the rationale behind.
Q1: Keyword Discovery. The command `-q1 keyword limit` performs the keyword discovery query. This allows users to identify the most prolific authors in the DBLP community for a given keyword. This requires to specify also the keyword to be used and the limit value for results. Example: `-q1 'multimedia' 10` will perform query 1 using multimedia as keyword and collecting top 10 results.

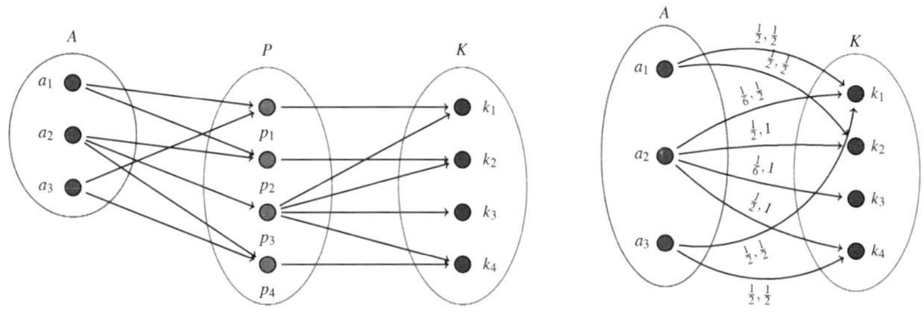

(a) (b)

Fig. 2: (a) Working example of (a) a tripartite graph with Authors (A), Publications (P) and Keywords (K) derived from the data model of Fig. 1, (b) HAS_RESEARCH_TOPIC relations computed on the graph of Fig.2a. The values for the score/relevance properties are shown on edges separated by commas.

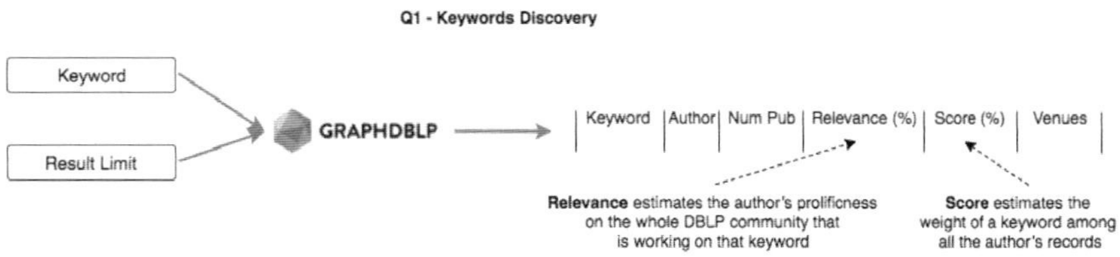

Fig. 3: Q1: Keyword Discovery

Q2: Author Publication Records Comparison. The command `-q2 author-name-surname limit similarity-threshold` runs the query. It begins from the keywords describing an author's research activities i.e., the keywords connected through the `has_research_topic` relationship. For each keyword, the most proficient author in the field is identified, and the related data are retrieved: (prolific) author name, score, relevance, and related keywords. This requires to specify also the keyword to be used, the max number of researchers to be considered for each keyword and the similarity threshold value for similar keywords. Example: `-q2 'John von Neumann' 3 0.4` will perform query #2 profiling the publication record of John von Neumann and retrieving up to 3 top researchers for each keyword appearing the in profile of John von Neumann. Only keywords with a similarity value grater than 0.4 will be returned.
Q3: Local Clustering Coefficient. The command `-q3 venue-name similarity-threshold` enables query #3 for computing local clustering coefficient on research communities[17]. This requires to specify the venue name and a threshold value for computing the similarity. Example: `-q3 'sebd' 10` percent will perform query 3 computing the community starting from sebd and considering venue with a similarity value with at least 10 percent. More specifically, here we are computing the *weighted Local Clustering Coefficient* (wLCC) [5]. Indeed, if on the one side Local Clus-

[5] it is inspired by [1] though they compute the weight of triples through arithmetic functions

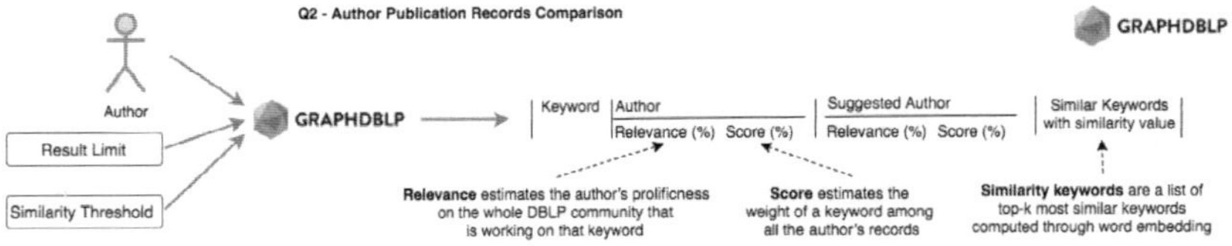

Fig. 4: Q2: Author Publication Records Comparison

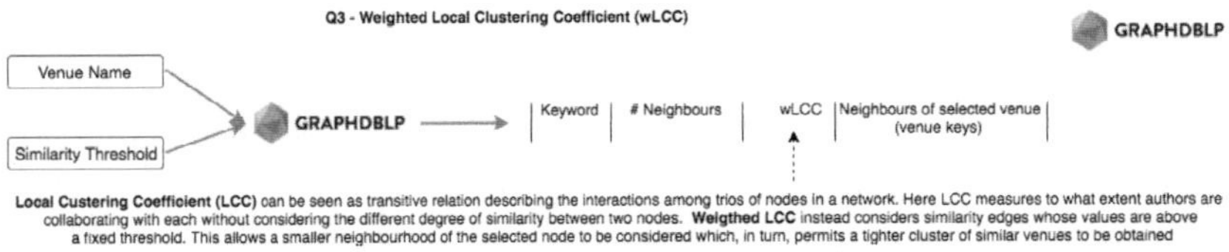

Fig. 5: Q3: Local Clustering Coefficient

tering Coefficient [22] computes the degree to which nodes in a graph tend to cluster together (aka transitivity coefficient), the weighted LCC explicitly takes into account the different *degree* of similarity between two nodes i.e., the triples are computed using all similarity relations on the basis of their degree. This allows a smaller neighbourhood of the node to be considered, which results in a tighter cluster of similar venues. Examples omitted due to space constraints can be found at [13].

4 Conclusion and Future Work

We have presented GraphDBLP, a tool that has been recently released as open source tool to perform graph-based queries on the DBLP community. GraphDBLP was implemented on top of a Neo4j graph database providing a shell interface to interact with the graph-db. To date, GraphDBLP is the first attempt to organise and reason with the DBLP data as a graph. The source code and datasets used has been made publicly available on Github with the idea that anyone might contribute to the project in a schema-free fashion, by adding node labels, new semantic similarities and metrics, and new features through graph-based queries as well. We are actually working for including the Arnet Miner citation within GraphDBLP. Indeed, to date, DBLP does not provide any information about citation relationships between papers, and this prevents the use of DBLP for performing influence analyses, such as community influence. On the graph-db side, we are planning to include graph-based reasoning, as community mining and expert finding, to the field of Labourt Market Intelligence (see, e.g. [12]) by including both language models and word embedding as graph properties, see, e.g. [19, 2].

References

1. Barrat, A., Barthelemy, M., Pastor-Satorras, R., Vespignani, A.: The architecture of complex weighted networks. Proceedings of the National Academy of Sciences of the United States of America **101**(11), 3747–3752 (2004)

2. Boselli, R., Cesarini, M., Mercorio, F., Mezzanzanica, M.: Using machine learning for labour market intelligence. In: ECML PKDD 2017, *LNCS*, vol. 10536. Springer (2017)
3. Chikhaoui, B., Chiazzaro, M., Wang, S.: A new granger causal model for influence evolution in dynamic social networks: The case of dblp. In: AAAI, pp. 51–57 (2015)
4. Consens, M.P., Mendelzon, A.O.: Graphlog: a visual formalism for real life recursion. In: Proceedings of the ninth ACM SIGACT-SIGMOD-SIGART, pp. 404–416. ACM (1990)
5. Deng, H., King, I., Lyu, M.R.: Formal models for expert finding on dblp bibliography data. In: ICDM'08, pp. 163–172. IEEE (2008)
6. Diederich, J., Balke, W.T., Thaden, U.: Demonstrating the semantic growbag: automatically creating topic facets for faceteddblp. In: ACM/IEEE-CS joint conference on Digital libraries, pp. 505–505. ACM (2007)
7. Du, N., Wu, B., Pei, X., Wang, B., Xu, L.: Community detection in large-scale social networks. In: Proceedings of the 9th WebKDD and 1st SNA-KDD 2007 workshop on Web mining and social network analysis, pp. 16–25. ACM (2007)
8. Elmacioglu, E., Lee, D.: On six degrees of separation in dblp-db and more. ACM SIGMOD Record **34**(2), 33–40 (2005)
9. Girvan, M., Newman, M.E.: Community structure in social and biological networks. Proceedings of the national academy of sciences **99**(12), 7821–7826 (2002)
10. Le, T., Zhang, D.: Dblpminer: A tool for exploring bibliographic data. In: Information Reuse and Integration (IRI), 2015 IEEE International Conference on, pp. 435–442. IEEE (2015)
11. Ley, M.: Dblp: some lessons learned. Proceedings of the VLDB Endowment **2**(2), 1493–1500 (2009)
12. Mezzanzanica, M., Mercorio, F.: Big data enables labor market intelligence. In: Encyclopedia of Big Data Technologies. Springer International Publishing (2018). DOI 10.1007/978-3-319-63962-8_276-1
13. Mezzanzanica, M., Mercorio, F., Cesarini, M., Moscato, V., Picariello, A.: Graphdblp: a system for analysing networks of computer scientists through graph databases. Multimedia Tools and Applications (2018). DOI 10.1007/s11042-017-5503-2
14. Mikolov, T., Chen, K., Corrado, G., Dean, J.: Efficient estimation of word representations in vector space. arXiv preprint arXiv:1301.3781 (2013)
15. Moreira, C., Calado, P., Martins, B.: Learning to rank academic experts in the dblp dataset. Expert Systems **32**(4), 477–493 (2015)
16. Nascimento, M.A., Sander, J., Pound, J.: Analysis of sigmod's co-authorship graph. ACM Sigmod record **32**(3), 8–10 (2003)
17. Newman, M.E.: Who is the best connected scientist? a study of scientific coauthorship networks. In: Complex networks, pp. 337–370. Springer (2004)
18. Papadopoulos, S., Kompatsiaris, Y., Vakali, A., Spyridonos, P.: Community detection in social media. Data Mining and Knowledge Discovery **24**(3), 515–554 (2012)
19. Pasi, G., Cesarini, M., Marrara, S., Mercorio, F., Viviani, M., Mezzanzanica, M., Pappagallo, M.: A language modelling approach for discovering novel labour market occupations from the web. In: 2017 IEEE/WIC/ACM International Conference on Web Intelligence (2017)
20. Tagarelli, A., Interdonato, R.: Ranking vicarious learners in research collaboration networks. In: International Conference on Asian Digital Libraries, pp. 93–102. Springer (2013)
21. Tang, J., Sun, J., Wang, C., Yang, Z.: Social influence analysis in large-scale networks. In: Proceedings of the 15th ACM SIGKDD international conference on Knowledge discovery and data mining, pp. 807–816. ACM (2009)
22. Watts, D.J., Strogatz, S.H.: Collective dynamics of 'small-world' networks. nature **393**(6684), 440–442 (1998)
23. Zaiane, O.R., Chen, J., Goebel, R.: Dbconnect: mining research community on dblp data. In: Proceedings of the 9th WebKDD and 1st SNA-KDD 2007 workshop on Web mining and social network analysis, pp. 74–81. ACM (2007)

Inverse Tree-OLAP: Definition, Complexity and First Solution

Domenico Saccà[1], Edoardo Serra[2], and Alfredo Cuzzocrea[3]

[1] University of Calabria, Italy
sacca@unical.it
[2] Boise State University, USA
edoardoserra@boisestate.edu
[3] University of Trieste and ICAR-CNR, Italy
alfredo.cuzzocrea@dia.units.it

Abstract. Count constraint is a data dependency that requires the results of given count operations on a relation to be within a certain range. By means of count constraints a new decisional problem, called the Inverse OLAP, has been recently introduced: given a flat fact table, does there exist an instance satisfying a set of given count constraints? This paper focus on a special case of Inverse OLAP, called Inverse Tree-OLAP, for which the flat fact table key is modeled by a Dimensional Fact Model (DFM) with a tree structure.

1 Introduction

Emerging "Big Data" platforms and applications call for the invention of novel data analysis techniques that are capable to handle large amount of data. There is therefore an increasing need to use real-life datasets for data-driven experiments but, as pointed out in a recent ACM SIGMOD Blog post by Gerhard Weikum [13], datasets used into research papers are often poor. Companies have their own interesting data, and industrial labs have access to such data and real-life workloads; however, such datasets are often proprietary and out of reach for academic research. In order to ensure high quality experimental findings, inverse mining techniques can be applied to generate artificial datasets that reflect the patterns of real ones: the patterns are first discovered by data mining techniques (or directly provided by domain experts) and then used to generate "realistic" privacy-preserving datasets.

A promising and important example of inverse mining is Inverse Frequent itemset Mining (`IFM`), first stated in [9], which consists of finding a transactional database $\mathcal{D}$ satisfying given support constraints on some itemsets, which are typically the frequent ones. As an example, given the items a, b, c, d, the itemsets $I_1 = \{a, b\}$, $I_2 = \{b, c\}$ and $I_3 = \{c, d\}$, the support constraints $\sigma_{I_1} = \sigma_{I_2} = 100$ and $\sigma_{I_3} = 50$, and a fixed database size equal to 170, a feasible transactional database $\mathcal{D}$ consists of the following (replicated) transactions: $\langle\{a, b, c\}, 70\rangle$ (i.e., there are 70 occurrences of the transaction $\{a, b, c\}$ in $\mathcal{D}$), $\langle\{b, c, d\}, 10\rangle$, $\langle\{a, b\}, 30\rangle$, $\langle\{b, c\}, 20\rangle$ and $\langle\{c, d\}, 40\rangle$. Observe that the support constraint $\sigma_{I_1} = 100$ is satisfied by $\mathcal{D}$ as there are 30 occurrences of I_1 in

SEBD 2018, June 24-27, 2018, Castellaneta Marina, Italy.

$\mathcal{D}$ and I_1 is a subset of $\{a, b, c\}$ occurring 70 times in $\mathcal{D}$ – it is easy to see that the other support constraints are satisfied as well.

Count constraints have been used in [12] to define a new integrity constraint decisional problem: given a relation scheme and a number of count constraints on it, does there exist a relation instance satisfying the count constraints? The problem has been called *Inverse OLAP* because the typical relation scheme dealt with is a *(flat) fact table*, whose attributes are dimensions (i.e., properties, possibly structured at various levels of abstraction) – no measure attributes are considered as the only aggregation operator is the count. We recall that a flat fact table can be represented as a *star schema* with additional tables for storing dimensions or a *snowflake schema*, which includes additional dimensional tables describing dimension hierarchies. This kind of fact table is called a *factless fact table* [7] and it arises in some scenarios storing many-to-many mappings in which no attribute qualifies as a measure – typical cases are event records, where an event is given by a combination of simultaneously occurring dimensional characteristics.

Inverse OLAP has a potential high relevance in synthesizing data cubes having predefined characteristics to be used in benchmarks of novel techniques for handling big data. Inverse OLAP has been proved in [12] to be NEXP-complete under various conditions: data complexity (i.e, the number of attributes and the size of constraints are constant), program complexity (i.e, the domains are constant) and combined complexity.

We are not discouraged by the high complexity and in this paper we present a solution approach of the Inverse OLAP problem for the case of a flat fact table, called *tree-fact table*, whose schema is a special case of Dimensional Fact Model (DFM) of [5]: it is a tree (and not a graph as in the general definition) having dimension hierarchy levels as nodes and the "rolls-up-t" relationships between them as edges.

This paper is the short version of the paper [11], where we present the main results of our research.

2 Inverse Tree-OLAP

In this section we define the *Inverse Tree-OLAP* problem. We assume that the flat fact table $\mathcal{R}$ has the following scheme (*tree-fact table*): $\mathcal{R}(B_1, \ldots, B_n, S^1, \ldots, S^n, M_1, \ldots, M_m)$, where $(B_1, \ldots, B_n)$ is the table key (*basic dimensions*), $S^i, 1 \leq i \leq n$, is a dimension hierarchy tree rooted on B_i, and $M_1, \ldots, M_m)$ are measures. We also assume that the all the once-to-many relationships in the subtrees $S^2, \ldots, S^n$ are stored as facts in ad-hoc additional domain tables (as in an ontology) whereas the first level of the one-to-many relationships in the subtree S^1 are not. In addition we assume that all the dimension domains are given in suitable tables except for the basic dimension B_1 (*aggregating basic dimension*), whose values are generated by means of a polynomial time function. Finally the values of measures are determined by means of a polynomial time function having the table key domains as range.

We make the following restrictions on the count constraints that can be applied to a tree-fact table:

- *Tree-Tuple Count Constraint*: the table key $\{B_1, \ldots, B_n\}$ must be contained in $\mathbf{X} \cup \mathbf{Y}$, being $\mathbf{X}$ and $\mathbf{Y}$ suitable subsets of dimensions, respectively;
- *Tree-Tuple Count Constraint-B_1*: $\mathbf{Y} = \{B_1\}$, $\mathbf{X}$ is a subset of dimensions in the subtree S^1 rooted at A_1 and all other basic dimensions $B_2, \ldots, B_n$ as well as the ones in the corresponding subtrees $S^2, \ldots, S^n$ must be contained in $\mathbf{Z}$, being $\mathbf{Z}$ a suitable subset of dimensions;
- *Tree-Group Count Constraint*: $\mathbf{W} = B_1$, $\mathbf{Y} = \{B_2, \ldots, B_n\}$ while all other dimensions must be in $\mathbf{Z}$ (being $\mathbf{Z}$ a suitable subset of dimensions), i.e., they are existentially quantified.

Observe that Tree-Group Count Constraints define an `IFM`-like subproblem, whose very objective is to model how the values of the basic dimensions can occur together in a many-to-many relationship. Restrictions on Tree-Tuple Count Constraints avoid the problem of handling duplicates on table projections. In fact, the projected tuples are guaranteed to be distinct as the table key $B_1, \ldots, B_n$ is included in the set of selection / projection attributes. The problem of removing duplicates from table projections has been recognized in [1] as the critical step for checking satisfaction of cardinality constraints. As for Tree-Tuple Count Constraint-B_1, distinctness of projected tuples will be guaranteed by our solution approach that group the tuples by the aggregation basic dimension.

We are now ready to define the specialization of Inverse OLAP.

Inverse Tree-OLAP Problem. Given a tree-fact table $\mathcal{R}$ on a DFM D and a set of 2D count constraints C, the *Inverse Tree-OLAP* problem consists of deciding whether there exists a relation r on $\mathcal{R}$ such that $r \models C \cup F$, where F are the functional dependencies corresponding to D. □

The next result shows that the (both data and combined) complexity of Inverse Tree-OLAP remains NEXP-complete.

Proposition 1. *Inverse Tree-OLAP is* NEXP*-complete.*

PROOF (*sketch*). Membership to NEXP derives from the fact that Inverse OLAP is in NEXP and Inverse Tree-OLAP is a specialization of Inverse OLAP. Actually satisfaction of FDs is not explicitly required in the general Inverse OLAP formulation as possible FDs are expressed as count constraints. Checking FDs can be obviously done in time polynomial in the size of a problem certificate and, therefore, the complexity remains in NEXP. To prove NEXP-hardness, it is sufficient to show that any instance x of $\mathtt{IFM_I}$ can be transformed in logarithmic space into an instance x' of Inverse Tree-OLAP, such that x is a YES-instance for $\mathtt{IFM_I}$ if and only if x' is a YES-instance for Inverse Tree-OLAP. We shall give some intuition on this part of the proof in the example below. □

Observe that NEXP-completeness only depends on the presence of Tree-Group Count Constraints. The fact that Tuple Constraints do not have high complexity is due to our restrictions that produce table projections without duplicates.

To get an intuition of our approach, consider a tree-fact table $\mathcal{R}(S, W, B, C, R, T, L, A, G, P)$ modeling a classical example of point-of-sales transaction application. Recall that the dimensions are: S (Sale), W (Ware), B (ware Brand), C (sale

Customer), R (customer Ranking), T (customer Town), L (sale Location), A (sale Area) and G (ware Group). The basic dimensions are S, W and B and S is the aggregating one. There is a unique measure: P (item Price), where an item is a pair ware-brand and its price may vary from one location to another. Then the value of P is univocally determined by the values of L, W and B – we assume that the function returning the price value is suitably stored to be used after a feasible solution has been produced. The domains of the dimensions, denoted by $\mathcal{D}_S$, $\mathcal{D}_W$ and so on, are given and they are finite tables; however, $\mathcal{D}_S$ is not explicitly stored but the values are generated as needed.

The prefixed one-to-many relationships are given and stored into the tables: $\mathcal{D}_{WG}$, $\mathcal{D}_{LA}$, and $\mathcal{D}_{CT}$. The other one-to-many relationships are not predefined.

A domain table $\mathcal{D}_{\{W\,B\}\sigma_1\sigma_2}$ stores a number of predefined itemsets (i.e., sets of items) and a range of admissible supports $\sigma_1 \leq \sigma_2$ for each of them. There are additional tables: $\mathcal{D}_{GA\,\alpha_1\alpha_2}$ storing the admissible numbers of ware groups that must be assigned for location areas, $\mathcal{D}_{BR\,\gamma_1\gamma_2}$ storing the admissible numbers of brands that must be sold to all customers of each ranking and $\mathcal{D}_{R\,\omega_1\omega_2}$ storing the admissible numbers of regions that must be interested to all customers of each ranking. Observe that the minimum value ω_1 for the lowest ranking is 0.

Enforcing the total number of sales

$$true \rightarrow s_1 \leq \#(\{\mathtt{S} : \mathcal{R}(\mathtt{S}, \mathtt{w}, \mathtt{b}, \mathtt{c}, \mathtt{r}, \mathtt{t}, \mathtt{l}, \mathtt{a}, \mathtt{g}, \mathtt{p})\}) \leq s_2 \tag{1}$$

where low letters represent existentially quantified variables and s_1, s_2 with $s_1 \leq s_2$ are two non negative integers, denoting respectively the minimal and the maximal number of sales in a feasible solution. Constraint (1) is a Tree-Tuple Count Constraint-B_1.

Enforcing frequency support constraints on itemsets

$$\mathcal{D}_{\{\mathtt{WB}\}\sigma_1\sigma_2}(\ddot{\mathtt{X}}, \ddot{\sigma}_1, \ddot{\sigma}_2) \rightarrow \\ \ddot{\sigma}_1 \leq \#(\{\mathtt{S} : \ddot{\mathtt{X}} \subseteq \{\mathtt{WB} : \mathcal{R}(\mathtt{S}, \mathtt{W}, \mathtt{B}, \mathbf{v})\}\}) \leq \ddot{\sigma}_2 \tag{2}$$

where $\mathbf{v}$ is the list of existentially quantified variables $[\mathtt{c}, \mathtt{r}, \mathtt{t}, \mathtt{l}, \mathtt{a}, \mathtt{g}, \mathtt{p}]$, dotted letters represent universally quantified variables and $\ddot{\sigma_1}$, $\ddot{\sigma_2}$ are the minimal and maximal support for frequent itemsets. Constraint (2) is a Tree-Group Count Constraint that enforces that all itemsets stored in $\mathcal{D}_{\{I\}\beta_1\beta_2}$ be frequent.

Enforcing infrequency support constraints on itemsets

$$\ddot{\mathtt{Y}} = \{W\,B : \mathcal{D}_W(W) \times \mathcal{D}_B(B)\} \wedge \mathcal{D}_{\{W\,B\}\sigma_1\sigma_2}(\ddot{X}, \ddot{\sigma}_1, \ddot{\sigma}_2) \wedge \\ \ddot{Y} \not\subseteq \ddot{X} \rightarrow \#(\{\mathtt{S} : \ddot{\mathtt{X}} \subseteq \{\mathtt{WB} : \mathcal{R}(\mathtt{S}, \mathtt{W}, \mathtt{B}, \mathbf{v}))\}\}) \leq \sigma \tag{3}$$

where σ is a non negative integer denoting the infrequency support threshold. Constraint 3 is a Tree-Group Count Constraint that enforces that all itemsets that are not a (not necessarily proper) subset of some itemset in $\mathcal{D}_{\{W\,B\}\sigma_1\sigma_2}$ must have a support below the threshold σ.

We point out that Constraints (1), (2) and (3) expresses the $\mathtt{IFM_I}$ problem – so they can be used in the NEXP-hardness proof of Proposition 1. Our formalism is rather powerful as it enable to define additional constraints to $\mathtt{IFM_I}$ – as an example, we next show how to enforce a size range for the fact table and a maximum number of items for transactions (the latter constraint has been analyzed in [3]).

Enforcing the total number of tuples in the fact table

$$true \;\rightarrow\; s_3 \leq \#(\{\mathtt{S\,W\,B} : \mathcal{R}(\mathtt{S},\mathtt{W},\mathtt{B},\mathbf{v})\}) \leq s_4 \tag{4}$$

where s_3, s_4 with $s_3 \leq s_4$ are two non negative integers, denoting respectively the minimal and the maximal cardinality of a feasible fact table instance. Constraint (1) is a Tree-Tuple Count Constraint.

Enforcing a maximum number of itemsets in a sale

$$\mathcal{D}_{\mathtt{S}}(\ddot{\mathtt{S}}) \;\rightarrow\; \#(\{\mathtt{W\,B} : \mathcal{R}(\ddot{\mathtt{S}},\mathtt{W},\mathtt{B},\mathbf{v})\}) \leq \lambda \tag{5}$$

where λ is a positive integer denoting the maximal transaction length. Constraint 5 is a Tree-Tuple Count Constraint.

We next define a number of additional Tree-Tuple Count Constraints (including type $B-1$) that involve also non-basic dimensions.

Enforcing prefixed one-to-many relationships Consider first the prefixed one-to-many relationship from G (ware Group) to W (Ware), defined by $\mathcal{D}_{W\,G}$. The following Tree-Tuple Count Constraint:

$$\begin{aligned}&\mathcal{D}_{W}(\ddot{\mathtt{W}}) \wedge \mathcal{D}_{\mathtt{S}}(\ddot{\mathtt{S}}) \wedge \mathcal{D}_{\mathtt{B}}(\ddot{\mathtt{B}}) \;\rightarrow\\ &\quad \#(\{\mathtt{G} : \mathcal{R}(\ddot{\mathtt{S}},\ddot{\mathtt{W}},\ddot{\mathtt{B}},\mathtt{c},\mathtt{r},\mathtt{t},\mathtt{l},\mathtt{a},\mathtt{G},\mathtt{p}) \wedge \neg\mathcal{D}_{\mathtt{W\,G}}(\ddot{\mathtt{W}},\mathtt{G})\}) = 0.\end{aligned} \tag{6}$$

excludes the possibility that any ware can take a group value different from the one that has been fixed in $\mathcal{D}_{W\,G}$. Observe that we have slightly modified the notation inside the function # by enabling a conjunction of the fact predicate with domain predicates – the semantics of this extension is obvious.

We add similar constraints for all other prefixed one-to-many relationships: from L (sale Location) to A (Area), from C (Customer) to T (Town) and from C to R (customer Ranking).

Distributing ware groups on areas

$$\begin{aligned}&\mathcal{D}_{GA\,\alpha_1\alpha_2}(\ddot{G},\ddot{A},\ddot{\alpha}_1,\ddot{\alpha}_2) \;\rightarrow\\ &\quad \ddot{\alpha}_1 \leq \#(\{\mathtt{S\,W\,B} : \mathcal{R}(\mathtt{S},\mathtt{W},\mathtt{B},\mathtt{c},\mathtt{r},\mathtt{t},\mathtt{l},\ddot{\mathtt{A}},\ddot{\mathtt{G}},\mathtt{p})\}) \leq \ddot{\alpha}_2.\end{aligned} \tag{7}$$

This Tree-Tuple Count Constraint fixes the number of wares of each group that must be sold to all locations of a given area.

Distributing sales on locations

$$\mathcal{D}_{\mathtt{L}}(\ddot{\mathtt{L}}) \;\rightarrow\; \gamma_1 \leq \#(\{\mathtt{S} : \mathcal{R}(\mathtt{S},\mathtt{W},\mathtt{B},\mathbf{v})\}) \leq \gamma_2. \tag{8}$$

where $\mathbf{v}$ has been defined above and γ_1, γ_2 with $\gamma_1 \leq \gamma_2$ are two non negative integers denoting the same distribution range for all locations. This is a Tree-Tuple Count Constraint-B_1.

Assigning brands to rankings

$$\begin{aligned}&\mathcal{D}_{\mathtt{B\,R}\,\tau_1\tau_2}(\ddot{B},\ddot{R},\ddot{\tau}_1,\ddot{\tau}_2) \;\rightarrow\\ &\quad \tau_1 \leq \#(\{\mathtt{S\,W\,\ddot{B}} : \mathcal{R}(\mathtt{S},\mathtt{W},\ddot{\mathtt{B}},\mathtt{c},\ddot{\mathtt{R}},\mathtt{t},\mathtt{l},\mathtt{a},\mathtt{g},\mathtt{p}\}) \leq \tau_2.\end{aligned} \tag{9}$$

This is a Tree-Tuple Count Constraint.

Assigning the numbers of sales to customers per ranking

$$\mathcal{D}_{\mathrm{R}\,\omega_1\omega_2}(\ddot{R},\ddot{\omega}_1,\ddot{\omega}_2) \;\rightarrow$$
$$\omega_1 \leq \#(\{\mathtt{S} :\ \mathcal{R}(\mathtt{S},\mathtt{w},\mathtt{b},\mathtt{c},\ddot{\mathtt{R}},\mathtt{t},\mathtt{l},\mathtt{a},\mathtt{g},\mathtt{p})\}) \leq \omega_2. \qquad (10)$$

This is a Tree-Tuple Count Constraint-B_1. Observe that a ranking dimension is considered in [8] to show an example of derived (hidden) dimensions.

3 Solving Inverse Tree-OLAP

In this section we present a method for finding an approximate solution of the Inverse Tree-OLAP. Given a instance x of the Inverse Tree-OLAP:

1. Construct an instance y of $\mathtt{IFM_I}$ using Tree-Group Count Constraints and possible Tree-Tuple Count Constraints (also in the variant B_1) for which all non-basic dimensions are existentially quantified. Any itemset is a set of $(n-1)$-tuples on the basic dimensions $B_2,\ldots,B_n$ that share the same value for the aggregating basic dimension B_1.
2. Solve y using the algorithm of [6] – let D be the transaction database computed by the algorithm, where a transaction is a set of items and each item is an element of $B_2 \times \cdots \times B_n$.
3. Represent the database D as a set of triples $(t, Z(t), \delta(t))$, where $Z(t)$ is an itemset occurring in D, $\delta(t)$ is the number of its duplicates in D and t is an identifier for the itemset $Z(t)$. Note that t is not a value in the domain of the aggregating basic domain B_1 but it represents a group of $\delta(t)$ distinct values for B_1.
4. Represent an instance r of the relation $\mathcal{R}$ by means of variables as follows: for each $(t, Z(t), \delta(t))$, introduce variables $x_{\hat{b}_1 b_2 \ldots b_n \mathbf{d}}$, where $b_2 \ldots b_n\,\mathbf{d}$ are all admissible values for $B_2,\ldots,B_n$, $\mathbf{d}$ is the list of all possible values for non-basic domains that are not determined by the prefixed one-to-many relationships and $\hat{b}_1$ represents the portion of t duplicates that are assigned to the values of the other subscript indices. Observe that this representation can be seen as a *chase*, which is a finite "canonical" database, witnessing the satisfiability of integrity constraints [2].
5. Use the Tree-Tuple Count Constraints and Tree-Tuple Count Constraints-B_1 involving non-basic dimensions to compute the variable values. To this end, we use linear equations that are solved using a linear program whose objective function is the cost of violating the above constraints.
6. Generate a flat table starting from the computed variable values by including the values for non-basic domains that are determined by the prefixed one-to-many relationships and by computing the measure values.

For presentation sake, we next illustrate our method by referring to the example described in Section 2.

As already mentioned, constraints (1), (2) and (3) encode an instance of $\mathtt{IFM_I}$, described in the following. We first present the formal definition of $\mathtt{IFM_I}$. Let:

1. $\mathcal{I}$ be a given set of n items and $\mathcal{U}_\mathcal{I}$ be the set of all non-empty itemsets over $\mathcal{I}$
2. S be a given set of m itemsets over the items in $\mathcal{I}$

3. S' denote $\{I \in \mathcal{U}_\mathcal{I} \mid I' \in S : I \subseteq I'\}$
4. $\Gamma_\sigma = \{(I, \sigma_1^I, \sigma_2^I) \mid I \in S,\ 0 \leq \sigma_1^I \leq \sigma_2^I\}$ be a given set of triples assigning a minimum and maximum support to each itemset in S
5. $\sigma' \geq 0$ be the maximum support threshold for all itemsets in S'
6. **size** $= (size_1, size_2)$, $0 \leq size_1 \leq size_2$, be the minimal and maximal number of transactions.

The *inverse frequent itemset mining problem with infrequency constraint* ($\mathtt{IFM_I}$) on $\mathcal{I}$, S, Γ_σ, σ' and **size** consists of finding a database D over $\mathcal{I}$ such that the following conditions hold (or of eventually stating that there is no such a database):

$$\forall I \in S : \sigma^I_{min} \leq \sigma^D(I) \leq \sigma^I_{max} \tag{11}$$

$$\forall I \in S' : \sigma^D(I) \leq \sigma' \tag{12}$$

$$size_1 \leq |D| \leq size_2. \tag{13}$$

By the anti-monotonocity property, constraints (12) can be replaced by:

$$\forall I \in B_{S'} : \sigma^D(I) \leq \sigma' \tag{14}$$

where $B_{S'} = \{I \in S' \mid I' \in S' : I' \subset I\}$ is the set of the bottom (i.e., minimal) elements of S'.

An instance of $\mathtt{IFM_I}$ is constructed by fixing: $\mathcal{I} = \{\langle \mathtt{w\,b} \rangle \mid \mathcal{D}_\mathtt{W}(\mathtt{w}) \times \mathcal{D}_\mathtt{B}\mathtt{b}\}$, $\Gamma_\sigma = \{(\mathtt{X}, \sigma_1, \sigma_2) \mid \mathcal{D}_{\{\mathtt{W\,B}\}\sigma_1\sigma_2}(\mathtt{X}, \sigma_1, \sigma_2)\}$, $\sigma' = \sigma$ (see constraint 3), $size_1 = s_1$ and $size_2 = s_2$ (see constraint 1). It is then straightforward to derive S and $B_{S'}$.

For the solution of the $\mathtt{IFM_I}$ instance, we adopt the approach of [6]. The instance is represented as an integer linear program with a linear number of constraints (corresponding to the support constraints of the itemsets in $S \cup B_{S'}$ and to the two database size constraints) and an exponential number 2^n of variables x_j, one for each possible transaction I_j, indicating to number of its occurrences in the database. The program is represented in a succinct format with size $\mathcal{O}(n\,(m + m'))$ – recall that a succinct problem is a problem whose instances are not given straightforward, but are themselves encoded using an a concise input with size logarithmic in the actual input size [10]. Then the integer constraint on the variables x_j are relaxed so that an approximate solution is obtained by solving a linear program. Because of the exponential number of variables, the *column generation* algorithm (see e.g [4]), which is a version of the simplex dealing with a large number of variables (large-scale linear programs). This method solves a linear program without explicitly including all columns (i.e., variables), in the coefficient matrix but only a subset of them with cardinality equal to the number of rows (i.e., constraints). Columns are dynamically generated by solving an auxiliary optimization problem called the *pricing problem.*

Observe that constraints (4) and (5) are not taken into account in the resolution algorithm of [6]. Constraint (4) can be easily handled by a simple additional constraint in the liar program. Constraint (5) states that for each itemset with length greater than λ, the associated variable x_j must be equal to zero. This restriction can be easily handled inside the pricing problem resolution.

The algorithm returns a transaction database D that is an approximate solution of the problem. The database D is represented in a succinct format: $(\hat{s}, Z, \delta)$, where Z is an itemset occurring in D, δ is the number of its duplicates and $\hat{s}$ is an identifier for Z. We stress that $\hat{s}$ is not a sale value in $\mathcal{D}_S$ as the itemset Z will be eventually assigned to δ distinct sale values. Let $\hat{S}$ the set of all identifiers $\hat{s}$. For each $\hat{s} \in \hat{S}$, $\delta(\hat{s})$ denotes the duplicate number for $\hat{s}$, $Z(\hat{s})$ is the itemset Z.

So far we have implemented steps (1)-(3). To implement step (4), we introduce the variables $x_{\hat{s}wblc}$ for each $\hat{s}$ in $\hat{S}$, for each ware w of the domain of W, for each brand b of the domain of B, for each location l of the domain L and for each customer c of the domain of C. There are no indices corresponding to non-basic domains that are defined by means of on-to-many fixed relationships. Indeed, because of constraints of type (6), once that a domain value is fixed, the value of its roll-up domain value is automatically fixed as well.

To make the computation effective, we relax the integer constraint on all variables; so they are defined on the domain of non-negative rational numbers. We introduce the following equations:

$$\sum_{l \in \mathcal{D}_L, c \in \mathcal{D}_C} x_{\hat{s}wblc} = \delta(\hat{s}) \qquad \forall \hat{s} \in \hat{S}\ \forall \langle w, b\rangle \in Z(\hat{s}) \tag{15}$$

$$x_{\hat{s}wblc} = 0 \qquad \begin{array}{c} \forall \hat{s} \in \hat{S}\ \forall l \in \mathcal{D}_L\ \forall c \in \mathcal{D}_C \\ \forall \langle w, b\rangle \in (\mathcal{D}_W \times \mathcal{D}_B) \setminus Z(\hat{s}) \end{array} \tag{16}$$

Equation (15) states that, fixed a transaction $\hat{z}$ and any item $\langle w, b\rangle$ of $Z(\hat{S})$, the sum of all assignments of the item to all possible locations and customers must be equal to the duplicate number $\delta(\hat{s})$. On the other hand, equation 16 enforces that $x_{\hat{s}wblc} = 0$ whenever the item $\langle w, b\rangle$ i is not part of any transaction $\hat{s}$.

Let us now implement step (5). To this end, we consider all constraints from (7) to (10).

Constraints (7) is implemented as:

$$\alpha_1^{ga} \le \sum_{\substack{\forall \hat{s} \in \hat{S}\ \forall c \in \mathcal{D}_C\ \forall l :\ \mathcal{D}_{LA}(l, a) \\ \forall \langle w, b\rangle \in Z(\hat{s}) :\ \mathcal{D}_{WG}(w, g)}} x_{\hat{s}wblc} \le \alpha_2^{ga} \qquad \begin{array}{c} \forall g \in \mathcal{D}_G \\ \forall a \in \mathcal{D}_A \end{array} \tag{17}$$

where $(\alpha_1^{ga}, \alpha_2^{ga})$ is the pair s.t. $\mathcal{D}_{GA\,\alpha_1\alpha_2}(g, a, \alpha_1^{lc}, \alpha_2^{lc})$ is true.

Constraints (8), (9) and (10) are implemented as:

$$\gamma_1 \le \sum_{\forall \hat{s} \in \hat{S}\ \forall \langle w, b\rangle \in Z(\hat{s})\ \forall c \in \mathcal{D}_C} x_{\hat{s}wblc} \le \gamma_2 \qquad \forall l \in \mathcal{D}_L \tag{18}$$

$$\tau_1^{br} \le \sum_{\substack{\forall \hat{s} \in \hat{S}\ \forall c :\ \mathcal{D}_{CR}(c, r) \\ \forall w \in \mathcal{D}_W :\ \langle w, b\rangle \in Z(\hat{s})}} x_{\hat{s}wblc} \le \tau_2^{br} \qquad \begin{array}{c} \forall b \in \mathcal{D}_B \\ \forall r \in \mathcal{D}_R \end{array} \tag{19}$$

$$\omega_1^r \le \sum_{\forall \hat{s} \in \hat{S}\ \forall \langle w, b\rangle \in Z(\hat{s})\ \forall c:\ \mathcal{D}_{CR}(c, r)} x_{\hat{s}wblc} \le \omega_2^r \qquad \forall r \in \mathcal{D}_R \tag{20}$$

where $(\tau_1^{br}, \tau_2^{br})$ and (ω_1^r, ω_2^r) are the pairs such that $\mathcal{D}_{BR\,\tau_1\tau_2}(b,\ r,\ \tau_1^{gr}, \tau_2^{gr})$ and $\mathcal{D}_{R\,\omega_1\omega_2}(r,\ \omega_1^r, \omega_2^r)$ are true.

Obviously equations (15)–(20) can be solved in time polynomial in the domain sizes. Nevertheless, there is a problem that must be dealt with: the equations could be too restrictive so that no solution exists. However, as we are interest in finding an approximate solution that has the minimal violation the problem can be solved by introducing two artificial variables for each equation. For instance, equation (18) is rewritten as:

$$w_1^l + \sum_{\forall \hat{s} \in \hat{S}\ \forall \langle w,b \rangle \in Z(\hat{s})\ \forall c \in \mathcal{D}_C} x_{\hat{s}wblc} \geq \gamma_1 \qquad \forall l \in \mathcal{D}_L$$

$$w_2^l - \sum_{\forall \hat{s} \in \hat{S}\ \forall \langle w,b \rangle \in Z(\hat{s})\ \forall c \in \mathcal{D}_C} x_{\hat{s}wblc} \geq -\gamma_2 \qquad \forall l \in \mathcal{D}_L$$

where w_1^l and w_2^l are non-negative artificial variables. We take the summation of all artificial variables as an objective function to be minimized. Therefore we obtain a linear program representation of the equation resolution problem. By solving the linear program we compute a solution minimizing the objective function – that is, the one with the minimal constraint violation.

We point out that the size of the linear program is not exponential as for the $\mathtt{IFM_I}$ linear program but polynomial. Nevertheless, the number of both rows and columns may be large. So, a row-column generation approach can be adopted: at each iteration step, the pricing problem has to also decide which row must be eventually expanded.

Once solved the linear equation system, we have to perform the last task (6) to construct a feasible instance r. To this end, for each positive basic variable $x_{\hat{s}wblc}$, say with value k, we select k distinct values $s_1, \ldots, s_k$ from the domain of S, add the values of non-basic domains R, T, A and G, compute the measure P and insert the so constructed tuples into r.

4 Conclusions

Inverse OLAP is the problem of deciding whether a given fact table satisfies a set of given count constraints [12]. In this paper we have defined a special case of this problem, called Inverse Tree-OLAP, for which the flat fact table key is modeled by a Dimensional Fact Model (DFM) with a tree structure. The count constraints define aggregation patterns to be respected by both the many-to-many relationship among the basic dimensions and the one-to-many relationships within dimension hierarchies.

References

1. Arvind Arasu, Raghav Kaushik, and Jian Li. Data generation using declarative constraints. In *Proceedings of the 2011 international conference on Management of data*, SIGMOD '11, pages 685–696, New York, NY, USA, 2011. ACM.

2. Catriel Beeri and Moshe Y. Vardi. Polynomial-time implication problems for unary inclusion dependencies. *J. of the ACM*, 37:15–46, 1990.
3. Toon Calders. The complexity of satisfying constraints on databases of transactions. *Acta Inf.*, 44(7-8):591–624, 2007.
4. George B. Dantzig and Mukund N. Thapa. *Linear Programming 2: Theory and Extensions*. Springer-Verlag, 2006.
5. Matteo Golfarelli, Dario Maio, and Stefano Rizzi. The dimensional fact model: A conceptual model for data warehouses. *Int. J. Cooperative Inf. Syst.*, 7(2-3):215–247, 1998.
6. Antonella Guzzo, Luigi Moccia, Domenico Saccà, and Edoardo Serra. Solving inverse frequent itemset mining with infrequency constraints via large-scale linear programs. *TKDD*, 7(4):18:1–18:39, 2013.
7. Ralph Kimball. *The Data Warehouse Toolkit: Practical Techniques for Building Dimensional Data Warehouses*. John Wiley & Sons, 1996.
8. Svetlana Mansmann, Nafees Ur Rehman, Andreas Weiler, and Marc H. Scholl. Discovering olap dimensions in semi-structured data. In Il-Yeol Song and Matteo Golfarelli, editors, *DOLAP*, pages 9–16. ACM, 2012.
9. T. Mielikainen. On inverse frequent set mining. In IEEE Computer Society, editor, *Proc. of 2nd Workshop on Privacy Preserving Data Mining (PPDM)*, pages 18–23, 2003.
10. Christos H. Papadimitriou. *Computational complexity*. Addison-Wesley, Reading, Massachusetts, 1994.
11. Domenico Saccà, Edoardo Serra, and Alfredo Cuzzocrea, editors. *IDEAS 2018: 22nd International Database Engineering and Applications Symposium, June 1820, 2018, Villa San Giovanni, Italy*. ACM, 2018.
12. Domenico Saccà, Edoardo Serra, and Antonella Guzzo. Count constraints and the inverse olap problem: Definition, complexity and a step toward aggregate data exchange. In *FoIKS*, pages 352–369, 2012.
13. Gerhard Weikum. Where's the Data in the Big Data Wave? 2013. *ACM Sigmod BLOG:* http://wp.sigmod.org/?p=786.

An Innovative Framework for Combining Set Similarity Join Algorithms and Clustering

Leonardo Andrade Ribeiro[1], Alfredo Cuzzocrea[2],
Karen Aline Alves Bezerra[3], Ben Hur Bahia do Nascimento[3], and Massimiliano Nolich[2]

[1] Instituto de Informática, Universidade Federal de Goiás, Goiânia, Goiás, Brazil
laribeiro@inf.ufg.br
[2] DIA Department, University of Trieste and ICAR-CNR, Italy
alfredo.cuzzocrea@dia.units.it, mnolich@units.it
[3] Departmento de Ciência da Computação, Universidade Federal de Lavras, Lavras, Brazil
karen.bezerra@posgrad.ufla.br, bhn@computacao.ufla.br

Abstract. Centered around the *data cleaning and integration* research area, in this paper we propose *SjClust*, a framework to integrate similarity join and clustering into a single operation. The basic idea of our proposal consists in introducing a variety of cluster representations that are smoothly merged during the set similarity task, carried out by the join algorithm. An optimization task is further applied on top of such framework. The framework exposes a wide number of application scenarios where it can be used effectively and efficiently.

1 Introduction

Data cleaning and integration (e.g., [11, 5]) found on *duplicate record identification* (e.g., [6, 20]), which aims at detecting duplicate records that represent the same real-world entity. This is becoming more and more relevant in emerging *big data research* (e.g., [21, 10, 18]), as a plethora of real-life applications are characterized by the presence of multiple records representing the same real-world entity, which practically plagues every large database. Such records are often referred to as *fuzzy duplicates* (duplicates, for short), because they might not be exact copies of one another. Duplicates arise due to a variety of reasons, such as typographical errors and misspellings, different naming conventions, and as a result of the integration of data sources storing overlapping information.

Duplicates degrade the quality of the data delivered to application programs, thereby leading to a myriad of problems. Some examples are misleading data mining models owing to erroneously inflated statistics, inability of correlating information related to a same entity, and unnecessarily repeated operations, e.g., mailing, billing, and leasing of equipment. Duplicate identification is thus of crucial importance in data cleaning and integration.

Duplicate identification is computationally very expensive and, therefore, typically done offline. However, there exist important application scenarios that demand (near) real-time identification of duplicates. Prominent examples are data exploration [8], where new knowledge has to be efficiently extracted from databases without a clear definition of the information need, and virtual data integration [5], where the integrated data is not materialized

SEBD 2018, June 24-27, 2018, Castellaneta Marina, Italy.

and duplicates in the query result assembled from multiple data sources have to be identified — and eliminated — on-the-fly. Such scenarios have fueled the desire to integrate duplicate identification with processing of complex queries [1] or even as a general-purpose physical operator within a DBMS [4].

An approach to realize the above endeavor is to employ *similarity join* in concert with a *clustering algorithm* [7]. Specifically, similarity join is used to find all pairs of records whose similarity is not less than a specified threshold; the similarity between two records is determined by a *similarity function*. In a post-processing step, the clustering algorithm groups together records using the similarity join results as input. For data of string type, *set similarity join* is an appealing choice for composing a duplicate identification operator. Set similarity join views its operands as sets — strings can be easily mapped to sets. The corresponding similarity function assesses the similarity between two sets in terms of their overlap and a rich variety of similarity notions can be expressed in this way [4]. Furthermore, a number of optimization techniques have been proposed over the years [15, 4, 2, 20, 14, 19] yielding highly efficient and scalable algorithms.

The strategy of using a clustering algorithm strictly for post-processing the results of set similarity join has two serious drawbacks, however. First, given a group of n, sufficiently similar, duplicates, the set similarity join performs $\binom{n}{2}$ similarity calculations to return the same number of set pairs. While this is the expected behavior considering a similarity join in isolation, it also means that repeated computations are being performed over identical subsets. Even worse, we may have to perform much more additional similarity calculations between non-duplicates: low threshold values are typically required for clustering algorithms to produce accurate results [7]. Existing filtering techniques are not effective at low threshold values and, thus, there is an explosion of the number of the comparisons at such values. Second, the clustering is a blocking operator in our context, i.e., it has to consume all the similarity join output before producing any cluster of duplicates as result element. This fact is particularly undesirable when duplicate identification is part of more complex data processing logic, possibly even with human interaction, because it prevents pipelined execution.

In this paper, we propose *SjClust*, a framework to integrate set similarity join and clustering into a single operation, which addresses the above issues. The main idea behind our framework is to represent groups of similar sets by a *cluster representative*, which is incrementally updated during the set similarity join processing. Besides effectively reducing the number similarity calculations needed to produce a cluster of n sets to $O(n)$, we are able to fully leverage state-of-the-art optimization techniques at high threshold values, while still performing well at low threshold values where such techniques are much less effective. Indeed, the resulting composed algorithm is even up to an order of magnitude faster than the original set similarity join algorithm for low threshold values. Moreover, we exploit set size information to identify when no new set can be added to a cluster; therefore, we can then immediately output this cluster and, thus, avoid the blocking behavior. Furthermore, there exists a plethora of clustering algorithms suitable for duplicate identification and no single algorithm is overall the best across all scenarios [7]. Thus, versatility in supporting a variety of clustering methods is essential. Our framework smoothly accommodates various cluster representation and merging strategies, thereby yielding different clustering methods for each combination thereof.

This paper is the short version of the papers [13, 12], where we present the main results of our research.

2 Fundamental Concepts and Background Knowledge

ncepts and definitions related to set similarity joins before present important optmization techniques. Then, we describe a general set similarity join algorithm, which provides the basis for our framework.

2.1 Basic Concepts and Definitions

We map strings to *sets of tokens* using the popular concept of *q-grams*, i.e., sub-strings of length q obtained by "sliding" a window over the characters of an input string v. We (conceptually) extend v by prefixing and suffixing it with $q-1$ occurrences of a special character "$" not appearing in any string. Thus, all characters of v participate in exact q q-grams. For example, the string *"token"* can be mapped to the set of 2-gram tokens {*t, to, ok, ke, en, n*}. As the result can be a multi-set, we simply append the symbol of a sequential ordinal number to each occurrence of a token to convert multi-sets into sets, e.g, the multi-set {a,b,b} is converted to $\{a\circ 1, b\circ 1, b\circ 2\}$. In the following, we assume that all strings in the database have already been mapped to sets.

We associate a weight with each token to obtain *weighted sets*. A widely adopted weighting scheme is the Inverse Document Frequency (*IDF*), which associates a weight $idf(tk)$ to a token tk as follows: $idf(tk) = ln(1+N/df(tk))$, where $df(tk)$ is the *document frequency*, i.e., the number of strings a token tk appears in a database of N strings. The intuition behind using IDF is that rare tokens are more discriminative and thus more important for similarity assessment. The weight of a set r, denoted by $w(r)$, is given by the weight summation of its tokens, i.e., $w(r) = \sum_{tk \in r} w(tk)$.

We consider the general class of set similarity functions. Given two sets r and s, a set similarity function $sim(r,s)$ returns a value in $[0,1]$ to represent their similarity; larger value indicates that r and s have higher similarity. Popular set similarity functions are defined as follows.

Definition 1 (Set Similarity Functions). *Let r and s be two sets. We have:*

- *Jaccard similarity:* $J(r,s) = \frac{w(r \cap s)}{w(r \cup s)}$.
- *Dice similarity:* $D(r,s) = \frac{2 \cdot w(r \cap s)}{w(r)+w(s)}$.
- *Cosine similarity:* $C(r,s) = \frac{w(r \cap s)}{\sqrt{w(r) \cdot w(s)}}$

We now formally define the set similarity join operation.

Definition 2 (Set Similarity Join). *Given two set collections $\mathcal{R}$ and $\mathcal{S}$, a set similarity function sim, and a threshold τ, the set similarity join between $\mathcal{R}$ and $\mathcal{S}$ returns all scored set pairs $\langle (r,s), \tau' \rangle$ s.t. $(r,s) \in \mathcal{R} \times \mathcal{S}$ and $sim(r,s) = \tau' \geq \tau$.*

In this paper, we focus on self-join, i.e., $\mathcal{R} = \mathcal{S}$; we discuss the extension for binary inputs in Section 2.3. For brevity, we use henceforth the term similarity function (join) to mean set similarity function (join). Further, we focus on the Jaccard similarity and the IDF weighting scheme, i.e., unless stated otherwise, $sim(r,s)$ and $w(tk)$ denotes $J(r,s)$ and $idf(tk)$, respectively.

Example 1. Consider the sets r and s below

$$r = \{\mathbf{A}, \mathbf{B}, C, \mathbf{D}, \mathbf{E}\}$$
$$s = \{\mathbf{A}, \mathbf{B}, \mathbf{D}, \mathbf{E}, F\}$$

and the following token-IDF association table:

tk	A	B	C	D	E	F
$idf(tk)$	*1.5*	*2.5*	*2*	*3.5*	*0.5*	*2*

Thus, we have $w(r) = w(s) = 10$ and $w(r \cap s) = 8$; thus $sim(r,s) = \frac{8}{10+10-8} \approx 0.66$.

2.2 Optimization Techniques

Similarity functions can be equivalently represented in terms of an *overlap bound* [4]. Formally, the overlap bound between two sets r and s, denoted by $O(r,s)$, is a function that maps a threshold τ and the set weights to a real value, s.t. $sim(r,s) \geq \tau$ iff $w(r \cap s) \geq O(r,s)$. The similarity join can then be reduced to the problem of identifying all pairs r and s whose overlap is not less than $O(r,s)$. For the Jaccard similarity, we have $O(r,s) = \frac{\tau}{1+\tau} \cdot (w(r) + w(s))$.

Further, similar sets have, in general, roughly similar weights. We can derive bounds for immediate pruning of candidate pairs whose weights differ enough. Formally, the weight bounds of r, denoted by $min(r)$ and $max(r)$, are functions that map τ and $w(r)$ to a real value s.t. $\forall s$, if $sim(r,s) \geq \tau$, then $min(r) \leq w(s) \leq max(r)$ [15]. Thus, given a set r, we can safely ignore all other sets whose weights do not fall within the interval $[min(r), max(r)]$. For the Jaccard similarity, we have $[min(r), max(r)] = \left[\tau \cdot w(r), \frac{w(r)}{\tau}\right]$. We refer the reader to [16] for definitions of overlap and weight bounds of several other similarity functions, including Dice and Cosine.

We can prune a large share of the comparison space by exploiting the *prefix filtering principle* [15, 4], which allows discarding candidate pairs by examining only a fraction of the input sets. We first fix a global order O on the universe $\mathcal{U}$ from which all tokens are drawn. A set $r' \subseteq r$ is a prefix of r if r' contains the first $|r'|$ tokens of r. Further, $pref_\beta(r)$ is the shortest prefix of r, the weights of whose tokens add up to more than β. The prefix filtering principle is defined as follows.

Definition 3 (Prefix Filtering Principle [4]). *Let r and s be two sets. If $w(r \cap s) \geq \alpha$, then $pref_{\beta_r}(r) \cap pref_{\beta_s}(r) \neq \varnothing$, where $\beta_r = w(r) - \alpha$ and $\beta_s = w(s) - \alpha$, respectively.*

We can identify all candidate matches of a given set r using the prefix $pref_\beta(r)$, where $\beta = w(r) - min(r)$. We denote this prefix simply by $pref(r)$. It is possible to derive smaller prefixes for r, and thus obtain more pruning power, when we have information about the set weight of the candidate sets, i.e., if $w(s) \geq w(r)$ [2] or $w(s) > w(r)$ [14]. Note that prefix overlap is a condition necessary, but not sufficient to satisfy the original overlap constraint: an additional verification must be performed on the candidate pairs. Finally, the number of candidates can be significantly reduced by using the *inverse document frequency ordering*, O_{idf}, as global token order to obtain sets ordered by decreasing IDF weight . The idea is to minimize the number of sets agreeing on prefix elements and, in turn, candidate pairs by

For ease of notation, the parameter τ is omitted.

A secondary ordering is used to break ties consistently (e.g., the lexicographic ordering).

shifting lower frequency tokens to the prefix positions — recall that higher IDF weights are associated to low-frequency tokens.

Example 2. Consider the sets r and s in Example 1 and $\tau = 0.6$. We have $O(r,s) = 7.5$; $[min(r), max(r)]$ and $[min(s), max(s)]$ are both $[6, 16.7]$. By ordering r and s according to O_{idf} and the IDF weights in Example 1, we obtain:

$$r = [D,B,C,A,E]$$
$$s = [D,B,F,A,E].$$

We have $pref(r) = pref(s) = [D]$.

2.3 Similarity Join Algorithms: Definitions and Usage

Similarity join algorithms based on inverted lists are effective in exploiting the previous optimizations [15, 2, 20, 14]. Most of such algorithms have a common high-level structure following a filter-and-refine approach.

Algorithm 1 formalizes the steps of a similarity join algorithm. The algorithm receives as input a set collection sorted in increasing order of set weights, where each set is sorted according to O_{idf}. An inverted list I_t stores all sets containing a token t in their prefix. The input collection R is scanned and, for each *probe set* r, its prefix tokens are used to find *candidate sets* in the corresponding inverted lists (lines 4–10); this is the *candidate generation phase*, where the map M is used to associate candidates to its accumulated overlap score os (line 3). Each candidate s is dynamically removed from the inverted list if its weight is less than $min(r)$ (lines 6–7). Further filters, e.g., filter based on overlap bound, are used to check whether s can be a true match for r, and then the overlap score is accumulated, or not, and s can be safely ignored in the following processing (lines 8–10). In the *verification phase*, r and its matching candidates, which are stored in M, are checked against the similarity predicate and those pairs satisfying the predicate are added to the result set. To this end, the *Verify* procedure (not shown) employs a merge-join-based algorithm exploiting token order and the overlap bound to define break conditions (line 11)[14]. Finally, in the *indexing phase*, a *pointer* to set r is appended to each inverted list I_t associated with its prefix tokens (lines 12 and 13).

Algorithm 1 is actually a self-join. Its extension to binary joins is trivial: we first index the smaller collection and then go through the larger collection to identify matching pairs. For simplicity, several filtering strategies such positional filtering [20] and min-prefixes [14], as well as inverted list reduction techniques [2, 14] were omitted. Nevertheless, these optimizations are based on bounds and prefixes and, therefore, our discussion in the following remains valid.

3 Our Proposal: The Innovative *SjClust* Framework

We now present *SjClust*, a general framework to integrate clustering methods into similarity joins algorithms. The goals of our framework are threefold: 1) *flexibility and extensibility* by accommodating different clustering methods; 2) *efficiency* by fully leveraging existing optimization techniques and by reducing the number of similarity computations to form clusters; 3) *non-blocking behavior* by producing results before having consumed all the input, preferably much earlier.

Algorithm 1: Similarity join algorithm

```
Input: A set collection R sorted in increasing order of the set weight; each set is sorted
       according to O_idf; a threshold τ
Output: A set S containing all pairs (r,s) s.t. Sim(r,s) ≥ τ
I_1, I_2, ... I_|U| ← ∅, S ← ∅
foreach r ∈ R do
    M ← empty map from set id to overlap score (os)
    foreach t ∈ pref(r) do                                  // can. gen. phase
        foreach s ∈ I_t do
            if w(s) < min(r)
                Remove s from I_t
            if filter(r, s, M(s))
                M(s).os ← −∞                                // invalidate s
            else M(s).os = M(s).os + w(t)
    S ← S ∪ Verify(r, M, τ)                                 // verif. phase
    foreach t ∈ pref(r) do                                  // index. phase
        I_t ← I_t ∪ {r}
return S
```

(a) Representation details. (b) Similarity evaluation.

Fig. 1. Cluster representation.

The backbone of *SjClust* is the similarity join algorithm presented in Section 2. In particular, *SjClust* operates over the same input of sorted sets, without requiring any pre-processing, and has the three execution phases present in Algorithm 1, namely, candidate generation, verification, and indexing phases. Nevertheless, there are, of course, major differences.

First and foremost, the main objects are now cluster of sets, or simply clusters. Figure 1 illustrates strategy adopted for cluster representation. The internal representation contains a list of its set element's ids, an (optional) auxiliary structure, and the cluster's *complete representation*, a set containing all tokens from all set elements. A cluster exports its external representation as the so-called *cluster representative* (or simply representative) (Figure 1(a)). Representatives are fully comparable to input sets and similarity evaluations are always performed on the representatives, either between a probe set and a cluster or between two clusters (Figure 1(b)). In the following, we use the term cluster and representative interchangeably whenever the distinction is unimportant for the discussion.

Figure 2 depicts more details on the *SjClust* framework. In the candidate generation phase, prefix tokens of the current probe set are used to find cluster candidates in the inverted lists (Figure 2(a)). Also, there is a *merging phase* between verification and indexing phases (Figure

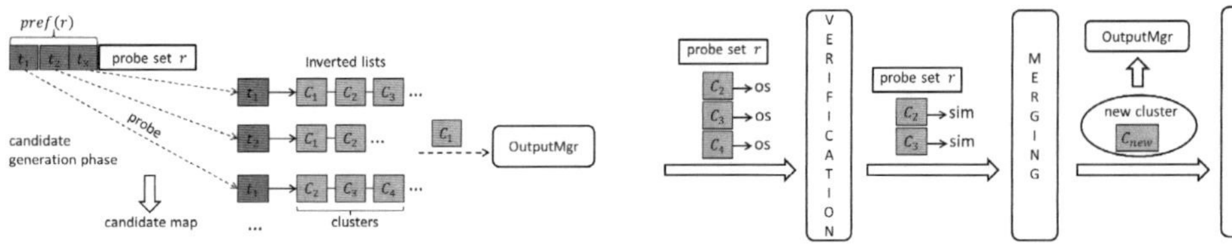

(a) Candidate generation. (b) *SjClust* course of evaluation.

Fig. 2. *SjClust* framework components.

2(b)). The verification phase reduces the number of candidates by removing false positives, i.e., clusters whose similarity to the probe set is less than the specified threshold. In the merging phase, a new cluster is generated from the probing set and the clusters that passed through the verification are considered for merging with it according to a *merging strategy*. In the indexing phase, references to the newly generated cluster are stored in the inverted lists associated with its prefix tokens. Finally, there is the so-called *Output Manager*, which is responsible for maintaining references to all clusters—a reference to a cluster is added to the Output Manager right after its generation in the merging phase (Figure 2(b)). Further, the Output Manager sends a cluster to the output as soon as it is identified that no new probing set can be similar to this cluster. Clusters in such situation can be found in the inverted lists during the candidate generation (Figure 2(a)) as well as identified using the weight of the probe set (not shown in Figure 2).

The aforementioned goals of *SjClust* are met as follows: flexibility and extensibility are provided by different combinations of cluster representation and merging strategies, which can be independently and transparently plugged into the main algorithm; efficiency is obtained by the general strategy to cluster representation and indexing; and non-blocking behavior is ensured by the Output Manager. Next, we provide details of each *SjClust* component.

4 Conclusions and Future Work

In this paper, we presented *SjClust*, a framework to integrate clustering into set similarity join algorithms. We demonstrated the flexibility of *SjClust* in incorporating different clustering methods by proposing several cluster representation and merging strategies. *SjClust* is an order of magnitude faster than the original set similarity join algorithm for lower thresholds, which are often needed in practice to obtain accurate results in duplicate identification. Furthermore, our proposal produces results earlier, thereby avoiding blocking behavior. We described *SjClust* and its main components in detail. Future work is mainly oriented towards enriching our framework with advanced features such as *uncertain data management* (e.g., [9]), *adaptiveness* (e.g., [3]), and *execution time prediction* (e.g, [17]).

Acknowledgments

This research was partially supported by the Brazilian agencies CNPq and CAPES.

References

1. Hotham Altwaijry, Sharad Mehrotra, and Dmitri V. Kalashnikov. Query: A framework for integrating entity resolution with query processing. *PVLDB*, 9(3):120–131, 2015.
2. Roberto J. Bayardo, Yiming Ma, and Ramakrishnan Srikant. Scaling up all pairs similarity search. In *Proc. of the WWW Conference*, pages 131–140, 2007.
3. Mario Cannataro, Alfredo Cuzzocrea, Carlo Mastroianni, Riccardo Ortale, and Andrea Pugliese. Modeling adaptive hypermedia with an object-oriented approach and xml. *WebDyn 2002*, 2002.
4. Surajit Chaudhuri, Venkatesh Ganti, and Raghav Kaushik. A primitive operator for similarity joins in data cleaning. In *Proc. of the 22nd Intl. Conf. on Data Engineering*, page 5, 2006.
5. AnHai Doan, Alon Y. Halevy, and Zachary G. Ives. *Principles of Data Integration*. Morgan Kaufmann, 2012.
6. Ahmed K. Elmagarmid, Panagiotis G. Ipeirotis, and Vassilios S. Verykios. Duplicate record detection: A survey. *TKDE*, 19(1):1–16, 2007.
7. Oktie Hassanzadeh, Fei Chiang, Renée J. Miller, and Hyun Chul Lee. Framework for evaluating clustering algorithms in duplicate detection. *PVLDB*, 2(1):1282–1293, 2009.
8. Stratos Idreos, Olga Papaemmanouil, and Surajit Chaudhuri. Overview of data exploration techniques. In *Proc. of the SIGMOD Conference*, pages 277–281, 2015.
9. Carson Kai-Sang Leung, Alfredo Cuzzocrea, and Fan Jiang. Discovering frequent patterns from uncertain data streams with time-fading and landmark models. *T. Large-Scale Data- and Knowledge-Centered Systems*, 8:174–196, 2013.
10. Hong Liu, Ashwin Kumar T. K, and Johnson P. Thomas. Cleaning framework for big data - object identification and linkage. In *Proc. of the Big Data Congress*, pages 215–221, 2015.
11. Arturas Mazeika and Michael H. Böhlen. Cleansing databases of misspelled proper nouns. In *Proc. of the VLDB Workshop on Clean Databases*, 2006.
12. Leonardo Andrade Ribeiro, Alfredo Cuzzocrea, Karen Aline Alves Bezerra, and Ben Hur Bahia do Nascimento. Incorporating clustering into set similarity join algorithms: The sjclust framework. In *Database and Expert Systems Applications - 27th International Conference, DEXA 2016, Porto, Portugal, September 5-8, 2016, Proceedings, Part I*, pages 185–204, 2016.
13. Leonardo Andrade Ribeiro, Alfredo Cuzzocrea, Karen Aline Alves Bezerra, and Ben Hur Bahia do Nascimento. Sjclust: Towards a framework for integrating similarity join algorithms and clustering. In *ICEIS 2016 - Proceedings of the 18th International Conference on Enterprise Information Systems, Volume 1, Rome, Italy, April 25-28, 2016*, pages 75–80, 2016.
14. Leonardo Andrade Ribeiro and Theo Härder. Generalizing prefix filtering to improve set similarity joins. *Information Systems*, 36(1):62–78, 2011.
15. Sunita Sarawagi and Alok Kirpal. Efficient set joins on similarity predicates. In *Proc. of the SIGMOD Conference*, pages 743–754, 2004.
16. Natália Cristina Schneider, Leonardo Andrade Ribeiro, Andrei de Souza Inácio, Harley Michel Wagner, and Aldo von Wangenheim. SimDataMapper: An architectural pattern to integrate declarative similarity matching into database applications. In *Proc. of the SBBD Conference*, pages 967–972, 2015.
17. Christiane Faleiro Sidney, Diego Sarmento Mendes, Leonardo Andrade Ribeiro, and Theo Härder. Performance prediction for set similarity joins. In *Proc. of the SAC Conference*, pages 967–972, 2015.
18. Nan Tang. Big RDF data cleaning. In *Proc. of the ICDE Conference Workshops*, pages 77–79, 2015.
19. Jiannan Wang, Guoliang Li, and Jianhua Feng. Can we beat the prefix filtering?: an adaptive framework for similarity join and search. In *Proc. of the SIGMOD Conference*, pages 85–96, 2012.
20. Chuan Xiao, Wei Wang, Xuemin Lin, Jeffrey Xu Yu, and Guoren Wang. Efficient similarity joins for near-duplicate detection. *TODS*, 36(3):15, 2011.
21. Feng Zhang, Hui-Feng Xue, Dong-Sheng Xu, Yong-Heng Zhang, and Fei You. Big data cleaning algorithms in cloud computing. *iJOE*, 9(3):77–81, 2013.

Deriving Local Internal Logic for Black Box Models

Eliana Pastor
Supervised by Elena Baralis

Politecnico di Torino, Italy
{eliana.pastor, elena.baralis}@polito.it

Abstract. Despite the widespread use, machine learning methods produce black box models. It is hard to understand how features influence the model prediction. We propose a novel explanation method that explains the predictions of any classifier by analyzing the prediction change obtained by omitting relevant subsets of attribute values. The local internal logic is captured by learning a local model in the neighborhood of the prediction to explain. The explanations provided by our method are effective in detecting associations among attributes and class label.

Keywords: Interpretability · Prediction Explanation · Local model.

1 Introduction

Machine learning algorithms are widely applied in every aspect of our society. Their growing popularity and their widespread use have made it increasingly important to understand why a classification model take a particular decision. The call for more explainable predictions comes also for institution. The European Union approved the GDPR, a regulation for ensuring personal data protection. It states that individuals have the right to receive "meaningful information about the logic involved" in case of automated decision-making. For some authors, this requirement legally mandates a "right to explanation" [2].

We propose a novel model-agnostic explanation method that explains the predictions made on single instances by any classifier. The explanation highlights the internal logic of the model in a neighborhood of the prediction. It is based on the knowledge of the local behavior of the model, captured by an interpretable local model.

2 Related Work

Many algorithms have been proposed for improving the interpretability of already existing classification models. Model-dependent solutions are proposed for

SEBD 2018, June 24-27, 2018, Castellaneta Marina, Italy.

handling only specific models. Model-agnostic solutions instead treat the machine learning model as a black box. Our research is focused on these approaches for their general applicability and the advantages derived from it. These methods in fact are applicable to any classification methods without making any assumption on their internal logic. Thus, the comparison among different techniques in terms of model interpretability is possible.

While some approaches try to explain the original model globally, others propose a general method for explaining individual predictions, i.e. why particular decisions are made. Ribeiro et al. [4] introduce a model-agnostic method for explaining individual prediction by learning an interpretable and linear model in the locality of the prediction to be explained. However, the linear approximation may not be faithful if the model is highly non-linear even in the locality of the prediction [4]. The locality is captured by randomly perturbed samples around the instance. Thus, non-existing configurations of attribute values can also be generated. Hence, the local model cannot be considered fully trustworthy.

Several works study how a prediction changes if parts of the input components are omitted. Lemaire et al. [3] and Robnik-Šikonja and Kononenko [5] consider how each attribute value is relevant for the prediction for tabular data, by omitting one attribute value at a time. Štrumbelj et al. study also the omission of more attribute values together, thus also addressing the attribute interaction [6]. The information of how attributes interact with the others is summarized in one single contribution for each attribute value. Hence, the information of interaction relevance is lost. Moreover, they compute the omission effect for the power set of the attributes. Hence, the method is affected by an exponential time complexity. We propose a novel solution that highlight not only the influence of each attribute value for a particular prediction but also of relevant attribute interactions. Moreover, we overcome the problem of exponential time complexity exploiting local properties of the original model to be explained.

3 Method

We propose a novel method applicable to explain individual predictions of any classification method. Given the particular prediction that we want to explain, we omit one or more attribute values at a time and we measure how the prediction changes. The relevance of the change is estimated as a difference of prediction probabilities with respect to a particular target class. The greater is this difference, the more the omitted attribute values are relevant for the prediction.

With respect to existing approaches, we are interested in understanding not only how each single attribute value is significant for the prediction but also how it interacts with the others. An attribute value can determine the prediction alone or only if it is in conjunction with others. In the latter case, we need to omit more attributes at the time for observing how the prediction changes. Omitting sets of attribute values allows also to deal with the disjunction case. The disjunction condition occurs when more than one configurations of attributes values determines the prediction. We can observe a change of the prediction probability only if we considered the omission of the attribute values together.

The feature values that in conjunction or disjunction are relevant for a prediction are highlighted by a local interpretable model. The local model is an associative classifier learned in the neighborhood of the prediction that we want to explain. The local rules, being understandable, provide preliminary insights of why a decision is made by the considered model. Each rule is in AND form. Thus, it gives the information of what attributes together determine the prediction. Moreover, a prediction may be determined by more rules. We can deal with the disjunction condition considering jointly the omission of the subsets highlighted by the local rules. Only the relevant attribute subsets provided by the local model are considered, instead of the complete power set of all attribute combinations. Hence, our approach overcomes the exponential time complexity.

4 Preliminary Results

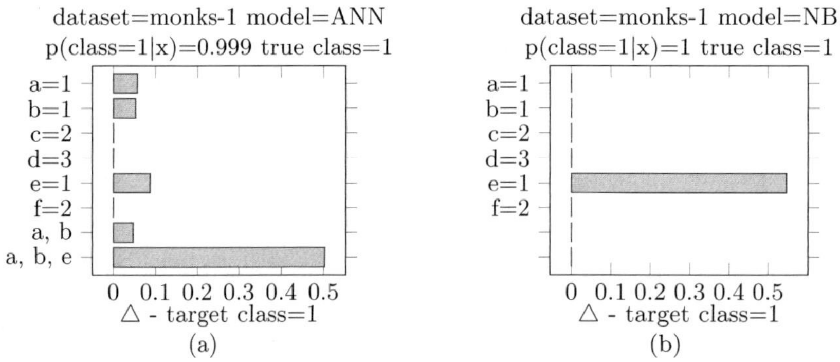

Fig. 1: Explanation of (a) the neural network and (b) the Naive Bayes prediction of a particular instance of the *monks-1* data set.

In this section, preliminary outcomes of our novel explanation method are presented. The *Monk1* data set is an artificial data set composed by 6 discrete attributes *a,b,c,d,e,f* and the class label can take value 1 or 0 [1]. Being artificial, the relation between the attributes and the class value is known. The class is 1 if *a=b* or if *e=1*, 0 otherwise. We train a MLP ANN using the *Monk1* data set. Let x = (a=1, b=1, c=2, d=3, e=1, f=2) be the instance that we want to explain. We know that the "true class" is 1 because *e=1* and *a=b*. The ANN correctly predicts the class label as 1. To estimate the relevant subsets of feature values, we train the associative classifier in the locality of instance x. The local model returns the following association rules: $\{e = 1\} \rightarrow class = 1$, $\{a = 1,\ b = 1\} \rightarrow class = 1$. Hence, if *e=1* the instance is assigned to the class 1 or if a and b are both equal to 1. These relations should indeed determine the class. Thus, the local behavior captures the true explanation. Once that the relevant subsets are determined, the prediction differences are computed. The estimation is made for each attribute value, for the relevant subset {*a=1,b=1*} and for the OR of the relevant rules, thus for {*a=1,b=1,e=1*}. The results are shown in Figure 1a. The terms *e=1*, *a=1* and *b=1* have alone a positive importance in the determination of the class. It is interesting to notice that {*a=1,b=1*} together have not a great prediction difference but it is comparable to the ones when they are considered alone. If a and b are removed together, the class label does not change. The prediction is in fact still 1 because of *e=1*. Same considerations can be made for *e=1*. Removing the rules in OR, the prediction probability drastically changes. Only if considered together, we can observe and quantify how these attributes interact.

If we explain the prediction for the same instance, made by another model, we may obtain a different result. The explanation should capture how the model behaves in the locality of the instance. Different models work differently. This difference may be on the predicted class label, but also on the feature values that drive the prediction. Consider the explanation of the same instance x and still built with respect to class 1, but classified by the Naive Bayes classifier (NB). The local model returns a single relevant rule: $\{e = 1\} \rightarrow class = 1$.
The results are shown in Figure 1b. The NB classifier assigns correctly the instance x to class 1, but only because *e=1*. The local model and the explanation highlight that the Naive Bayes classifier has not learned the association that if *a=b* then *class=1*. Because of its assumption of independence between features, it is not able to learn the importance that a and b have together. Hence, the local model and the explanation in this case successfully reflect the model behavior.

5 Conclusions and Future Work

Preliminary tests show that our technique is able to capture the diverse internal logic of classification techniques. Differently than existing approaches, the importance of relevant subsets of feature values to the prediction is computed. Thus, our method provides to end users the information of what attributes together determine the prediction and the quantification of their influence.

As future work we plan to (*i*) formalize our approach proposing formal definitions of the prediction change estimation, (*ii*) evaluate the effect of the neighborhood in the local rules and the resulting explanations and (iii) apply the proposed method to real-world data sets, validating explanations through the assistance of domain experts.

Acknowledgements This work is partially funded by SmartData@PoliTO.

References

1. Dheeru, D., Karra Taniskidou, E.: UCI machine learning repository (2017)
2. Goodman, B., Flaxman, S.: European union regulations on algorithmic decision-making and a "right to explanation". arXiv preprint arXiv:1606.08813 (2016)
3. Lemaire, V., Feraud, R., Voisine, N.: Contact personalization using a score understanding method. In: 2008 IEEE Int. Joint Conf. on Neural Networks. pp. 649–654
4. Ribeiro, M.T., Singh, S., Guestrin, C.: "Why Should I Trust You?": Explaining the Predictions of Any Classifier. In: Proc. of the 22Nd ACM SIGKDD Int. Conf. on KDD. pp. 1135–1144. KDD '16, ACM, New York, NY, USA (2016)
5. Robnik-Šikonja, M., Kononenko, I.: Explaining classifications for individual instances. IEEE Trans. Knowl. Data Eng. **20**(5), 589–600 (2008)
6. Štrumbelj, E., Kononenko, I., Robnik Šikonja, M.: Explaining instance classifications with interactions of subsets of feature values. DKE **68**(10) (2009)

On the Incremental Computation of Argumentation Frameworks

Gianvincenzo Alfano
supervised by Prof. Sergio Greco

Department of Informatics, Modeling, Electronics and System Engineering (DIMES)
University of Calabria, Rende (CS), Italy
{g.alfano,greco}@dimes.unical.it

Abstract. We tackle the problem of efficiently recomputing extensions of dynamic Argumentation Frameworks (AFs) under well-known semantics, namely frameworks able to model human ability to argue. We introduce an incremental approach that, given an initial argumentation framework, an initial extension for it, and an update, computes an extension of the updated framework.
The proposed approach is then extended to different kinds of argumentation frameworks (i.e., abstract, bipolar, extended, structured), and is able to incorporate existing AF-solvers in order to compute an extension of the updated framework.

Keywords: Argumentation · Knowledge Representation · Incremental Algorithm.

1 Introduction

Argumentation has emerged as one of the major fields in Artificial Intelligence [10,17,7]. In particular, abstract argumentation frameworks (AFs) [11] are simple and powerful formalism for modelling disputes between two or more agents. The formal meaning of an AF is given in terms of argumentation semantics, which intuitively tell us the sets of arguments (called *extensions*) that can be exploited to support a point of view in a discussion. Although the idea underlying AFs is very simple and intuitive, most of the argumentation semantics proposed so far suffer from a high computational complexity [12]. Complexity bounds and evaluation algorithms for AFs have been deeply investigated in the literature, as also witnessed by the International Competition on Computational Models of Argumentation (ICCMA, *http://argumentationcompetition.org*) whose aim is encouraging research and development of efficient algorithms for computational models of AFs. However, most research focused on 'static' frameworks, whereas in practice AFs are dynamic systems [9,8]. In fact, typically an AF represents a temporary situation, and new arguments and attacks can be added/retracted to take into account new available knowledge.

2 Argumentation Frameworks

Literature offers several formalism for modeling disputes between two or more agents. Each of them belongs to one of the two major argumentation categories, namely *ab-*

SEBD 2018, June 24-27, 2018, Castellaneta Marina, Italy.

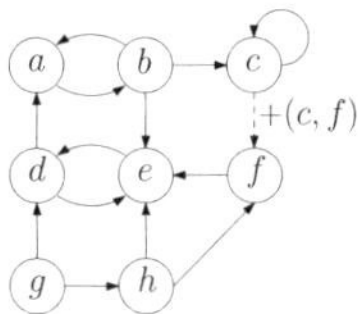

Fig. 1. AFs $\mathcal{A}_0$ and $\mathcal{A} = +(c, f)(\mathcal{A}_0)$.

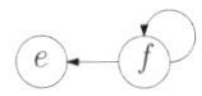

Fig. 2. R-AF

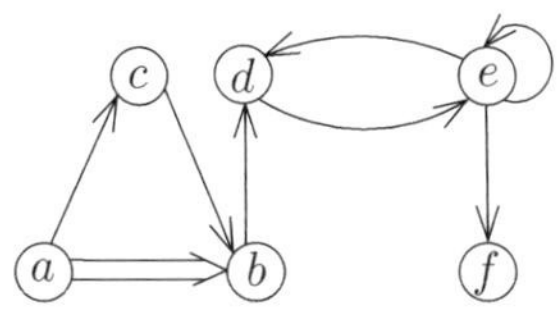

Fig. 3. BAF for weather example.

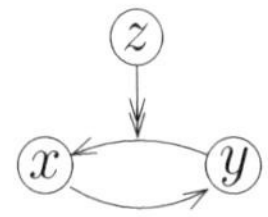

Fig. 4. EAF for weather example.

stract, where arguments are abstract entities (i.e., words, phrases, etc.) since we abstain on where it comes from, and *structured*, where the structure describing how an argument is built is also provided in the framework. Here we briefly introduce those frameworks over which we proposed an incremental technique for recomputing extensions after a change operation performed over the framework.

Abstract Argumentation Frameworks. An argument is an abstract entity whose role is entirely determined by its relationships with other arguments. We assume the existence of a set Arg of *arguments*. An AF is a pair $\langle A, \Sigma \rangle$, where $A \subseteq Arg$ and $\Sigma \subseteq A \times A$ is a binary relation over A whose elements are called *attacks*. Thus, an AF is a directed graph where nodes correspond to arguments and edges correspond to attacks. An argumentation semantics specifies the criteria for identifying a set of arguments that can be considered "reasonable" together, called *extension*. Some of the well-known semantics for abstract argumentation are *complete*, *preferred*, *stable*, *grounded* and *ideal*.

Bipolar Abstract Argumentation Frameworks. Bipolar argumentation frameworks (BAFs) extend Dung's argumentation frameworks to explicitly represent the notion of support between arguments, in addition to that of attack. An *abstract bipolar argumentation framework* (*BAF* for short) [6] is a triple $\langle A, \Sigma, \Pi \rangle$, where $\Pi \subseteq A \times A$ is a binary relation over A whose elements are called *supports*, and $\Sigma \cap \Pi = \emptyset$. Thus, a Dung's argumentation framework (AF) [11] is a BAF of the form $\langle A, \Sigma, \emptyset \rangle$. A BAF can be viewed as a directed graph where each node corresponds to an argument and each edge in the graph corresponds to either an attacks($\rightarrow$) or a support($\Rightarrow$). An example is reported on Figure 3.

Extended Abstract Argumentation Frameworks. Extended argumentation frameworks (EAFs) extend Dung's argumentation frameworks (AFs) to represent a kind of defeasible attack in addition to the Dung's classical notion of attack.Consider the following arguments about weather forecast: argument x is "*The week-end will be dry in Rome since AccuWeather forecasts sunshine*", while argument y is "*The week-end will be wet in Rome since The Weather Channel forecasts rain*". These arguments attack each other, as they claim contradictory conclusions. One could be persuaded that AccuWeather is recognized to be more trustworthy than The Weather Channel, meaning that y *does not successfully attack* x. This kind of situations can be modelled in EAFs that incorporate *second-order attacks* (i.e., attacks to classical Dung's attacks) whose intuitive meaning is "deactivating" the attacked attack whenever the argument from which the second-order attack originates is accepted. The resulting EAF is shown in Figure 4.

Defeasible Logic Programming. DeLP incorporates a defeasible argumentation formalism for the treatment of contradictory knowledge. A *dialectical process* is used for deciding which information prevails as warranted. This dialectical process involves the construction and evaluation of arguments that either support or interfere with the query under analysis. A DeLP program $\mathcal{P} = (\Pi, \Delta)$ is a set of *facts*, *strict rules* and *defeasible rules*. Intuitively, facts and strict rules represent non-defeasible information, while defeasible rules represent tentative information, that is, information that can be used if nothing could be posed against it. In a program $\mathcal{P}$, we will distinguish the subset Π of facts and strict rules, and the subset Δ of defeasible rules.

3 Research Focus

Argumentation is an inherently dynamic process which springs accordingly argumentation frameworks that changes over time. Performing an update on an AF $\mathcal{A}_0$ means modifying it into an AF $\mathcal{A}$ by adding or retracting arguments or attacks. We first proposed a technique for incrementally computing extensions of dynamic abstract argumentation frameworks (AFs): given an initial extension and a set of updates, our algorithm computes an extension of the updated AF under most popular argumentation semantics [13,15,14,2]. The algorithm consists of the following three main steps: (*i*) identification of a (smaller) sub-AF, called *reduced* AF (R-AF for short), on the basis of the update and additional information provided by the initial extension (*ii*) using *any* non-incremental algorithm to compute an extension of the reduced AF; and (*iii*) getting the final extension by merging a portion of the initial extension with that computed for the reduced AF. To make an example, consider the AF reported on Figure 1, and consider the update operation $u = +(c, f)$. The reduced framework (the sub-AF affected by the change) consists of only arguments e and f, having as initial grounded extension $\{f, g\}$. The reduced AF is reported on Figure 2.

From an experimental analysis, the algorithm performs two orders of magnitude faster than the best solvers computing the semantics from scratch. This allowed us to extend the technique to cope with other different kinds of (abstract) argumentation frameworks. Particularly, in [1] we applied this technique after that a bipolar argumentation framework is mapped into a Dung's equivalent one using additional meta-knowledge. Using the meta-argumentation approach, namely a procedure to convert a framework into a Dung's equivalent one, we envisage the possibility to apply the incremental technique to compute extensions over EAFs [3] , where they are firstly mapped into an abstract equivalent one by adding pieces of knowledge (i.e., using meta-arguments and meta-attacks) useful to convert second-order attacks into 'classical' attacks.

Our current research is to identify similar approach for structured argumentation frameworks. A first attempt was proposed in [5] where DeLP formalism is taken into account to model structured information, and updates consisting on adding a defeasible/strict rule. Although the workflow is similar to the algorithm for abstract frameworks, different problems arise when we deal with structured argumentation. One of the major problem is that arguments are not given as input, but they should be build according to the knowledge-base given. For this purpose we envisage the use of an hyper-graph which maps a DeLP-program, and using a particular notion of reachability on hyper-graphs we identify only those portion of the program which needs to be recomputed after that a rule is just added.

4 Conclusion and Future Work

Continuing on studying incremental algorithm for structured argumentation frameworks is our primary goal. Particularly, we are currently working on extending our technique for both (strict and defeasible) rule deletion and addition in the DeLP-framework [4]. Additionally, we should also investigate the possibility to find analogous incremental approach to cope with other structured formalisms like $ASPIC^{+}$ [16]. Another important aspect that reserve more investigation is to extend the technique to enumerate the whole set of extensions when a multiple-status semantics is called over an updated abstract argumentation framework, more precisely, returning the whole set of extensions after that an update is computed.

References

1. Alfano, G., Greco, S., Parisi, F.: Computing stable and preferred extensions of dynamic bipolar argumentation frameworks. In: Proc. of Workshop on Advances In Argumentation In Artificial Intelligence (AI^3), co-located with AI*IA. pp. 28–42 (2017)
2. Alfano, G., Greco, S., Parisi, F.: Efficient computation of extensions for dynamic abstract argumentation frameworks: An incremental approach. In: Proc. of IJCAI. pp. 49–55 (2017)
3. Alfano, G., Greco, S., Parisi, F.: Computing extensions of dynamic abstract argumentation frameworks with second-order attacks. In: Proc. of IDEAS. pp. 183–192 (2018)
4. Alfano, G., Greco, S., Parisi, F., Simari, G.I., Simari, G.R.: An incremental approach to structured argumentation over dynamic knowledge bases. In: Proc. of KR (to appear) (2018)
5. Alfano, G., Greco, S., Parisi, F., Simari, G.I., Simari, G.R.: Incremental computation of warranted arguments in dynamic defeasible argumentation: The rule addition case. In: Proc. of ACM Symposium on Applied Computing (SAC). pp. 911–917 (2018)
6. Amgoud, L., Cayrol, C., Lagasquie-Schiex, M.: On the bipolarity in argumentation frameworks. In: Proc. of NMR. pp. 1–9 (2004)
7. Baroni, P., Caminada, M., Giacomin, M.: An introduction to argumentation semantics. The Knowledge Engineering Review **26**(4), 365–410 (2011)
8. Baroni, P., Giacomin, M., Liao, B.: On topology-related properties of abstract argumentation semantics. A correction and extension to dynamics of argumentation systems: A division-based method. Artificial Intelligence **212**, 104–115 (2014)
9. Baumann, R.: Splitting an argumentation framework. In: Proc. of LPNMR. pp. 40–53 (2011)
10. Bench-Capon, T.J.M., Dunne, P.E.: Argumentation in artificial intelligence. Artificial Intelligence **171**(10 - 15), 619 – 641 (2007)
11. Dung, P.M.: On the acceptability of arguments and its fundamental role in nonmonotonic reasoning, logic programming and n-person games. Artificial Intellig. **77**(2), 321–358 (1995)
12. Dunne, P.E., Wooldridge, M.: Complexity of abstract argumentation. In: Argumentation in Artificial Intelligence, pp. 85–104 (2009)
13. Greco, S., Parisi, F.: Efficient computation of deterministic extensions for dynamic abstract argumentation frameworks. In: Proc. of ECAI. pp. 1668–1669 (2016)
14. Greco, S., Parisi, F.: Incremental computation of deterministic extensions for dynamic argumentation frameworks. In: Proc. of JELIA. pp. 288–304 (2016)
15. Greco, S., Parisi, F.: Incremental computation of grounded semantics for dynamic abstract argumentation frameworks. In: Proc. of ECAI Workshop COREDEMA. pp. 66–81 (2016)
16. Modgil, S., Prakken, H.: The *ASPIC*$^{+}$ framework for structured argumentation: a tutorial. Argument & Computation **5**(1), 31–62 (2014)
17. Rahwan, I., Simari, G.R.: Argumentation in Artificial Intelligence. Springer Publishing Company, Incorporated, 1st edn. (2009)

Efficient and Effective Source Selection in the Web of Data: a Smart Caching Approach

PhD Session Paper

Francesco De Fino
Supervised by: Barbara Catania, Giovanna Guerrini

University of Genoa, Italy
francesco.defino@dibris.unige.it

1 Problem Statement and Motivation

In the last decade, the traditional Web is evolved in the *Web of Data*, where huge collections of structured data are gathered over distributed, heterogeneous sources. These datasets are often exploited much below their potential due to difficulties in accessing them. Processing complex requests on diverse and dynamic sources requires: (i) source selection; (ii) actual processing of the request on the relevant, and usually big in size, sources. The overall process may not guarantee user satisfaction, since the request may be processed on inaccurate, incomplete, unreliable data; or the processing time may be inadequate to the query urgency. In [1], the authors claimed that user profiles and request contexts, data and processing quality, and information about similar requests recurring over time could be exploited to inform query processing and cope with these issues.

In this thesis, we focus on recurring retrieval needs for improving query processing. Recurring retrieval needs have been considered in query processing for a very long time in terms of materialized views and caching approaches. Both of them suffer from some problems when applied to the reference scenarios. Materialized views associate a result with a given query even if, for improving efficiency, additional information could be of interest (e.g., the set of used data sources). On the other hand, caching approaches usually rely on precise query matching, not always suitable in the reference environments, and, similarly to materialized views, cached queries are usually associated with query results.

The aim of the thesis is to exploit how information about similar requests recurring over time can be exploited in order to efficiently and effectively process complex requests on heterogeneous and dynamic data sources, while guaranteeing user satisfaction and limiting as much as possible user interactions. In particular, we propose a new smart caching technique that gets over the limitations of current approaches by: (i) taking advantage of prior processing in order to obtain *shortcuts* to different points in the query processing stack, with a special emphasis on source selection, thus providing a multilayer caching approach;

SEBD 2018, June 24-27, 2018, Castellaneta Marina, Italy.

(ii) relying on relaxed matches; (iii) providing a human-in-the-loop solution by which user feedback as well as query and data contexts are taken into account in cache management.

We claim that the proposed approach could be quite effective in processing complex requests on diverse and dynamic sources. Indeed, by maintaining not only query results but also more general processing information collected during processing, like the set of selected sources, in distinct but related caches, we will be able to cope with the trade-off between data dynamicity and accuracy of the result. By exploiting relaxation, performance can also be improved, since the number of cache hits will increase. Relaxation, as well as the adoption of a human-in-the-loop solution, can finally increase user satisfaction, in terms of both quality of data (accuracy and completeness of the result) and quality of service (execution time).

Our smart cache approach is also quite innovative: as far as we know, no multilayer caching approach, taking into account source selection, has been proposed so far. The exploitation of relaxation and human-in-the-loop features in cache management is also quite original, moving to a traditional physical task features that are typical of higher level processing steps.

The proposed approach is an instantiation of the framework proposed in [2,3] in the context of Linked Data but we claim it can be easily extended to other graph-based contexts. Data sources correspond to RDF data sources[1] and queries are represented in SPARQL.

2 A Relaxed Caching Approach for Source Selection

We first introduce the reference architecture for source selection caching we rely on in the overall multilayer approach. Then, a preliminary proposal for relaxed cache matches is discussed.

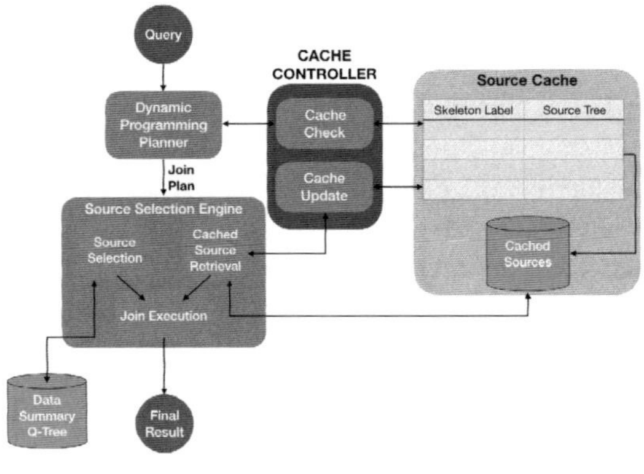

Fig. 1. Query processing architecture

[1] A RDF set of triples available on the Web.

Reference architecture. We extend the caching framework for RDF data and SPARQL queries in [6] to deal with source selection. It represents query graphs through canonical labels generated by a variation of the *Bliss* algorithm [5].

Fig. 1 shows the resulting reference architecture. Given a query Q as input, the *Dynamic Programming Planner* module, from [6], identifies the best query plan relying on a dynamic programming approach. Query plan components correspond to connected subgraphs of Q, whose results have then to be joined for generating the final result. For each connected subgraph, a cache look up is performed; if no match is found, the subgraph will be executed by a traditional graph query processing engine. The cost model takes into account the cost for the cache look up and the cost for traditional graph query execution.

In order to design a cache for source selection, we first modified the cache module with the aim of associating sets of source identifiers, instead of sets of data items, to cached queries. All cached queries sharing a common structure (called *skeleton*) are cached together, relying on a tree structure. The processing engine has then been modified to cope with source selection execution. To this aim, we relied on the index-based source selection approach proposed in [7] (but any other source selection technique can be used as well): a data summary, called QTree, is used to index available sources by representing triples as points in a three-dimensional space and source portions as hyper-rectangles in such a space. Preliminary results show that our smart caching framework outperforms the approach in [7] for different types of recurring SPARQL queries.

Relaxation. Exact matching can represent a limitation to fully exploit caching potential in speeding up source selection. If cached queries represent recurrent requests, exact matching precludes the planner to choose entries that are similar but not exactly equal to the current user request. For this reason, we propose to extend our smart caching approach with query relaxation to fully exploit the cache. The idea is to exploit a reference ontology $\mathcal{O}$ expressed by RDFS [4] and to consider relaxed matches w.r.t. the ontology. As a starting point, we consider $\mathcal{O}$ as a predicate taxonomy, i.e., a taxonomy in which predicates are related by a *rdfs:subPropertyOf* relationship.

The problem is now the following: given a query Q and n cached queries Q_1,...,Q_n, find $\overline{Q} \in \{Q_1, ..., Q_n\}$ such that $\overline{Q}$ generalizes Q and it has the minimum relaxation cost $relax\_\mathcal{C}$ from Q, i.e., $relax\_\mathcal{C}(Q, \overline{Q}) = min_{i=1}^{n} relax\_\mathcal{C}(Q, Q_i)$. The relaxation cost is defined on query canonical representations. $relax\_\mathcal{C}(Q_1, Q_2)$ returns ∞ if Q_2 does not generalize Q_1 (i.e., it is not possible to find in Q_2, for each triple pattern in Q_1, a triple pattern with a more general predicate, according to the taxonomy $\mathcal{O}$, and with the same subject and object). Otherwise, the returned value depends on how "far" is each triple pattern in Q_2 from the corresponding one in Q_1. Distance is defined in terms of the path length between predicates in the taxonomy $\mathcal{O}$.

In order to efficiently select query $\overline{Q}$ as described above, we assume that cached queries are indexed by a tree, where each node corresponds to a query triple pattern and each path from the root to a leaf corresponds to a cached query. The cached query at the minimum cost is then selected by a variation of the A^* algorithm.

We are currently working on an extension of this algorithm to take into account not only the generalization cost but also the cost for accessing sources. To this purpose, we plan to associate some statistics related to sources with each index leaf and use them, combined with the generalization cost, in computing the total cost. Another relevant extension concerns the usage of more generic ontologies for defining relaxed matches.

3 Future Research Plan

We plan to extend the work presented in Section 2 in several directions:

- Integrating the relaxation approach in the reference architecture.
- Integrating the source cache with a traditional cache for query processing over Linked Data and defining specific cache policies for a combined usage of both caches, depending on data dynamicity and target result accuracy, for both precise and relaxed queries.
- Extending the proposed smart caching approach so that the choice of the queries to cache is not only based on a recurrence principle, but also on a diversification principle, thus avoiding to keep in cache queries that are too similar or one is a slight relaxation of the other.
- Extending the proposed smart caching approach to bring the human in the loop, through the usage of specific cache management policies taking care of user feedbacks as well as query and data contexts.
- Experimentally evaluating the proposed approach, with reference to Linked Data sets, different query patterns, and different recurrence patterns. We will start with a synthetic workload but we will then look for a real workload. The main aim of the evaluation will be to measure the increase in efficiency (in terms of source selection and overall query processing costs), with varying amounts of available space, and the result accuracy due to the degree of approximation introduced by relaxation.

References

1. B. Catania et al. Wearable Queries: Adapting Common Retrieval Needs to Data and Users. *DBRank Workshop* (co-located with VLDB 2013), 2013.
2. B. Catania et al. Recurring Retrieval Needs in Diverse and Dynamic Dataspaces: Issues and Reference Framework. *EDBT/ICDT Workshops* 2017.
3. F. De Fino et Al. Exploiting Recurrent Retrieval Needs in Querying Heterogeneous and Dynamic Graph Dataspaces. *SEBD* 2017.
4. R. Frosini et al. Flexible Querying for SPARQL. *Semantic Web* 8(4), 2017.
5. T. Junttila et al. Engineering an Efficient Canonical Labeling Tool for Large and Sparse Graphs. *ALENEX. Society for Industrial and Applied Mathematics*, 2007.
6. N. Papailiou et al. Graph-aware, Workload-adaptive SPARQL Query Caching. *ACM SIGMOD* 2015.
7. J. Umbrich. et al. Comparing Data Summaries for Processing Live Queries over Linked Data. *World Wide Web* 14(5-6), 2011.

A methodology for GDPR compliant data processing

Domenico Desiato and supervised by Genoveffa Tortora

Department of Computer Science, University of Salerno,
via Giovanni Paolo II n.132, 84084 Fisciano (SA), Italy
ddesiato@unisa.it

Abstract. Nowadays new laws and regulations to prevent the privacy of users have been proposed. For instance, the General Data Protection Regulation (GDPR) is taking effect in Europe, requiring organizations to define privacy policies complying with the preferences of their users. One way to abide by GDPR is to obscure sensitive data. However, in order not to limit the usage of data, it is vital to limit the amount of data to be obscured. To this end, we propose a methodology exploiting relaxed functional dependencies (RFDs) to automatically identify attributes from which sensitive values can be derived. The methodology prescribes to partially encrypt database values causing data privacy threats, identified through the automatically discovered RFDs.

Keywords: Data privacy, Anonymity, Data management

1 Introduction

When a user provides personal data to use a services on the web, s/he will no longer own them, rather they became property of the organization running the services. To this end, the European Community has issued the *General Data Protection Regulation (GDPR)*, in order to ensure the protection of personal user data while they are processed by organizations.

Standard privacy prevention techniques, such as cryptography and anonymity, could lead to the impossibility of using the data, even if part of them do not represent sensitive data. For this reason, it is necessary to detect the data to be considered sensitive, and those that would not affect user's privacy.

In this paper we present a new methodology that analyzes data correlations detected by means of relaxed functional dependencies RFDs [2], aiming to identify potentially sensitive data that could break privacy preservation. In particular, the proposed methodology aims to: (1) classify the data potentially yielding violations users' anonymity, and (2) enhance privacy prevention, by determining whether data declared as sensitive could be implied by identifying data that could imply the values of sensitive data.

The paper is organized as follows. In Section 2 we provide a formalization of the privacy prevention problem, based on which the proposed methodology is described Section 3. In Section 4 we present the results of several experiments in order to validate the proposed methodology. Finally, conclusions and future research directions are discussed in Section 5.

2 Problem description

The two main concerns in data privacy are: *anonymity* and *information confidentiality*. Anonymity can be intended as non-identifiability. Thus, organizations must prevent the possibility to associate data to legitimate owners when letting third parts access them [4]. To formalize the concept of *anonymity*, we define the concept of *anonimity-violating attribute set*.

Anonimity-violating attribute set. Given a relation schema R containing user personal data, an attribute set $X = \{X_1, \ldots, X_k\}$, $X \subseteq attr(R)$, and a relation instance r of R, X represents an *anonimity-violating* attribute set if and only if it permits to *identify* data tuples in r (we denote this set by X_δ).

A relation R preserves the anonymity if and only if R does not contain an anonymity-violating attribute set X_δ. For instance, if a third-part knows an identifier value, then s/he is able to identify a user with a certainty degree of 100%. However, in order to limit third-part's power, we must also deny access to attributes enabling user's identification with a high certainty degree, even if less than 100%.

Information confidentiality is more a general concept. Here, the user would protect data s/he considers as *sensitive*. In this case, starting from a set of user specified sensitive data, we need to detect attributes from which it is possible to derive them. To formalize the concept of *information confidentiality*, we introduce the concept of *confidentiality-violating attribute set*.

Confidentiality-violating attribute set. Given a relation schema R containing user personal data, a relation instance r of R, and two attribute sets $X, Y \subseteq attr(R)$, where $Y = \{Y_1, \ldots, Y_h\}$ is the set of user specified sensitive attributes by user, then X represents a confidentiality-violating attribute set, if and only if it is not a key, but it determines at least one Y_i, one $Y_i \in Y$ (we denote this set by X_ς).

A relation R preserves the information confidentiality if and only if (i) it does not contain user specified sensitive attributes or (ii) they are obscured and R does not contain *confidentiality-violating* attribute sets X_ς. To this end, we use the concept of *functional determination* in order to exclude the possibility to derive values of attributes declared as sensitive. Thus, given a sensitive attribute A, if a third-part knows values of attributes determining those of A, then s/he could be able to discover values of A with a certainty degree of 100%, and with a maximum accuracy degree. However, it would be useful to limit third-part's power not only by decreasing the certainty degree (as defined for anonymity violations), but also by excluding the possibility to use values that are similar to those determining sensitive ones, i.e. by considering similarity-based matches.

For this reason, in this case we can identify a confidentiality violating attribute set X_ζ by using: (i) the above defined measure Ψ and a threshold ε, and (ii) a set of constraints Φ containing similarity-based matching predicates.

3 Methodology

We propose a methodology that guarantees user privacy for both *anonymity* and *information confidentiality* while permitting to continue use data. It exploits Relaxed Functional Dependencies (RFDs) [2], which enable us to detect sensitiveness of data, and to reduce the encryption processes only to them.

RFDs extend Functional Dependencies (FDs) by relaxing some constraints of their definition. In particular, they might relax on the *attribute comparison* method, and or on the fact that the dependency must be satisfied by the entire database. Relaxing on the attribute comparison method means adopting an approximate tuple comparison operator, instead of the "equality" operator. In order to define the type of attribute comparison used within an RFD, we use the concept of *constraint*. Instead, a dependency holding for "almost" all tuples or for a "subset" of them is said to relax on the extent. In this case, a *coverage measure* or a *condition* is specified to quantify the subset of tuples on which the RFD holds.

More formally, the following RFD

$$X_{\Phi_1} \xrightarrow{\Psi \geq \varepsilon} Y_{\Phi_2} \tag{1}$$

holds on a relation instance r of R iff: $\forall\ (t_1, t_2) \in r$, if $t_1[X]$ and $t_2[X]$ agree with the constraints specified by Φ_1, then $t_1[Y]$ and $t_2[Y]$ agree with the constraints specified by Φ_2 with a degree of certainty (measured by Ψ) greater than ε.

Our methodology exploits RFDs discovered from data to identify sensitive data, using block ciphers to encrypt a minimal set of attributes among those containing sensitive data. Then, ranking techniques are applied to discovered RFDs, in order to detect a minimal set of attributes to be encrypted to guarantee *anonymity* and *information confidentiality.*

Anonimity. Given a relation R, we need to identify all of its sets X_δ, defining a way to make them no longer accessible on R. Formally, to identify such set of attributes X_δ we map the concept of anonymity to that of *key dependency.* In particular, since a set X_δ identifies a user, it will also be the Left-Hand-Side (LHS) of a key dependency, to preserve the anonymity of R we need to identify the minimum attribute set $Z \subseteq attr(R)$, such that by obscuring all attributes in Z from R, then no anonymity violation can be found. To automatically obtain Z we must use a metric to rank RFDs discovered from data. We defined two simple and effective ranking metrics, but they do not always guarantee the minimality of the attribute set to be encrypted in order to satisfy privacy requirements, due to the fact that this problem can be reduced to the Minimum Feedback Vertex Set [3] that is NP-Complete.

Information confidentiality. Given a relation R, we need to identify all the confidentiality violating attribute sets X_ζ in R, and define a way through which

X_ς is no longer accessible on R. Formally, to identify a set X_ς, we map the concept of *information confidentiality* to RFDs relaxing on the extent by a coverage measure, and to attribute comparison by means of similarity constraints. The latter represents the required accuracy degree.

Given the set of all X_ςs in R, to preserve the confidentiality of R we need to identify a minimal set of attributes $Z \subseteq attr(R)$, such that by obscuring Z from R, no more confidentiality violation can be found.

The cryptographic technique that we use in the proposed methodology is *block cipher* [5]. In particular, given the set of "sensitive" attributes calculated for the i-th user (according to the user choices and the application of RFDs), denoted by $X^i = X^i_1, \ldots X^i_m$, we encrypt each X^i with a different key. The user's key permits to decrypt his/her set of sensitive data.

4 Evaluation

We validated the proposed methodology, by conducting experiments on six datasets derived from the real-world datasets *Customers*, *Cancer*, *Job*, *Votes*, *WholeSale* and *Echocardiogram*, available from the UCI machine learning repository, to which we added same personal data. They show that the number of attributes to be encrypted is in general small, and that the proposed methodology can effectively help to detect anonymity and/or confidentiality threats.

5 Conclusions and Future Work

We have proposed a new methodology to automatically identify and partially encrypt "sensitive" data in order to guarantee anonymity and information confidentiality. It can help organizations comply with the GDPR privacy prevention regulations. The identification procedure exploits automatically discovered RFDs [1], in order to derive the minimal set of data to be encrypted.

In the future, we would like to apply this methodology in the context of data manipulation processes that can potentially break data privacy, such as data integration [2], and schema evolution.

References

1. Caruccio, L., Deufemia, V., Polese, G.: On the discovery of relaxed functional dependencies. In: IDEAS. pp. 53–61 (2016)
2. Caruccio, L., Deufemia, V., Polese, G.: Relaxed functional dependencies - A survey of approaches. IEEE TKDE **28**(1), 147–165 (2016)
3. Fomin, F.V., Gaspers, S., Pyatkin, A.V., Razgon, I.: On the minimum feedback vertex set problem: Exact and enumeration algorithms. Algorithmica **52**(2), 293–307 (2008)
4. Mohammed, N., Fung, B., Hung, P.C., Lee, C.K.: Centralized and distributed anonymization for high-dimensional healthcare data. ACM TKDD **4**(4), 18 (2010)
5. Stallings, W.: The offset codebook (ocb) block cipher mode of operation for authenticated encryption. Cryptologia **42**(2), 135–145 (2018)

https://archive.ics.uci.edu/ml/index.php

AUTHOR INDEX

AUTHOR INDEX